REVISION SYMBOLS

 W9-BHT-060

The symbols below indicate a need to make revisions in the areas designated. Boldface numbers and letters refer to handbook sections.

ab	abbreviation 31a–e
ad	form of adjective/adverb 11, 7c
agr	agreement 10
awk	awkward diction or construction 21, 15, 7b
ca	case 8
cap	capitalization 30a–d
coh	coherence 4i, 5d
coord	coordination 19a, 18a, 7f
cs	comma splice 13
d	diction, word choice 21, 22
dm	dangling modifier 15h
dev	development needed 3, 4, 18d
emph	emphasis needed 19, 20
frag	sentence fragment 12, 7b
fs	fused sentence 13
hyph	hyphen 32
inc	incomplete construction 16g–h, 7b
ital	italics 30e–g
k	awkward diction or construction 21, 15, 7b
lc	lower-case letter 30a–d
log	logic 6, 37a, 38a, 39a
mm	misplaced modifier 15, 7d
ms	manuscript form 4k, Appx. B
mix	mixed construction 16e–f
no ¶	no paragraph needed 5
num	number 31f–h
¶	paragraph 5
¶ dev	paragraph development needed 5

ref	unclear pronoun reference 14
rep	unnecessary repetition 17a
sp	spelling error 23
shift	inconsistent, shifted construction 16
sub	sentence subordination 19b, 7f
t	verb tense error 9e–f
trans	transition needed 5a, 5f
var	sentence variety needed 19, 20
vb	verb form error 9, 17b
w	wordy 17a
ww	wrong word; word choice 21, 22
//	faulty parallelism 18
. ? !	end punctuation 24
:	colon 29a
ⱽ	apostrophe 27
—	dash 29b
( )	parentheses 29c
[ ]	brackets 29d
. . .	ellipsis 29e
/	slash 29f
;	semicolon 26
" "	quotation marks 28
⋀	comma 25
⌒	close up
⋀	insert a missing element
ℯ	delete
⎣⎤	transpose order

THE
Allyn & Bacon
HANDBOOK

LEONARD J. ROSEN
Bentley College

LAURENCE BEHRENS
University of California, Santa Barbara

Allyn & Bacon

Boston London Toronto Sydney Tokyo Singapore

*For Jonathan and Matthew—
teachers both.*

Executive Editor: Joseph Opiela
Series Editorial Assistant: Amy Capute
Developmental Editor: Allen Workman
Production Administrator: Susan McIntyre
Editorial-Production Service: Deborah Schneck
Copy Editor: Kathy Smith
Cover Administrator: Linda Dickinson
Composition Buyer: Linda Cox
Manufacturing Buyer: Louise Richardson

Laser imagery by LASERIUM/Laser Images, Inc.
Pages 1, 51, 201, 285, 341, 391, 441, 509, 539, 649, 719

Allyn & Bacon
A Division of Simon & Schuster, Inc.
160 Gould Street
Needham Heights, MA 02194

Copyright © 1992 by Leonard J. Rosen. All rights reserved. No part of the
material protected by this copyright notice may be reproduced or utilized in
any form or by any means, electronic or mechanical, including photocopying,
recording, or by any information storage and retrieval system, without the
written permission of the publisher.

Library of Congress Cataloging-in-Publication Data

Rosen, Leonard J.
  The Allyn & Bacon handbook / Leonard J. Rosen, Laurence Behrens.
    p. cm.
  Includes bibliographical references and index.
  ISBN 0-205-13348-7
  1. English language—Rhetoric—Handbooks, manuals, etc.
2. English language—Grammar—Handbooks, manuals, etc.
I. Behrens, Laurence.   II. Title.   III. title: Allyn and Bacon handbook
PE1408.R677 1992
808'.042—dc20   91-37817
                                                                  CIP

Printed in the United States of America
10 9 8 7 6 5 4 3 2   96 95 94 93 92

CONTENTS

X Writing and Reading in the Disciplines 649

PREFACE TO THE INSTRUCTOR

What do today's students need from a composition handbook? Have student needs in recent years outgrown the generally competent, currently available selection of handbooks? Answering these questions was foremost in our minds when we began what evolved into *The Allyn & Bacon Handbook*. Based on our classroom experiences and on consultations with colleagues across the curriculum, we each had for several years seen the need for a book that directly addressed the writing of students both within and *beyond* the composition classroom and that at the same time introduced foundational skills of critical thinking. We believed that handbooks should give increased attention to these important matters. We also believed that a handbook should be something more than a collection of loosely affiliated discussions: it should function as *one* book in which strong, unifying themes help users to perceive the writing process as a whole. Motivated by these concerns, we embarked on our project and chose four mutually reinforcing themes to make a single, coherent text that would cover the ground of traditional handbooks and break new ground as well.

Critical Thinking

With its opening chapters—"Critical Thinking and Reading" and "Critical Thinking and Writing"—*The Allyn & Bacon Handbook* marks a departure in the world of handbooks. Other books begin with chapters on the writing process. We open with strategies for reading thoughtfully and for thinking about sources *through* writing. This approach follows our conviction that writing is a process of clarifying thought. Much of what students write is based on sources, and much of the often-heard lament that students are neither thinking nor writing well is made in reference to students working with sources. Our book is unique in the extent of the coverage devoted to critical thinking.

- Chapter 1 introduces critical reading as a fundamental college-level skill that in the long run *saves* a student time. Students learn to read closely in order to understand sources, and then to evaluate, analyze, reflect, or infer relationships as the occasion demands.
- Chapter 2 presents varieties of writing and thinking that correspond to differing strategies for reading: summary, evaluation, analysis, and synthesis.

Chapters 1 and 2 are based on a survey of current research in the field and undergird all subsequent discussions of thinking and writing developed in the text: in Part II, on the Writing Process; in Part IX, on the Research

Process; and in Part X, on Writing and Reading across the Curriculum. **We approach critical thinking as decision making at *all* stages of the writing process.** Indeed, one cannot write well without thinking well. Writing aids thinking; thinking aids writing. In these opening, foundational chapters, we work to make this connection explicit for students.

Writing as a Process

Chapters 2 through 6 on the writing process are designed to serve both as a quick-reference tool and as a mini-rhetoric, with assignments that call on students to write and revise paragraphs and whole papers. Throughout Part II—and extending to our discussion of the sentence and word choice in Parts III, IV, V, and VI—we **emphasize the role of revision in clarifying meaning and achieving a clean, spare style.** Students learn to identify potential problems and then to revise—to think critically about an essay as a whole and about its component sections, paragraphs, and sentences. In chapters 3 and 4, students observe a sample paper evolve from an initial assignment and meandering first thoughts into a polished, final draft. **We present revision as an effort continually directed at one purpose: a clearly expressed thought.** At every turn in the process, writers make decisions in the hope of clarifying thinking. We want students to trust in this process and to learn that writing, though initially messy, will through revision yield a competent product.

Because we have found that writing improves significantly when students give careful and sustained attention to a paper's governing sentence, **we have made our discussion of thesis more extensive than those found in existing handbooks.**

- We approach thesis as inference-making and relate the types of inference that writers make to patterns of development (e.g., comparison) discussed in chapter 5, on Writing and Revising Paragraphs.
- We tie these same inferences to relationships that students make while reading source materials.
- We stress that certain theses lead to informative papers while others lead to argumentative ones.
- We discuss how, through a choice of thesis, writers communicate their ambitions for a paper.

One feature unique to this handbook is found in chapter 5, Writing and Revising Paragraphs, where **students will find a strategy for building from single paragraphs to a whole essay.** Too often, in our experience, students arrive at the end of the planning stage with little more than an outline and good intentions, without ever having learned strategies for piecing together paragraphs to form sections and sections to form whole papers.

Argumentation

Chapter 6, an outgrowth of the attention given throughout the book to critical thinking, focuses both on writing and on evaluating arguments. *The Allyn & Bacon Handbook* is the first handbook to adapt the **Toulmin model** of argument for students in the composition classroom. The choice of the widely respected Toulmin approach is especially important for this book not only because the approach is an excellent one for teaching the component parts of argument but also because it is without parallel in its ability to bring coherence to a discussion of writing—particularly, arguing—across the curriculum.

- Toulmin emphasizes the elements of argument common to persuasion in any discipline.
- Toulmin also explains how the form an argument takes, as well as the evidence used, depends heavily on the discipline (or context) in which a writer works.

We present the elements common to all arguments in chapter 6; we discuss the discipline- (or context-) specific elements of argument in chapters 37 through 39. Throughout, we have worked to make Toulmin's language accessible to students—using, for instance, the word *inference* in place of *warrant* and tying the core logic of argument making to the logic of thesis making.

Writing and Reading across the Curriculum

Having seen the need to give sustained attention to the writing and reading that students do beyond their first composition course, we set out to write cross-curricular chapters that would be unique among handbooks. These chapters—on reading and writing in the Humanities (chapter 37), in the Social Sciences (chapter 38), and in the Sciences (chapter 39)—not only introduce students to particular assignments they will encounter, but also show how writing, reading, and thinking change from one discipline area to the next. We have grounded our cross-curricular coverage both theoretically and practically in the material on argument and critical thinking from the first two parts of the book. We wanted our discussion to be a *coherent* extension of principles developed earlier—principles with which students who have used the book will be familiar. In this effort, Toulmin's approach to argument proved invaluable. After a general introduction devoted to characteristic assumptions and questions, each chapter reviews patterns for writing to inform and for making arguments in the discipline area; it reviews typical kinds of reading and audience situations; and it presents types of assignments found in the discipline, a sample student paper, and a listing of specialized reference materials.

To demonstrate how writing is used in different academic contexts, we present **in each cross-curricular chapter a research paper on the topic of** *alcohol,* **written from a particular disciplinary perspective.** One paper is a lab report on the fermentation of wine; another is a sociological investigation of women alcoholics; the third is an analysis of a character's alcohol use in a story by James Joyce. In chapter 35, on research, a fourth paper is written on the advisability of alcohol and drug testing—from a business perspective. Students who read these papers will appreciate the ways in which a researcher's point of view helps to determine the types of investigations that are carried out, the types of evidence that are called for, and the types of arguments that are made.

Other Concerns

Critical thinking, writing as a process, argumentation, and writing across the curriculum are themes we feel give *The Allyn & Bacon Handbook* a distinctive, unifying focus. These themes emphasize the value of careful decision making at all stages of the writing process. In showing students the importance of thinking clearly at the levels of the essay, paragraph, and sentence, **we have worked hard to achieve a tone that is clear, direct, and authoritative while at the same time** *respectful.* This tone reflects our view of students as fellow writers who in important respects are our peers: for whom the tensions in producing a first draft parallel our own and for whom commitment to a topic provides the motivating energy to revise and refine until words exactly express thoughts.

Any experienced writer knows that there is often more than one solution to a common sentence error. Therefore, when appropriate, we discuss alternative solutions and encourage students *in their role as writers* to make decisions. When usage is a matter of strict convention, we offer firm, clear guidelines. Throughout, we have worked to make our text enjoyable. Students will find real academic writing used as a basis for more than ninety percent of the exercises *and* example sentences. **Both exercises *and* examples almost always feature connected discourse from a variety of disciplines—** on topics as various as Van Gogh's life, Newton's separation of visible light into a spectrum, and the origins of the first World War. We wanted a book that would provide interesting and useful reading, as well as a clear guide to eliminating common errors and understanding key concepts of grammar, usage, and style. We also wanted a book that would be easy to use as a reference tool and visually appealing as well. To this end we have created numerous boxes that summarize important information or provide useful lists.

From the smallest details to the broadest themes that motivated us to undertake this project, we have aimed to make *The Allyn & Bacon Handbook* a single, coherent text that both demonstrates and celebrates the rich variety of academic writing.

Supplements for the Student

A student workbook—*The Allyn & Bacon Workbook* by Kathleen Shine Cain of Merrimack College—supplements the handbook with abridged topical explanations keyed to handbook sections and a new set of illustrative examples. The objective of the workbook is to provide an abundance of additional exercise work in basic grammar, sentence faults, punctuation, mechanics, and effective sentence construction. The workbook further provides supplementary work on the writing process, vocabulary, critical thinking, and argumentation.

The Allyn & Bacon Workbook is also published in an ESL version—developed by Judith Garcia of Miami-Dade Community College—which contains additional explanations, special topics, and additional exercises aimed at students for whom English is a second language. Finally, special workbooks are available to prepare students for the CLAST and TASP competency tests in Florida and Texas.

A compact collection of readings—*Thinking and Writing in the Disciplines: A Reader* by Mary McGann of the University of Indianapolis—is also available to students at an economical price for use in courses that explore some of *The Allyn & Bacon Handbook*'s themes. Focused on three major discipline areas, the reader includes examples from professional journals, popular writing, and student writing, each accompanied by pre-reading and study questions.

Supplements for the Instructor

The *Instructor's Annotated Edition* of the handbook—by Kathleen Shine Cain of Merrimack College—features succinct annotations in the margins of each chapter, offering a wide variety of useful information pertinent to teaching from the text. The *Instructor's Resource Manual* by Kathleen Shine Cain provides additional material for new and experienced instructors.

Testing and exercise instruments in computerized form as well as in booklet form are also available to support the instructor's composition program. First, two Allyn and Bacon *Diagnostic Tests* are keyed to the text, each containing a fifty-item test on grammar and mechanics with an essay component. Second, a computerized *Exercise Bank* contains hundreds of exercise examples keyed to the grammar and usage sections of the handbook for students needing supplementary practice, either independently in a learning laboratory or in a class setting.

Software and Audiovisual Supplements

Software is available to students through special packaging options with this handbook. For example, a widely used Macintosh on-line guide for writers, the **Editorial Advisor,** provides instant reference advice to writers as they work on a word processor. It is available at special pricing either separately, by license to a college department, or for sale in combination with the text. Other software packages and options are available through consultation with local Allyn and Bacon representatives.

A package of twenty acetate **Transparencies,** available to adopting instructors, presents key text diagrams in four-color, two-color, and one-color form, along with several special lecturing examples and demonstration pieces for use in focusing classroom discussions. A separate booklet of transparency masters also accompanies the text.

A series of professionally-produced video teaching lessons, forming *The Allyn & Bacon Video Grammar Library,* is available free to adopters. Each 10–minute lesson presents a separate topic in grammar, mechanics, sentence structure, or on such topics as sexist language and plagiarism.

Acknowledgments

Special thanks go to Kathleen Shine Cain of Merrimack College for her fine work on the *Instructor's Annotated Edition,* the companion *Allyn & Bacon Workbook,* and the *Instructor's Resource Manual.* To the many reviewers who took the time to critique our work, we give warm thanks. The following colleagues were both generous and tough with their comments. Whenever we did not, for our own hard-headed reasons, accept their advice, we had to construct good arguments, since our reviewers invariably argued with force and insight. Many thanks to Chris Anson, University of Minnesota; Phillip Arrington, Eastern Michigan University; Kathleen Shine Cain, Merrimack College; Barbara Carson, University of Georgia; Thomas Copeland, Youngstown State University; Sallyanne Fitzgerald, University of Missouri, Saint Louis; Dale Gleason, Hutchinson Community College; Stephen Goldman, The University of Kansas; Donna Gorrell, St. Cloud State University; Patricia Graves, Georgia State University; John Hanes, Duquesne University; Kristine Hansen, Brigham Young University; Bruce Herzberg, Bentley College; Vicki Hill, Southern Methodist University; Jeriel Howard, Northeastern Illinois State University; Clayton Hudnall, University of Hartford; David Joliffe, University of Illinois at Chicago; Kate Kiefer, Colorado State University; Nevin Laib, Franklin and Marshall University; Barry Maid, University of Arkansas at Little Rock; Thomas Martinez, Villanova University; Mary McGann, University of Indianapolis; Walter Minot, Gannon University; Jack Oruch, University of Kansas; Twyla Yates Papay, Rollins College; Richard Ramsey, Indiana/Purdue University at Fort Wayne; Annette Rottenberg, University of Massachusetts, Amherst; Mimi Schwartz, Stockton State College; Louise Smith, University of Massachusetts, Boston; Sally Spurgin, Southern Methodist University; Judith Stanford, Rivier College; Barbara Stout, Montgomery College; Ellen Strenski, University of California, Los Angeles; Christopher Thaiss, George Mason University; Michael Vivion, University of Missouri, Kansas City; Barbara Weaver, Ball State University; and Richard Zbracki, Iowa State University.

Many others helped us along the way. While their particular contributions are too numerous to mention here, we gratefully acknowledge their assistance. From Bentley College, we thank Tim Anderson, Christy Bell, Lindsey Carpenter, Sarika Chandra, Robert Crooks, Nancy Esposito, Barbara Gottfried, Sherman Hayes, Tom Heeney, Richard Kyte, Donald McIntyre, Kathy Meade, and George Radford. We thank other colleagues as well: John Clarke of the University of Vermont, whose work on critical thinking aided the formulating of our pedagogy, and Carol Gibbens of the University of California, Santa Barbara, for suggestions on the reference unit. Thanks go to Burke Brown, University of Southern Alabama; Eric Godfrey, Ripon College; Clarence Ivie, University of Southern Alabama; John Laucus, University Librarian, Boston University; William Leap, The American University; Larry Renbaum, Georgetown University Law School; Carol G. Schneider, Association of American Colleges; and Arthur White, Western Michigan University.

Writers are fortunate, indeed, to work with an editorial and production staff as fine as the team at Allyn and Bacon. Joe Opiela, Executive Editor for English, shared and helped to shape our vision for this book. Throughout the manuscript's writing and rewriting, Joe proved himself a tireless advocate and a steady source of helpful ideas. Allen Workman, with his more than twenty years of experience, is surely one of the industry's premier developmental editors. With his crisp line-by-line edits and his astonishingly detailed analysis of the features that make a handbook useful, Allen earned his last name with honesty and great distinction. Susan McIntyre shepherded the manuscript through production with an unfailing eye for detail. She cluttered her living room floor working over manuscript pages just as we did ours. Her advice on rewordings and on page layouts was always expert. Kathy Smith did an admirable job of copyediting, and Elaine Ober oversaw the process of designing and coordinating production schedules. Deborah Schneck designed the book and handled the incredible array of details in the day-to-day production process. With enthusiasm and creativity, Rick Bassett, Sandi Kirshner, and Nancy Forsyth helped to focus attention on the themes that make this book distinctive. John Isley, President of Allyn and Bacon, and Bill Barke, Vice President and Editorial Director, generously agreed to devote the editorial and production resources needed to make this a project that all concerned could take pride in. Editorial assistant Amy Capute was able, with ease and good humor, to help make the writing process move ahead smoothly. To all we give hearty and warm thanks.

Leonard Rosen, *Bentley College*

Laurence Behrens, *University of California, Santa Barbara*

Special Acknowledgment. During the writing of this book, Linda Rosen managed to bear a child, work a demanding job, and maintain faith (sometimes firmer than my own) that what started as a fragment of a seed of an idea so long ago would one day come to fruition. To Linda goes my most deeply felt and lasting thanks. Thank you, Linda. Thank you.   L.R.

PREFACE TO THE STUDENT

As a student, you will find yourself writing papers well beyond your composition and literature courses. A chemistry professor may ask you to explain in paragraph form the changes that occur in a chemical reaction. A physics professor may ask you to read and summarize an important journal article. Beyond college, you will discover that writing is an essential tool for anyone who must make decisions and document them. Many business people generate more than twenty memos or letters a week, in addition to drafting periodic reports and proposals. In school or out, you will have many occasions to write. Writing well—with confidence—will always serve your interests and make you a valued colleague, whatever the endeavor.

Writing as Thinking

One of the underlying goals of *The Allyn & Bacon Handbook* is to make you aware of the connections between good writing and clear thinking. Successful writers are problem solvers: they are critical thinkers who pose questions about their own work, spot difficulties that block communication, and devise strategies for resolving those difficulties. A writer who is a problem solver is much like any other competent worker. Think of a musician or an athlete. A guitarist having trouble mastering a song will not practice mindlessly for hours on end but will, rather, pose questions to make practice more focused and productive: "Why am I having trouble? What should I be understanding that I'm not?" The athlete faced with a bad day on the playing field might wonder: "My rhythm was off today—what went wrong?" Athletes especially intent on improving will videotape themselves in action and later study those tapes. To gain competence, a person must think critically about his or her performance, first by gaining distance from the performance and then by posing questions that help pinpoint difficulties and set corrective courses of action. *The Allyn & Bacon Handbook* will help you to analyze your written work and, if need be, take corrective action.

Writing and Reading in the Disciplines

On a typical day you will take courses in and read about a number of different subjects. Traveling from one subject area (or discipline) to the next, you will realize that certain features of good writing are essential to your success as a writer, whatever the context. For instance, all writing must be well organized. At the same time certain features of writing change as you move from one subject area to another. In a literature class you will be asked to interpret certain products of culture—stories, poems, or plays—and to support your interpretations with references to particular lines of text. By contrast, the goal of a biology or chemistry class will be to understand the workings of the natural world. In support of the statements you make, you will present carefully gathered measurements or observations based on your work in a laboratory or field setting. The questions that professors expect you to ask as well as the evidence they expect you to produce in support of arguments will change from discipline to discipline. To succeed as a writer in college, you should understand something of these shifting expectations.

The Allyn & Bacon Handbook will help you master skills that are common to the disciplines, and at the same time will encourage you to appreciate some of the significant ways in which skills of writing, reading, and thinking change as you move from one part of the curriculum to the next. When you are assigned writing in your various courses, you will find it helpful to read, as appropriate, chapter 37 (Writing and Reading in the Humanities), 38 (Writing and Reading in the Social Sciences), and 39 (Writing and Reading in the Sciences). In your composition course, you will likely work through the first six chapters of the book. You will be able to apply the material in these early chapters to writing in *any* context.

How to Use This Handbook

Those who need to find information in a handbook may not know the formal terminology by which certain matters are covered, particularly matters of grammar and punctuation; without knowing terminology, some writers cannot find their way into the book and thus will have trouble using it. How can you gain access to a handbook when you are unfamiliar with its terminology and coverage?

First, be assured that you do not need to memorize rules or definitions. What you will need, though, is to make a modest investment of time—say, one hour. Take an hour to review the various parts of *The Allyn & Bacon Handbook*. Learn how it categorizes information; become familiar with its contents by reading each chapter's introductory paragraph, which defines and discusses the significance of the topics covered. Be sure to locate the appendices as well, including the glossaries of usage and grammar. The Glossary of Usage will help you to use words about which you have questions. (Would you write "I feel *bad*" or "I feel *badly*"? Consult the glossary for this and other such questions.) The Glossary of Terms defines in one convenient place those terms that appear throughout the text but may not be defined with every use. Each term is boldfaced on first use in the text itself.

After your hour-long review, ask your teacher's help in identifying two or three elements of writing that are potentially troubling for you. Read, from start to finish, the pertinent discussion of these subjects. Having done this much, having invested perhaps three or four hours of your time, you will be able to reach for the handbook and know in an approximate way what information it contains, where the information is located, and at what point in the writing process this information is helpful.

You will find in two places the correction symbols your professor might use in commenting on your papers. Look to the inside front cover of the book and you will see each symbol defined and cross-referenced to pertinent discussions. For ease of reference, these same symbols appear on the chapter tabs throughout the book. On the inside back cover you will find a brief table of contents, which provides an overview of the book's organization.

Our first goal as authors was to make *The Allyn & Bacon Handbook* an authoritative, useful guide to writing; but we also wanted the book to be enjoyable. Throughout, we have tried to provide examples of writing that are in themselves interesting. Rarely will you find an example sentence or an exercise that does not draw on some bit of information you are likely to encounter in one or another of your courses. For instance, one exercise is built on a discussion of Newton's use of prisms in studying light; a typical example paragraph relates the process of building a silicon chip. On virtually every page we have tried to give you information about the world that is altogether independent of the point concerning grammar, usage, style, or structure we happen to be making.

As you become a more accomplished writer who makes decisions and solves problems, use *The Allyn & Bacon Handbook* as you would a familiar tool: to help fix what is broken and strengthen what is weak. While this handbook will assist you, it will not provide shortcuts around the writing process. Good writers write, and they revise. The more you know, the more you will want to revise, and the messier your papers will become as you work your way toward final drafts. For this effort you will produce letters, essays, and papers that communicate clearly and that earn the respect of your colleagues. Persevere and you *will* succeed.

Leonard Rosen, *Bentley College*

Laurence Behrens, *University of California, Santa Barbara*

Thinking Critically

CHAPTER 1

Critical Thinking and Reading

O ne of your important tasks in college will be to take your innate problem-solving abilities and to adapt and expand them to academic circumstances, so that you can take on intellectual challenges as a student— and, later, as a professional. Research shows that the insights of talented people in all walks of life—writers, musicians, biologists, mathematicians, business people—tend not to come as bolts from the blue. Creative minds (those that generate new ideas and information) and critical minds (those that are adept at analyzing and evaluating existing knowledge) are developed through hard work. If you would be creative, you must first be willing to evaluate problems and to investigate what others have done to resolve them. Striking a thoughtful pose and then waiting for good ideas to drop from the sky is seldom a good strategy. Creativity is more mundane than this: usually, you will need to work your way through to insights. The good news is that no special genius is necessary to become the sort of student who consistently asks thoughtful questions in class or who explores compelling ideas in papers. What *is* required is a certain attitude in the face of intellectual problems, along with a willingness to read and write in self-aware, strategic ways. As you will come to appreciate, reading and writing are tools that will help you to think creatively and critically.

1a Critical reading: Effort that *saves* time

Much of what you write in college will depend on reading. A professor of contemporary American history may ask you to analyze transcripts of Richard Nixon's conversations in the Oval Office during the Watergate scandal. A professor of biology might ask you to read from Darwin's journals and comment on his methods of observation. In an English literature course you might read Brontë's *Wuthering Heights,* along with five interpretive essays about the novel, and be asked to synthesize this material with your own critical responses. In almost all your courses you will read textbooks. Once you have finished your college career, you will probably read reports and correspondence at your job. And after hours, both in college and at work, there will be the magazines, books, and newspapers that you will read for leisure and information.

As you sit down with a selection in hand, determine its importance and focus your energies accordingly. If you are beginning a research project and are conducting a broad, initial reading to learn about possible topics, read quickly and take only the most preliminary notes (see The Research Process, 33d). If you are reading a newspaper or magazine to keep up with current events, again read quickly, and do not take notes unless some item is of interest for a course. If you read an article or a book in order to write a paper, identify the parts important for your purposes and read with care: take notes, since your reading will provide the basis for later writing. Assigned reading selections for class will prepare you for lectures and discussions; later you may be tested on the material, so once again you should read with care.

Critical, careful reading requires effort. Not every reading needs to be the kind of close, critical reading described in this chapter, but when you need to master the material you read, the strategies offered here will be helpful. A note on terminology: critical reading is also called *close* reading in the sense that you are reading attentively (very near the page, so to speak) and can see what an author is up to. Regardless of its name, critical reading takes more time—perhaps 30 percent more—than casual reading because you will be pausing to reflect on what you read and to integrate new information with what you already know. In the long run, though, critical reading saves time by relieving you from having to reread material in order to reconstruct an author's main points or your response to those points.

1b   Reading to understand a source

To read well you will need to focus your attention. The length and difficulty of an article, the time of day when you read, and your general mood will all affect your attention span. If you have many pages ahead of you, divide the task into manageable sections. Pace yourself. Take a break between sections, and give yourself a realistic goal each time you sit down to read.

1   Before reading: Look ahead

Research shows that people perceive the world in terms of categories: groupings of related items. The name you attach to a category is a general term describing all of the more specific items in the category. For example, you have a category for *trees*. When you encounter some new object that has bark, branches, and leaves, you at once identify it as belonging to the class of things called *trees*. You start looking for other details to see whether they fit this category; that is, you begin to make predictions, as well as observations based on those predictions. Similarly, you can prepare for reading and new learning by thinking about the topic of a selection in terms of an appropriate

1b

category. You do this type of thinking *before* reading; then you make predictions, read, and observe details. Specifically, you can prepare for understanding what you read in two ways:

■ *Preview the selection.* Read the title. Read an article's or chapter's opening paragraphs with care. Then skim the selection, reading all headings and the first sentence of each paragraph. For a book, read the preface (if there is one), the table of contents, and the introductory paragraphs of each chapter. Based on this preview, *predict* what you will learn from the reading. Predictions are important: on the basis of these you will monitor your progress toward understanding.

■ *Pose questions.* Stimulate your thoughts on a topic (further activate the mind's categories) by posing questions: What do I know about the topic? What is my experience with it? What do I think about it? What are my emotional reactions to it?

2   During reading: Make notes and monitor progress

In college, you will read to summarize, evaluate, link sources, and reflect; whatever your purpose, your first goal is to understand the information and ideas that an author presents. All subsequent activities assume that you understand the material you have read. Two activities can help: make content notes to identify main points and to follow their development; and monitor your reading, stopping periodically to ask yourself how well you understand the reading. (For an example, see the practice reading at the end of this section.) A method for making notes follows, but this is by no means the only method available. Try to develop your own shorthand for reading carefully.

Make content notes

■ *Underline* or otherwise highlight important information.

■ *Write notes to summarize* an author's important points. Your brief notes in the margins, together with your highlighting, will make the important information of the passage stand out, both while you are reading and later, while you are reviewing. (This method is appropriate for your own textbook, but not for original library sources.)

■ *Write section headings* if the author does not. Indicate with brief phrases how paragraphs are grouped to form recognizable sections. These notes will help you to follow how the author develops ideas and information.

■ *Highlight difficult passages.* Identify what you do not understand. Highlight unfamiliar vocabulary words whose meanings you cannot infer from context; also highlight ideas you do not fully grasp. (For a demonstration of these techniques, see the practice reading at the end of this section.)

Monitor your progress

1b

An essential element of critical thinking is your ability to stop periodically to monitor your progress toward understanding and to redirect your efforts if necessary. You will monitor your progress as a critical thinker whether you are reading a chapter of a textbook or are playing Sherlock Holmes, solving a mystery. As you read, pause periodically and ask:

- Do I understand?
- How does what I am reading compare with what I expected to read?
- Do I need to redirect my efforts and read differently?

Based on your answers, make *new* predictions about the reading you have yet to complete. Try integrating what you have read with what you already know about the topic. If the fit is not easy—if the selection presents you with ideas and information that you cannot incorporate with what you know—pay special attention. Work to discover the source of your troubles. If the language of the selection is difficult and the ideas are completely new, slow the pace of your reading. Divide the selection into several sections. In any one reading, take one section and reread it until you understand the material—or understand enough to identify what you *do not know*. With difficult subjects, realizing what you do not know marks an excellent beginning in the learning process.

3   After reading: Consolidate information

Capitalize on the attention you have given your reading by spending a few minutes consolidating what you have learned. Focus on the content of the passage and its structure. Understand the pattern by which the author has presented ideas and information. The additional minutes of review that you devote now will crystallize what you have learned and be a real help later on, when you are asked to refer to and *use* the selection, perhaps for an exam or paper.

- *Review your notes.* Flip through the passage and reread your content notes. Clarify them, if necessary, so that they accurately represent the selection. Reread and highlight (with boxes or stars) what you consider to be the author's significant sentences or paragraphs.

- *Organize your questions.* Review the various terms and concepts you have had trouble understanding. Organize your questions concerning vocabulary and content. Use dictionaries; seek out fellow students or a professor to clarify especially difficult points. Even if you do not pursue these questions immediately, you should clarify what you do not understand. Your questions, gathered into one place, such as a journal, will be an excellent place to begin reviewing for an exam.

1b

A Strategy for Critical Reading

Before Reading

Look ahead.
 Preview the selection.
 Pose questions.

During Reading

Make comment notes.
 Underline.
 Write notes to summarize.
 Write section headings.
 Highlight difficult passages.

Monitor your progress.
 Ask: Do I understand?
  How does the material compare with what I predicted?
  Do I need to redirect my efforts?

After Reading

Consolidate information.
 Review your notes and highlight important passages.
 Organize your questions.

---

4   Practice close reading.

Here is an illustration of the notes you can make to aid your understanding of a selection. The paragraphs that follow form the first part of an analysis of the movie classic, *The Wizard of Oz*. Before reading the selection, think about the movie for a bit. What images does it conjure up for you? As a child, what were your reactions to the wicked witch? (Remember the theme music for the witch?) Dr. Harvey Greenberg views the movie as a psychiatrist would, using theories of psychoanalysis to reveal what he believes are the hidden meanings of Dorothy Gale's dream-journey to the Land of Oz. Exercises that follow this example, as well as other examples in this chapter, will continue with a portion of Greenberg's analysis.

In your reading of this selection, feel free to disagree with Greenberg. You may find the essay difficult at times. The selection was chosen precisely because it treats familiar material (a movie you have seen) in unfamiliar ways. To incorporate new information about *The Wizard of Oz*, you will have to stretch the present categories by which you understand the movie and, perhaps, make new ones.

In 1939, MGM delivered two of the all-time movie   1
greats—*Gone With the Wind* and *The Wizard of Oz*. Both pictures
spoke directly to the American heartlands and were instant

box office smashes; the heroine of each is a gutsy teenager (Scarlett O'Hara is sixteen at the start of GWTW, Dorothy Gale about thirteen in *Wizard*) whose serene life is shattered—in Scarlett's case by the hammerblows of fate during the Civil War, in Dorothy's by a concussion sustained during a savage Kansas twister. Each young lady has her mettle fiercely tested in a succession of compelling trials and tribulations: Scarlett emerges from economic and romantic disaster in post-bellum Georgia older and no wiser—bullheaded, scheming as ever. But Dorothy Gale returns from her Oz-dream only a few moments older, and—as we shall see—matured far beyond her years.

[margin note: trials and tribulations make D. wiser]

Dorothy's "trip" is a marvelous metaphor for the psychological journey every adolescent must make. Contrary to popular misconception, psychoanalysts do not believe that the core of personality is fixed, immutable, in earliest childhood. Those years are certainly crucial, but we remain open to change and healing every day of the rest of our lives. At no other stage of development is this more true than adolescence, when the enormous thrust of physical, intellectual and sexual growth literally propels the youngster out of the family nest. Simultaneously, the half-buried conflicts of childhood are resurrected to be resolved or haunt us forever. A poignant and infuriating mixture of regressive and progressive tendencies, the adolescent is exquisitely vulnerable to further emotional injury and terrifically capable of self-repair.

[margin note: 2]

[margin note: Greenberg's point of view]

[margin note: D's psychological journey = journey of every teenager]

With the onset of puberty, the parents, previously viewed from below as supreme authorities, are now confronted at eye level—and who ever enjoyed *that* view? After all, if one admits that one's progenitors are simply human, then the very human wish to be cared for and protected indefinitely must go out the window. This possibility terrifies the adolescent, until it is recognized that realistic power can be acquired over one's affairs, that one is neither omnipotent nor absolutely helpless in shaping personal destiny. Before this saving recognition is firmly rooted within the psyche, the quixotic teenager will alternately badger his folks with outrageous demands to be treated like the ruler of the nursery, or else rake them with withering blasts of contempt and go out questing for substitutes to redeem their "failure," some superhero to worship and imitate.

[margin note: 3]

[margin note: conflicts: teenager balanced between childhood & adulthood]

These substitutes take many shapes, and are traded in with bewildering frequency: rock stars; sports and other media idols; teachers; gang leaders; these are all sought with one idea in mind: the "hero" is put back on the pedestal vacated by the parents, endowed with a special mightiness—athletic, romantic, spiritual, etc.—to remedy the sense of a perceived lack within the self. In other words, *everyone wants a Wizard during adolescence,* but the wanting will cease when the youngster begins to tap his own unique abilities.

[margin note: 4]

[margin note: Hero/wizard becomes substitute for parents]

1b

Forswearing childhood wishes, giving up worn-out at-   5
tachments to one's parents, produces a profound feeling of
loss, a deep sorrow that is an important ingredient in the
periodic "blues" afflicting teenagers so inexplicably. The inner
vacuum may loom as large as outer space, until it is filled by
solid new relationships away from the family. This takes time;
in our particular culture, which grants its youth a great deal of
leeway for experimentation, one may be well into the twenties
before the establishment of satisfying peer relationships and
the consolidation of identity can occur. It is comforting for an
adolescent to have the real parents around during this period
of subtle psychic shifts, to know that one *can* go home again
to touch comfortable emotional bases. But when the youngster
must re-mourn a mother or father *already* lost, the tendency to
cling to an idealized image of the dead parent increases and
the pain of letting go and growing up can be intolerable.

Longing for hero eases when teenager's identity made solid

Reference to Dorothy – an orphan

¶s 1-5 These ¶s: the adolescent from the psychoanalyst's point of view – confusion transforming itself into solid identity

EXERCISE 1

Choose any two reading assignments from one of your courses. The selections should be approximately the same length. Read one assignment without making any notes. Conduct a close, critical reading of the second assignment, following the steps just discussed, remembering that one by-product of a critical reading is a well marked-up selection. In a brief paragraph, compare the advantages and disadvantages of each type of reading.

EXERCISE 2

Conduct a close reading of the next several paragraphs of Harvey Greenberg's analysis. Based on the example of close reading shown previously, make some predictions about the paragraphs that follow. What do you expect Greenberg to say? Underline important sentences, make content notes, jot down your questions, and monitor your progress.

Such is the case with Dorothy Gale, who throughout *The Wizard*   6
of Oz is desperately trying to come to terms with her orphanhood.
Neither the film, nor the L. Frank Baum classic, explains how, when, or
in what sequence her parents died. Permit me to speculate, on the basis
of my analyses of a number of grown-up Dorothies, that her father died
first—probably before her eighth year, thereby impelling her into an
extraordinarily close relationship with her mother. When her mother
passed away, Dorothy suffered an overwhelming spiritual wrenching.
Every sign in *Wizard* points to enormous desolation over parental loss,
more specifically over maternal loss, and terrible dread of its repetition.

It is perverse paradox that the mother, giver of life, is uncon-   7
sciously perceived at the very beginning of life as the destroyer of life.
Insofar as we can fathom the mental activity of the very young child, it
appears that the infantile mind splits the image of mother in twain. The
Good Mother nourishes and cherishes, the Bad Mother abandons and

devastates. This primitive doubling is often found in religion. The Hindus, for instance, believe the Mother-goddess Kali is the source of fertility as well as the harbinger of death and chaos.

In folklore and fairy tale, the Bad Mother is the witch who snares 8 the children strayed from home, then enslaves or murders them. To the unconscious, which thrives on opposites, the Bad Mother kills either by abandonment or binding so close that one strangles in her clutches. (Often, the victim is devoured, the ultimate "closeness"!) The Good Mother is the bounteous fairy godmother, the lovely gossamer queen who makes everything copacetic with a wave of her wand.

Good and Bad Mother are, of course, *one and the same*. The child, 9 given time, growth and understanding, comes to appreciate that Mom isn't abandoning because she cannot be around constantly to gratify every whim. But a host of natural shocks compromise the ability to integrate and reconcile the Good and Bad Mother-images within. Maternal death is the most severe of these: the mother who dies is blamed by the child; she is supremely bad for leaving the child so exposed and vulnerable. *Mutatis mutandis*, the child also believes that it was bad and drove mother away; kids are pathetically prepared to take the burden of death and divorce upon themselves: if I was bad, then if I am good, maybe it will be all right again. . . .

At the dawn of adolescence, the very time she should start to 10 distance herself from Aunt Em and Uncle Henry, the surrogate parents who raised her on their Kansas farm, Dorothy Gale experiences a hurtful reawakening of her fear that these loved ones will be rudely ripped from her, especially her Aunt (Em—M for Mother!). Dorothy is seriously hung up on her ambivalence towards Em: she wants Em to be the Good Mother, but frets that Em will turn Bad, die, go away forever. Dorothy's fear goes hand in hand with her rage—rage at the abandonment by her dead mother, displaced upon her equally guiltless aunt.

The voice of her conscience cries: *How can you be so wicked, so* 11 *ungrateful? It wasn't mother's fault she had to go! Doesn't Em always do her best?* So, to keep her dead mother all good, all giving, and safe from her wrath, Dorothy takes the bad potential of the mothering figure and projects it wholesale into a fantasy of a malevolent persecutrix—a witch!—one can't have any trouble hating. But if this pseudoresolution persists, it must only perpetuate her problem by reinforcing her ambivalence. For it is only when she can view Em and all the grown-ups in her life for who they really are, not as wizards *or* witches, that she will be able to join them as a mature adult herself. The drama of Dorothy's search for her authentic, autonomous self is delightfully played out during her adventures in the Land of Oz.

1c Reading to evaluate a source

Not everything you read will be of equal value: equally interesting, equally accurate, equally well written, or equally useful. You may agree heartily with an author, or you may disagree. As a critical reader, you must therefore read to evaluate—reading, primarily, with two questions in mind: Is what I'm reading dependable? Do I agree with the author? In response to these questions, you will need to distinguish between an author's facts and opinions and between his or her assumptions, or basic views on a topic, and your own. As well, you will need to determine how thoroughly and logically an author has presented the material.

1   Distinguish facts from opinions.

Before you can evaluate a statement, you should know whether it is being presented to you as a fact or an opinion. A **fact** is any statement that can be verified.

Nationwide, the cost of college tuition is rising.

New York lies at a more southerly latitude than Paris.

Andrew Johnson was the seventeenth President of the United States.

The construction of the Suez Canal was completed in 1869.

These are statements that, if challenged, can through appropriate research be established as true or false. As a reader evaluating a selection, you may doubt the accuracy of a fact. You might question how the fact was established, how it was shown to be true. You could challenge the accuracy of the fact or question the method by which it was determined. You might doubt, for instance, that Paris is a more northerly city than New York. The argument is quickly settled by reference to a map. You can generally accept facts when they are common knowledge, capable of being checked in an encyclopedia or other standard references.

But you should, however, question the validity of facts when an author has something to gain from them. For instance, an author affiliated with a drug manufacturer might claim that "ninety percent of the doctors surveyed are confident of Product X's safety." As a critical reader you would want to know how many doctors were surveyed. If the answer were ten, you would have the right to be suspicious. If all the doctors surveyed worked for the pharmaceutical company, you could reject the so-called fact as unworthy of your trust.

An **opinion** is a statement of interpretation and judgment. Opinions are not true or false in the way that a statement of fact will be. Rather, an opinion is more or less well supported. You evaluate an opinion based on the level of support provided for it and on the extent to which you agree with its bearer. If a friend says, "That movie was terrible," this is an opinion. If you ask why and your friend responds, "Because I didn't like it," you are faced with a statement that is unsupported and that makes no real claim on you for a response. Someone who writes that the majority of U.S. space missions should not have astronaut crews is stating an opinion. Someone who refers to the *Challenger* disaster is referring to a fact, a matter of historical record.

Opinions are judgments based on facts. If an opinion is supported by an entire essay, then the author is, in effect, demanding a response from you. Do you agree or not, and on what basis do you agree or disagree?

Identify the strongly stated opinions in what you read, and then write a **comment note:** in the margin, jot down a brief note summarizing your response to the opinion. Agree or disagree. Later, your note will help you crystallize your reactions to the selection.

Distinguishing Fact from Opinion

Fact: a statement, the accuracy of which can be checked
Ask: Is this fact dependable?
      How could I check the accuracy of this fact?

Opinion: an interpretation of facts
Ask: Is this opinion well supported?
      If so, do I agree or disagree? Why?

---

2 Distinguish your assumptions from those of an author.

An **assumption** is a core belief, often unstated, that shapes the way people see the world. When you closely examine an opinion that you read or hear, you find that ultimately it rests on one or more assumptions. Take the following statement: "The majority of U.S. space missions should not have astronaut crews." In trying to understand this opinion, you would want to examine the assumptions of the person who holds it. You might ask: What does this person believe about the world, about space exploration, and about human technology that would lead to such a view? Whenever you read a work, two sets of assumptions come into play: yours and the author's. The extent to which you agree with an author will depend on the extent to which you and the author share assumptions. The following are two assumptions on which the opinion about space exploration might be based:

- Human life is so precious that it should not be risked on space missions.
- The *exploration* of space is important, and exploration can and should be accomplished without astronaut crews.

Assumptions often go unstated. You might read an article in which the author firmly holds an opinion, and yet nowhere in the article will you find the assumptions on which the opinion is based. To be a critical reader, you must understand the assumptions, stated or not, that underlie an author's presentation, as well as your own assumptions with respect to those of an author.

1c

Three types of assumptions merit your special attention:[1] **Value assumptions** are core beliefs about the way the world *should* work. They are based on the intensity with which a person believes in certain fundamental values, such as the dignity of human life, the proper role of government, or the obligation to make moral decisions. The objection that astronauts should not be placed on routine space flights because of the dangers involved is based on the value assumption that human life is too precious to risk for space missions that could be accomplished by machines alone. The more strongly people believe in a value assumption, the more firmly they will hold to opinions based on that assumption.

Descriptive assumptions are accounts of how the world *in fact* works—how people interact, how things get done—accounts that an author assumes to be true. In a discussion of space exploration, an author might observe that it is unrealistic to think that machines could completely replace astronauts, however sensible that might be. This observation would be based on a descriptive assumption, a recognition of how the world of funding large projects has worked in the past and is likely to work in the future: (1) that the public quickly loses interest in machines and gadgets, but not in people—especially heroic types, such as astronauts; and (2) that if the public begins to lose interest in a government-sponsored project, the project is doomed because it will soon lose its funding.

Definitional assumptions are, as the term implies, definitions that an author holds to be true. Consider this statement: *Machines can explore space as well as and in some respects better than humans.* What do the words *as well as and in some respects better than* mean? If an author defines these words one way and you define them another, you and the author are sure to disagree.

Types of Assumptions, Stated and Unstated, to Search for When Reading

1. **Value assumptions:** beliefs about what the world ought to be, about the way people ought to behave.

2. **Descriptive assumptions:** beliefs about the way the world is, about what is true.

3. **Definitional assumptions:** definitions of key terms on which a presentation rests.

In both academic and non-academic contexts, assumptions provide the principles on which decisions are made and opinions developed. Often

---

[1]This classification of assumptions is based on the work of M. Neil Brown and Stuart M. Keeley, *Asking the Right Questions: A Guide to Critical Thinking*, 2nd ed., Englewood Cliffs: Prentice Hall, 1986.

assumptions will be stated directly, as Anna Freud and Dorothy Burlingham do in the introduction to their book, *War and Children*. Note in the first sentence the phrase *is based on the idea,* and see later the phrases *it is generally recognised* and *it is not generally recognised*. Such phrases signal an assumption.

> Work in the War Nurseries is based on the idea that the care and education of young children should not take second place in wartime and should not be reduced to wartime level. Adults can live under emergency conditions and, if necessary, on emergency rations. But the situation in the decisive years of bodily and mental development is entirely different. It has already been generally recognised, and provision has been made accordingly, that the lack of essential foods, vitamins, etc., in early childhood will cause lasting bodily malformation in later years, even if harmful consequences are not immediately apparent. It is not generally recognised that the same is true for the mental development of the child. Whenever certain essential needs are not fulfilled, lasting psychological malformations will be the consequence. These essential elements are: the need for personal attachment, for emotional stability, and for permanency of educational influence.

Both a value assumption and a descriptive assumption are explicitly made in this paragraph. On the basis of these directly stated assumptions, Freud and Burlingham, directors of three wartime nurseries in England during World War II, presented in their book several case studies on children and their reactions to war.

VALUE ASSUMPTION	(what an author wants the world to be like) "The care and education of young children should not take second place in wartime and should not be reduced to wartime level."
DESCRIPTIVE ASSUMPTION	(how an author believes the world works) "Whenever certain needs are not fulfilled, lasting psychological malformations will be the consequence."

Assumptions may not be stated at all, in which case you will need to make inferences.

The basic pattern of inference making

An **inference** is a conclusion you reach that is based on and is consistent with available evidence. An inference about assumptions is developed in a pattern like this:

> I have read one or several facts.
> or
> I have read one or several points of view.

What new statement underlies these facts or points of view—a statement that the author does *not* make explicitly?

1c

In an editorial about U.S. military involvement in some distant part of the world, you might find an author making a statement in which an underlying assumption is *implied*, that is, hidden or not stated directly.

STATEMENT WITH A "HIDDEN" ASSUMPTION

> In no way does a conflict 7,000 miles from our border threaten this nation, and we are therefore not justified in fighting.

The author of this statement is making a definitional assumption concerning the word *justified*. Clearly, the writer has a definition in mind, yet the definition is *implicit*, that is, indirect (as opposed to the *explicit*, or directly stated, assumptions of Freud). Suppose you disagree with this statement concerning the reasons a nation should go to war. To understand your disagreement, compare your assumptions with those of the author. First, clarify the author's definitional assumption.

THE AUTHOR'S IMPLIED ASSUMPTION

> A nation is justified in going to war when hostile forces threaten its borders.

This is the definition of *justified* with which the author is operating, an assumption that underlies the statement about distant threats not justifying a nation's going to war. You, or government officials, might hold a different assumption.

A COMPETING ASSUMPTION

> A nation is justified in going to war when hostile forces threaten its interests anywhere in the world.

Based on this competing assumption, you or a government official *could* justify military involvement based on a threat 7,000 miles from this nation's borders. Having identified competing assumptions, you have established a foundation on which to evaluate the reading. When you disagree with an author, challenge the author's assumptions. If you can show that the assumptions are flawed, then you can argue that all opinions based on them are flawed and should be rejected.

Your ability to identify assumptions, both an author's and your own, will play an important role in your ability to evaluate what you read. Evaluation is based both on your review of facts (their trustworthiness) and on your agreement or disagreement with an author's opinions. Agreement and disagreement turn out to depend on how closely your assumptions match those of an author. Sometimes, authors will state their assumptions directly; other times, you will need to infer them. In either case, you should identify assumptions as part of a close, critical reading.

3   Practice reading to evaluate.

In the example paragraphs that follow, observe how Harvey Greenberg continues with his analysis of *The Wizard of Oz*. Once again, based on your familiarity with the movie—and based *also* on what you have read already of

Greenberg's analysis—make some predictions about what follows. What treatment of Dorothy Gale do you expect to see? How did your prior reading of Greenberg's material go? If you had difficulty, pinpoint the source of the difficulty. Try to make adjustments in your reading strategy . . . and push on.

The opening scenes of *Wizard* are shot in listless black-and-white, rendering the Kansas landscape absolutely prosaic. Dorothy and her little dog, Toto, come hurrying down the road:

> *Dorothy (breathlessly):* She isn't coming yet, Toto—did she hurt you? . . . We'll go tell Uncle Henry and Aunty Em!

12

The farm is bustling: an old incubator has broken down, Em and Henry are laboring desperately to save some newly hatched chicks. Dorothy spills out her story: Toto got into Miss Gulch's garden, chased her cat, Miss Gulch hit him with a rake. Em is abstracted [sic], can't be bothered with such foolishness. Dorothy wanders over to the pigpen where three farmhands—Zeke, Hickory and Hunk—are bickering. They can't spare Dorothy more than off-handed advice. Hunk tells her to use her head—*"it's not made of straw"*—don't walk home near Miss Gulch's house, then Toto won't get the chance to bother her. Zeke tells Dorothy not to "let that old Gulch heifer bother ya—she ain't nothin' ta be afraid of—*have a little courage, that's all!"*

13

[margin note:] Fragments of life in Kansas that show up in D's dream. Scarecrow, lion.

She balances precariously on the railing, falls into the pen and is almost trampled. Zeke pulls her out and collapses with fright at his own bravery. Out of patience, Em rousts the boys back to work, sternly chiding Dorothy to find a place where she won't get into more trouble. Crestfallen, Dorothy muses: "Do you suppose there is such a place, Toto? There must be . . . far, far away . . . behind the moon, beyond the rain . . ." and sings the famous "Over the Rainbow." (This lovely song was almost removed by studio pundits who thought audiences would find it unrealistic to have the heroine singing in a barnyard. So much for creative thinking at the executive level!)

14

Just as the first dream recalled in therapy often encapsulates a person's entire neurosis, just as the first words uttered by a patient coming through the office door often strike the theme of an entire analytic session, the opening sequences of *Wizard* adroitly capture Dorothy's central preoccupation with whether the child within her will be cherished

15

[margin note:] * G's assumption: a movie can be viewed exactly as a patient under psychoanalysis.

1c

or abandoned, and whether the adult stirring within her can dare to leave the nest. Toto, her dog, becomes an extension of herself—perky, mischievous, nosing into things that don't concern him, forever *running away* when he should stay put. He has been bad, and that manifestly bad woman, Miss Gulch, may be coming to take him from the farm. The incubator is broken, the newborn chicks are threatened by the failure of their mechanical womb and Em and Henry are struggling to help them survive. Dorothy herself nearly perishes, and is rescued by an obviously weak, cowardly man. The characters are deftly sketched in: Aunt Em, harried, decisive; Uncle Henry, kind but vague; the three handymen, lovable bumblers all. The farm is a matriarchy, Em obviously rules the roost. Dorothy, rejected by Em and everyone, conjures up a place where happiness springs eternal and the dreams you dare to dream *do* come true.... One recalls the many myths of Utopias overflowing with lavish sustenance granted on nothing more substantial than a wish—the Big Rock Candy Mountain, or the German *Schlaraffenlandt,* where preroasted chickens obligingly walked themselves into your mouth.

Dorothy's fantasies are interrupted as Miss Gulch sweeps in on her bicycle with a court order for Toto, and proclaims that she'll take the whole farm if she doesn't get him. Dorothy's identification with the mutt is underscored: she offers to take Toto's place, and when Miss Gulch refuses, she cries— *"You go away, or I'll bite you myself . . . you wicked old witch!"* Em and Henry put up only token resistance, and Dorothy is forced to part with Toto. Henry is particularly ineffective, mumbling a few inarticulate words of small comfort. *After* Dorothy runs out sobbing, Emily dresses down Miss Gulch, the Good Mother contending with the Bad. Henry stands silent. In Dorothy's realm, as I have suggested, it would seem that power resides on the distaff side.

As Miss Gulch pedals away, the redoubtable Toto leaps out of the basket and scoots back to Dorothy's room. Without a moment's hesitation she packs her things and takes off. Ostensibly, she is worried that Gulch will return to claim her pound of pooch, but actually Toto's escape has given Dorothy the excuse she needed to spread her wings and quit the farm.

16

17

Handwritten margin notes:

D's conflict: can she hold on to the child in her & still become an adult who goes out into the world?

Farm ruled by a woman

Toto: extension of D?

 Good/Bad mother. I don't buy it.

The drama of D's adolescence begins.

EXERCISE 3

Continue your reading of Harvey Greenberg's analysis of *The Wizard of Oz*. As you read, highlight sentences important for your understanding of the passage. Make notes about the content. As well, underline any sentences that you feel bear evaluation. Make notes in which you comment on these sentences. Finally, identify any important assumptions Greenberg seems to be making.

1c

Just down the road, the runaways encounter an engaging old   18
carny faker, toasting hot dogs near his wagon: PROFESSOR MARVEL—AC-CLAIMED BY THE CROWNED HEADS OF EUROPE—LET HIM READ YOUR PAST, PRESENT AND FUTURE!!!" The "Perfessor" easily reads her very obvious plight: "They don't understand you at home . . . they don't appreciate you . . . you want to see other lands—big cities, big mountains, big oceans!" He sits her down before his crystal ball—". . . the same genuine authentic crystal used by the priests of Isis and Osiris in the days of the Pharoahs [sic] of Egypt, in which Cleopatra first saw the approach of Julius Caesar and Mark Antony, and so on. . . ." While Dorothy has her eyes closed, Marvel rummages through her basket, comes up with a picture of Em, and describes a painful vision: "A woman . . . her face is careworn . . . she is crying . . . someone has just about broken her heart . . . someone she loves very much . . . someone she's taken care of in sickness . . . she's putting her hand down on her heart . . . she's dropping down on the bed. . . ."

Rather cruelly (or so I've always thought), Marvel addresses   19
Dorothy's dread both of losing and hurting her aunt. Strangely enough, all too often the child will believe that the sheltering parent can be harmed if *it* grows up and goes away. The more intense the relationship between mother and child, the more the child is likely to be worried about the ill effects the rupture of the charmed partnership will have upon *both* parties. Dorothy is evidently only too willing to believe that her absence can kill Em, so she starts back down the road for home immediately after Marvel's "revelation." From our first glimpse of them, Dorothy and Toto have been ping-ponging back and forth between the safety of the farm and the mysterious, seductive world that lies outside the fence. . . .

Now Dorothy's fear of separation becomes a desperate reality. As   20
she draws near the farm, a tornado twists evilly in the gray distance. The wind rises to an insane howl. Em, screaming hysterically for Dorothy, is dragged down into a storm cellar by the menfolk, and Dorothy is left utterly alone and unprotected. Calling after Em, she stumbles back into her room. A shutter flies loose and smacks her temple; she drops, unconscious upon the bed. Intriguingly, *she* has taken Em's place in Marvel's prophecy, suffering for having made Em suffer, paying for her "badness" by being brought to the brink of death, the ultimate separation.

The house rises dizzily into the twister's spout. Dorothy awakens,   21
peers out the window and sees, whizzing merrily by, an old lady in a

1c

wheelchair (undigested memory of Em's "sickness"?), a cow, two gentlemen rowing a boat, and Miss Gulch, pedaling furiously. In the twinkling of an eye, Gulch metamorphoses into the witch of every child's darkest nightmare, and flies off on a jet-propelled broom, cackling hideously.

The house descends with a sickening jolt. Dorothy opens the door   22
in the sudden stillness and, as a female choir sings wordlessly, she whispers—in what has to be one of the great understatements of cinema—"Toto, I have a feeling we're not in Kansas anymore!"—as she steps into a Technicolor Fairyland.

We are, and we aren't, for this is the landscape of the dream. Freud   23
found that dreams take the characters and events of the preceding day—down to indifferent details—and weave them into a strange, meaningful tapestry. The characters of Kansas reality reappear in the dream Dorothy dreams, while she lies unconscious during the tornado, clad in the costume of her fantasies.

EXERCISE 4

Read the passages that follow. Infer (or restate) the author's assumptions by completing sentences, as directed.

1. [T]his is the landscape of the dream. Freud found that dreams take the characters and events of the preceding day—down to indifferent details— and weave them into a strange, meaningful tapestry. The characters of Kansas reality reappear in the dream Dorothy dreams, while she lies unconscious during the tornado, clad in the costume of her fantasies.

   Restate the author's descriptive assumption.

   Dreams _____ .

2. The democratic ideology that "all men are created equal" has been a central value throughout American history. We are often reminded by politicians, editorial writers, and teachers that ours is a society where the equality of every person is highly valued. This prevailing ideology, however, does not mesh with reality. Slavery was once legal and racial discrimination against Blacks was legal until the 1960s. Women were not permitted to vote until this century. Native Americans had their land taken from them and were then forced to locate on reservations. Japanese Americans were interned against their will during World War II. Even today people often find that their race, gender, and lack of resources place them at risk in the courts and at a disadvantage in the job market. And, at a time when the richest 400 Americans in 1986 had an average net worth of $390 million (*Forbes*, 1986), there were 33 million Americans living below the official poverty line. Clearly, as George Orwell wrote in his classic, *Animal Farm*, "all . . . are equal but some are more equal than others" (1946: 123).

   Infer the author's implicit definitional assumption by completing this sentence.

   A *consistent* social order is one in which _____ .

   Infer the author's implicit value assumption by completing this sentence.

   In America, we should _____ .

1d

3. Of course, I have moments of incredible intimacy with my husband, . . . And they are just moments. I have that kind of intimacy with my women friends all the time, whenever we meet and talk. I feel so hungry for that kind of talk with my husband, and I've told him. He tries. He listens to my problems and soothes my hurts, but he doesn't know how to give back and forth. He's afraid to take off his armor except for a few minutes at a time.

Infer the author's implicit definitional assumption by completing this sentence.

An *intimate* marriage is one in which _____ .

1d   Reading to infer relationships among sources

You have seen in the discussion on evaluating sources that you can make inferences based on an individual reading (see 1c-2). When writing essays, term papers, experimental reports, and proposals, you often face the challenge of inferring relationships among several sources. Assume you have read five assigned articles on the topic of marriage. Your professor will expect you to be able to state how these sources are related; further, your professor will expect you to develop your own position on the topic. If you are asked to write about the topic, *your* position will predominate, and you will use information from the five sources in order to support and develop the points that you wish to make. (See Writing a Synthesis: A Paper Based on Sources, 2d.)

You first need to know what individual sources say about a topic and how the sources are related. Identification of relationships involves special skills in critical thinking. All successful efforts begin with your ability to understand the ideas and information of the individual essays, articles, chapters, or books that you have read. Obviously, it is impossible to relate what is not well understood; however, if you can make good content notes for each reading selection, you will be able to lay sources on a table before you and infer relationships among them. The thinking that you do will be developed in several steps.

1   Follow a strategy for making inferences among sources.

1. *Read multiple sources on one topic.* It is very likely that the authors will have different observations to make. Because you are working with the different sources, you are in a unique position to draw relationships among them.

2. *Subdivide the topic into parts and give each a brief title.* We will call the topic that the several authors discuss X. What are all the parts, or the subdivisions, of X that they discuss? List the separate parts on a sheet of paper, giving each a brief title. Leave room to make notes. In the

1d

example shown in Exercise 5, five authors discuss the topic of *marriage*. The parts of this topic that are discussed include *intimacy, hostility,* and *satisfaction.* Several authors also *define* marriage. Four words, then, become part "titles."

3. *Write cross-references for each part.* For each subdivision of the topic, list *specific* page references to whichever sources discuss that part. This task is called **cross-referencing.** Once you have cross-referenced each of the topic's parts, you will have created an index to your reading selections.

4. *Summarize author's information or ideas about each part.* Now that you have generated cross-references that show you which authors discuss which parts of topic *X*, take up one part at a time and reread all passages you have cross-referenced. On a clean sheet of paper, make notes—something like this:

    p.____(Author 1):

Following each page reference, write a note that summarizes what the author has written about this one part of topic *X*.

5. *Infer relationships among reading selections.* Study your notes and make inferences among sources for each part of the topic. Here are several inferences that you might consider:

Comparison: One author *agrees* with another.

Contrast: One author *disagrees* with another.

Example: Material in one source *illustrates* a statement in another.

Definition: Material from several sources, considered together, may help you *define* or redefine a term.

Cause and effect: Material from one source may allow you to *explain directly* why certain events occur in other sources.

Personal response: You find yourself agreeing or disagreeing with points made in one or more sources. Ask yourself *why* and then develop an answer by referring to specific passages of one or more selections.

2   Read multiple sources on a topic.

Identifying relationships among lengthy selections may seem a formidable task. Realize, though, that as a critical reader you do not make relationships among whole articles, chapters of books, or entire books; you make relationships among *specific parts* of these works. In the same way, as a strategically minded writer, you never write an entire essay or paper at any one time; you write *parts*. The key to your success as a critical reader and writer lies in your ability to divide the treatment of a topic into parts. When reading multiple sources, you will soon discover that other authors discuss the same parts of the topic, although they may use different terms to do so. Once you begin to make cross-references and generate your own private index to your reading selections, you will become a critical reader.

EXERCISE 5

Five brief selections follow, all on the general topic of marriage. Read each one closely, following the method described in section 1b. (See the box on page 6.) Underline or otherwise highlight words, phrases, and sentences important to understanding the selections. Make notes in the margins. Also, write down any questions you have concerning vocabulary or content.

1d

1. The popular notion about marriage and love is that they are synonymous, that they spring from the same motives, and cover the same human needs. Like most popular notions this also rests not on actual facts, but on superstition.

   Marriage and love have nothing in common; they are as far apart as the poles; are, in fact, antagonistic to each other. No doubt some marriages have been the result of love. Not, however, because love could assert itself only in marriage; much rather is it because few people can completely outgrow a convention. There are today large numbers of men and women to whom marriage is naught but a farce, but who submit to it for the sake of public opinion. At any rate, while it is true that some marriages are based on love, and while it is equally true that some love continues in married life, I maintain that it does so regardless of marriage, and not because of it.

   —EMMA GOLDMAN

2. Of course, I have moments of incredible intimacy with my husband, . . . And they are just moments. I have that kind of intimacy with my women friends all the time, whenever we meet and talk. I feel so hungry for that kind of talk with my husband, and I've told him. He tries. He listens to my problems and soothes my hurts, but he doesn't know how to give back and forth. He's afraid to take off his armor except for a few minutes at a time.

   —ANONYMOUS

3. All happy families resemble one another, but each unhappy family is unhappy in its own way.

   Everything was upset in the Oblonskys' house. The wife had discovered an intrigue between her husband and their former French governess, and declared that she would not continue to live under the same roof with him. This state of things had now lasted for three days, and not only the husband and his wife but the rest of the family and the whole household suffered from it. They all felt that there was no sense in their living together, and that any group of people who had met together by chance at an inn would have had more in common than they.   —LEO TOLSTOY

4. Marriage [is] a socially recognized and approved union between two individuals of the opposite sex made with the expectation of permanence and usually with the aim of producing offspring. There are societies that recognize other kinds of unions: the Shiite Muslims of Iran and Afghanistan permit temporary marriages under certain circumstances; . . . Although many societies permit divorce, all regard permanence as the ideal. In some societies a union is not given the status of marriage until the birth of a child, and in some societies failure to produce a child is considered valid grounds for divorce, especially if one of the partners is opposed to having children.

   —ELIZABETH E. BACON

1d

5. [The] mutual inward moulding of husband and wife, this determined effort to perfect each other, can in a very real sense . . . be the chief reason and purpose of matrimony, provided matrimony be looked at not in the restricted sense as instituted for the proper conception and education of the child, but more widely as the blending of life as a whole and the mutual interchange and sharing thereof.

By this same love it is necessary that all the other rights and duties of the marriage state be regulated as the words of the Apostle: "Let the husband render the debt to the wife, and the wife also in like manner to the husband, not only a law of justice, but of charity."

—Pope Pius XI

3 Divide the topic into parts.

Your ability to divide a topic into parts depends *entirely* on the quality of your reading. If you read selections with care and make notes in the margins, you can depend on those notes when the time comes to relate the sources to one another. The five brief selections concern the topic of marriage. If you have read closely, you have seen that the authors discuss different parts, or aspects, of marriage: *intimacy, hostility, satisfaction/dissatisfaction,* and *definitions.* It is very likely that different readers will subdivide a topic differently, based on a reading of their sources. You might be able to suggest a fifth or sixth subdivision of the topic. As long as you can make subdivisions and create cross-references for them, you should be able to infer relationships among your sources. Once you have divided a topic into constituent parts, you will discover that not every author discusses every part.

4 Cross-reference each part and summarize.

In actual course work, your reading selections will come from different journals, newspapers, and books—and cross-referencing should prove a useful technique. Assume that you have identified parts of your topic (marriage) and have listed page numbers from your sources that relate to each part. Following the page references, you would write a brief note summarizing the author's information or ideas, as illustrated next.

EXERCISE 6

Based on your close reading of the selections in Exercise 5, complete the note-making started here. If you find that notes you wish to make are appropriate for more than one category, make two entries.

Intimacy/love in marriage

Goldman: "Marriage and love have nothing in common"

Anonymous: intimacy in marriage is partial; does not have with husband what she has with friends.

Tolstoy:

Bacon:

Pius XI:

Hostility in/farce of marriage

Goldman: many marriages a farce—only reason marriage survives is that "few people can completely outgrow a convention"

Tolstoy:

Satisfaction/dissatisfaction in marriage

Tolstoy: Everyone in the Oblonsky household unhappy

Anonymous:

Pius XI:

Definition of marriage

Goldman: marriage is a social convention

Bacon:

Pius XI:

1d

5   **Identify relationships among ideas and information presented in the readings.**

Based on your close reading of each selection and on your cross-references and notes, you should be able to establish relationships among the readings. Five general questions should get you started.

EXERCISE 7

Develop an answer for each specific question concerning the readings on marriage.

1. Which authors agree?

   How do Anonymous and Pope Pius XI agree, concerning what marriage is or should be? (You might want to refer to an answer in Exercise 4, in which you made an inference concerning the thoughts of this writer.)

   In what ways do Emma Goldman and Elizabeth Bacon agree on a definition of marriage?

2. Which authors disagree?

   Who obviously disagrees about the definition of marriage? On what points do they disagree?

3. Are there any examples in one source of statements made in another?

   Which author provides an example of what Emma Goldman calls the "farce" of marriage?

   Pius XI offers an ideal definition of marriage in which partners seek to "perfect each other." Two sources offer *negative* examples of this ideal. Which sources are they—and how do the two negative examples differ?

4. Can you offer any definitions?

   How can you define the term *intimacy,* based on your reading?

   Longing is a word that suggests an intense emotional desire for something unattainable or, for the moment, not present. To which reading(s) does the term *longing* apply?

1e

5. Are any readings related by cause and effect?

Re-examine three readings: Pius XI, who sets out an ideal for marriage; Tolstoy, who shows a marriage fallen apart; and Anonymous, who reveals a marriage under strain. Based on these selections, make a cause-and-effect statement about one way in which a marriage can dissolve.

1e   Reading to reflect on a source

Reading often prompts personal reflection. Professors will assign stories, poems, reports, articles, and films that challenge you personally and extend the way you think about a subject. Reading to reflect can be an intimate, moving experience. You might find yourself shaken or made joyful or pensive by what you read. Your reactions are of great value, for by virtue of them you enter the circle of other people who have thought hard about life and have committed their thoughts to paper. It is as if when you read and are moved by another's writing, the spirit of that person (living or dead) stirs: the author's ideas have come alive and made a connection with you over time and space. Posing the following questions will not guarantee that you will be moved by a reading. Only you have control over that by remaining open, even vulnerable, to what others write. These questions can, however, help you to articulate how and why a reading has moved you.

Questions for reflective reading

What do I feel when reading this material?

Why do I feel this way?

What are the implications, for me, in reading this material? How am I changed or how could I imagine myself changing?

How relevant is what the author writes about to my own experience?

Why is this material important to me?

EXERCISE 8

Following is a letter written by Major Sullivan Ballou to his wife, Sarah, one week before he was killed at the first Battle of Bull Run. This letter, read during the acclaimed documentary *The Civil War*, prompted thousands of calls to public television stations across the country. What is your response? Read and reflect on the letter; use any of the previously given questions to stimulate your thinking; and write out your thoughts in a few paragraphs.

July 14, 1861
Camp Clark, Washington
My very dear Sarah:

The indications are very strong that we shall move in a few days—perhaps tomorrow. Lest I should not be able to write again, I feel

1e

impelled to write a few lines that may fall under your eye when I shall be no more.

I have no misgivings about, or lack of confidence in, the cause in which I am engaged, and my courage does not halt or falter. I know how strongly American Civilization now leans on the triumph of the Government, and how great a debt we owe to those who went before us through the blood and sufferings of the Revolution. And I am willing—perfectly willing—to lay down all my joys in this life, to help maintain this Government, and to pay that debt . . .

Sarah, my love for you is deathless, it seems to bind me with mighty cables that nothing but Omnipotence could break; and yet my love of Country comes over me like a strong wind and bears me unresistibly on with all these chains to the battle field.

The memories of the blissful moments I have spent with you come creeping over me, and I feel most gratified to God and to you that I have enjoyed them so long. And hard it is for me to give them up and burn to ashes the hopes of future years, when, God willing, we might still have lived and loved together, and seen our sons grown up to honorable manhood around us. I have, I know, but few and small claims upon Divine Providence, but something whispers to me—perhaps it is the wafted prayer of my little Edgar, that I shall return to my loved ones unharmed. If I do not, my dear Sarah, never forget how much I love you, and when my last breath escapes me on the battle field, it will whisper your name. Forgive my many faults, and the many pains I have caused you. How thoughtless and foolish I have often times been! How gladly would I wash out with my tears every little spot upon your happiness . . .

But, O Sarah! If the dead can come back to this earth and the unseen around those they loved, I shall always be near you; in the gladdest days and in the darkest nights . . . always, always, and if there be a soft breeze upon your cheek, it shall be my breath, as the cool air fans your throbbing temple, it shall be my spirit passing by. Sarah, do not mourn me dead; think I am gone and wait for thee, for we shall meet again.

CHAPTER 2

Critical Thinking and Writing

Four forms of writing and thinking will recur throughout your academic career: summary, evaluation, analysis, and synthesis. A **summary** provides a brief, neutral restatement of a source and answers the question: What are the main points of the author's discussion? An **evaluation** reviews a source and answers the question: How effective is this author's presentation? An **analysis** uses a clearly defined set of principles to investigate something and is used to answer many questions, among them: How does X (a particular topic) work? What does X mean? A **synthesis** draws material from several sources into a single presentation. It, too, is used to answer many questions, for instance: What are my views on a topic? What views do various authors have on this topic? How can I weave together my views with those of the authors?

The patterns of writing discussed in this chapter will vary somewhat depending on the courses you take, but the logical form of each pattern will remain consistent: a summary requires the same skills in critical thinking whether you are summarizing a source in philosophy or physics; an evaluation is, regardless of discipline, a critical assessment of another's work; an analysis retains its investigative character whether you are applying a set of principles from economics or literary theory; and a synthesis is always a drawing together of source materials, based on a specific purpose that you have defined. Because you will use them so often, these forms of academic writing and thinking deserve careful attention.

2a Writing a summary

Summary writing is a skill fundamental to working with written sources. To write a summary, you must understand the source you are reading. The best way to ensure understanding is to read "closely." (See 1b for a review of strategies for close reading.) Before commenting on or otherwise making use of a reading, you are obligated to restate without comment (that is, neutrally) the main points of that reading. A summary focuses on the source material, *not* on your reactions to it. Thus, writing summaries is an excellent tool for learning in that it can demonstrate both to you and to professors your level of understanding. As you will discover, the summary is far more than an instructional tool: like any complex piece of writing, it calls for you to make decisions and to plan, draft, and revise. While useful in itself, a summary also appears as a key element in evaluating, analyzing, and synthesizing source materials. The following are some assignments that call for summary preparation.

2a

MATHEMATICS   Read the article "Structuring Mathematical Proofs," by Uri Leron (*The American Mathematical Monthly*, 90, March 1983: 174–185). In two to four typed pages, summarize the concept of linear proof, giving one good example from the course.

FILM STUDIES   Summarize Harvey Greenberg's discussion of *The Wizard of Oz*.

SOCIAL PSYCHOLOGY   Write a summary of your textbook's discussion of the "realistic conflict theory." Make sure that you address the theory's explanation of prejudice as an intergroup conflict.

1 Challenges in writing a summary

The main challenge of writing a summary is to identify the main points of a presentation and thus distinguish them from the less important ones. If a piece is at all well written, its principal purpose will be clear. The author may identify this purpose for you in the title and will almost certainly state it directly in the opening or closing paragraphs. Distinguishing important from unimportant supporting information is more difficult, however, for your ability to make such distinctions depends largely on your understanding of the topic. Reading and summarizing are far easier when you are familiar with a topic.

Still, it is possible to identify a selection's main points even if a topic is new to you: First, you will need to read closely (as discussed in 1b). In your reading, search for repeated phrases and terms, a sure sign that these words and the concepts associated with them are important and should find their way into your summary. Next, identify all examples in the selection and ask of each: what point is being illustrated here? Points that an author thinks are worthy of illustrating are usually important enough to include in your summary. A third strategy is to identify the author's thesis. (A *thesis*, an author's one-sentence summary of his or her work, crystallizes the main purposes of a reading and suggests its main parts.) Read the thesis carefully and consider what points the author is obligating himself to discuss. Then look to the selection for signs of this discussion. Expect the author to devote a group of paragraphs, or one section, to the development of a single important point. Any well-structured reading will be developed in sections, and the choice of these sections will be determined by the thesis. If you can identify

2a

the major sections and match them with the thesis, you can be confident of having identified the reading's main points.

If these three strategies fail, try thinking about the selection in terms of the questions familiar to reporters: *who, what, when, where, how,* and *why*. Responding to these questions will certainly give you a good start toward writing a competent summary.

Writing a Summary

■ Read your source material with care, putting into practice strategies discussed in 1b, "Reading to understand a source."

■ Based on the sentences you have highlighted and the marginal notes you have made, restate the author's main point, in your own words.

■ For relatively brief selections of six to ten pages, write a one- or two-sentence summary, a restatement in your own words of every paragraph.

If the selection is long:

■ Identify sections of the passage. For each section, write a two- or three-sentence summary. (This technique also works with brief passages.)

■ Join your paragraph summaries with your summary of the main point.

■ Revise for clarity and style. Provide transitions where needed.

---

2   Building a summary

The techniques for writing a summary can now be applied to the extended example in chapter 1, Dr. Harvey Greenberg's analysis of *The Wizard of Oz*. Specifically, see pages 6–8, the first example of close reading. There you will see sentences underlined and notes placed in the margin. One test of a close reading is your ability to return to a selection days or weeks after having read it and to understand the main thrust of the author's presentation without rereading the entire piece. Thoughtful underlining and note making will help in this regard. As you will see, each sentence in the summary is an extension of a note originally made in the margin.

> Begin with a restatement of the author's main point, in your own words.

Harvey Greenberg psychoanalyzes *The Wizard of Oz* and draws a parallel between Dorothy Gale's trip to Oz and the journey of every adolescent into adulthood.

2a

Write a one- or two-sentence summary of every paragraph.

¶1 Dorothy Gale in *The Wizard of Oz* undergoes a trial that, in just a short span of dream time, makes her older and wiser.

¶2 *Conflict* is a key to understanding the film: adolescence is a time of emotional, sexual, and intellectual turmoil during which teenagers are vulnerable to hurt and open to healing.

¶3 Adolescents want to stay safely at home, with reassuring and all-powerful parents. Adolescents realize their parents have flaws.

¶4 Adolescents belittle or reject their parents and look for heroes or wizards who have exceptional qualities and who can replace the parents as idols worth imitating.

¶5 Letting go of childhood and dependence on parents is profoundly painful to adolescents. In order to emerge as an adult with a solid identity, an adolescent must form relationships outside of the family. For Dorothy Gale, an orphan, letting go of childhood to become an adult is especially painful.

Join your paragraph summaries with your summary of the main point.

(In the following example of a student summary, revisions for clarity and style, along with transitions, are underlined.)

In "The Wizard of Oz—Little Girl Lost—and Found," Harvey Greenberg psychoanalyzes the 1939 film classic and draws a parallel between Dorothy Gale's trip to Oz and the journey of every adolescent into adulthood. Greenberg bases his interpretation of the film on the notion of conflict. Adolescence is a time of emotional, sexual, and intellectual conflict during which teenagers are both vulnerable to hurt and open to healing. On the one hand, adolescents want to stay safely at home, with reassuring and all-powerful parents; on the other, adolescents realize their parents have flaws and are capable of being rejected or belittled. Once they knock parents off the pedestal, teenagers look for "wizards" who have exceptional qualities and can replace parents as models. Abandoning childhood dependence on parents is profoundly painful to an adolescent, who must form relationships outside of the family in order to emerge with a solid adult identity. For Dorothy Gale, particularly because she is an orphan, abandoning childhood and becoming an adult is painful in that she idealizes her dead parents. Nonetheless, Dorothy emerges from her trial "matured far beyond her years."

—FELICIA ARGUILAR

Like any writing, summary writing occurs in stages: planning, writing, and revising. Placed together in the actual summary, the one- and two-sentence paragraph summaries presented problems with style and emphasis. With respect to style, the word *adolescent* appeared far too many times. In addition, sentences were choppy and somewhat repetitive. In the second draft, emphasis was given to the word *conflict* with the parallel phrasings *on the one hand* and *on the other.* You will also have noticed that the summary of paragraph 1 was shifted to the end of the overall summary to provide greater emphasis. The transitional *nonetheless* helps the reader to see that even though Dorothy's relinquishing of childhood was made especially painful because of orphanhood, she rallied and "matured far beyond her years." This last quotation, which did not appear in the sentence summary, added emphasis as well.

Writing a summary is more than merely stitching together paragraph- or section-summaries. Summary writing involves *decision making:* understanding the material read, thinking of a reader's needs, and manipulating sentences—all the while remaining faithful to information in the source. For a more detailed discussion of decisions involved in the writing process, see chapter 3.

EXERCISE 1

Write a summary of the remaining sections of Harvey Greenberg's analysis of *The Wizard of Oz.* Three additional sections of the article appear in chapter 1: in Exercise 2, pages 8–9; in the example reading for evaluation, pages 15–16; and in Exercise 3, pages 17–18. If you have completed the exercises, you will have written notes and highlighted sentences, which will greatly help your preparations for summary.

2b Writing an evaluation

Consider the following typical college assignments:

SOCIOLOGY — Write a review of Christopher Lasch's *Culture of Narcissism.*

BUSINESS ETHICS — In "Good Riddance to Corporate America," Mary Shea argues that highly credentialed women MBAs are beginning to quit corporate America because of its "essential emptiness." How convinced are you by Shea's argument?

HISTORY — In "Everyman His Own Historian," Carl L. Becker argues for a definition of history as "the memory of things said and done." Based on your reading in this course, evaluate Becker's definition.

PHYSICS — Write a review of *Surely You're Joking, Mr. Feynman!*

2b

These assignments call for writers to evaluate sources. Writing an evaluation formalizes the process of *reading* to evaluate. (See the discussion at 1b and 1c.) When evaluating a source, you are interested in two issues: determining how dependable the author's presentation is and expressing the extent to which you agree with the author. *Dependable* is a subjective term, of course: what you reject as superficial, others will accept as adequate, and vice versa. For this reason you will need to be as clear as possible about the *criteria*, or standards, you use to evaluate a source. Agreement and disagreement depend on the extent to which you and the author share assumptions (see 1c-2). In an evaluation, state assumptions when you can: yours and those of the author. Clarifying assumptions will explain the *basis* for agreement or disagreement.

To prepare for an evaluation, make two sets of notes, which you can organize as answers to these questions: How dependable is this author's presentation? and Do I agree with this author? Making two sets of notes allows you to evaluate a presentation on its merits and, as a separate matter, to agree or disagree with the author's views.

1 Making preparatory notes

Your opinions aside for the moment, how good a job has the author done in presenting material? There are several criteria, or standards, to bear in mind when making this judgment.

ACCURACY	Are the author's facts accurate?
DEFINITIONS	Have terms important to the discussion been clearly defined—and if not, has lack of definition confused matters?
LOGIC	Has the author adhered to standards of logic? Is the presentation coherent? Is it well focused and consistent?
DEVELOPMENT	Does each part of the presentation seem well developed, satisfying to you in the extent of its treatment? Is each main point adequately illustrated and supported with evidence?
FAIRNESS	If the issue discussed is controversial, has the author represented opposing points of view fairly?

In most cases, these criteria should get you started on evaluating a source. Remember that in this set of notes, you are evaluating *only* the effectiveness of a presentation, not your agreement or disagreement.

2 Identifying and responding to an author's assumptions

A well-written presentation notwithstanding, you may disagree with an author about assumptions. If you accept that a work of art can be psychoanalyzed since it is the expression of a human mind, which can also be psychoanalyzed, then you will have little trouble accepting Harvey Greenberg's interpretation of Dorothy Gale's dream-journey to Oz (see chapter 1, Exercise 2). You might disagree with one or another of Greenberg's specific interpretations: for example, concerning Dorothy's splitting of Aunt Em into a Good Mother and Bad Mother. At the same time, you might enthusiastically endorse his analysis that Dorothy's story *is* a metaphor for every adolescent's journey into adulthood. Of course, if you reject the value of psychoanalysis for people as well as for works of art, you will not have much use for Harvey Greenberg's work-up of *The Wizard of Oz.* It is important, therefore, that you understand both your assumptions concerning a topic and those of the author as you conduct your reading and plan your evaluation. See the discussion at 1c-2.

As part of your preparations for writing an evaluation, list the author's opinions concerning a topic and then note your reactions, making a special effort to understand both your assumptions and those of the author. Here is a format you might consider:

Author's opinion:

Assumption underlying the opinion:

My reaction:

Assumption underlying my reaction:

3 Writing your evaluation

Once you have prepared for writing an evaluation by making notes, review your material and try to develop an overall impression of the reading. In writing an evaluation, you will have space enough to review at least two, but probably not more than four or five, aspects of an author's work. Therefore, you must be selective in the points you choose to evaluate. Review your notes concerning quality of the presentation and extent of your agreement with the author; then select the points that will best support your overall impression of the reading. As with any piece of formal writing, plan your evaluation with care. If you expect to discuss three points concerning a selection, do so in a particular order, for good reasons. Readers will expect a logical, well-developed discussion.

An evaluation will consist typically of five parts, as presented in the box. These parts need not, and probably will not, be single paragraphs. Evaluations will vary greatly in length, depending on your occasion for writing. As with the writing of any documents, drafting and revising an evaluation will be a messy business. The steps presented here may look neat enough in their sequential order, but the actual writing will come as a result of multiple drafts in which you refine your ideas as you refine your writing.

2b

Writing an Evaluation

- Introduce the topic and author: one paragraph.

    One sentence in the introduction
    should hint at your general impression
    of the piece.

- Summarize the author's work: one to three paragraphs.

    If brief, the summary can be joined to the
    introduction.

- Briefly survey the key points in the author's work that you will evaluate:
  one paragraph.

- Identify key points in the author's presentation; discuss each in detail:
  three to six paragraphs.

    If you are evaluating the quality of the author's presentation, state
    your criteria for evaluation explicitly; if you are agreeing or dis-
    agreeing with opinions, try to identify assumptions (yours and the
    author's) underlying these.

- Conclude with your overall assessment of the author's work.

The order of parts in the written evaluation may not match the actual order of writing. For instance, many writers would be unable to write the third section, a survey of the main points they will discuss, without first having evaluated the author's key points.

4   Practicing writing evaluations

Harvey Greenberg's analysis of *The Wizard of Oz* provides an opportunity to practice evaluating a source. Both preparatory notes and the actual evaluation are begun here, and you will be asked to complete the effort. The first order of business is to prepare notes for an evaluation, based on a careful *re*reading of the selection. Read once to follow the presentation and to understand your general, if vague, reactions to it. Read a second time to focus your reactions, bearing two questions in mind: How dependable is the author's presentation? Do I agree with the author?

How dependable is the author's presentation?

LOGIC

Greenberg is methodical in his treatment of *The Wizard of Oz*. After introducing the movie in ¶1, he sets out in ¶s 2–5 to establish the principles on the basis of which he will later interpret the movie. Every interpretation he subsequently offers is carefully based on principles of psychoanalysis. (He

2b

does not define these principles, but this is not a problem—see Definition next.) Greenberg's organization is logical and tight. Having set the terms by which he will conduct his analysis, he works through the scenes of the movie in order, interweaving a summary of the Oz tale with his psychoanalytic insights. Greenberg has earned the right to his interpretation of the movie.

DEFINITION

Greenberg never defines psychoanalysis—but then he does not need to. The principles are well known (even if not to individual readers) and are a matter of public record.

DEVELOPMENT/FAIRNESS

Greenberg stays within the boundaries of psychoanalysis to develop the points he makes. Each point gets attention, especially his interpretation of Aunt Em being split into the Good Mother and Bad Mother. He does not offer alternative views, which seems a conscious choice, not an oversight. This will be a psychoanalytic interpretation of *The Wizard of Oz*. For other interpretations, he seems to say, go to other sources. He is challenging the reader, in effect, to agree or not.

Do I agree with the author?

AUTHOR'S OPINION #1

Dorothy Gale's dream-journey in *The Wizard of Oz* is a metaphor for the psychological journey every adolescent makes into adulthood.

AUTHOR'S ASSUMPTION

Greenberg assumes that the principles of psychoanalysis can be applied to the interpretation of a movie.

MY REACTION

Why not? Psychoanalysis certainly gives him the tools to write intelligently about the movie. He takes the movie seriously and reveals things not in plain view (just as psychoanalysis shows patients aspects of themselves they never consciously acknowledge).

MY ASSUMPTION

I can accept a set of principles that, applied to a movie, can make its meaning more accessible.

AUTHOR'S OPINION #2

Dorothy unconsciously divides Aunt Em into a Good Mother and a Bad Mother. This conflict is the primary one that gets resolved in Dorothy's dream-journey to Oz. "[O]nly when she can view Em and all the grown-ups in her life for who they really are, not as wizards *or* witches, [will she] be able to join them as a mature adult herself." (¶11)

AUTHOR'S ASSUMPTION

This "primitive doubling" (¶7) is an established psychological fact, demonstrated in "the mental activity of the very young child" and in religion.

MY OPINION

I don't buy it. Greenberg's general interpretation of *The Wizard of Oz* as a story of an adolescent emerging through conflict into adulthood does help me make sense of the movie. But the analysis of Dorothy's splitting of Em into the Good Mother and Bad Mother seems way too obscure for me. The movie as a story of adolescent conflict can still work without this "primitive doubling."

MY ASSUMPTION

I don't accept as "key" any argument that can be removed from a presentation and still leave the major points intact.

2b

EXERCISE 2

Identify one opinion, other than the one just expressed, that you have responded to in Harvey Greenberg's article. Write notes to prepare yourself for an evaluation, following the format used thus far:

Author's opinion:

Author's assumption:

My opinion:

My assumption:

Also, make one comment regarding the quality of Greenberg's presentation. As above, clearly state your criterion for evaluation (definition, development, etc.) before commenting.

Here is the beginning of an evaluation of Greenberg's article on *The Wizard of Oz,* written by student Felicia Arguilar. The last part of Felicia's evaluation has been deleted so that you can add your own observations (in Exercise 3).

```
              Evaluation of Harvey Greenberg's

        "The Wizard of Oz--Little Girl Lost--and Found"

      Virtually everyone in America can recall terror as

a child in watching Margaret Hamilton's Wicked Witch

threaten Dorothy Gale in The Wizard of Oz. Even the        Introduction

witch's theme music--Da-da Da-da da-Dah-da--conjures

scenes of flying monkeys and scarecrows on fire. Ameri-

cans share a culture, one of the pillars of which is

movie going. Of the tens of thousands of movies made in

this century, only a handful have been seen by most ev-

eryone. Without question, The Wizard of Oz is one such

movie.
```

2b

What makes Wizard a classic? In a psychoanalysis of
the movie (which he subtitles "Little Girl Lost--and
Found"), Harvey Greenberg offers some answers. Greenberg
finds Dorothy Gale's trip to Oz a "metaphor for the psychological journey every adolescent must make." At the
heart of this journey lies the notion of conflict. Adolescence, says Greenberg, is a time of emotional, sexual, and intellectual conflict during which teenagers
are both vulnerable to hurt and open to healing. On the
one hand, adolescents want to stay safely at home, with
reassuring and all-powerful parents; on the other, adolescents realize their parents have flaws and are capable of being rejected or belittled. Once they knock
parents off the pedestal, teenagers look for "wizards"
who have exceptional qualities and can replace parents
as models. Abandoning childhood dependence on parents is
profoundly painful to an adolescent, who must form relationships outside of the family in order to emerge with
a solid adult identity. For Dorothy Gale, particularly
because she is an orphan, abandoning childhood and becoming an adult is painful in that she idealizes her dead
parents. Nonetheless, Dorothy emerges from her trial "matured far beyond her years."

Certainly the tools of psychoanalysis help
Greenberg to explain The Wizard of Oz, and his main
point rings true: that Dorothy's story is a metaphor for
every adolescent's difficult journey through conflict
and into adulthood. And if Wizard is a metaphor, then unconsciously we watch our own emergence into adulthood as
we watch Dorothy work her way down the yellow brick road
to Oz and, eventually, home. Without question, Greenberg
makes his point that the story is psychologically rich.
Less convincing, however, is his attempt to anchor his
analysis of the movie in Dorothy's conflicts with her
dead mother. This effort seems strained, at least to a
non-psychiatrist, and appears in no way crucial to the
more general point that the Wizard is a rich psychological tale.

> Summary

> Survey of key
> points to be
> made in evalu-
> ation

36

[You will add a sentence here, anticipating *your* contributions to the evaluation. See Exercise 3.]

Any adolescent, or anyone who can recall adolescence, well knows that conflict is one word that describes those years. Teenagers, after all, are on their way to becoming adults: they are in the process of leaving home, psychologically if not physically, to discover their place in the world not as their parents' children but as their own adult selves. Part of the journey inevitably involves rejecting parents and looking toward some substitute figure of authority. Harvey Greenberg makes this general pattern of adolescent conflict a central feature of his interpretation of Wizard. Because we as readers of his article and viewers of the movie have lived through our own conflicts, his interpretation of Dorothy's conflict rings true. The language of psychoanalysis seems to unlock the movie and make it more intelligible: for instance, identification is a term that psychiatrists use to describe the psychological need a patient has to be like someone else. In Dorothy's case, the someone is a some "thing": Toto, her dog, who is "perky, mischievous,...forever running away when he should stay put." Prior to reading Greenberg, Toto seemed--well, just a dog. But when Dorothy says to Miss Gulch: "You go away, or I'll bite you myself," it seems that Greenberg's interpretation is on the mark. The language of psychoanalysis does help enrich appreciation of the movie, and any approach that succeeds in this must be given credit.

Throughout the analysis, Greenberg assumes that a character in a movie can be analyzed in just the same way as a psychoanalyst's patient on a couch:

> Just as the first dream recalled in therapy often encapsulates a person's entire neurosis,...the opening sequences of Wizard adroitly capture Dorothy's central preoccupation with whether the child within her will be cherished or abandoned, and whether the adult stirring within her can dare to leave the nest.

2b

First of Greenberg's points to be evaluated

Assumption underlying Greenberg's point is evaluated

2c

> You do not need to be a psychoanalyst to appreciate that the opening scenes of the movie do in fact lay out Dorothy's conflict and that this conflict is more than her own: it is the viewer's as well, replaying, as Greenberg believes, the universal conflicts of adolescence. Thus the use of psychoanalysis to interpret *Wizard* generally succeeds. However, the effort becomes strained when Greenberg insists that Dorothy has unconsciously "doubled" her Aunt Em into a Good Mother and a Bad Mother....

Transition to second point to be evaluated

EXERCISE 3

Your job is to complete this evaluation. Assume that a discussion of two more points follows: The first is Greenberg's use of psychoanalysis to explain Dorothy's doubling of Aunt Em into the Good Mother and Bad Mother. If you agree with Greenberg's analysis, say so and explain why. (Also identify which sentences in the preceding sample evaluation would need to be changed.) If you disagree with the analysis, you can use the notes on pages 34–35 to help explain your position. Your second point should be one that you defined in Exercise 2. Add a sentence to the end of the third paragraph in this evaluation (at the bracketed note) to set up your later discussion. Finally, write a concluding paragraph to the evaluation in which you sum up the points made (yours included). If you have not already done so, you will need to reread the sections of Greenberg's article in chapter 1 beginning in 1b-4.

2c Writing an analysis

An analysis is an investigation conducted by systematically applying a set of principles. When conducting an analysis, your job is to take something apart to see how it works. Following are four assignments from different disciplines that call for analysis. Notice the common feature of these assignments: each asks the student to apply a well-defined set of principles to some new (at least for the student) topic in order to gain insight into that topic.

SOCIOLOGY Write an essay in which you place yourself in American society by locating both your absolute position and relative rank on each single criterion of social stratification used by Lenski & Lenski. For each criterion, state whether you have attained your social position by yourself or if you have "inherited" that status from your parents. (Alternately, your status might have a genetic origin.)

LITERATURE   Apply principles of Jungian psychology—that is, an Archetypal approach to literature—to Hawthorne's "Young Goodman Brown." In your reading of the story, apply Jung's concepts of the *shadow, persona,* and *anima.*

PHYSICS   Use Newton's Second Law ($F = ma$) to analyze the acceleration of a fixed pulley, from which two weights hang: m_1 (.45 kg) and m_2 (.90 kg). Having worked the numbers, explain in a paragraph the principle of Newton's law and your method of applying it to solve a problem. Assume your reader is not comfortable with mathematical explanations: do not use equations in your paragraph.

FINANCE   Using Guilford C. Babcock's "Concept of Sustainable Growth" [*Financial Analysts Journal* 26 (May–June 1970): 108–114], analyze the stock price appreciation of the XYZ Corporation, figures for which are attached.

The most common error in analysis writing, and one that is fatal to an essay, is to offer a summary only. When writing an analysis, you will need to summarize the topic you are investigating; and if your principles of analysis are not widely known you will need to summarize those as well. To conduct an analysis, you will need to apply those principles to a new context. You have seen Harvey Greenberg do exactly this in his discussion of *The Wizard of Oz.*

What permits Greenberg to interpret the movie as he does is psychoanalysis—an elaborate theory developed by Sigmund Freud to explain the unconscious workings of the mind. The great power of an analysis lies in its ability to focus our vision, like a pair of glasses. Without the work of Freud we would not be reading about *The Wizard of Oz* in the terms that Greenberg suggests. The theory and its application have allowed for a unique interpretation of the movie. If you found yourself flinching at Greenberg's treatment of Dorothy, you have caught on to the inherent weakness of analyses: in the very act of focusing our vision, they direct and thereby limit what we see. Thus the strengths and weaknesses of an analysis are two sides of the same coin. You must decide, both when reading and when writing analyses, the extent to which a set of principles or a theory, once applied, reveals or obscures what is being examined. Different analyses of the same topic can yield very different results. For example, in one "economic" interpretation of *The Wizard of Oz,* a critic saw in the film a conscious attempt to put a world of fantasy before an American public that was still struggling with the Great Depression. When reading an analysis, be aware that other analyses of the same topic are possible.

1   Preparing to write an analysis

Regardless of the discipline, professors will want to see that you have understood abstract principles and can apply them. A professor of history, for

2c

instance, might ask that you take two theories on what constitutes historical evidence and apply those theories to a recent event. When the moment comes, you must remember to write an analysis, not a summary. You can prepare yourself by arranging your notes as shown in the box.

Preparing for an Analysis

What are the key parts, the central and most important ideas, of the theory you have been asked to use?

Write several sentences, each of which expresses *one* of these key ideas.

Convert each sentence into a specific question.

Use each question as a basis to investigate your topic.

An analysis should focus carefully on specific parts of the topic being examined, and posing specific questions drawn from a theory will help you do this. The theory of psychoanalysis used by Greenberg is rooted in conflict between parts of the psyche: the id, the ego, and the superego. It follows that Greenberg would pose the following question of *The Wizard of Oz:* What is the conflict here? Greenberg offers two answers. In ¶s 2–5 (see pages 7–8), Greenberg focuses on adolescent conflict in general, according to psychoanalytic theory. In ¶s 6–11 (see pages 8–9), he then poses a more particular question: What is Dorothy's conflict? He responds with his discussion about Dorothy's unconscious splitting of Aunt Em into the Good Mother and the Bad Mother. Another question arising from Greenberg's use of psychoanalysis is this: How do early moments in the movie provide insight into Dorothy's psychological condition? His answer:

> Just as the first dream recalled in therapy often encapsulates a person's entire neurosis, just as the first words uttered by a patient coming through the office door often strike the theme of an entire analytic session, the opening sequences of *Wizard* adroitly capture Dorothy's central preoccupation with whether the child within her will be cherished or abandoned, and whether the adult stirring within her can dare to leave the nest.

Greenberg's analysis proceeds, question by specific question, with each question based directly on the theory he is using and aimed specifically at the parts of the movie he is analyzing.

In summary, preparatory notes for analysis should be based on questions that you build from your understanding of a theory or set of principles you have been asked to apply. Pose a question and use it to focus on one specific part of the thing you are examining. Jot down your thoughts and move on to the next question. Once you have assembled a page or two of such questions and responses, choose the three or four questions that best (that is, most specifically) enable you to examine your topic. You will construct your formal analysis by linking these questions and responses together in some meaningful way.

2 A strategy for writing analyses

2c

The process of writing an analysis remains the same regardless of the discipline in which you are working. Whether it is for a literature or a biology course, you will develop an analysis by taking a theory and applying it systematically.

Writing an Analysis

- Introduce and summarize the topic that will be analyzed.

- Introduce and summarize key points of the theory to be applied.

- Systematically apply key points of the theory to specific parts of the topic.

- Conclude. Review the ways in which you have applied the theory. Answer this question: To what extent has your application of a theory generated new and important insights into the topic you have analyzed?

EXERCISE 4

In making psychoanalysis the lens through which he analyzed *The Wizard of Oz*, Harvey Greenberg applied a complex set of principles with a long history. Greenberg's lens is not the only one that can be used to analyze the movie, however. Following is another theory—we will call it the "Heroic Needs" theory—which is nothing to match psychoanalysis in scope or explanatory power, but is nonetheless a broad statement that can be used to analyze a number of movies or novels. First, read the theory as stated here. Then, using key parts of the theory that you convert to questions, write out preparatory notes for an analysis of *The Wizard of Oz*. The goal of this exercise is for you to appreciate that when different theories are applied to the same topic, they will yield completely different interpretations. Feel free to disagree with the "heroic needs" theory. A theory's usefulness is determined by its explanatory power; if this one does not seem to explain much (if it does not help you to answer the questions How does X work? and What does it mean?), then reject it in favor of another one.

THE HEROIC NEEDS THEORY

No society can support too many heroes. If a majority was bent on adventure, too few would be left behind to mind the stores, to run the factories, to work the farms, and to care for children. In order to function, a society must consist, primarily, of unheroic workers; a society of heroes would likely be no society at all. The question, therefore, is why do we Americans so value stories with heroes? In stories and legends, we celebrate free-spirited heroes who are quick to set out on their own and find new lands and opportunities. These stories seduce us into believing that every American is potentially heroic, when the fact is that most of us are anything but. It is the *illusion* of heroism (the thought that we are capable of great feats at any moment) that we cherish.

From an economic point of view, the great mass of Americans must be dependable workers willing to stay at home and tend to business. Economically, we have no choice if we want to live well (both individually and as a society). Still, we seem to need more than our predictable, workaday lives; so we tell stories to soothe our souls and to express the wish that we were someone else. The stories that Americans tell each other can be seen in the context of this wishing.

2d Writing a synthesis

The writing that you do in college will exist in the context of other writing. Whatever the subject area, you can be sure that over the years many people have devoted themselves to the study of that subject. Often, you will be assigned research: you will be asked to locate and to use the work of others. This effort will require that you synthesize sources and in the process answer at least three questions: Which authors have written on the topic? How are their comments related? How can I best weave the views of others and my *own* views into a meaningful whole?

A synthesis may be devoted partly to summary, partly to evaluation, or partly to analysis. The purpose of synthesizing sources may be to inform or to persuade your reader. Regardless of its content and purpose, or the subject area in which you are writing, a synthesis will require that you develop two particular skills: an ability to infer relationships among sources and an ability to use sources according to *your own* design. The following assignment calls for a synthesis.

This semester we have read a number of books, articles, and essays on the general topic of marriage. Following are excerpts from the material you were responsible for reading. In a take-home essay, reflect on these five passages and discuss any three or four in ways that crystallize your thoughts about the topic.

The key components of synthesis are evident in this assignment. Were you the writer (which you will be if you complete Exercise 5), you would need to infer relationships among sources and to use these inferences in support of your original thinking. (See 1d.) It is impossible to infer relationships among sources if you do not understand the material in individual sources. As for using sources according to your own design, professors want to read papers to learn what you think about a topic and how you pull together source materials according to your own purpose. It will seldom be acceptable, when writing a paper based on sources, to stitch together four or five summaries (or one summary for however many sources you have read) and call that your paper. Usually, you will need to become more involved than this.

Your first concern about "speaking up" in your papers may involve a question of authority. "Who am I," you might ask, "to add my views to a paper in which I am quoting four world experts?" Rest assured that no one expects you to speak with the authority of a world expert. Nonetheless, your personal observations about an issue *are* valuable. In studying the question "What is a good marriage?" experts will have something to say, but so will you: perhaps you are married; certainly you have observed many marriages, among these your parents' marriage. The goal of a synthesis is for you to set your own views about a topic in a broader discussion in which both you and experts participate. Experts, too, were novice writers at some point; they got their start in the same way you are getting yours. What is needed early on in your career is a willingness to see your own ideas as legitimate and worthy of expression.

Following is a method for preparing and writing syntheses in which you "speak up." First, recall that in chapter 1 you read and inferred relationships among the comments of five authors, all of whom wrote on the topic of marriage. Refer to pages 21–22 and read the passages again.

1 Preparing to write a synthesis

Synthesis writing formalizes the process of reading to infer relationships among sources. The simplest possible synthesis will involve little more than the stitching together of summaries such as the following:

¶1 Several authors have discussed the topic of marriage. Emma Goldman believes that . . .

¶2 An anonymous writer cited in a book on the feminization of America writes that . . .

¶3 The Russian novelist Tolstoy began his novel *Anna Karenina* with a scene describing a greatly troubled Oblonsky family. . . .

¶4 Elizabeth Bacon, writing for *Collier's Encyclopedia*, states . . .

¶5 And Pope Pius XI, in his encyclical letter "On Christian Marriage," offers the Church's view. . . .

For most purposes, a synthesis by summary is unacceptable because it shows no effort to merge ideas. You as the writer are invisible in a synthesis by summary.

Cross-referencing ideas

In contrast to a synthesis by summary, a synthesis organized by *ideas* shows you to be intellectually present and involved with the material you have gathered. To organize a paper by ideas, you need first to divide the topic into the component parts that the various authors take up in their discussions. These component parts then become the key ideas around which you organize your paper. You can follow this method when your writing is based on library research. Cross-referencing is a necessary step in the process (see chapter 1, page 22); once you have identified a component part of a topic and have cross-referenced authors' discussions, you are nearly ready to write. In response to Exercise 6 in chapter 1, you worked on completing a note sheet.

2d

If you have not completed this assignment, turn back to pages 22–23 and do so now.

A Strategy for Making Inferences among Sources

1. Read multiple sources on a topic.
2. Subdivide the topic into parts and give each a brief title.
3. Cross-reference your sources for each part.
4. Summarize authors' information or ideas about each part.
5. Identify connections among readings, which may be related by comparison, contrast, example, definition, cause-and-effect—or by the extent of your agreement or disagreement with particular selections.

Clarifying relationships among authors

Your cross-referenced notes enable you to lay out and examine what several authors have written about *particular* parts of a topic, in this case marriage. Working with what your sources say on a particular point, you can now infer relationships. Sources can be related in a variety of ways, but you will find that patterns emerge, which can be identified by asking several questions.

Which authors agree?

Which authors disagree?

Are there any examples in one source of statements made in another?

Can you offer any definitions?

Are any readings related by cause and effect?

In addressing these questions, you need not be limited by the parts of the topic you have already defined (for example, satisfaction/dissatisfaction, intimacy, hostility). Pose these questions to all the readings as well to see if any new relationships emerge. Refer to pages 23–24 (Exercise 7, chapter 1) for specific questions for the five passages on marriage. Your responses to these questions will help you prepare to write a paper based on sources.

Ensuring that your voice is heard

When working with source materials, you may be tempted to forget the larger reason that you have sought out the observations of others. From time to time you may need to remind yourself that any references to source materials should *help to make your own points.* This advice presupposes that you have a point to make. If you have no point, you must try to find one, as well as a way to be committed to it. (See 3d for a discussion on generating ideas.) Unless you claim a paper as your own by having a reason for writing that is evident, your paper will inevitably lack interest for you and, subsequently, for your reader.

Do Not Become Invisible in Your Papers

The danger signs:

1. Your paragraphs are devoted wholly to the work of the authors you are synthesizing.
2. Virtually every sentence introduces someone else's ideas.
3. The impulse to use the first-person *I* never arises.

Instead of writing a string of paragraphs organized around the work of others, write paragraphs organized around statements that you make about a topic. In the context of the paper on marriage, a discussion organized by summary (see page 43) would leave you invisible. Generally, one needs to read no further than a statement such as the one that follows to know that the writer will never appear.

Several authors have discussed the topic of marriage.

This statement is *source* based and exhibits all the danger signals mentioned in the preceding box: it is focused on sources, not on a subject, and the writer is bound to disappear. Nowhere is the writer's purpose or direction evident. By contrast, a paper in which the author is present will show an active, interested mind engaged with the reading material and headed in some clear direction, with a purpose:

Definitions of marriage are so varied that no one definition seems adequate to all cases. Clearly, humans have created an institution that isn't entirely understood.

This statement is *writer* based. The writer's purpose and direction are made known. The reading material does not overshadow the writer. If you find source materials monopolizing your work, reexamine your thesis and make a more ambitious assertion (see 3f-2, 3).

2 A strategy for writing syntheses

A paper in which you draw on source materials will usually involve your inferring a number of relationships among sources. In a paper on marriage, for instance, one section might be devoted to defining terms, another section to comparing or contrasting various views on intimacy in marriage, and a third section to establishing a cause-and-effect relationship. Each section might show examples. When you know you will be referring to sources in a paper, consider carefully before you begin writing how various authors will contribute to the points you wish to make. Draw from your preparatory notes. Generally, you can use the following guidelines for writing a paper that synthesizes source materials.

2d

Writing a Paper Based on Sources

- Read sources on the topic; subdivide the topic into parts and infer relationships among parts, cross-referencing sources when possible.

- Clarify relationships among authors by posing these questions:

  Which authors agree?

  Which authors disagree?

  Are there any examples in one source of statements made in another?

  Can I offer any definitions?

  Are any readings related by cause and effect?

- Write a thesis (see 3f) that allows you to develop sections of the paper in which you refer to sources.

- Sketch an outline of your paper, organizing your discussion by *idea*, not by summary. Enter the names of authors into your outline along with notes indicating how these authors will contribute to your discussion.

- Write a draft of your paper and revise, following strategies discussed in chapter 4.

---

3 Practicing synthesis writing

To help you practice working on a synthesis, we will examine a response to the following essay assignment that began our discussion on synthesis.

> This semester we have read a number of books, articles, and essays on the general topic of marriage. Following are excerpts from the material you were responsible for reading. In a take-home essay, reflect on these five passages and discuss any three or four in ways that crystallize your thoughts about the topic.

You have read the source materials carefully; you have made notes on each; you have divided the topic of marriage into parts and cross-referenced those parts; and you have posed questions of these parts in an attempt to infer relationships among sources. Now make notes. Following are notes that would prepare you for developing a cause-and-effect relationship among the three authors cross-referenced under the category "Satisfaction/Dissatisfaction in Marriage" (page 23): Anonymous, Pius XI, and Tolstoy. Specifically, what comments do these authors make about satisfaction and dissatisfaction? The responses of student Leon Thompson follow.

> **Anonymous:** It seems clear that Anonymous is troubled by the relationship with her husband. She doesn't say so directly, but she seems frustrated. She knows what she wants in a marriage, in terms of emotional openness, yet

she enjoys only moments of such openness with her husband. Why is Anonymous frustrated? *Why* is the core question in a cause-and-effect relationship. Turning to Pius XI provides one answer.

2d

Pius XI: Writing in the encyclical "On Christian Marriage," Pope Pius creates an image of what a marriage can be: a "mutual inward moulding of husband and wife, . . . [in a] determined effort to perfect each other." Here is marriage as an ideal, as a spiritual as well as physical state.

Tolstoy: A marriage showing the very opposite of a "mutual inward moulding" is the Oblonsky marriage, in which the whole reason for union seems to have dissolved. There is no love in this house. The husband is having an affair with the governess; the wife feels she can't live with the man a moment longer; no one in the house seems to have much in common with anyone else, save a desire to leave.

Cause and effect: In terms of the degrees of satisfaction in the marriages they are discussing, the three authors can be set in the following order.

TOLSTOY	ANONYMOUS	PIUS XI
ideal shattered	ideal threatened	ideal defined
dissatisfied	troubled	satisfied

The inference: The ideal that Pius discusses links these three authors and is related to the level of satisfaction in marriage: The Oblonsky marriage in Tolstoy is terrible—in it, the spiritual ideal of marriage is dead. Anonymous's marriage is troubled but far from dead. Anonymous seems to operate with a definition of marriage very close to that of Pius. To the extent she reaches this ideal (moments at a time) with her husband, she is satisfied; to the extent she and her husband do not reach this ideal (most of the time), she is "hungry."

A STATEMENT OF CAUSE AND EFFECT

A marriage will dissolve when partners operate with different definitions of what a marriage should be.

On the basis of this sentence, you could argue for a cause-and-effect relationship among the three sources. *Argue* is the proper word here, for your inferences about sources, at least your more ambitious inferences, will not be readily apparent to readers. You will therefore need to support your inferences with evidence: direct references to your sources that make clear your reasoning. The cause-and-effect relationship inferred earlier would probably form one section of a larger paper. To determine the other sections of that paper, you would need to step back from all your sources to see if some large, comprehensive pattern emerges. This is the point at which you examine all that you have learned about your topic: reviewing your own thoughts; reviewing the thoughts of individual authors; and reviewing relationships inferred among sources. From this mix you can make a statement—a thesis.

THESIS

Newlyweds had better understand which of the many definitions of marriage they are working with before they exchange vows.

Based on this thesis, the following outline can be generated:

2d

I. The numerous, conflicting definitions of marriage are confusing and suggest radically different relationships between husband and wife. (Discuss sources in a three-way comparison-contrast)

    A. Emma Goldman

    B. Elizabeth Bacon

    C. Pope Pius

II. *Whatever* the definition, a marriage can work if both partners agree to it.

    A. Pius XI (partners work toward mutual perfection)

    B. Bacon (childless marriage nullified in some cultures—no apparent discussion of husband and wife perfecting each other; focus is on children)

III. A marriage will dissolve when partners operate with different definitions of what a marriage should be. (Cause and effect)

    A. Tolstoy

    B. Anonymous

    C. Pius XI

The sentences at sections I, II, and III show that the outline is organized by three *ideas,* which represent subdivisions of the major idea in the paper—the thesis. The three sections become "mini-papers" within the larger paper. In each section, the writer refers to source materials to help make his own point. It is the *writer's* ideas that dominate this paper—not those of the sources. Here is the final section to Leon Thompson's paper, based on the preceding outline and preparatory notes.

    Given the radically different definitions of marriage, I believe that a marriage will dissolve when partners do not share a definition. Take, for example, the view of marriage by Pope Pius XI as a determined effort by husband and wife to perfect each other. If one partner holds to this definition and the other does not, dissatisfaction is sure to result. This we see in the marriage of "Anonymous," a woman who agreed to discuss her private life with Elinor Lenz and Barbara Meyerhoff, authors of The Feminization of America. Here is what Anonymous said:

        Of course, I have moments of incredible intimacy with my husband,... And they are just moments. I have that kind of intimacy with my women friends all the time, whenever we meet and talk. I feel so

Organization by idea

Cause-and-effect relationships

hungry for that kind of talk with my husband, and
I've told him. He tries. He listens to my problems
and soothes my hurts, but he doesn't know how to
give back and forth. He's afraid to take off his
armor except for a few minutes at a time. (43)

Anonymous's marriage is in trouble because she
seems to operate with a definition of marriage that her
husband does not share. Intimacy for her is crucial in a
marriage, and in this respect her definition is reminis-
cent of Pope Pius's. Surely the "mutual inward moulding"
of husband and wife requires a full commitment to intimacy by both partners. Anonymous is willing: she thrives
on intimacy, yet she knows only moments of it with her
husband. She speaks with him about her need, he tries,
but "he doesn't know how to give back and forth."
Clearly he does not understand his wife's definition of
marriage and, hence, her expectations. Perhaps he cannot
understand; perhaps he is operating with some other definition of which she (and perhaps even he) is unaware.
This marriage would seem to be in trouble and headed for
more, because the spouses are not in sync concerning the
core definition of what their union should be.

In the opening to Anna Karenina, Tolstoy paints a
vivid picture of family life that has come completely un-
raveled:

Everything was upset in the Oblonskys' house. The
wife had discovered an intrigue between her husband
and their former French governess, and declared
that she would not continue to live under the same
roof with him. This state of things had now lasted
for three days, and not only the husband and his
wife but the rest of the family and the whole household suffered from it. They all felt that there was
no sense in their living together, and that any
group of people who had met together by chance at
an inn would have had more in common than they. (1)

Reference to two sources

Reference to third source

2d

From this passage alone we cannot know, specifically, what went wrong in the Oblonsky marriage such that
the husband would develop "an intrigue" with the French
governess. More precisely put, if both husband and wife
agreed that intrigues were permissible--if this were
their shared definition of a marriage, then there would
have been no problem. But clearly husband and wife do
not share such a definition, and (to say the least) problems result. The marriage, apparently, is loveless. "Everything [is] upset." Everyone is suffering.

Definitions of what a marriage is or ought to be
can evolve; still, newlyweds would be wise to discuss in
advance of the ceremony what each means, exactly, when
he or she says "I do." [At this point the paper would
stop drawing on source materials and would turn toward a
conclusion.]

Restatement
of thesis
Move to con-
clusion

EXERCISE 5

Make notes for and write a draft of the first *or* second section of the outline
at 2d-3. If the topic of this particular paper on marriage doesn't suit you,
then write an outline (including a thesis) for a different paper based on the
five passages you read on the topic. Your outline should have distinct
sections, organized by *idea*. Make preparatory notes and write the draft of
one section of your outline.

PART II

Writing as a Process

CHAPTER 3

Planning and Developing the Paper

Contrary to what you may think, you will arrive at a satisfactory final draft of your papers more quickly by writing them two or three times than you will by writing them once and waiting for perfection. Good writing generally requires that you narrow your focus and gain precision *as* you revise. Points you want to make do not exist in your head in some "perfect" but unarticulated form, waiting for you to find just the right words. Your thoughts come into being through the very act of writing and rewriting. Revision is the key; revision brings clarity and precision of thought.

3a Thinking and writing: An overview

The following box provides an overview of the thinking and writing process that will be developed in this chapter and the next.

The Writing Process

Preparing to Write

3c-1 **Identifying a purpose:** A clear purpose in writing provides you with a course by which you can generate and organize ideas, and then write and refine those ideas. In college, you will write primarily for two reasons: to inform and to persuade.

3c-2 **Defining an audience:** A writer's job is to communicate *with* someone. If you want documents to succeed, identify your audience. Anticipate and then try to satisfy your reader's needs; choose content, level of coverage, examples, and tone according to the requirements of your audience.

3d **Generating ideas and information:** Generating pertinent ideas and evidence for a paper can be difficult. Paper topics seldom spring to mind fully formed. Many writers use strategies such as reading, brainstorming, free writing, or journal writing to generate ideas and information, both before and during the writing of a first draft and during revision.

3e & 3f

Organizing material and writing a thesis: Once the purpose and audience are clarified and the ideas are generated, give form and direction to your work by outlining the paper you plan to write. Devise a *thesis*, a single sentence that states clearly the point of your writing. Select and organize ideas and information in the outline so as to develop and fully explain your thesis.

3a

dev

Writing a first draft

4a-1

Adopting a strategy for writing: The object of the first draft is to *create* and to *finish* one entire version of your document. When you accept that what you write in a first draft will not be final, you can give yourself permission to push on, knowing that you will return to rough spots. Complete one section of the document at a time, until you have finished.

Writing a second draft

4e

Revising for purpose, structure, and content: In your initial rereading of the first draft, reconsider your purpose for writing and the extent to which your draft achieves that purpose. Check for unity: do all elements of the document develop and complete some part of your purpose? Check for coherence: have you carefully ordered the sections of your discussion so that each section leads logically to the next? Check for development: are all important elements of the paper adequately developed with pertinent and convincing details? You may need to devote several drafts to clarifying purpose, structure, and content.

4i

Editing for grammar, punctuation, style, and tone: With the large-scale elements of your paper in place, you are ready to polish your work and make it ready for public view. Turn your attention to sentence-level concerns such as grammar, punctuation, style, and tone.

1 Writing: A recursive activity

You will not work through the stages of writing from beginning to end in a simple sequence. Much more likely, you will stop and pause, moving forward through one or two stages, stopping and pausing to move backward to an earlier stage, stopping and pausing again before continuing on with a new stage. Writing is *recursive*, a backward- and forward-looping activity. In actual writing you will to some extent generate, evaluate, and revise your work at every stage of the process, from first draft to last. You still will do well to save your most substantial revisions of a paper until *after* you have completed a first draft. In this way you allow yourself freedom to write without being overcritical. To be sure, good writing is not possible without criticism—yours and someone else's. But given at the wrong time, criticism may block you from completing the all-important first draft.

3a

dev

2   The thinking wheel and writing

A wheel is a useful metaphor in describing the writing process. Stages of writing are like points on a circle around which a writer loops and loops again in the process of preparing to write, drafting, and revising. Variations on the wheel in the illustration will be offered throughout this chapter to help you visualize the writing process. In these wheels, thinking *is* writing: spiraling in toward the main idea of your paper.

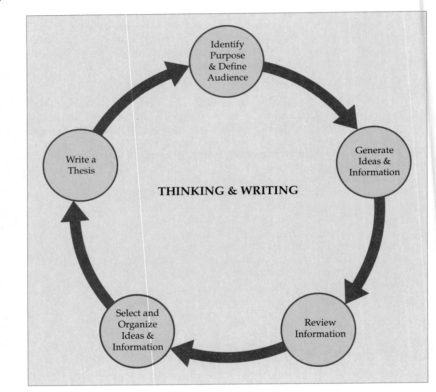

EXERCISE 1

Think of two essays, letters, or reports you have written: one that came easily and one that did not. Write a paragraph describing each effort. Discuss the topic, your attitude toward the topic, your purpose for writing, and your reader(s). Once you have written these two paragraphs, write a third in which you try to define what makes writing relatively easy or difficult for you.

EXERCISE 2

Arrange to interview three nonstudents who work more than twenty hours a week. Ask about the writing they do at their jobs. Write three paragraphs, summarizing your discussions with your interviewees. Possible questions include: Do you need to write on the job, and if so, would you describe the variety of writing you do? To what extent is writing an important factor in job advancement? What are your attitudes toward writing? Was the writing you did in school useful for your job?

3b   Discovering a topic

In your college career and beyond, you can expect to be assigned topics for writing and to be asked to devise your own topics. In either case, you should be prepared to act efficiently, which you can do by adhering to three precepts: write about what you know or can learn about in a reasonably brief period of time; make the topic your own; and narrow a topic so that you can develop it fully in a work of manageable and appropriate length.

1   Writing about what you know

The more you know about a topic, the more you will find to write about it. You can prove this point easily. Think of some topic you know little about, for instance: nuclear fission, U.S. defense policy, or metaphysical poetry. If asked to speak or write on that topic, you would quickly fall silent, unable to penetrate much beyond a few superficial observations. Now think of the activity you do best or enjoy most, such as swimming, skiing, reading, climbing, camping, writing computer programs, or playing the cello. Can you divide that activity into several parts? Can you discuss those parts in any detail? The request probably poses no great challenge because you understand the activity and can appreciate subtleties that nonexperts cannot.

In the example paper that will be developed through this and the next chapter, *football* proved to be the topic that student writer Sean Hannan knew well. Sean had thought a great deal about his ambivalent feelings toward the sport. Before coming to college he played on a championship high school team, and based on that experience, he decided never to play organized football again. Sean needed three drafts to write his paper. You will see his paper take shape through various stages, progressing from initial and sketchy thoughts, to a rough outline, to a draft, and after two full revisions to a final, successful essay. Here is a second-draft paragraph on its way to final form.

The paragraph introduces Sean's essay:

3b

dev

"This team has more character than any team I've had the pleasure

of working with." My football coach spoke honestly to the audience of

players, parents and local officials, but ~~the irony that flowed from~~ *hearing him*

~~his mouth~~ filled me with disdain. I glanced across the table to catch

~~one of my~~ *a* teammate's reactions. He simply shook his head, disgusted ~~at~~

and shamed by how we were being made into heroes.
~~our glorification which he knew to be a shameful misrepresentation.~~

understood   *traits*
All of the players ~~realized~~ that the ~~character~~ referred to by our

were   *were*   *were*
coach ~~was~~ nothing to be proud of, nothing to celebrate, and certainly

gave us an ovation
nothing to cheer about, but the crowd ~~did~~ anyway. To these people,

watching our football team had been a source of pride and entertain-

The fans turned to us. They needed us. And during the
ment. ~~Unfortunately, winning, with all of its benefits, creates mon-~~
season, the members of the team turned to each other. We
~~sters of the very players it glorifies.~~
were a tightly-knit group. We stood up for each other, and,
as the season unfolded, we lost our souls together. Though
being a member of a group has its benefits, group living
can usurp an individual's conscience.

Paragraph #1 from Sean Hannan's essay: "The Win Justifies the Means" (The essay's design, development, and revision will be traced through this chapter and the next.)

2 Making the topic your own

Effective writing is produced by those who understand *and* are committed to a topic. As you have seen (and will continue to see), Sean Hannan writes with conviction. You should as well. If you find yourself feeling indifferent or worse toward a topic, find another topic; otherwise, you will condemn yourself and your reader to boredom. Of course, you may not have the luxury of changing a topic that is assigned. If this is the case, then find a way to make the topic your own. In the end, it is *your* responsibility to be interested in what you write and to make it interesting to others. You may find the following suggestions helpful.

- *Stretch the topic to fit your interests.* Redefine the assignment in such a way that it touches on your experience and at the same time is acceptable to your professor.

- *Read about the topic.* If you do not know the topic well, read several sources, and review class notes and textbook selections. The more you know, the more likely it is you will find some element of a topic that interests you.

- *Identify a debate concerning the topic and choose sides.* Try to understand why the topic is debatable (if it is) and whom the topic affects, as well as the merits and limitations of each side of the debate. To stimulate interest, personalize the debate. Imagine yourself affected by it and take a position.

3b

dev

3   Narrowing the topic to make it manageable

You would be hard pressed to discuss the topic of "college life" in a five-page essay. If to cover the territory of a topic you must move quickly from one general point to the next, then the topic is too broad and should be narrowed. When beginning the writing process, be aware of the length limitations attached to an assignment and choose a topic accordingly. Imagine someone writing on "college life" who had never attended or even visited a college. The writer might produce a five-page paper on the topic, but the discussion could well turn superficial as the writer devotes two or three breezy sentences to major subtopics like "dorm life" or "studying habits." Any of these subtopics could become the focus of a five-page paper.

Try narrowing a topic with either of the strategies listed in the box below. Both strategies assume that you will first review what you know of the topic. If you know a great deal, your efforts at narrowing will soon yield results. If you are unfamiliar with the topic, you will need to conduct enough research to find out if the topic can be meaningfully subdivided.

Narrow Your Topic

- *Divide the topic into constituent parts.* Ask yourself: What are the component parts of this topic? What parts (or subtopics) do I know most about? Can I link subtopics together in meaningful ways? In which subtopic am I most interested?

- *Ask a journalist's questions.* Narrow a topic to a subtopic that interests you by posing questions, as appropriate: who, what, where, when, why, how? Often, a response to one or more of these questions can become the focus for a paper.

Sean Hannan and his classmates were given a series of assignments that ended with the final draft of a five-page paper. The following is the first assignment that Sean and his classmates received.

3b

dev

With this assignment you will begin the process of writing a five-page paper on a topic you know well. List three topics with which you are intimately familiar and about which you can write for *public* view. Subdivide each topic into as many parts as you can. Eventually, you will select from these parts a focus for your paper.

Sean knew at once what his topic would be: his championship football season in high school. Here is how Sean completed the first assignment.

Sean Hannan's Paper
Narrowing a Topic

```
Broad topic: my championship season

Topic divided into parts:

    the game--our strategy for winning

    our hopes for football scholarships to college

    the intensity needed to win

    pressure to devote all energy to football

    *the public's reaction to our season: they loved us

    *my reactions to our season: I hated myself by the end

Narrowed topic:

    Reactions (mine and the public's) to the team's championship

    season
```

EXERCISE 3

If you are writing a paper as you work through this chapter, begin with this assignment: List three topics with which you are intimately familiar and about which you can write for *public* view. Subdivide each topic into as many parts as you can. Eventually, you will select from these parts a focus for your paper. As preparation for subdividing topics of your choice, subdivide the following topics and compare your divisions with those of your classmates: politics, evolution, work, and corporations.

(In this chapter the following exercises parallel the sequence of assignments that led to Sean Hannan's paper: 3, 4, 6, 7, 9, 11, 12, 15, and 17.)

EXERCISE 4

Of the topics you have narrowed in Exercise 3, which one do you care most about? In which topic are you most interested? Write a brief paragraph in which you explain to yourself the *reasons* you are interested in one of these narrowed topics.

3c Purpose and audience: Considering the occasion for writing

dev

Immediately after (and often simultaneously with) your having discovered a **topic** for writing, you will need to understand the two other elements that will bear significantly on your work: your main reason for writing—your **purpose**; and your **audience,** the person or people who will be reading. The topic, purpose, audience—and you, the writer—constitute the **writing occasion.**

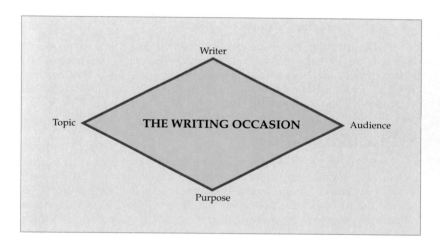

Understanding the occasion for writing requires that you read an assignment with care and understand your professor's expectations of the paper's purpose and audience. (See chapter 41 on essay exams.) Professors will also set expectations in terms of formal elements such as length and format. Several minutes spent considering these variables can help you enormously in preparing to write.

1 Identifying your purpose

Think of an object, an idea, an emotion, a relationship, or an institution: think of anything at all and you can probably explain it, argue about it, reflect on its significance, or make it the subject of an artistic work. There are four basic purposes or aims for writing: to *inform,* to *persuade,* to *express,* and to *entertain.* Since you will generally be asked to produce informative and persuasive pieces in college, this book is devoted primarily to these types of writing.

Informative writing

When writing to *inform*, your job is to present a topic and to explain, define, or describe it so that the reader understands its component parts, its method of operation, its uses, and so on. The following assignments call for informative writing.

LITERATURE   Cite three examples of metaphor in *Great Expectations* and explain how each works.

CHEMISTRY   Explain the chemical process by which water, when boiled, becomes steam.

PSYCHOLOGY   What is "cognitive dissonance" and in what ways does it contribute to the development of personality?

What the reader already knows about the topic will in large part determine the level of language you use and the difficulty of the information that you present. A professor of aeronautical engineering discussing the flight of planes would use one vocabulary with engineering students and another vocabulary with an audience that had no technical background. (See 3c-2.)

Persuasive writing

When you write to *persuade*, your job is to change a reader's views about a topic. As with informative writing, the persuasive writer must carefully consider the reader's prior knowledge in order to provide the background information necessary for understanding. If you lacked a background in international business, for instance, you might not be persuaded about the need to master a foreign language in college. The person urging you to learn Spanish or Japanese would need to inform you, first, of certain facts and trends. As a persuasive writer, you will provide information both to establish understanding and to provide a base for building an argument. (See chapter 6, which is devoted entirely to argumentation.) The following assignments call for persuasive writing.

PHILOSOPHY   In *The Myth of Sisyphus* Albert Camus writes, "From the moment absurdity is recognized, it becomes a passion, the most harrowing of all." Explain this statement, with respect to Camus's philosophy. Then, in a brief argument, present reasons for accepting or rejecting the statement.

ASTRONOMY   Given limited government money available for the construction and updating of astronomical observatories, which of the projects discussed this semester deserve continued funding? Argue for your choices based on the types of discoveries you expect the various projects to make in the next five years.

SOCIOLOGY   You have read two theories on emotions: the Cannon-Bard theory and the James-Lange theory. Which seems the more convincing to you? Why?

MARKETING   Select three ads that describe similar products. Which ad is most effective? Why?

Expressive writing and writing to entertain

Expressive writing—sometimes private and recorded as journal entries, sometimes written for public view—focuses on an exploration of your own ideas and emotions. When it is private, expressive writing can lead you to be more experimental, less guarded, perhaps even more honest than in a paper meant for others. When it is public, expressive writing will not be a journal entry, but rather an essay in which you reflect on your impressions. In many composition courses, the first part of a semester or an entire semester will be devoted to expressive writing. The least frequent purpose of academic writing is to *entertain*. Possibly you will write a poem, story, or play in your college career; and certainly you will read forms of writing that are intended to entertain readers. What makes a piece of writing entertaining is itself a subject for debate. It suffices to say here that writing to entertain need not be writing that evokes smiles.

Purposes for writing may overlap: in a single essay, you may inform, persuade, and entertain a reader. But if an essay is to succeed, you should identify a *single,* primary purpose for writing. Otherwise, you risk having a document that tries to do all things but does none well. Sean Hannan chose an informative purpose for his paper.

3c

dev

**Sean Hannan's Paper
Determining a Purpose**

```
    I want to write an informative paper that explains how I became an
animal during the course of a championship football season and how
what happened to me happens to other people--in and out of football,
wherever groups exert pressure. I'll need to tell the story of my
season, and I may bring in some sources to make a larger point about
groups.
```

EXERCISE 5
In chapter 1, Exercise 5, you will find five brief passages on the topic of marriage. Determine which paragraph is intended to inform, which to entertain, which to persuade, and which to express or reflect. Explain your choices by referring to particular features of each paragraph.

EXERCISE 6
Return to the writing you produced for Exercises 3 and 4, in which you divided broad topics into subtopics and then selected one narrowed topic as particularly interesting. This (or the topic suggested below) will become

3c

dev

your topic for a five-page paper. Write a brief paragraph explaining your purpose for this paper. Although purposes may overlap to some extent, decide on one of two primary purposes for this paper: to inform *or* persuade your reader. If the topics in Exercises 3 and 4 left you uninspired, you may want to try this one:

> Imagine yourself a student at a college or university where the Board of Trustees has voted to institute a curfew on dormitory visitors. After 11 PM on weekdays and 1 AM on weekends, no student may have a guest in his or her dormitory room. The rule simply put: no overnight guests.

2 Defining your audience

Unless you are making a journal entry, you will write in order to communicate *with* someone: whether your intent is primarily to inform or persuade, you must know your audience since what you write will depend greatly on who will read it. With readers who understand your topic, you can assume a common base of knowledge. For instance, if you were preparing a paper on gene splicing for an audience of nonbiologists, you would be obliged to cover rudimentary concepts in language that nonspecialists would understand. In preparing a paper on the same topic for fellow biology majors, you would be free to use technical terms and to discuss higher level material. Questions that you ask about an audience *before you write a first draft* can help you make decisions concerning your paper's content and level of language.

Audience Needs Analysis

Pose these general questions, regardless of your purpose:

- Who is the reader? What is the reader's age, sex, religious background, educational background, and ethnic heritage?
- What is my relationship with the reader?
- What impact on my presentation—on choice of words, level of complexity, and choice of examples—will the reader have?
- Why will the reader be interested in my paper? How can I best spark the reader's interest?

If you are writing to inform, pose these questions as well:

- What does the reader know about the topic's history?
- How well does the reader understand the topic's technical details?
- What does the reader need to know? want to know?
- What level of language and content will I use in discussing the topic, given the reader's understanding?

If you are writing to persuade, pose both sets of questions above as well as the following:

- What are the reader's views on the topic? Given what I know about the reader (from the preceding questions), is the reader likely to agree with my view on the topic? to disagree? to be neutral?

- What factors are likely to affect the reader's beliefs about the topic? What special circumstances (work, religious conviction, political views, etc.) should I be aware of that will affect the reader's views?

- How can I shape my argument to encourage the reader's support, given his or her present level of interest, level of understanding, and beliefs?

Sean Hannan's Paper
Audience Analysis

```
        I assume that my readers will be high school or college students

or older. Religious background and ethnic heritage should not have any

bearing on what I write or the way I write. Though my readers will

know about the game of football, they probably will not be experts. In

my paper, I will build on the reader's basic, minimal knowledge. I

will explain the raw emotional intensity and the violence of football

from a high-school player's perspective.
```

3 Writing for an unspecified audience

One of the few times in life that you may write when an audience is *not* apparent may be in college. If your audience for writing is not clearly stated, then you should regard your professor as the main reader. Do not think that because she is an expert on the topic of your paper you are relieved of developing points thoroughly. Many writing assignments are developed expressly to gauge what you know about a topic; in these instances, to omit information intentionally so as to not bore your reader (the professor) will prove disastrous.

When writing for a professor, one approach that ensures thoroughness is to assume the professor functions as an expert editor who will review your paper before passing it on to another reader. This second reader is *not* an expert on your topic and must therefore rely fully on your powers of explanation. Assume this reader is skeptical and neutral regarding your topic. Being a skeptic, the reader will hear you out, but will probe with questions and will require that you develop general statements with specific illustrations and that you defend any assertions needing support. Being neutral, the reader will be poised to accept your position, but only if you present it reasonably.

3c

dev

One danger of considering your professors to be the audiences for your papers is that you can gradually lose your voice, or identity, as a writer. Papers can become long essay exams; your tone in one course can sound exactly like your tone in another; you can forget the ways in which the context of your writing will affect what is written; and you can come to disregard the importance of style, since "only the professor" is reading. Avoid these dangers by recognizing them. When no audience is specified, consciously work to maintain your identity as a writer (see 2d-1).

When Does Your Audience Need to Know More?

Consider these points when deciding whether your audience needs to know more about a key term or person.

- Major personalities referred to in textbooks or in lectures will help constitute the general, shared knowledge of a discipline. In all cases, *refer to people in your papers either by their* last *names or by their first* and *last names.* Do not identify "giants of a field" with explanatory tags like *who was an important inventor in the early part of the 20th century.*

- Terms that have been defined at length in a textbook or lecture also constitute the general, shared knowledge of a discipline. Once you have understood these terms, use them in your papers—but do not define them. Demonstrate your understanding by using the terms accurately.

- The same people and terms not requiring definition in an academic context may well need to be defined in a nonacademic one. Base decisions about what information to include in a paper on a careful audience analysis.

EXERCISE 7

Return to the topic you selected in Exercise 6, where you wrote a paragraph explaining your purpose for a proposed five-page paper. Working with your topic and your purpose (to inform or persuade), answer questions in the Audience Needs Analysis box three times, once for each of three different audiences: a friend at another school, your parents, and some other audience of your choosing. Select one of these audiences as the one to whom you will direct your paper.

4   Matching tone with purpose and audience

Tone is the term used to summarize a writer's general attitude toward the reader and the subject. Through an accumulation of signals, some subtle and others not, readers can tell whether you are interested in your topics; whether you have prepared adequately; or whether you are committed, engaged, humble, proud, irritable, or defensive. Appreciate that a paper *will* have, and cannot help but have, a characteristic tone. English offers numerous ways of saying the same thing, and the fact that you write a sentence one way and not another reflects a choice about language and the reasons underlying that choice. The most simple request can be worded to reflect a variety of tones.

May I have the salt?   Give me that salt!   Salt!

Pass the salt.   Pass the salt, please.

Formal writing adheres to all the rules and conventions of writing expected in the professional and academic worlds. Formal writing is precise and concise; it avoids colloquial expressions, and it is thorough in content and tightly structured. **Informal writing,** the writing of personal correspondence and of journals, tends to be conversational. Word choice is freely colloquial and structure need not be as tightly reasoned as in a formal paper. Occasional lapses in grammar, usage, spelling, or punctuation matter little in personal correspondence and not at all in personal journal writing. **Popular writing,** the writing typical of most general interest magazines, adheres to all conventions of grammar, usage, spelling, and punctuation; it is also carefully organized. The language, however, is more conversational than that found in formal writing. Heavy emphasis is placed on engaging readers and maintaining their interest.

Register is the term describing the level of language or tone used in a paper. Versatile writers can shift registers, moving from informal to popular to formal language as the writing occasion requires. You can inform or persuade a reader in *any* register, but once a register is chosen, use it consistently.

EXERCISE 8

Write a series of three brief letters to a mail-order business. Ask why you have not received the computer software you ordered and paid for. The letters should show a change in tone, moving from a neutral inquiry in the first letter to annoyed concern in the second to controlled anger in the third. In each case, maintain a formal tone. Avoid using colloquial expressions.

EXERCISE 9

Given the audience and the purpose you have chosen for the paper you are planning (see your answers to Exercises 6 and 7), decide on the tone you should adopt.

3d Generating ideas and information

It is not easy to generate ideas about a topic. In most academic writing, a combination of efforts is usually needed: you will reflect on your own experience and think a topic through to get ideas for writing; and you will

3d

dev

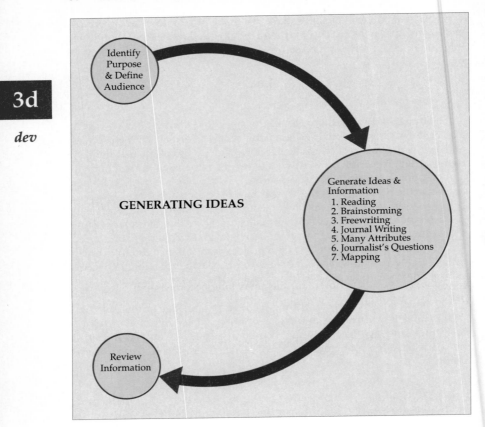

Identify Purpose & Define Audience

GENERATING IDEAS

Generate Ideas & Information
1. Reading
2. Brainstorming
3. Freewriting
4. Journal Writing
5. Many Attributes
6. Journalist's Questions
7. Mapping

Review Information

conduct research in a library, in a lab, or in the field. At times you may stare at your topic, a word on a blank page, and feel as though there is *nothing* to write about.

To succeed as a writer you need to be both a creator and a critic; but you need these qualities in different measures at different times. Too often, the critic in you is quick to reject ideas at the early stages of writing. The critic does not understand that in the creative process good ideas are often scattered among not-so-good ones. You must strike a deal with the critic in you, saying in effect: "Take a break. When I need you, I'll call." If you are generating ideas using the strategies discussed next and the critic in you snaps, "That one's no good!" remind yourself that you are creating. Tough judgments about what you create will come later.

As you review the following strategies for generating ideas, bear in mind this "User's Manual" for generating information:

- No one method will work for all topics.
- Some methods may not suit your style of discovery.
- Some methods work well when paired.
- Move quickly to a new strategy if one does not work.
- Tell your critic to take a vacation.

3d

dev

1 Reading

Most academic writing is based on reading. Early in the writing process, when you are still not precisely sure of what your topic will be, reading can be an excellent stimulus. Even if you do not plan to depend heavily on sources in a paper, reading about your tentative topic will help you to generate ideas. Source materials may present compelling facts or strongly worded opinions with which to agree or disagree. Above all, read to *respond*. Be alert to your responses and jot them down, for they may later become important to your paper. (See chapter 1 and the discussion of strategies for reading effectively.) If you are writing a paper that will not draw heavily on sources, use your reading mainly as a stimulus. If you are writing a research report, read to generate the information you will then use to write the paper.

At the time Sean Hannan was preparing to write, he was enrolled in an introductory social psychology course. He browsed through the index of his textbook and found that the entries on *aggression* and *compliance* sparked his interest. Recall Sean's tentative topic: "Reactions (mine and the public's) to the team's championship season." Sean made the following notes, based on his initial reading.

Sean Hannan's Paper
Reading

According to my textbook, human aggression is an intensely studied problem and much on people's minds. Group members can be particularly aggressive because few members of a group are willing to speak up and call aggression wrong. There are powerful psychological and social incentives in belonging to a group. For a football team to be a team, everyone must sacrifice for each other physically and emotionally. A close bond forms that no one will break--even if his conscience calls on him to do so. My problem on the football field was not just my problem, I've discovered. Everyone is susceptible to group pressures and can lose individuality.

2   Brainstorming

Brainstorming is a technique to get you thinking through writing. The idea is to write quickly and, once finished, to return to your work with a critical eye. Place your topic at the top of a page, and then list any related phrase or word that comes to mind. Set a time limit of five or ten minutes, and list items as quickly as you can. All items are legitimate for your list, since even an allegedly bad idea can spark a good one. To brainstorm in a small group, a technique that allows the ideas of one person to build on those of another, write your topic on a board or sheet of easel paper. (If you have no topic, see "Freewriting," 3d-3). Sit in a circle and ask each member of the group to offer two or three words or phrases for your list. Work about the circle a second time, asking each member to add another one or two ideas, based on an item already mentioned. Finally, open the floor to anyone who can add more ideas. As a ground rule, urge each group member to understand that all ideas are equally useful.

After you have generated your list, group related items and set aside items that do not fit into a grouping. Groupings with the greatest number of items indicate areas that should prove fertile in developing your paper. Save the results of your brainstorming session for your next step in the planning process: selecting, organizing, and expanding information.

Sean divided his topic into three parts and brainstormed separately about each part (my reactions to the championship season, the public's reactions, the season).

Sean Hannan's Paper
Brainstorming

```
My reactions

elation--winning was a high

fear--about the person I was becoming

anger, hostility--about the person I was becoming

numbness--couldn't let these thoughts in during a game

coach--frightened me with his intensity sometimes

intensity--team's, coach's

winning--at all costs

media attention--I loved it

close bond with team, like we shared this secret, were brothers

loved the glory--made me feel important

tackle--broke a guy's thigh, terrible

tackle--wrecked a guy's knee, mean, felt like an animal
```

Sean grouped the list as follows. The question mark denotes the "left-over" category. Sean was unsure how to group "tackles."

```
            My Reactions


Negatives       Positives        ?

fear            elation          tackles

anger           winning

numbness        bond with team

intensity       glory

winning         media
```

3 Freewriting

Freewriting is a technique to try when you are asked to write but have no topic. Think for a moment about the subject area in which you have been asked to write. Recall lectures or chapters read in textbooks. Choose a broad area of interest and then start writing for some predetermined amount of time—say, five or ten minutes. Alternately, you can write until you have filled a certain number of pages (typically one or two). As you write, do not stop to puzzle over a word choice or punctuation. Do not stop to cross words out because they do not capture your meaning. Push on to the next sentence. Freely change thoughts from one sentence to the next, if this is where your thinking takes you. If you are stuck, write: "Stuck, stalled, can't write, stuck . . . " Then push through to more sentences. Write quickly, even furiously, but in any event *write*. Once you have reached your time limit or page allotment, read over what you have done. Circle ideas that lend themselves to possible paper topics. To generate ideas about these specific topics, you may then try a more focused strategy for invention: brainstorming, focused freewriting, or any of the other strategies that will be discussed in later sections.

Focused freewriting gives you the benefits of freewriting, but on a *specific* topic. The end result of this strategy is the same as brainstorming, and so the choice of invention strategies is one of style: do you prefer making lists or writing sentences? Begin with a definite topic. Write for five or ten minutes; reread your work; and circle any words, phrases, or sentences that look potentially useful. Draw lines that link circled words, and make notes to explain the linkage. Then clarify these linkages on a separate sheet of paper. The result will be a grouping of items, some in sentence form, that looks a great deal like the result of brainstorming. Save your work for the next step in the planning process: selecting, organizing, and expanding information.

Following is a portion of Sean's focused freewrite around the second part of his topic: the public's reaction to his team's championship season.

Sean Hannan's Paper
Focused Freewriting

Winning only one game got the (town all excited) about how our team

was going to win a league championship. I never realized how important

winning was to my neighbors. We were only a high school team after

all (Why should they be so excited?) They were. After we had won a cou-

ple of games, it seemed we were holding more interviews than prac-

tices. And then there were the (people erecting signs) in storefront

windows and the (headlines,) not just on the sports pages either, of our

local paper. It was getting out of hand. At the end of the season, the

coach was on a platform with us--the town gave us a (banquet)--and he

spoke about the team like we were national heroes. Stuff that made no

sense to me, about character, poise, dedication. To football, maybe.

But what about the (people who got hurt along the way)--some not by acci-

dent? The town loved us. They loved the (animals we became.) I didn't.

It scared me, to see the (evil I was capable of,) and what scared me

even more, I think, was that (people on the outside didn't see it at all.)

(They wanted heroes,) and they got them. But the cost was too high.

We started the season as young men. I felt something like a criminal

by the end of it.

Sean organized his freewriting into these notes:

```
Town excited              Why?

-people erecting signs    -wanted heroes
-headlines in local paper -didn't see our ugly side
-banquet
We became animals
-hurt people intentionally
-I was capable of evil
-others didn't see, all the more frightening
```

4 Journal writing

You might keep a journal in conjunction with your writing course. A *journal* is a set of private, reflective notes that you keep, in which you describe your reactions to lectures, readings, discussions, films, current events—any topic touching on your course work. A journal borrows from both diary writing and course notebooks. As in a diary, your journal entries are private, reflective, and "safe" in the sense that you know no one is looking over your shoulder; thus, you are free to experiment with ideas and to express your thoughts honestly without fear of consequences. Unlike a diary, a journal focuses on matters relating to your course work and not on matters of your private family and social lives, unless observations concerning these tie in with your course work. Journal writing gives you an opportunity to converse with yourself in your own language about what you have been studying. You pose questions, develop ideas, reflect on readings, speculate and explore, and try to pinpoint confusions. The more you write, the more you clarify what you know and, equally important, what you do not know. The language of your journal entries should reflect your voice: use the words, expressions, and rhythms of your vocabulary as when you chat with friends. Punctuation is a minor matter in journal entries: as long as you can reread your entries, do not concern yourself with rules for placing commas and such. Periodically review journal entries, looking for ideas in which you seemed particularly interested. As with freewriting, use these ideas as the basis for a more focused strategy of invention.[1]

---

[1]Discussion of journal writing here is based on Toby Fulwiler, ed. *The Journal Book* (Portsmouth, NH: Boynton/Cook-Heinemann, 1987), 1–7.

3d

dev

5 The "many attributes" strategy[2]

Another method for generating ideas about a topic is to list attributes, or features, that a topic possesses. Number the items of your list. Then ask: "What are the uses of Number 1? Number 2? Number 3?" and so on. If the *uses of* question does not seem to work for the attributes of the topic you are exploring, try *consequences of*: "What are the consequences of Number 1?" The *many attributes* strategy gets you thinking about *parts* of a topic, and lets you be far more specific and imaginative than you can be, typically, in thinking about the topic as a whole. Once you have responded to your questions about the uses or consequences of some attribute, you might pursue the one or two most promising responses in a focused freewrite.

Sean Hannan's Paper
The "Many Attributes" Strategy

```
 I. What are the attributes of a championship season?

    1 student, teacher pride

    2 town pride

    3 something to talk about, besides weather

    4 way to divert attention from problems

    5 intense players

    6 coach keeps job and is known as winner


One attribute, explored:

II. What are the consequences of students' and teachers' showing
    pride?

    focus on school as a positive place

    increase students' awareness of behaving in ways that don't
       reflect poorly on school--good for administration & teachers

    some students let pride go to their heads--they brag

    pride also creates burden--students, teachers, administrators
       begin to cut us slack and we begin to think we're as great
       as everybody tells us

    school's pride creates respect for players
```

---

[2]This strategy is adapted from John C. Bean and John D. Ramage, *Form and Surprise in Composition: Writing and Thinking Across the Curriculum* (New York: Macmillan, 1986), 170–171.

6 The journalist's questions

You have read or heard of the journalist's questions: *who, what, when, where, why,* and *how.* In answering the questions, you can define, compare, contrast, or investigate cause-and-effect. Again, the assumption is that by thinking about parts you will have more to write about than if you focused on a topic as a whole. The journalist's questions can help you to narrow a topic (see 3b-3), giving you the option to concentrate, say, on any three parts of the whole: perhaps the *who, what,* and *why* of the topic. Under mapping, next, you will find Sean Hannan's notes made in response to three of the journalist's questions.

7 Mapping

If you enjoy thinking visually, try **mapping** your ideas. Begin by writing your topic as briefly as possible (a single word is best). Circle the topic and draw three, four, or five short spokes from the circle. At the end of each spoke place one of the journalist's questions, making a major branch off the spoke for every answer to a question. Now, working with each answer individually, pose one of the six journalist's questions once again. After you have completed the exercise, you will have a page that looks something like a map.

Sean Hannan's Paper
Mapping the Journalist's Questions

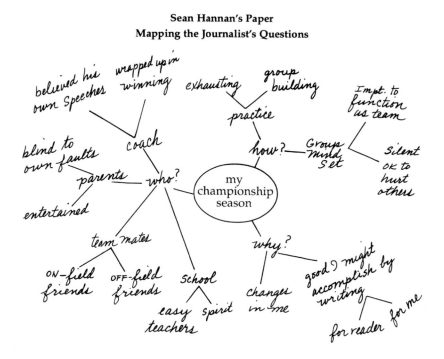

You can map ideas to make thinking visual for the "many attributes" strategy as well as for the journalist's questions. One clear advantage of mapping is that the map groups and subordinates ideas for you, distinguishing between major points and supporting information just as you will do in your papers.

EXERCISE 10

Generate ideas about three of the following topics, using *two* of the previously mentioned methods of invention for each idea. The results of this exercise will provide the basis for your answer to Exercise 14.

river rafting	the symphony	dorm life
a cousin	compulsory draft	space flight

EXERCISE 11

If you are preparing a paper as you read this chapter, use any *three* methods of invention to generate ideas about your topic. The end result of your work should be several categories of grouped ideas.

3e   Selecting and organizing ideas and information

Not all of the information you have generated will be equally useful. Therefore, your next task in the writing process is to select from among your ideas those that look most promising for your paper. *Promising* in this context is an inexact term, and at this stage of the writing process there is no way to be exact: until you have completed a first draft, you cannot know for certain the content of your paper. Despite the plans you make when preparing to write, your *actual* writing is where you will discover much of your content. For this reason, the choices you make about which ideas and information to include in a paper must be based on hunches: informed guesses about what will work.

1   Selecting ideas and making meaningful categories

After you have used various methods to generate ideas, your challenge is to gather and make sense of them by creating categories. A *category* is akin to a file drawer into which you place related information. When you brainstormed, you generated lists and grouped like items; when you completed a focused freewrite and analyzed your work by drawing and linking circles, you again generated and grouped ideas. Ideas generated by different methods usually reinforce one another. *The task facing you now is to consolidate: to take* all *your prior groupings of ideas and information and to make new, more exact categories.* It is on the basis of these categories that you will arrive at the core idea of your paper. To facilitate your thinking later on, write a brief sentence or phrase that defines each of your consolidated categories.

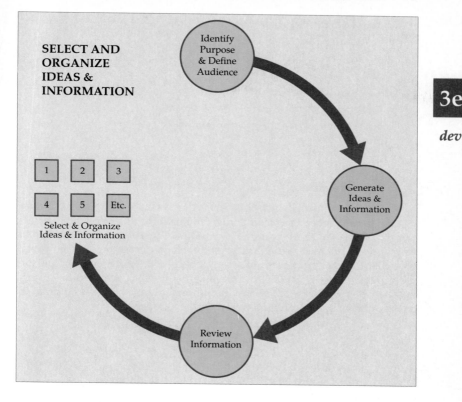

Sean Hannan generated five categories of information on which he could base a paper: playing has advantages; playing has disadvantages; the story of my season; my reactions; the public's reactions. Following is one of these categories, with information consolidated from the results of four different methods for generating information.

Sean Hannan's Paper
Selecting Information into Categories

Playing has disadvantages.

winning became a burden--we had to win league title

intensity: games, lockers, coach was hard to handle

fear of becoming an animal, a criminal

adulation made us cocky

we felt like we deserved special treatment in restaurants

I broke a kid's leg on a tackle, unintentionally

```
I took one kid out of a game, intentionally--in retro-
  spect, terrible
one team mate banged his head on a wall to prepare--
  scary
every game, pressure built to keep win streak alive
couldn't sleep before game nights, sometimes
teachers gave some players easy treatment on tests
```

2   Organizing information *within* categories

Organize information within categories to clarify your ideas and their relation to each other. Once you understand patterns of relation within each category, then you can see patterns of relation *across* categories, at which point you will be prepared to write a thesis and then the first draft. First, however, you will need to identify main, or *general,* points within each category and the subordinate, or *specific,* points supporting them, which is exactly what you will do when writing a paper. Use an informal outline or a tree diagram to organize major and supporting points within a category.

Sean Hannan's Paper
Organizing Information within Categories

Organization by informal outline

```
Playing had real disadvantages.

Major point: winning became a burden--we had to win league title
  Supporting points: (1) every game, pressure built to keep win
  streak alive; (2) couldn't sleep before game nights, sometimes
Major point: intensity--games, lockers, coach was hard to handle
  Supporting points: (1) one team mate banged his head on a
  wall to prepare--scary
Major point: fear of becoming an animal, a criminal
  Supporting points: (1) I broke a kid's leg on a tackle uninten-
  tionally; (2) I took one kid out of a game, intentionally--in
  retrospect, terrible
Major point: adulation made us cocky
  Supporting point: (1) we felt like we deserved special treatment
  in restaurants; (2) teachers gave some players easy treatment
```

Organization by tree diagram

3   Expanding information: Filling in gaps

Organizing material within a category is an excellent technique for revealing which of your main points will need further development once you begin writing a first draft. When Sean Hannan organized his category on the disadvantages of playing football, he realized that he had neglected to generate enough supporting materials for his point about the season's intensity. When Sean asked, "What other examples of intensity can I point to?" answers came quickly. An asterisk marks the two additions to the category.

```
Major point: intensity: games, lockers, coach was hard to handle
  Supporting points: one team mate banged his head on a wall
    to prepare--scary
  *coach gave inspiring speeches in which he ignored or downplayed
    the fact of kids getting seriously hurt
  *during games, nothing else existed except playing football--I
    locked every other part of myself away
```

Look to each of your main points to see how you might add supporting points. Developing categories fully at this stage will maximize the information you will have to work with when devising a thesis.

4   Expanding information: Using source materials

Virtually any paper can benefit when a writer refers to the work of others. Essay writing like Sean Hannan's is primarily devoted to the writer's own insights, but the insights of others are welcome when they expand the frame of reference or the context of the essay. Up until this point, Sean Hannan has limited his observations to his own experience, but by seeking out source materials, Sean purposely broadens the topic of his essay to include not just football but the behavior, generally, of people in groups.

When writing an essay, you may draw on a limited number of sources (if you use sources at all) to accent your own insights. When writing a research paper, you will rely on sources more heavily, using them as a foundation on which to write. In both cases, however, *your* ideas should predominate. (See 2d on writing a synthesis.)

Sean's reading in social psychology resulted in his going to the library to find (among other sources) a book by social psychologist Solomon Asch, from which he quoted in the final version of his paper.

EXERCISE 12

Select the most promising information from your efforts to generate ideas about your topic, as defined in Exercise 11. *Form categories:* consolidate information that resulted from your using all three invention strategies. Write a brief sentence or phrase of definition for each category. *Organize each category* into a main point and supporting points. Finally, *expand information:* fill in gaps, if need be; and if you are interested (or if your professor requires it) seek out source material that you can use in your paper. At the conclusion of this exercise, each category should have a main point supported by at least two specific, subordinate points.

3f   Devising a working thesis

All your effort in identifying a topic, defining an audience, generating ideas, grouping ideas into categories, and organizing categories leads in one direction: to devising a thesis. A *thesis* is a general statement that you make about your topic, a one-sentence summary of your paper. Just as you cannot write a definitive summary of an article that you have only partially read, you cannot produce a fully accurate thesis of a paper you have not finished writing. Before sitting down to a first draft, you will at best have a **working thesis:** a statement that, based on everything you know of your topic, should prove to be a reasonably accurate summary of what you will write. However, it is only after you have produced a complete draft that you will be in a position to write a **final thesis,** the accurate one-sentence summary of your work that will appear in your final draft.

3f

dev

In the act of writing, you will discover, discard, and revise ideas. Before you write, you simply cannot tell how your draft will evolve and how, subsequently, your working thesis will need to change in order to become final. Suffice it to say that the working thesis *will* change. Even so, you will depend on it to get you started on your draft.

1   Narrowing the subject of your thesis

Like any sentence, a thesis consists of a subject and a predicate (that is, a verb and its associated words). The subject of a thesis identifies the subject of your paper. The predicate represents the claim or assertion you will make about the subject. To the extent possible, before you begin the first draft, you will want to narrow the subject of your working thesis such that you can discuss it thoroughly within the number of pages allotted. Given that you have generated (and, if you have conducted library research, gathered) a great deal of information, how will you narrow your subject?

Build on the fact that you have organized your information into categories. To settle on a subject for your thesis, review your categories and *select* from among them your most promising and interesting material that appears related (see 3f-2). You might physically lay all your notes in front of you. These notes represent the broadest possible paper you could write. Most likely, you will use only a fraction of your material.

One useful way to narrow the subject of your thesis is to pose a journalist's questions: *who, what, when,* and *where.* To these questions you might add *which aspects.* For instance, if you were planning to write a paper on the topics of *the wilderness* or *voter registration drives,* you would want to narrow your focus considerably (assuming a five-page paper).

Subject (too broad): voter registration drives

Limiting questions: where, when, who?

Narrowed subject: voter registration drives among the urban poor in the 1991 elections

Subject (too broad): wilderness

Limiting questions: which aspects?

Narrowed subject: wilderness camping

2   Basing your thesis on an inference

Once you have narrowed your subject, you must make an assertion about it; that is, you must complete the predicate part of your thesis. If you have ever written a paper before, you recognize this as the moment of chaos coalescing into order. If you have generated ideas on your own, you have several pages of notes; if you have conducted research, you have filled out perhaps fifty file cards. You cannot write until you have begun to make relationships among the ideas and information that you have generated. It is only *in the process* of making relationships—trying to make logical connections one way, seeing that a certain tactic does not work, trying other tactics, and constantly making adjustments—that sense emerges and you come to know what you think about your material. Once you know what you think, you can make an assertion and complete your working thesis. This thesis, in turn, will allow you to plan and write the first draft of your paper.

Represented visually, the process of devising a thesis from your categories of information can be represented as a triangle. At the triangle's base is the raw and uncategorized information you have generated for your topic, referred to as *data* here.

Assuming comprehensive research and idea generating on your part, this data would consist of facts, opinions, statistics, examples, and quotations. You may have invented some or all of this material; you may have researched some or all of it. At this stage the logical processes involved in getting from your information to a working thesis are the same. As the triangle (and your focus) narrows, you find the categories you have created by selecting and organizing your data. At the tip of the triangle is the thesis: the statement that you make by selecting material from your categories.

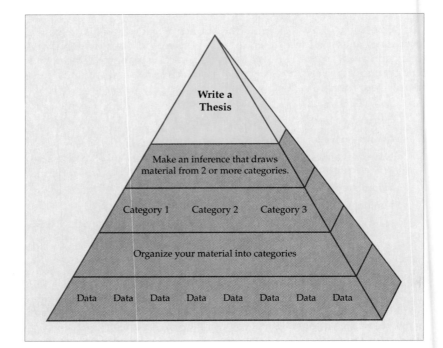

The diagram shows that in narrowing your focus and getting from a review of your categories to a thesis you must make an **inference,** a logical leap to a conclusion, based on available information. You make inferences countless times every day, so automatically that you are often unaware of them. If you see black smoke curling from a window, you make an inference— fire!—based on available information. *The inference that you make about a subject based on the information in your categories will become the* predicate part *of your thesis.* In deciding on this predicate, you will make visible a connection you have inferred from your assembled information. In examining the notes you have set out in categories, ask yourself: What *new* statement, what conclusion, can I make that is consistent with my material? Your answer will be the predicate part of your working thesis.

3f

dev

3 Varieties of inference

In principle, an unlimited number of relationships may exist among the categories you have gathered, but experience teaches that a few patterns of relation tend to recur. Recognizing these patterns can help you to make an inference and complete the predicate part of a thesis. Recall (from 3c-1) that most academic writing is devoted to informing or persuading a reader. Your decision to inform, primarily, or to persuade is communicated in the predicate part of your thesis. Certain inferences lead to informative writing; others lead to persuasive writing.

Inferences that lead to informative writing

SEQUENTIAL ORDER   In reviewing notes across categories, you find that you can place certain information in a logical order. You infer a *sequence*—a pattern of first, second, third. . . . A sequence might suggest a *process*. Based on your notes, you might infer the process of how creative thinkers typically approach a problem. (Steps in a process do not suggest cause. Causal explanations form another inference—see pages 81–82.)

DEFINITION   Certain notes may enable you to define a term. Given your observations and reading over the course of a semester, you might be able to define the term *creativity*. (An inference concerning definitions can at times lead to making an argument. For example, see ¶44 in chapter 5, page 151.)

CLASSIFICATION   You may find such abundant examples of a term that you can recognize different varieties, or classes. Working with the term *creativity,* you may be able to classify types: visual, verbal, mathematical, or musical.

COMPARISON	After a review of the classifications, you can compare or show similarities among various elements of the same class. Thus, you would be able to explain the particular ways in which visual, verbal, mathematical, and musical creativity are similar.
CONTRAST	Upon review of classifications, you can also contrast or show differences among various elements of the same class. Thus, you would be able to explain the particular ways in which visual, verbal, mathematical, and musical creativity differ.

Inferences about sequence, definition, classification, comparison, and contrast become the predicate parts of thesis statements that *inform* readers. Informative writing places a subject before the reader and explains it—shows how it works, what it is made of, what its uses are, and so on. Following are five thesis statements. The predicate part of each is italicized and based on one of the preceding inferences.

Thesis statements that lead to informative papers

SEQUENTIAL ORDER	A creative thinker *will study a problem, arrive at a solution, and then hold off on accepting that solution until she has explored alternatives.*
DEFINITION	Creativity *is the act of recognizing problems and finding solutions.*
CLASSIFICATION	The four types of creativity *are visual, verbal, musical, and mathematical.*
COMPARISON	Of the four types of creativity, musical and mathematical *are most alike.*
CONTRAST	Of the four types of creativity, visual and verbal *differ the most.*

Inferences that lead to argumentative writing

In a thesis that informs, you say: Here is how subject X works, here is what it is made of, here is what its uses are. In a thesis that persuades, you say: Here is my *opinion* on subject X. Usually an argumentative paper includes a good deal of information. The writer provides information, however, to express an opinion. The following four inferences—based on generalization, causation, sign, and analogy—expressed as the predicate part of a thesis, lead to an argument. In chapter 6, on argumentation, these inferences (and one other) are called "lines of argument." The four statements that follow will illustrate how persuasive theses differ from informative ones. Once again, the predicate part of each statement, based on an inference, is italicized.

Thesis statements that lead to persuasive papers

GENERALIZATION   Creative students *are the life blood of any classroom.*

CAUSATION   The causes of creativity *are complex and involve a rich mixture of inheritance and learning.*

SIGN   Risk taking *is a sign of creativity.*

ANALOGY   In the same way that athletes who train vigorously for one sport may be out of shape for others, people who are creative in one sphere—visually, verbally, musically, or mathematically—*will not necessarily be creative in others.*

3f

dev

4   Inferences as patterns of development

Once you express an inference in the predicate part of your thesis, you must develop that inference by giving examples and providing support. In Section 5e-2, patterns of development, including sequential order, definition, classification, comparison/contrast, cause and effect, and analogy are discussed.

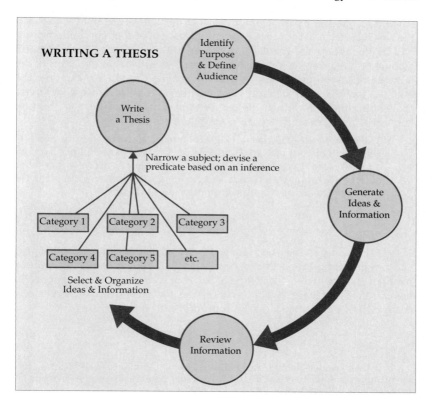

The types of paragraphs you write in a paper are tied directly to the inferences that you express in your thesis. For instance, if your thesis states that you have inferred a sequence concerning your subject, then surely at least several of the paragraphs that you write will be introduced with *first, second, third,* and so on. If in your thesis you suggest a comparison, then surely you will organize a certain number of paragraphs in one of the two ways discussed under "comparison/contrast" in Section 5e-2. Your papers will consist of many paragraphs, of course; and only certain ones will directly develop the inference in the predicate part of your thesis, but these will be the key paragraphs of your paper. Others will prepare for or will lead away from these key paragraphs. Once you decide on a thesis and you understand the inference you will make, turn to chapter 5 for examples of how an inference is made explicit and developed in the writing of paragraphs.

3f

dev

5 The thesis and your ambitions for a paper

Whether you intend to inform or persuade, your assertion about a subject (the predicate part of your thesis) can be more or less ambitious: when the assertion is ambitious, your thesis and the paper that you build from it will be, too. The legal scholar and Supreme Court justice Oliver Wendell Holmes (1841–1935) once characterized intellectual ambition in terms of the number of levels, or stories, in a building. His description captures the qualities that distinguish barely adequate theses from competent and more challenging ones. Although his use of *men* should read *men and women,* Holmes offers an excellent guide to writing thesis sentences:

> There are one-story intellects, two-story intellects, and three-story intellects with skylights. All fact collectors who have no aim beyond their facts are one-story men. Two-story men compare, reason, generalize, using the labor of fact collectors as their own. Three-story men idealize, imagine, predict— their best illumination comes from above the skylight.[3]

One-story thesis

A one-story thesis leads to informative writing and demonstrates that you can gather and report facts. Any paper that follows from such a thesis requires little more than a stitching together of summaries. Strong papers do not use one-story theses. Only on some essay exams will a paper developed in support of a one-story thesis be appropriate in college writing.

---

[3]Oliver Wendell Holmes, cited in Esther Fusco, "Cognitive Levels Matching and Curriculum Analysis," ed. Arthur L. Costa. *Developing Minds: A Resource Book for Teaching Thinking* (Alexandria, VA: ASCD, 1985), 81.

One-story thesis:

There were many voter registration drives among the urban poor in the 1991 elections.
—Registration drive #1
—Registration drive #2, etc.

Wilderness camping poses many challenges.
—Challenge #1
—Challenge #2, etc.

3f

dev

Two-story thesis

Holmes suggests that a thinker is someone who compares facts, generalizes from them, or reasons with them: that is, a thinker *argues* or *informs* with some degree of sophistication. Someone who reasons will define, order, classify, delineate a process, or establish cause and effect—all types of thinking and writing discussed in this book. When you can reason with facts, you are working with a two-story thesis because you are seeing facts *in relation to one another;* you are making inferences and seeing implications. By contrast, the writer of a one-story thesis sees and can write about only one set of facts at a time. A two-story thesis shows an engaged mind at work, *making connections* where none existed previously.

Two-story thesis:

In the 1991 elections, there were three reasons why voter registration drives among the urban poor succeeded where earlier drives had not. [Notice the connection made between voter registration drives in the 1991 elections and such drives in previous elections.]

Like holding a mirror to your personality, wilderness camping shows you to yourself—for better *and* worse. [Notice the connection between wilderness camping and self-reflection.]

Three-story thesis

In addition to making connections where none existed previously, a three-story thesis with a skylight shows a writer willing to take intellectual risks: that is, the writer is willing to expand the scope of the paper, widening its context in order to take up a broader, more complex, and (if executed well) more important discussion. A three-story thesis will create tension among its parts, setting opposites against each other in order to create a contrast.[4] In a thesis with tension, you often find the conjunctions *although* and *even if*. The writer's job is to navigate between opposites. The reader, sensing tension,

---

[4]The term *tension,* as it relates to the thesis statement, is borrowed from John C. Bean and John D. Ramage, *Form and Surprise in Composition: Writing and Thinking Across the Curriculum* (New York: Macmillan, 1986), 168–169.

wants to know what happens and why. A thesis with tension motivates readers.

The three-story thesis, clearly the most ambitious of the three types, can be enormously satisfying as you set out to "idealize, imagine, [or] predict." Holmes remarks that illumination for such a thinker comes "from above the skylight." The metaphor does not suggest someone waiting to be inspired by mysterious agents; rather, the skylight metaphor suggests a mind that lets light in, that is open to a world outside itself and is ready to learn and question. The very best papers are built on three-story theses. These papers tend to be argumentative.

Three-story thesis with a skylight:

> Even though voter registration drives were more successful in 1991 than in previous elections, many urban poor have given up on the American political system—and for good reason.

Compared to the two-story thesis on the same subject, the context of this thesis is broadened, and the paper built on it will discuss more than various elections. Tension is introduced in the contrast between successful registration drives and the attitudes of urban poor.

Three-story thesis with a skylight:

> Wilderness camping teaches that we must preserve what is brutal in Nature, even at the expense of public safety.

Compared to the two-story thesis on the same subject, the context of this thesis is broadened beyond the individual and relates wilderness camping to society at large. Tension is introduced by placing a higher value on "brutality" than on "public safety." A reader's natural response to such tension will be *why*?

Know what sort of paper you are writing

As you create a working thesis, consider whether you are writing a one-, two-, or three-story thesis. By no means should you feel compelled to write a three-story thesis (and a three-story paper) for every assignment. Many writing tasks are one-story jobs: summaries, for instance, and responses to certain essay questions do not call for imaginative engagement on your part. Then again, you may not have time enough to develop a three-story thesis, or you may not know enough about the material to write ambitiously on it. When you have the opportunity, though, try at least for a two-story thesis.

The point of the Holmes metaphor is for you to realize what sort of paper you will write *before* you sit down to a draft. How ambitious will you be? This is the decision you will reflect in your thesis. Experiment with different versions of a thesis, showing in each a different level of ambition. Write the sentences, read them, and see what each requires by way of commitment to the topic and mastery of material. Then choose your thesis, realizing that your choice will set your agenda in the paper to follow.

Generating a Working Thesis

1. Narrow your subject so that you will be able to write specifically on it in the number of pages allotted.
2. Assemble the notes—arranged in categories—that you have generated for your paper.
3. Study the categories you have generated for your subject. *Selectively* draw ideas and information from across categories in order to narrow your subject.
4. Ask: What inference can I make concerning the material I have generated? How will this inference allow me to draw on information and ideas from two or more categories? The answer to these questions will become the predicate of your thesis.
5. Ask: How ambitious will I be with my thesis—and in my paper?

3g

dev

EXERCISE 13

Following are three theses concerning *The Wizard of Oz*. Classify each as a one-, two-, or three-story thesis and explain your reasons for your classifications.

1. In the Depression, a cyclone takes a girl from her family's Kansas farm to the mythical land of Oz; after a series of adventures, she returns home.
2. An adolescent who must soon face the adult world yearns for a return to the simple world of childhood, but she eventually accepts the demands of adulthood.
3. A girl dreams of leaving home to escape her troubles; only after she leaves does she realize how much her home means to her.

EXERCISE 14

Refer to your results of Exercise 10, where you chose three topics from a list and generated ideas about them. Choose one of these topics and narrow it by posing a journalist's questions, as described in 3d-6, so that it would be appropriate for a five-page paper. Then, given the ideas you generated in Exercise 10, write one-, two-, and three-story theses for this topic.

EXERCISE 15

Working with your results of Exercise 11, write one-, two-, and three-story theses for your topic.

3g Shaping and outlining the essay

Look to your working thesis for clues about the ideas you will need to develop in your essay. For an academic paper to succeed, a writer must develop all directly stated or implied ideas in the thesis. You may want to regard your thesis as a contract. In the final draft, the contract exists between you and your reader; the thesis promises the reader a discussion of certain material, and the paper delivers on that promise. As a tool used in writing a first draft, your working thesis is a provisional contract between you and yourself: the thesis represents your best hunch about what direction your paper will take; as you write the paper and investigate the terms of that contract, you will accept some terms (probably most) but will reject others.

3g

dev

1 Identifying and developing significant parts of your thesis

The first step in creating an outline of your first draft is to study your working thesis and to identify all significant elements, stated directly or indirectly. You are obliged to develop each of these elements and to explain how it is related to others. It may be helpful to write the working thesis at the top of a page and to circle its significant words. You can then ask these development questions of each circled element, as appropriate.

Asking These Questions of a Thesis Will Identify Major Sections of Your Paper.

how does/will it happen?
how to describe?
what are some examples?
what are the reasons for?
what is my view?
compared to what?
what is the cause?
any stories to tell?

what has/will prevent it from happening?
who is involved?
what are the key features?
what are the reasons against?
how to define?
possible to classify types or parts?
what is the effect of this?

These questions will help to identify major sections of your paper. Once you have written a draft, you can sharpen the focus of each section by recalling your purpose for writing it. Generally, your purpose (in response to the questions in the box) will be to *explain a process,* to *describe,* to *illustrate,* to *define,* to *classify,* to *establish cause and effect,* or to *tell a story.* These patterns of development directly match the types of inference you can make in formulating the predicate part of your thesis. (The patterns are discussed and illustrated in 5e-2).

When you circle significant words or phrases in your working thesis, presumably you will be able to answer the development questions you pose, given all your effort in generating information. It is quite possible, though, that a development question may leave you without answers. In this case, you will then need to generate more information either by reflecting on your own or by conducting research in the library.

What are the key features?

What are the reasons for?

How will it happen?

(Establishing colonies on the moon)(will be possible by the early 21st century.)

who's involved?

what will prevent it from happening?

3g

dev

2 Conceiving an overall design for the paper

Once you have identified the major parts of your paper, you need to arrange these parts according to some plan. Whatever the plan, make sure that it meets the requirements of unity (see 5c) and coherence (see 5d). These terms will guide your first major revision of the paper; for the moment you should dwell on them only long enough to understand how they can help you write the strongest possible first draft. A *unified paper* will meet two tests: it will develop all significant parts of your thesis, and it will avoid developing any topic not closely related to your thesis. In a *coherent paper,* all parts that you develop will lead logically from one to the next. As you write the first draft, be mindful of the requirements for unity and coherence. Remember, however, that in a first draft you must give yourself freedom to discover. Thus, you may well veer away from the plan you set yourself, and the result will be a temporary *lack* of unity and coherence. Do not worry. In your first draft, you *should* veer off and discover whenever the opportunity presents itself. You will address problems of unity and coherence during revision.

Now that you are aware of the general need for unity and coherence in a paper, as well as your paper's major parts, you can sketch a plan. In terms of its broad organization, a paper can be arranged chronologically, spatially, or logically. A single paper, well planned, can incorporate all three types of arrangement. A **chronological arrangement** begins at one point in time and proceeds in sequence, forward or backward, to some other point. A chronological organization lends itself to papers in which you want to narrate a story; track a process; trace the development or emergence of some thing or person; or report on events as they have occurred, if you feel timing is significant. If you plan to devote large parts of your paper to description, you might consider a **spatial arrangement.** Such an arrangement can lend an overall coherence to your descriptions: for instance, in discussing a painting or photograph, you might organize your writing into three sections: one focused on the foreground, the next on the middle ground, and the third on the background.

Logical arrangement is by far the most common design for academic papers. In arranging a paper logically, you commit yourself to dividing a topic into its constituent parts and discussing one part at a time in an order that will make sense to your readers. In your discussion of each part, you will present material in a variety of ways, selecting from among several methods of development as your needs dictate: you will define terms, illustrate points, compare and contrast, classify, delineate a process, and/or analyze cause and effect.

3g

dev

3 Outlining the paper

An outline is the map you give yourself of the territory you are about to enter as you sit down to write a first draft. Personal preference will dictate how thorough a map you need in order to feel secure about beginning. Depending on the situation and the person, a rough sketch will often do—a general plan noting major sections of your paper and their placement. You (or your professor) may prefer a formal outline. With either approach you must appreciate that your outline is *provisional*, a best guess. The actual writing of your paper may reveal elements of a topic that you did not intend to explore but that seem worth exploring nonetheless. Outlines are useful for getting you started; but do not hesitate to revise the outline if you discover new or better routes to your goal.

Informal outline

In an informal outline, you do little more than note the major sections of your paper and their placement, relative to each other. You may also want to note the type of arrangement you plan to use in each part of the paper.

Thesis:

> Establishing colonies on the moon will be possible by the early 21st century.

- Describe a moon colony. (spatial arrangement)
- Identify the people and agencies involved in design and construction of the colony. (logical arrangement)
- Review the challenges to building a colony: financial, technical, political. (logical arrangement)
- Present a realistic timetable for construction, detailing the developmental milestones that will need to be met. (chronological arrangement)

Formal outline

A formal outline establishes the major sections and subsections of your paper. The outline shows how each section is supported by points you plan to discuss (see 18e-2). It also shows how these points are themselves supported. The goal of a formal outline is to make visible the material you plan to use in the paper. Standard outline form is as follows: uppercase roman numerals indicate the most general level of heading in the outline; these headings correspond with major sections of your paper. Upper case letters mark the major points you will use in developing each heading. Arabic numbers mark the supporting points you will use in developing main points. Lowercase letters mark further subordination—support of supporting points. Note that the entries at each level of heading are grammatically parallel (see 18e-2); that each level of heading has at least two entries; and that only the first letter of an entry is capitalized. A formal outline need not show plans for your introduction or conclusion.

3g

dev

You can also use a formal outline as a tool for revision. Once you have written your paper, outline its parts. Your outline will help reveal to you the extent to which your writing is unified and coherent. Following is a partial outline of a paper on colonizing the moon.

Thesis: Establishing colonies on the moon will be possible by the early 21st century.

I. Colonizing the moon
   A. Base
   B. Missions
      1. Science
         a. Astronomy
         b. Geology
      2. Industry
         a. Mining
         b. Crystal growth
   C. Inhabitants
      1. Specialists
      2. Nonspecialists

II. Designing and building the base
   A. Designers
      1. Architects
      2. Psychologists
      3. Engineers
   B. Construction
      1. Materials
      2. Methods
      3. Crews
      4. Dangers

Each item of a formal outline can also be written as a sentence, which you may prefer in your efforts to begin writing. The following is one section of the preceding outline, written in sentence form.

B. There will be two broad missions for a Moon Base.
   1. The first mission will be scientific.
      a. By setting up telescopes on the far side of the moon, astronomers will have an unparalleled view of the universe.

b. Geologists studying samples of lunar soil will be able to learn both about earth's origin and the origin of the solar system.

2. The second mission will be industrial.

a. Mining companies will be able to begin commercial operations almost immediately.

b. In the light moon gravity, technicians will be able to grow superior crystals.

3g

dev

Sean Hannan's Paper
Informal Outline

```
Working thesis:

   Fans do not know how the raw emotion and violence required of a

   football player can turn him into an animal.

   -What's in it for the fans (logical arrangement)

   -Football games: tell story of the winning season, describing

    emotional intensity and violence (chronological arrangement)
```

4   Working collaboratively

In assigning a writing project, your professor may ask you to work collaboratively—that is, in a group. The great advantage of creating a document collaboratively is that you can put the power of several minds to work on a task that for one person might prove overwhelming. Both in content and presentation, however, your group's work should read as though *one* person had written it even if several people have been involved in the actual writing.

- To minimize rewriting, meet with group members before any writing takes place. Agree on a structure for the overall document and then assign parts to individual group members. Agree on a consistent point of view for the paper.

- At a second meeting after writing has just begun, ask each group member to outline his or her section and to discuss its structure. As a group, think specifically of the ways in which one section will build from and lead to another. Also raise and address any problems encountered thus far in the writing.

- At the completion of a first draft, distribute the assembled document to the entire group and have each member revise for content and consistency of perspective.

- Incorporate all revisions in a single version of the document. *One* member of the group should then take responsibility for rewriting the paper so as to ensure continuity of style and voice.

Whether you write a paper individually or collaboratively, you may be asked to *revise* your work with the aid of other people. (See 4j, "Giving and Receiving Editorial Advice.")

EXERCISE 16

Following are four theses that you have seen earlier. For any three, circle significant words and phrases, pose development questions (see 3g-1), and write an informal outline of a paper that would develop the thesis. For the remaining thesis, circle words and phrases, pose development questions, and develop a formal outline. Invent information as needed to complete the assignment.

3g

dev

1. In the 1991 elections, there were three reasons why voter registration drives among the urban poor succeeded where earlier drives had not.

2. Like holding a mirror to your personality, wilderness camping shows you to yourself—for better *and* worse.

3. Even though voter registration drives were more successful in 1991 than in previous elections, many urban poor have given up on the American political system—and for good reason.

4. Wilderness camping teaches that we must preserve what is brutal in Nature, even at the expense of public safety.

EXERCISE 17

Reread the results of Exercise 15 in which you devised a one-, two-, and three-story thesis for the paper you are planning. Choose a two- or three-story thesis. Circle significant words or phrases, pose development questions, and prepare an informal or formal outline of your paper.

CHAPTER 4

Drafting and Revising the Paper

Your working thesis and your sketch or outline are essential for giving you the confidence to begin a first **draft.** Realize, however, that your final paper will *not* be identical to your original plans, even if they were carefully prepared. Once begun, writing will lead you to discard and revise your original ideas and will lead to new ideas as well. Through writing you will *explore* your subject. As you do, obstacles and opportunities will present themselves: by keeping your eyes open, you will be ready to avoid one and seize the other.

4a Adopting a strategy for writing

Following are three strategies for using your outline as a basis for writing. None of these strategies is *correct* in the sense that one produces a better draft than the others. All will get you a first draft, and all have advantages and disadvantages. How you choose to use an outline is a matter of your temperament as a writer.

 1 Adhering closely to your outline

Writing from the "outside–in" closely follows the outline you made prior to actual drafting. To make full and frequent use of the detailed outline you have assembled makes a great deal of sense, as long as you are aware that your paper *will* deviate from the outline.

Advantages

By regularly consulting your outline, you will feel that you are making regular progress toward the completion of your paper.

Disadvantages

A comprehensive outline can so focus your vision that you will not allow yourself to stray and discover the territory of your paper. The paper planned will be the paper written, for better or worse.

 2 Adhering loosely to your outline

Some writers prefer to use an outline exclusively as a strategy for preparing; in the actual drafting of the paper, they abandon the outline in favor of one that they generate *while* writing the draft. This is drafting from the "inside–out," letting your progress in the draft direct you. Following this strategy, you examine your outline, studying its first section carefully, and then begin writing. The outline is set aside and, once writing is under way, a new outline for each section of the paper you are about to write is created, based on the material you have just written. As you complete each section, you update and adjust your outline of the entire paper. Written from the inside–out, your outline is constantly evolving.

4a

dev

Advantages

This strategy gives you the best chance of discovering material, since each new section of the paper is based on the writing you have just completed and not on an outline prepared in advance.

Disadvantages

The same freedom that gives you room to be creative can result in a draft's being incoherent and lacking unity: paragraphs may not lead logically from one to the next and whole groupings of paragraphs may drift away from the working thesis.

3 Combining strategies

Some writers like to give themselves more freedom than close adherence to a pre-draft outline allows; but at the same time they prefer more structure than the outline-as-you-go approach provides. These writers borrow from both methods. First, they carefully review their pre-draft outline for each section of the paper before writing it; then they write the section *without* further reference to the outline. At the end of each section, they compare their work against the outline and plan to add or delete material as needed. They also look ahead to the next section and revise the outline, if necessary. As you might expect, the advantages and disadvantages of the two preceding strategies are merged in this combined strategy.

Strategies for Drafting

Working with your pre-draft outline

1. Follow the outline closely, but remain aware of the need to deviate.
2. Abandon the pre-draft outline in favor of an outline that you create and continually update as you are drafting.
3. Combine methods 1 and 2: study a section of the outline; turn away from the outline to write a draft of the section; and then compare your draft with the outline, making adjustments as needed.

EXERCISE 1

Select one of the preceding strategies, or some variant of your design, for writing a rough draft of your paper. Reflect on the strategy you usually use when writing a paper and in a brief paragraph compare or contrast your usual strategy with the one you will be adopting for this paper.

4b

dev   **4b**   Beating writer's block

Journalists, novelists, beginning writers, writing teachers, graduate students, business people, students in freshmen composition: *everybody* avoids writing at some point or another. Odd as it may seem, this information can be of comfort: for if you avoid writing, be assured that avoidance does *not* mean you have done things poorly or that you do not "have what it takes" to be a competent writer. Avoidance and the anxiety that causes it are fundamental, natural parts of the writing process. By no means are they ever-present parts, and if you devote sufficient time to preparing yourself to write (attending to the various tasks discussed in chapter 3), then you minimize the danger of writer's block. Still, preparing is not the same as writing a draft, and you inevitably face a moment in which you decide to take a step—or not. Think about the feelings you get when you do not want to write. When you are stuck as a writer, what might you be telling yourself? And how might you get unstuck?

STUCK   *I cannot get started.* I am afraid of the blank page—or its electronic equivalent, the empty screen: However fully formed ideas for writing may come to me, I write one letter at a time, one word after the next. And as I do, what I *have not* written seems so vast that I cannot make a beginning.

UNSTUCK   *Prepare yourself mentally to write* one *section of the paper, not the entire paper.* Three-page papers, just like 500-page books, get written one section at a time. When you sit down to write a draft, identify a *section*: a grouping of related paragraphs that you can write in a single sitting. Choose a section, write it, and take a break. Sooner than you realize, the pages will add up. (For detailed advice on writing sections of a paper, see 5a.)

STUCK   *I want my writing to be perfect.* My early attempts to express anything are messy. I get a sinking feeling when I reread my work and see how much revision is needed. Sometimes, completing the first draft seems impossible. Whenever I cannot think of the right word, I freeze up.

UNSTUCK   *Accept* two *drafts, minimum, as the standard for writing any formal paper.* When you understand that you will rewrite the first draft of all formal papers or letters, you can give yourself permission to write a first draft quickly and at times imprecisely. More important than getting a word choice correct in a first draft is getting the entire draft completed.

STUCK *Why advertise my problems?* I worry about grammar, punctuation, and spelling, and I do not want to embarrass myself before teachers, fellow students, or employers.

UNSTUCK *Use a writer's reference tools.* Many people are nervous about exposing the extent to which they have not mastered fundamentals of writing. The fear is real, but not one that should prevent you from producing a first draft. As long as you know how to use standard desk references—a dictionary and a handbook—there is no need to memorize rules of grammar, punctuation, and spelling. Of course, knowing the rules *does* save you time.

4c

dev

Strategies for Drafting

Working yourself through the draft

1. Write *one* section of the paper at a time: write a general statement that supports some part of your thesis, then provide details about the supporting statement. Once you have finished a section, take a break. Then return to write another section, working incrementally in this fashion until you have completed the draft. See 5a.

   * Alternately, write one section of the paper and take a break. Then reread and revise that one section before moving to the next. Continue to work in this fashion, one section at a time, until you complete the draft.

2. Accept *two* drafts, minimum, as the standard for writing any formal paper. In this way, you give yourself permission to write a first draft that is not perfect.

3. If you have prepared adequately for writing, then trust that you will discover what to write *as* you write.

4. Save for later substantial revisions concerning grammar, punctuation, usage, and spelling. In your first drafts, focus on content.

EXERCISE 2

In a paragraph or two, discuss a time you were asked to write but could not. Based on the discussion in this section, analyze that writing situation. Explain, if you can, why you were unable to write.

4c Identifying and resolving problems in mid-draft

It is likely that at some point in the writing process you will find yourself unable to steam ahead, one section after the next. You will encounter obstacles, which you can recognize as follows: you are aware that your work in one section of the paper is not as good as it is elsewhere, or you make several attempts at writing a section and find that you simply cannot do it. When you are feeling especially frustrated, stop. Step back from your work and decide how you will get past this obstacle. Ask: Why am I having trouble? Here are several possibilities:

Potential obstacles in writing a draft

1. You do not have enough information to write. You have not gathered the information or, if you have, you may not thoroughly understand it.

2. You do not understand the point you planned to make or its relation to the rest of your paper.

3. The point you planned to make no longer seems relevant or correct, given what you have discovered about your subject while writing.

4. You recognize a gap in the structure of your paper, and you suddenly see the need to expand an existing section or to write an entirely new section.

5. The material in the section seems inappropriate for your audience.

6. You have said everything you need to in a page, but the assignment calls for six to ten pages.

7. At the moment, you do not have the attention span to write.

Each of these obstacles can frustrate your attempts at writing, and only you can know what is for you a normal and abnormal level of frustration. Whatever your tolerance, develop sensors to let you know when things are not going well. Frustration usually occurs for a good reason, so you should trust the reaction and then act on it. You will come of age as a writer the moment you can realize you are having trouble and can then step away to name your problem and find a solution.

The wheel in this diagram gives you a visual representation of the writing process and the backward and forward looping you will do as you write a draft and pause, periodically, to identify obstacles and decide on courses of action. A variation on the thinking and writing wheel introduced in chapter 3, this diagram shows each part of the writing process up until drafting:

- identifying your purpose and defining your audience
- generating ideas and information
- selecting and organizing ideas and information
- writing the working thesis

The diagram shows that your writing of a draft takes place in an abbreviated wheel, an "inner loop." Working from your thesis and with information already present and organized, you write one section of your draft at a time. When you encounter an obstacle, you leave this inner loop and return to some earlier, preparatory stage of the process: possibly to reconsider your purpose or audience, possibly to generate more information,

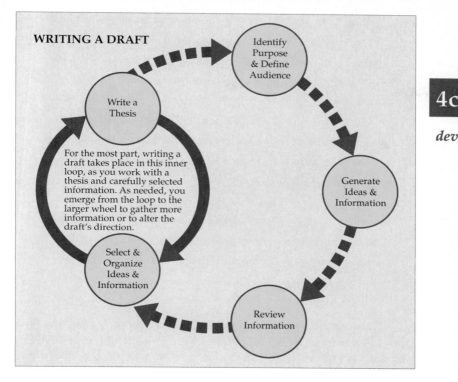

WRITING A DRAFT

Identify Purpose & Define Audience

Write a Thesis

For the most part, writing a draft takes place in this inner loop, as you work with a thesis and carefully selected information. As needed, you emerge from the loop to the larger wheel to gather more information or to alter the draft's direction.

Generate Ideas & Information

Select & Organize Ideas & Information

Review Information

4c

dev

possibly to choose a better example, or possibly to rethink ways you have selected and grouped information. Once you have located necessary material or have otherwise thought your way through the problem, you return to the inner loop to continue with your draft.

EXERCISE 3

Using the strategy you selected in Exercise 1, write a draft of your paper. Remember to write one section of your paper at a time. (See 5a for advice.)

REVISING

Most of the sentences and paragraphs in this handbook went to reviewers and editors only after going through revisions such as you see here:

nothing will change this fact: writing is

~~A first step you can take is to appreciate how utterly~~ messy,the

~~process of writing truly is. Messiness groping its way towards~~

~~order is a condition of the writer's life—of the beginner's work~~

~~and the expert's. Writing is always messy.~~ *Early versions of whatever you write will seem terrible to you.*

4d

dev

Writing is an exceedingly messy,—though necessary and often very gratifying—business. Nothing that anyone will ever tell you about writing will change the fact that early versions of whatever you're writing will likely seem terrible to you, *and you cannot go to later, more polished, drafts without first writing a messy initial one.* Nothing anyone will ever tell you will change the fact *that writing is a* early versions of whatever you're working on will often seem terrible *messy process* to you; and you cannot go to later, more polished versions without first writing a messy initial one.

Nothing anyone will ever tell you about writing will change the fact that writing is a messy process. Early versions of whatever you're working on will be flawed; but you cannot get to later, more polished versions without first writing an initial messy one.

Certainly writing *is* messy business, a statement as true for professional writers as it is for novices. "But," you say, "a professor of composition can whip off a better-looking first draft of a report than I can." Most likely, yes. But you can be sure this first draft will look as flawed to the professor as your first draft looks to you—for as writers become more proficient, their expectations rise. In this way, writers at all levels are forever finding fault with early versions of their work. The beginning writer, ironically, is often the one who has not yet developed the ability to spot correctable problems and to address them. The more you know about writing and the writing process, the more you will see **revision** as a natural extension of writing a first draft.

4d Clarifying your purpose and thesis

Having written a first draft, you are in a position to reread your work and see what you have accomplished. But first get some distance from your writing. If possible, let an entire day go by before returning to the draft. Fresh eyes allow you to see your draft for what it is, as opposed to what you intended it to be. If you relied heavily on your outline, then you transferred your working thesis to your draft. The mere presence of the thesis, however, in no way guarantees the sound organization of your draft. Underline what you assume is your working thesis. Then read your draft carefully, looking for some other sentence that may more accurately describe what you have written. Often, such a "competing thesis" appears toward the end of the draft, where in your conclusion you forced yourself to summarize.

Sean Hannan's draft, pages 106–110, led him to a competing thesis. He began his draft (see the end of paragraph 1) with the following working thesis.

> Fans don't know how the raw emotion and violence required of a football player can turn him into an animal.

4d

dev

Sean's final paragraph pointed the way to a competing thesis. In rereading the draft, he agreed with his instructor that while he had started the draft with one thesis, he had ended with another that more precisely stated what he had achieved in his writing.

> Winning at football, with all of its obvious benefits, creates monsters out of the very players it glorifies.

Writing a draft enabled Sean Hannan to clarify his purpose. In no way did he waste effort by beginning his first draft with a thesis he did not, in fact, end up developing. His draft started him on a process of discovery. As a first step in the revision process, reread your draft to see what you have discovered and to determine the extent to which your discovery merits changing your thesis.

Choosing a title

On the basis of your final thesis, devise a title for your paper. Sean Hannan chose " The Win Justifies the Means," a play on the phrase "the end justifies the means." In writing his first draft, Sean realized that it was an adherence to this philosophy, not the game of football itself, that had transformed him and his teammates into animals. The phrasing of his title therefore directly captures the sense of his paper and is an example of an *evocative* title: a playful, intriguing, or otherwise indirect title meant to pique a reader's interest. A *descriptive* title directly announces the content of a paper and is appropriate for reports and write-ups of experiments: occasions when you are expected to be direct. Sean gave his third and final draft a descriptive title: "Group Life and the Loss of Conscience." Both evocative and descriptive titles should be brief (no longer than ten words).

Revise to Clarify Your Purpose and Thesis

1. Before rereading your draft, recall your original purpose for writing. If this purpose was set for you in an assignment, reread the assignment.

2. Reread your first draft. Underline your working thesis and then ask this question: To what extent has the paper I have written developed this sentence? If your answer is *to a large extent*, then you wrote the draft more or less according to plan and your working thesis, after some tinkering, will become your final thesis.

(continued)

dev

Revise to Clarify Your Purpose and Thesis (Continued)

3. If your answer to the question is *only slightly*, then search for a competing thesis—some other sentence that is developed in the draft. Underline this sentence. If no one sentence will do, underline several sentences and summarize them. Some version of this new sentence will become your final thesis.

EXERCISE 4

Reread your draft. Clarify the purpose and thesis of your rough draft, following the strategies discussed.

4e Using your thesis to revise for unity and coherence

Structurally, the goal of formal, academic writing is to produce a close, logical fit between the sections of a paper and the paper's thesis. Only after you have determined a final thesis can you settle down to the business of creating this fit.

1 Unity

Begin your structural revision of a paper by posing questions of your final thesis, just as you did of your working thesis. The goal here is to clarify exactly what you should discuss in order to make good on your obligations to the reader, as implied by the thesis. On page 88, you will find fifteen development questions, among them: *who is involved? what are the key features? how to define?* Once again pose these questions, as appropriate. Here are development questions from 3g-1, as applied to Sean Hannan's final thesis.

Though being a member of a group has its benefits, group life can usurp an individual's conscience—a lesson I learned all too well playing football on a championship team.

What are some examples of the benefits of belonging to a group? *By what process* can a group usurp an individual's conscience? *What causes* the loss of individual conscience? *Are there any stories* to tell about playing on a championship team? Sean must respond to these questions if his paper is to deliver on the promise of his thesis. For the reader, a thesis is like a contract. The reader reads the statement, forms expectations about what will follow, and then reads with these expectations in mind. The content of a paper exhibits **unity** when a writer discusses only those aspects of the subject that are implied by the thesis.

Sections of a paper, just like the paper itself, can be unified or not. In a section of the paper discussing events prior to the football season, it would disorient the reader to find sentences referring to the conclusion of the season. Similarly, a paragraph is unified when all sentences pertain to the same topic. Unity is a principle of logic that applies with differing levels of generality to the whole essay, to sections within the essay, and to paragraphs within sections. Once you have settled on a final thesis, begin your revision by checking for overall unity at the level of the essay. Check next for unity among the paragraphs in each section. Finally, check for unity within paragraphs.

4e

2   Coherence

dev

Coherence describes the clarity of the relationship between one unit of meaning and another. If readers are to follow a discussion, they need to understand how you move, logically, from one thought to the next: one sentence to the next, within paragraphs; one paragraph to the next, within sections; and one section to the next, within the essay. Thus coherence, like unity, is a principle of logic that applies to all levels of writing in a paper. You establish coherence by building logical bridges, or transitions, between your thoughts. A **transition** may be a word, a sentence, or a paragraph devoted to building a smooth logical relationship between parts. In all cases, a transition reminds readers of what they have just read and simultaneously forecasts what is to come. Often, these bridges may be individual words within a paragraph:

> In the finished film [*Serpico*] the protagonist develops from a clean-shaven police officer to a shaggy hipster. In production, *however,* the film was shot in reverse order. The star, Al Pacino, began with long hair and a beard; *then* for each scene, his hair and beard were trimmed bit by bit until he became clean-cut. *Thus* the last episodes to be shot were the first the audience would eventually see.

However, then, and *thus* are one-word transitions that implicitly ask the reader to summarize preceding information. Sentence-length transitions make this request explicitly:

> Film production has been our principal concern, but the social institution of cinema also depends on distribution and exhibition.

The first part of this sentence explicitly casts the reader backwards by summarizing material that has just been presented. The second part of the sentence casts the reader forward by announcing a new, though related, topic. At times, a writer may devote an entire paragraph to building a logical link from one section of a paper to the next. (See 5d-3 for an example.) Whatever form it takes—word, sentence, or paragraph—a transition establishes coherence by setting adjacent elements (words, sentences, or paragraphs) in clear relation to one another. Once you are sure that your paper is unified, turn your attention to coherence. Ask yourself:

> Which sections of this paper should come first, second, third . . . ?
> How can I use transitions to facilitate understanding?

Ask the same questions of paragraphs within a section and sentences within a paragraph. When a paper is coherent, your reader will be able to follow your discussion from sentence to sentence, paragraph to paragraph, and section to section.

4e

dev

Revise for Unity and Coherence

- Reread your draft and identify your final thesis: the one sentence that your paper spends most of its time developing. Often, your original working thesis—with modifications—will become your final thesis. At times, you will identify a new sentence, discovered in the act of writing, that more nearly captures the content of your paper.

- Rewrite your final thesis until it is as precise as possible. Then ask development questions of it (3g-1) to identify all major sections you are obligated to discuss in your paper. Based on your final thesis, choose a title for your paper.

The Paper

- Revise the entire paper for unity: work through the draft methodically, identifying sections, or groupings of paragraphs, you have developed. (One technique for doing this is to outline your paper. Topics off the point will quickly become apparent.) Retain all sections that develop some part of thesis, as defined previously. Cut any sentence, paragraph, or group of paragraphs that does not develop some part of the thesis.

- Revise the entire paper for coherence: arrange the sections of the paper into a logical order, providing transitions between each section.

The Section

- Revise each section for unity; retain all paragraphs that develop the main point being developed in the section. Delete or transfer to a different section any paragraph or sentence that does not develop the main point.

- Revise each section for coherence: arrange paragraphs within each section so that paragraphs follow logically from one to the next. Provide transitions between paragraphs.

The Paragraph

- Revise each paragraph for unity: retain all sentences that develop the main point of the paragraph. Delete or transfer to another paragraph any sentence that does not develop the main point.

- Revise each paragraph for coherence: arrange sentences within each paragraph so that there is a logical order. When needed, provide transitions between sentences or use repetition or pronouns (see 5d) to establish coherence.

- As a final check that your revised draft is both unified and coherent, outline your draft. You should see a clear and unified progression of ideas, each of which develops some part of your final thesis.

EXERCISE 5

Revise your first draft for unity and coherence, following the guidelines discussed.

4f Revising for balance

4g

dev

First drafts are typically uneven in the amount of attention given to each section of a paper. In the early stages of a draft you cannot know, precisely, what will follow: whether the point you are writing at the moment will be developed later; whether the point you are writing now will even appear in the final draft. In revision, one of your jobs is to review the weight (the extent of development) you have given each of the topics you have discussed and to determine how appropriate that weight is to the importance of that particular point. At times, you will need to **expand:** to add material, in which case you will need to return to the notes you made in preparing to write. You may need to generate new information by reflecting on your subject, by conducting additional library research, or both. At times, you will need to **condense:** to take a lengthy paragraph, for example, and reduce it to two sentences. At other times you will need to **cut:** to delete sentences because they are off the point or because they give too much attention to a subordinate point.

Revise for Balance: Expand, Condense, and Cut

1. In conjunction with your revision for unity and coherence, reread your paper to determine how evenly you have developed each section.
2. Expand discussions that are underdeveloped.
3. Condense discussions that are overdeveloped.
4. Cut extraneous material or material that gives too much weight to minor points.

EXERCISE 6

Revise your draft for balance, following the guidelines discussed. Prepare a clean copy of your revised draft for your instructor.

4g Responding to an instructor's requests for revision

Instructors often want to see an early draft of your papers in order to make comments that you can take into account during the revision process. The earlier the draft that instructors see, the more likely they are to focus on large-scale matters such as the accuracy of content as well as unity, coherence, and balance. You will make best use of your instructor's time if you submit a paper that you have already revised to the best of your ability (as Exercises 4, 5, and 6 ask you to do). To submit true first draft pages that you have not reread or corrected in any way will result in your instructor's commenting on the obvious: for instance, that an important supporting point in your paper had been left undeveloped. You might know this; but the instructor, not knowing that you knew, would feel obligated to comment, thus taking time from other observations that might have been more helpful to you. Revise the paper yourself, first; concentrate on unity, coherence, and balance; and then see what your instructor has to say. Without question, the more seasoned an early draft you submit, the more useful the comments you will get in return.

dev

4h   Preparing the first draft

Here is the first *clean* draft of Sean Hannan's paper, preparations for which you followed in chapter 3. Sean revised as best he could to clarify matters of purpose, unity, coherence, and balance before submitting the draft to his instructor for review. You will find the instructor's comments written throughout.

```
                    Rough Draft

          Football is a challenging sport. To win,

     players must sacrifice physically and mentally.

     I know this because in my senior year of high

     school, I played on a championship team. The

     raw emotion and violence of the game which had

     dominated our lives for four months had mani-

     fested into an evil unparalleled by any good

     that could have been derived from winning. Fans

     don't know how the raw emotion and violence re-

     quired of a football player can turn him into

     an animal.

          The first game of the year served as intro-

     duction to both the horrors and advantages of

     winning. At the beginning of the second half we
```

Expand. What about before the season?

You are planning to discuss how a football player can become an animal. Does the process begin on the first game of the year? before this?

were beating the opposition handily. They were visibly fatigued and getting desperate, calling trick plays and misdirections. I was playing linebacker, when a reverse was run to my side. I had read the play from the snap and was waiting for the runner. My heart raced and adrenaline pumped as he ran directly at me. I lunged at him and planted my helmet into his thigh. Halfway through the tackle I felt his leg give under my helmet and heard the sound of bone breaking. We landed hard and were immediately covered by my teammates who were trying to make the same play. My arms were still wrapped around his knees and my helmet still laid against his crooked thigh, when he began crying.

Expand. a horrifying moment!

You must have been torn with conflicting emotions. How did you feel after breaking this player's leg?

After winning only one game the team and the media already talked of a league championship. What's more, our town which had been deprived of the title for thirty years began to vehemently support us. Signs were erected in store fronts to encourage us, and we made headlines in the local paper.

Expand.
How else did the town support you, and what were your reactions to this support?

4h

dev

Expand. You have me wanting more! What happened during the season? A process shows steps along the way, from beginning to end.

We had won all our games, and with each win the town's support grew until it reached a fever pitch at the last game. We were scheduled to play the league's only other undefeated team. Before the game, players were putting on their pads and taping their knees seemingly unaware of what they were about to go through. The coach soon entered and told us to be ready in a half hour. Immediately, as if in one motion, helmets went on, chin straps were tightened, and the stereo was turned on. The mood became deadly serious as players began to zombie about trying to unlock a rage within themselves. I focused on the words of the heavy metal music playing. I had my eyes closed thinking about the game when one of my teammates grabbed me and embraced me. Tears began to flow.

Cut or condense?

I'm concerned that your story of the season is becoming just — that is, only — a story. Your narration is compelling, but too much narration causes difficulties. See my note at the end.

My heart was filled with absolute hatred when we took the field and I raged at the sight of our opponents. But, as the game began it became clear that our opposition wanted to win just as bad as we did. They matched us in intensity and will to win. On a kick-off one of our players named Jason had five ribs broken away from the play, and for the first time I feared being seriously hurt. The game was tied at 0

going into the fourth quarter. I was in charge
of blocking their best player. His name was
Hunter. He was over six feet tall and weighed
about two hundred and fifty pounds. He was also
the one responsible for injuring my teammate.
Toward the end of the game we were able to get
the ball inside their twenty. I was having trouble blocking Hunter. He made two big tackles
that stalled our drive. It was third and seven
and we called a time out. My teammates confronted me. Mark, who was apparently speaking
for the whole group, looked directly into my
eyes and asked: "Did you notice Hunter's knee
brace." Nothing else was said, I knew what I
had to do. On the next play I didn't even try
to block Hunter. Instead, I stayed back. He
stood up and exposed the weakness. When his leg
was firmly planted I rushed him. I lowered my
shoulder and planted it into the side of his
right knee. It collapsed easier than I thought,
but he did not scream or cry or even fall. Instead he hobbled off the field squinting. The
game had made Hunter tough and I respected him
but I also knew that he wouldn't be back. In
the huddle I was met with thankful nods and
pats on the back. Everyone knew that what had
happened was no accident. Revitalized, the team
went on to score and eventually win. Elation
was in the air as fans poured onto the field.

The intensity of this game and of our opponents had given us perspective, though. In playing, we were forced to look into a mirror.

4h

dev

While the town celebrated, my teammates and I began to question what we were doing and why we were doing it. Throughout the next week I thought about the people that had been hurt in our climb to the league championship. I had also discovered what evil I was capable of. And now that we had achieved our goal, I could no longer rationalize the monster I had become. Winning, with all of its benefits, had created monsters out of us.

4h

dev

Have you discovered a new thesis here? I can't help but think that you've ended at a more significant place than where you began.

General comments: The writing here is immediate and forceful. You have a talent for describing violence with sensitivity. The essay tells a story of conversion, of how you changed. Two points to bear in mind that might improve the telling: Your story locks you into a strict time sequence in which you must present all information chronologically. A full accounting of how playing football turned you into an animal would therefore be very long. The second, related difficulty, is that your "narrator" mode locks out your "observer" mode, and the observer has some shrewd things to say. To sum up: Compress the narration when you can; add comments and interpretations when you can. This is a strong beginning—speaking of which, your introduction could be more imaginative. And what about a title?

4i Editing

Editing is rewriting at the sentence level: the level at which you attend to style, grammar, punctuation, and word choice. Depending on their preferences, writers will edit (just as they revise) throughout the writing process, from the first draft through to the last. It would be misleading to state flatly that the process of sentence-level rewriting should wait until all issues of unity and coherence are resolved. Still, to the extent that you *can* hold off, save editing until the later drafts, once you are relatively confident that your paper has a final thesis and that the major sections of the paper are in order. In any event, don't allow sentence-level concerns to block your writing process early on—especially since the sentence you are fretting over may not even make it to the final draft.

4i

coh

Checklist for Punctuation

1. Have you used a period, a question mark, or (rarely) an exclamation point—but *not* a comma—to end sentences? (See 24a-c.)
2. Have you placed a comma after introductory elements in your sentences? (See 25a.)
3. Have you remembered to use a *second* comma to mark the end of a non-essential word, phrase, or clause appearing in the middle of a sentence? (See 25d.)
4. Have you checked for consistent and correct use of the apostrophe (see 27a-d) and quotation marks (see 28a-c)?
5. Have you used a colon after a complete sentence? (See 29a.)
6. Have you used semicolons to separate grammatically equal elements? (See 26a-g.)
7. Have you used hyphens correctly? (See 32a.)
8. Have you used elements of mechanics correctly: capitals, abbreviations, numbers, and italics? (See chapters 30 and 31.)

Matters of precision are not so easily held off, however. Precise wording means precise thinking; and no doubt your ability to think clearly at any point in the draft will affect your subsequent writing. Use your judgment. If you find yourself struggling with the wording of an especially important sentence, take the time to edit and get it right. But if you are groping for a word in a sentence that is not central to your thinking, hold off your editing. Later in the writing process you will have time enough to settle questions of style, grammar, punctuation, usage, and spelling. By no means must you memorize rules concerning these matters as long as you can recognize problems and know you can seek help in a handbook and a dictionary.

Use the cross-referenced checklists in this chapter to help edit your sentences. The checklists assume you are aware of terms common to discussion of grammar, punctuation, and style. A suggestion made in the preface is worth repeating here: take an hour to read the introductions to each of the chapters in the handbook. If such a review is not realistic, then read the introductions to the chapters on sentence errors (see 12–16), effective sentences (see 17–20), and punctuation (see 24–29). Your review will give you a sense of the types of errors to watch for when editing.

4j

coh

Checklist for Avoiding Common Sentence and Grammar Errors

1. Have you identified and corrected fragments? (See 12a-d.)

2. Have you identified and corrected comma splices and fused sentences? (See 13a-b.)

3. Have you corrected misplaced or dangling modifiers? Watch especially in sentences beginning with an *ing* phrase that you follow with the noun being modified. (See 15a-h.)

4. Have you avoided shifts in person, number, tense, and tone? (See 16a-c.)

5. Have you avoided mixed constructions and incomplete sentences? (See 16e-h.)

6. Have you checked tense endings? Have you used tenses consistently? (See 9e-f.)

7. Have you maintained agreement between subjects and verbs (see 10a) and between pronouns and antecedents (see 10b)?

8. Have you used correct pronoun cases (See 8a-f.) Have you reviewed each use of a pronoun and clarified its reference? (See 14a-e.)

9. Have you distinguished properly between adjectives and adverbs? Have you positioned them correctly? (See 11a-g.)

4j   Giving and receiving editorial advice

One of your jobs as a writer is to learn how to give and receive editorial advice. All writers can benefit from an editor, a person whose fresh perspective can identify trouble spots that escaped the writer's view. If you are working collaboratively with your peers you will discover this quickly. There are two basic ground rules for giving and receiving editorial advice: the first concerns ego and the second, honesty.

1 Receiving advice

Without question, it is difficult and sometimes painful to be told by an instructor or fellow student that your paper needs a major reworking. As the writer of an effort that does not yet succeed, you should be aware that critical comments, provided they come from a responsible source, are being directed at your work and not at you. By understanding that it is your *writing* that is being criticized, you can ease the blow a little; still, you wrote the paper and so a slap at it is bound to raise a few welts across your cheek. To the extent possible, disengage your ego from the editorial review and respond not according to your hurt feelings but to the substance of the comments directed at your paper.

4j

coh

Checklist for Writing Effective Sentences

1. Have you been precise at every opportunity, stating your *exact* meaning? (See 21a-d.)
2. Have you been concise, eliminating *all* words, phrases, and sentences that do not add directly to your meaning? Have you made sentences brief when possible? (See 17a.)
3. Have you used parallel structures to add balance and emphasis to your writing? (See 18a.)
4. Have you varied sentence openings in order to create rhythmically pleasing paragraphs? (See 20a-b.)
5. Have you used vivid and concrete language to create immediacy in your writing? (See 21c-d.)
6. Have you correctly subordinated and coordinated sentence parts? (See 19a.)
7. Have you used strong verbs that keep your sentences lively and direct? (See 19b.)
8. Have you used the passive voice sparingly, and for good reason? (See 19c and 9g.)
9. Have you avoided sexist language or pronoun use? (See 21g and 10c.)
10. Have you maintained a consistent tone, appropriate to the occasion for writing? (See 3c-5 and 21b.)

As a writer, you have the absolute prerogative to accept, to accept partially, or to reject editorial advice. Of course you will also bear the burden of rejecting advice. But if you truly disagree with your editor, even one who will at some point be grading you, then you should hold your ground and thoughtfully explain what you were trying to do in the paper, what you would like to do, and why you cannot accept a particular suggestion for revision. *Thoughtfully* is the key here. First, give your editor the benefit of any doubt and assume that the advice offered is well founded. If the advice seems wrong, say: "I don't understand . . . Could you explain again. . . ." If you understand the editor's advice and continue to disagree, say so—and give your reasons. But remember that if the editor is responsible, he or she has the interests of your paper in mind and is making suggestions to improve your effort. These suggestions deserve an honest hearing.

4j

coh

2 Giving advice

As an editor, you will want to be similarly mindful of ego and honesty. First, you must allow the writer his or her topic and interest in it. Do not criticize because a topic does not interest you. Next, realize that this is not

---

Guidelines for Peer Editing

1. Understand your role as an editor. Disinvest your ego and work to improve the paper according to the author's needs, not your own.

2. Ask the writer to identify elements of the paper to which you should pay special attention.

3. Questions you might consider as you are reading:
   Is the writer helping me to become interested in this topic?
   Do all the parts of this paper seem to be present? Are general points backed up with specific examples?
   Is the writing at the sentence level sharp?
   How much help does the writer need with the nuts and bolts of grammar and punctuation?

4. Begin with the positive. Whether you are writing your editorial comments or are delivering them in conference, begin with the parts of the paper that you liked. If at all posible, find *something* that is worthy of a compliment.

5. Be specific with criticism. Identify sections or sentences that you particularly like and state why you like them. When you see room for improvement, identify specific words, sentences, or paragraphs, and state specifically what you think needs changing and why. If possible, build your constructive criticisms on earlier strengths:
   Avoid statements like, "This is vague."
   Strive for statements like "Your sentences in this section don't have the same vivid detail as your earlier sentences."

6. End your editorial advice with a summary of what you have observed. Then suggest a point-by-point action plan for the writer. That is, advise the writer on specific steps to take that will lead to an improved paper.

your paper that you are commenting on. Disinvest your ego from the job so that you do not attempt in your comments to make the paper yours. Realize as well the power of your criticism. Many people feel fragile about their writing, and when you must criticize, be respectful. Most writing has something good in it. Start there and be specific with your praise. State "I like this sentence," and say why. If possible, build your criticisms with your compliments. Say, for instance, "These sentences in the other part of the paper don't do what you did earlier. Here's why. . . ." You must be honest with your criticism. To be otherwise is a disservice to the writer and compromises you in the process.

The better you edit other people's work, the more proficient you will become at editing your own. Whatever your editorial skills, you still can benefit from the editorial advice of others precisely because they are not you and can therefore offer a fresh perspective. In developing your own guidelines for giving editorial advice, you may want to build on the notes in the preceding box.

4k

ms

EXERCISE 7

Edit the draft of your paper that you revised for purpose, coherence, and unity. Realize that you may need to make several passes at your draft to put it into final form.

4k When is a final draft *final*?

1 Making the judgment

At some point you must determine that your paper is finished. In the age of word processing, this is not always so easy a decision since, with relative ease, you can make that one last correction and have the computer print a new page. If you work with a typewriter and not a computer, then the decision about your final draft is more clear cut. At some point you will refuse to retype another page if the change you are making does not seem worth the effort.

When changes seem not to improve the product, then you have reached an end to revision and editing. To consider a draft final, you should be satisfied that your paper has met these standards:

- The paper has a clearly stated main point to communicate.
- It has met all requirements of unity and coherence at the levels of the paper, section, and paragraph.
- It is punctuated correctly and is free of errors in grammar and usage.

Stylistically, you could edit your papers *ad infinitum*. For especially important papers, take extra time to ensure that your writing is crisp and direct and that your sentence rhythms are pleasing. But once you have met your obligations in the final draft, any changes you make will amount to refinements of an already competent work. To be sure, stylistic editing can mean the difference between a good work and an excellent one. Eventually, however, you will reach a point at which changes do not improve the quality of your paper. When you reach this point, stop.

41

ms

2 Proofreading

Before you call a paper finished, check for minor errors that may annoy readers and embarrass you. Reread your paper to identify and correct misspelled words; words (often prepositions) omitted from sentences; words that have been doubled; punctuation that you tend to forget; and homonyms (writing *there* instead of *their*). If you have trouble spotting these minor errors in your writing, find a way to disrupt your usual pattern of reading so that the errors will become visible to you. One technique is to photocopy your work and have a friend read it aloud. You read along and make corrections. Another technique is to read each line of your paper in reverse order, from the last word on the line to the first. This approach forces you to focus on one word at a time. Besides checking for minor errors, review your occasion for writing one last time to make sure you have prepared your manuscript in an appropriate form. (See Appendix B on Manuscript Form.)

41 Sample paper: Final draft

Sean Hannan wrote three drafts of his paper, developing in each a successively more ambitious thesis. In early revisions, he settled large-scale matters of unity and coherence. Then, in a final effort he corrected errors in grammar, punctuation, and usage. As you will see, Sean spent time refining his sentences so that they would read effortlessly. You will find in his essay the paradox evident in all good writing: when sentences are clear and easy to read, they mask the considerable effort that went into their making. Good writing looks to a reader as though it took no work at all; but of course the writer knows otherwise.

Group Life and the Loss of Conscience

"This team has more character than any team I've had

the pleasure of working with." My football coach spoke hon-

estly to the audience of players, parents and local offi-   Introduction
                                                                frames the
cials, but hearing him filled me with disdain. I glanced   paper

across the table to catch a teammate's reactions. He simply
shook his head, disgusted and shamed by how we were being
made into heroes. All of the players understood that the
traits referred to by our coach were nothing to be proud
of, were nothing to celebrate, and certainly were nothing
to cheer about. But the crowd gave us an ovation anyway.
During the season, as fans had turned to us as a source of
pride and entertainment, members of the team had turned to
one another for different, darker reasons. We had become a
tightly knit group. We stood up for each other: played together, won together and--as the season unfolded--lost our
souls together. Though being a member of a group has its
benefits, group life can usurp an individual's conscience--
a lesson I learned all too well playing football.

The social psychologist Solomon Asch observed that
groups behave according to laws that have little resemblance to the laws governing individual behavior:

> [W]hen men live and act in groups there arise
> forces and phenomena that follow laws of their own and
> which cannot be described in terms of the properties of
> individuals composing them. (242)

Asch was describing the "Group Mind Thesis" here, the validity of which I proved to myself during the football season.
I do not think of myself as a thug. In fact, people have described my manner as gentle. But as a member of my football
team, I became something else. Before the season even
started the team attended practices that conditioned both
bodies and minds. These practices thoroughly stripped us of
our personal identities, and we were taught like soldiers
to be obedient and to define ourselves by becoming part of

Sean
returns to
the banquet
in his
conclusion

41

ms

Reference
to a source
that sets
the discus-
sion of foot-
ball in a
broader
context

the team. In this way, the success of the team became my
success, and the failure of the team became my failure. The
team became my family and winning became my only goal.

41

ms

The first game of the year served as an introduction
to both the horrors and advantages of winning. At the beginning of the second half we were beating the opposition handily. They were visibly fatigued and getting desperate,
calling trick plays and misdirections. I was playing linebacker, when a reverse was run to my side. I had read the
play from the snap and was waiting for the runner. My heart
raced and adrenaline pumped as he ran directly at me. I
lunged at him and planted my helmet into his thigh. Halfway
through the tackle I felt his leg give under my helmet and
heard the sound of bone breaking. We landed hard and were
immediately covered by my teammates who were trying to make
the same play. My arms were still wrapped around his knees
and my helmet still laid against his crooked thigh, when he
began crying. I wanted to get up and away from what I had
done but the weight of my teammates held me down. When I
was finally let up I stood with the team trying to disasso-
ciate myself from the scene. I felt sick. I didn't want to
play football anymore. I wanted to tell the injured boy how
sorry I was. But I didn't; instead I listened to a rabble
rousing speech from the coach ("That's the kind of hit that
wins games!") and attempted to play. I was tentative; the
whole team was. Luckily, the other team was just as disturbed as we were and made no attempt to come back.

My initiation into the group had been cemented by that
tackle. In retrospect, I see that the team gained its identity that afternoon. No one stepped forward to say: "That
was a lousy thing that happened." Publicly, at least, no

Narration:
the story
of Sean's
season

one dared violate what was becoming the group ethic: hit
hard, make opponents fear us, and win! Why didn't anyone object? According to recent research in social psychology, individuals become members of groups because of two strong
desires. The first desire is to be liked. Known as "norma-
tive social influence," this desire causes people to agree
because agreement brings approval. In the locker room,
after the game, no one was willing to bring down the anger
of the whole team on his head by saying what he and the
rest of us felt. The second desire is to be right. Known as
"informational social influence," this desire causes people
to agree because agreement confirms the correctness of certain behaviors. I broke an opposing player's leg. If no one
spoke against the injury, then the circumstances that
caused it--circumstances in which we all played a part--
must have been acceptable (Baron and Byrne, 323).

The violence of our first game was no doubt horrifying, but at the same time the glory of winning was mon-
strously pleasurable. After winning only one game the team
and the media already talked of a league championship.
What's more, our town, which had been deprived of the title
for thirty years, began to vehemently support us. Signs
were erected in store fronts to encourage us, and we made
headlines in the local paper. As we continued to win, support for the team intensified. One game after the next we
beat our opponents. Everywhere we went people stopped to
wish us luck. At restaurants we got free food. At school,
at least one key player who had been struggling academically was kept eligible to play by the generosity of understanding teachers. Gradually, we grew accustomed to our
special treatment, until winning and its benefits became

Reference to
a second
source

41

ms

Return to
narration

something we expected and needed--like a drug. Sadly, no
one seemed to notice how our characters were being transformed.

41

ms

Loyalty to the team became my passionate concern. <u>That</u>
was the warning sign I should have heeded; for when a
group's interests overwhelm an individual's, trouble is
sure to follow. Our public life is filled with stories of
an individual's conscience being usurped by a group. Two examples come to mind. In the Watergate scandal, John Dean
and others lied and went to jail in order to protect President Nixon. In the E. F. Hutton check-kiting scandal, a
major brokerage house regularly overdrew its accounts by as
much as a million dollars in order to collect on the interest illegally earned. Numerous employees knew of the fraud,
but no one dared speak up. In both cases, the need to be
liked and the need to be right were operating--and were
overwhelming individual conscience. These same needs were
so strong in me that by the end of the football season I
knew I would do anything to help my team win the championship.

Two non-
football
examples of
a group
usurping an
individual's
conscience

Our obsession with winning and our popularity peaked
at the same time: the end of the regular season when our
team, in true movie-script form, was scheduled to play the
only other undefeated team in the league. The night before
the game several members of the team went out for dinner at
a local restaurant. No one mentioned the game during our
meal, but we seemed to prolong leaving as if waiting for
some significant thing to happen. Mark, who sat across the
table from me, raised his hand. My hand met his. He gripped
it tightly and said: "I would do anything to win this game:
this is my only chance to do anything important."

Return to
narration

The next day the game was to start at one o'clock, but I went early to get ready. The pregame ritual that had been developed over the season aided in transforming young men into monsters whose sole purpose was winning, no matter what the consequences. In our locker room, the heavy metal music was loud and the mood, deadly serious. One teammate began to knock his bare head against a cinder block wall in order to bang away whatever civilized parts of him remained. I kept my eyes closed, thinking about the game, when one of my teammates grabbed and embraced me. The others joined in, and as a team we exited the locker room possessed by an evil more powerful than any good that could have come from winning a football game.

Narration continued

41

ms

My heart was filled with absolute hatred when we took the field, and I raged at the sight of our opponents. But as the game began it became clear that our opposition wanted to win every bit as much as we did. They matched us in intensity and will. On a kick-off one of our players named Jason had five ribs broken away from the play, and for the first time I feared being seriously hurt. The game was tied at 0 going into the fourth quarter. I was in charge of blocking their best player. His name was Hunter. He was over six feet tall and weighed about two hundred and fifty pounds. He was also the one responsible for injuring my teammate.

Toward the end of the game we were able to get the ball inside their twenty yard line. I was having trouble blocking Hunter. He made two big tackles that stalled our drive. It was third and seven and we called a time out. My teammates confronted me. Mark, who was apparently speaking for the whole group, looked directly into my eyes and

Narration continued

41

ms

asked: "Did you notice Hunter's knee brace?" Nothing else was said. I knew what I had to do. On the next play I didn't even try to block Hunter. Instead, I stayed back. He stood up and exposed the weakness. When his leg was firmly planted I rushed him. I lowered my shoulder and planted it into the side of his right knee. It collapsed easier than I thought, but he did not scream or cry or even fall. Instead he hobbled off the field squinting. The game had made Hunter tough and I respected him, but I also knew that he wouldn't be back. In the huddle I was met with thankful nods and pats on the back. Revitalized, the team went on to score and eventually win.

By the evening of our victory banquet, I had thought a good deal about the intensity of that game and the intensity of our opponents. They craved that win every bit as much as we craved it. In Hunter's team we had met ourselves and were forced to look into a mirror. While the town celebrated, my teammates and I began to question what we were doing and why we were doing it. Winning had become so fierce an addiction that we would do anything, including hurting people, to win. We rationalized our behavior with a dangerous philosophy--that the end justifies the means. We had become monsters, capable of inflicting great harm; and for this, people cheered us as heroes.

An individual's conscience, it turns out, is a fragile thing both on the football field and off. This is what I learned in my championship season, and this is what I remember whenever I look at my trophy. I have hurt people. But I don't think I ever will again--not knowingly, anyway, because my conscience is far stronger now for having lost it once.

Conclusion: ends the "banquet frame" begun in the introduction

Works cited

Asch, Solomon. Social Psychology. New York: Prentice, 1952.

Baron, Robert A., and Donn Byrne. Social Psychology: Understanding Human Interaction. 6th ed. Boston: Allyn and
Bacon, 1991.

41

ms

CHAPTER 5

Writing Paragraphs

A **paragraph** is a group of related sentences organized by a single, controlling idea. Marked with an indented first word (typically five spaces from the left margin), a paragraph can be as brief as a sentence or longer than a page. Paragraphs rarely stand in isolation: they are extended units of thought that, pieced carefully together, build the content of a paper. In this chapter you will learn about the characteristics of a well-written paragraph and the relationship of individual paragraphs to larger units of thought.[1]

5a The relationship of single paragraphs to a whole paper

At times, you may feel that generating a paragraph is easy enough, but that writing an entire essay, paper, or report lies beyond your abilities. (How will I *ever* write twenty pages?) In these moments, you need to rediscover that whole documents are written one paragraph at a time and whole paragraphs, one sentence at a time. This section presents a strategy for writing an entire paper by writing groups of related paragraphs.

1 The relationship of paragraphs to sections

Just as sentences are the units that comprise individual paragraphs, paragraphs are the units that comprise whole letters, essays, and reports. Aside from specialized occasions for writing such as summaries and short-answer essay exams, you will seldom write a single, isolated paragraph. Usually, any paragraph will be situated in a grouping—a **section**—that constitutes part of the larger document. Except for the beginning of a paper and the end (see 5f), any one paragraph will be involved directly with at least two others: the one immediately preceding and the one that follows. If in a single sitting you can write a group of three related paragraphs, then you will be able to piece together an entire paper.

---

[1]Example paragraphs from various sources are consecutively numbered throughout the chapter for ease of reference.

How to Write One Section of a Paper

1. **Prepare to write.** Identify purpose and define audience; generate and organize ideas and information; and devise a working thesis: see 3a.

2. **Identify sections of the paper.** Ask of your thesis: What parts must I develop in order to deliver on the promise of this statement? Your answer of perhaps three or four points will identify the sections you need to write to complete that statement.

3. **Plan to write one section of your paper at a sitting.** If a section is long, divide it into manageable parts and write one part at a sitting.

4. **Write individual paragraphs.** Each paragraph will be related to others in the section. As you begin a second paragraph, clearly relate it to the first; relate the third paragraph to the second, and so on until you finish writing the section. Then take a break.

5. **Write other sections, one at a time.** Continue writing, building one section incrementally on the next, until you complete your first draft.

5a

trans

The paragraphs that follow form a section—one part of a chapter—of Helen Keller's autobiography. At the age of nineteen months, Keller was stricken by a disease that left her deaf and blind. Not until she was seven, with the arrival of her teacher Anne Sullivan, did Keller discover language. The moment described in these famous paragraphs is one of extraordinary awakening: the realization that things in the world have names. These paragraphs are related; they read as a carefully written section, as if they appeared from the pen of the author all at the same instant. Be assured, however, that Keller wrote this section of her autobiography one paragraph at a time, one sentence at a time. She was twenty-two and a sophomore at Radcliffe College when *My Life Story* was published.

1

The morning after my teacher came she led me into her room and gave me a doll. The little blind children at the Perkins Institution had sent it and Laura Bridgman had dressed it; but I did not know this until afterward. When I had played with it a little while, Miss Sullivan slowly spelled into my hand the word "d-o-l-l." I was at once interested in this finger play and tried to imitate it. When I finally succeeded in making the letters correctly I was flushed with childish pleasure and pride. Running downstairs to my mother I held up my hand and made the letters for doll. I did not know that I was spelling a word or even that words existed; I was simply making my fingers go in monkey-like imitation. In the days that followed I learned to spell in this uncomprehending way a great many words, among them *pin*, *hat*, *cup* and a few verbs like *sit*, *stand* and *walk*. But my teacher had been with me several weeks before I understood that everything has a name.

2

One day, while I was playing with my new doll, Miss Sullivan put my big rag doll into my lap also, spelled "d-o-l-l" and tried to make me understand that "d-o-l-l" applied to both. Earlier in the day we had had a tussle over the words "m-u-g" and "w-a-t-e-r." Miss Sullivan had tried to impress it upon me that "m-u-g" is *mug* and that "w-a-t-e-r" is *water*, but I persisted in confounding the two. In despair she had dropped the subject for the time, only to renew it at the first opportunity. I became impatient at her repeated attempts and, seizing the new doll, I dashed it upon the floor. I was keenly delighted when I felt the fragments of the broken doll at my feet. Neither sorrow nor regret followed my passionate outburst. I had not loved the doll. In the still, dark world in which I lived there was no strong sentiment or tenderness. I felt my teacher sweep the fragments to one side of the hearth, and I had a sense of satisfaction that the cause of my discomfort was removed. She brought me my hat, and I knew I was going out into the warm sunshine. This thought, if a wordless sensation may be called a thought, made me hop and skip with pleasure.

3

We walked down the path to the well-house, attracted by the fragrance of the honeysuckle with which it was covered. Someone was drawing water and my teacher placed my hand under the spout. As the cool stream gushed over one hand she spelled into the other the word *water*, first slowly, then rapidly. I stood still, my whole attention fixed upon the motions of her fingers. Suddenly I felt a misty consciousness as of something forgotten—a thrill of returning thought; and somehow the mystery of language was revealed to me. I knew then that "w-a-t-e-r" meant the wonderful cool something that was flowing over my hand. That living word awakened my soul, gave it light, hope, joy, set it free! There were barriers still, it is true, but barriers that could in time be swept away.

4

I left the well-house eager to learn. Everything had a name, and each name gave birth to a new thought. As we returned to the house every object which I touched seemed to quiver with life. That was because I saw everything with the strange, new sight that had come to me. On entering the door I remembered the doll I had broken. I felt my way to the hearth and picked up the pieces. I tried vainly to put them together. Then my eyes filled with tears; for I realized what I had done, and for the first time I felt repentance and sorrow.

5

I learned a great many new words that day. I do not remember what they all were; but I do know that *mother, father, sister, teacher* were among them—words that were to make the world blossom for me, "like Aaron's rod, with flowers." It would have been difficult to find a happier child than I was as I lay in my crib at the close of that eventful day and lived over the joys it had brought me, and for the first time longed for a new day to come.

—HELEN KELLER, *My Life Story*

2

The relationship of sections to the whole paper

A **thesis** explicitly states the topic you will address in a paper and either directly or indirectly suggests the points you will make about that topic (see 3f). You will probably devote one section of your paper to discussing each point you wish to develop. For each section of your paper you will write a **section-thesis,** a statement that explicitly announces the point you will address in the section and either directly or indirectly suggests what you will discuss relating to this point. You will organize your discussion in paragraphs.

The section-thesis organizing the paragraphs by Helen Keller appears at the end of ¶1: *"But my teacher had been with me several weeks before I understood that everything has a name."* The next four paragraphs focus on and develop various aspects of this statement.

5a

trans

¶2 Events leading to the moment of discovery: an account of Sullivan's frustrated attempts to teach Keller.

¶3 The moment of discovery: clearly the most famous in the autobiography, Keller realizing the mystery of language.

¶4 Consequence 1 of the discovery: objects quivering with life and Keller knowing repentance and sorrow for the first time.

¶5 Consequence 2 of the discovery: joy in having learned that everything has a name.

These five paragraphs form a distinct section of one chapter in Keller's autobiography. The section as a whole is *unified* and *well developed* in that all paragraphs focus on and amply discuss a single controlling idea: the section-thesis highlighted previously. Each paragraph is unified and well developed; each focuses on and amply discusses its own more narrowly defined controlling idea. And because each paragraph builds on the one that precedes it and is positioned according to a clear plan, the whole section is *coherent.* In the same way, every paragraph in the section is itself coherent since the sentences of each lead from one to the next and establish a clear pattern of relation.

EXERCISE 1

Use the strategies just discussed to make the transition from writing a single paragraph to writing a group of related paragraphs. In a single sitting, write the first draft of one section (or a well-defined part of one section) of a paper you are developing in connection with an assignment in chapter 3 or chapter 6 or with some other assignment. Reread the section after you have written it: (1) Check for a controlling idea (a section-thesis). (2) Reread the paragraphs to determine how thoroughly you have developed the controlling idea. (3) Determine how successfully you have moved from one paragraph to the next with a clear plan.

EXERCISE 2

Choose *one* section of a textbook chapter to study in depth. (Define a *section* as a group of related paragraphs preceded by a subheading.) Closely read each paragraph in this section, and prepare an analysis by responding to three points: (1) Identify the controlling idea (the section-thesis) of the

trans

> ### Unity, Coherence, and Development
>
> Each *paragraph* of a paper consists of *sentences* that are
>
> **Unified:** the sentences are all concerned with a central, controlling idea.
>
> **Coherent:** the sentences are arranged in a clear order, according to a definite plan.
>
> **Well developed:** the sentences provide details that explain and illustrate the paragraph's controlling idea.
>
> Each *section* of a paper consists of *paragraphs* that are
>
> **Unified:** the groups of paragraphs are devoted to one controlling idea, a section-thesis that develops some part of the thesis.
>
> **Coherent:** the groups of paragraphs within a section are arranged in a clear order, according to a definite plan.
>
> **Well developed:** the groups of paragraphs provide details that explain and illustrate the section's controlling idea.
>
> Every *paper* consists of *sections* (groups of related paragraphs) that are
>
> **Unified:** each section is devoted to developing one part of the thesis, the central organizing idea of the paper.
>
> **Coherent:** the sections are arranged in a clear order, according to some definite plan.
>
> **Well developed:** each section of the paper provides details important for developing the thesis.

section. (2) Explain how the entire section is unified, developed, and coherent. (3) Discuss the way in which the section fits into the overall structure of the chapter.

EXERCISE 3

Read the following letter written by Anne Sullivan, describing from her vantage point Helen Keller's discovery that everything has a name. Analyze Sullivan's paragraphs as follows: (1) Identify the controlling idea (the section-thesis). (2) Explain how the entire section is unified, developed, and coherent.

April 5, 1887

6   I must write you a line this morning because something very important has happened. Helen has taken the second great step in her education. She has learned that *everything has a name, and that the manual alphabet is the key to everything she wants to know.*

7   In a previous letter I think I wrote you that "mug" and "milk" had given Helen more trouble than all the rest. She confused the nouns with the verb "drink." She didn't know the word for "drink," but went through the pantomime of drinking whenever she spelled "mug" or "milk." This morning, while she was washing, she wanted to know the name for "water." When she wants to know the name of anything, she points to it and pats my hand. I spelled "w-a-t-e-r" and thought no more about it until after breakfast. Then it occurred to me that with the help of this new word I might succeed in straightening out the "mug-milk" difficulty. We went out to the pump-house, and I made Helen hold her mug under the spout while I pumped. As the cold water gushed forth, filling the mug, I spelled "w-a-t-e-r" in Helen's free hand. The word coming so close upon the sensation of cold water rushing over her hand seemed to startle her. She dropped the mug and stood as one transfixed. A new light came into her face. She spelled "water" several times. Then she dropped on the ground and asked for its name and pointed to the pump and the trellis, and suddenly turning round she asked for my name. I spelled "Teacher." Just then the nurse brought Helen's little sister into the pump-house, and Helen spelled "baby" and pointed to the nurse. All the way back to the house she was highly excited, and learned the name of every object she touched, so that in a few hours she had added thirty new words to her vocabulary. Here are some of them: *Door, open, shut, give, go, come,* and a great many more.

8   P.S.—I didn't finish my letter in time to get it posted last night; so I shall add a line. Helen got up this morning like a radiant fairy. She has flitted from object to object, asking the name of everything and kissing me for very gladness. Last night when I got in bed, she stole into my arms of her own accord and kissed me for the first time, and I thought my heart would burst, so full was it of joy.

—ANNE SULLIVAN

5b   The paragraph: Essential features

In important ways, a paragraph and an essay are essentially alike. Both must be *unified* if they are to be comprehensible: all sentences of a paragraph must refer to one organizing idea, just as all paragraphs of an essay must concern one organizing idea. Both an essay as a whole and its individual paragraphs must be *well developed:* sentences in a paragraph must amply explain or defend the main point of a paragraph just as paragraphs of an essay must explain or defend a thesis. As well, both a paragraph and an essay must be *coherent:* sentences of a paragraph must be arranged in some order, just as paragraphs in an essay must follow from one to the next according to some clear progression of ideas. If you can master the techniques necessary for making a single paragraph unified, well developed, and coherent, then by adapting these same techniques and by expanding your focus you will be able to write and organize an entire essay.

5b

¶ *dev*

The following is an example of a well-written paragraph that appears in a biology text.

5b

¶ *dev*   9

Life on this planet began in water, and today, almost wherever water is found, life is also present. There are one-celled organisms that eke out their entire existence in no more water than that which can cling to a grain of sand. Some species of algae are found only on the melting undersurfaces of polar ice floes. Certain species of bacteria and certain blue-green algae can tolerate the near-boiling water of hot springs. In the desert, plants race through an entire life cycle—seed to flower to seed—following a single rainfall. In the jungle, the water cupped in the leaves of a tropical plant forms a microcosm in which a myriad of small organisms are born, spawn, and die. We are interested in whether the soil of Mars and the dense atmosphere surrounding Venus contain water principally because we want to know whether life is there. On our planet, and probably on others where life exists, life and water have been companions since life first began.

—HELENA CURTIS, "Water"

Examine the qualities that make this grouping of sentences a paragraph, a unit of thought. First, each of the six sentences constituting the body of Curtis's paragraph is narrowly focused by a single, controlling idea: *water* and its relation to life. Given this focus, the grouping of sentences is unified. Observe as well that Curtis develops her central idea with six sentences arranged according to a clear plan. In the first five of these, she associates water with life on earth. Notice how she moves from an extreme presented in one sentence to an opposite extreme presented in the next.

Curtis's next-to-last sentence about water on Mars or Venus extends observations made concerning water and life on earth to other planets, and once again she drives home her point, which she repeats by way of summary in the paragraph's last sentence. She has taken care to present eight *unified* sentences that *develop* a central idea and which are arranged in a meaningful, *coherent* order. Thus, Curtis has written a paragraph: a well-developed unit of thought organized around a single idea and arranged according to some definite plan.

EXERCISE 4

Read the following group of sentences and explain why it can justifiably be called a paragraph. In your explanation (1) identify the central, organizing idea that unifies the sentences, (2) identify the parts of the paragraph that explain or defend this central idea, and (3) explain how the sentences are organized according to a definite, coherent plan.

What the canoeist gets, instead of an impression of the river's speed, is an impression of its power. Or, more exactly, an impression of the *voluminousness* of its power. The sense of the volume alone has come to me when, swimming in the summertime, I have submerged mouth and nose so that the plane of the water spreads away from the lower eyelid; the

awareness of its bigness that comes then is almost intolerable; one feels how falsely assuring it is to look down on the river, as we usually do. The sense
10 of the power of it came to me one day in my boyhood when I attempted to swim ashore in a swift current, pulling an overturned rowboat. To check the downstream course of the boat I tried grabbing hold of the partly submerged willows along the shore with my free hand, and was repeatedly pulled under as the willows bent, and then torn loose. My arms stretched between the boat and the willow branch might have been sewing threads for all the holding they could do. It was the first time I realized that there could be circumstances in which my life would count for nothing, absolutely nothing—and I have never needed to learn that again.

—Wendell Berry, "The Rise"

5c

¶ *dev*

5c   Writing and revising to achieve paragraph unity

A unified paragraph will focus on, will develop, and will not stray from a paragraph's central, controlling idea or **topic sentence.** Recall that a *thesis* announces and controls the content of an entire essay, and that a *section-thesis* announces and controls the content of a section. Just so, a *topic sentence* announces and controls the content of sentences in a single paragraph. Think of the topic sentence as a paragraph-level *thesis,* and you will see the principle of unity at work at *all* levels of the paper. At each level of the essay, a general statement is used to guide you in assembling specific, supporting parts.

ESSAY-LEVEL UNITY   The thesis (the most general statement in the essay) governs your choice of sections in a paper.

SECTION-LEVEL UNITY   Section-theses (the second-most general statements in the essay) govern your choice of paragraphs in a section.

PARAGRAPH-LEVEL UNITY Topic sentences (the third-most general statements in the essay) govern your choice of sentences in a paragraph.

Within a paragraph, a topic sentence can appear anywhere, provided that you recognize it and can lead up to and away from it with some method in mind. If you have read the example paragraphs in this chapter thus far, you have seen topic sentences placed at virtually all locations in a paragraph: at the beginning, one sentence after the beginning, the middle, the end, and both the beginning *and* end. The basic positions of a paragraph's topic sentence are discussed below.

1   Placing the topic sentence at the beginning of a paragraph

Very often, a topic sentence is placed first in a paragraph. You will want to open your paragraphs this way when your purpose is to inform or persuade a reader and you wish to be as direct as possible, as in the following example.

5c

¶ dev

11

> Factory farm animals need liberation in the most literal sense. Veal calves are kept in stalls five feet by two feet. They are usually slaughtered when about four months old, and have been too big to turn in their stalls for at least a month. Intensive beef herds, kept in stalls only proportionately larger for much longer periods, account for a growing percentage of beef production. Sows are often similarly confined when pregnant, which, because of artificial methods of increasing fertility, can be most of the time. Animals confined in this way do not waste food by exercising, nor do they develop unpalatable muscle.
> —PETER SINGER, "Animal Liberation"

Peter Singer begins the paragraph with a direct statement: *Factory farm animals need liberation in the most literal sense.* Every subsequent sentence focuses on and develops this topic sentence. The second and third sentences are devoted to the confinement of veal calves; the fourth sentence to the confinement of intensive beef herds; and the fifth sentence to the confinement of sows. The paragraph's final sentence explains the rationale of confinement.

2 Placing the topic sentence in the middle of a paragraph

When you need to provide readers with background information necessary for them to understand a paragraph's main point, then you might hold off a paragraph's topic sentence until you have provided such information. This is exactly what Anne Sullivan does in ¶7 (page 129). She opens with the remark: "In a previous letter . . ." and then proceeds to bring her reader up to date on the " 'mug-milk' difficulty." Only after Sullivan provides sufficient information to establish her reader's understanding does she offer a topic sentence.

> Then it occurred to me that with the help of this new word I might succeed in straightening out the "mug-milk" difficulty.

The rest of the paragraph is devoted to Sullivan's description of both her method for "straightening out the . . . difficulty" and the dramatic consequences of the successful application of this method.

3 Placing the topic sentence at the end of a paragraph

When in an essay you wish to tell a story—to recount some event or events narratively—the point of telling often lies in the story itself. Not only would it be anticlimactic, but also it would ruin the story to tell the reader your point, to write your topic sentence first. You have two choices in this case: not to tell at all (to let the reader infer your topic sentence) or to delay telling until the very end of your narrative. Helen Keller chose the second strategy in ¶1 (page 125).

A more academically oriented occasion for delaying a topic sentence until the end of a paragraph is to convince a reader to accept a debatable statement. The strategy is to avoid beginning a paragraph with a topic sentence that might alienate readers and disincline them to read the remainder of the paragraph. To make sure that readers will consider your reasons *before* responding to a debatable statement, place the topic sentence last, as in the following example:

5c

¶ *dev*

> The place of history in the world of learning and its relation to the various other fields of study can be argued without end. History is sometimes classed with the humanities, along with literature, the arts, and philosophy, as an aspect of the human achievement over the centuries. However, it differs from all of these subjects in being based on fact rather than on imagination and feeling. More often history is included among the social sciences, together with economics, political science, sociology, anthropology, and some branches of geography and psychology. One may
> 12   question whether any of these fields deserves to be called a "science" in the sense we associate with the natural or exact sciences, but history is particularly resistant to a strictly scientific approach. It tries to explain by particular description rather than by general analysis and laws; its aim is to depict the significant historical individual or situation in all its living detail. History is defined by its focus on time, but it also has the characteristic of embracing all aspects of human activity as they occurred in the past. History, accordingly, is able to serve as the discipline that integrates the specialized work of the other fields of social science. (32)
> —ROBERT V. DANIELS, *Studying History: How and Why*

If you place the last sentence of this paragraph first, you see that subsequent sentences support and develop the idea that *History . . . is able to serve as the discipline that integrates the specialized work of the other fields of social science.* This statement is debatable. In fact, it is a position taken up in an argument that Daniels acknowledges at the beginning of the paragraph. By delaying his topic sentence, Daniels ensures that his audience will have read his survey of the debate concerning history's place in the world of learning. The survey is important to the reader's accepting Daniels's point, so delaying the topic sentence is an effective strategy. See ¶25 for another example of this arrangement.

4   Omitting the topic sentence from the paragraph

In narrative and descriptive papers, and much less frequently in informative and persuasive papers, writers will occasionally omit the topic sentence from a paragraph. In a narrative paragraph in which you are telling a story, including the topic sentence may be too heavy handed and may ruin an otherwise subtle effect. In descriptive writing, including a topic sentence will sometimes seem redundant, so obvious is the main focus of a paragraph. When you decide to omit a topic sentence from a paragraph, take care to write the paragraph as though a topic sentence were present. With respect to unity, this means that you should focus each sentence on the implied topic and should not include any sentence that strays from that implied topic. Helen Keller does exactly this in ¶2 (page 126). Had she written a topic sentence for this paragraph, it might have read: *The events immediately leading up to my discovery of language showed how thoroughly difficult and insensitive a child I was.*

5c

¶ dev

The following is an example of an informative paragraph with an implied topic sentence, rather than a directly stated one.

13   Etiquette books used to teach that if a woman had *Mrs.* in front of her name then the husband's name should follow because *Mrs.* is an abbreviated form of *Mistress* and a woman couldn't be a mistress of herself. As with many arguments about "correct" language usage, this isn't very logical because *Miss* is also an abbreviation of *Mistress.* Feminists hoped to simplify matters by introducing *Ms.* as an alternative to both *Mrs.* and *Miss,* but what happened is that *Ms.* largely replaced *Miss* to became a catch-all business title for women. Many married women still prefer the title *Mrs.,* and some resent being addressed with the term *Ms.* As one frustrated newspaper reporter complained, "Before I can write about a woman, I have to know not only her marital status but also her political philosophy." The result of such complications may contribute to the demise of titles which are already being ignored by many computer programmers who find it more efficient to simply use names; for example in a business letter: "Dear Joan Garcia," instead of "Dear Mrs. Joan Garcia," "Dear Ms. Garcia," or "Dear Mrs. Louis Garcia."

—ALLEEN PACE NILSEN, "Sexism in English: A 1990s Update"

The sentence that comes closest to being a topic sentence is the paragraph's long final sentence. But this sentence, with its opening "The result of such complications," assumes another sentence, not written: *There has been a great deal of confusion about the politically correct title of address for women.* Placed at the head of Nilsen's paragraph, this would function adequately as a topic sentence. The paragraph's final sentence is actually built on the validity of this implied topic sentence. Nilsen's choice of every sentence is governed by the implied topic sentence just as if that sentence had actually been included in the paragraph.

EXERCISE 5

Reread several paragraphs you have recently written for one of your classes. Choose one paragraph to revise for unity: add, delete, or modify sentences as needed.

EXERCISE 6

The following paragraphs form one section of a psychology textbook. Read each paragraph and identify its topic sentence. If a paragraph's topic sentence is not stated directly, then write an appropriate one. For any two of the seven paragraphs, explain how the paragraph is unified around the topic sentence.

5c

EXERCISE 7

Explain how ¶s 14–20 function as a *section*, a group of related paragraphs. What is the section thesis? What parts make up the section?

¶ *dev*

14 Most jobs involve some degree of stress. Yet somehow, the persons performing them manage to cope; they continue to function despite their daily encounters with various stressors. Some individuals, though, are not so fortunate. Over time, they seem to be worn down (or out) by repeated exposure to stress. Such persons are often described as suffering from **burnout,** and they demonstrate several distinct characteristics.

15 First, victims of burnout suffer from *physical exhaustion*. They have low energy and feel tired much of the time. In addition, they report many symptoms of physical strain such as frequent headaches, nausea, poor sleep, and changes in eating habits (e.g., loss of appetite). Second, they experience *emotional exhaustion*. Depression, feelings of helplessness, and feelings of being trapped in one's job are all part of the picture. Third, persons suffering from burnout often demonstrate *mental* or *attitudinal exhaustion*. They become cynical about others, hold negative attitudes toward them, and tend to derogate themselves, their jobs, their organizations, and even life in general. To put it simply, they come to view the world around them through dark gray rather than rose-colored glasses. Finally, they often report feelings of *low personal accomplishment*. Persons suffering from burnout conclude that they haven't been able to accomplish much in the past, and assume that they probably won't succeed in this respect in the future, either. In sum, burnout can be defined as a syndrome of emotional, physical, and mental exhaustion coupled with feelings of low self-esteem or low self-efficacy, resulting from prolonged exposure to intense stress. . . .

16 What are the causes of burnout? As we have already noted, the primary factor appears to be prolonged exposure to stress. However, other variables also play a role. In particular, a number of conditions within an organization plus several personal characteristics seem to determine whether, and to what degree, specific individuals experience burnout. For example, job conditions implying that one's efforts are useless, ineffective, or unappreciated seem to contribute to burnout. Under such conditions, individuals develop the feelings of low personal accomplishment which are an important part of burnout. Similarly, poor opportunities for promotion and the presence of inflexible rules and procedures lead employees to feel that they are trapped in an unfair system and contribute to the development of negative views about their jobs. One of the most important factors contributing to burnout, however, is the *leadership style* adopted by employees' supervisors.

17   Evidence concerning this relationship has been reported by Seltzer and Numerof. These researchers asked over 800 M.B.A. students to report on their own levels of burnout, the leadership style of their supervisors, and several other factors (e.g., their position within their organization, their age, marital status). Results indicated that the lower the amount of consideration demonstrated by their supervisors (i.e., the lower their concern with employee's welfare or with maintaining friendly relations with them), the higher employees' reported levels of burnout. Among the other variables studied, only marital status exerted significant effects: married individuals reported lower levels of burnout than those who were single. . . .

18   Whatever the precise causes of burnout, once it develops, it has important consequences. First, it may lead individuals to seek new jobs or careers. In one study concerned with the impact of burnout, Jackson, Schwab, and Schuler asked several hundred teachers to complete a questionnaire designed to measure burnout and to report on the extent to which they would prefer to be in another job or career. As expected, the greater the teachers' degree of burnout, the more likely they were to prefer another job and to be actively considering a change of occupation.

19   Second, persons suffering from burnout may seek administrative roles where they can hide from jobs they have grown to hate behind huge piles of forms. While this pattern certainly occurs, it appears to be relatively rare. Most victims of burnout seem either to change jobs or to withdraw psychologically and mark time until retirement.

20   Before concluding, we should comment briefly on one final question: can burnout be reversed? Fortunately, growing evidence suggests that it can. With appropriate help, victims of burnout can recover from their physical and psychological exhaustion. If ongoing stress is reduced, if individuals gain added support from friends and co-workers, and if they cultivate hobbies and other outside interests, at least some persons, it appears, can return to positive attitudes and renewed productivity. Such results can only be attained, however, through active efforts designed to overcome burnout and to change the conditions from which it develops.

—ROBERT A. BARON AND JERALD GREENBERG

5d   Writing and revising to achieve paragraph coherence

Your job in ensuring the overall coherence of a paragraph is to make clear the logic by which you position sentences in the paragraph. When your paragraphs are coherent, readers will understand the logic by which you move from one sentence to the next, toward or away from your topic sentence. When writing the first draft of a paper, you may not have a plan to ensure paragraph coherence; you may not even have a clear idea of every paragraph's main point. Revision is the time when you sort these matters out, when you can make certain that each paragraph has a clear purpose and a clear, coherent plan for achieving that purpose.

1   Arranging sentences to achieve coherence

There are standard patterns available to you for arranging paragraphs. The most common are arrangements by space, by time, and by importance. If it occurs to you as you are writing a first draft that one of these patterns lends itself to the particular point you are discussing, then by all means write your paragraph with the pattern in mind. It is not necessary, though, that you map out patterns of coherence ahead of time.

Arrangement by space

You can help readers visualize what you are describing by arranging a paragraph spatially. Start the reader at a well-defined position with respect to the object being described and then move him or her from that position to subsequent ones by taking systematic steps, one at a time, until your description is complete. In planning the paragraph, you might divide the object into the parts that you will describe; next, devise a definite plan for arranging these parts. Your description could proceed from front to back, right to left, top to bottom, outside to inside, and so on: the choice is yours. Once you choose a plan for organizing details, stick to the plan and you will help your readers to visualize your topic, as in this paragraph on the Brooklyn Bridge.

> Brooklyn Bridge belongs first to the eye. Viewed from Brooklyn
> Heights, it seems to frame the irregular lines of Manhattan. But across the
> river perspective changes: through the narrow streets of lower Manhattan
21   and Chinatown, on Water Street or South Street, the structure looms above
> drab buildings. Fragments of tower or cable compel the eye. The view
> changes once again as one mounts the wooden walk of the bridge itself. It
> is a relief, an open space after dim, crowded streets.
> —ALAN TRACHTENBERG, *Brooklyn Bridge: Fact and Symbol*

This description of the bridge is arranged by the various perspectives from which it is viewed: from Brooklyn Heights, the bridge has one appearance; viewed from lower Manhattan, the structure "looms above drab buildings"; viewed from the wooden walkway of the bridge, the view provides a "relief."

Arrangement by time

You can arrange a paragraph according to a sequence of events. Start the paragraph with a particular event and move forward or backward in time in some definite order. Give your readers signals in each sentence that emphasize the forward or backward movement. In this example paragraph on the increase of cigarette consumption in the United States during the first half of this century, Thomas Whiteside moves the reader forward in time with these words: *First World War, the mid-twenties, between 1920 and 1930, latter half of the thirties . . . forties, between 1950 and 1952.*

5d

coh   22

The merchandising of cigarettes on a large scale became practical with the development, around the time of the First World War, of a slightly acid cigarette tobacco, which allowed smokers to inhale without an immediate unpleasant effect. (Tobacco smoke that is alkaline produces an automatic cough reflex when inhaled.) Mass production of cigarettes really got under way in the mid-twenties, with the help of big advertising campaigns that, in further expanding the market, employed such slogans as "Reach for a Lucky Instead of a Sweet" and "Blow Some My Way," by way of encouraging women as well as men to take up the habit. Pushed by such campaigns in the press, the per-capita consumption of cigarettes in the adult population of the United States doubled between 1920 and 1930. Between the latter half of the thirties and the latter half of the forties cigarette consumption, urged on now by hard-driving advertising campaigns on network radio as well as in the press, approximately doubled again. The increase continued in the formative period of commercial television; between 1950 and 1952, for example, the per-capita consumption of cigarettes in the adult population increased from thirty-five hundred and twenty-two cigarettes a year to thirty-eight hundred and eighty-six.

—THOMAS WHITESIDE, *Selling Death*

Arrangement by importance

Just as you discuss different parts of a thesis at different locations in a paper, you will discuss different parts of a topic sentence at different locations in a paragraph. When revising, be aware of a paragraph's component parts so that you can arrange these parts in the most logical, accessible order. Arrangement is largely determined by your positioning of the topic sentence. How will your sentences lead to and away from the topic sentence? You should be aware of two general patterns: general to specific and specific to general.

GENERAL TO SPECIFIC: WHEN THE TOPIC SENTENCE BEGINS THE PARAGRAPH

By far the most common method for arranging sentences in a paragraph is to begin with your topic sentence and follow with specific, supporting details. When beginning a paragraph this way, decide how to order the information that will follow. You might ask: What does this paragraph's topic sentence obligate me to discuss? What are the *parts* of this paragraph and in what order will I discuss them? Arthur C. Clarke discusses three parts of his topic, the portable electronic library—the library's top half, its bottom half, and its overall size—in the following paragraph.

23

The great development in your near future is the portable electronic library—a library not only of books, but of films and music. It will be about the size of an average book and will probably open in the same way. One half will be the screen with high-definition, full-color display. The other will be a keyboard, much like one of today's computer consoles, with the full alphabet, digits, basic mathematical functions, and a large number of special keys—perhaps 100 keys in all. It won't be as small as some of today's midget calculators, which have to be operated with toothpicks.

—ARTHUR C. CLARKE, "Electronic Tutors"

In this example, Clarke is informing readers. In the next example, Peter Farb is making an argument. Farb also opens the paragraph with his topic sentence, a debatable statement he wants to support.

5d

coh

24

The most probable explanation for the disappearance of the Neanderthals, though, is simply that they evolved by degrees into modern humans. Evidence that this might be so comes from caves in Israel, where many generations of Neanderthals lived less than 45,000 years ago, and where they left their fossil remains. The skulls found there reveal a great diversity of types, ranging from undisputed Neanderthals to others who would be virtually indistinguishable from humans today. The change from Neanderthal to *Homo sapiens sapiens* must have been imperceptible to the people concerned.

—PETER FARB, *Humankind*

Farb follows his topic sentence with two sentences of evidence. The first locates the reader at the site of the evidence he wants to present; the second sentence presents specific evidence: varied skull types. From these sentences of support, Farb draws his conclusion—the last sentence of his paragraph, which is essentially a restatement of the topic sentence: that Neanderthals "evolved by degrees into modern humans."

SPECIFIC TO GENERAL: WHEN THE TOPIC SENTENCE ENDS THE PARAGRAPH

When you are writing a description or narration and when you are arguing a point, you may want to delay your topic sentence until the final sentence of a paragraph. Here you reverse the standard arrangement of a paragraph and move from specific details to a general, concluding statement. The goal is to build one sentence on the next so securely that the final sentence strikes the reader as inevitable.

25

We drink it, use it to wash, and use it to grow farm products and manufacture goods. We almost take for granted that rain will replenish whatever amount of water we may use up. Water, however, is no longer the infinitely renewable resource that we once thought it was. Consider the giant Ogallala aquifer, which stretches nearly 800 miles under eight states from the Texas panhandle to South Dakota. The aquifer provides about 30 percent of the total irrigation needs in the United States and serves as the water source for 200,000 wells in 180 counties and for 40 percent of the nation's beef cattle. Water is being drawn from the Ogallala aquifer eight times faster than nature can replenish the supply, creating huge sinkholes in the Texas panhandle. Economists believe that part of the problem is that water has traditionally been underpriced. The law of demand indicates that a higher price of water will reduce the quantity of water used. One solution for the rapidly decreasing water resources, therefore, would be to make it more expensive for consumers to use the water.

—SEMOON CHANG, *Modern Economics*

In this paragraph, Chang is making an argument by moving from specific facts to a general conclusion, or topic sentence. Chang begins with facts concerning water use about which no one could disagree. His second sentence builds on the first by generalizing about attitudes concerning water use: we "almost take for granted" that water is an infinitely renewable resource. The third sentence builds on the second by making another, though debatable, statement of fact that (1) sets up a contrast with the second sentence and (2) is itself supported by several subsequent sentences about the Ogallala aquifer. Chang builds sentence on sentence, leading us to the paragraph's climax in which he applies economic theory to the problem of "decreasing water resources." The solution to this problem is the paragraph's final, topic sentence.

2   Achieving coherence with cues

When sentences are arranged with care, you need only to highlight this arrangement to ensure that readers will move easily through a paragraph. To highlight paragraph coherence, use **cues:** words and phrases that remind readers as they move from sentence to sentence that (1) they continue to read about the same topic and (2) that ideas are unfolding logically. Four types of cues help to highlight sentence-to-sentence connections: pronouns, repetition, parallel structures, and transitions (which will be discussed in the next section). Accomplished writers usually combine techniques in order to highlight paragraph coherence, often not adding cues to a paragraph until the revision stage, when they are better able to discern a paragraph's shape.

Pronouns

The most direct way to remind readers that they continue to examine a certain topic as they move from sentence to sentence is to repeat the most important noun, or the subject, of your topic sentence. To prevent repetition from becoming tiresome, use a pronoun to take the place of this important noun. Every time a pronoun is used, the reader is *cued,* or reminded, about the paragraph's main topic. In the following example, *he* and *his* take the place of the name *Herbert Hoover.* These pronouns are repeated eight times, tying the paragraph together without dulling the reader with repetition.

Herbert Hoover was a perfect symbol of the ideals and hopes of the American business community in the 1920s. He showed that to succeed in the United States and to be elected President you did not have to come from a rich, upper-class family. His life proved that in America character, intelligence, and hard work could make a national leader. Born of Quaker parents on a small farm in Iowa in 1874, he had been orphaned at the age of ten. He worked his way through Stanford University, where he studied engineering. Then he made his fortune as a mining engineer—in Australia, Africa, China, Latin America, and Russia. He was a millionaire by the time he was 40.

> —Daniel Boorstin and Brooks Mather Kelley,
> *A History of the United States*

26

5d

coh

Repetition

While unintentional repetition can make sentences awkward, planned repetition can contribute significantly to a paragraph's coherence. The strategy is to repeat identically or to use a substitute phrase to repeat an important word or words in a paragraph. As with pronoun use, repetition cues readers, reminding them of the paragraph's important information. In the example that follows, concerning the word *meter*, combinations of the following four words are repeated sixteen times: *meter, define/definition, bar, standard*. Skillful use of repetition ties sentences together without boring the reader. Repetition helps to make this paragraph coherent.

The fundamental unit of length in the metric system is the meter. Originally, the meter was defined to be 10^{-7} of the distance from the North Pole to the equator. Later, a platinum-iridium bar was constructed whose length was as close as possible to the original definition. This bar, which became known as the *standard meter*, is kept at the Bureau of Weights and Measures near Paris. A similar bar was installed at the U.S. Bureau of Standards in Washington, D.C. All rulers, meter sticks, and other length-measuring devices were in the past calibrated by comparison with the

27

standard meter bar. An even more precise standard is currently being used. The meter is now defined to be a length equal to the distance light travels in a vacuum in 1/299,792,458 of a second. The number of digits in this figure shows the great precision with which such measurements can be made.

—PAUL S. COHEN AND MILTON A. ROTHMAN, *Basic Chemistry*

5d

coh

Parallelism

Chapter 18 is devoted entirely to a discussion of **parallelism:** the use of grammatically equivalent words, phrases, and sentences to achieve coherence and balance in your writing. A sentence whose structure parallels that of an earlier sentence has an echo-like effect, linking the content of the second sentence to the content of the first. As with pronoun use and skillful repetition, parallel structures cue readers by highlighting the paragraph's important information.

Of course, it cannot be literally true that what the sculptor imagines and carves out is already there, hidden in the block. And yet the metaphor tells the truth about the relation of discovery that exists between man and nature; and it is characteristic that philosophers of science (Leibniz in particular) have turned to the same metaphor of the mind prompted by a vein in the marble. In one sense, everything that we discover is already there: a sculptured figure and the law of nature are both concealed in the raw material. And in another sense, what a man discovers is discovered *by* him; it would not take exactly the same form in the hands of someone else—neither the sculpture figure nor the law of nature would come out in identical copies when produced by two different minds in two different ages. Discovery is a double relation of analysis and synthesis together. As an analysis, it probes for what is there; but then, as a synthesis, it puts the parts together in a form by which the creative mind transcends the bare limits, the bare skeleton, that nature provides.

—J. BRONOWSKI, *The Ascent of Man*

28

Bronowski writes two sets of sentences in parallel.

In one sense, everything that we discover . . . .
And in another sense, what a man discovers is discovered . . . .

Later in the paragraph you find the following set of sentences.

Discovery is a double relation of analysis and synthesis together. As an analysis, it probes for what is there; but then, as a synthesis, it puts the parts together . . . .

5d

coh

The fourth type of cue that highlights paragraph coherence, the transition, is discussed next.

3 Highlighting coherence with transitions

Transitions are words that establish logical relationships between sentences, between paragraphs, and between whole sections of an essay. A transition can take the form of a single word, a phrase, a sentence, or an entire paragraph. In each case it functions the same way: first, it either directly summarizes the content of a preceding sentence (or paragraph) or it implies that summary. Having established a summary, transitions then move forward into a new sentence (or paragraph), helping the reader anticipate what is to come. For example, when you read the word *however,* you are immediately aware that the material you are about to read will contrast with the material you have just read. In so brief a transition, the summary of the preceding material is implied—but present. As the reader, *you* do the summarizing.

Transitions also act as cues by helping readers to anticipate what is coming *before* they read it. Within a paragraph, transitions tend to be single words.

The survival of the robin, and indeed of many other species as well, seems fatefully linked with the American elm, a tree that is part of the history of thousands of towns from the Atlantic to the Rockies, gracing their streets and their village squares and college campuses with majestic archways of green. Now the elms are stricken with a disease that afflicts them throughout their range, a disease so serious that many experts believe all efforts to save the elms will in the end be futile. It would be tragic to lose the elms, but it would be doubly tragic if, in vain efforts to save them, we plunge vast segments of our bird populations into the night of extinction. Yet this is precisely what is threatened.

—RACHEL CARSON, *Silent Spring*

29

Transitions placed between paragraphs help readers move through sections of your paper. If you have done a good job of arranging paragraphs so that the content of one leads logically to the next, then by using a transitional expression you are highlighting a relationship that already exists. By summarizing the previous paragraph and telegraphing something of the content of the paragraph that follows, a transition helps to move the reader through your paper. A transition between paragraphs can be a word or two—*however, for example, similarly*—a phrase, or a sentence. In ¶s 16 and 17 you will find a sentence-length transition between paragraphs (at the end of ¶16). The following is a sentence-length transition used to join two sections of a chapter in a textbook.

> *Just as through* formal religion and civic life the Sumerians at the dawn of recorded history, created a new kind of human experience, *so through* writing and figurative art they found a new way to represent that experience. Writing had been invented by the simplifying of pictures into signs, . . .
> —*Gardner's Art Through the Ages,* 5th ed.

The first half of this paragraph's lead sentence explicitly summarizes the preceding section of a chapter. The second half of the sentence is the paragraph's topic sentence and points the reader forward to a new discussion on writing and figurative art. If the relationship between sections of a paper is complex, you may want to take some time and write a paragraph-length transition, as in this example.

> **30** So Grant and Lee were in complete contrast, representing two diametrically opposed elements in American life. Grant was the modern man emerging; beyond him, ready to come on the stage, was the great age of steel and machinery, of crowded cities and a restless burgeoning vitality. Lee might have ridden down from the old age of chivalry, lance in hand, silken banner fluttering over his head. Each man was the perfect champion of his cause, drawing both his strengths and his weaknesses from the people he led.
>
> **31** Yet it was not all contrast, after all. Different as they were—in background, in personality, in underlying aspiration—these two great soldiers had much in common. Under everything else, they were marvelous fighters. Furthermore, their fighting qualities were really very much alike.
>
> **32** Each man had, to begin with, the great virtue of utter tenacity and fidelity. Grant fought his way down the Mississippi Valley in spite of acute personal discouragement and profound military handicaps. Lee hung on in the trenches at Petersburg after hope itself had died. In each man there was an indomitable quality . . . the born fighter's refusal to give up as long as he can still remain on his feet and lift his two fists.
> —BRUCE CATTON, "Grant and Lee: A Study in Contrasts"

Whatever its length, a transition will establish a clear relationship between sentences, parts of sentences, paragraphs, or entire sections of an essay. Transitions serve to highlight relationships already present by virtue of a writer's having positioned sentences or paragraphs next to one another.

Whenever you have trouble finding a word or sentence to serve as an effective transition, reexamine the sentences or paragraphs you are trying to link: it may well be that they are not arranged coherently, and thus are in need of revision. The following box lists the most common transitions, arranged by type of relationship.

5d

coh

Transitional Expressions	
To show addition	additionally, again, also, and, as well, besides, equally important, further, furthermore, in addition, moreover, then
To show similarity	also, in the same way, just as . . . so too, likewise, similarly
To show an exception	but, however, in spite of, on the one hand . . . on the other hand, nevertheless, nonetheless, notwithstanding, in contrast, on the contrary, still, yet
To indicate sequence	first, second, third, . . . next, then, finally
To show time	after, afterwards, at last, before, currently, during, earlier, immediately, later, meanwhile, now, recently, simultaneously, subsequently, then
To provide an example	for example, for instance, namely, specifically, to illustrate
To emphasize a point	even, indeed, in fact, of course, truly
To indicate place	above, adjacent, below, beyond, here, in front, in back, nearby, there
To show cause and effect	accordingly, consequently, hence, so, therefore, thus
To conclude or repeat	finally, in a word, in brief, in conclusion, in the end, on the whole, thus, to conclude, to summarize

4 Combining techniques to achieve coherence

Experienced writers will often combine the four techniques just discussed to establish coherence within a paragraph. A skillful mix of pronouns, repeated words and phrases, parallel structures, and transitions will help to maintain the focus of a paragraph and to provide multiple cues, or signposts, that help readers find their way from one sentence to the next. The following paragraph on the settling of the Kansas frontier in the mid-nineteenth century illustrates the use of all four techniques for establishing paragraph coherence.

> Beautiful and bountiful, the land was the great lure of Kansas. Some settlers sought freedom, some yearned for prosperity, some craved adventure, but in the end it was the promise of the land that drew them halfway across a continent. Here they could build their own homes, cultivate their own fields and develop their own communities. Undoubtedly, it took a special kind of fortitude to adjust to this harsh terrain. Yet with hard work, imagination and tenacity, the future was theirs to mold. In this new land, God's own country, they reached to the stars through the wilderness.
>
> —JOANNA STRATTON, *Pioneer Women*

In this paragraph, the word *land* is repeated in six ways. As well, the term for the main actors of the paragraph—the *settlers*—is repeated with six pronouns. In three different sentences, Joanna Stratton makes effective use of parallel structures. Stratton also makes use of transitional expressions: *but, here, undoubtedly,* and *yet.*

EXERCISE 8

Reread ¶s 14–20 in Exercises 6 and 7. For each paragraph, identify the techniques that the author uses to establish coherence. Show the use of pronouns, repetition, parallel structures, and transitions. In addition, identify the use of transitions between paragraphs.

EXERCISE 9

Reread a paragraph you have recently written, and circle all words that help to establish coherence. If few words suggest themselves to you for circling, this may be a sign that your paragraph lacks coherence. Photocopy your paragraph and then revise it for coherence, using the techniques discussed previously: arrange sentences according to a pattern and then highlight that arrangement with pronouns, repeated words, parallel structures, and transitions. When you are done revising, write a clean copy of the paragraph and make photocopies of both the original and the revision for classmates in a small-group discussion. Prepare a brief presentation in which you discuss the changes you have made.

5e Writing and revising to achieve well-developed paragraphs

One important element of effective writing is the level of detail you can offer in support of a paragraph's topic sentence. To *develop* a paragraph means to devote a block of sentences to a discussion of its core idea. Sentences that develop will explain or illustrate, and will support with reasons or facts. The various strategies presented here will help you to develop paragraphs that inform and persuade.

1   **Balancing the general and the specific in a paragraph**

To write a paragraph, you must appreciate the mix of general sentences and detailed specific sentences that work in tandem to create meaning. Read the following sentence, written by a psychiatrist. Certainly it is accurate to make this statement about the behavior of obsessive-compulsive people.

> In general, obsessive-compulsive people feel that any relaxation of deliberateness or purposeful activity is improper, unsafe, or worse.

This sentence may be true, but why should we accept it if the writer has offered no reasons? And how useful is the sentence if we are not given specific information that shows us how obsessive-compulsive people behave? Here is how writer and psychiatrist David Shapiro develops a paragraph around this sentence.

> In general, obsessive-compulsive people feel that any relaxation of deliberateness or purposeful activity is improper, unsafe, or worse. If they are not working, they usually feel that they should at least be thinking (that is, worrying) about some problem, and the prospect of not worrying about a problem that exists, even if it is one that they can do nothing about, seems quite foolhardy to them. They do not feel comfortable with any activity that lacks an aim or a purpose beyond its own pleasure, and usually they do not recognize the possibility of finding life satisfying without a continuous sense of purpose and effort, a continuous sense of advancing the career, making money, writing papers, or the like.

34

> —DAVID SHAPIRO, *Neurotic Styles*

By providing explanatory details about obsessive-compulsive behavior, Shapiro clarifies and makes meaningful his opening, general statement—which in relation to more specific details that follow now functions as a topic sentence. A paragraph consisting only of details will seem narrow-minded and even confusing to readers, who look to a writer to provide a statement that sets a general framework within which to read and understand. Conversely, a paragraph of general statements that lack supporting details will strike readers as vague and possibly arrogant in the sense that the writer is assuming his ideas are so clearly put and self-evidently true that they need no clarification. A writer's aim, surely, must be to balance vivid, clarifying detail with broader statements that argue a point or seek to inform. An analogy would be to a filmmaker who pulls the camera's lens back to give a general view and then zooms close to study specific details. As a writer moving from paragraph to paragraph, you are repeatedly pulling the lens back and then zooming close, making general statements and then developing them with details. Balancing the general with the specific will allow you to "think large"—to get a core, governing idea for a paragraph, but at the same time the right to express that idea by supplying detailed information.

Developing Paragraphs: Essential Features

In determining whether a paragraph is well or even adequately developed, you should be able to answer three questions without hesitation:

- **What is the main point of the paragraph?**
- **Why should readers accept this main point?** (That is, what reasons or information have you provided that would convince a reader that your main point is accurate or reasonable?)
- **Why should readers *care* about the main point of this paragraph?**

---

2 Using patterns of development

When writing the first draft of a paper, you may not stop to think about how you are developing the central idea of every paragraph. There is no need in first-draft writing to be this deliberate. By the second draft, however, you will want to be conscious of developing your paragraphs. The most common technique is **topical development,** that is, announcing your topic in the opening sentence; dividing that topic into two or three parts (in the case of chronological arrangement, into various *times*); and then developing each part within the paragraph.

In revision, and even in first-draft writing, you may be conscious of wanting to develop a paragraph's core idea by following specialized patterns: by narrating a story, by describing an event or scene, by offering an example, by offering a definition, by comparing or contrasting, by delineating a process, by establishing cause and effect, or by analyzing and classifying. While in principle there are limitless ways in which to develop a paragraph, these patterns are especially useful and tend to recur. Within a paper, writers may employ a variety of development strategies. One paragraph may offer a definition; two more may be developed topically; a fourth may provide an example; a fifth and sixth may present a comparison and contrast, and so on.

The patterns of paragraph development that follow mirror the varieties of inference that can underlie a paper's thesis. You make certain inferences about material you have gathered in planning a paper and these inferences become a key component of your working thesis (see 3f). The key paragraphs of any paper will be the ones that express and develop the patterns of relation—the inferences—that lie at the core of either the working thesis or a section thesis. In chapter 3 you saw that these inferences were of several types: sequential order, definition, classification, comparison and contrast, causation, and analogy. These same patterns of relation can be used to develop ideas in individual paragraphs.

Narration and Description

Stories that you tell (**narration**) and events or scenes that you describe (**description**) are two strategies for development that can give a paper vivid detail.

5e

¶ *dev*

Narration

Narratives usually involve descriptions; a narrative's main purpose is to recount for readers a story that will have a point pertinent to the larger essay. Brief stories are often used as examples. Most often, narratives are sequenced chronologically and will occur in an essay either as a single paragraph or as a grouping of paragraphs. The challenge in writing a narrative is to keep readers involved both in the events you are relating and in the people involved in those events. In the example that follows, Annie Dillard manages to do both. These paragraphs appear in her autobiography, in a chapter devoted to joke telling in her family.

35　　There was another very complicated joke, also in a select category, which required a long weekend with tolerant friends.

　　You had to tell a joke that was not funny. It was a long, pointless story about a construction job that ended with someone's throwing away a brick.
36　There was nothing funny about it at all, and when your friends did not laugh, you had to pretend you'd muffed it. (Your husband in the crowd could shill for you: " 'Tain't funny, Pam. You told it all wrong.")

　　A few days later, if you could contrive another occasion for joke telling, and if your friends still permitted you to speak, you set forth on another joke, this one an old nineteenth-century chestnut about angry passengers on a train. The lady plucks the lighted, smelly cigar from the man's mouth and flings it from the moving train's window. The man seizes the little black poodle from her lap and hurls the poor dog from the same window. When
37　at last the passengers draw unspeaking into the station, what do they see coming down the platform but the black poodle, and guess what it has in its mouth? "The cigar," say your friends, bored sick and vowing never to spend another weekend with you. "No," you say, triumphant, "the brick." This was Mother's kind of joke. Its very riskiness excited her. It wasn't funny, but it was interesting to set up, and it elicited from her friends a grudging admiration.

　　　　　　　　　　　　—ANNIE DILLARD, *An American Childhood*

Description

All writers must make observations and describe what they see. What counts as an accurate and worthwhile description will vary according to circumstance, but generally it can be said that a writer who can evoke in us a clear sense of sight, feeling, smell, hearing, or taste earns our admiration. Consider this sentence from Bruce Chatwin's *In Patagonia:* "The wind blew the smell of rain down the valley ahead of the rain itself, the smell of wet earth and aromatic plants." This is a fine sentence. It evokes in us not only a feeling for the scene that Chatwin saw but also a recollection of our own experience. Everyone has smelled rain coming in advance of a storm. Everyone has smelled wet earth and an aromatic plant, perhaps an orchid or gardenia on prom night. Now mingle these smells as Chatwin does and have the scent carried on a moist wind, in a valley that is likely lush with vegetation. If one sentence can evoke such a clear sense of place, think what a well-written paragraph can do! Following is a description of the promenade—the walk-way—on the Brooklyn Bridge. The author does a fine job of letting us see the bridge, even if we have never been there.

5e

¶ dev

> On most traffic bridges the only foot passage is a pavement alongside rushing vehicles. Here the walk is a promenade raised above the traffic; one can lean over the railing and watch cars speeding below. The promenade is wide enough for benches—for walkers and for cyclists. Old-fashioned lamp posts remind the walker that it is, after all, a thoroughfare. But the walk is narrow enough for the promenader to reach over and touch the large, round cables, wrapped in wire casing, or the rough wire rope of the vertical suspenders. Crossing the verticals is a rigging of diagonal wire ropes—stays, attached somewhere below to the floor of the roadway.
>
> —ALAN TRACHTENBERG, *Brooklyn Bridge: Fact and Symbol*

38

Example

An example is a particular case of a more general point. After topical development, development by example is probably the most common method of supporting the core idea of a paragraph. Examples *show* readers what you mean; if an example is vivid, readers will have a better chance of remembering your general point. The topic sentence of a paragraph may be developed with one extended example or several briefer ones. It is very common for writers to include an example along with other strategies for developing a paragraph. Several transitions are commonly used to introduce examples: *for example, for instance, a case in point, to illustrate.* In the following paragraph, Rachel Carson describes how methods of insect control can affect fish.

> Wherever there are great forests, modern methods of insect control threaten the fishes inhabiting the streams in the shelter of the trees. One of the best-known examples of fish destruction in the United States took place in 1955, as a result of spraying in and near Yellowstone National Park. By the fall of that year, so many dead fish had been found in the Yellowstone River that sportsmen and Montana fish-and-game administrators became alarmed. About 90 miles of the river were affected. In one 300-yard length

39

of shoreline, 600 dead fish were counted, including brown trout, whitefish, and suckers. Stream insects, the natural food of trout, had disappeared.

—RACHEL CARSON, *Silent Spring*

Sequential order/process

If you have ever cooked a meal by following a recipe, you have read paragraphs patterned as a sequence of steps, as a process. Such a paragraph will not explain the causes of a particular outcome—it will not, for instance, explain the chemical reactions that cake batter undergoes when placed in an oven. A paragraph that presents a process will show carefully sequenced events. The range of possibilities is endless: what is the process by which people fall in love? by which children learn? by which steel is made? by which a poem is written? by which a computer chip is manufactured? Each of these cases, different as they are, requires a clear delineation of steps. In paragraphs organized as a process, you will typically use transitions that show sequence in time: *first, second, after, before, once, next, then,* and *finally.*

Making a chip is a complex process. Most manufacturers now use what Heilmeier calls the "dip and wash" technique. A diagram of electronic circuitry is designed by a scientist on a computer terminal. Photographic machines produce hundreds of reproductions of the display and reduce them in size until their individual components are in the micron range. A photographic negative, or mask, is made of the patterns. Ultraviolet light is then projected through the mask onto a thin, 4-inch wafer of silicon that has been treated with photo resist, a light-sensitive material. Just like a film, the photo resist is developed, and the tiny patterns of the chips' circuitry emerge on the silicon's surface. The wafer is dipped in acid, which eats away the silicon where there is no photo resist. A layer of metal can be deposited for the interconnections between circuits, then another layer of photo resist. Some wafers take ten or more etched layers. Once all the layers are formed on the wafer, the chips are sawed out, fine wire leads are connected and they are ready for use in electronic devices.

40

—MERRILL SHEILS, "And Man Created the Chip"

Definition

Paragraphs of definition are always important. In informative writing, readers can learn the meaning of terms needed for understanding difficult concepts. In essays intended to persuade, writers define terms in order to establish a common language with the reader, an important first step toward gaining the reader's agreement. Certainly it is impossible to argue about the role of *civil disobedience* in a democracy if a writer is vague about the term or if the writer and reader do not agree on the how the term should be defined. With a paragraph of definition, the writer has a chance to explain a term in ways advantageous to the argument. Once a term is defined, it can be clarified with examples, comparisons, or descriptions. The paragraph that follows is informative in character—more or less announcing its definition.

5e

¶ *dev*

When we are hungry, we think of McDonald's or Godfather's Pizza. When we actually go to these fast food places, we never worry about whether they will have enough Big Macs or pizzas for us. Shouldn't we worry about it? How do they know that we are coming? Of course, they do not know that *we* are coming, but they know that someone will. In a market economy, stores tend to carry products that customers want and customers usually find products that they want at their favorite stores. A market economy is one in which competition works through the interaction of supply and demand. Individual sellers pursue private interests by selling the quantity and charging the price that will maximize their profits. Individual buyers, on the other hand, pursue private interests by selecting the bundle of goods and services that will maximize their satisfaction. There is no order imposed from above, but there is a sense of orderliness in the market.

—SEMOON CHANG, *Modern Economics*

Paragraphs that define can also be argumentative in character, attempting to persuade readers that the writer's definition of a term is the correct or most useful one. In any argument, a writer is obligated to provide reasons, and this standard holds for paragraphs of definition. The example paragraph that follows is far longer than any you will normally write, but it provides an excellent illustration of a definition that is *argued* for, as opposed to being merely announced. For reasons of length alone, the writer might easily have divided the paragraph into three parts. Presenting definitions can be complex; for this reason entire essays are sometimes devoted to their development.

[History is a word] that I wish to reduce to its lowest terms. In order to do that I need a very simple definition. I once read that "history is the knowledge of events that have occurred in the past." That is a simple definition, but not simple enough. It contains three words that require examination. The first is knowledge. Knowledge is a formidable word. I always think of knowledge as something that is stored up in the *Encyclopaedia Britannica* or the *Summa Theologica:* something difficult to acquire, something at all events that I have not. Resenting a definition that denies me the title of historian, I therefore ask what is most essential to knowledge. Well, memory, I should think (and I mean memory in the broad sense, the memory of events inferred as well as the memory of events observed); other things are necessary too, but memory is fundamental: without memory no knowledge. So our definition becomes, "History is the memory of events that have occurred in the past." But events—the word carries an implication of something grand, like the taking of the Bastille or the Spanish-American War. An occurrence need not be spectacular to be an event. If I drive a motor car down the crooked streets of Ithaca, that is an event—something done; if the traffic cop bawls me out, that is an event—something said; if I have evil thoughts of him for so doing, that is an event—something thought. In truth anything done, said, or thought is an event, important or not as may turn out. But since we do not ordinarily speak without thinking, at least in some rudimentary way, and since the psychologists tell us that we cannot think without speaking, or at least not without having anticipatory vibrations in the larynx, we may well combine thought events and speech events under one term; and so our definition becomes, "History is the memory of things said and done in the past." But the past—the word is both misleading and unnecessary: misleading, because the past, used in connection with history, seems to imply the distant past, as if history ceased before we were born; unnecessary, because after all everything said or done is already in the past as soon as it is said or done. Therefore I will omit that word, and our definition becomes, "History is the memory of things said and done." This is a definition that reduces history to its lowest terms, and yet includes everything that is essential to understanding what it really is.

—CARL BECKER, "Everyman His Own Historian"

5e

¶ *dev*

Division and classification

Division (also called *analysis*) and classification are closely related operations. A writer who divides a topic into parts to see what it is made of performs an analysis. This is exactly the strategy used by Carl Becker in the preceding example to argue for a particular definition of "history." Becker's analysis begins early in the paragraph with the claim that three words in the commonplace definition of history "require examination." Becker evaluates these words—*history, events, past*—and then dispenses with them in favor of his own definition of history. An entire paper, as well as a single paragraph, can be organized as an analysis. (See chapter 1 for an analysis of *The Wizard of Oz*.)

Analysis is an act of critical thinking that can be put to several ends. You have just seen analysis used in the service of a definition. The careful study of parts can also be instrumental in comparing and contrasting, in understanding a process, and in inferring cause and effect. While a paragraph may emphasize a definition, comparison, process, or cause, in each case this emphasis is made meaningful at least in part through analysis.

A *classification* is a grouping of like items. The writer begins with what may appear at first to be bits of unrelated information. Gradually, patterns of similarity emerge and the writer is able to establish categories by which to group like items. (See 3e-1 for a discussion of creating categories.) In the example that follows, Brian Fagan considers the various locations at which archaeological digs are made and then classifies or groups the digs according to common features. Because establishing categories is a matter of judgment, another writer might well classify archaeological sites differently. Fagan's paragraph begins with his topic sentence. Notice that once he defines various classes, he devotes a sentence or two to developing each.

Archaeological sites are most commonly classified according to the activities that occurred there. Thus, cemeteries and other sepulchers like Tutankhamun's tomb are referred to as **burial sites.** A 20,000-year-old Stone Age site in the Dnieper Valley of the Ukraine, with mammoth-bone houses, hearths, and other signs of domestic activity, is a **habitation site.** So too are many other sites, such as caves and rockshelters, early Mesoamerican farming villages, and Mesopotamian cities—in all, people lived and carried out greatly diverse activities. **Kill sites** consist of bones of slaughtered game animals and the weapons that killed them. They are found in East Africa and on the North American Great Plains. **Quarry sites** are another type of specialist site, where people mined stone or metals to make specific tools. Prized raw materials, such as obsidian, a volcanic glass used for fine knives, were widely traded in prehistoric times and profoundly interest the archaeologist. Then there are such spectacular **religious sites** as the stone circles of Stonehenge in southern England, the Temple of Amun at Karnak, Egypt, and the great ceremonial precincts of lowland Maya centers in Central America at *Tikal,* Copán, and Palenque. **Art sites** are common in southwestern France, southern Africa, and parts of North America, where prehistoric people painted or engraved magnificent displays of art.

—BRIAN FAGAN, *Archaeology*

Comparison/contrast

To *compare* is to discuss the similarities between people, places, objects, events, or ideas. To *contrast* is to discuss differences. The writer developing such a paragraph conducts an analysis of two or more subjects, studying the parts of each and then discussing the subjects in relation to each other. Specific points of comparison and contrast make the discussion possible. Suppose you are comparing and contrasting a computer and the human brain. Two points you might use to make the discussion meaningful are the density with which information is packed and the speed with which information is processed. You could analyze a computer and a human brain in light of these two points, and presumably your analysis would yield similarities *and* differences.

Paragraphs of comparison and contrast should be put to some definite use in a paper. It is not enough to point out similarities and differences; you must *do* something with this information: three possibilities would be to classify, evaluate, or interpret. When writing your paragraph, consider two common methods of arrangement: by subject or point-by-point.

ARRANGEMENT BY SUBJECT Following a topic sentence in which you signal that a comparison is coming, you discuss each subject separately within the paragraph. First you discuss computers—their density of information, and then the speed with which they process information. Next, you discuss the human brain—its density of information, and then the speed with which it processes information. Either in the separate discussions within the paragraph or at the end you would review similarities and differences.

ARRANGEMENT, This method allows you to mingle observations about computers
POINT-BY-POINT and brains. After your topic sentence, raise your first *point* of comparison and contrast—density of information. Then follow with a discussion of *both* computers and brains. Next, raise your second point of comparison and contrast—speed at which information is processed. Again, follow with a discussion of *both* computers and brains.

5e

¶ *dev*

When the comparisons you want to make are relatively brief, arrangement by subject works well. Readers are able to hold in mind the first part of the discussion as they read the second. When comparisons are longer and more complex, a point-by-point discussion helps the reader to focus on specific elements of your comparative analysis. Paragraphs developed by comparison and contrast use transition words such as: *similarly, also, as well, just so, by contrast, conversely, but, however, on the one hand/on the other,* and *yet.*

Organizing a Paragraph of Comparison and Contrast

Comparison and contrast is a type of analysis in which parts of two (or more) subjects are studied and then discussed in terms of one another. Particular points of comparison and contrast provide the means by which to observe similarities and differences between subjects. A comparative analysis is usually arranged in one of two ways.

Arrangement by subject

Topic sentence (may be shifted to other positions in the paragraph)

Introduce Subject A
  Discuss Subject A in terms of the first point to be discussed
  Discuss Subject A in terms of the second point to be discussed

Introduce Subject B
  Discuss Subject B in terms of the first point to be discussed
  Discuss Subject B in terms of the second point to be discussed

Conclude with a summary of similarities and differences.

Arrangement, point-by-point

Topic sentence (may be shifted to other positions in the paragraph)

Introduce the first point to be compared and contrasted
  Discuss Subject A in terms of this point
  Discuss Subject B in terms of this point

Introduce the second point to be compared and contrasted
  Discuss Subject A in terms of this point
  Discuss Subject B in terms of this point

In the following paragraph, Carl Sagan uses a point-by-point arrangement to compare and contrast the human brain with a computer. First, he examines the two subjects with respect to the density with which their information is packed; next, he examines the two subjects with respect to the speed with which they process information.

¶ dev

44   How densely packed is the information stored in the brain? A typical information density during the operation of a modern computer is about a million bits per cubic centimeter. This is the total information content of the computer, divided by its volume. The human brain contains, as we have said, about 10^{13} bits in a little more than 10^3 cubic centimeters, for an information content of $10^{13}/10^3 = 10^{10}$, about ten billion bits per cubic centimeter; the brain is therefore ten thousand times more densely packed with information than is a computer, although the computer is much larger. Put another way, a modern computer able to process the information in the human brain would have to be about ten thousand times larger in volume than the human brain. On the other hand, modern electronic computers are capable of processing information at a rate of 10^{16} to 10^{17} bits per second, compared to a peak rate ten billion times slower in the brain. The brain must be extraordinarily cleverly packaged and "wired," with such a small total information content and so low a processing rate, to be able to do so many significant tasks so much better than the best computer.

—CARL SAGAN, *The Dragons of Eden*

In the following paragraph, John Morreall organizes his comparative discussion by subject. First, he discusses his Subject A: the person with a sense of humor and the traits associated with this view of the world. Then Morreall discusses his Subject B: the person who lacks a sense of humor and the traits associated with this view of the world. Morreall concludes the paragraph with a topic sentence that makes a general point about humor and places the comparison and contrast in a larger perspective.

45   When the person with a sense of humor laughs in the face of his own failure, he is showing that his perspective transcends the particular situation he's in, and that he does not have an egocentric, overly precious view of his own endeavors. This is not to say that he lacks self-esteem—quite the contrary. It is because he feels good about himself at a fundamental level that this or that setback is not threatening to him. The person without real self-esteem, on the other hand, who is unsure of his own worth, tends to invest his whole sense of himself in each of his projects. Whether he fails or succeeds, he is not likely to see things in an objective way; because his ego rides on each of the goals he sets for himself, any failure will constitute personal defeat and any success personal triumph. He simply cannot afford to laugh at himself, whatever happens. So having a sense of humor about oneself is psychologically healthy. As A. Penjon so nicely said, it "frees us from vanity, on the one hand, and from pessimism on the other by keeping us larger than what we do, and greater than what can happen to us."

—JOHN MORREALL, *Taking Laughter Seriously*

Analogy

An **analogy** is a comparison of two topics that, on first appearance, seem unrelated. An analogy gains force by surprising a reader, by demonstrating that an unlikely comparison is not only likely but in fact is illuminating. Well-chosen analogies can clarify difficult concepts. In the following example, the process of learning is compared with a symphony orchestra. The words *like* or *analogous to* typically signal the beginning of an analogy. After describing the first of the two topics in the comparison, the writer follows with an expression such as *just so* or *similarly* and then continues with the second part of the comparison.

5e

¶ *dev*

> In closing, we might describe learning with an analogy to a well-orchestrated symphony, aimed to blend both familiar and new sounds. A symphony is the complex interplay of composer, conductor, the repertoire of instruments, and the various dimensions of music. Each instrument is used strategically to interact with other instruments toward a rich construction of themes progressing in phases, with some themes recurring and others driving the movement forward toward a conclusion or resolution. Finally, each symphony stands alone in its meaning, yet has a relationship to the symphonies that came before and those that will come later. Similarly, learning is a complex interaction of the learner, the instructional materials, the repertoire of available learning strategies, and the context, including the teacher. The skilled learner approaches each task strategically toward the goal of constructing meaning. Some strategies focus on understanding the incoming information, others strive to relate the meaning to earlier predictions, and still others work to integrate the new information with prior knowledge.
>
> —BEAU FLY JONES, ET AL., "Learning and Thinking"

46

Cause and effect

Development by cause and effect shows how an event or condition has come to occur. Inferring a causal relationship between events requires careful analysis. As discussed elsewhere (see 6d-2), causes are usually complex, and a writer must avoid the temptation to oversimplify. In particular, avoid the mistake of suggesting that because one event precedes another in time, the first event causes the second. A causal relationship is not always so clear cut, a point that James Watts and Alan Davis acknowledge in the following paragraph on the Depression of the 1930s. Paragraphs developed by cause and effect frequently use these transition words: *therefore, thus,* and *consequently.*

> The depression was precipitated by the stock market crash in October 1929, but the actual cause of the collapse was an unhealthy economy. While the ability of the manufacturing industry to produce consumer goods had increased rapidly, mass purchasing power had remained relatively static. Most laborers, farmers, and white-collar workers, therefore, could not afford to buy the automobiles and refrigerators turned out by factories in the 1920s, because their incomes were too low. At the same time, the federal government increased the problem through economic policies that tended to encourage the very rich to over-save.
>
> —JAMES WATTS AND ALAN F. DAVIS,
> *Your Family in Modern American History*

47

Combining methods of development

Writers may combine methods of developing a paragraph's core idea, as needed. The same paragraph that shows an example may also show a comparison or contrast. You have seen a paragraph of definition (¶42) developed partially on the strength of an analysis. No firm rules constrain you in developing a paragraph. Let your common sense and an interest in helping your reader understand your subject be your guides. A number of example paragraphs in this chapter have been developed by using two or more methods of development. (See ¶s 10, 16, and 43.)

5e

¶ dev

EXERCISE 10

Turn to the paragraphs in Exercise 6 (¶s 14–20), which you have already analyzed for unity and coherence. Identify the principal method by which the core idea or topic sentence of each paragraph is developed. To summarize the options: paragraphs will be developed topically, by narration, description, example, process, definition, division, classification, comparison/contrast, analogy, or cause and effect—or by a combination of these methods.

EXERCISE 11

Return to Exercise 2 (page 127) in which you outlined one chapter of a textbook and selected one section of that chapter to study in depth. If you have not done so, complete that exercise, and then for that same block of paragraphs perform the analysis requested in Exercise 10: that is, analyze each paragraph and identify its pattern of development.

EXERCISE 12

In one paragraph compare and contrast your first day as a student at your present school with your first day in any other circumstance. Take care to choose two or three points on the basis of which you will generate your comparison and contrast. Be sure your comparison and contrast is put to some purpose (perhaps you will classify, interpret, or evaluate). Express this purpose in your paragraph's topic sentence. See ¶s 44 and 45 for possible models.

EXERCISE 13

Reread a paper you have recently written and select a paragraph to revise so that its topic sentence is thoroughly developed. Use any of the patterns of development presented here so that you are able, without hesitation, to answer the three questions in the box on page 148. Make photocopies of your original paragraph and your revision; plan to address a small group of classmates and explain the choices you have made in revision.

5f Writing and revising paragraphs of introduction and conclusion

The introduction and conclusion to a paper can be understood as a type of transition. Transitions provide logical bridges in a paper: they help readers to move from one sentence to another, one paragraph to another, and one section to another (see 5d-3). At the beginning of a paper, the introduction serves as a transition by moving the reader from the world outside of your paper to the world within. At the end of the paper, the conclusion works in the opposite direction by moving readers from the world of your paper back to their own world—with, you hope, something useful gained by their effort.

1 Introductions

Writing an introduction is often easier once you know what you are introducing; for this reason many writers choose not to work seriously on an introduction until they have finished a draft and can see the overall shape and content of a paper. Other writers need to begin with a carefully written introduction. If this is your preference, remember not to demand perfection of a first draft, especially since the material you will be introducing has yet to be written. Once it is written, your introduction may well need to change.

The introduction as a frame of reference

Introductions establish frames of reference. On completing an introduction, readers know the general topic of your paper; they know the disciplinary perspective from which you will discuss this topic; and they know the standards they will use in evaluating your work. Readers quickly learn from an introduction if you are laboratory researcher, a field researcher, a theorist, an essayist, a reporter, a student with a general interest, and so on. Each of these possible identities implies for readers different standards of evidence and reasoning by which they will evaluate your work. Consider the paragraph that follows, which introduces a paper that you will find in chapter 37 of this book, which is devoted to writing in the Humanities. The introduction, explicitly in the thesis and implicitly in the writer's choice of vocabulary, establishes a frame of reference that alerts readers to the type of language, evidence, and logic that will be used in the subsequent paper. Thus situated, readers are better able to anticipate and evaluate what they will read.

5f

trans   **48**

James Joyce's "Counterparts" tells the story
of a man, Farrington, who is abused by his boss
for not doing his job right. Farrington spends
a long time drinking after work; and when he finally arrives home, he in turn abuses--he beats--
his son Tom. In eleven pages, Joyce tells much
more than a story of yet another alcoholic vent-
ing failures and frustrations on family members. In "Counterparts," Farrington turns to
drink in order to gain power--in much the same
way his wife and children turn to the Church.

Language of literary analysis

Evidence: based on close reading of a story

Logic : generalization

Drinking and church going related to a need for power

Also comparison/ contrast

By comparison, read the following introduction to a paper written from a sociological perspective. This paragraph introduces a paper you will find in chapter 38, Writing in the Social Sciences.

49

Currently in the United States there are at
least two million women alcoholics (Unterberger,
1989, p. 1150). Americans are largely unaware
of the extent of this debilitating disease
among women and the problems it presents. Numerous women dependent on alcohol remain invisible
largely because friends, family, coworkers, and
the women themselves refuse to acknowledge the
problem. This denial amounts to a virtual conspiracy of silence and greatly complicates the
process of diagnosis and treatment.

Language of sociology

Evidence: based on review of sociological literature

Logic: cause and effect. Will show how denial complicates diagnosis and treatment.

The introduction as an invitation to continue reading

Aside from establishing a frame of reference and set of expectations about language, evidence, and logic, an introduction is also the place where you will—or will not—establish in your reader a desire to *continue* reading. A complete introduction will provide background information needed to understand a paper. An especially effective introduction will gain the reader's attention and gradually turn that attention toward the writer's thesis and the rest of the paper. Writers typically adopt specialized strategies for introducing their work. In the discussion that follows you will learn several of these strategies, all of which can be developed in one or two paragraphs, at the end of which you will place your thesis. The examples that follow by no means exhaust the possible strategies available to you for opening your papers; they should, however, give you a taste for the variety of techniques available.

5f

trans

Strategies for Writing Introductions

1. Announce your topic, using vocabulary that hints at the perspective from which you will be writing. On completing your introduction, readers should be able to anticipate the type of language, evidence, and logic you will use in your paper.

2. If readers lack the background needed to understand your paper, then provide this background. In a paragraph or two, choose and develop a strategy that will both orient readers to your subject and interest them in it:
    define terms
    present a brief history
    review a controversy

3. If readers know something of your subject, then devote less (or no) time to developing background information and more time to stimulating interest. In a paragraph or two, choose and develop a strategy that will gain the reader's attention:
    raise a question
    quote a source familiar to the reader
    tell a story
    begin directly with a statement of the thesis

4. Once you have provided background information and gained the reader's attention with an opening strategy, gradually turn that attention toward your thesis, which you will position as the last sentence of the introductory paragraph(s).

A revolutionary event took place at Raleigh Tavern in 1776, an event that has added an important dimension to my life at college. In fact, nearly all American undergraduates are affected in some way by the actions of several students from the College of William and Mary on December 5, 1776. The formation of the first Greek-letter fraternity, Phi Beta Kappa, started the American college fraternity-sorority tradition that today can be an important addition to your undergraduate education.

50

—Daniel Burke, "Defense of Fraternities"

5f

trans

In this example, student writer Daniel Burke provides pertinent historical information that sets a context for the paper. By linking a "revolutionary event" in 1776 to his own life over two hundred years later, Burke captures the reader's interest. In this next introduction, student writer Jim Roddy provides background information of another sort: specifics about a novel he intends to analyze.

E. L. Doctorow's *Ragtime* is considered a classic of American contemporary literature. Set at the turn of the century, it is a unique and innovative look at American transformation. The fact that *Ragtime* was published the year before the American bicentennial might lead some to believe that it is a celebration of our great American culture. However, large portions of the book deal with some of the more atrocious and barbarous elements of our society. One cannot help feeling that Doctorow wants to remind us of the many inhumane aspects of life in the United States. Indeed, *Ragtime* challenges the view that much of white America has toward this country.

51

—Jim Roddy, "Images of America in Doctorow's *Ragtime*"

The following example begins with a question, the response to which leads to the author's thesis. (The reference to "Valenti" is to Jack Valenti, head of the Motion Picture Production Association when Stephen Farber wrote his book.)

How are [movie] ratings actually determined? Official brochures on the rating system provide only very brief general definitions of the four categories, and I do not believe the categories can or should be defined much more specifically. It is impossible to set hard-and-fast rules; every film is different from every other film, and no precise definition could possibly cover all films made. Valenti has frequently toyed with the idea of more detailed definitions, though any rigid demarcations between the categories inevitably seem hopelessly arbitrary.

52

—Stephen Farber, *The Movie Rating Game*

See 5f-3 for two additional strategies for opening a paper: using a quotation and telling a story.

2 Conclusions

One important job in writing a paper is to explain to readers what you have accomplished and why your ideas are significant. Minimally, a conclusion will summarize your work, but often you will want to do more than write a summary. Provided you have written carefully and believe in what you have written, you have earned the right to expand on your paper's thesis in a conclusion: to point the reader back to the larger world and to suggest the significance of your ideas in that world. A conclusion gives you an opportunity to answer a challenge that all readers raise—*So what? Why does this paper matter to me?* A well-written conclusion will answer these questions and will leave readers with a trace of your thinking as they turn away from your paper and back to their own business.

Strategies for Writing Conclusions

1. **Summary.** The simplest conclusion is a summary, a brief restatement of your paper's main points. Avoid conclusions that repeat exactly material presented elsewhere in the paper.

2. **Summary and Comment.** More emphatic solutions build on a summary in one of several ways. These conclusions will:
   set ideas in the paper in a larger context
   call for action (or research)
   speculate or warn
   purposefully confuse or trouble the reader
   raise a question
   quote a familiar or authoritative source
   tell a story

The example conclusions that follow do not exhaust the strategies for closing your papers; these examples should, however, give you a taste for the variety of techniques available. Here is a paragraph that presents the simplest possible conclusion: a summary.

53 One can see by the number of steps involved in the legislative process that the odds are very great against an average bill becoming law. At almost every turn a bill may be killed. Hundreds of bills may start out, but only a few survive to become law.

—KEVIN COSTELLO, "Long Odds: How a Bill Becomes Law"

A more ambitious conclusion will move beyond a summary and call for involvement on the reader's part. For instance, you might ask the reader to address a puzzling or troubling question, to speculate on the future, or to reflect on the past. In this next example, the reader is asked to help resolve a problem plaguing college sports. (This example appears in an essay located in chapter 6, pages 190–195.)

54

```
We don't need to eliminate college sports. We probably
couldn't anyway, what with all the money being made. Eliminating
sports would do more harm than good, taking away both a source
of pride in college life and an important source of revenue.
Changing the admissions process to deny marginally prepared stu-
dent-athletes would not be fair, since for many of these kids
sports is their only avenue of exposure to college life and the
possibility of a higher education. To eliminate the chance to at-
tend college for marginal student-athletes would be heartless,
because it places on them a burden they did not make, a burden
that should and can be lifted with the proper approach. That's
why a plan that modifies the present system, not destroys it,
makes the most sense. Let's take advantage of all the money that
college sports generates and use that money to really educate
the student-athlete. The proposals I have made would not only
allow student-athletes to gain access to college but would also
increase the chances of their actually receiving an education.
```
—JENAFER TRAHAR, "Athletes and Education"

A final example shows an author speculating on the benefits of addressing and the dangers of ignoring the need for Americans to be proficient in at least two languages.

55
We have 29 years, nearly triple the time President Kennedy allowed when he committed us to reaching the moon. By comparison, the expenditures required to create a linguistically proficient nation would be insignificant. The benefits, not only in economic terms but also in terms of enhancing our understanding of other cultures and of ourselves, would be beyond measure. The costs, should we fail to act decisively, could eventually prove to be catastrophic.
—DANIEL SHANAHAN, "The Usefulness of Studying a Second Language"

Two additional strategies for concluding a paper are discussed next: using a quotation and telling a story.

3   The opening and closing frame

You might consider creating an introductory and concluding frame for your papers. The strategy is to use the same story, quotation, question—any device that comes to mind—as an occasion both to introduce your subject and, when the time is right, to conclude emphatically. Provided the body of a paper is unified, coherent, and well developed, an opening and closing frame will give the paper a pleasing symmetry. In the following example, Rachel L. Jones works with a quotation.

Introduction

56   William Labov, a noted linguist, once said about the use of black English, "It is the goal of most black Americans to acquire full control of the standard language without giving up their own culture." He also suggested that there are certain advantages to having two ways to express one's feelings. I wonder if the good doctor might also consider the goals of those black Americans who have full control of standard English but who are every now and then troubled by that colorful, grammar-to-the-winds patois that is black English. Case in point—me.

5g

¶ *dev*

Conclusion

57   I would have to disagree with Labov in one respect. My goal is not so much to acquire full control of both standard and black English, but to one day see more black people less dependent on a dialect that excludes them from full participation in the world we live in. I don't think I talk white; I think I talk right.

—RACHEL L. JONES, "What's Wrong with Black English"

EXERCISE 14

Locate a collection of essays and or articles: any textbook that is an edited collection of readings will work. Read three articles and examine the strategies the authors use to introduce and conclude their work. Choose one article to analyze more closely. Examine the strategies for beginning and ending the selection and relate these strategies to the selection itself. Why has the writer chosen these *particular* strategies? Be prepared to discuss your findings in a small group.

EXERCISE 15

In connection with a paper you are writing, draft *two* opening and *two* closing paragraphs, using different strategies. Set your work aside for a day or two and then choose which paragraphs appeal to you the most. Be prepared to discuss your choices in a small group.

5g Determining paragraph length

Paragraphs vary greatly in length. As long as the governing idea of a paragraph remains clear, all sentences are unified, and the paragraph is coherent, then in theory a paragraph can be one sentence, five sentences, or twenty. This said, you should realize that readers will tire of a paper whose paragraphs are consistently one typewritten page or longer. If for no other reason than to give readers visual relief, keep paragraphs moderate in length. *Moderate* is a variable and personal term. Perhaps you decide that visually your paragraphs should average one-third to two-thirds of a typewritten page. If your sentences tend to be brief, then your average number of sentences per paragraph may be ten or twelve; if your sentences tend to be long, then the average of sentences per paragraph may drop to six.

Devote your energies to the content of your paragraphs first. Turn to paragraph length in the later stages of revision when you are relatively satisfied with your work. Then think of your reader and the way your paragraphs appear on the page. Visually, does the length of your paragraphs invite the reader into your paper? Consistently short paragraphs may send the signal that your ideas are not well developed. Consistently long paragraphs may give the impression that your writing is dense or that your ideas are not well differentiated. You should freely divide a long paragraph for reasons of length alone. As you will see in this next example, a new paragraph created because of length does not need its own topic sentence, provided this paragraph is a clear continuation of the one preceding it.

5g

¶ *dev*

58   When I investigated the Bay of Pigs invasion and other fiascoes, I found that there were at least six major defects in decision-making which contributed to failures to solve problems adequately.

59   First, the group's discussions were limited to a few alternatives (often only two) without a survey of the full range of alternatives. Second, the members failed to re-examine their initial decision from the standpoint of non-obvious drawbacks that had not been originally considered. Third, they neglected courses of action initially evaluated as unsatisfactory; they almost never discussed whether they had overlooked any non-obvious gains.

60   Fourth, members made little or no attempt to obtain information from experts who could supply sound estimates of losses and gains to be expected from alternative courses. Fifth, selective bias was shown in the way the members reacted to information and judgments from experts, the media and outside critics; they were only interested in facts and opinions that supported their preferred policy. Finally, they spent little time deliberating how the policy might be hindered by bureaucratic inertia, sabotaged by political opponents or derailed by the accidents that happen to the best of well-laid plans. Consequently, they failed to work out contingency plans to cope with foreseeable setbacks that could endanger their success.

—IRVING JANIS, "Groupthink"

Brief paragraphs of one, two, or three sentences can be useful for establishing transitions between sections of a paper (see ¶34) and, as illustrated in this next example, for creating emphasis.

61   A coyote also eats avocados, oranges, melons, berries, chickens, small dogs, livestock and fowl with relish. The rare but rising number of attacks on small children indicates that once certain coyotes overcome their inherent fear of man, very young human specimens also look like food. And if his own offspring or mate is killed, he might well snack off the carcass. A meal's a meal.

62   To Brother Coyote, it's truly a dog-eat-dog world.

63   Coyotes, it was discovered, are so intelligent they can learn from their own mistakes and the mistakes of fellow coyotes. Remarkably, they also teach their young to avoid those mistakes.

—MICHELLE HUNEVEN, "The Urban Coyote"

If in revising a first draft you find that your paragraphs are consistently two or three sentences, consider ways in which you can further develop each paragraph's topic sentence. Unless you are writing in a journalism class or in some other context where consistently brief paragraphs are valued, once again the advice is to maintain a moderate length and only rarely—for clear reasons—use very brief or very long paragraphs.

5g

¶*dev*

EXERCISE 16

Reread ¶ 42 and mark the places that, for reasons of length, you would begin new paragraphs.

EXERCISE 17

Reread the draft of one of your essays and pay close attention to the length of your paragraphs. What observations can you make? How often are your paragraphs longer than one-half of a page? How often are they shorter? Are there any generalizations you can draw, based on an analysis of your own work? Be prepared to discuss your findings in class.

CHAPTER 6

Writing and Evaluating Arguments

In the broadest sense, every time you speak or write, you argue, because arguments are implicit in the very structure of the English sentence. A sentence consists of two parts: a **subject,** which states who or what is acting or being described, and a **predicate,** a verb and its related parts that make some claim about the subject—who or what the subject is, how it appears, or what it does. The arguments implicit in everyday speech go unnoticed until an occasion for debate arises: you and a friend disagree on the merits of a book or movie; a door-to-door canvasser asks you to donate money to a cause; or you negotiate the cost of moving a family heirloom across the country. In each instance, the context in which the argument takes place will determine what counts as a reasonable point to make and what counts as evidence in support of that point. Formal arguments in academic disciplines similarly depend on context.[1]

6a   Arguments as a way of knowing

1   Arguing in everyday life

Both inside and outside of academics, arguments provide a way of knowing about and participating in the world, primarily because they require that you be *active.* Consider this scenario: you want to attend the main campus of a state university one hundred miles from home, but your parents urge you to attend a satellite campus of the university ten miles from home. An argument ensues. You and your parents state your positions; everyone offers reasons. You will attend college someplace: the question is *where,* and the answer to this question relies on how persuasive you can be. Here is an argument that would have very real consequences for your life, and you would therefore want to argue well: you would want to convince your parents that your position was reasonable.

---

[1]The approach to argument taken here is based on the work of Stephen Toulmin, as developed in *The Uses of Argument* (Cambridge: The University Press, 1958).

To argue well requires that you know your subject. You might need to conduct research to discover exactly how much more expensive living away from home would be. To argue well you must also have an opinion about your subject and, if possible, be genuinely committed to that opinion. And then you must consider the needs of the people you are trying to persuade. In the debate over college, do you think your parents are concerned about the extra expense of living away? Do you suspect other concerns, such as your living on your own in a dorm? Do they fear loss of contact with you? Do they *trust* you? Identifying issues important to your audience will help you as you plan to argue your position. Once you present an argument, you may meet opposition; and thus you must be prepared to present well-organized evidence. In sum, making a successful argument requires that you take an active stance from beginning to end.

6a

log

2   Arguing in academic contexts

Making arguments is a way of knowing: of learning about your needs, the needs of others, and the importance of assembling evidence. Within the world of academics this statement is especially true. In each of your courses knowledge is built *through* arguments, as you can see from the following examples.

Example A

A marine biologist from Jamaica reports the death of coral reefs in the Caribbean basin.

CLAIM	The biologist claims that the general warming of ocean water worldwide is the cause and *argues* the case.
DATA	The biologist has used agreed-upon procedures to gather information on ocean warming and on the condition of coral life in the Caribbean.
LOGIC	On the basis of her data, the biologist infers patterns and sees a relationship between water temperature and the health of marine life.
CONCLUSION	The biologist draws a conclusion that she is willing to argue before an audience of her peers.

Example B

On examining the novels and short stories of Nathaniel Hawthorne, a literary critic is convinced that some deep and abiding shame blotted Hawthorne's conscience.

CLAIM	The critic, steeped in a tradition of psychoanalysis, *argues* that certain psychological factors have caused Hawthorne to invest his characters with sin.
DATA	The critic has read Hawthorne's work and made observations; he has researched Hawthorne's life and made further observations.

LOGIC   In a crucial link, the critic has *connected* what has gone on in the life with what was written in the fiction.

CONCLUSION   The critic draws a conclusion about Hawthorne's psychological life, based on the evidence of biography and the fictional works.

6a

log

Through argumentation researchers build knowledge about the world. They conduct experiments, they read documents closely, they administer surveys: then, studying the information they have generated, they search for patterns and make statements, or claims. A **claim** is an arguable thesis, a debatable statement about which people will disagree. An arguer presents a claim to readers or listeners, who in turn accept or reject the claim or urge that it be modified.

As you move from the study of one discipline to the next, you will find that forms of argumentation and what counts as evidence in argumentation will vary. In one discipline, an argument may take the form of a lab report; in another, an essay; in a third, a review of statistics; in a fourth, a proposal; in a fifth, a computer program; in a sixth, a series of equations. Very often when you argue you will be expected to draw on source materials, weaving them into your argument as you work to convince your readers. Do not expect any single discipline to exhibit only one type of argument. Sociologists, for instance, may present arguments by using five of the six formats just men-

---

Writing an Argument

The classic five-part structure

1. Introduce the topic to be argued. Establish its importance.

2. Provide background information so that readers will be able to follow your discussion.

3. State your claim (your argumentative thesis) and develop your argument by making a logical appeal based on the following factors (discussed in 6d-2 and 6d-3): generalization, causation, sign, analogy, parallel case, or authority. Support your claims with facts, opinions, and examples. If appropriate, mix an emotional appeal or an appeal to authority with your logical appeals.

4. Acknowledge counterarguments and treat them with respect. Rebut these arguments. Reject their evidence or their logic or concede some validity and modify your claim accordingly. Be flexible: you might split the counterarguments and rebut them one at a time at different locations in the paper; or you might begin the paper with a counterargument, rebut it, and then move on to your own claim.

5. A useful way to conclude is to summarize the main points of your argument. Then remind readers of what you want them to believe or do.

Note: This five-part structure for argument does not suggest, necessarily, a five-paragraph argument. Arguments can be considerably longer than five paragraphs.

Writing an Argument

Writing an argument: The problem-solution structure

I.   There is a serious problem.
  A. The problem exists and is growing.
      (Provide support for this statement.)
  B. The problem is serious.
      (Provide support.)
  C. Current methods cannot cope with the problem.
      (Provide support.)

II. There is a solution to the problem. (Your argumentative thesis, or claim, goes here.)
  A. The solution is practical.
      (Provide support.)
  B. The solution is desirable.
      (Provide support.)
  C. We can implement the solution.
      (Provide support.)

Note: This six-part structure for argument does not suggest, necessarily, a six-paragraph argument. A problem-solution argument can be considerably longer than six paragraphs.

Source: Adapted from Richard D. Rieke and Malcolm O. Sillars, *Argumentation and the Decision Making Process* (Glenview: Scott, Foresman, 1984) 163.

6a

log

tioned, along with associated types of evidence. The particular variety of sociology practiced, as well as the audience the sociologist is writing for, will determine the type of argument made.

Expect variety in the arguments you will read and write in college. (For a sampling of that variety, see chapters 37–39, devoted to Writing in the Disciplines.) Expect also that arguments will share certain essential features. Whatever the context, an argument will have a claim; all will be supported by evidence (though types of evidence will change from subject to subject); and all evidence will be presented according to fundamental patterns of logic. These recurring features of argumentation—claims, evidence, and logic—are reviewed in this chapter.

EXERCISE 1

In a paragraph, recall an argument that you have had recently in which some issue of importance to you was being debated. With whom did you argue? What positions did you and the other person (people) argue? What was the outcome? To what extent did your powers of persuasion affect the argument's outcome?

6b The argumentative thesis (or claim)

Any paper that you write in college will have a **thesis,** a single statement that crystallizes your purpose for writing and governs the logic and development of the paper. The thesis of an argument, also called a **claim** (the terms will be used interchangeably), will express not only the subject you are writing on but also the view that you hold about that subject. In an argument, your thesis is your conclusion, which you can present earlier or later in the discussion depending on your strategy. Your goal in the argument is to defend your thesis as being true, probable, or desirable. Because the argumentative thesis is a specialized case of thesis statements for all varieties of writing, the discussion here assumes that you have read chapter 3, section f.

1 Answering questions with the argumentative thesis

Arguments provide answers to one of three types of questions: questions of *fact, value,* or *policy.*

Argumentative thesis answering a question of fact

A *question of fact* can take the following forms:

Does X exist?

Does X lead to Y?

How can we define X?

The first question can be answered with a *yes* or *no.* The second question leads to an argument about cause and effect. If one thing leads to or causes another, the writer must show how this happens. The third question is an argument about definitions. At times, definitions can be presented without debate; at other times, writers will argue to define a term in a particular way and then will build an entire presentation based on that definition. (For an excellent example of definition by argument, see Carl Becker's definition of *history,* ¶42 in chapter 5.)

Once established as true, a statement of fact can be used as evidence in other arguments. For instance, in a problem-solution argument (see the preceding box and the sample argument at 6g) the writer must establish that a problem exists; once this fact is established, the writer can make a second argument in support of a particular solution. The tests for determining whether something exists will change from discipline to discipline and even within disciplines.

> *Example theses*
>
> Extrasensory perception does not exist.
>
> Far from being an imaginary "yuppie" disease, chronic fatigue syndrome *is* real, though its causes are not entirely understood.

Stories describing near-death experiences have not withstood scientific scrutiny.

Argumentative thesis answering a question of value

A *question of value* takes the form: *What is X worth?* You make an argument about values when at the conclusion of a hearty meal you pat your belly and smile. In more academic circumstances, scholars argue about value when they review and comment on one another's work—for instance, calling a theory *powerful* or elegant. Determinations of value are based on standards called *criteria* that are explicitly stated and then used to judge the worth of the object under review. (See 2b, "Writing an evaluation.")

Example theses

So-called "cold fusion," if it proves practical, will have tremendous economic and humanitarian value.

Though it raises useful questions, Eric Smith's research linking intelligence and birth order is flawed.

Nabokov's *Lolita* is a great novel, notwithstanding the opinion of one editor who, rejecting it, commented that the manuscript should be "buried under a stone for a thousand years."

Argumentative thesis answering a question of policy

A *question of policy* takes the form: *What action should we take?* Politics is a major arena for arguments of policy. In this arena, arguments help to determine which legislative actions are taken and how huge sums of money are spent. *Should the legislature raise taxes? Should the United States support totalitarian regimes?* These questions about what *ought* to be done prompt arguments based on claims of policy.

Example theses

Funding decisions for NASA should be based on a coherent, long-term approach to space exploration.

Eventually, taxes will have to be raised if the government cannot reduce our massive national debt.

More businesses should provide on-site daycare facilities.

EXERCISE 2

Choose two subjects and pose questions of fact, value, and policy about them. Of each topic, ask: Does X exist? (or Does X lead to Y? or How can we define X?) What is the value of X? and What should we do with regard to X? Answer these questions with statements that could serve as claims for later arguments.

6b

log

Example subject: self-restraint

What is self-restraint?

> Self-restraint is the act of denying yourself a momentary desire in order to satisfy some larger goal.

What is the value of self-restraint?

> Self-restraint is valuable in that it can teach you discipline and can help you achieve desired results, such as losing weight, improving grades, or increasing stamina.

What action should we take with respect to self-restraint?

> The many school committees around the nation eager to promote excellence should consider a curriculum that emphasizes self-restraint.

2 Defining terms in the argumentative thesis

In order to provide the basis for a sound argument, all words of a claim must be carefully defined so that people are debating the same topic. Consider this claim, which answers a question of policy: *The United States should not support totalitarian regimes.* Unless the term *totalitarian regimes* is clearly defined (and distinguished, say, from authoritarian regimes), the argument could not succeed. The writer, the reader, and various experts referred to in the argument might define and use the word *totalitarian* differently. If this happened, a reader could not be sure about what is being argued and no meaningful exchange of ideas would take place. Take care to examine your claims and, if one term or another requires it, actually write a paragraph of definition into your argument. If you suspect that your audience will not accept your definition, then you will need to argue for it. Entire arguments are sometimes needed to define complex terms, such as *honor.* If a key term in your claim is not complicated, then a paragraph or even a sentence of definition will suffice. With terms well defined, argumentation can begin.

EXERCISE 3

Circle any terms needing definitions in the following claims. Choose any two of the terms you have circled and briefly define them.

> Funding decisions for NASA should be based on a coherent, long-term approach to space exploration.
>
> A "coherent, long-term" approach would seek to define NASA's objectives for the next fifteen years and would commit funds to meet those objectives. NASA's funding should not be subject to a year-by-year review in which a year's political considerations can end up affecting scientific goals.

1. Far from being an imaginary "yuppie" disease, chronic fatigue syndrome *is* real.

2. Stories describing near-death experiences have not stood up to scientific scrutiny, although a great deal of anecdotal evidence for such experiences is mounting.

3. So-called "cold fusion," if it proves practical, will have tremendous economic and humanitarian value.

4. Nabokov's *Lolita* is a great novel, notwithstanding the opinion of one editor who, rejecting it, commented that the manuscript should be "buried under a stone for a thousand years."

5. The saucer-shaped flying object in the sky that thousands of New Jersey residents saw on the evening of July 18, 1988, was swamp gas.

6c Types of evidence

log

Evidence consists of the facts, opinions, and examples that you assemble and offer as support for your claim. What counts as evidence will change not only as you move from one discipline to another but also, frequently, as you move from course to course *within* a discipline. Within disciplines there are usually several types of arguments that take place. In some contexts, only information learned in an experimental setting will be considered as evidence in an argument. In other contexts, evidence consists of ideas, trends, or themes one is able to point to in the written work of others. Other arguments use information learned from interviews or questionnaires as evidence.

By understanding the context in which argumentation takes place, you will understand what your listeners or readers will accept as evidence. Do not assume that in any one discipline only a single sort of evidence is legitimate. One literature professor may accept references to an author's life, believing as you do that such references bear on the novel or play you are reading; another literature professor may not accept these references and may insist that your study of a work be limited to the work itself. Such disagreement about what counts as evidence does not occur because standards are arbitrary but because researchers (your professors) commonly train and operate within different traditions, each of which has a distinctive approach to argumentation. In order to understand what will count as evidence for your arguments, you will need to be aware of individual preferences as you move from discipline to discipline, and course to course.

You can offer three types of evidence in an argument: facts, opinions, and examples. A **fact** is a statement that can be verified, proven true or false. As a writer you should be able to verify facts on demand, and most often you will do this by referring to an authoritative source. (This is one of the reasons for documenting your papers.) In most circumstances once facts are presented and accepted by experts in a given field, the rest of us can be content to accept them as well. Facts are constantly being updated and revised as a consequence of research. It is therefore essential that you refer to the most recent sources possible.

An **example** is a particular instance of a statement you are trying to prove. The statement is a generalization, and by offering an example you are trying to demonstrate that the generalization is correct. For instance, if you stated that the behavior of hypochondriacs (people who always think they are ill) is often humorous, you would want to offer examples that demonstrate the accuracy of your statement. A story about your Uncle Alfred who thought that every ache of his body signaled some dread disease would provide one such example. Or suppose you want to convince your parents that a car you are about to buy is safe. Your parents would have a much clearer image of what you mean by *safe* if you could offer at least one well-chosen example in support of your generalization. You might therefore describe an accident in which all the passengers traveling in this car were spared serious injury, primarily because the car was built so well. Vivid examples are memorable and help to legitimize your general statements about a topic.

An **opinion** is a statement of interpretation and judgment. Opinions are themselves arguments and should be based on evidence in order to be convincing. Opinions are not true or false in the way that statements of fact are. Rather, opinions are more or less well supported. You do your own argument a great service by referring to the opinions of experts who happen to agree with you. An example: In arguing to a parent that buying Car A makes the most sense, you could quote a brief paragraph from *Consumer Reports* or *Road and Track Magazine,* some independent reviewer of cars that has no vested interest in endorsing one or another product. The endorsement would then lend credibility to your argument.

> **EXERCISE 4**
>
> Provide paragraph-length examples for two of the following general statements. If you feel that the statement is inaccurate, revise it to your liking. Then provide an example based on your own experience.
>
> 1. During the first weeks of a semester, freshmen are unsure of themselves socially.
> 2. Assignments at the college level are much more demanding than those in high school.
> 3. My friend _____ (you provide the name) usually offers sound advice.
>
> **EXERCISE 5**
>
> With pen in hand, reread the paragraphs you wrote in answer to Exercise 4. Circle your statements of opinion. Underline your statements of fact. Do any patterns emerge? (Instead of working with your own paragraphs, you might work with the paragraphs of a classmate.)

6d Lines of argument: Appeals to logic, authority, and emotion

Once you have determined that a claim will answer a question of fact, value, or policy and once you have assembled a variety of evidence in support of your claim, you will devise arguments. Arguments are based on appeals to reason, authority, and emotion. Each of these appeals rests on certain inferences you make concerning the evidence you have assembled.

1   Understanding lines of argument and inferences

In chapter 3 you saw that at the core of any thesis lies an inference. Informative theses, and informative papers, are built on inferences that define, order, classify, compare, and contrast material that you have previously gathered into categories—the various "file drawers" into which you placed related ideas and information (see 3f-1, 2). To write an informative thesis, you selected material from across categories, relating the information by using one of the five varieties of inference (see 3f-3).

To write an argumentative thesis, you also select material from across categories, but you relate that information with a different set of inferences: these include generalization, causation, sign, analogy, definition (in some instances), and parallel case. The very same information and ideas that one person draws on to write an informative paper can provide another person with material to write an argument. Inference making resides in the *writer*, not in the material. Thus you find lawyers in a courtroom arguing different positions (making different inferences) based on the same facts. In your courses you will be asked to write papers based on material that could lend itself equally well to an informative paper or to an argument. The sort of paper you write will depend on what you have been asked to do with the material and how you have interpreted it.

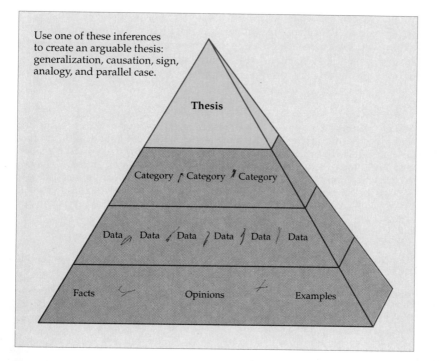

Use one of these inferences to create an arguable thesis: generalization, causation, sign, analogy, and parallel case.

Thesis

Category / Category / Category

Data / Data / Data / Data / Data / Data

Facts   Opinions   Examples

6d

log

6d

log

2 Appealing to reason

An appeal to reason is by far the most common basis for arguing in the academic world. This section demonstrates five of the most common types of appeal you can make, each representing evidence organized by a different pattern of inference. These crucial inferences are called *lines of argument*. You can argue from generalization, from causation, from sign, from analogy, or from parallel case. The persuasiveness of your argument will depend on how carefully you can re-create for readers the major inference(s) that enabled you to make a claim.

Argument from generalization

Given several representative examples of a group (of people, animals, paintings, trees, washing machines, whatever), you can infer a general principle or **generalization**—a statement that applies to other examples of that group. Assume you have examined several backpack designs over the past several years. Based on your experience with ten different packs, you derive the following general principle: packs with internal frames provide more comfort when you carry light loads than do packs with external frames; but packs with external frames are better for carrying heavy loads. You have not tried out every backpack currently on the market; but based on your sampling, you can make a generalization. In order for a generalization to be fair, you must select an adequate number of examples that are typical of the entire group; you must also acknowledge the presence of examples that apparently disprove the generalization. Arguments from generalization allow you to support claims that answer questions of fact and value.

Example

You are planning to buy a car. In your research you investigated six economy cars and found them to have three defining features: they are lightweight, and they have undersized engines and plain interiors. Assume now that you read a report that a new car is being introduced to the market. The car is advertised as having an efficient engine and a "rugged" interior. Based on the ad you might decide to include the car in your list of possibilities, since the car meets your tests for being an "economy car." An argument from generalization allows you to support a claim of fact:

QUESTION OF FACT	Is Car X an economy car?
ARGUMENTATIVE THESIS	Car X is an economy car, and I should therefore consider it in my search.
INFERENCE (FROM GENERALIZATION)	Economy cars are lightweight, with an undersized engine and plain interior. Car X is advertised as efficient with a rugged interior. Therefore, I can probably consider Car X an economy model.

Argument from causation

In this type of argument you begin with a fact or facts about some person, object, or condition. (If readers are likely to contest these facts, then you must make an argument to establish them before pushing on with an argument from causation.) A causal inference or argument from **causation** enables you to claim that an action created by that person, object, or condition leads to a specific result, or effect: Sunspots cause the aurora borealis. Dieting causes weight loss. Smoking causes lung cancer. Working in the opposite direction, you can begin with what you presume to be an effect of some prior cause: the swing of a pendulum, inattention among school children, tornadoes. Of this presumed effect, you ask: "What causes this?" If you are a scientist or social scientist, you might perform an experiment. Establishing a direct causal link is seldom easy, for usually multiple causes will lead to a single condition (think of the inattentive child at school). In arguing causation, therefore, you need to be sensitive to complexity. Arguments of causation allow you to support a claim that answers a question of fact or a claim that answers a question of policy. Cause-and-effect reasoning also allows you to use a problem-solution structure in your arguments. (See the box on page 171 and the sample paper at 6g.)

Example

Your research on cars suggested that during certain years of the last two decades cars were designed with small engines. You assume the small engine design was the consequence of some decision. What factor(s) caused that decision? You happened in your economics class to be reading about the availability of oil during the oil embargo of the 1970s. You made a causal inference that enabled you to answer a question of fact.

QUESTION OF FACT   Does a causal relationship exist between engine size and availability of oil?

ARGUMENTATIVE THESIS   In the early 1970s, the availability of oil from the Middle East partially determined the size of engines for cars produced in Detroit.

NOTE: The inference of cause and effect is stated directly in this thesis. Proving the inference here would be complicated and would require that you make direct links between the availability of oil, the price of gas, and the decision to make smaller engines. Very possibly, more than the availability of oil affected the decision about engine size. In the early 1970s, the country suffered from a recession, and consumers had less buying power than in earlier years. Perhaps the recession figured importantly in the decision about engine size. If you could prove that the oil crisis was one cause of the recession and if you could also prove that the lack of oil and the jump in gas prices affected the decision on engine size, you could reasonably argue that the availability of oil was a *partial* cause.

Argument from sign

A sore throat and fever are signs of flu. Black smoke billowing from a window is a sign of fire. Risk taking is a sign of creativity. In an argument from **sign,** two things are correlated; that is, they tend to occur in the presence of one another. When you see one thing, you tend to see the other. A sign is *not* a cause, however. If your big toe aches at the approach of thunderstorms, your aching toe may be a sign of approaching storms, but it surely does not cause them. Economists routinely look to certain indexes (housing starts, for instance) as indicators, or signs, of the economy's health. Housing starts are *correlated with* economic health, often by means of a statistical comparison. If a sign has proven a particularly reliable indicator, then you can use it to support a claim that answers a question of fact.

Example
You are leaning toward buying Car A, and you are particularly pleased that the manufacturer has attended to little details that suggest for you an overall commitment to excellence. You use an argument from sign to answer a question of fact:

QUESTION OF FACT	Has Car A been carefully built?
ARGUMENTATIVE THESIS	Car A has been carefully built.
INFERENCE (FROM SIGN)	The manufacturer has attended to little details of passenger comfort and quality of finish, reliable signs that the car was well designed and constructed.

Argument from analogy

An argument from **analogy** sets up a comparison between the topic you are arguing and another topic that initially appears unrelated. Assume you are a member of a campus group that formed to address the needs of homeless people in areas near your campus. After several months of mixed success, you feel some frustration that, for all your individual efforts, the group has not been as effective as you had hoped. At your regular monthly meeting, you argue in favor of the group's finding a faculty advisor: "Actors on a stage need a director to coordinate their individual efforts," you say. "And our group needs an advisor: someone who can help make sense of the different directions we've been going in and who can help us to define a clear mission."

While suggestive and at times persuasive, an analogy actually proves nothing. There is always a point at which an analogy will break down. (Actors, for instance, follow a script written by a playwright. In the preceding example, the group is very much discovering its own script.) It is usually a mistake to build an argument on analogy alone. Use analogies as you would seasonings in cooking. As one of several attempts to persuade your reader, an analogy spices your argument and makes it memorable. You can use analogies in support of claims that answer questions of fact, value, or policy.

Example

In your research you discovered that several auto manufacturers are dragging their feet on installing air bags, which tests have shown to be effective in preventing crash fatalities. You write a letter to your state representative in support of a bill requiring manufacturers to install these safety devices. You could at one point argue from analogy:

QUESTION OF POLICY	What action should we take with respect to air bags in passenger vehicles?
ARGUMENTATIVE THESIS	The government should require the installation of air bags on all passenger vehicles.
INFERENCE (FROM ANALOGY)	Just as the government required that hard hats be worn in construction areas to reduce construction-related deaths, so too the government should require the installation of air bags in all passenger vehicles to reduce traffic-related deaths.

Argument from parallel case

While an analogy argues a relationship between two apparently unrelated people, objects, conditions, or events, an argument from parallel case argues a relationship between directly related people, objects, events, or conditions. The implicit logic is this: the way a situation turned out in a closely related case is the way it will (or should) turn out in this one. Lawyers argue from parallel case whenever they cite a prior criminal or civil case in which the legal question involved is similar to the question involved in a current case. Because the earlier case ended a certain way (with the conviction or acquittal of a defendant, or with a particular monetary award), so too should the present case have this outcome. An argument from parallel case requires that situations presented as parallel be alike in essential ways; if this requirement is not met, the argument loses force. The argument would also be weakened if someone could present a more nearly perfect parallel case than yours. You can use a parallel case in support of claims that answer questions of fact, value, or policy.

Example

You are aware that a particular design team was responsible for work on Car A. Research shows that the same team, ten years ago, designed Car Z—which in its day was a state-of-the-art, uniformly well-accepted automobile. You can use this information to argue from parallel case to answer a question of value:

QUESTION OF VALUE	What is the worth of Car A?
ARGUMENTATIVE THESIS	Car A will be highly praised.
INFERENCE (FROM PARALLEL CASE)	The last time that design team came together to create a product, they produced Car Z, famous for its elegance, pricing, and performance. It is very likely that this time the team has produced a similar success.

6d

log

3 Appealing to authority and to emotion

Appeals to authority

Appeals to authority rely on your and the reader's respect for expert opinion. As a writer, you greatly help your cause when you can quote experts on a subject who support your point of view. Realize, though, you are likely to find that experts disagree. For instance, in court cases both prosecution and defense present expert witnesses, sworn to tell the truth. One expert says "up"; the other says "down." The first says, "in"; the second says "out." No doubt, the experts *are* telling the truth. But expert *opinions* are just that: interpretations of facts. Facts usually lend themselves to multiple interpretations, and you should not be discouraged when authorities seem to contradict one another.

Whether you find contradictions or not, sources of authority must in fact be authoritative. If they are not, any argument built on an appeal to authority will falter. One of your important challenges, then, both as a writer of arguments and as a critical reader, is to evaluate the worthiness of sources that you and others use. Is the expert testimony that you or others are drawing on truly expert? If you are not an expert in the field, how can you tell? A number of general guidelines should help you make this determination.

Use *Authoritative* Sources

1. Prefer acknowledged authorities to self-proclaimed ones.
2. Prefer an authority working within his or her field of expertise to one who is reporting conclusions about another subject.
3. Prefer first-hand accounts over those from sources who were separated by time or space from the events reported.
4. Prefer unbiased and disinterested sources over those who can reasonably be suspected of having a motive for influencing the way others see the subject under investigation.
5. Prefer public records to private documents in questionable cases.
6. Prefer accounts that are specific and complete to those that are vague and evasive.
7. Prefer evidence that is credible on its own terms to that which is internally inconsistent or demonstrably false to any known facts.
8. In general, prefer a recently published report to an older one.
9. In general, prefer works by standard publishers to those of unknown or "vanity" presses.
10. In general, prefer authors who themselves follow [standard] report-writing conventions. . . .

11. When possible, prefer an authority known to your audience to one they have never heard of.

Source: This material is quoted from Thomas E. Gaston and Bret H. Smith, *The Research Paper: A Common-Sense Approach* (Englewood Cliffs: Prentice Hall, 1988) 31–33.

6d

log

Once you have determined to the best of your ability that an expert whom you wish to quote is indeed expert, you must then identify those points in your discussion where appeals to authority will serve you well. You may want to mix appeals to authority with appeals to reason and, perhaps, to emotion. Appeals to authority can be used to support claims that answer questions of fact, value, and policy.

Example

QUESTION OF VALUE	What is the worth of Car A?
ARGUMENTATIVE THESIS	Car A is a good buy for the money.
INFERENCE (FROM AUTHORITY)	Lee Iacocca, chairman of Chrysler, is on record as saying that "Car A is a terrific, economical car." Car A is not made by Chrysler—so Iacocca is not promoting the car for his own benefit. Iacocca's endorsement carries weight.

Appeals to emotion

Appeals to reason are based on the force of logic; appeals to authority are based on the reader's respect for the opinions of experts. By contrast, appeals to emotion are designed to tap the needs and values of an audience. Arguments based on appeals to reason and authority may well turn out to be valid; but validity does not guarantee that readers will *endorse* your position. For instance, you might establish with impeccable logic that the physical condition of your community's public schools has deteriorated badly, to the point of affecting the performance of students. While true, your claim may not carry force enough to persuade the Town Council to vote on a bond issue or to raise taxes—two actions that would generate the requisite money to renovate several buildings. To succeed in your effort or in any appeal to emotion, you must make your readers feel the same urgency to act that you do. The following would be an emotional appeal.

> Our children are sitting in schools where paint is flaking off the walls, where the heating plant works sixty percent of the time, where plumbing backs up repeatedly, where windows are cracked or broken and covered by cardboard to keep out the winter. No member of the Town Council would for a moment consider working in an office with such appalling conditions.

You each would be indignant and would claim that the environment endangered your welfare. Yet these are precisely the conditions our children contend with now. To vote against a tax hike will be to condemn our children to circumstances that you personally would find intolerable.

6d

log

On the basis of an audience analysis (see 3c-2), you can sketch a profile of your readers and consider strategies suited to win their emotional support. Plan your emotional appeal by beginning with a claim that has already been supported by an appeal to reason. In your efforts to raise taxes for school renovation, you could show photographs, produce a list of items in need of repair, and quote expert witnesses who believe that children's learning suffers in deteriorating environments. Having argued by an appeal to reason, you can then plan an emotional appeal. Emotional appeals can help support claims that answer questions of value and policy; they have no bearing on questions of fact, however.

Making an Emotional Appeal

1. List the needs of your audience with respect to your subject: these needs might be physical, psychological, humanitarian, environmental, or financial.

2. Select the category of needs best suited to your audience and identify emotional appeals that you think will be persuasive.

3. In your appeal, place the issue you are arguing in your reader's lap. Get the reader to respond to the issue emotionally.

4. Call on the reader to agree with you on a course of action.

The limits of argument

In the real world, the best of arguments may sometimes fail to achieve its objective. Some subjects—for example, abortion or capital punishment—are so controversial or so tied to preexisting religious or moral beliefs that many people have long since made up their minds one way or the other and will never change them. Such subjects are so fraught with emotion that logical arguments are ineffective in persuading people to rethink their positions. Sometimes, also, your audience has a vested interest in *not* being persuaded by your arguments. Perhaps your audience has a financial stake in holding to an opposing position. A union representative might offer unassailable arguments that wages should be increased at least 10 percent, and yet fail to persuade the employer—who will bear the cost of giving a raise. In such cases, when your audience feels significantly threatened by the prospect of your victory, you must realize that it is futile, perhaps even dangerous, to continue insisting on the validity of your argument. In these situations you would be well-advised either to make your claim to a more objective audience or switch to a topic in which your audience has less invested.

4 Choosing a line of argument

The following chart summarizes the main lines of argument (which types of logic) you can use in presenting claims of fact, value, and policy. In presenting a claim, you will typically offer several lines of argument. Each line would be based on an inference that allows you to select and organize evidence. Thus, to support a claim of fact, you would look to the chart and see that you could argue in any of six ways. There are five ways to argue for claims of value and five for claims of policy. In presenting a claim of fact, you might review the chart; review the facts, opinions, and examples you have gathered; and then decide you have enough material to argue in more than one way.

Matching lines of argument with types of claims

	Claims of Fact	Claims of Value	Claims of Policy
Appeals to Reason			
generalization	x	x	
causation	x		x
sign	x		
analogy	x	x	x
parallel case	x	x	x
Appeals to Authority	x	x	x
Appeals to Emotion		x	x

Adapted from Wayne Brockriede and Douglas Ehninger, "Toulmin on Argument: An Interpretation and Application," *Quarterly Journal of Speech* 46 (1960): 53.

In the sample argument that you will find in section 6g, Jenafar Traher argued a claim of policy by appealing to reason (with an argument from cause) and, in her conclusion, appealing to emotion. Once you know what sort of claim you are arguing, this chart can help you plot a strategy for convincing your readers.

EXERCISE 6

Write the sketch of an argument, based on the claim: "Car X represents a good value for the money, and I want to buy it." Substitute the name of an actual car in this sentence. Assume that you will be making an argument to your parents (or other benefactors), who have offered to split the down payment with you provided you make the monthly payments. Consult the chart on "Matching Lines of Argument with Types of Claims," and plan a discussion in which you argue three ways in support of your choice of car. (Make sure these arguments are consistent with the type of claim you are making—see the chart.) For each line of argument, write a sentence or two that will indicate the particular type of appeal you will be making.

6e   Rebuttals and strategies

1   Making rebuttals

By definition, arguments are subject to challenge, or to counterarguments. Because reasonable people will disagree, you must be prepared when arguing to acknowledge differences of opinion—for two reasons. First, by raising a challenge to your own position you force yourself to see an issue from someone else's perspective. This can be a valuable lesson in that challenges can prompt you to reevaluate and refine your views. In addition, challenges pique a reader's interest. Research shows that when tension (that is, disagreement) exists in an argument, readers maintain interest: they want to know what happens or how the argument is resolved.

Once you acknowledge opposing views, respond with a **rebuttal,** an argument of opposition. One type of response is to reject the counterargument by challenging its logic. If the logic is flawed, the counterargument will not weaken the validity of your argument. Another response would be to find some merit in the counterargument and to modify your position accordingly. Thus, you make a concession and in the process show yourself to be reasonable. When you are confident in the position you are arguing, raise the most damaging argument against your position that you can, and then neutralize that challenge. If you do not raise objections, your readers inevitably will; better that you raise them on your terms so that you can control the debate.

In response to the example argument in Exercise 6, your parents (or benefactor) may object if you decide to buy a sports car. They might say: "Wait a minute. People buy sports cars to drive fast. We don't want you getting hurt, and we're not going to support your buying that car." You would now be in the position of responding to, or rebutting, the counterargument. Because you need your parents' half of the down payment, you must regard the objection as a serious one and you must plan a response. Ideally, you would have anticipated the objection and addressed it. Here are some possible responses to the claim that sports cars are dangerous.

1. Buying a sports car will not *cause* me to speed. The two are not related. Every car made is capable of exceeding the speed limit. Cars do not speed; people do. I have never gotten a speeding ticket. You can count on me not to speed.

2. If you do not contribute to the down payment, which is your right, I have decided to postpone buying a car until I can make the full down payment myself.

3. Ultimately, this is a matter of trust. Do you trust me?

6e

log

The first rebuttal is based on logic: you are arguing that your parents have incorrectly claimed that buying a sports car causes speeding. Then you are making a generalization that *people* speed, not cars. (This logic parallels that used by members of the National Rifle Association, who oppose the banning of firearms: People kill, not guns.) The second rebuttal is based on authority. You are saying, in effect, that your parents do not have the authority to change your mind on this decision. This rebuttal could prove offensive, and you would want to word it with care. You might begin this way: "While I respect your opinion and am grateful for your concern, . . ." The third rebuttal is clearly an appeal to emotion. Such statements raise issues about the relationship between you and your parents that go well beyond the purchase of a car. Emotional issues such as trust are potentially explosive, so you will want to think carefully about making this type of rebuttal.

Parents might raise other objections: sports cars are small; other cars are large. The laws of physics dictate that in a crash (which you would never cause, being the safe driver you are), sports cars will lose every time. There would be still other objections, and you would want to anticipate and neutralize them as best you could. If you do not raise and address challenges in an argument, readers will be wary. They will sense that you are hiding information or that you are not well informed enough to know that challenges exist. Either reaction will undermine the success of your argument.

2 Devising strategies

See the boxed information on pages 170–171 for two time-honored strategies for arranging arguments: the classic five-part structure and the problem-solution structure. The following are some of the decisions you face in planning a strategy for your argument: Where will you place your claim (thesis)? In what order will you present arguments in support of your claim? You can position the claim in your argument at the beginning, middle, or end of the presentation. In the problem-solution structure, you see that the claim is made only after the writer introduces a problem. Working with the five-part structure, you have more flexibility in positioning your claim. One factor that can help determine placement is considering the members of your audience and the likelihood of their agreeing with you. When an audience is likely to be neutral or supportive, you can make your claim early on with the assurance that you will not alienate readers. When an audience is likely to disagree, plan to move your claim toward the end of the presentation, in that way giving yourself space to build consensus with your readers, step by step, until you reach a conclusion.

6f

log

Readers tend to remember most clearly what they read last. Thus, you may want to present your reasons in support of your claim in the order of least to most emphatic. Conversely, you may want to offer your most emphatic reasons in support of a claim at the very beginning of the argument. In one strong move you might gain the reader's agreement and then cement that agreement with reasons of secondary importance. Any argument can be arranged in a variety of ways. Decisions you make about placing your claim and arranging your points of support will depend on your assessment of the members of your audience and their probable reactions to your views.

EXERCISE 7

1. In light of the discussion in this section, return to the argument you outlined in Exercise 6 and introduce at some point in the outline an argument counter to your own. In a paragraph, discuss how you would rebut the counterargument or accept it in part so as to neutralize any damage it could do to your own claim.

2. In light of the discussion in this section, review the placement of your argument's claim. Given your parents as an audience, have you positioned the claim correctly? Also review the order in which you arranged supporting arguments. In a few sentences, justify your positioning of claim and support.

6f Preparing to write an argument

Writing an argument is more a re-creation of thinking than an exploration. Exploration—through writing or through talking with friends—comes prior to writing a first draft. You should know your views on the subject you are arguing *before* you sit down to write the draft. As you begin the draft, you would do well to understand your claim and the lines of argument you will use. As well, you should have a sound sense of the evidence you will present. You will flesh out your discussion as you write; but the backbone of your argument—your appeals to reason, authority, and emotion—should be carefully thought out ahead of time. The thinking you do to prepare for an argument might well be written. Many writers need a discovery draft or extended notes to learn what they will argue. Simply realize that in the preparatory stage you are writing to *explore* possible lines of argument, not to write a draft.

Gathering Materials for Your Argument

1. Gather material on your subject. Generate information on your own—see 3d; if necessary, conduct research—see 1b and 1d on reading sources closely and on inferring relationships among sources. See also Part IX on library research.

2. Review the material you have gathered. Decide what you think about the topic, and in a single sentence answer a question of fact, value, or policy. (To decide, you may need to do some brainstorming. See 3d-2.) Your one-sentence answer to the question will be the claim of your argument, your thesis.

3. Understand your audience: What do they know about the topic? What do they need to know? To what sorts of appeals will they respond?

4. Plan out the reasons, the lines of argument, you will present in support of your claim.

5. Identify strong counterarguments and plan to rebut and neutralize them.

6. Sketch your argument, deciding on placement of your claim and arrangement of your lines of argument.

7. Write a draft of your argument, realizing that you will need to backtrack on occasion to get new information or to rethink your strategy. As with the writing of any paper, writing an argument will be a messy, backward-looping activity that often requires mid-course corrections. See chapters 3 and 4 on the necessary uncertainties in preparing for and writing a first draft.

8. Revise two or three times. See chapter 4 for advice.

6g

log

EXERCISE 8

Based on your outline in Exercise 7, write the draft of a five-page argument. Or read the following scenario (which you may have worked on in chapter 3). Take a position for or against the stated policy. Carefully plan and then write a five-page argument.

Imagine yourself a student at a college or university where the Board of Trustees has voted to institute a curfew on dormitory visitors. After 11 P.M. on weekdays and 1 A.M. on weekends, no student may have a guest in his or her dormitory room. The rule simply put: no overnight guests.

6g   Sample argument

The following argument on "Athletics and Education" follows (with some modifications) the problem-solution format presented on page 171. You will find that Jenafer Trahar answers a question of policy with her argument and that she argues, primarily, from cause. She defines a problem—the exploitation of student-athletes—and traces that problem back to its causes. Change the conditions that caused the exploitation of these athletes, she reasons, and the exploitation (the effect) will end.

6g

log

Athletes and Education

There have always been athletics on college campuses, but the presence of athletes posed no problems until the late nineteenth century. It was around this time that many colleges and universities began to rely on financial support from the alumni. What the alumni wanted was for their alma mater to be a winner. Sports became part of an important fund-raising activity for many campuses, particularly at midwestern and southern universities. Northeastern schools could always rely on their academic reputations for maintaining the flow of alumni money. Midwestern and southern schools, however, did not have a ready-made source of contributions and needed some attraction other than academics to get alumni interested in making donations (Naison 493-94). For many years, schools turned to building their sports programs at the expense of their academic ones.

> Background

Today, schools that field major football or basketball teams stand to make tens of thousands of dollars every time a game is played, not only from ticket sales but also from television revenue. Every time a game is televised, the schools involved make money. The payoff for the very best teams is enormous. For example, each team that advances to the Final Four of the NCAA basketball tournament earns its institution one million dollars.

One major problem with the commercialization of college sports is the exploitation of student-athletes, many of whom come to school on athletic scholarships. Frequently, student-athletes don't deserve to be admitted to a school. Many colleges routinely lower admission

> Statement of the problem

requirements for their ball players, and some schools
will even waive requirements for that exceptional athlete who, without his sports abilities, might not have
had a place on a college campus. Most kids not interested in academics would normally shun a college education. But for gifted athletes, college appears to be a
road that leads to the pros. Or so they think. According
to Richard Lapchick of the Center for the Study of Sport
in Society, twelve thousand high school athletes participate in sports in any one year, but only one will subsequently play for a professional team. But the news gets
even more grim:

> [O]nly 1 in 50 will get a scholarship to play in
> college. And of the top players who receive scholar-
> ships in big-money sports like football and basket-
> ball, fewer than 30 per cent will graduate from
> college after four years. (xv)

Academically qualified or not, what these young men
and women may not realize in coming to college is that
athletics is the only service their school is offering
them. These kids spend so much time practicing and then
studying play books that they barely have enough time to
attend their required classes, let alone do the work for
them. One football player described his schedule this
way: "[T]wo to six, practice. Seven to eight, watch
films. Eight to 10:30, go to study hall—where you just
get plays from coaches" (Lichtenstein 47). The result of
this preoccupation with sports is too often a player who
has played through his athletic eligibility and who
loses his scholarship because he has done poorly in his
course work. The scholarship is revoked, and the student-
athlete leaves the university without a degree. He was
too busy to get one.

Though many reformers have sought to correct the exploitation of student-athletes, no one has come up with
a workable solution. Some have suggested that big-time
sports be cut entirely out of colleges. The logic of
this argument is that since sports seem inevitably to

6g

log

Rebuttal of
counter-
argument

lead to commercialization, and since commercialization
of sports leads inevitably to students being exploited,
the only way to end exploitation is to take the money entirely out of college sports. This approach amounts to
wishing for the purity--the amateur status--of an earlier time. Simply put, there is too much money involved
now to ever go back. The days of amateurism are gone;
sports have become too integral a part of college life,
especially now that many schools depend heavily on the
revenue their teams bring in.

The NCAA's Proposition 48 requires athletes to have
a certain grade point average, SAT score, and achievement scores in order to be accepted as students at a
school. As John Thompson, basketball coach at Georgetown
University, pointed out when Proposition 48 was initially discussed, the idea is not particularly fair to
student-athletes who come from poor school districts
where education suffers due to a lack of funding. Student-athletes should not be held responsible for their
lack of achievement if that lack is due, in part, to
overcrowded and underfunded classes (Asher B4).

The system of college athletics has been in place
for so long now that it's almost too late for change. Almost, but not quite. <u>After nearly a century of student-
athlete exploitation, the time has come not for a
de-emphasis on sports but for a re-emphasis on education.</u> What follows is a four-step outline of a reasonable, workable solution to addressing the exploitation
of student-athletes. The first step we must take, before
we can expect a change in the admission process, is to
teach our educators that they must demand more from student-athletes. Study time must come to equal, if not exceed, playing time. There should be a required GPA for
student-athletes. It should be a reasonable one, however:
perhaps 2.0, taking into account the fact that student-
athletes do have heavy athletic schedules. Athletics
should be taken into account, not used as an

Rebuttal of
counter-
argument

Claim
(Argumenta-
tive thesis)

Proposed
Policy, step 1

excuse to defend unacceptable student performance in the
classroom.

The second step in resolving the problem is to eliminate the sympathetic professor who is a "friend" to the
student-athlete. Professors and administrators need to
learn that the education of athletes is more important
than the score of Saturday's game. All those people who
think they're helping by letting student-athletes slide
are really doing more harm than good. If it takes punishment to teach professors and administrators this, then
punishment is what's needed. First, the grading process
used for "helping" student-athletes should be reviewed.
Any professor caught scaling for a student should be punished. (The punishment should be left up to the school
to decide.) Second, efforts must be made to supervise
student-athletes. Tutors can be assigned to each athlete, and an administrator from outside the athletic department can be assigned to organize (and enforce) study
schedules for entire teams. Athletes who do not study
will lose their eligibility. Professors who scale will
be punished. With these strategies in place, the problem
of poor academic performance among student-athletes
should diminish over time.

Proposed
Policy, step 2

6g

log

The third step in addressing the exploitation of
student-athletes is to reduce practice time. Schools
must not trust coaches to see to it that students are
studying enough. There needs to be a rigidly fixed
amount of time on the field; once that time is over, so
is practice. Period. No excuses for longer practice or
sports-related study halls should be tolerated.

Proposed
Policy, step 3

The final step in addressing the problem, perhaps
the most important, is the creation of a special education center for the student-athlete. Such a center would
be a place where an athlete could get honest help, from
honest students who want to see athletes get an educa-
tion--not a touchdown or home run. Of course the student
tutors in these facilities would need supervision, but

Proposed
Policy, step 4

6g

log

this could be easily arranged if the college administration were committed to helping the student-athlete.

Some might find fault in these recommendations,
claiming that there isn't enough money available to make
all these changes. But, of course, the money would come
from the ticket sales and proceeds from televised games.
Television contracts with the NCAA should be written to
guarantee that a certain percentage of sports revenue be
spent directly on supervising the education of student-
athletes. Colleges with nationally competitive teams
should each form a special committee from the Board of
Trustees to oversee and to implement the recommendations
I have offered.

We don't need to eliminate college sports. We probably couldn't anyway, what with all the money being made.
Eliminating sports would do more harm than good, taking
away both a source of pride in college life and an important source of revenue. Changing the admissions process
to deny marginally prepared student-athletes would not
be fair, since for many of these kids sports is their
only avenue of exposure to college life and the possibility of a higher education. To eliminate the chance to attend college for marginal student-athletes would be
heartless, because it places on them a burden they
didn't make, a burden that should and can be lifted with
the proper approach. That's why a plan that modifies the
present system, not destroys it, makes the most sense.
Let's take advantage of all the money that college
sports generates and use that money to <u>really</u> educate
the student-athlete. The proposals I have made would not
only allow student-athletes to gain access to college
but would also increase the chances of their actually receiving an education.

Conclusion
(with an
emotional
appeal)

Works Cited

Asher, Mark. "The Rule Doesn't Kill the Problem." Washington Post 18 June 1985: B4.

Lapchick, Richard E., with Robert Malekoff. On the Mark: Putting the Student Back in Student-Athlete. Lexington, MA: Lexington Books, 1987.

Lichtenstein, Grace. "Playing for Money." Rolling Stone 30 Sep. 1982: 44-48.

Naison, Mark. "Scenario for Scandal." Commonweal 24 Sep. 1982: 493-497.

6h

log

6h Evaluating arguments

Whether you are evaluating your own arguments or someone else's, there are several common blunders to watch for. Correct these blunders in your own writing, and raise a challenge when you find them in the writing of others.

1 Defining terms

Your evaluation of an argument should begin with its claim. Locate the claim and be sure that all terms are well defined. If they are not, determine whether the lack of definition creates ambiguities in the argument itself. For example, the term *generosity* might appear, without definition, in a claim. If that term and the claim itself were later illustrated with the example of a mall developer's "generously offering the main corridors of the mall for exhibitions, during the Christmas Season, of waste recycling demonstrations by Scouting troops," you might justifiably question the validity of the argument. If you define *generosity* as the giving of oneself freely and without any expectation of return, then you might wonder how generous the mall developer is really being. Certainly the increased traffic flow through the mall would boost business, and the supposed generosity might be an advertising ploy. As the reader of this argument, you would be entitled to raise a challenge; if you were the writer, you could by carefully defining terms avoid later challenges to your implied view of the word *generosity*. For instance, you could define the word as "any action, regardless of its motive, that results in the greatest good for the greatest number of people." This one sentence (specifically, the phrase *regardless of its motive*) lets you fend off the challenge, which you could rebut by saying: "Sure, the mall developer is increasing traffic to the mall, and probably profits as well; the developer is also educating an entire community about the importance of recycling. Here is a situation in which everyone wins. To be generous, you don't need to be a martyr."

2   Examining inferences

As you have seen, the inferences that a writer makes—generalization, causation, and so on—establish logical support for a claim. If you as the reader feel that the argument's inferences are not valid, then you are entitled to raise a challenge because if these inferences are flawed, the validity of the claim may be in doubt. Any of the following seven types of fallacies, or flaws, will undermine an argument's logic. The first four flaws specifically address the inferences you will use to make arguments from generalization, causation, sign, and analogy.

1. *Faulty generalization.* Generalizations may be flawed if they are offered on the basis of insufficient data. It would not be valid, for instance, to make the generalization that left-handed people are clumsy because all three lefties of your acquaintance are clumsy. A more academic example: Assume you had administered a survey to students in your dorm. In studying the results you discovered that attitudes toward joining fraternities and sororities were evenly split. Slightly more than 50 percent wanted to join, a bit less than 50 percent did not. It would be a faulty generalization to claim on the basis of this one survey that students on your campus are evenly split on joining Greek organizations. In order for your generalization to be accurate, the survey would need to have been administered campus-wide, if not to every student, then at least to a representative cross-section.

2. *Faulty cause and effect.* Two fallacies can lead a writer to infer incorrectly that one event causes another. The first concerns the ordering of events in time. The fact that one event occurs before another does *not* prove that the first event caused the second. (In Latin, this fallacy is known as *post hoc*, a brief form of *post hoc, ergo propter hoc*—after this, therefore because of this.) If the planets Venus and Jupiter were in rare alignment on the morning of the Mt. St. Helens eruption, it would not be logical to argue that an alignment of two planets caused the volcano to erupt. The second flaw in thinking that leads to a faulty claim of causation is the belief that events must have *single* causes. Proving causation is often complicated, for many factors usually contribute to the occurrence of an event. What caused the layoff of production-line workers at the General Motors plant in Framingham, Massachusetts? An answer to this question would involve several issues, including increased competition from foreign auto manufacturers, a downturn in the economy, the

cost of modernizing the Framingham assembly line, a need to show stockholders that there were fewer employees on the payroll, and a decision to build more cars out of the country. To claim that *one* of these is the sole cause of the plant shutdown would be to ignore the complexity of the event.

3. *Confusing correlation with causation.* There is a well-known saying among researchers that *correlation does not imply causation.* In one study on creativity, researchers correlated *risk taking* and *a preference for the unconventional* with groups of people classified as creative. It would not be logical to infer from this correlation that creativity *causes* risk taking or a preference for the unconventional or that these traits *cause* creativity. The most that can be said is that the traits are associated or correlated with—they tend to appear in the presence of—creative people. Arguments made with statistical evidence are usually subject to this limitation.

4. *Faulty analogy.* The key components of an analogy must very nearly parallel the issues central to the argument you are making. The wrong analogy not only will *not* clarify, but also it will positively confuse. For instance, an attempt to liken the process of writing to climbing a flight of stairs would create some confusion. The analogy suggests that the writing process occurs in clearly delineated steps, when progress in actual writing is seldom so neat. The stages of writing do not progress "step by step" until a final draft is achieved. It is more accurate to say that the process of writing loops back on itself and that the process of revision takes place not just at the end of writing (the last step) but throughout. So the stairs analogy might confuse writers who, reflecting on their own practices, do not see neat linear progress and therefore assume they must be doing something wrong. Analogies should enhance, not obscure, understanding.

5. *Either/or reasoning.* Assume that someone is trying to persuade you that the United States ought to intervene militarily in a certain conflict many thousands of miles from U.S. territory. At one point in the argument you hear this: "Either we demonstrate through force that the United States continues to be a world power or we take a back-seat, passive role in world affairs. The choice is clear." Actually, the choice is not at all clear. The person arguing has presented two options and has argued for one. But many possibilities for conducting U.S. foreign policy exist besides going to war or becoming passive. An argument will be flawed when its author pre-selects two possibilities from among many and then attempts to force a choice.

6. *Personal attacks.* Personal attacks, known in Latin as *ad hominem* arguments, challenge the person presenting a view rather than the view itself. You are entitled to object when you read or hear this type of attack: "The child psychologist on that talk show has no kids, so how can he recommend anything useful to me concerning my children?" Notice

that the challenge is directed at the person who is presenting ideas, not at the ideas themselves. The psychologist's advice may well be excellent, but the *ad hominem* attack sidesteps the issues and focuses instead on personality. Here is a variant on the *ad hominem* argument: "The speaker is giving what sounds like good advice on child rearing, but she is neither a psychologist nor an educator, so we really shouldn't base our actions on her views." In this case, the critic is dismissing a statement because the speaker is not an acknowledged expert. This kind of criticism can be legitimate if an argument is being directly based on the authority of that speaker's expertise, and you *should* give preference to sources that are authoritative. Nonetheless, it is sidestepping the other issues in an argument to dismiss an apparently useful observation by dismissing the person who holds it. At the very least, statements should be evaluated on their merits.

7. *The begged question.* Writers who assume the validity of a point that they should be proving by argument are guilty of begging the question. For instance, the statement "All patriotic Americans should support the President," begs a question of definition: what *is* a patriotic American? The person making this statement assumes a definition that he should in fact be arguing. By making this assumption, the writer sidesteps the issue of definition altogether. The point you want to make must be addressed directly through careful argument.

3 Examining evidence

Arguments also can falter when they are not adequately or legitimately supported by facts, examples, statistics, or opinions. Refer to the following guidelines when using evidence.

Facts and examples

1. *Facts and examples should fairly represent the available data.* An example cannot be forced. If you find yourself needing to sift through a great deal of evidence *against* a point you wish to make in order to find one confirming fact or example, take your difficulty as a sign and rethink your point. Suppose ten sources compare riding in Car A to riding on the bare metal floor of a flat-bed truck. It would be less than ethical to take a lone eleventh example and to offer it as evidence supporting Car A's comfortable ride.

2. *Facts and examples should be current.* Facts and examples need to be current, especially when you are arguing about recent events or are drawing information from a field in which information is changing rapidly. If, for example, you are arguing a claim about the likelihood of incumbent politicians being reelected, you should find sources that

report on the most recent elections. If in your argument you are trying to show a trend, then your facts and examples should also be drawn from sources going back several years, if not decades.

3. *Facts and examples should be sufficient to establish validity.* A generalization must be based on an adequate number of examples and on representative examples. To establish the existence of a problem concerning college sports, for instance, it would not do to claim that because transcripts were forged for a handful of student-athletes at two schools a problem exists nationwide.

6h

log

4. *Negative instances of facts and examples should be acknowledged.* If an argument is to be honest, you should identify facts and examples that constitute evidence *against* your position. Tactically, you are better off being the one to raise the inconvenient example than having someone else do this for you in the context of a challenge. For example, an argument might conclude that a particular advertising company has consistently misrepresented facts about its products. The arguer would be less than ethical to omit from the discussion several advertisements that were entirely legitimate in their treatment of facts. The wiser strategy would be for the arguer to address these negative examples (negative in the sense that they apparently disprove the claim), either turning them to advantage or at the very least neutralizing them.

Statistics

5. *Use statistics from reliable and current sources.* Statistics are a numerical compression of information. Assuming you do not have the expertise to evaluate procedures by which statistics are generated, you should take certain common-sense precautions when selecting statistical evidence. First, cite statistics from reliable sources. If you have no other way of checking reliability, you can assume that the same source cited in several places is reliable. The U.S. government publishes volumes of statistical information and is considered a reliable source. Just as with facts and examples, statistics should be current when you are arguing about a topic of current interest.

6. *Comparative statistics should compare items of the same logical class.* If you found statistical information on housing starts in New England in one source and in a second source found information on housing starts in the Southwest, you would naturally want to compare the numbers. The comparison would be valid only if the term "housing starts" was defined clearly in both sources. Lacking a definition, you might plunge ahead and cite the statistics in a paper, not realizing that one figure included apartment buildings in its definition of "housing" while the other included only single-family homes. Such a comparison would be faulty.

Expert opinions

7. *"Experts" who give opinions should be qualified to do so.* Anyone can speak on a topic, but experts speak with authority by virtue of their experience. Cite the opinions of experts in order to support your claims. Of course you will want to be sure that your experts are, in fact, expert; and evaluating the quality of what they say can be troublesome when you do not know a great deal about a topic. You can trust a so-called expert as being an authority if you see that person cited as such in several sources. For experts who are not likely to be cited in academic articles or books, use your common sense. If you were arguing that birchbark canoes track better in the water than aluminum canoes, you would want to seek out a person who has considerable experience with both. (See the box in 6d-3 for more on evaluating expert opinions and choosing authoritative sources.)

8. *Experts should be neutral.* You can disqualify an expert's testimony for possible use in your argument if you find that the expert will profit somehow from the opinions or interpretations offered. Returning to the example of the birchbark canoe: you would want to cite as an authority in your paper the person who has paddled hundreds of miles in both aluminum and birchbark canoes, not the one who earns a living making birchbark canoes.

EXERCISE 9

Read the following scenarios and evaluate the statements associated with each for logical fallacies. Name the fallacy and briefly explain how the statement illustrates it.

1. Sam's acquaintance writes all her papers the evening (and early morning) before they are due, and she is forever getting good grades. Sam concludes: "For my next paper, I won't start writing until twenty-four hours before it's due."

2. Louise flies to a distant city to visit a friend who attends school there. The taxi driver who takes her from the airport to a bus depot is surly. At the depot, the ticket agent seems more intent on reading the paper than on helping Louise find her way to the suburban campus. When she finally arrives at her friend's school, Louise remarks, "The people in this town aren't very friendly."

3. As part of your research on a paper you are writing, you watch a State House debate on universal health care. One state representative makes this remark: "We will adopt the universal health care bill as written and give everyone in this state equal access to medical facilities, or we will say to the poor among us that their good health is less important than ours. Distinguished members of this governing body, the choice is yours."

PART III

Understanding Grammar

CHAPTER 7

Constructing Sentences

If you are a lifelong speaker of English, then you are an expert in the language—in its grammar, its vocabulary, its sentence structures, and the proper relationships among its words. When you speak, people understand. You *know* English, but in all likelihood your knowledge is *implicit*. That is to say, you can do just fine communicating verbally, and yet you may probably not be able to recite a textbook definition of *participle*, for instance—even though you use participles correctly every day. To be sure, there is seldom need to talk of participles; still, if you want to become fully confident as a writer, you will gain by making your implicit knowledge *explicit*.

7a   Understanding sentence parts

The sentence is our basic unit of communication. Sentences, of course, are composed of words, each of which can be classified as a part of speech. As you review definitions of nouns, verbs, and the other parts of speech, remember that these are parts of a whole: meaning in language is built on the *relationship* among words.

1   The basics: Recognizing subjects and predicates

The fundamental relationship in a sentence is the one between a subject and its predicate. Every sentence has a **subject**: a noun or word group serving as a noun that engages in the main action of the sentence or is described by the sentence. In addition, every sentence has a **predicate**: a verb, and other words associated with it, that states the action undertaken by a subject or the condition in which the subject exists.

A **simple subject** is the single noun or pronoun that identifies what the sentence is about or produces the action of the sentence. The **simple predicate** is the main sentence verb. You can gain a great deal of confidence from your ability to divide a sentence into its subject and predicate parts; you will improve your ability to avoid fragments and to write sentences with varied, interesting structures. Again, recall that subjects and predicates consist of nouns, verbs, and other parts of speech. Learning these parts of speech and their functions will help you understand how sentences operate. In the sentences that follow, the simple subject is marked "ss" and the simple predicate, "sp."

Subject	Predicate
ss In small doses, alcohol	*sp* acts as a stimulant.
ss Large doses	*sp* act as a depressant.
ss Individuals under the influence	*sp* often become more aggressive.
ss Alcohol consumption	*sp* interferes with one's ability to foresee negative consequences.
ss A person's actions	*sp* can grow extreme in the presence of this drug.

7a

2 Nouns

A **noun** (from the Latin *nomen*, or name) is the part of speech that names a person, place, thing, or idea.[1] Only nouns can be introduced by an **article** or a **determiner,** the words, *a, an,* and *the*: a rock; an animal; the truth. The **indefinite article,** *a* or *an*, introduces a generalized noun: *a* person can be any person. The indefinite article *a* appears before nouns beginning with a consonant; *an* is placed before nouns beginning with a vowel or unpronounced *h*—as in *hour*: *a* book, *an* hour. The **definite article,** *the,* denotes a specific noun: *the* book. Nouns can also be accompanied by certain classes of words that limit what they refer to. The most common limiting words (and their categories) are these: *this, that, these, those* (demonstrative); *any, each, some* (indefinite); *one, two, first, second,* etc. (numerical); *which, that, whose,* etc. (relative).

Nouns change their form to show **number**; they can be made singular or plural: *boy/boys, child/children, herd/herds.* They also undergo limited change in form to show **possession,** but, unlike pronouns (discussed next), they do this only with the addition of an apostrophe and usually an *s*: *girl's, children's, herd's.* Finally, nouns can be classified according to categories of meaning that affect the way they are used, as shown in the following box.

---

[1] We owe our discussions on the parts of speech to Hulon Willis, *Modern Descriptive English Grammar* (San Francisco: Chandler, 1972).

7a

Classification of Nouns

Proper nouns, which are capitalized, name particular persons, places, or things:

Sandra Day O'Connor, Chevrolet, "To His Coy Mistress"

Common nouns refer to general persons, places, or things and are not capitalized:

judge, automobile, poem

Count nouns can be counted:

cubes, cups, forks, rocks

Mass nouns cannot be counted:

sugar, water, air, dirt

Concrete nouns name tangible objects:

lips, clock, dollar

Abstract nouns name an intangible idea, emotion, or quality:

love, eternity, ambition

Animate versus **inanimate nouns** differ according to whether they name something alive:

fox and *weeds* versus *wall* and *honesty*

Collective nouns are singular in form but plural in sense:

crowd, family, group, herd

Specific uses of nouns are addressed in several places in this handbook.

Nouns: as modifiers 11g

Nouns: agreement with verbs 10a

Nouns: as complements 7b

Nouns: as clauses 7e-3

Nouns: as objects 7b

Nouns: phrases 7d 2 and 3

Nouns: showing
    possession 27a, 8c

Nouns: as subjects 7b

3 Verbs

A **verb,** the main word in the predicate of a sentence, expresses an action, expresses an occurrence, or establishes a state of being.

ACTION   Eleanor *kicked* the ball.

OCCURRENCE   A hush *descended* on the crowd.

STATE OF BEING Thomas *was* pious.

Verbs change form on the basis of their **principal parts.** Building from the **infinitive** or **base form** (often accompanied by **to**), these parts are the **past tense,** the **present participle,** and the **past participle.**

Base form	Past tense	Present participle	Past participle
to escape	escaped	am escaping	escaped
to ring	rang	am ringing	rung

The principal parts of a verb have a major role in how the verb shows **tense,** the change in form that expresses the verb's action in time relative to a present statement. See chapter 9 for details on the principal parts and other form changes of verbs.

7a

There are three varieties of verbs in English, and each establishes a different relationship among sentence parts. **Transitive verbs** such as *kick, buy, kiss,* and *write* transfer action from an actor—the subject of the sentence—to a person, place, or thing receiving that action, as in: *Harold invested his money.* **Intransitive verbs** such as *laugh, sing, smile, fall,* and *sit* show action, yet no person, place, or thing is acted upon, as in: *Stock prices fell.* The same verb may be transitive in one sentence and intransitive in another: she *runs* every day; she *runs* a good business. **Linking verbs** such as *is, feel, appear,* and *seem* allow the word or words following the verb to complete the meaning of the subject, as in: *Felix is a cat; Felix seems unhappy.* **Auxiliary verbs** such as *be, will, can, do, shall,* and *may* are sometimes called **helping verbs** because they help to show tense and mood. Compare: I *am* going. I *will* go. I *could* go. I *did* go. I *should* go. I *might* go.

See chapter 9 for a detailed discussion of verbs. The following list provides a brief index to more information on verb use.

Verbs: active and passive voices   9g

Verbs: agreement with subjects   10a

Verbs versus verbals   7a-4

Verbs: mood   9h

Verbs: regular and irregular   9a, b

Verbs: (avoiding) shifts   16a, b

Verbs: strong vs. weak   9g–h, 17b

Verbs: tense   9e, f

Verbs: thesis statements   3f-2, 3, 4

4   Verbals

A **verbal** is a verb form that functions in a sentence as an adjective, an adverb, or a noun. There are three types of verbals: gerunds, participles, and infinitives. A **gerund,** the *-ing* form of a verb without its helping verbs, functions as a noun.

Editing is both a skill and an art. [The gerund is the subject of the sentence.]

I am tired of *editing*. [The gerund is an object of a preposition.]

A **participle** is a verb form that functions as an adjective. Its present and past forms make up two of the verb's principal parts, as shown previously.

The *edited* manuscript was 700 pages. [The past participle functions as an adjective.]

The man *editing* your manuscript is Max Perkins. [The present participle functions as an adjective.]

An **infinitive,** often preceded by **to,** is the base form of the verb (often called its *dictionary form*). An infinitive can function as a noun, adjective, or adverb.

7a

To edit well requires patience. [The infinitive functions as the noun subject of the sentence.]

The person *to edit* your work is Max Perkins. [The infinitive functions as an adjective.]

He waited *to edit* the manuscript. [The infinitive functions as an adverb.]

The following is a brief index to other information on verbals:

Important Relationships between a Subject and Verb

A sentence must have a *complete* subject and verb.

A word grouping that lacks a subject, a verb, or both is considered a fragment. See chapter 12 on fragments and chapter 16 for a special class of fragments—grammatically "mixed" constructions.

INCOMPLETE   At the beginning of the meeting. [There is no verb.]

REVISED   At the beginning of the meeting, the treasurer reported on recent news.

INCOMPLETE   The fact that this is an emergency meeting. [The use of *that* leaves the statement incomplete, without a verb.]

REVISED   This is an emergency meeting of the board.

A sentence must have a *logically compatible* subject and verb.

A sentence in which a subject is paired with a logically incompatible verb is sure to confuse readers, as you will see in chapter 16.

INCOMPATIBLE   The meeting room is sweating. [A room does not normally sweat.]

REVISED   Those gathered in the meeting room are sweating.

A sentence must have a subject and verb that *agree in number.*

A subject and verb must both be singular or plural. The conventions for ensuring consistency are found in chapter 10.

INCONSISTENT	The treasurer are a dynamic speaker. [The plural verb does not match the singular subject.]
REVISED	The treasurer is a dynamic speaker.

A sentence must have a subject close enough to the verb to ensure clarity.

Meaning in a sentence can be confused if the subject/verb pairing is interrupted with a lengthy modifier. See chapter 15 for a discussion of misplaced modifiers.

7a

INTERRUPTED	We because of our dire financial situation and our interests in maintaining employee welfare have called this meeting.
REVISED	We have called this meeting because of our dire financial situation and our interests in maintaining employee welfare.

5 Adjectives

By modifying or describing a noun or pronoun, an **adjective** provides crucial defining and limiting information in a sentence. It can also provide nonessential but compelling information to help readers see, hear, feel, taste, or smell something named. Adjectives include the present and past participle forms of verbs, such as *fighting* Irish, *flying* wing, *baked* potato, and *written* remarks. The single-word adjectives in the following sentences are italicized.

Climate plays an *important* part in determining the *average* numbers of a species, and *periodical* seasons of *extreme* cold or drought I believe to be the most *effective* of *all* checks.

CHARLES DARWIN, *On the Origin of Species*

6 Adverbs

An **adverb** can modify a verb, adjective, adverb, or an entire sentence. Adverbs describe, define, or otherwise limit, generally answering these questions: *when, how, where, how often, to what extent,* and *to what degree.* Although most adverbs in English are formed by adding the suffix -*ly* to an adjective, some are not: *after, ahead, already, always, back, behind, here, there, up, down, inside, outside.* **Descriptive adverbs** describe individual words within a sentence.

The poor *unwittingly* subsidize the rich. [The adverb modifies the verb *subsidize.*]

Poverty *almost* always can be eliminated at a higher cost to the rich. [The adverb modifies the adverb *always.*]

Widespread poverty imposes an *increasingly* severe strain on our social fabric. [The adverb modifies the adjective *severe*.]

Conjunctive adverbs, a particular class of adverbs, establish adverb-like relationships between whole sentences. These words—*moreover, however, consequently, thus, therefore, furthermore,* and so on—have a special role to play in linking ideas and sentences. (See chapter 19 for more information.) Chapter 11 provides a detailed discussion of adjectives and adverbs. The following is a brief index to more information on adjectives and adverbs.

7a

Adjectives: clauses as 7e-2
Adjectives: coordinate 25c-2
Adjectives: and hyphenation 32a
Adjectives: phrases as 7d-1, 2, 3
Adjectives: as subject
  complements 11d

Adjectives: positioning 15a–g
Adverbs: and hyphenation 32a
Adverbs: phrases as 7d-1, 2
Adverbs: positioning 15a–g

7 Pronouns

Pronouns substitute for nouns. The word that a pronoun refers to and renames is called its **antecedent.** Like a noun, a pronoun shows **number**—it can be singular or plural. Depending on its function in a sentence, a pronoun will change form—that is, its **case:** it will change from **subjective,** to **objective,** to **possessive.** The following examples show this change in case for the pronoun *he,* which in each instance is a substitute for the noun *Jake.*

Jake reads a magazine. *He* reads a magazine.
antecedent   pronoun
                                (subjective)

The magazine was given to Jake. The magazine was given to *him.*
                                antecedent   pronoun
                                                      (objective)

Jake's subscription is running out. *His* subscription is running out.
antecedent   pronoun
                                    (possessive)

There are eight classes of pronouns.

Personal pronouns (*I, me, you, us, his, hers,* etc.) refer to people and things.

When sugar dissolves in water, the sugar molecules break *their* close connection within the sugar crystal.

Relative pronouns (*who, whose, which, that,* etc.) begin dependent clauses (see section 7e) and refer to people and things.

The presence of the sugar, *which* is now in solution, changes many of the properties of the water.

Demonstrative pronouns (*this, these, that, those*) point to the nouns they replace.

These changes involve the water's density, boiling point, and more.

Interrogative pronouns (*who, which, what, whose,* etc.) form questions.

What does boiling sugar water have to do with coating caramel apples?

Intensive pronouns (*herself, themselves,* and other compounds formed with *self* or *selves*) repeat and emphasize a noun or pronoun.

The sugar *itself* can be recovered from the water by the simple act of boiling.

7a

Reflexive pronouns (*herself, themselves,* and other compounds formed with *self* or *selves*) rename—reflect back to—a preceding noun or pronoun.

The ease of recovery demonstrates that sugar molecules do not bind *themselves* strongly to water molecules.

Indefinite pronouns (*one, anyone, somebody, nobody, everybody,* etc.) refer to general, or nonspecific, persons or things.

Anyone who has stained a shirt with salad dressing knows that water will not dissolve oil.

Reciprocal pronouns (*one another, each other*) refer to the separate parts of a plural noun.

The many solvents available to chemists complement *one another.*

The following is a brief index to more information on pronouns.

 Prepositions

   A **preposition** links a noun (or word group substituting for a noun) to other words in a sentence—to nouns, pronouns, verbs, or adjectives. *In, at, of, for, on, by,* are all prepositions. Many common prepositions are shown in the following box. Along with the words that follow them, prepositions form **prepositional phrases,** which function as adjectives or adverbs. In the following sentence, an arrow leads from the (three) prepositional phrases to the (three) words modified. Note that the middle prepositional phrase modifies the first prepositional phrase.

The theory *of evolution* *by natural selection* was proposed *in the 1850s.*

7a

Common Prepositions

Single-word prepositions

about	beyond	off
above	by	on
across	concerning	onto
after	despite	out
against	down	outside
along	during	over
among	except	through
around	for	to
as	from	toward
before	in	under
behind	into	until
below	like	up
beneath	near	with
between	of	

Multi-word prepositions

according to	contrary to	on account of
along with	except for	on top of
apart from	in addition to	outside of
as for	in back of	owing to
because of	in case of	with regard to
by means of	in spite of	with respect to

The following is a brief index to more information on prepositions.

Prepositions: and fragments   12c-2

Prepositions: and mixed
   constructions   16g-3, 18a

Prepositions: using objective-
   case pronouns   8b-1

Prepositions: punctuating
   introductory phrases   25a

Prepositions: punctuating
   nonessential phrases   25d

9   Conjunctions

Conjunctions join sentence elements, or entire sentences, in one of two ways: either by establishing a coordinate or *equal* relationship among joined parts or by establishing a subordinate *unequal* relationship. (Subordinate conjunctions are discussed in detail in 7e. Coordinate and correlative conjunctions are discussed in chapter 19.) Briefly, conjunctions are classified in four ways: as coordinate conjunctions, conjunctive adverbs, correlative conjunctions, or subordinate conjunctions.

Coordinate conjunctions join parallel elements from two or more sentences into a single sentence: *and, but, or, nor, for, so*

Infants only cry at birth, *but* within a few short years they speak in complete sentences.

Conjunctive adverbs create special logical relationships between the clauses or sentences joined: *however, therefore, thus, consequently,* etc.

> Infants can only cry at birth. Within a few short years, *however,* they can speak in complete sentences.

Correlative conjunctions are pairs of coordinate conjunctions that place extra emphasis on the relationship between the parts of the coordinated construction: *both/and, neither/nor, not only/but also,* etc.

> Three-year-olds *not only* speak in complete sentences, *but* they *also* possess vocabularies of hundreds or even thousands of words.

Subordinate conjunctions connect subordinate clauses to main clauses: *when, while, although, because, if, since, whereas,* etc.

> *When* children reach the age of three, they can usually carry on complete conversations with their peers and with adults.

7a

10 Interjections

An **interjection** is an emphatic word or phrase. When it stands alone, it is frequently followed by an exclamation point. As part of a sentence, the interjection is usually set off by commas.

> Oh, they're here.   Never!

11 Expletives

An **expletive** is a word that fills a slot left in a sentence that has been rearranged. *It* and *there* function as expletives—as filler words without meanings of their own—in the following examples.

> BASIC SENTENCE   A sad fact is that too few Americans vote.
>
> WITH EXPLETIVE   It is a sad fact that too few Americans vote.
>
> BASIC SENTENCE   Millions of people are not voting.
>
> WITH EXPLETIVE   There are millions of people not voting.

Expletives are used with the verb *to be* in sentences with a delayed subject. Sentences with expletives can usually be rearranged back to their basic form. Try to delete expletives from your writing in the interest of achieving a spare, concise style. (See chapter 17.)

EXERCISE 1

Place a slash (/) between the subject and predicate parts of the following sentences. Identify the simple subject and simple predicate of each sentence with the abbreviations "ss" and "sp." Circle prepositions.

>   ss   sp
> *Example:* The physics(of)particle behavior / is important(for)designing safe and efficient processing plants.

1. Farmers frequently store tons of grain in large metal silos.
2. Unlike silos for liquids, grain silos occasionally collapse.
3. We do not know exactly the cause of this failure.
4. Simple fluid dynamics applied to sand flow does not predict the instability of grain particles.
5. Silo manufacturers still must include some details of the physics of particle flows in their design criteria.

7b

frag/fs

7b Understanding basic sentence patterns

There are five basic sentence patterns in English, from which are built virtually all of the sentences you read in this and other books. Each of the five sentence patterns consists of a subject and predicate. Depending on the sentence's structure, the predicate may contain a direct **object,** an **indirect object,** or a (subject or object) **complement.** The basic pattern diagrams that follow include definitions of these key terms and concepts.

┌─*Predicate*─┐
Pattern 1: Subject   verb
         We   *read.*

SUBJECT: a noun or word group serving as a noun that produces the main action of the sentence or is described by the sentence.
PREDICATE: a verb and other words associated with it, that states the action undertaken by the subject or the condition under which the subject exists.

┌────── *Predicate* ──────┐
Pattern 2: Subject   verb (tr.) direct object
         Stories   *excite the imagination.*

DIRECT OBJECT: a noun, or group of words substituting for a noun, that receives the action of a transitive verb (tr.). A direct object answers the question *What or who is acted upon?*

┌────── *Predicate* ──────┐
Pattern 3: Subject   verb (tr.) indirect object   direct object
         Stories   *offer us relief.*

INDIRECT OBJECT: a noun, or group of words substituting for a noun, that is indirectly affected by the action of a verb. Indirect objects typically follow transitive verbs such as *buy, bring, do, give, offer, teach, tell, play,* or *write.* The indirect object answers the question *To whom or for whom has the main action of this sentence occurred?*

┌──────── *Predicate* ────────────────┐
Pattern 4: Subject   verb (tr.) direct object object complement
  They   *make us tense.*

OBJECT COMPLEMENT: an adjective or noun that completes the meaning of a direct object by renaming or describing it. Typically, object complements follow verbs such as *appoint, call, choose, consider, declare, elect, find, make, select,* or *show.*

┌──────── *Predicate* ────────┐
Pattern 5: Subject   verb (linking) subject complement
  We   *are readers.*

7c

ad

SUBJECT COMPLEMENT: a noun or adjective that completes the meaning of a subject by renaming or by describing it. Subject complements follow linking verbs such as *appear, feel, seem, remain,* as well as all forms of *be.*

EXERCISE 2

Working with a topic of your choice, write a paragraph in which you use each of the five basic sentence patterns.

Example: The trumpeter played music. [Sentence Pattern 2] The couple listened. [Sentence Pattern 1] A waiter brought them a drink. [Sentence Pattern 3] The trumpeter was sizzling. [Sentence Pattern 5] The couple found the music excellent. [Sentence Pattern 4]

7c Modifying a sentence with single words

Principles of sentence expansion can be found at work in virtually any paragraph you read. The first technique for expanding sentences is to add modifiers—descriptive, modifying information. The nouns and verbs in the five basic sentence patterns can be modified by adjectives and adverbs.

1 Modifying nouns and verbs with adjectives and adverbs

VERB MODIFIED   I read *thoroughly.*
BY ADVERB

NOUN MODIFIED   A novel will engage an *active* imagination.
BY ADJECTIVE

2 Positioning modifiers

The position of an adverb can be shifted in a sentence from beginning to middle to end. Depending on its location, an adverb will change the meaning of a sentence or the rhythm. When moving an adverb, take care that it modifies the word you intend it to modify.

SHIFTED   I am *only* moving my bed (that is, nothing more important than the bed).
MEANING   I am moving *only* my bed (that is, no other furniture).

SHIFTED   *Sometimes,* stories can provide emotional relief.
RHYTHM   Stories *sometimes* can provide emotional relief.

              Stories can provide emotional relief *sometimes.*

7d

mm

A single-word adjective is often positioned directly before the noun it modifies, although writers make many variations on this pattern. When more than one noun in the sentence could be described by the adjective, take particular care to place the adjective closest to the noun it modifies. See chapter 15 on editing to correct misplaced modifiers.

A *good* story will excite a reader.   [*Story* is the word modified.]
A story will excite a *good* reader.   [*Reader* is the word modified.]

EXERCISE 3

Use one-word adjectives or adverbs to modify the nouns and verbs in the following sentences.

> *Example:* A man walked down a street.
>   An *old* man walked *slowly* down a *tree-lined* street.

1. The couple listened. [Sentence Pattern 1]
2. The trumpeter played music. [Sentence Pattern 2]
3. A waiter brought them a drink. [Sentence Pattern 3]
4. The couple found the music excellent. [Sentence Pattern 4]
5. The trumpeter was sizzling. [Sentence Pattern 5]

EXERCISE 4

Take the paragraph you wrote for Exercise 2 and modify its nouns and verbs as you have done in Exercise 3.

7d   Modifying and expanding sentences with phrases

A **phrase** does not express a complete thought, nor can it stand alone as a sentence. Phrases consist of nouns and the words associated with them, or verb forms not functioning as verbs (called *verbals)* and the words associated with them. Phrases function in a sentence as modifiers and as objects, subjects, or complements. As such, they can be integrated into any of the five sentence patterns (see 7b) to add detail.

1 Adding prepositional phrases

A preposition links nouns and pronouns to other words in a sentence. (See 7a-8 for a list of commonly used prepositions.) Together with its noun, called an *object*, a preposition forms a **prepositional phrase,** which functions in a sentence as a modifier—either as an adjective or as an adverb.

ADJECTIVE   Stories can excite the imaginations *of young people.*

ADVERB   Paul reads *in the evening.*

NOTE: A pronoun that functions as the object of a preposition must be written in the objective case. See chapter 8 for a discussion of pronoun case.

FAULTY   Between you and *I,* that movie was terrible.

REVISED   Between you and *me,* that movie was terrible.

7d

mm

2 Adding verbals: Infinitive phrases

A verbal is a verb form functioning not as a verb but instead as a noun, adjective, or adverb. An infinitive—the base form or dictionary form of a verb—often is preceded by the word *to.* Infinitives function as adjectives, adverbs, or nouns, but behave as verbs in that they can be modified with adverbs and can be followed with direct and indirect objects. Infinitives and the various words associated with them form **infinitive phrases.**

NOUN SUBJECT   *To read in the evening* is a great pleasure.

NOUN OBJECT   Some children start *to read at an early age.*

ADJECTIVE   Stories offer us a chance *to escape dull routines.*

ADVERB   We read *to gain knowledge.*

3 Adding verbals: Gerund and participial phrases

When appearing without its helping verbs, the *-ing* form of the verb functions as a noun and is called a *gerund.* Without its helping verb, the present or past participle can function as an adjective. Like infinitives, both gerunds and participles form phrases by taking objects and modifiers. A noun or pronoun appearing before a gerund is often called the subject of the gerund; this pronoun or noun must be written in its possessive form. In the following sentences, the gerund phrase functions as the object of the preposition *of.*

GERUND   We did not approve of *Paul's* reading all night. [The gerund phrase functions as the object of the preposition *of.* A noun in the possessive case is used before the gerund.]

FAULTY   We did not approve of *him* reading all night. [The pronoun before the gerund does not use the possessive case.]

REVISED   We did not approve of *his* reading all night.

7d

mm

4 Adding noun phrases

A **noun phrase** consists of a noun accompanied by all of its modifying words. A noun phrase can be quite lengthy, but it always functions as a single noun—as the subject of a sentence, as the object of a verb or preposition, or as a complement.

SUBJECT *Even horror stories with their gruesome endings* can delight readers.

DIRECT OBJECT A tale of horror will affect *anyone who is at all suggestible.*

COMPLEMENT Paul is *someone who likes to read horror stories.* [The phrase is a subject complement.]

5 Adding absolute phrases

Unlike other phrases, **absolute phrases** consist of both a subject and a predicate—although an incomplete predicate. Absolute phrases modify entire sentences, not individual words. When you use an absolute phrase, set it off from your sentence with a comma or pair of commas. (See chapter 25.) An absolute phrase is formed by deleting the linking verb *to be* from a sentence.

SENTENCE His hands were weak with exhaustion.

ABSOLUTE PHRASE his hands weak with exhaustion

NEW SENTENCE His hands weak with exhaustion, Paul lifted the book off its shelf. [The phrase modifies the basic sentence, *Paul lifted. . . .*]

An absolute phrase may also be formed by changing the main verb of a sentence to its *-ing* form, without using an auxiliary.

SENTENCE His hands trembled with exhaustion.

ABSOLUTE PHRASE his hands trembling with exhaustion

NEW SENTENCE His hands trembling with exhaustion, Paul lifted the book off its shelf.

6 Adding appositive phrases

Appositive phrases rename nouns. The word *appositive* describes the positioning of the phrase *in apposition to,* or beside, the noun. Appositives are actually "clipped" sentences—the predicate part (minus the verb) of Sentence Pattern 5.

Pattern 5: Subject Linking verb subject complement
Paul *is* *an old college friend.*
——————— Predicate ———————

APPOSITIVE PHRASE   an old college friend

NEW SENTENCE   Paul, an old college friend, is an avid reader.

EXERCISE 5

In the sentences that follow, circle all single-word modifiers and all modifying phrases.

> *Example:* Recently, Stephen W. Hawking published a popularized version of his ideas about space and time.

- *Recently* is an adverb and modifies the verb *published.*
- *Popularized* is an adjective and modifies the noun *version.*
- Two prepositional phrases—*of his ideas about space and time*—function as an adjective by modifying the noun *version.*
- The second prepositional phrase, *about space and time,* functions as an adjective by modifying the object of the preceding phrase, *ideas.*

1. On a clear, moonless night, he says, the brightest objects in the sky are the planets nearest Earth.
2. Looking more closely, we can see that the stars near Earth appear to be fixed, but are not.
3. To measure the distance of a star from Earth, scientists calculate the number of years it takes the star's light to reach us.
4. His calculations having proved it, Sir William Herschel confirmed that our galaxy (the Milky Way) forms a spiral.
5. We now know our galaxy is only one of some hundred thousand million galaxies.
6. Each of those hundred thousand million galaxies contains a hundred thousand million stars.

7e

sub

7e Modifying and expanding sentences with dependent clauses

A **clause** is any grouping of words that has both a subject and a predicate. There are two types of clauses. An **independent** (or **main) clause** can stand alone as a sentence. Any sentence fitting one of the five structural patterns reviewed in 7b is an independent clause. A **dependent** (or **subordinate) clause** cannot stand alone as a sentence because it is usually introduced either with a subordinate conjunction (e.g., *while)* or with a relative pronoun (e.g., *who).* There are four types of dependent clauses: adverb, adjective, noun, and elliptical clauses.

1 Adding dependent adverb clauses

Dependent **adverb clauses** that modify verbs, adjectives, and other adverbs begin with subordinate conjunctions and answer the questions *when,* *how, where, how often, to what extent,* or *to what degree.* Subordinate conjunctions establish a distinct logical relationship between the clauses joined.

Subordinate Conjunctions and the Logical Relationships They Establish

To show condition: *if, even if, unless,* and *provided that*
To show contrast: *though, although, even though,* and *as if*
To show cause: *because* and *since*
To show time: *when, whenever, while, as, before, after, since, once,* and *until*
To show place: *where* and *wherever*
To show purpose: *so that, in order that,* and *that*

Placed at the head of a clause, a subordinate conjunction makes one sentence grammatically dependent on another. When the subordinate conjunction *if,* for example, is placed at the head of a sentence, it renders that sentence grammatically dependent, unable to stand alone.

MAIN CLAUSE PLUS SUBORDINATE   *if* + There is a fixed amount of water in a given
CONJUNCTION   area.

DEPENDENT CLAUSE   if there is a fixed amount of water in a given area

Although it consists of a subject and predicate, this last grouping of words is no longer a sentence. To make sense, this clause must be set in a dependent relationship with an independent clause.

If there is a fixed amount of water in a given area, water like any other commodity can be described by the law of supply and demand.

For guidance on punctuating sentences with subordinate conjunctions, see 25a-1, 2, and the boxed information at 20b-1.

2   Adding dependent adjective clauses

Like adjectives, **adjective clauses** modify nouns. The clauses usually begin with the relative pronouns *which, that, who, whom,* or *whose.* The following examples show an adjective clause modifying the subject of a sentence.

People *who lived through the Depression of the 1930s* remember it well.

A country *that had prospered in the first two decades of the century* now saw massive unemployment and hardship.

For a discussion of when to use which relative pronoun, see 8f.

3   Adding dependent noun clauses

Noun clauses function exactly as single-word nouns do in a sentence: as subjects, objects, complements, and appositives. Noun clauses are introduced with the pronouns *which, whichever, that, who, whoever, whom, whomever,* or *whose* and with the words *how, when, why, where, whether,* or *whatever.*

SUBJECT   *That a beam of light is not a continuous wave but rather a stream of wave packets* was a new and revolutionary idea.

DIRECT OBJECT   In the early part of this century, physicists could not explain *how the energy of electrons knocked out of a metal surface was directly proportional to the frequency of the light waves irradiating the surface.*

SUBJECT COMPLEMENT   The presence of this theoretical problem was *why Albert Einstein devised his theory of quanta.*

sub

4   Working with elliptical clauses

An **elliptical clause** is one in which a word or words have been omitted, though the sense of the clause remains clear. Often, the words omitted are relative pronouns and the logically parallel second parts of comparisons. An elliptical clause functions exactly as a clause would, were all its words restored. In the following example, the words in parentheses are usually omitted.

English speakers, with their verb tenses and numerous words for divisions of years, weeks, and days, have a far different concept of time than the Hopis (have a concept of time).

EXERCISE 6

Combine each of the sentence pairs that follow by using a subordinate conjunction.

    Example: Colonial America could support its many needs with its own population. It could not so much as hope for independence.
           Unless colonial America could support its many needs with its own population, it could not so much as hope for independence.

1. One hundred years of colonization had passed. Seventeenth-century America held only 250,000 people.
2. In the eighteenth century, America's population exploded. Immigration and birth rates increased.
3. So many white settlers had come from England. It was not surprising that the English language, English customs, and English ways of government dominated the land.

4. Britons moved. They faced the challenges of living with Africans, Scots, Scotch-Irish, Irish, Portuguese Jews, Swedes, Finns, Swiss, and even a few Austrians and Italians.
5. Conflict had to give way to cooperation. New communities might flourish.

7f   Classifying sentences

7f

coord/
sub

1   Functional definitions

Sentences are classified by structure and by function. There are four functional types: declarative, interrogative, exclamatory, and imperative. The **declarative** sentence, by far the most common of the four types, makes a statement or assertion about a subject. An **interrogative** sentence poses a question and is formed either by inverting a sentence's usual word order (*She did sing./Did she sing?*) or by preceding the sentence with words such as *who, whom, which, when, where, why,* and *how.* **Exclamatory** sentences, used rarely in academic writing, are used as a direct expression of a speaker's or writer's strong emotion. **Imperative** sentences are an expression of a command addressed to a second person.

DECLARATIVE   The driver turned on the ignition.

INTERROGATIVE   Was the engine flooded?

EXCLAMATORY   What an awful fire! How terrible!

IMPERATIVE   Get back! Don't you go near that!

2   Structural definitions

As you expand sentences by adding phrase- and clause-length modifiers, or by combining two or more sentences, you change the structural relationships within sentences. There are four structural classes of sentences in English: simple, compound, complex, and compound-complex. Good stylistic sense dictates that you vary sentence types and lengths. See the discussion in chapter 20.

Each of the five basic sentence patterns discussed in section 7b qualifies as a **simple sentence,** for each has a single subject and a single predicate. The designation "simple" refers to a sentence's structure, not its content. A simple sentence, with all its modifying words and phrases, can be long.

For thousands of years, waves of migrating people had moved slowly across the great Eurasian steppes down into the Mediterranean. [This sentence consists of one subject, *waves,* and one simple predicate, *had moved.*]

Compound sentences have two subjects and two predicates. They are created when two independent clauses are joined with a coordinate or correlative conjunction or with a conjunctive adverb. Coordinate conjunctions express specific logical relations between the elements they join. *Or* and *nor* suggest choice, one positive and the other negative. *And* joins elements by addition. *But* and *yet* join elements by establishing a contrast. *For* and *so* are the only coordinate conjunctions that must join entire sentences. The others may join sentence elements and entire sentences. *For* suggests a cause of an occurrence. *So* suggests a result of some action. Correlative conjunctions such as *either/or* and conjunctive adverbs such as *however* can also be used to create compound sentences. For details on how coordination can be used to create sentence emphasis, see 19a.

7f

> In the second century A.D. the Goths moved southward from the Baltic regions, and they settled on the north shore of the Black Sea. [The conjunction *and* joins two independent clauses.]

coord/ sub

Complex sentences consist of an independent clause and one or more dependent clauses. As shown in section 7e, the four kinds of dependent clauses can be introduced with subordinate conjunctions or relative pronouns. For details on how complex sentences help to create sentence emphasis, see 19b.

> The Goths met and defeated the Vandals, who retreated toward central Europe. [The relative pronoun *who* signals a dependent adjective clause in this complex sentence.]

> After they met and defeated the Vandals, the Goths forced that tribe to retreat toward central Europe. [The subordinate conjunction *after* signals a dependent adverb clause.]

Compound-complex sentences consist of at least two independent clauses and one subordinate, dependent clause.

> Rome had for centuries been able to withstand migratory incursions along its northern borders, but in A.D. 376 the Emperor Valens and nearly two-thirds of his army were killed in a battle with the Visigoths at Adrianople, which marked the last real Roman resistance to the barbarian nations. [The coordinating conjunction *but* here signals a compound sentence, and the relative pronoun *which* signals a dependent clause in a complex sentence.]

EXERCISE 7

Use the clauses and phrases provided to build up the core sentence. Add conjunctions when they are necessary to the logic of your expanded sentence.

> *Example:*   Athol Fugard is a South African playwright.
> plays confront difficulties
> interracial relations
> his troubled country

Athol Fugard is a South African playwright whose plays confront the difficulties of interracial relations in his troubled country.

1. A common thread connects Fugard's work.

   respect for humanity
   search for human dignity
   struggle to cultivate faith, trust, and hope in a demeaning, demoralizing world.

2. Fugard's looks reflect his struggles.

   a mix of tenacity, decency, and empathy
   a weathered, chiseled visage
   the face of an ancient mariner who has dealt with the burden of the albatross and won

3. Fugard handwrites his plays.

   in this computer age
   with a tortoise-shell Parker pen
   which include *A Lesson from Aloes, The Road to Mecca,* "Master Harold" *. . . and the Boys,* and *My Children, My Africa,* all successfully produced in America

4. South Africa is changing.

   for Fugard there are signs
   the freeing of Nelson Mandela
   the lifting of the ban on the African National Congress
   the government's willingness to negotiate
   which he discusses with a mixture of caution and reverence

5. Fugard continued writing.

   during the mid-1960s
   he staged classic plays with the Serpent players
   the country's first non-white theater troupe
   they suffered constant political persecution
   including arrest and the revoking of passports

CHAPTER 8

Case in Nouns and Pronouns

The term **case** refers to a noun or pronoun's change in form, depending on its function in a sentence. Nouns do not change their form when their function changes from subject to object.

SUBJECT   Edmund Hillary climbed Mt. Everest in 1953. [*Edmund Hillary* is the subject.]

OBJECT   Leaders the world over congratulated Edmund Hillary on the achievement. [*Edmund Hillary* is the object of the verb.]

By contrast, pronouns *do* change form when they change function.

SUBJECT   *He* climbed Mt. Everest in 1953. [*He* as the subject of the sentence takes the form of the subjective case.]

OBJECT   Leaders the world over congratulated *him* on the achievement. [*Him* as the object of the verb takes the form of the objective case.]

Nouns and pronouns *both* change form when they show possession.

> *Hillary's* feat has since been accomplished by other mountaineers. [To show possession, a noun takes an apostrophe and the letter *s*.]

> *His* feat has since been accomplished by other mountaineers. [*His* is a possessive pronoun.]

Writers are always making choices in a sentence. Some of these choices concern stylistic matters. Others, like selecting a noun or pronoun's case, concern the fundamental meaning of a sentence. Above all, your obligation to your reader is to be clear, and choosing the correct case for your sentences helps to ensure clarity. The primary concern with case involves changes in a pronoun's form to reflect its function. Especially when revising, you may change a pronoun's function—say, from object to subject. By understanding this change, you will be prepared to make a corresponding change to the pronoun's form, which readers will expect. There are eight classes of pronouns. *Case* proves most troublesome with **personal pronouns,** which refer to people and things, and these will be the focus of discussion here.

8a   Using pronouns in the subjective case

8a

ca

Subjective Case Pronouns		
	Singular	*Plural*
1st person	I	we
2nd person	you	you
3rd person	he, she, it	they

Use the subjective case when a pronoun functions as a subject, a subject complement, or as an appositive that renames a subject.

SUBJECT OF AN
INDEPENDENT CLAUSE
Abigail Adams was brilliant and much admired; *she* ran the family farm and business while her husband attended the Continental Congress.

SUBJECT OF A
DEPENDENT CLAUSE
While *she* lived in the capital, Abigail Adams repeatedly approached her husband on behalf of American women.

SUBJECT COMPLEMENT
John Adams was a pacifist, and it was largely *he* who kept the country from going to war with France in 1798.

APPOSITIVE THAT
RENAMES A SUBJECT
Adams retired from public life in 1801; only one President of the United States—*he*, alone—has lived to see a son elected president.

Use the subjective case for pronouns with the linking verb "to be."

In a sentence whose main verb is a linking verb, the pronoun following the verb refers directly to (is the "complement" of) the noun preceding the verb. Because the noun before the verb functions as the subject of the sentence, the pronoun after the verb must be in the subjective case. This requirement is clear enough with normal (that is, subject-verb-complement) word order; but the requirement also applies when the linking-verb construction is reversed.

NORMAL   *He* was the only president whose son became president.

REVERSED   The only president whose son became president was *he*, John Adams.

In nonstandard usage it is fairly common to hear a linking-verb construction using an objective case: as in "It's me" or "This is her." But in academic English these constructions should be revised using a subjective-case pronoun that maintains sentence logic and consistency: "It's I" and "This is she."

NONSTANDARD It isn't *me* in the White House; the decision makers are never *us* ordinary folks.

REVISED It isn't *I* in the White House; the decision makers are never *we* ordinary folks. [These linking-verb constructions require the same subjective case they would have required in a sentence with normal word order.]

To some writers, the word order in this revised sentence sounds stilted. If this is your view, the best remedy is to reorder the sentence in question.

REORDERED *I* am not in the White House; *we* ordinary folks never make decisions. [Use normal order and subjective-case pronouns.]

The decision-makers don't consult *us*. [Use normal word order and an objective-case pronoun.]

8b

ca

8b Using pronouns in the objective case

Objective Case Pronouns		
	Singular	*Plural*
1st person	me	us
2nd person	you	you
3rd person	him, her, it	them

1 Use the objective case for pronouns functioning as objects.

Pronouns functioning as the object of a preposition, as the object or indirect object of a verb, or as the object of a verbal take the objective case.

Object or indirect object of verb

Babe Ruth started as a pitcher in 1915, when the Boston Red Sox gave *him* a contract. [*Him* is the indirect object of *gave*.]

Ruth so impressed *them* with his hitting that between the games he pitched he was asked to play first base and outfield. [*Them* is the direct object of *impressed*.]

Object of preposition

Ruth pitched 25 games in 1916 and won 23 of *them*.

Appositive that renames the object

Hank Aaron eventually broke Ruth's home run record of 714; a place in the Hall of Fame has been reserved for both legends—Aaron and *him*.

Object of verbal

Even though teams opposing *him* could not hit his pitching, Ruth gave up the pitcher's mound to concentrate on hitting. [*Him* is the direct object of the participle *opposing*.]

For twelve years Ruth either led the American League in hitting home runs or was tied for hitting *them*. [*Them* is the object of the gerund *hitting*.]

2 Use the objective case for pronouns functioning as the subject of an infinitive.

When a pronoun appears between a verb and an infinitive, the pronoun takes the objective case. In this position, the pronoun is called the subject of the infinitive.

WITH INFINITIVE His 60 home runs in 1927 helped *him* to reach a level of stardom unmatched by athletes of his era. [The objective-case pronoun appears between the verb *helped* and the infinitive *to reach*.]

8c Using nouns and pronouns in the possessive case

Use a possessive noun or pronoun before a noun to indicate ownership of that noun (or noun substitute). A pronoun's possessive form also has other distinctive uses.

Eleanor Roosevelt gave the Civil Works Administration *her* enthusiastic support for hiring 100,000 women by the end of 1933.

Possessive Case Pronouns

	Singular	*Plural*
1st person	my, mine	our, ours
2nd person	your, yours	your, yours
3rd person	his, her, hers, its	their, theirs

1 Certain possessive pronouns are used as subjects or subject complements to indicate possession.

The possessive pronouns *mine, ours, yours, his, hers, theirs* are used in place of a noun as subjects or subject complements.

Ours is a country of opportunity for both men and women, she argued. This land of opportunity is *ours*. (*mine, yours, his, hers, theirs*)

2   Use a possessive noun or pronoun before a gerund to indicate possession.

When appearing before a gerund, an *-ing* word that functions as a noun, a pronoun should take the possessive case.

GERUND   *Her* lobbying helped to legitimize the role of women in government. [The pronoun before the gerund specifies whose *lobbying*.]

Problems with pronouns before gerunds occur when the *-ing* word is confused with a participle, which has the same *-ing* form but functions as an adjective. A participle is often preceded by an objective-case pronoun.

8c

PARTICIPLE   In Babe Ruth's most famous game, fans saw *him* pointing to the spot where, moments later, he hit a home run. [*Him*, a direct object of *saw*, is modified by the participle *pointing*, which functions as an adjective.]

ca

In a similar construction, *pointing to the spot . . .* can be preceded by the possessive-case *his*.

GERUND   Fans saw *his* pointing to a spot in the left-field bleachers as a sign of confidence, not arrogance. [The gerund phrase *pointing to a spot . . .* functions as the object of *saw*; the possessive *his* indicates Ruth's ownership of this act.]

The focus in this last sentence is no longer on *him* (on Ruth) but on *his pointing*—an important difference in meaning. Since gerunds and participles both have distinctive uses in sentences, be sure to choose the correct pronoun case to help convey your meaning. Confusion between an *-ing* word's function—as a gerund or as a participle—can create errors.

FAULTY   American women were eager to work; Eleanor Roosevelt's efforts resulted in *them* getting government jobs in unprecedented numbers. [*Getting* is mistakenly treated as a participle and is incorrectly preceded by an objective-case pronoun.]

REVISED   American women were eager to work; Eleanor Roosevelt's efforts resulted in *their* getting government jobs in unprecedented numbers. [*Their* indicates possession of the gerund *getting . . . jobs*.]

EXERCISE 1

Based on your analysis of each of the following sentences, fill in the blanks with an appropriate subjective-, objective-, or possessive-case pronoun: *I/we, you, he/she/it/they; me/us, you, him/her/it/them; my/mine/our/ours, your/ yours, his/her/hers/its/their/theirs.*

> *Example:* _____ changing costumes, mid-performance, amused the audience.
>
> *Changing costumes* is a gerund phrase and functions as the subject of the verb *amused*. Gerunds take possessive-case pronouns. Therefore, the sentence can be completed as follows: *His* (or *her*) changing costumes, mid-performance, amused the audience.

1. Delegates to the convention watched _____ changing positions on important issues and deserted the candidacy.
2. Delegates wanted _____ to remain steadier under challenges from contenders.
3. After _____ left the convention, the delegates searched for a restaurant.
4. The newly elected president arrived and said the delegates had worked so effectively that she wanted to give _____ a banquet.
5. "_____ is an organization that recognizes honest effort," the president said.

EXERCISE 2

Complete the sentences that follow by filling in the blanks with pronouns or nouns of the appropriate case.

1. Presenting the newly discovered evidence—the intruder's gloves— to the district attorney, the chief inspector said: "These are _____."
2. It is _____ who has won.
3. It is _____ who have won.
4. This is _____ contest.
5. Mark answered the phone and, listening to a person asking for him, said: "Yes, this is _____."

In a compound construction, use pronouns in the objective or subjective case according to their function in the sentence.

The coordinate conjunction *and* can create a compound construction—a multiple subject or object that sometimes obscures how a pronoun functions in a sentence. Whenever you have difficulty choosing between a subjective- or objective-case pronoun in a compound construction, try this test: *Create a simplified sentence by dropping out the compound;* then *try choosing the pronoun.* With the compound gone in the simpler construction, you should be able to tell whether the pronoun operates as a subject or an object.

Compound subject

Pierre and Marie Curie worked collaboratively; together Marie and *he* discovered polonium and radium. [The subjective-case pronoun forms the second part of a compound subject.]

CONFUSED Marie and *him* received the Nobel Prize in physics in 1903. [The pronoun subject is mistakenly put in the objective case in the compound construction.]

SIMPLIFIED Marie received the Nobel Prize; *he* also received it. [In the simplified construction the need for the subjective pronoun is clear.]

REVISED Marie and *he* received the Nobel Prize in 1903.

8e

ca

Compound object

The 1903 Nobel Prize in physics was awarded to Pierre and *her* for their work on radioactivity. [The objective-case pronoun is the object of a preposition in a compound construction.]

CONFUSED An award was presented to Pierre and *she* in 1903, based on their work on radioactivity. [In this construction, the pronoun functions as part of the preposition's compound object. Mistakenly, the pronoun is made subjective.]

SIMPLIFIED The award was presented to Pierre; it was also presented to *her*.

REVISED An award was presented to Pierre and *her* in 1903.

8e Pronouns paired with a noun take the same case as the noun.

1 For first-person plural pronouns paired with a noun, use the same case as the noun.

The first-person plural pronoun *we* or *us* is sometimes placed before a plural noun to help establish the identity of the noun. Use the subjective-case *we* when the pronoun is paired with a noun subject and the objective-case *us* when the pronoun is paired with an object of a verb, verbal, or preposition. In nonstandard usage the case of these paired pronouns may become confused, but this can be avoided in academic writing by testing for and choosing the correct pronoun. Simplify the sentence and *drop out* the paired noun. In the simpler sentence remaining, you should be able to determine which pronoun case is required.

NONSTANDARD	*Us* strikers demand compensation. [*Strikers* is the subject of the sentence and the pronoun paired with it should be the subjective-case *we*.]
SIMPLIFIED	*We* . . . demand compensation. [The need for subjective-case *we* is now clear.]
REVISED	*We* strikers demand compensation.

NONSTANDARD	Give *we* strikers a fair share. [*Strikers* in this sentence is the indirect object of the verb *give,* and the pronoun paired with it should be the objective-case *us*.]
SIMPLIFIED	Give *us* . . . a fair share. [The need for objective-case *us* is now clear.]
REVISED	Give *us* strikers a fair share.

ca

2 In an appositive, a pronoun's case should match the case of the noun it renames.

Pronouns may occur in an **appositive**—a word or phrase that describes, identifies, or renames a noun in a sentence. If so, the pronoun must take the same case as the noun being renamed. Once again you can test for pronoun choice by simplifying the sentence: *Drop the noun being renamed out of the sentence.* The simpler sentence that remains will usually reveal what pronoun case is required.

RENAMED SUBJECT	For years Babe Ruth held the home run record; only one player—*he* alone—had hit the magic 714 home runs.
CONFUSED	Only one player—*him* alone—had hit the magic number.
SIMPLIFIED	*He* alone had hit the magic number.
RENAMED OBJECT	Hank Aaron eventually broke Ruth's home run record of 714; a place in the Hall of Fame has been reserved for both legends—Aaron and *him*. [A simplification—". . . for Aaron" and ". . . for him"—will show the need for the objective case here.]

8f Choose the appropriate form of the pronouns *whose, who, whom, whoever,* and *whomever* depending on the pronoun's function.

The basic forms of the relative pronouns *whose, who, whom, whoever,* and *whomever* are shown in the following box. These forms are used to begin questions and dependent (adjective) clauses. The subjective and objective forms in questions and dependent clauses will function either as the subject of the clause (using *who* and *whoever*), or as an object in the clause (using *whom* and *whomever*).

> ### Case Forms of the Relative Pronoun "Who(m)/Who(m)ever"
>
> | Subjective | Objective | Possessive |
> |------------|-----------|------------|
> | who | whom | whose |
> | whoever | whomever | — — |

Writers are often in doubt when to use *who* and *whom* partly because questions and dependent clauses can be quite complex in structure, and also because the objective forms may be seldom or inconsistently used in conversation. When in doubt, remember that the pronoun's case depends on its function within its own clause.

8f

ca

1   In a question, choose a subjective, objective, or possessive form of *who(m)* or *who(m)ever* according to the pronoun's function.

To test the correct choice for these pronouns at the beginning of a question, mentally *answer* the question, substituting the personal pronouns *I/me, we/us, he/him,* or *she/her* for *the relative pronoun.* Your choice of the subjective or objective case in the answer sentence will likely be quite clear, and it will be the same choice to make for the case of *who(m)* or *who(m)ever.*

QUESTION   (Who/whom) are you addressing?

ANSWER   You are addressing (he/*him*). [The choice of the objective case is clear.]

REVISED   *Whom* are you addressing? [The objective case is correct.]

QUESTION   For (who/whom) are you writing?

ANSWER   You are writing for (she/*her*). [The choice of the objective case is clear.]

REVISED   For *whom* are you writing? [The objective case is correct.]

QUESTION   (Who/Whom) wrote this story?

ANSWER   *She* wrote this story? [The choice of the subjective case is clear.]

REVISED   *Who* wrote this story?

The possessive form *whose* can begin a question if the pronoun must show possession of the noun that immediately follows. To determine whether a possessive pronoun is correct for a sentence, replace the initial pronoun in the question with *what* and then mentally answer that question: If the answer requires that you use *his, her, their,* or *its* in place of the relative pronoun, then choose the possessive form, *whose.*

QUESTION   What name goes on the envelope? [Is a pronoun in the possessive case—his/her/their/its—needed?]

POSSESSIVE   *Whose* name goes on the envelope?

> **2** In a dependent clause, choose the subjective, objective, or possessive form of *who(m)* or *who(m)ever* according to the pronoun's function within the clause.

To choose the correct case for a relative pronoun in a dependent clause, eliminate the main clause temporarily; consider the pronoun's function *only* in the dependent clause. When deciding between the subjective or objective forms, apply the following tests.

8f

ca

Determine whether the relative pronoun functions as the subject of a dependent clause.

If the relative pronoun is followed immediately by a verb, you should probably use the subjective-case *who* or *whoever*. To be sure that the choice of pronouns is correct, substitute the words *I, we, you, he,* or *she* for *who* or *whoever*. Does this yield a legitimate sentence? If so, the choice of the subjective case is correct.

SUBJECTIVE   Your request will be of concern to (whoever/whomever) gets it.

SIMPLIFIED   (Whoever/whomever) gets it. [The pronoun is followed by a verb, *gets,* so the likely choice of pronouns will be *whoever*. As a second test, the subjective-case pronoun *she,* substituted for *whoever,* yields the sentence "*she* gets it." The choice of the subjective case is correct.]

REVISED   Your request will be of concern to *whoever* gets it.

SUBJECTIVE   John Maynard Keynes, *who* taught economics at Cambridge University, is best known for his *General Theory of Employment, Interest, and Money* (1936). [The pronoun is followed by a verb, *taught,* so the likely choice of pronouns will be *who.* A second test: The subjective-case pronoun *he,* substituted for *who,* yields a sentence, "*He* taught economics. . . ."]

Determine whether the relative pronoun functions as an object in the dependent clause.

If the relative pronoun is followed immediately by a noun or by the pronouns *I, we, you, he, she, few, some, many, most, it,* or *they,* you should probably use the objective-case *whom* or *whomever*. To be sure of the choice, consider the dependent clause as if it were a sentence by itself (without the main clause). Rearrange the clause into normal word order and then substitute the words *him, her,* or *them* for the relative pronoun. If one of these newly substituted pronouns fits into the sentence as an object of a verb, verbal, or preposition, then the choice of the objective-case *whom* or *whomever* is correct.

OBJECTIVE   Please send this to *whom* it may concern. [The relative pronoun is followed by the pronoun *it,* so the choice of pronoun will likely be objective case. A second test: The objective-case pronoun *them,* substituted for *whom,* yields a rearranged sentence "It may concern *them.*"]

OBJECTIVE   Keynes, *whom* many regard as the preeminent economist of the twentieth century, broke with classical concepts of a free economy when he
endorsed a government public works program to promote employment. [The relative pronoun is followed by the pronoun *many*, so the
choice of pronoun will likely be objective case. A second test: The
objective- case *him* yields a rearranged sentence "Many regard *him* as
the. . . ."]

Determine whether the relative pronoun needs to show ownership.

If the relative pronoun beginning a dependent clause needs to show
possession, then you should use the possessive-case *whose*. Confirm the choice
by substituting the words *his, her, their,* or *its* for the relative pronoun. A
sentence should result when the dependent clause is considered by itself.

8g

ca

POSSESSIVE   Keynes, *whose* theories prompted entire nations to change the course
of their economic policy, believed that during periods of recession
deficit spending and easier monetary policies could stimulate business activity. [The possessive-case *his* yields a sentence: *"His* theories
prompted. . . ."]

 **Choose the case of a pronoun in the second part of a
comparison depending on the sense intended.**

The words *than* and *as* create a comparison. Often, the second part of a
complete comparison is omitted for brevity's sake. The result is an elliptical
(or clipped) sentence that has the potential to create confusion.

COMPLETE   Psychologists knew their colleague William James better than they
knew his brother Henry.

COMPLETE   Psychologists knew their colleague William James better than his
brother Henry knew him.

CLIPPED   Psychologists knew their colleague William James better than
(he/him). [This sentence is correct with either pronoun. The pronoun
chosen will have *one* of the preceding meanings.]

In clipped comparisons like this, choosing the wrong pronoun case will
convey the wrong meaning. It is important, therefore, to choose a pronoun
for the second part of a comparison as if the comparison were being written
out fully. This means that you should mentally recreate the omitted verb in
the second part of the comparison. The meaning of your sentence will depend
on whether the pronoun you choose functions as the subject or object of that
verb.

CLIPPED   Psychologists knew their colleague William James better than *him*. [i.e.,
. . . better than they knew *him*, his brother *Henry*].

CLIPPED   Psychologists knew their colleague William James better than *he*. [i.e., . . . better than *he, Henry,* knew William].

When the omitted verb in the second part of a clipped comparison is intransitive and thus does not take an object, then you have no choice: the pronoun will be in the subjective case.

FAULTY   She was as fast as *him*. [The verb can take no object.]

REVISED   She was as fast as *he*. [i.e., . . . *as fast as he was fast*.]

8g

ca

EXERCISE 3

In the following sentences, correct the usage of the italicized pronouns. If a pronoun choice is correct, circle the pronoun.

> *Example:*   Anne told me it was Simon's fault; but between you and *I*, she's as much to blame as *him*.
>
> Anne told me it was Simon's fault; but between you and *me*, she's as much to blame as *he*. [Pronouns that follow a preposition must be objective case: thus, <u>between you and me</u>. The second part of the comparison requires a subjective-case pronoun: <u>She is to blame as much as *he* is to blame</u>.]

1. It was *me* who asked Helen to go to the museum.
2. It was not *him* who called.
3. "*Whom* may I ask is calling? Yes, this is *her*."
4. "To *Who* It may Concern" is not an especially effective opening for a business letter.
5. He gave the present to both *you* and *she*.
6. *You* and *she* have been friends for many years.
7. A group that can't afford cutbacks in health care is *us* salaried employees.
8. *Whomever* the people elect is the person *who* we depend upon.
9. Richard Nixon, *who* was elected, resigned from office.
10. *Him* resigning was the first presidential abdication in *our* history.
11. Frank could read a newspaper more quickly than *him*.
12. Abraham Lincoln, *who* many regard as one of our great presidents, was often gloomy despite his reputation for telling good jokes.
13. *Whoever* can provide a direct answer should step forward.
14. Clearly, there is motivation for *you* and *I* to do well.
15. Euclid was a Greek scholar *whose* work in geometry is still studied today.

CHAPTER 9

Verbs

The smoke hovers.   The smoke is coiling.
The smoke billowed.   The smoke might have drifted.

Hovers, is coiling, billowed, might have drifted: meaning in a sentence depends on the form of the verb you choose as much as on the selection of the verb itself. (See 17b on effective verb use.) The verb forms you select will convey three important messages that are the focus of this chapter: *tense*—an indication of when an action or state of being occurs; *mood*—your judgment as to whether a statement is a fact, a command, or an occurrence contrary to fact; and *voice*—your emphasis on the actor of a sentence or on the object acted upon.

VERB FORMS

 9a Using the principal parts of regular verbs consistently

All verbs other than *to be* have two basic forms and three principal parts; these five forms and parts are the foundation for all the varied aspects of verbs. A dictionary entry presents these forms and parts: base form *-s* form, past tense, past participle, and present participle.

The Principal Parts of Regular Verbs				
BASE FORM	**PRESENT TENSE** (*-S* **FORM**)	**PAST TENSE**	**PAST PARTICIPLE**	**PRESENT PARTICIPLE**
share	shares	shared	shared	sharing
start	starts	started	started	starting
climb	climbs	climbed	climbed	climbing

Most verbs in the dictionary are **regular** in that they follow the simple, predictable pattern shown in the box, in which the past tense and past participle are identical.

235

9a

vb

1 Recognizing the forms of regular verbs

Base form + the -s form = present tense

The **base** (or infinitive) **form** of a verb—often called its **dictionary form**—is the base from which all changes are made. Use the base form of a verb with *no* ending for occasions when the action of a verb is present for plural nouns or for the personal pronouns *I, we, you,* or *they.*

> Alaska's Pacific mountains *create* a region of high peaks, broad valleys, and numerous island fjords.

The **-s form** of a verb (creates, tries, loves) occurs with third-person, singular subjects when an action is in the present. A verb's *-s* form (add *-s* or *-es* to a verb) is used in three instances: with the personal pronouns *he, she,* or *it;* with any noun that can be replaced by these pronouns; and with a number of indefinite pronouns (such as *something* or *no one*), which are often considered singular.

> Alaska's north slope *consists* of the plateaus and coastal regions north of the Brooks mountain range.

Difficulties with subject-verb agreement occur when a writer is unsure whether to use a verb's base form or *-s* form in a sentence. For a discussion of subject-verb agreement, see chapter 10.

Past-tense form

The **past tense** of a verb indicates that an action has been completed in the past. The regular verbs follow a predictable pattern in forming the past tense by taking the suffix *-ed* or *-d.*

> Secretary of State William H. Seward *arranged* for the purchase of Alaska from Russia in 1867.

Irregular verbs follow no such pattern: their base forms change their root spelling to show the past tense (see 9b).

Two participle forms

For regular verbs, the form of the **past participle** is identical to that of the past tense. A verb's past participle is used in three ways: paired with *to have,* the past participle functions as a main verb of a sentence; paired with *to be,* the past participle forms a passive construction; and, paired with a noun or pronoun, the past participle functions as an adjective.

> With the Russian treasury *depleted* [adjective] after the Crimean War, the Tsar *had decided* [main verb] to sell the western-most part of his empire, which *was colonized* [passive construction] very sparsely by Russians.

The **present participle,** the *-ing* form of the verb, has three uses: it functions as a main verb of a sentence and shows continuing action when paired with *to be;* it functions as an adjective when paired with a noun or pronoun; or it functions as a noun, in which case it is called a *gerund* (see 7a).

The *decimating* [gerund] of seal herds *was proceeding* [main verb] at an *alarming* [adjective] rate.

 2 Revising nonstandard verb forms by using standard *-s* and *-ed* forms

In rapid conversation, many people skip over *-s* and *-ed* endings. In some dialects the base (or infinitive) form of the verb is used in place of verbs with *-s* and *-ed* endings. Writers of standard academic English, however, need to observe the regular forms.

NONSTANDARD   She was *ask* to read this assignment. She *like* to stay up late and she *be* still wide awake.

REVISED   She was *asked* to read it. She *likes* to stay up late and she *is* still wide awake. [Base forms have been replaced by standard verb forms with *-s* and *-ed* endings.]

9b

vb

9b   Learning the forms of irregular verbs

Most verbs are regular in that they form the past tense and past participle with the suffixes *-ed* or *-d*. An irregular verb will form its past tense and past participle by altering the spelling of the base verb, as in *build/built* or *bring/brought*. A dictionary entry for an irregular verb shows the principal parts and basic forms of a verb as the first information in the entry. This will show you when a verb is irregular—when it does not take an *-ed* ending in its past tense and past participle forms. Because irregular verbs are some of the most commonly used words in the language, most speakers and readers are accustomed to, and expect, them. You should take care to use correct irregular forms. Memorize troublesome forms or look them up as necessary.

To be

The most frequently used verb in our language, *to be,* is also the only verb with more than five forms. It functions both as the main verb in a sentence and as a frequently used auxiliary verb (see 9c and 7a-3). The eight principal parts of *to be* are shown in the box on page 238.

9b

vb

The Principal Parts of *be*

BASE FORM	PRESENT TENSE	PAST TENSE
(to) be	he, she, it *is* I *am* we, you, they *are*	he, she, it, *was* I *was* we, you, they *were*

PAST PARTICIPLE	PRESENT PARTICIPLE
been	*being*

The following box contains a partial list of irregular verbs. Remember that the past participle is the form of the verb used with the auxiliary *have*—or, without the auxiliary, it is the form that functions as an adjective.

Some Irregular Verb Forms

BASE FORM	PAST TENSE	PAST PARTICIPLE
arise	arose	arisen
be (is, am, are)	was, were	been
bear	bore	borne, born
beat	beat	beaten
become	became	become
begin	began	begun
bend	bent	bent
bind	bound	bound
bite	bit	bit, bitten
bleed	bled	bled
blow	blew	blown
break	broke	broken
bring	brought	brought
build	built	built
burn	burned, burnt	burned, burnt
burst	burst	burst
buy	bought	bought
catch	caught	caught
choose	chose	chosen
cling	clung	clung
come	came	come
cost	cost	cost
cut	cut	cut
dig	dug	dug
dive	dove, dived	dived

BASE FORM	PAST TENSE	PAST PARTICIPLE
do (does)	did	done
draw	drew	drawn
drink	drank	drunk
drive	drove	driven
eat	ate	eaten
fall	fell	fallen
feed	fed	fed
feel	felt	felt
fight	fought	fought
find	found	found
fling	flung	flung
flee	fled	fled
fly	flew	flown
forbid	forbade, forbad	forbidden, forbid
forget	forgot	forgot, forgotten
freeze	froze	frozen
get	got	got, gotten
give	gave	given
go	went	gone
grow	grew	grown
hang[1]	hung	hung
have (has)	had	had
hear	heard	heard
hide	hid	hidden
hit	hit	hit
keep	kept	kept
know	knew	known
lay	laid	laid
lead	led	led
leave	left	left
lend	lent	lent
lie[2]	lay	lain
lose	lost	lost
make	made	made
mean	meant	meant
pay	paid	paid
prove	proved	proved, proven
read	read	read
ride	rode	ridden
ring	rang	rung
rise	rose	risen

9b

vb

[1] *Hang* as an irregular verb means to *suspend*. When *hang* means to *execute*, it is regular: *hang, hanged, hanged.*

[2] *Lie* as an irregular verb means to *recline*. When *lie* means to *deceive*, it is regular: *lie, lied, lied.*

(continued)

9c

vb

Some Irregular Verb Forms (continued)

BASE FORM	PAST TENSE	PAST PARTICIPLE
run	ran	run
say	said	said
see	saw	seen
seek	sought	sought
send	sent	sent
set	set	set
shake	shook	shaken
shine[3]	shone	shone
sing	sang	sung
sink	sank	sunk
sit	sat	sat
sleep	slept	slept
speak	spoke	spoken
spend	spent	spent
spring	sprang, sprung	sprung
stand	stood	stood
steal	stole	stolen
stick	stuck	stuck
strive	strove	striven
swear	swore	sworn
swim	swam	swum
swing	swung	swung
take	took	taken
teach	taught	taught
tear	tore	torn
tell	told	told
think	thought	thought
throw	threw	thrown
wake	woke, waked	waked, woken
wear	wore	worn
wind	wound	wound
wring	wrung	wrung
write	wrote	written

[3]*Shine* as an irregular verb means to *emit light*. When *shine* means to *polish*, it is regular: *shine, shined, shined.*

9c Using auxiliary verbs

An **auxiliary** (or helping) **verb** is combined with the base form of a verb or the present or past participle forms to establish tense, mood, and voice in a sentence. This combination of verbs creates a **verb phrase.** The most frequently used auxiliaries are *to be, to have,* and *to do. To be* functions as an auxiliary when it combines with the *-ing* form of a verb to create the progressive tenses (as in I *am going*). *To have* functions as an auxiliary when it combines with the past participle form of a verb to create the perfect tenses (as in I *have gone*). *To do* functions as an auxiliary when it combines with the base form of a verb to form questions, to show emphasis, and to show negation. (*Do* you care? I *do* care. I *don't* care.)

1 **Use modal auxiliaries to refine meaning.**

When paired with the base form of a verb, a **modal auxiliary** expresses urgency, obligation, likelihood, possibility, and so on: *can, could, may, might, must, ought to, should, would.* Unlike the auxiliaries *to be, to have,* and *to do,* these modal auxiliaries do not change form. They follow singular or plural subjects in the first, second, or third persons. Modal auxiliaries can follow the pronouns *I, we, you, he, she, one, they.* Observe how meaning in a sentence changes depending on the choice of modal auxiliary.

I must resign.	I ought to resign.	I would resign.
I could resign.	I can resign.	I might resign.

Modal auxiliaries can combine with other auxiliaries to create complex verbal phrases that require careful use.

I ought to have resigned.

I might have been resigning.

The auxiliaries *will* and *shall* establish the future tense.

Shall I resign?

She will resign.

2 **Revise nonstandard auxiliaries by using standard forms of** *be.*

Some dialects form present-tense auxiliary constructions with variations on the base form of *be.* For written academic English, these forms must be revised.

NONSTANDARD She *be* singing beautifully. [The base form of *be* is a nonstandard usage here. The *-s* form of the verb is needed.]

NONSTANDARD She singing a beautiful melody. [The *be* form has been dropped.]

REVISED She *is* singing a beautiful melody. [The base form of *be* in the auxiliary has been replaced by the standard *-s* form.]

9d

vb

EXERCISE 1

Identify the main verb and any auxiliary verb associated with it in the sentences that follow.

> *Example:* Almost 300 years ago, Isaac Newton separated visible light into a spectrum of colors. (The verb is *separated*.)

1. Newton had let light pass through a prism.
2. The experiment showed the following.
3. White light consists of different colors, ranging from violet at one end of the spectrum to red at the other.
4. Light of different colors will bend at different angles in passing through a prism.
5. Newton believed that light was a stream of particles.

EXERCISE 2

In the sentences that follow, fill in the numbered blanks with the appropriate form of *be*.

> *Example:* In the nineteenth century, through the genius of James Clerk Maxwell (1831–1879), it came __1__ known that what we experience as light __2__ in truth a very small part of a vast continuous spectrum of radiation, the electromagnetic spectrum.

1. It came *to be* known. . . .
2. What we experience as light *is*. . . .

Radiation in the spectrum travels in waves, and wavelengths vary—from X-rays, which __1__ exceedingly short, to low frequency radio waves, which __2__ measured in miles. The energy of a short wavelength __3__ greater than that of a long wavelength. A feature that all electromagnetic radiations have in common __4__ that, in a vacuum, they travel at the same speed—186,000 miles per second. By 1900, however, it had become clear that the wave theory of light __5__ not adequate.

9d Using transitive and intransitive verbs

Action verbs are classified as *transitive* and *intransitive*. A **transitive verb** (marked with the abbreviation **tr.** in the dictionary) transfers an action from a subject to an object; the action of an **intransitive verb** is limited to the subject of a sentence.

1 **Distinguish between verbs that take direct objects and those that do not.**

A large number of verbs regularly take a direct object and are always transitive; others never take an object and are always intransitive.

TRANSITIVE	The politician kissed the baby. [The transitive verb *kissed* transfers action from *politician* to *baby*.]
INTRANSITIVE	The politician smiled. [An action is performed, but no object is acted upon.]

Many verbs can have both a transitive and an intransitive sense. Such "two-way" verbs will take a direct object or not depending on their use.

INTRANSITIVE	She runs every day. [The verb takes no object.]
TRANSITIVE	She runs a big business. [The verb has changed meaning and now takes an object.]

9d

2 Avoid confusion between the verbs *sit/set, lie/lay, rise/raise.*

vb

Difficulties in distinguishing between transitive and intransitive verbs lead to misuse of *sit/set, lie/lay,* and *rise/raise.* The forms of these verbs are shown in the following box. Because the meaning of the verbs in each pairing is somewhat similar, the verbs are sometimes used interchangeably in speech. In formal writing, however, careful distinctions should be maintained: the first verb in each pair is intransitive—it takes no object, while the second verb is transitive.

Sit is normally an intransitive verb; its action is limited to the subject.

You sit *on the bench.*
          adverb

Set is a transitive verb. It transfers action to an object, which must be present in the sentence.

You set *the papers on the bench.*
          object   **adverb**

Lie is an intransitive verb; its action is limited to the subject.

I lie *on the couch.*
      adverb

Lay is a transitive verb. It transfers action to an object, which must be present in the sentence.

I lay *the pillow on the couch.*
       object   **adverb**

Rise is an intransitive verb; its action is limited to the subject.

I rise *in the morning.*
        adverb

Raise is a transitive verb. It transfers action to an object, which must be present in the sentence.

I raise *the flag each morning.*
         object   **adverb**

The Principal Parts of *sit/set, lie/lay,* and *rise/raise*

BASE FORM	PRESENT TENSE	PAST TENSE	PAST PARTICIPLE	PRESENT PARTICIPLE
sit	sits	sat	sat	sitting
set	sets	set	set	setting
lie	lies	lay	lain	lying
lay	lays	laid	laid	laying
rise	rises	rose	risen	rising
raise	raises	raised	raised	raising

9d

vb

EXERCISE 3

Choose the appropriate form of *sit/set, lie/lay,* or *rise/raise* in these sentences.

Example: A squirrel was (*sit/set*) _____ on a picnic table.

A squirrel was *sitting* on a picnic table.

1. A man walked by and (*sit/set*) _____ a newspaper on a nearby table.
2. He then (*sit/set*) _____ down and unfolded the paper.
3. From one pocket he produced a tomato, which he (*lie/lay*) _____ on the paper.
4. From another pocket came a salt shaker, which he (*rise/raise*) _____ ceremoniously.
5. The squirrel (*rise/raise*) _____ at the scent of food.
6. The man was quick; he had (*lie/lay*) _____ a napkin over the tomato and turned to face the squirrel.

EXERCISE 4

Fill in the blanks in the following sentences with the appropriate form of the verb indicated in parentheses.

Example: The First World War _____ (begin) as an Old World War.

The First World War *began* as an Old World War.

1. Everything about the war expressed the world that Americans _____ (hope) they had _____ (leave) behind.
2. That Old World _____ (be) a battlefield of national ambitions, religious persecutions, and language barriers.
3. European armies had _____ (fight) over whether a nation's boundary should _____ (be) on one side or the other of a narrow river.
4. Old World monarchs had _____ (transfer) land from one flag to another, _____ (barter) people as if they _____ (be) mere real estate.

5. In the 1800s, the English, French, and German empires _____ (expand) across the globe.
6. Each empire _____ (send) out its own merchants and colonial settlers.

TENSE

9e Understanding the uses of verb tenses

9e

t

A verb's tense indicates when an action has occurred or when a subject exists in a given state. There are three simple tenses in English: *past, present,* and *future*. Each has a **perfect** form, which indicates a completed action; each has a **progressive** form, which indicates ongoing action; and each has a **perfect progressive** form, which indicates ongoing action that will be completed at some definite time. The following box summarizes the use of auxiliaries and suffixes in forming verb tenses.

The Tenses of Verbs

Present: I start the engine.
Present perfect: I have started the engine.
Present progressive: I am starting the engine.
Present perfect progressive: I have been starting the engine.

Past: I started the engine.
Past perfect: I had started the engine.
Past progressive: I was starting the engine.
Past perfect progressive: I had been starting the engine.

Future: I will start the engine.
Future perfect: I will have started the engine.
Future progressive: I will be starting the engine.
Future perfect progressive: I will have been starting the engine.

---

1 The varied uses of the present tense

The simple present

A verb's base form is the present-tense form for first- and second-person subjects, singular or plural (*I, we, you* play), as well as plural third-person subjects (*they* play). A present-tense verb for a third-person, singular noun or pronoun ends with the suffix *-s* (*he* plays). The **simple present tense** primarily indicates an action taking place in the writer's present time: *You see these words.* But the present tense in combination with other time-specific words indicates other time references, such as the future.

After I arrive, I will call.

Before I arrive, I will call.

When I arrive, pretend you don't know me.

Next week, Nelson *dances* at the White House.

The historical present

The so-called **historical present tense** is used when referring to actions in an already existing work: a book, a report, an essay, a movie, a television show, an article, and so on. Action in an existing work is always present to a reader or viewer.

In *The Songlines,* Bruce Chatwin *explores* the origins and meanings of Aboriginal "walkabouts" in Australia.

The historical present tense is also used when referring to movies.

In *Blade Runner,* Harrison Ford *plays* a world-weary detective whose job it *is* to disable renegade, human-like robots.

Additionally, the present tense is used to express information that, according to current scientific knowledge or accepted wisdom, is true or likely to be true.

Evidence *indicates* that Alzheimer's patients *show* a decrease in an important brain transmitter substance.

Absence *makes* the heart grow fonder.

She *is* an excellent dentist.

The present tense is also used to indicate a repeated action.

Each Tuesday I *walk* to the bakery.

The present perfect tense

The **present perfect tense** is formed with the auxiliary *have* or *has* and the verb's past participle. This tense indicates an action completed at an indefinite past time.

I *have returned* and she *has left.*

The present perfect tense also indicates an action that, although begun at some past time, continues to have an impact in the present.

He *has* recently *given* support to museums.

The present progressive tense

The **present progressive tense** is formed with the auxiliary *is, am,* or *are* and the verb's present participle. This tense indicates a present, ongoing action that may continue into the future.

She *is considering* a move to Alaska.

The present perfect progressive tense

The **present perfect progressive tense** is formed with the auxiliary *has been* or *have been* and the verb's present participle. This tense indicates an action that began in the past, is continuing in the present, and may continue into the future.

She *has been considering* a move to Alaska.

 ### The past and future tenses

PAST TENSES

The simple past tense

Regular verbs form the **simple past tense** by adding *-d* or *-ed* to the infinitive of the verb; irregular verbs form the past tense in less predictable ways and are best memorized or verified in a dictionary. The simple past tense indicates an action completed at a definite time in the past.

In 1867, the United States *bought* Alaska from Russia for $7.2 million.

The past perfect tense

The **past perfect tense** is formed with the auxiliary *had* and the verb's past participle. This tense indicates a past action that has occurred prior to another action.

Relatively few Americans *had visited* Alaska.

The past progressive tense

The **past progressive tense** is formed with the auxiliary *was* or *were* and the verb's present participle. This tense indicates an ongoing action conducted—and completed—in the past.

Britain, France, and Russia *were vying* for control of Alaska.

The past perfect progressive tense

The **past perfect progressive tense** is formed with the auxiliary *had been* and the verb's present participle. This tense indicates a past, ongoing action completed prior to some other past action.

Before the first Russian settlers, native Americans *had been living* in Alaska.

FUTURE TENSES

The simple future tense

The **simple future tense** consists of the base form of the verb along with the auxiliary *will* for all nouns and pronouns. This tense indicates an action

9e

t

or state of being that will begin in the future. In very formal writing, the first person *I* and *we* have traditionally taken the auxiliary *shall*; increasingly, this word is reserved for opening (first-person) questions: "Shall I?"

> Alaska *will celebrate* fifty years of statehood in the year 2009. I think I *will* attend the celebration. Shall I go? I *shall* attend. (This last sentence is reserved for the most formal writing.)

The future perfect tense

The **future perfect tense** is formed with the verb's past participle and the auxiliary *will have*. This tense indicates an action occurring in the future, prior to some other action.

> By the time the cleanup of the *Exxon Valdez* spill is completed, the federal government *will have spent* hundreds of millions of dollars.

The future progressive tense

The **future progressive tense** is formed with the auxiliary *will be* (or *shall be)* and the verb's present participle. This tense indicates an ongoing action in the future.

> Government officials in Alaska *will be monitoring* oil shipments very carefully.

The future perfect progressive tense

The **future perfect progressive tense** is formed with the auxiliary *will have been* and the verb's present participle. This tense indicates an ongoing action in the future that will occur before some specified future time.

> By the year 2000, the Alaska pipeline *will have been transporting* crude oil for twenty-three years.

9f Sequencing verb tenses

Although it will always have a main verb located in its independent clause, a sentence may have other verbs as well: a complex sentence will have a second verb in its dependent clause, and a sentence with an infinitive or participle (verb forms that function as adjectives, adverbs, and nouns) will also have at least two verbs. Since every verb shows tense, any sentence with more than one verb may indicate actions that occur at different times. Unless the sequence of these actions is precisely set, confusion will result.

UNCLEAR Before I leave, I reported on my plans. [The logic of this sentence suggests that two events (one in each clause) are related, but the time sequencing of the events—one future, the other past—makes the relationship impossible.]

CLEAR   Before I leave, I will report on my trip. [The two actions take place in the future, one action earlier than the other.]

CLEAR   Before I left, I reported on my plans. [The two actions take place in the past, one action earlier than the other.]

1 Sequence the events in complex sentences with care.

A complex sentence joins an independent clause with a dependent clause. Generally, look to the logical relationship between events in the two clauses and choose verb tenses that clarify that relationship—as in the immediately preceding example. Be especially mindful of the sequences in time established by subordinate conjunctions. As shown previously, when the conjunction *before* is paired with a present-tense verb, it establishes a future sense in the sentence's dependent clause. Paired with a past-tense verb, the conjunction establishes not only a past tense but also a definite moment in the past—before and after which other events are sequenced. This same tense-establishing quality is true of other subordinate conjunctions expressing time: *after, once, since,* and *until.* Be sure to make the sense of time in the independent clause consistent with the sense of time established in the dependent clause.

UNCLEAR   After she proposed her amendment, I speak against it. [The subordinate conjunction paired with the past-tense verb establishes a definite past time in the dependent clause. The verb's action in the independent clause takes place in the present time.]

CLEAR   After she proposed her amendment, I spoke against it. [The action in both clauses is now set in the past. One event—*proposing an amendment*—occurs before the other—*speaking;* thus, the subordinate conjunction establishes the sense of the past perfect tense without the need to use the auxiliary *had.*]

Troublesome tense sequences tend to involve complex sentences in which the verb tense of the main clause is either past or past perfect. In the box on page 250 you will find the likely sequences of tenses for such sentences.

2 Choose verb tense in an infinitive phrase based on your choice of verb in the main clause.

An **infinitive phrase** begins with the word *to* placed before a verb such as *see, want, watch, wish, need, go, like,* and *hope.* A present infinitive shows an action that occurs at the same time as or later than the action of the main verb. In the following sentences, the main verb is underlined.

Once Hull House became known as a center of social reform, admiring visitors from all over the world <u>arrived</u> *to see* the work of Jane Addams and her colleagues. [*To see* shows an action at the same time as *arrived.*]

9f

t

9f

t

To establish a relationship between two events, both of which occur in the past:

- Use the simple past tense in the independent clause—and any of the four past tenses in the dependent clause.

    The settlers *lived* where the land *supported* them. [past/past]

    Frank *called* the doctor who *had operated* on him. [past/past perfect]

    Shelly *wrote* her letters while she *was traveling* to Moscow. [past/past progressive]

    We *believed* that she *had been working* on a solution for years. [past/past perfect progressive]

- Use the past perfect tense in the independent clause and the simple past tense in the dependent clause.

    Lucy *had* almost *decided* to quit smoking when she *visited* her sister. [past perfect/past]

To establish a relationship between a past event and a future event:

- Use the past tense in the independent clause and the simple future, future progressive, or simple present tense in the dependent clause.

    We *reserved* tickets for the play that *will open* on Saturday night. [past/future]

    We *reserved* tickets for the play that *will be opening* on Saturday night. [past/future progressive]

    We *reserved* tickets for the play that *opens* on Saturday night. [past/present]

To establish a relationship between a past event and an acknowledged fact or condition:

- Use the simple past tense for the main clause and the simple present tense in the dependent clause.

    The study *concluded* that few people *trust* strangers. [past/present]

    Helen *contacted* the lawyer who *has* the best reputation. [past/present]

    We *found* evidence that the theory *is* correct. [past/present]

- Use the past perfect tense for the main clause and the simple present tense in the dependent clause:

    Smith *had argued* that everyone *needs* basic services. [past perfect/present]

A number of people wanted *to see* Addams properly recognized for her work—perhaps with a Nobel Prize. [*To see Addams* . . . shows a possible action in the future, later than *wanted.*]

A perfect infinitive is formed by placing the auxiliary *have* between the word *to* and the past participle of the verb. A perfect infinitive phrase shows an action that occurs before the action of the main verb.

To have participated in the programs at Hull House profoundly <u>changed</u> the lives of Jane Addams and her co-residents—Julia Lathrop and Florence Kelley. [The *change* in people is past; their *participation* occurred earlier than, and encouraged, the change.]

3 Choose the verb tense of a participle based on your choice of verb in the main clause.

Participles, past and present, function as adjectives in a sentence. A participle in its present (*-ing*) form indicates an action that occurs at the same time as the action of the sentence's main verb. The main verb in each of the following examples is underlined.

Starting with efforts to improve the immediate neighborhood, the Hull House group <u>became</u> involved with a city- and state-wide campaign for better housing. [The efforts at improvement occurred at the same time as the involvement in another campaign. Both actions occur in the past.]

A participle's present perfect form (the past participle preceded by the auxiliary *having*) shows an action that occurs before that of the main verb.

Having given twenty-five years of her life to Hull House, Addams <u>turned</u> in 1915 to the peace movement. [Addams gave of her time to Hull House before turning to the peace movement. Both actions occur in the past.]

A participle in its past form (the base form + *-ed* for regular verbs) shows an action that occurs at the same time as or earlier than the action of the main verb.

Resented for her pacifist views, Addams nonetheless <u>lobbied</u> for an end to international conflict and founded the Women's International League for Peace and Freedom. [Addams was likely resented for her pacifist views both before and during her efforts to end war.]

EXERCISE 5

In each sentence that follows, identify the tense of the italicized verb. Then choose the appropriate tense for subsequent verbs in each sentence.

> *Example:* Personality *is* the unique but stable set of characteristics and behavior that _____ (set) each individual apart from all others.
>
> *is*   present tense   *sets*   present tense

1. Most people *have accepted* the view that human beings _____ (possess) specific traits that _____ (be) fairly constant over time.
2. You *may be* surprised _____ (learn) that until recently a heated debate _____ (exist) in the behavioral sciences over the definition's accuracy.

3. On one side of this debate *were* scientists who _____ (contend) that people _____ (do) not _____ (possess) lasting traits.

4. According to these researchers (whom we *will term* the "anti-personality" camp), behavior _____ (be) shaped largely by external factors.

5. On the other side of the controversy *were* scientists who _____ (hold), equally strongly, that stable traits _____ (do) exist.

6. The weight of scientific opinion *has swung* strongly toward the view that behavior _____ (do) often stem, at least in part, from stable traits.

VOICE

9g Using the active and passive voices

Voice refers to the emphasis a writer gives to the actor in a sentence or to the object acted upon. Because only transitive verbs (see 9d) transfer action from an actor to an object, these verbs exhibit the active and passive voices. The **active voice** emphasizes the actor of a sentence.

Brenda scored the winning goal.

Thomas played the violin.

In each case, an actor, or agent, is *doing* something. In a **passive voice** sentence, the object acted upon is emphasized.

The winning goal was scored by Brenda.

The violin was played by Thomas.

The emphasis on the object of a passive voice sentence is made possible by a rearrangement of words—the movement of the object, which normally follows a verb, to the first position in a sentence. A passive voice construction also requires use of the verb *to be (is, are, was, were, has been, have been)* and the preposition *by.*

The winning goal was scored by Brenda.

In a further transformation of the active voice sentence, you can make the original actor/subject disappear altogether by deleting the prepositional phrase.

The winning goal was scored.

1 Prefer a strong active voice for clear, direct assertions.

In active-voice sentences, people or other agents *do* things. Active-voice sentences attach ownership to actions and help you create a direct, lively attitude toward the subject and the reader. By contrast, passive-voice sentences are inherently wordy and reliant on the weak verb *to be*. Unintended overuse of the passive voice gives prose a flat, dull finish. Unless you have a specific reason for choosing the passive voice (see the following discussion), use the active voice.

You can make a passive-voice sentence active by restoring a subject/verb sequence. Rewording will eliminate both the preposition *by* and the form of *to be*. Note that if an actor of a passive-voice sentence is not named, you will need to provide a name.

9g

vb

PASSIVE
(weak)
In 1858, Stephen Douglas was challenged to a series of historic debates. [The "challenger" is not named.]

ACTIVE
(stronger)
In 1858, Abraham Lincoln challenged Stephen Douglas to a series of historic debates.

PASSIVE
(weak)
The senate race was won by Douglas, but a national reputation was established by Lincoln.

ACTIVE
(stronger)
Douglas won the senate race, but Lincoln established a national reputation.

2 Use the passive voice to emphasize an object or to de-emphasize an unknown subject.

While you should generally prefer the active voice for making direct statements, you will find the passive voice indispensable on two occasions: to emphasize an object and to de-emphasize an unknown subject.

Emphasize an object with a passive construction.

When the subject/actor of a sentence is relatively unimportant compared to what is acted upon, use the passive voice both to de-emphasize the subject/actor and to emphasize the object. The passive voice will shift the subject/actor to a prepositional phrase at a later position in the clause. You may then delete the phrase.

ACTIVE
We require twelve molecules of water to provide twelve atoms of oxygen.

PASSIVE
(subject retained)
Twelve molecules of water are required by us to provide twelve atoms of oxygen.

PASSIVE
(subject deleted)
Twelve molecules of water are required to provide twelve atoms of oxygen.

De-emphasize an unknown subject with the passive voice.

You may de-emphasize or delete an *unknown* subject by using the passive voice. Instead of writing an indefinite subject/actor (such as *someone* or *people*) into a sentence, use the passive voice to shift the subject/actor to a prepositional phrase. You may then delete the phrase.

ACTIVE	People mastered the use of fire some 400,000 years ago.
PASSIVE (subject retained)	The use of fire was mastered by people some 400,000 years ago.
PASSIVE (subject deleted)	The use of fire was mastered some 400,000 years ago.

vb

> **EXERCISE 6**
>
> Change the passive-voice sentences that follow to the active voice and change active-voice sentences to passive. Invent a subject if need be for the active-voice sentences.
>
> *Example:* Stocks and securities are bought by an arbitrageur and then quickly sold for a profit. [The passive voice involves two verbs: *"are bought . . .* and *. . . sold."*]
>
> An arbitrageur buys stocks and securities and then quickly sells them for a profit. [changed to active voice]
>
> 1. In the 1980s, an increase in the number of stock broker arbitrageurs was seen.
> 2. Originally, companies were invested in by arbitrageurs after a merger was announced.
> 3. Investments were based on the relationship between the stock prices of the two firms involved and the probabilities that the two firms would merge.
> 4. In the mid-1980s, investments were made in firms that *might* be candidates for mergers.
> 5. Arbitrageurs hoped to make a profit on the price increases at the time of the merger announcement.
> 6. Rumors of impending mergers were therefore very important and were listened to carefully.
> 7. Conflicts of interest arose because the investment banking firms that employed arbitrageurs also advised firms involved in mergers.

MOOD

9h Understanding the uses of mood

The **mood** of a verb indicates the writer's judgment as to whether a statement is a fact, a command, or an occurrence contrary to fact. In the

indicative mood, a writer states a fact, opinion, or question. Most of our writing and speech is confined to the indicative mood.

> The mayor has held office for eight years. [fact]
>
> The mayor is not especially responsive. [opinion]
>
> Did you vote for the mayor? [question]

In the **imperative mood,** a writer gives a command, the subject of which is "you," the person being addressed. In this book, for example, the imperative addresses readers with specific guidelines for writing or making revisions. An imperative uses the verb in its base form. Often, the subject of a command is omitted from a sentence but occasionally it is expressed directly.

9h

vb

> Follow me!
>
> Do not touch that switch.
>
> Don't you touch that switch!

By using the **subjunctive mood,** a writer shows that he or she does not believe an action or situation to be factual. With a subjunctive verb, a writer makes a recommendation or expresses a wish, requirement, or statement contrary to fact. The **present subjunctive** uses the base form (infinitive) of the verb, for all subjects.

> I recommend that he *develop* his math skills before applying.
>
> I recommend that they *develop* their skills.

The **past subjunctive** uses the past-tense form of the verb—or, in the case of *to be*—the form *were*.

> If the management *assumed* traveling costs, the team would not grumble.
>
> He wished he *were* four inches taller.

The **past perfect subjunctive** uses the past perfect form of the verb.

> If I *had been* faster, I would have made the team.
>
> I wish I *had prepared* more thoroughly.

1   Use the subjunctive mood with an *if* construction.

When an *if* clause expresses a condition contrary to fact, use the subjunctive mood. In a subjunctive *if* construction, the modal auxiliary *would, could, might,* or *should* is used in the main clause. (See 9c for a discussion of modals.)

FAULTY   If Tom was more considerate, he would have called. [Clearly, Tom was not considerate (he did not call), and so the indicative or "factual" mood is at odds with the meaning of the sentence.]

SUBJUNCTIVE   If Tom *were* more considerate, he would have called.

SUBJUNCTIVE   If I *were* elected, I might raise taxes.

NOTE: When an *if* construction is used to establish a cause-and-effect relationship, the writer assumes that the facts presented in a sentence either are true or could very possibly be true; therefore the writer uses an indicative ("factual") mood with normal subject-verb agreement.

FAULTY If I were late, start without me.

REVISED If I am late, start without me. [The lateness is assumed to be a likely or possible fact.]

9h

vb

2 Use the subjunctive mood with *as if* and *as though* constructions.

When an *as if* or *as though* construction sets up a purely hypothetical comparison that attempts to explain or characterize, use the subjunctive mood.

FAULTY She swims as if she *was* part fish. [But since the speaker knows she is not, the indicative ("factual") mood is inconsistent.]

REVISED She swims as if she *were* part fish.

SUBJUNCTIVE He writes quickly, as though he *were* running out of time. [The sentence assumes that he is not running out of time.]

3 Revise to eliminate auxiliary *would* or *could* in subjunctive clauses with *if*, *as if*, or *as though*.

In subjunctive constructions like those shown previously, the modal auxiliary verbs *would*, *could*, or *should* may appear in the main clause to help indicate that its action is contrary to fact or is conditional. The auxiliaries *would* and *could* cannot appear in the *if* clause, however, since this creates a kind of "double conditional"; these auxiliaries must be replaced with the appropriate subjunctive form.

FAULTY If the mate at the wheel *would have* been alerted, the oil spill would have been avoided.

REVISED If the mate at the wheel *had* been alerted, the oil spill would have been avoided.

FAULTY He could have acted as though he *could have* seen the reef.

REVISED He could have acted as though he *had* seen it.

4 Use the subjunctive mood with a *that* construction.

Use the subjunctive mood with subordinate *that* constructions expressing a requirement, request, urging, belief, wish, recommendation, or doubt. In each of these constructions, the word *that* may be omitted.

The rules require that we *be* present.

I wish that I *were* a painter.

We recommend that he *accept* the transfer.

We recommend he *accept* it.

EXERCISE 7

Use the subjunctive mood, as appropriate, in revising the sentences that follow.

> *Example:* If I was a carpenter, I would have a trade and a steady job.
>
> If I *were* a carpenter, I would have a trade and a steady job.

1. First-semester freshman students are often very earnest about their studies, as if they are resolved not to let the social attractions of college life drag them down.
2. One unwritten rule of fraternity and sorority life requires that one talks like a member of the group.
3. If my analysis were right, then we can begin the project next week.
4. The professor recommends that she takes the course.
5. If I would have prepared for the exam, I wouldn't have flunked.

9h

vb

CHAPTER 10

Agreement

Agreement is a term that describes two significant relationships in a sentence: the relationship between a subject and verb and that between a pronoun and its antecedent. These elements *always* occur in pairs. The subject of a sentence must be paired with a verb to make a complete assertion, and a pronoun derives meaning from its relation to the noun, or antecedent, that it renames. If you change one element in these pairs, you must often change the corresponding element:

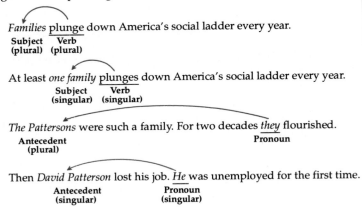

Families plunge down America's social ladder every year.

Subject   **Verb**
(plural)   **(plural)**

At least *one family* plunges down America's social ladder every year.

         Subject   **Verb**
         (singular)   **(singular)**

The Pattersons were such a family. For two decades *they* flourished.

   Antecedent   **Pronoun**
   (plural)

Then *David Patterson* lost his job. *He* was unemployed for the first time.

     Antecedent   **Pronoun**
     (singular)   **(singular)**

This chapter is divided into two broad sections that will help you to make subjects agree with verbs and pronouns agree with antecedents.

SUBJECT-VERB AGREEMENT

Subjects and verbs must agree in both number and person. The term **number** indicates whether a noun is singular (denoting one person, place, or thing) or plural (denoting more than one). The term **person** identifies the subject of a sentence as the same person who is speaking (the first person), someone who is spoken to (the second person), or someone who is being spoken about (the third person). Both pronouns and nouns are classified according to person.

	First-person subject	Second-person subject	Third-person subject
Singular	I	you	he, she, it
Plural	we	you	they

Agreement between a verb and first- or second-person pronoun subject does not vary. The pronouns *I*, *we*, and *you* take verbs *without* the letter *s*.

I walk.   We walk.   You walk.

I scream, you scream, we scream—for ice cream.

Problems of confusion sometimes occur, however, in the forms of agreement for third-person subjects and verbs.

10a

agr

10a Make a third-person subject agree in number with its verb.

He, she, they do this. The suffix -*s* or -*es*, affixed to a verb, indicates action for a singular third-person subject; the suffix -*s* or -*es*, affixed to most third-person nouns, indicates a plural.

The "tradeoff" principle

To remember the basic forms of third-person agreement in the present tense, you may find it helpful to visualize something like a balanced tradeoff of -*s* endings between most noun subjects and their verbs: if one ends with an -*s*, then the other does not. Thus if the noun subject is singular and lacks an -*s* ending, then it is the singular verb that takes the -*s* ending. If the subject is a noun that forms an -*s* plural, then it takes the -*s* and the plural verb loses the ending.

SINGULAR   A boy__ hikes. A girl__ swims. A kid__ does it.

PLURAL   The boys hike__. The girls swim__. Kids do__ it.

If a noun or pronoun has a plural sense, even if it does not end with an -*s*, (e.g., children, oxen, geese, they, these), the tradeoff principle still applies. Since the noun or pronoun is plural (just as it would be if it were a word made plural with an -*s* ending), the verb is also plural—that is, the verb loses its -*s* ending.

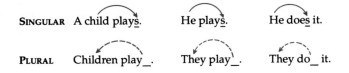

SINGULAR   A child plays.   He plays.   He does it.

PLURAL   Children play_.   They play_.   They do_ it.

Revising nonstandard verb and noun forms to observe -s and -es endings

10a

agr

In rapid conversation people sometimes skip over the -s or -es endings of verbs that are paired with singular nouns. In some English dialects, the base (or infinitive) form of the verb is used for singular nouns. Standard academic English, however, requires that writers observe subject-verb agreement.

NONSTANDARD	He read the book.
STANDARD	He reads the book.
NONSTANDARD	She do it.
STANDARD	She does it.

Determining the Number of a Third-Person Subject

One way to establish the number of a third-person subject is to apply a simple test. Any noun in the third person can be replaced by a corresponding third-person pronoun: the singular pronouns *he, she,* or *it,* or the plural *they.* When you are uncertain about the number of a noun subject, reread the sentence and, based on its context, replace the subject with a third-person pronoun. Read the sentence once more. In most cases, you can fairly easily choose an appropriate verb that agrees with the pronoun.

UNSURE?   *The experience of downwardly mobile people* (*seem* or *seems*?) a strange subject for an anthropologist.

REPLACE   *It* <u>seems</u> a strange subject for an anthropologist. [Replacing the subject *experience* and its modifying phrase with the singular *it* clarifies the need for a singular verb.]

1   A subject agrees with its verb regardless of whether a phrase or clause separates them.

Often a subject may be followed by a lengthy phrase or clause that comes between it and the verb, confusing the basic pattern of agreement. To clarify the matching of the subject with the verb, mentally strike out or ignore phrases or clauses separating them. Verbs in the following examples are underlined; subjects are italicized.

Downward mobility—because of its severe impact on families—poses an immediate and pressing problem. [The verb *poses* agrees with its singular subject, *downward mobility*, not with the plural *families* in the interrupting phrase.]

Each of my friends in three nearby towns has heard this. [The prepositional phrases must be ignored to make the singular *each* agree with *has*.]

NOTE: Phrases beginning with "in addition to," "along with," "as well as," "together with," or "accompanied by" may come between a subject and its verb. Although they add material, these phrases do *not* create a plural subject; they must be mentally stricken out to determine the correct number of the verb.

10a

agr

FAULTY *The anthropologist,* as well as social researchers such as statisticians and demographers, are always looking for indicators of change in status. [The interrupting phrase before the verb gives a false impression of a plural subject.]

REVISED *The anthropologist,* as well as social researchers such as statisticians and demographers, is always looking for indicators of change in status. [The singular subject *anthropologist* agrees with the singular verb.]

2 A compound subject linked by the conjunction *and* is in most cases plural.

When a compound subject linked by *and* refers to two or more people, places, or things, it is usually considered plural.

PLURAL *Statistical information* and *the analysis based upon it* allow an anthropologist to piece together significant cultural patterns. [The compound subject has a plural sense. Thus the verb, *allow*, is plural.]

Exception: When a compound subject refers to a single person, place, or thing, it is considered singular.

SINGULAR Whatever culture she studies, *this anthropologist* and *researcher* concerns herself with the relations among husbands, wives, children, kin, and friends. [The compound subject has a singular sense—it refers to one person and can be replaced by the singular pronoun *she*. Thus the verb, *concerns*, is singular.]

3 When parts of a compound subject are linked by the conjunction *or* or *nor*, the verb should agree in number with the closest part of the subject.

When all parts of the compound subject are the same number, agreement with the verb is fairly straightforward.

Either John or *Maria* sings today.

Either the Smiths or the *Taylors* sing today.

When one part of the compound subject is singular and another plural there can be confusion; the subject nearest the verb determines the number of the verb. If the nearest subject is singular, the verb is singular.

SINGULAR According to popular wisdom, either poor habits or *ineptitude* is responsible when an individual fails to succeed in American culture. [The singular subject, *ineptitude*, is nearest to the verb; therefore the verb, *is*, is singular.]

When the subject nearest the verb is plural, the verb is plural.

PLURAL Neither the downwardly mobile individual nor the *people* surrounding him realize that losing a job is often due to impersonal economic factors. [The plural subject, *people*, is nearest to the verb; therefore the verb, *realize*, is plural.]

NOTE: Subject/verb agreement in this situation may appear to be mismatched unless the plural part of the compound subject is placed closest to the verb. Avoid such awkwardness by revising to place the plural part closest to the verb.

4 **Most indefinite pronouns have a singular sense and take a singular verb.**

Indefinite pronouns (such as *any* and *each*) do not have specific antecedents—they rename no particular person, place, or thing and thus raise questions about subject-verb agreement. The following indefinite pronouns have a singular sense:

another	every	none, no one
any	everybody	nothing
anybody	everyone	one
anyone	everything	somebody
anything	more	someone
each	much	something
each one	neither	
either	nobody	

SINGULAR For every five men working in America, *one* skids down the occupational ladder sometime during his career.

SINGULAR While our culture provides stories that give meaning and shape to the lives of the upwardly mobile, *nothing* of this sort is available to once-prosperous individuals who suddenly lose their positions.

The indefinite pronouns *both, ones,* and *others* have a plural sense and take a plural verb.

PLURAL Occasionally, the downwardly mobile are heroes who find ways to rise above their circumstances; *others* are lost souls, wandering the social landscape without direction.

10a

agr

The indefinite pronouns *all, any, more, many, enough, none, some, few,* and *most* have a singular or plural sense, depending on the meaning of a sentence.

Try substituting *he, she, it, we,* or *they* for the indefinite pronoun. The context of a sentence will give you clues about the number of its subject.

PLURAL   After losing their jobs, *some* people <u>are</u> highly self-critical. [*Some* (people) has a plural sense—it can be replaced by the pronoun *they* and thus takes a plural verb, *are.*]

SINGULAR   Self-doubt is a common reaction among the downwardly mobile; at least *some* of this reaction <u>is</u> unwarranted. [*Some* can be replaced by *it,* has a singular sense, and thus takes a singular verb, *is.*]

10a

agr

5 | **Collective nouns have a plural or a singular sense, depending on the meaning of a sentence.**

When a collective noun, such as *audience, band, bunch, committee, crew, crowd, faculty, family, group, staff, team,* and *tribe,* refers to a single unit, the sense of the noun is singular and the noun takes a singular verb. The context of a sentence will give you clues about the number of its subject.

SINGULAR   *The tribe* of the downwardly mobile <u>consists</u> of four subgroups: white-collar managers; workers with special expertise (such as air-traffic controllers); blue-collar workers in the middle class; and divorced women who were white-collar and middle-class during marriage. [*Tribe* is a single unit, subdivided; thus, it has a singular sense and takes a singular verb.]

When the collective noun refers to individuals and their separate actions within a group, the sense of the noun is plural and the noun takes a plural verb.

PLURAL   *The tribe* of the downwardly mobile <u>have</u> diverse reactions to losing their jobs, depending on their subgroup membership. [*Tribe* here emphasizes the action of individual members; thus, it has a plural sense and takes a plural verb.]

6 | **Nouns plural in form but singular in sense take singular verbs.**

The nouns *athletics, economics, mathematics, news, physics,* and *politics* all end with the letter *-s,* but they nonetheless denote a single activity. **Note:** *Politics* can be considered plural, depending on the sense of a sentence.

News of a layoff <u>causes</u> some people to feel alone and blame themselves.

Politics often <u>comes</u> into play. [*Politics* has a singular sense and takes a singular verb.]

7 A linking verb agrees in number with its subject.

In a sentence with a linking verb, identify the singular or plural subject when deciding the number of the verb. Disregard any phrase or clause that interrupts the subject and verb; also disregard the subject complement *following* the linking verb.

SINGULAR   According to Adam Smith's laissez-faire doctrine, *the cause* of downward mobility is market conditions. [The singular verb, *is,* agrees in number with the singular subject, *the cause,* not with the plural subject complement, *market conditions.*]

10a

agr

PLURAL   *Market conditions,* according to the laissez-faire doctrine, are the cause of downward mobility. [The plural verb, *are,* agrees in number with the plural subject, *market conditions*—not with the singular subject complement, *the cause,* or with the singular noun, *doctrine.*]

8 In sentences with inverted word order, a verb should agree in number with its subject.

Typically, the subject of a sentence in English is placed before a verb. When this order is reversed, the subject and verb continue to agree in number.

NORMAL   *Two reasons* are evident for abandoning the laissez-faire response to downward mobility. [The subject of the sentence, *two reasons,* is plural; therefore the verb is plural.]

REARRANGED   Here are *two reasons* for abandoning the laissez-faire response to downward mobility.

SINGULAR   Here is *a reason* for abandoning the laissez-faire response to downward mobility.

Expletives

It and *there* are **expletives,** words that fill gaps in a sentence when normal word order is reversed (see 7a-11). Disregard the expletive *there* when determining whether the verb will agree in number with a singular or plural subject.

PLURAL   There are *two reasons* for abandoning that approach. [*There* is disregarded; the verb, *are,* agrees with the plural subject, *reasons.*]

SINGULAR   There is at least *one* good *reason.*

Notice that the expletive *it* is always followed by a singular verb.

SINGULAR   It is a very good *idea* to give up that approach.

Questions

Inverting a sentence's word order is one method of forming a question. The relocated verb must still agree in number with the subject.

QUESTION <u>Does</u> *he* really <u>want</u> to hold on to that idea? [The verb *does want* agrees with the subject *he*.]

SINGULAR What <u>is</u> *the cost* to him of abandoning it?

PLURAL What <u>are</u> *the costs* aside from that?

 9 The verb of a dependent clause introduced by the pronoun *which, that, who,* or *whom* should agree in number with the pronoun's antecedent.

In such a dependent clause, both the pronoun subject (*which, that,* etc.) and verb are dependent for their number on an antecedent in the main clause. The number of that antecedent determines the number of both the pronoun subject and the verb in the dependent clause.

PLURAL In the long run society suffers from the *costs* of downward mobility, *which* <u>are</u> measured in damaged psyches more than in dollars and cents. [The relative pronoun, *which,* renames the plural antecedent, *costs*; the relative pronoun has a plural sense and the verb following must be plural.]

SINGULAR *The ethic* of the American workplace, *which* in many ways <u>is</u> a definition of America, will be undermined when the mutual commitment between workers and employers dissolves. [The relative pronoun, *which,* renames the singular antecedent, *ethic*; the relative pronoun has a singular sense and the verb following must be singular.]

10 Phrases and clauses that function as subjects are treated as singular and take singular verbs.

Often a noun clause, or a phrase with a gerund or infinitive, will act as the subject of a sentence. Such a construction is always regarded as a singular element in the sentence.

SINGULAR *To live in a society that closely connects occupation to self-worth* <u>places</u> us at emotional risk when we lose our jobs. [The long infinitive phrase that functions as the subject of this sentence has a singular sense. It therefore takes a singular verb, *places*.]

SINGULAR *That honest effort and ability can go unrewarded* <u>strikes</u> many as unfair. [The noun clause introduced by *that* functions as the subject of this sentence and takes a singular verb, *strikes*.]

11 Titled works, key words used as terms, and companies are treated as singular in number and take singular verbs.

Titles of works, names of companies or corporations, underlined or italicized words referred to as words, numbers, and units of money are regarded as singular entities in a sentence and take singular verbs.

10a

agr

SINGULAR   *Falling from Grace: The Experience of Downward Mobility in the American Middle Class* <u>is</u> the title of Katherine Newman's book.

SINGULAR   *Savage dislocation* <u>is</u> the term Newman uses to describe the experience of the downwardly mobile.

SINGULAR   *Fifty thousand dollars* per year <u>provides</u> for a solidly middle-class life-style; unemployment checks do not.

EXERCISE 1

In the following sentences, determine whether a subject is singular or plural. Choose the correct form in parentheses and be able to explain your choice.

Example: How (do/does) we get other people to agree with us?

How *do* we get other people to agree with us? [The subject of the sentence is the plural pronoun, *we*. Even though the auxiliary part of the verb, *do*, is placed before the subject to form a question, the full verb (including the auxiliary) and the subject must agree in number.]

1. One reason for making a purchase (is/are) a buyer's emotional needs.
2. There (is/are) no single method that (assure/assures) success in persuading others; still, several methods (seem/seems) helpful.
3. One effective way of getting a "yes" from other people (is/are) to get them to like us.
4. Flattery, an extremely common tactic for gaining compliance, (has/have) a long history.
5. Both flattering people and getting them to talk about themselves (work/works) in surprisingly consistent ways.
6. Maintaining high levels of eye contact (is/are) also an effective strategy.
7. The cautious and wary individual (has/have) little patience for insincere displays of good will.
8. But even the cautious (appreciate/appreciates) techniques that (is/are) skillfully blended.

PRONOUN-ANTECEDENT AGREEMENT

An **antecedent** is a word—usually a noun, sometimes a pronoun—that is renamed by a pronoun. Pronouns in the following examples are underlined and antecedents are italicized.

Van Leeuwenhoek called the microorganisms that he found everywhere
Antecedent   **Pronoun**
in vast numbers "little animals."

A pronoun's antecedent must be clearly identified in order for the
pronoun itself to have a meaningful reference (see chapter 14 on pronoun
reference); a pronoun and antecedent must also agree in *number, person,* and
gender. (See the definitions before 7a.) **Gender** refers to whether a noun or
pronoun is feminine, masculine, or neuter.

Mary flies planes.	She flies planes. (feminine)
Bob rides trolleys.	He rides trolleys. (masculine)
A trolley runs on tracks.	It runs on tracks. (neuter)

10b

In most cases, as in the preceding examples, a pronoun is easily matched to
its antecedent in terms of person (first, second, or third), number (plural or
singular), and gender (masculine or feminine). At times, however, the choice
of the right pronoun requires careful attention.

agr

10b Pronouns and their antecedents should agree in number.

Of the three components that determine pronoun selection, agreement
in number causes the most difficulty—for the same reason that subject-verb
agreement is sometimes difficult: the *number* of a noun (either as subject or
antecedent) is not always clear. The following conventions will help you to
determine whether an antecedent is singular or plural.

1 A compound antecedent linked by the conjunction *and* is usually plural.

PLURAL   In all early attempts at classification, living things were separated into
two major groups—*the plant kingdom* and *the animal kingdom.* These were
then subdivided in various ways. [The compound antecedent has a
plural sense; therefore the pronoun renaming it is plural in form.]

PLURAL   In the 4th century B.C., *Aristotle* made a study of the animal kingdom and
Theophrastus studied plants; their systems for classifying animals and
plants began the scientific effort of classifying all living things. [The
compound antecedent has a plural sense; therefore the pronoun renaming it is plural in form.]

EXCEPTIONS: When a compound antecedent with parts joined by the
conjunction *and* has a singular sense, use a singular pronoun.

SINGULAR   *An English naturalist* and *writer,* probably the first to call groupings of
like organisms *species,* used his new system of classification to identify
more than 18,000 different types of plants. [The compound antecedent
refers to one person; therefore the pronoun renaming it is singular.]

When an antecedent joined by the conjunction *and* is preceded by the word *every* or *each,* use a singular pronoun.

SINGULAR   Each *visible organism* and *microscopic organism* has <u>its</u> own distinctive, two-word Latin name according to the system designed by Carolus Linnaeus in the early eighteenth century.

10b

agr

2 When parts of a compound antecedent are linked by the conjunction *or* or *nor,* a pronoun should agree in number with the closest part of the antecedent.

This pattern of agreement with *or* or *nor* follows the same convention as with subject-verb agreement (10a-3).

SINGULAR   Of the several approaches to classifying organisms in nature, neither the traditional two-kingdom systems nor the recent five-kingdom *system* is complete in <u>its</u> account. [The pronoun is closest to the singular "system" and so agrees in the singular.]

NOTE: Avoid awkward pronoun use by revising to place the plural part of the compound antecedent closest to the pronoun.

REVISED   Of the several approaches to classifying organisms in nature, neither the five-kingdom system nor the traditional two-kingdom *systems* are complete in <u>their</u> accounts. [The plural part of the antecedent is revised to fall closest to the pronoun; the sentence is no longer awkward in its agreement.]

3 Make pronouns agree in number with indefinite pronoun antecedents.

Indefinite pronouns (such as *each, anyone,* and *everyone*) do not refer to particular persons, places, or things. Most often, an indefinite pronoun used as an antecedent will have a singular sense. When it does, rename it with a singular pronoun.

SINGULAR   *Each* of the millions of organisms now living has <u>its</u> own defining features.

When an indefinite pronoun (such as *both* or *others*) functions as an antecedent and has a plural sense, rename it with a plural pronoun.

PLURAL   Some organisms are readily classified as animal or plant; *others,* most often the simplest single-cell organisms, find <u>themselves</u> classified in different ways, depending on the classification system used.

A few indefinite pronouns (such as *some, more,* or *most*) can have a singular or a plural sense, depending on the context of a sentence. Determine the number of an indefinite pronoun antecedent before selecting a pronoun replacement.

PLURAL   *Some* of the simplest living organisms defy classification, by virtue of their diversity. [*Some* has a plural sense.]

SINGULAR   *Some* of the recent research made possible by microscopes is startling in its findings that certain unicellular organisms like the euglena have both plantlike and animal-like characteristics. [*Some* has a singular sense.]

  4 **Make pronouns agree in number with collective noun antecedents.**

10c

Collective nouns will be singular or plural depending on the meaning of a sentence. When a collective noun such as *audience, band, group,* or *team* refers to a *single unit,* the sense of the noun as an antecedent is singular and takes a singular pronoun.

ww/
agr

SINGULAR   A *group* of similar organisms that interbreed in nature is called a species and is given its own distinct Latin name. [*Group* has a singular sense.]

When a collective noun refers to individuals and their *separate actions* within a group, the sense of the noun as an antecedent is plural and takes a plural pronoun.

PLURAL   Human beings are the only *group* of primates who walk on two legs, without the aid of their hands. [*Group* has a plural sense.]

10c **Rename indefinite antecedents with gender-appropriate pronouns.**

Indefinite pronouns that have a singular sense and refer to people (as opposed to places or things) will likely refer to both males *and* females. Traditionally, the **generic *he*** or *his* was used to rename an indefinite antecedent, such as *each* or various nouns without specific gender identity.

OFFENSIVE   To some extent, *a biologist* must decide for himself which system of classification he will use.

The use of *himself* and *he* in this sentence would exclude female biologists, of whom there are many. In addition to being inaccurate, this exclusion will offend anyone sensitive to the ways in which language can be used as a weapon as well as a tool. Writers have available five techniques for avoiding unintentional sexism.

1. **Use the constructions *he or she, his or her,* and *him or her* in referring to an indefinite pronoun or noun.** Choose this option when the antecedent of a pronoun must have a singular sense. Realize, however, that some readers will object to the *he or she* device as cumbersome. The variants *(s)he* and *he/she* are considered equally cumbersome. The *he or*

she device can work, provided it is not overused in any one sentence or paragraph:

AWKWARD   To some extent, *a biologist* must decide for <u>him or herself</u> which system of classification <u>he or she</u> will use.

REVISED   To some extent, *a biologist* must decide which system of classification <u>he or she</u> will use.

2. **Make a pronoun's antecedent plural.** If the accuracy of a sentence will permit a plural antecedent, use this device to avoid unintentional sexism in pronoun selection.

PLURAL   To some extent, *biologists* must decide for <u>themselves</u> which system of classification *they* will use.

3. **Use the passive voice to avoid gender-specific pronouns—but only if it is appropriate to de-emphasize a subject.** Note, however, that using the passive voice creates its own problems of vague reference. (See 9g-2 and 17b-1.)

NEUTRAL   It is every biologist's responsibility to specify which system of classification *is being used.*

4. **Reconstruct the entire statement so as to avoid the problem.** Often it is easier to rewrite sentences to avoid pronouns altogether.

NEUTRAL   When choosing among competing systems of classification, the biologist makes a choice that greatly affects later work both in the field and in the lab. [*Later work* is left without a limiting, gender-specific modifier.]

5. **Link gender assignments to specific indefinite antecedents.** Some writers will arbitrarily assign a masculine identity to one indefinite antecedent and a feminine identity to another. The gender assignments are then maintained throughout a document.

ALTERNATE GENDER ASSIGNMENTS   A *biologist* must decide which system of classification <u>she</u> will use. An *anthropologist* must also choose when selecting the formal, stylistic, and technological attributes <u>he</u> will use in distinguishing ancient objects from one another.

Writers can combine two or more of these methods within a paragraph. The best way to avoid offensive gender-specific references or omissions is to become sensitive to the language you read and write. Be aware that language can be used to exclude and marginalize as well as to empower. For more discussion on gender reference, see 21g.

EXERCISE 2

Revise the following sentences to ensure agreement between pronouns and antecedents. Eliminate uses of, or avoid using, the generic *he.* Place a check before the sentences in which a pronoun agrees in number with its antecedent.

Example: Like land mammals, marine mammals have ears which it uses to receive impressions of its environment.

Like land mammals, marine mammals have ears which *they use* to receive impressions of *their* environment.

1. The clicks, groans, and creaking of whales have impressed researchers with its variations.
2. A dolphin produces his sound by blowing air through the nasal passageway and over two flap-like structures in his blowhole.
3. Anyone who wants to communicate with dolphins must turn his attention to patterns of whistles, squeaks, and yelps that constitute his vocabulary.
4. When dolphins are angry, they bark.
5. The neurophysiologist and marine mammal specialist John Lilly has spent a great deal of their time attempting to communicate with dolphins.
6. Each mother dolphin communicates with their baby by whistles and barks.

10c

ww/ agr

EXERCISE 3

Revise the following gender-biased sentences so that they do not stereotype males or females or otherwise restrict references to males. When you make singular nouns plural, other words in the sentence will change.

Example: The behaviorist theory in psychology assumes that man's response to his environment is similar to the response of other animals.

The behaviorist theory in psychology assumes that humans respond to their environment in the same ways that other animals do.

1. Each operator answers her phone.
2. As part of her job, a nurse prepares injections for her patients.
3. A miner would take a canary below ground to make sure the air was safe for him to breathe.
4. A pilot, today, takes much of his training in flight simulators.
5. Recent research has suggested a relationship between the amount of time a child watches television and his later performance in school.
6. An astronaut's wife must endure a great deal of stress.

EXERCISE 4

Revise the following paragraph to ensure agreement between subject and verb and between pronoun and antecedent. Also, revise any sentence in which the generic *he* is used.

A manager or others who delivers bad news performs two functions. First, he delivers the news and makes certain the message is received and understood. To accomplish this task require an ability to be both blunt and supportive. This trait allows the giver of news to fulfill his responsibilities to management and at the same time protect workers when he or she is about to be laid off. Either the person delivering bad news or his colleagues has as one of his responsibilities the job of helping the worker cope with the event. The role of compassionate helper involve identifying resources and writing letters of recommendation, which can sometimes take the sting out of a dismissal, especially ones caused by downturns in the economy and not by the worker's individual performance.

CHAPTER 11

Adjectives and Adverbs

Adjectives and adverbs are **modifiers**—*descriptive* words, phrases, or clauses that enliven sentences with vivid detail. Compare two versions of a sentence about Nicholas II, Tsar of imperial Russia in 1894:

> Nicholas II ruled Russia.

> From the Baltic city of St. Petersburg, Nicholas II now ruled an imperial Russia covering one-sixth of the globe.

In the second sentence, the phrase *from the Baltic city of St. Petersburg* is a prepositional phrase that functions as an adverb by modifying the verb *rule.* Within the phrase, we find the single-word adjective *Baltic.* The verb is modified by the single-word adverb *now,* while the noun *Russia* is modified by the adjective *imperial* as well as by the adjectival clause beginning with *covering.* As you can see from reading this pair of sentences, most of the interest and substance of writing is to be found in modifiers. The sentence comes alive with detail once modifiers are added to the basic skeleton of subject and verb. The adjective and adverb modifiers of a sentence typically come all in a mix—as single words, phrases, and clauses. In chapter 7 you learned how phrases and clauses function as modifiers. But even when dealing with one-word modifiers, as in this chapter, you can see that the effectiveness of modifiers depends on keeping straight the two main types: adjectives and adverbs.

11a Distinguishing between adjectives and adverbs

Some basic distinctions between the use of adjectives and adverbs are summarized in the following box.

Distinguishing Adjectives from Adverbs

An **adjective** modifies a noun or pronoun and answers these questions:
Which: The *latest* news arrived.
What kind: An *insignificant* difference remained.
How many: The *two* sides would resolve their differences.

(continued)

Distinguishing Adjectives from Adverbs (continued)

An **adverb** modifies a verb and answers these questions:
When: *Tomorrow,* the temperature will drop.
How: The temperature will drop *sharply.*
How often: Weather patterns change *frequently.*
Where: The weather patterns *here* change frequently.

An **adverb** also modifies adjectives, adverbs, and entire clauses:
Modifying an adjective: An *especially* large group enrolled.
Modifying a clause: *Consequently,* the registrar closed the course.
Modifying an adverb: Courses at this school *almost* never get closed.

11a

ad

When choosing between an adjective and adverb form for a sentence, identify the word being modified and determine its part of speech. Then follow the conventions presented in this chapter.

1 Identifying and using adjectives

An **adjective** modifies a noun or pronoun by answering these questions: **which?** the *tall* child; **what kind?** the *artistic* child; **how many?** *five* children. Pure adjectives are not derived from other words: *large, small, simple, difficult, thick, thin, cold, hot.* Many adjectives, however, are derived from nouns.

BASE NOUN	SUFFIX	ADJECTIVE
science	-ic	scientific
region	-al	regional
book	-ish	bookish

Adjectives are also derived from verbs.

BASE VERB	SUFFIX	ADJECTIVE
respect	-ful	respectful
respect	-ed	respected (past participle)
respect	-ing	respecting (present participle)
demonstrate	-ive	demonstrative
hesitate	-ant	hesitant

Writers frequently build up their desired meanings by taking a word and adapting its base form, thereby converting the word into the part of speech needed for a new sentence.

The audience maintained a (respect + ful) silence.

The (region + al) conference was about to begin.

Placement

A single-word adjective is usually placed before the word it modifies. On occasion an adjective can appear after a noun or pronoun—which is usually the case when the adjective is formed by a phrase or clause.

The speaker was received with *enthusiastic* applause.

The speaker, *bookish* and *hesitant,* approached the podium.

2 ### Identifying and using adverbs

11a

ad

An **adverb** modifies a verb by answering several questions: **When?** *Yesterday,* the child sang. **How?** The child sang *beautifully.* **How often?** The child sings *regularly.* **Where?** The child sang *here.* Adverbs modify adjectives: The child sang an *extremely* intricate melody. Adverbs can modify other adverbs: The child sings *almost* daily. Certain adverbs can modify entire sentences: *Consequently,* the child's voice has improved.

Pure adverbs are not derived from other words: *again, almost, always, never, here, there, now, often, seldom, well.* Many adverbs, however, are formed from adjectives (some of which took their meaning from nouns or verbs). These adverbs may be formed simply by adding the suffix *-ly* to adjectives.

ADJECTIVE	ADD *-ly*	ADVERB
beautiful		beautifully
strange		strangely
clever		cleverly
respectful		respectfully

However, an *-ly* ending alone is not sufficient to establish a word as an adverb, since certain adjectives show this ending: a friend*ly* conversation, a love*ly* afternoon. Any standard dictionary will distinguish between the adjective and adverb forms of a word. (Look for the abbreviations **adj.** and **adv.**) Thousands of words in our language have both adjective and adverb forms. Consider the noun *grace,* defined by the *American Heritage Dictionary* as "seemingly effortless beauty or charm of movement, form, or proportion." *Graceful* and *gracious* are adjectives, and *graciously, gracefully,* and *gracelessly* are adverbs.

Placement

The location of an adverb may be shifted in a sentence, depending on the rhythm a writer wants to achieve. An adverb (as a word, phrase, or clause) can appear in the sentence's beginning, middle, or end.

Formerly, Zimbabwe was known as Rhodesia.

Zimbabwe was *formerly* known as Rhodesia.

Zimbabwe was known as Rhodesia, *formerly.*

A note of caution: lengthy adverb phrases and clauses should not split sentence elements that occur in pairs, such as a subject and verb or a verb and its object (see 15d).

11b

ad

EXERCISE 1

Identify the single-word adjectives and adverbs in the following sentences; also identify the words being modified.

> *Example:*   As night began to fall on the *Russian* Empire's *western*
> Adj.   Adj.
>
> borders, day was *already* breaking on the *Pacific* coast.
> Adv.   Adj.

1. Through the depth of Russian winters, millions of tall pines stood silently in heavy snows.
2. In summer, clusters of white-trunked birches gently rustled in the slanting rays of the afternoon sun.
3. Rivers, wide and flat, flowed peacefully through the grassy plains of European Russia.
4. Eastward, in Siberia, mightier rivers rolled northward to the Arctic.
5. Here and there, thinly scattered across the broad land, lived one hundred and thirty million subjects of the Tsar.

EXERCISE 2

Convert the following nouns and verbs to adjectives and adverbs; convert the adjectives to adverbs. (Use a dictionary for help, if necessary.) Then use each newly converted word in a sentence.

> *Example:*   courtesy (noun)   courteous (adjective)
> extreme (adjective)   extremely (adverb)
> The driver was extremely courteous.
>
> substance   wonderful
> reason   colossal
> argue

11b   Use an adverb (not an adjective) to modify verbs as well as verbals.

Adverbs are used to modify verbs even when a direct object stands between the verb and its modifier.

FAULTY   If you measure an object in Denver *precise,* it will weigh somewhat less than the same object measured in Washington. [The adjective *precise*— following a direct object—is used incorrectly to modify the verb *measured.*]

REVISED   If you measure an object in Denver *precisely,* it will weigh somewhat less than the same object measured in Washington.

FAULTY   A *precise* measured object in Denver will weigh somewhat less than the same object measured in Washington. [The adjective *precise* incorrectly modifies the participle *measured*.]

REVISED   A *precisely* measured object in Denver will weigh somewhat less than the same object measured in Washington.

FAULTY   An object's weight can be determined by measuring it *careful* against a known weight. [The adjective *careful* incorrectly modifies the gerund *measuring*.]

REVISED   An object's weight can be determined by measuring it *carefully* against a known weight.

ad

11c Use an adverb (not an adjective) to modify another adverb and an adjective.

Although informal or nonstandard usage occasionally finds adjectives like *real* or *sure* functioning as adverbs ("a real bad time," "it sure was good"), standard academic usage requires that adverbs modify adjectives and other adverbs.

NONSTANDARD   A *reasonable* accurate scale can measure hundredths of a gram. [The adjective *reasonable* incorrectly modifies the adjective *accurate*.]

REVISED   A *reasonably* accurate scale can measure hundredths of a gram.

FAULTY   An object on the Moon weighs *significant* less than it does on Earth. [The adjective *significant* incorrectly modifies the adverb *less*.]

REVISED   An object on the Moon weighs *significantly* less than it does on Earth.

11d Use an adjective (not an adverb) after a linking verb to describe a subject.

The following verbs are linking verbs: forms of *be* (*is, are, was, were, has been, have been*), *look, smell, taste, sound, feel, appear, become, grow, remain, seem, turn,* and *stay.* A sentence with a linking verb establishes, in effect, an equation between the first part of the sentence and the second:

$\underline{\quad A \quad}$ LINKING VERB $\underline{\quad B \quad}$, or $\underline{\quad A \quad}$ = $\underline{\quad B \quad}$.

In this construction, the predicate part, *B*, is called the *subject complement*. The function of a **subject complement** is to rename or modify the subject of a sentence, which is a noun. The subject complement may be a noun, pronoun, or adjective—but **not** an adverb. In these examples, the linking verbs are followed by adjectives that describe a subject.

LINKING   The dessert looks *delicious.*

The crowd turned *violent.*

The pilots were *thirsty.*

Important Exceptions: Several linking verbs, especially those associated with the five senses, can also express action. When they do, they are considered *action* (not linking) *verbs* and are modified by adverbs.

11d

ad

ACTION   Palmer looked *menacingly* at the batter. [*Looked* is an action verb with an adverb modifier.]

LINKING   Palmer looked angry and *menacing.* [*Looked* is a linking verb, with the adjective *menacing* describing the subject's apparent attitude.]

ACTION   The storm turned *violently* toward land. [*Turned* is an action verb with an adverb modifier.]

LINKING   The storm turned *violent.* [*Turned* is now a linking verb meaning "became." The adjective *violent* is linked as a modifier to *storm.*]

Good, well, bad, badly

The words *good* and *well, bad* and *badly* are not interchangeable in formal writing (though they tend to be in conversation). The common linking verbs associated with well-being, appearance, or feeling—*looks, seems, appears, feels*—can cause special problems. The rules of usage are as follows:

1   Good and well

Good is an adjective, used either before a noun or after a linking verb to describe the condition of a subject.

ACCEPTABLE   Kyle looks good. [After a linking verb, *good* describes the subject's appearance.]

Kyle is a good dancer. [*Good* modifies the noun *dancer.*]

NONSTANDARD   Susan drives good. [*Drives* is an action verb and requires an adverb as modifier.]

REVISED   Susan drives well.

The word *well* can be used as either an adjective or an adverb. It has limited use as an adjective only after certain linking verbs (*looks, seems, be/am/is/are*) that describe the subject's good health.

ACCEPTABLE   Robert looks well. [*Looks* is a linking verb. The sense of this sentence is that Robert seems to be healthy.]

Well functions as an adverb whenever it follows an action verb.

NONSTANDARD   Janet sings good. [*Sings* is an action verb and requires an adverb as modifier.]

REVISED   Janet sings well.

 2   **Bad and badly**

11d

Bad is an adjective, used before a noun and after a linking verb to describe a subject. Again, the linking verbs that involve appearance or feeling—*looks, seems, appears, feels*—can cause special problems.

ad

FAULTY   Marie feels badly. [*Feels* is a linking verb and must tie the subject *Marie* to an adjective.]

REVISED   Marie feels bad. [As an adjective, *bad* is linked to the subject to describe *Marie* and her mental state.]

EXCEPTION: The verb *feels* could possibly be an action verb indicating a sense of touch rather than a linking verb indicating well-being: "The blind reader feels braille letters carefully and well." Only in this limited meaning would the phrases "feels badly" or "feels well" be used properly to show how that sense is operating.

Badly is an adverb, used after an action verb or used to modify an adjective or adverb.

NONSTANDARD   John cooks bad. [*Cooks* is an action verb and must be modified by an adverb.]

REVISED   John cooks badly.

EXERCISE 3
Browse through a dictionary and locate five words that have both adjective and adverb forms. Write a sentence for the two uses of each word—ten sentences in all. Draw an arrow from each adjective or adverb to the word modified.

Example: *patient*   The people in the waiting room were patient.

patiently   The people waited patiently.

EXERCISE 4
Fill in the blank in each sentence with *good, well, bad,* or *badly* and draw an arrow from the word chosen to the word modified.

Example: The team's prospects are _____ .

The team's prospects are *good.*

1. Tom has been looking _____ .
2. If he were under a doctor's supervision, he might look _____ .
3. He certainly sleeps _____ .
4. A _____ sleeper can put in eight hours a night.
5. Sleeping _____ can make one feel old in a hurry.

11e

ad

11e The uses of comparative and superlative forms of adjectives and adverbs

Both adjectives and adverbs change form to express comparative relationships. The base form of an adjective or adverb is called its **positive** form. The **comparative** form is used to express a relationship between two elements, and the **superlative** form is used to express a relationship among three or more elements. Most single-syllable adverbs and adjectives, and many two-syllable adjectives, show comparisons with the suffix *-er* and superlatives with *-est.*

	POSITIVE	COMPARATIVE	SUPERLATIVE
ADJECTIVE	crazy	crazier	craziest
	crafty	craftier	craftiest
ADVERB	near	nearer	nearest
	far	farther	farthest

Adverbs of two or more syllables and adjectives of three or more syllables change to the comparative and superlative forms with the words *more* and *most.* Adjectives and adverbs show downward (or negative) comparisons with the words *less* and *least* placed before the positive form. If you are uncertain of an adjective's or adverb's form, refer to a dictionary.

	POSITIVE	COMPARATIVE	SUPERLATIVE
ADJECTIVE	elegant	more/less elegant	most/least elegant
	logical	more/less logical	most/least logical
ADVERB	beautifully	more/less beautifully	most/least beautifully
	strangely	more/less strangely	most/least strangely

1 Use irregular adjectives and adverbs with care.

A number of adjectives and adverbs are irregular in forming comparatives and superlatives, and they must be memorized. Consult the box for these basic forms.

Irregular Forms of Comparison

	POSITIVE	COMPARATIVE	SUPERLATIVE
ADJECTIVE	good	better	best
	bad	worse	worst
	little	less	least
	many	more	most
	much	more	most
	some	more	most
ADVERB	well (also adj.)	better	best
	badly	worse	worst

ad

NOTE: Degrees of downward comparison among nouns that can be **counted** must be made with the adjectives *few, fewer,* or *fewest* rather than with *little, less,* or *least,* which are used before **mass** nouns.

FAULTY   Frozen yogurt has *less* calories than ice cream. [Since *calories* can be counted, *less* is the wrong comparative term.]

REVISED   Frozen yogurt has *fewer* calories than ice cream.

FAULTY   "Dieter's Delight" candy has *fewer* sugar than regular candy. [Since *sugar* is a mass noun and cannot be counted, *fewer* is the wrong comparative term.]

REVISED   "Dieter's Delight" candy has *less* sugar than regular candy.

Use the adjective *many* with nouns that can be counted and use the adjectives *much* and *some* for mass nouns.

FAULTY   Ice cream has *much* calories. [Since *calories* can be counted, *much* is the incorrect adjective form.]

REVISED   Ice cream has *many* calories.

2 Express comparative and superlative relationships accurately, completely, and logically.

Accuracy

Use the comparative form of adverbs and adjectives to show a relationship between two items; use the superlative form when relating three items or more.

TWO ITEMS   John is funnier than his brother Frank.

TWO ITEMS   Walking is less strenuous than running.

MULTIPLES   IBM is the world's largest manufacturer of computers.

Completeness

If the elements of a two- or three-way comparison are not being mentioned explicitly in a sentence, be sure to provide enough context so that the comparison makes sense.

INCOMPLETE   John is funnier. [Funnier than what? who?]

REVISED   John is the funnier brother. [Two brothers are being compared.]

or

John is funnier than his brother Frank.

11f

ad

Logic

Certain adjectives have an absolute meaning—they cannot be logically compared. It makes no sense, for instance, to discuss greater or lesser degrees of *perfect* (although in advertising and in conversation, people often try). *Perfect* represents a logical endpoint of comparison, as do the words *unique, first, final, last, absolute, infinite,* and *dead.* Note, though, that a concert performance might be *nearly* perfect or a patient on an operating table *almost* dead. Once *perfection* or *death* is reached, comparisons literally make no sense.

ILLOGICAL   The story was submitted in its most final form.

REVISED   The story was submitted in its final form.

or

The story was submitted in nearly final form.

11f Avoid double comparisons, double superlatives, and double negatives.

Double comparisons/superlatives

Adjectives and adverbs show comparative and superlative relationships either with a suffix (*-er/-est*) *or* with the words *more, most, less, least.* It is redundant and awkward to use the *-er/-est* suffix with *more/most* or *less/least.*

FAULTY   The World Trade Center is more taller than the Chrysler Building.

REVISED   The World Trade Center is taller than the Chrysler Building.

FAULTY   That is the least likeliest conclusion to the story.

REVISED   That is the least likely conclusion to the story.

Double negatives

Double negatives—the presence of two modifiers that say "no" in the same sentence—are redundant and sometimes confusing, though fairly common in nonstandard usage. A clear negation in a sentence should be expressed only once. Combine the negatives *not, never, neither/nor, hardly,* or *scarcely* with *any, anything,* or *anyone.* Do not combine these negatives with the negatives *no, none, nothing,* or *no one.*

NONSTANDARD	I didn't have none.
	I didn't have no cash. [These double negatives risk the implication that the speaker in fact has cash.]
REVISED	I had none.
	I didn't have any cash.
NONSTANDARD	I hardly had none.
REVISED	I hardly had any.
NONSTANDARD	I never had nothing.
REVISED	I never had any.
	I had nothing.

11g

k

11g Avoid overusing nouns as modifiers.

Several words that have the form of a noun will modify verbs and function as adverbs: Judith walked *home*. (This usage may be a time-worn shortcut for "toward home" or "homeward.") More often, a noun will modify another noun and thus will function as an adjective. A few examples include *gate* keeper, *toll* booth, *cell* block, *beauty* parlor, *parlor* game, *finger* puppet, and *tax* collector. Certainly, *toll booth* is more concise than *a booth where tolls are collected.* Noun modifiers provide handy shortcuts, but when two or more nouns are stacked before a third noun to function as adjectives, the result is logically and stylistically disastrous.

UNCLEAR   The textbook Civil War chapter review questions are due tomorrow.

Logically, the sentence falters because we are given five seemingly unrelated nouns from which to choose a subject: *textbook, Civil War, chapter, review,* or *questions.* Momentarily, at least, we are left to guess the subject. Could the last noun be the subject and the others modifiers? Stylistically, the sentence shows no appreciation for the varying relationships a writer can give to parts of a sentence in order to facilitate a reader's understanding. Unstack noun modifiers by using possessive forms and prepositional phrases.

REVISED   The *review questions from the textbook's chapter on the Civil War*
　　　　　　　　　subject　　　　prep. phrase with possessive　　　prep. phrase
are due tomorrow.

11g

k

EXERCISE 5

Correct the problems with comparative and superlative forms in the following sentences.

> *Example:*   Of three books I read recently on life in nineteenth-century England, Hardy's *Far from the Madding Crowd* is the more engaging.
>
> Of the three books I read recently on life in nineteenth-century England, Hardy's *Far from the Madding Crowd* is the <u>most</u> engaging. [The superlative is needed for differentiating three or more items.]

1. Hardy is better known for *Tess of the d'Urbervilles*.
2. Hardy is sometimes called the most last of the Victorians.
3. He was one of the prolifickest writers of the nineteenth century, with several major novels and more than one thousand poems to his credit.
4. Scholarship on Hardy's life and work is so bountiful that no one should have no trouble in finding ample analyses of his works.
5. Of the many editions of Hardy's work now available, the more notable is the Macmillan Wessex edition.

Writing Correct Sentences

CHAPTER 12

Sentence Fragments

A **sentence fragment** is a partial sentence punctuated as if it were a complete sentence with an uppercase letter at its beginning and a period, question mark, or exclamation point at its end. Because it is only a partial sentence, a fragment leaves readers hanging; the result is likely to be confusion as readers try to guess at what claims or statements are being made. To be a sentence, a group of words must first have a subject and a predicate (see 7a-1). A sentence fragment may often lack either a subject or a predicate—and sometimes both. A fragment may also be a dependent clause (see 7e) that has not been joined to an independent (or main) clause.

FRAGMENT   Stressing unity of effect as the story's most characteristic feature. [The clause lacks both a subject and a verb, since *stressing* is a verbal. (See 12c.)]

REVISED   *Edgar Allen Poe stressed* unity of effect as the story's most characteristic feature. [A subject and verb are added to create a sentence.]

FRAGMENT   Although storytelling is one of the oldest arts. [This unit is a dependent clause.]

REVISED   Although storytelling is one of the oldest arts, *the short story* as a narrative form *is* comparatively new in literature. [The clause is joined to an independent clause.]

 Check for completeness of sentences.

Avoid writing fragments by checking your sentences for grammatical completeness. There are three tests you can conduct:

1. Locate a verb.
2. Locate the verb's subject.
3. Check for subordinate conjunctions or relative pronouns.

First test: Locate a verb.

Disqualify Verbals: Many words—called verbals—look like verbs but do not function as main sentence verbs. Be sure that the word you settle on as the verb of the sentence is not a verbal (see 7a-3). There are three types of verbals you should disqualify when looking for sentence verbs: verb forms ending in *-ing*, verb forms ending in *-ed* (when not paired with a subject), and verb forms introduced with the infinitive *to.*

Verb forms ending in *-ing* must be preceded by a form of *to be* (e.g., *is, was, has been*, etc.) in order to function as sentence verbs.

FRAGMENT His arguing a long and tiresome case without any sensitivity to his readers.

REVISED *He was* arguing a long and tiresome case without any sensitivity to his readers.

Verb forms ending in *-ed* may be called *participles* and function as adjectives, not as verbs, when they are preceded by an article (*a, an,* or *the* [see 7a-2]), by a noun or pronoun in its possessive form (e.g., *Paul's, his*), or by a preposition (*of, by, for,* etc.). To function as a verb, such a form must be paired with a subject.

12a

frag

FRAGMENT The calculated, highly dangerous risk. [*Calculated* functions as a participle describing risk.]

REVISED *Susan calculated* the highly dangerous risk. [*Calculated* is paired with a subject to become a verb.]

REVISED Susan's *calculated risk* paid off. [*Calculated* is a participle describing Susan's risk. A verb has been added.]

FRAGMENT A series of legislated revolutionary reforms. [*Legislated* is a participle describing reforms.]

REVISED *Congress legislated* revolutionary reforms. [*Legislated* is a verb with a subject, *Congress.*]

Verb forms introduced with the infinitive marker *to* never function as sentence verbs; another verb must be added to make a sentence:

FRAGMENT To appreciate the alternative.

REVISED *Frank failed* to appreciate the alternative. [The verb *failed* has been added to accompany the subject *Frank.*]

For more information on verbs and verbals, see 7a-3 and 7a-4.

Second test: Locate the verb's subject.

Once you have located a verb, ask *who* or *what* makes its assertion or action and you will find the subject.

FRAGMENT Separated visible light into a spectrum of colors.

REVISED *Isaac Newton* separated visible light into a spectrum of colors. [The subject, *Isaac Newton,* is needed to answer the question *Who separated?*]

FRAGMENT First attempted an analysis of the short story.

REVISED *Edgar Allan Poe* first attempted an analysis of the short story. [A subject, *Edgar Allan Poe,* is added to answer the question *who first attempted an analysis?*]

Imperative sentences—commands—often lack a subject; still, they are considered sentences since the implied subject is understood to be *you.*

IMPERATIVE SENTENCE	UNDERSTOOD AS
Open the door!	You open the door.
Come here, please.	You come here, please.

12a

frag

Third test: Check for subordinate conjunctions or relative pronouns.

Be certain that a subject and verb are not preceded by a subordinate conjunction or that a relative pronoun taking the place of a subject does not make the clause dependent. If a word grouping consists of a subject and predicate, it is a sentence *unless* it contains a subordinating word, either an opening subordinate conjunction or a relative pronoun taking the place of its subject.

Checking for Sentence Completeness

1. **Locate a verb.**
   Every sentence has a verb. As you look for the sentence verb, *disqualify verbals:*
   verb forms ending in *-ing*: Eugene laugh*ing* to himself.
   verb forms ending in *-ed*: A suspec*ted* terrorist
   verb forms beginning with *to*: *To* visit the country
   Once you have located what you think is the sentence verb, see if you can *change its ending* by placing the pronouns *I* and *she* before it and by making it refer to both a past event and a present event. If the word changes form, it is a verb.

2. **Locate the verb's subject.**
   Every verb in a sentence has its subject. Ask of the verb *who* or *what* makes the verb's assertion or action, and you will have located the subject.

3. **Check for subordinate conjunctions or relative pronouns.**
   A unit of words with both a verb and a subject is a *clause.* If a clause contains a subordinate conjunction (e.g., *because, since*) the clause will *not* be a sentence. If a relative pronoun (e.g., *which, who*) takes the place of the subject of a clause, the clause will also *not* be a sentence.

SUBORDINATE CONJUNCTIONS

after	although	as if	because	before	how
if	once	since	until	while	

A subordinate conjunction placed at the beginning of an independent clause renders the clause dependent, so that it cannot stand alone as a complete sentence. If the conjunction is eliminated, the clause will stand as a sentence. If the clause is combined with another sentence, the new dependent clause will function as an adverb.

FRAGMENT Though people may have a personality disorder. [The conjunction *though* makes the clause dependent on another assertion.]

REVISED ~~Though~~ People may have a personality disorder. [Dropping the conjunction makes a simple sentence.]

REVISED Though people may have a personality disorder, *they may see their behavior as normal.* [The dependent clause now functions as an adverb.]

12a

frag

RELATIVE PRONOUNS

that	which	whichever	who
whoever	whom	whomever	

If a relative pronoun takes the place of a subject in a clause, this signals that the clause is dependent and cannot stand alone as a complete thought. If the pronoun is eliminated, the clause will stand as a sentence. If it is combined with another sentence, the dependent clause will function as an adjective:

FRAGMENT People who have a personality disorder. [*Who* takes the place of the subject *people,* creating a dependent clause.]

REVISED People ~~who~~ have a personality disorder. [Eliminating *who* leaves a simple sentence.]

REVISED People who have a personality disorder *see their behavior as acceptable.* [*People* is the subject of a verb *see,* with a *who* clause as adjective modifier.]

EXCEPTION: When a relative pronoun introduces a question, the construction is not considered to be a fragment: *Who has a personality disorder?*

EXERCISE 1

Use the three-part test to identify fragments and to explain the cause of each fragment. Place a check before complete sentences, and circle the numbers of items that are fragments.

Example: In the Near East, five thousand years of history.
Fragment—fails test 1 (no verb)

1. Recorded in government archives in inscriptions and on thousands of clay tablets.

2. The lists of kings and genealogies in Egyptian archives record dates in years that go back to at least 3000 B.C.
3. Recorded history starts in about 750 B.C. in the central Mediterranean.
4. About 55 B.C. the start of historical records in Britain.
5. The first historical records for the New World long thought to begin with the Spanish conquest.
6. Parts of Africa entered "history" in A.D. 1890.
7. Historical records covering but the very smallest fraction of the human experience.

12b Eliminate fragments: Revise dependent clauses set off as sentences.

12b

frag

A dependent clause that has been set off incorrectly as a sentence can be corrected in one of two ways: by converting the clause to an independent clause or by joining the clause to a new sentence.

 1 Convert the dependent clause to an independent clause.

If the dependent clause begins with a subordinate conjunction, delete the conjunction and you will have an independent clause—a sentence:

FRAGMENT   After Teddy Roosevelt was hit in the eye while boxing.

REVISED   ~~After~~ Teddy Roosevelt was hit in the eye while boxing. [The conjunction is deleted.]

If a dependent clause uses a relative pronoun, eliminate the relative pronoun, replacing it with a noun or personal pronoun, and you will have an independent clause:

FRAGMENT   The President, who went blind in his left eye from the incident.

REVISED   The President ~~who~~ went blind in his left eye from the incident. [The eliminated relative pronoun leaves the noun as subject.]

REVISED   ~~The President, who~~ *He* went blind in his left eye from the incident. [The eliminated relative pronoun is replaced by a personal pronoun.]

2 Join the dependent clause to a new sentence.

The dependent clause introduced by a subordinate conjunction can be made to function as an adverb by joining it to an independent clause. When the dependent clause introduces a sentence, set it off with a comma (see 25a-1). When the clause ends a sentence, it is typically not set off with a comma.

FRAGMENT   When Teddy Roosevelt had his first chance to show how a President should lead.

REVISED   *Hardly had Teddy Roosevelt moved into the White House* when he had his first chance to show how a President should lead.

A dependent clause fragment that uses a relative pronoun can be made to function as an adjective (a relative clause) by attaching it to an independent clause. If the new relative clause is not essential to a definition of the noun that it modifies, set the clause off with a *pair* of commas. If the new relative clause *is* essential to the definition, do not use commas. (See 25d-1.)

FRAGMENT   Roosevelt the champion of the ordinary American, who had gotten striking coal miners a "square deal." [The noun and modifying clause have no verb.]

REVISED   Roosevelt, who had gotten striking coal miners a "square deal," *emerged as* the champion of the ordinary American. [The *who* clause functions as an adjective in a sentence with a new verb *emerged*.]

FRAGMENT   A large holding company that controlled all rail traffic in the Northeast. [The noun and its modifying clause have no verb.]

REVISED   He showed solidarity for the powerless *by busting a large holding company that controlled all rail traffic in the Northeast.* [The noun and its modifying clause become part of a new sentence (as objects of the verbal *busting*).]

12b

frag

EXERCISE 2

Identify fragments in the following pairs of sentences. Correct fragments by converting dependent clauses to independent clauses or by joining dependent clauses to independent clauses.

Example: Because Charlemagne was eager to reestablish the imperial past.

He encouraged the revival of Roman building techniques.

Because Charlemagne was eager to reestablish the imperial past, *he* encouraged the revival of Roman building techniques.

1. Although in early medieval northern Europe several Roman colonial towns contained many impressive stone structures. The Germanic tribes had always relied on their vast forests to supply them with building materials.
2. Northern architecture was a timber architecture. Which continued to be so well into the Middle Ages.
3. Charlemagne's adoption of southern building principles for the construction of his palaces and churches was epoch-making. Since his reliance on models in Rome and Ravenna changed the development of architecture in northern Europe.
4. Although it is true that Charlemagne's builders abandoned rectangular, wooden-framed structures for more elaborate geometrical forms. They were careful to adapt Roman and Byzantine prototypes into a distinctive Carolingian style.

5. The design of Charlemagne's buildings of the eighth century foreshadows later architecture. Eleventh- and twelfth-century buildings that we now call Romanesque.

Eliminating Fragments from Your Writing

1. Revise dependent clauses set off as sentences.
Convert the dependent clause to an independent clause:

FRAGMENT Although computers may be revolutionizing the world.

REVISED ~~Although~~ Computers may be revolutionizing the world.

Join the dependent clause to a new sentence.

FRAGMENT Although computers may be revolutionizing the world.

REVISED Although computers may be revolutionizing the world, *relatively few people understand how they function.*

2. Revise phrases set off as sentences.
There are various kinds of phrases: verbal, prepositional, absolute, and appositive. None can stand alone as a sentence.

FRAGMENT After years of drought.

REVISED ~~After~~ Years of drought *can devastate a national economy.*

REVISED After years of drought, *a nation's economy can be devastated.*

3. Revise repeating structures or compound predicates set off as sentences.
Repeating elements and compound predicates cannot stand alone. Incorporate such structures into an existing sentence or add words to construct a new sentence.

FRAGMENT College sports has long been conducted as a business. A profitable business. [The repeating element is a fragment.]

REVISED College sports has long been conducted as a business—*a* profitable business. [The repeating element has been incorporated into an existing sentence.]

FRAGMENT Some coaches achieve legendary status on campus. And are paid legendary salaries. [The second element is part of a compound verb.]

REVISED Some coaches achieve legendary status on campus *and* are paid legendary salaries. [The second verb and its associated words are incorporated into an existing sentence.]

Eliminate fragments: Revise phrases set off as sentences.

12c

Phrases consist of nouns and the verbs associated with them or verb forms not functioning as verbs (called *verbals*) and the words associated with them. Phrases function as sentence parts—as modifiers, subjects, objects, and complements—but never as sentences. The various kinds of phrases are defined in chapter 7, section d. As with dependent clauses that form fragments, you may either convert phrases to complete sentences by adding words, or you may join phrases to independent clauses.

1 Verbal phrases

12c

frag

Participial and gerund phrases (functioning as modifiers or nouns)

FRAGMENT   Reviving the Sherman Antitrust Act.

REVISED   *Roosevelt* -reviving- *revived* the Sherman Antitrust Act. [The phrase is rewritten as a sentence.]

REVISED   Reviving the Sherman Antitrust Act, *Roosevelt brought suit against the Northern Securities Company.* [The participial phrase, functioning as an adjective, is joined to an independent clause.]

REVISED   Reviving the Sherman Antitrust Act *was one way to fight Northern Securities Company.* [The phrase is used as a gerund, functioning as a noun, to become the subject of an independent clause.]

Infinitive phrases (functioning as nouns)

FRAGMENT   To sue Northern Securities rather than deal.

REVISED   *Roosevelt decided* to sue Northern Securities rather than deal. [The phrase is rewritten as a sentence.]

2 Prepositional phrases (functioning as modifiers)

FRAGMENT   In 1904 by a very narrow vote of 5 to 4.

REVISED   In 1904 by a very narrow vote of 5 to 4, *the Supreme Court held that the Northern Securities Company did violate the Sherman Antitrust Act.* [The phrase is joined to an independent clause.]

3 Absolute phrases (modifying an entire sentence)

FRAGMENT   Roosevelt's instincts leaning to public protection.

REVISED   His instincts ~~leaning~~ *leaned* to public protection. [The phrase is rewritten as a sentence.]

REVISED   His instincts leaning to public protection, *Roosevelt tolerated trusts that benefited ordinary Americans.* [The phrase is joined as modifier to an independent clause.]

4 Appositive phrases (renaming or describing other nouns)

FRAGMENT   A bill designed to give federal officials the right to inspect all meat shipped in interstate commerce.

REVISED   *The Meat Inspection Act was* a bill designed to give federal officials the right to inspect all meat shipped in interstate commerce. [The phrase is rewritten as a sentence.]

REVISED   *Roosevelt went on to advocate the Meat Inspection Act,* a bill designed to give federal officials the right to inspect all meat shipped in interstate commerce. [The phrase is joined to an independent clause.]

12c

frag

EXERCISE 3

Identify the numbered units that are fragments, and correct them by joining them to independent clauses. Then specify what type of phrase the fragment has become in the new sentence. Place a check before any sentence needing no revision.

Example: (1) In order to comprehend the nature of stress, we must consider three related issues. (2) *Physiology, the nature of stressors, and personality.*

(1) In order to comprehend the nature of stress, we must consider three related issues: physiology, the nature of stressors, and personality. [The fragment is joined with the independent clause to become an appositive renaming *issues.*]

(1) Physiologically, the body prepares itself for stress. (2) By eliciting an immediate and vigorous alarm reaction. (3) Alarm is soon replaced by resistance. (4) A state in which activation remains relatively high but at levels a person can sustain over a long period of time. (5) If stress persists, the body's resources may become depleted. (6) Exhaustion occurs. (7) The ability to cope decreasing sharply over time. (8) A person risks severe biological damage by remaining exhausted for too long. (9) *Stressors* can be defined as those elements in the environment that produce an urge in the individual to approach a stressful activity. (10) To flee from it as well.

12d Eliminate fragments: Revise repeating structures or compound predicates set off as sentences.

Repetition can be an effective stylistic tool (see 19c-2). Repeated elements, however, are not sentences but sentence parts and should not be punctuated as sentences. Use a comma or dashes to set off repeated elements.

FRAGMENT   Children begin for the first time to differentiate themselves from others as they enter adolescence. *As they begin to develop a personal identity.* [The subordinate *as* clause cannot stand alone.]

REVISED   Children begin for the first time to differentiate themselves from others as they enter adolescence, as they begin to develop a personal identity. [The clause is subordinated.]

FRAGMENT   An adolescent has much more concern than adults about fitting in. *About finding where he or she belongs in the social order.* [The phrase and clause need a connection.]

REVISED   An adolescent has much more concern than adults about fitting in—about finding where he or she belongs in the social order. [The structure repeats and parallels the previous *about* phrase.]

12d

frag

Compound predicates consist of two sentence verbs (and their associated words) joined with a coordinate conjunction, such as *and* or *but*. The two predicates share the same subject and are part of the same sentence. When one half of the compound predicate is punctuated as a sentence, it becomes a fragment. To correct the fragment, join it to a sentence that contains an appropriate subject or provide the fragment with its own subject.

FRAGMENT   The process of maturation is lifelong. *But is most critical during the adolescent years.* [The last unit has no subject.]

REVISED   The process of maturation is lifelong. But *the process* is most critical during the adolescent years. [The unit is given its own subject.]

REVISED   The process of maturation is lifelong but is most critical during the adolescent years. [The phrase is joined to the preceding sentence as a compound predicate.]

EXERCISE 4

Identify which of the following units below are fragments. Correct each by writing a new sentence or by joining the fragment to an independent clause.

    Example: At very low temperatures, many materials behave in unfamiliar ways. *And display properties much different from those we expect.* [The second unit lacks a subject.]

At very low temperatures, many materials behave in unfamiliar ways and display properties much different from those we expect. [The second unit is attached as a compound verb to the preceding sentence.]

1. When cooled in liquid nitrogen, a banana becomes extremely hard. So hard that it can be used as a hammer.
2. A rubber ball becomes brittle. And will shatter like glass when dropped onto the floor.
3. When certain metals are cooled to low temperatures, they gain the ability to conduct electric currents with no resistance at all. And are called superconductors.
4. Once the current is set up, a superconducting ring can carry current for a long time. For thousands of years with no further source of energy.

12e

frag

12e   Use fragments intentionally on rare occasions.

Aside from the accepted use of apparent fragments in questions (*Who is coming for dinner?*) and commands (*Come to dinner!*), experienced writers will occasionally use sentence fragments by design. These intentional uses are always carefully fitted to the context of a neighboring sentence, sometimes answering an implied question or completing a parallel structure that has been separated for emphasis. Such intentional uses occur mainly in personal or expressive essay writing or in fiction, when writers want to alter the rhythm of paragraphs and thereby call attention to fragments or to reproduce the staccato rhythms of speech or thought. A fragment should be used rarely if at all in academic prose, where it will probably be regarded as a lapse, not as a stylistic flourish.

INTENTIONAL USE OF FRAGMENT

Dick and Elsie backed the skiff in to the little island beach. Joxer helped Miss Perry and Sally and the baby. The other guests took off their shoes and went over the sides, calling heartily to Joxer and Joxer's wife. They were as cheerful as Joxer. *Amused too.*

JOHN CASEY, *Spartina*

EXERCISE 5

Correct each sentence fragment either by joining it with an independent clause or by rewriting it as an independent clause.

Example: When the influential scholar Ulrich B. Phillips declared in 1918 that slavery in the Old South had impressed upon African savages the glorious stamp of civilization. He set the stage for a long and passionate debate. [The first unit is a dependent clause.]

When the influential scholar Ulrich B. Phillips declared in 1918 that slavery in the Old South had impressed upon African savages the glorious stamp of civilization, he set the stage for a long and passionate debate. [The dependent clause is connected to the sentence that follows it.]

1. As the decades passed and the debate raged on. One historian after another confidently professed to have deciphered the real meaning of slavery. That "peculiar institution."
2. The special situation of the female slave remained unexamined. Amidst all this scholarly activity.
3. Because the ceaseless arguments about her "sexual promiscuity" or her "matriarchal" proclivities obscured the condition of Black women during slavery.
4. If and when a historian sets the record straight on the experiences of enslaved Black women. She (or he) will have performed an inestimable service.
5. It is not for the sake of historical accuracy alone that such a study should be conducted. For lessons can be gleaned from the slave era. That will shed light upon Black women's and all women's current battle for emancipation.
6. The enormous space that work occupies in Black women's lives today. Follows a pattern established during the very earliest days of slavery.
7. Compulsory labor overshadowed every other aspect of women's existence. The slave system defined Black people. As chattel. Since women, no less than men, were viewed as profitable labor units. They might as well have been genderless as far as the slaveholders were concerned.

12e

frag

CHAPTER 13

Comma Splices and Fused Sentences

S entence grammar is built on the fundamental rule that independent clauses—complete sentences—are the basic units for making a statement. Sentences must be kept distinct from one another. When sentence boundaries are blurred, statements become confused; readers must turn away from the content of a paper and struggle to decipher which combinations of words might form meaningful units. Difficulties at this level of comprehension can sabotage a message, frustrating and confusing readers.

To keep your statements distinct and clear, remember this: independent clauses must be separated with a period, a semicolon, or a colon, or they must be carefully linked with a conjunction and the appropriate punctuation.

Five Ways to Mark the Boundary between Sentences

Mark a sentence boundary with punctuation.

1. Use a period: He laughed. He danced. He sang.
2. Use a semicolon: He laughed; he danced and sang.

Mark a sentence boundary with a conjunction and punctuation.

3. Use a coordinating conjunction: He laughed, and he danced.
4. Use a subordinating conjunction: While he laughed, he danced.
5. Use a conjunctive adverb: He laughed; moreover, he danced.

Sentence boundaries can become blurred in two ways: with comma splices or with fused (run-on) sentences. In the **fused** (or **run-on**) **sentence**, the writer fails to recognize the end of one independent clause and the beginning of the next.

FUSED SENTENCE   The blurring of sentence boundaries can create a comprehension problem readers must often stop to decipher which combinations of words form meaningful units. [*Readers* is a new subject of a new independent clause; a period or semicolon should precede it.]

The writer of a **comma splice** recognizes the end of one independent clause and the beginning of the next, but marks the boundary between the two incorrectly—with a comma.

COMMA SPLICE   The blurring of sentence boundaries can create a comprehension problem, readers must often stop to decipher which combinations of words form meaningful units. [The first independent clause ends at the comma, which should instead be a period or semicolon, with *readers* beginning a new sentence.]

13a   Identify fused sentences and comma splices.

Before submitting a draft of your work to be read or reviewed by others, read your sentences aloud. When you listen to your writing, you can often catch errors that go undetected when you read silently. Look for long sentences that seem to consist of two or more separate statements, or those that seem so long they force you to stop midway to take a breath. Be on the alert, especially, for the following three circumstances in which fused sentences and comma splices are found.

13a

cs/fs

1. **A sentence of explanation, expansion, or example** is frequently fused to or spliced together with another sentence that is being explained, expanded on, or illustrated. Even if the topics of the two sentences are closely related, the sentences themselves must remain distinct.

   FUSED SENTENCE   Tobacco smoking is an ancient habit of humankind studies on the effects of smoking have appeared in medical journals over the last 100 years.

   COMMA SPLICE   Tobacco smoking is an ancient habit of humankind, studies on the effects of smoking have appeared in medical journals over the last 100 years.

   REVISED   Tobacco smoking is an ancient habit of humankind. Studies on the effects of smoking have appeared in medical journals over the last 100 years. [The sentences are separated.]

2. **The pronouns *he, she,* and *they,*** when renaming the subject of a sentence, can signal a comma splice or a fused sentence. Even when the subject named or renamed in adjacent sentences is identical, the sentences themselves must be kept distinct.

   FUSED SENTENCE   Raphael was a painter he was also a muralist.

   COMMA SPLICE   Raphael was a painter, he was also a muralist.

   REVISED   Raphael was a painter, and he was also a muralist.

3. **Conjunctive adverbs** (words such as *however, furthermore, thus, therefore,* and *consequently*) **and transitional expressions** (phrases such as *for example* and *on the other hand*) are commonly found in fused or spliced clauses. Conjunctive adverbs and transitions always link complete sentences. Writers must reflect this linkage with appropriate punctuation: a period or semicolon.

FUSED SENTENCE | Hispanics have emerged as a nationally influential group of voters in presidential politics furthermore, 90 percent of the Hispanic vote is concentrated in nine states that cast 71 percent of all electoral ballots.

COMMA SPLICE | Hispanics have emerged as a nationally influential group of voters in presidential politics, furthermore, 90 percent of the Hispanic vote is concentrated in nine states that cast 71 percent of all electoral ballots.

REVISED | Hispanics have emerged as a nationally influential group of voters in presidential politics; furthermore, 90 percent of the Hispanic vote is concentrated in nine states that cast 71 percent of all electoral ballots. [*Furthermore* starts a new main clause.]

13b

cs/fs

EXERCISE 1

Use a slash mark (/) to identify the points at which the following sentences are fused or spliced together.

Example: The American farmer and his family had avoided the Great Plains, it was a strange place at first they did not like it.

The American farmer and his family had avoided the Great Plains, / it was a strange place / at first they did not like it.

1. They were accustomed to the wooded lands of the East, some had become acquainted with the flat prairies that stretched from Illinois to Iowa and from Canada to Texas the prairies were known for rich soil, regular rainfall, and tall grass.
2. The Great Plains were different, however, out there trees were rare.
3. The grass was short worst of all there was very little rain, it is not surprising that for a while the farmer had gladly left the West to others.
4. Finally farmers decided to move onto the plains, they faced new problems.
5. Since there was no wood for houses, they had to learn to make houses of sod, to their astonishment they found that sod houses could be warm and cozy in winter they could be cool in summer.

13b Correct fused sentences and comma splices in one of five ways.

1 Separate independent clauses with a period (and sometimes a colon).

Using a period is the most obvious way to repair a fused or spliced construction, especially when the first independent clause is not very closely related in content to its neighbor, and when you do not want to link the two with a conjunction. But when using a period to repair faulty constructions, take care that your paragraphs do not become choppy. See the discussion on sentence variety in chapter 20.

Occasionally, writers use a colon between independent clauses when the first sentence is a formal and emphatic introduction to an explanation, example, or appositive in the second sentence.

FUSED SENTENCE   Logging is often the first step in deforestation it may be followed by complete clearing of trees and a deliberate shift to unsound land uses.

COMMA SPLICE   Logging is often the first step in deforestation, it may be followed by complete clearing of trees and a deliberate shift to unsound land uses.

REVISED   Logging is often the first step in deforestation. It may be followed by complete clearing of trees and a deliberate shift to unsound land uses.

REVISED   Logging is often the first step in deforestation: it may be followed by complete clearing of trees and a deliberate shift to unsound land uses. [The colon gives the opening clause an emphatic introductory function.]

13b

cs/fs

---

 2   Link clauses with a comma and a coordinate conjunction.

Use a comma placed *before* a coordinate conjunction—*and, but, or, nor, for, so,* and *yet*—to link sentences that are closely related in content and that are equally important. Like all conjunctions, coordinate conjunctions establish clear and definite logical relationships between the elements joined, so choose conjunctions with care. (See 19a for a detailed discussion of coordinate conjunctions.)

FUSED SENTENCE   Deforestation has a severe environmental impact on soil in heavy tropical rains soil erodes quickly.

COMMA SPLICE   Deforestation has a severe environmental impact on soil, in heavy tropical rains soil erodes quickly.

REVISED   Deforestation has a severe environmental impact on soil, for in heavy tropical rains soil erodes quickly.

---

3   Link clauses with a semicolon.

Use a semicolon in place of a comma and a coordinate conjunction to link sentences that are closely related and equally important. The semicolon links independent clauses without making the relationship between them explicit. You might choose a semicolon to repair a fused or spliced construction either when the relationship between clauses is crystal clear and a conjunction would be redundant or when you wish to create anticipation—leaving your readers to discover the exact relationship between clauses.

FUSED SENTENCE	Experience reinforces the argument that deforestation has not been a path to economic development in most tropical countries it has instead been a costly drain on resources.
COMMA SPLICE	Experience reinforces the argument that deforestation has not been a path to economic development, in most tropical countries it has instead been a costly drain on resources.
REVISED	Experience reinforces the argument that deforestation has not been a path to economic development; in most tropical countries it has instead been a costly drain on resources.

13b

cs/fs

4 Link clauses with a semicolon (or period) and a conjunctive adverb.

Use conjunctive adverbs—words such as *however, consequently, therefore,* and *moreover*—to link closely related, equally important clauses. (See 19a-3 for a discussion of conjunctive adverbs.) Conjunctive adverbs establish the same relationships, such as addition, contrast, and cause, as do coordinate conjunctions. The conjunctive adverbs, however, are more formal and a little stiffer, but also more rigorous and forceful than coordinate conjunctions. As well, conjunctive adverbs and coordinate conjunctions create different rhythms in the sentences you are linking. Choose conjunctions based on the tone and rhythm you wish to establish in your paragraphs.

Place a period between clauses when you want a full separation of ideas. Place a semicolon between clauses when you want to emphasize the link between ideas. As with most adverbs, a conjunctive adverb can shift its location in a sentence. If placed at the beginning, the conjunctive adverb is followed (usually) by a comma. If placed in the middle, it is usually set off by a pair of commas. And if placed at the end, it is preceded by a comma. Wherever you place the adverb, be sure to use a period or a semicolon between the two clauses you have linked.

FUSED SENTENCE	Deforestation is not inevitable it is the consequence of poor stewardship.
COMMA SPLICE	Deforestation is not inevitable, it is the consequence of poor stewardship.

REVISED   Deforestation is not inevitable; ultimately, it is the consequence of poor stewardship. [The semicolon emphasizes the link between ideas.]

REVISED   Deforestation is not inevitable. Ultimately, it is the consequence of poor stewardship. [The period makes a full separation.]

REVISED   Deforestation is not inevitable. It is the consequence, ultimately, of poor stewardship.

REVISED   Deforestation is not inevitable. It is the consequence of poor stewardship, ultimately.

5   Link clauses with a subordinate conjunction or construction.

Use a subordinate conjunction or construction to join fused or spliced independent clauses. By placing a subordinate conjunction at the beginning of an independent clause, or by using a relative pronoun such as "who," "whom," "which," or "that," you render that clause dependent, unable to stand alone as a complete thought. The new dependent clause will function as a modifier. Be aware of comma use with these constructions: when the clause begins a sentence, a comma follows it; but when a main clause begins a sentence, the dependent clause that follows very often does not use a comma. (See 19b for a discussion of subordination.)

13b

cs/fs

FUSED SENTENCE   International development-assistance agencies have begun to lend help a number of governments are now strengthening their forest-management programs.

COMMA SPLICE   International development-assistance agencies have begun to lend help, a number of governments are now strengthening their forest-management programs.

REVISED   Because international development-assistance agencies have begun to lend help, a number of governments are now strengthening their forest-management programs. [A dependent clause begins the sentence.]

REVISED   A number of governments are now strengthening their forest-management programs because international development-assistance agencies have begun to lend help. [A dependent clause ends the sentence.]

REVISED   A number of governments are now strengthening the forest-management programs that have begun to get help from international development-assistance agencies. [A dependent relative clause ends the sentence, creating a different meaning.]

Choose the Right Conjunction

Coordinate Conjunctions

and but so or for nor yet

Use coordinate conjunctions with punctuation in this pattern:

Independent clause **,** CONJUNCTION independent clause

FUSED SENTENCE Newton developed calculus he discovered laws of gravity.

COMMA SPLICE Newton developed calculus, he discovered laws of gravity.

REVISED Newton developed calculus, and he discovered laws of gravity.

Conjunctive Adverbs

however moreover furthermore therefore thus consequently

Use conjunctive adverbs with punctuation in these patterns:

Independent clause **;** CONJUNCTION **,** independent clause
Independent clause **.** CONJUNCTION **,** independent clause

REVISED Newton developed calculus; moreover, he discovered laws of gravity.

REVISED Newton developed calculus. Moreover, he discovered laws of gravity.

Subordinate Conjunctions

after although because once since though while

Use subordinate conjunctions with punctuation in these patterns:

CONJUNCTION clause **,** independent clause
Independent clause CONJUNCTION clause

REVISED After Newton developed calculus, he discovered laws of gravity.

REVISED Newton discovered laws of gravity after he developed calculus.

13b

cs/fs

EXERCISE 2

Correctly punctuate the following fused sentences in two different ways.

Example: In addition to a system of moats, gates were important elements in the defense of the Japanese castle gates were established at the foot of the castle side of a bridge. [This example is a fused or run-on sentence.]

In addition to a system of moats, gates were important elements in the defense of the Japanese castle: gates were established at the foot of the castle side of a bridge. [The colon introduces what follows as an explanation.]

In addition to a system of moats, gates were also important elements in the defense of the Japanese castle; usually, gates were established at the foot of the castle side of a bridge. [The conjunctive adverb makes a close link between the two main clauses.]

1. Guards on duty around the clock scrutinized all comers and goers gatekeeping rotated among the daimyos it was one of the most important duties daimyos performed for the shogun.
2. At one time there were more than ninety gates at Edo Castle because the gates were strictly ranked daimyos and vassals had to use the bridge permitted them by their status at the apex of the hierarchy was Ote Gate.
3. One gate was for the exclusive use of women who worked in the castle there was also a gate dubbed the Fujo ("Impure") Gate because it was used by criminals all of whom were expelled from the castle.
4. Hanzo Gate was named for the head of the ninja clan who protected the castle during the reign of Tokugawa Ieyasu his mansion was located near the gate.
5. The ninja were another important element in the defense of the castle Ieyasu had great faith in their ability their forte was scaling walls and mountains by means of a rope ladder.
6. The gates were strictly guarded all of the gates were usually opened at six in the morning and closed at six in the evening.

13b

cs/fs

EXERCISE 3

Correct the following sentences, each of which is spliced with a comma. Use any of the five strategies discussed in this chapter.

Example: At the center of the virtually impregnable Edo Castle was the Honmaru, the main citadel and palace of the shogun, daimyos and vassals lived outside the castle and walked to it from their residences.

At the center of the virtually impregnable Edo Castle was the Honmaru, the main citadel and palace of the shogun. Daimyos and vassals lived outside the castle and walked to it from their residences. [The spliced sentences are separated into two sentences.]

1. However, a number of officials, servants, wives of the shogun, and ladies-in-waiting lived in the Honmaru, thus the Honmaru was designed to accommodate the needs of a range of people.
2. The official route to the front entrance of the Honmaru began at the Ote Gate and led through three more gates, the route, intentionally complicated to confuse unwelcome visitors, included several turns to the right and left.
3. The Honmaru consisted of three main parts, government offices, the palace of the shogun, and the shogun's private residence, although there were fewer women than warriors in the castle town, the shogun's private residence was a woman's world that only the shogun himself could enter.

4. In the Honmaru palace there were a number of rooms partitioned by sliding doors, as well as offices and anterooms for officials, these rooms were linked by many small and large corridors, and several rooms could be turned into a single room by fully opening the sliding doors.

EXERCISE 4

Correct the fused sentences and comma splices in the following paragraphs, making use of all five strategies discussed in this chapter. One consideration governing your choice of corrections should be sentence variety. Avoid repeating sentence structures in consecutive sentences by varying methods for correcting fused and spliced clauses.

We primates are very social animals watch a troop of baboons crossing the African savanna, or a group of gorillas preparing their overnight bivouac, and you soon realize the importance of communal living. Human behavior centers on the social group, too, the profusion of modern and extinct societies offers a bewildering variety of ways and means of ordering social relations. These have spawned an anthropological jargon that tries to divide and place other cultures into neat groupings.

13b

cs/fs

CHAPTER 14

Pronoun Reference

A **pronoun** substitutes for a noun, allowing us to talk about something without having to repeat its name over and over (see 7a-7). To do this, a pronoun must take on meaning from a specific noun; the pronoun must make a clear and unmistakable linkage or reference to the noun for which it substitutes—called its **antecedent.** When the reference is not clearly made to a specific noun, the meaning of the whole sentence can become vague or confused.

UNCLEAR   Michelangelo had a complex personality, as did Raphael, though *his* was the more complex. *His* art was not nearly so typical of the High Renaissance, and *he* was frequently irascible—as impatient with the shortcomings of others as with *his* own.

To whom do the pronouns *he* and *his* refer in these sentences? No one can tell, and in this case frustrated readers might helplessly backtrack in search of the references to noun antecedents that should give the pronouns meaning. The sentences need to be revised, and the pronouns and antecedents must be placed with care to keep readers moving forward.

REVISED   Michelangelo had a complex personality, as did Raphael, though *Michelangelo's* was the more complex. *His* art was not nearly so typical of the High Renaissance, and *he* was frequently irascible—as impatient with the shortcomings of others as with *his* own. [The proper noun replaces an unclear pronoun, providing a reference point for all the pronouns that follow.]

14a   Make pronouns refer clearly to their antecedents.

Revise a sentence whenever a pronoun can refer to more than one antecedent. Use a noun in place of a pronoun, if needed for clarity; or reposition a pronoun so that its reference to an antecedent is unmistakable.

CONFUSING   In 1806, Andrew Jackson dueled with Charles Dickinson, a successful lawyer who had learned his profession from Chief Justice John Marshall. *He* was fine southern gentleman—and a crack shot, too. [Does the pronoun *he* refer to Jackson, Dickinson, or Marshall?]

REVISED   Dickinson was a fine southern gentleman—and a crack shot, too. [A noun is substituted for the unclear pronoun.]

Describing a person's speech indirectly can lead to unclear pronoun reference. Occasionally, if you can document what was said, you can convert indirect quotations to direct ones in order to clarify a pronoun's reference. Otherwise, you can restate the sentence carefully to avoid confusion among the nouns.

CONFUSING   First Dickinson, then Jackson, fired. Jackson later told a friend *he* thought *he* had been killed.

DIRECT   Jackson later told a friend, "I thought I had been killed."
STATEMENT

RESTATEMENT   As he later told a friend, Jackson at that moment felt himself to be mortally wounded.

14b

14b   Keep pronouns close to their antecedents.

ref

Even when pronoun choice is correct, too many words between a pronoun and its antecedent can confuse readers. If in a long sentence or in adjacent sentences several nouns appear between a pronoun and its proper antecedent, these nouns will incorrectly claim the reader's attention as the word renamed by the pronoun.

CONFUSING   *Prehistoric peoples* used many organic substances, which survive at relatively few archaeological sites. Bone and antler were commonly used, especially in Europe some fifteen thousand years ago. *They* relied heavily on plant fibers and baskets for their material culture. [The pronoun *they* must refer to *prehistoric peoples*, since only people can *rely*, but the intervening nouns distract from this reference.]

CLOSER   *Prehistoric peoples* use many organic substances, which survive at
ANTECEDENT   relatively few archaeological sites. *They commonly used* bone and antler, especially in Europe some fifteen thousand years ago. *They* also relied heavily on plant fibers and baskets for their material culture. [The pronoun subject, *they*, is added to the second sentence in order to maintain a clear antecedent. The pronoun subject of the third sentence is thereby made clear.]

PRONOUN   *Prehistoric peoples* used many organic substances, which survive at
REPLACED   relatively few archaeological sites. Bone and antler were commonly used, especially in Europe some fifteen thousand years ago. *The desert peoples of western North America* relied heavily on plant fibers and baskets for their material culture. [A new subject replaces the confusing pronoun.]

The relative pronouns *who, which,* and *that,* when introducing a modifying adjective clause, should be placed close to the noun they modify (see 19b-2).

CONFUSING   Prehistoric peoples used many organic substances difficult to find at archaeological sites, which included bone and antler. [Does *which* refer to *sites* or *substances*?]

CLOSER
ANTECEDENT
Prehistoric peoples used many organic substances, including bone and antler, which survive at relatively few archaeological sites.

EXERCISE 1

Rewrite the sentences that follow so that pronouns are replaced or are close to and refer clearly to the nouns they rename. Place a check beside the sentences that need no revision.

> *Example:* Edmond Halley as well as Isaac Newton studied the motions of comets, and in 1705 he published calculations relating to 24 cometary orbits. [Is Halley the clear antecedent, or could *he* refer to Newton?]
>
> Edmond Halley as well as Isaac Newton studied the motions of comets, and in 1705 Halley published calculations relating to 24 cometary orbits. [The pronoun is replaced with a noun.]

1. In particular, he noted that the elements of the orbits of the bright comets of 1531, 1607, and 1682 were so similar that a single comet could have produced all of the orbits.
2. Halley predicted that only one object existed and it should return about 1758.
3. Alexis Clairaut calculated the variations a comet should experience in passing near the planet Jupiter and also near Saturn and predicted that it should first make its appearance very late in 1758.
4. The comet that Clairaut identified was first sighted by an amateur astronomer, George Palitzsch, on Christmas night, 1758, exactly in accordance with his calculations.
5. The comet has been named *Halley's comet* in honor of the man who first recognized it to be a permanent member of the solar system.
6. Halley's comet last appeared in 1986 and is due to appear next in 2061. Observational records exist by the thousands for every other comet, though it is the most famous.

14c

ref

14c A pronoun's antecedent should be stated directly, not implied.

To be clear, a pronoun's antecedent should be stated directly, either in the sentence in which the pronoun appears or in an immediately preceding sentence. If the antecedent is merely implied, the pronoun's meaning will be weak or imprecise and the reader will probably be confused.

Make a pronoun refer to a specific noun antecedent, not to a modifier that may imply the antecedent.

Although an adjective may imply the antecedent of a pronoun, an adjective is not identical to and thus cannot serve as that antecedent. Revise sentences so that a *noun* provides the reference for a pronoun.

CONFUSING Two glass rods will repel each other when they are electrified. *It* is created from a buildup of positive and negative charges in the rods. [What does *it* refer to?]

NOUN ANTECEDENT Two glass rods will repel each other when they carry *electricity. It* is created from a buildup of positive and negative charges in the rods.

PRONOUN REPLACED Two *electrified* glass rods will repel each other. *Electricity* arises from the buildup of positive and negative charges in the rods.

2 Make a pronoun refer to a noun, not the possessive form of a noun.

14c

ref

Although the possessive form of a noun may imply the noun as the intended antecedent of a pronoun, this form is not identical to and thus is not clear enough to serve as that antecedent. Revise sentences so that a *noun* provides the reference for a pronoun.

CONFUSING The *Greeks'* knowledge of magnetic forces was evident before 600 B.C. *They* observed how certain minerals, such as loadstone, have the ability to attract pieces of iron.

NOUN ANTECEDENT The *Greeks* had knowledge of magnetic forces before 600 B.C. *They* observed how certain minerals have the ability to attract iron. [The possessive form—*Greeks'*—is eliminated to provide an antecedent for the pronoun *they.*]

PRONOUN REPLACED The *Greeks'* knowledge of magnetic forces was evident before 600 B.C. *The Greeks* observed how certain minerals, such as loadstone, have the ability to attract pieces of iron.

3 Give the pronouns *that, this, which,* and *it* precise reference.

The pronouns *that, this, which,* and *it* should refer to specific nouns. Avoid having them make vague reference to the overall sense of a preceding sentence.

CONFUSING Magnets have two poles—called north and south poles—and these poles obey the same kind of rule as electric charges: like poles repel each other and unlike poles attract each other. *This* was not well understood until the twentieth century. [What, exactly, does *this* refer to?]

ANTECEDENT PROVIDED Magnets have two poles—called north and south poles—and these poles obey the same kind of rule as electric charges: like poles repel each other and unlike poles attract each other. *This phenomenon* was not well understood until the twentieth century.

CONFUSING Knowledge of atomic structure was advanced in the late nineteenth century by British scientist J. J. Thompson, *which* established that one component of the atom, electrons, are negatively charged. [The pronoun *which* does not refer to a particular noun.]

ANTECEDENT PROVIDED   Knowledge of atomic structure was advanced in the late nineteenth century by British scientist J. J. Thompson, *who* established that one component of the atom, electrons, are negatively charged.

CONFUSING   Thompson believed atoms of matter contain two kinds of particles, intermingled: negatively charged electrons and positively charged protons. *That* was the impetus other physicists needed to refine even further the structural model of the atom. [The pronoun *that* has no single antecedent.]

PRONOUN REPLACED   Thompson believed atoms of matter contain two kinds of particles, intermingled: negatively charged electrons and positively charged protons. *Thompson's theory* was the impetus other physicists needed to refine even further the structural model of the atom.

4   Avoid indefinite antecedents for the pronouns *it, they,* and *you.*

14c

ref

Expressions such as "you know," "they say," and "it figures" are common in speech and informal writing. The pronouns in these expressions do not refer to particular people—or, in the case of *it*, to a particular object. These pronouns are said to have *indefinite* reference. In academic writing, pronouns should refer to specific antecedents. *You* should be used either to address the reader directly or for a direct quotation; *it* and *they* should refer to particular things, ideas, or people.

NONSTANDARD   Today, *they say* that an atom has a nucleus, consisting of neutrons and positively charged protons, around which circle negatively charged electrons.

STANDARD   Today, *physicists believe* that an atom has a nucleus, consisting of neutrons and positively charged protons, around which circle negatively charged electrons.

NONSTANDARD   Because physicists conduct experiments and propose models based on tools and mathematical languages only specialists can understand, *you* must almost take what physicists say as an item of faith.

STANDARD   Because physicists conduct experiments and propose models based on tools and mathematical languages only specialists can understand, *nonscientists* must almost take what physicists say as an item of faith.

How to Revise Unclear Pronoun Reference

1. Provide a clear, nearby antecedent.
2. Replace the pronoun with a noun and thereby eliminate the problem of ambiguous reference.
3. Totally recast the sentence to avoid the problem of ambiguous reference.

5   Avoid using a pronoun to refer to the title of a paper in the paper's first sentence.

A pronoun should have a reference in the sentence in which it appears or in an immediately preceding sentence. A title, while directly related to a paper or essay, does not occur *within* the paper or essay and thus cannot function appropriately as an antecedent.

A TITLE	"Eliot's Desert Images in *The Waste Land*"
A FIRST SENTENCE	They are plentiful, and their cumulative effect is to leave readers thirsty—in both body and soul.
FIRST SENTENCE REVISED	Desert images in T. S. Eliot's *The Waste Land* are plentiful, and their cumulative effect is to leave readers thirsty—in both body and soul.

ref

14d   Avoid mixing uses of the pronoun *it*.

The word *it* functions both as a pronoun and as an expletive (see 7a-11)—that is, as a space filler in a rearranged sentence.

AS AN EXPLETIVE	*It* is clear that the committee is resisting the initiative.
AS A PRONOUN	Although the committee voted, *it* [i.e., the committee] showed no leadership.

Avoid using the word *it* both as an expletive and as a pronoun in the same sentence.

CONFUSING	*It* is clear that *it* is shirking *its* responsibilities.
WEAK	*It* is clear that the committee is shirking *its* responsibilities.
CLEAR	Clearly, the committee is shirking *its* responsibilities.

14e   Use the relative pronouns *who*, *which*, and *that* appropriately.

1   Selecting relative pronouns

Relative pronouns (see 7e-2) introduce dependent clauses that usually function as adjectives. The pronouns *who*, *which*, and *that* rename and refer to the nouns they follow. The pronoun *who* can refer to people or to personified divinities or animals.

Nobel laureate Gabriel García Márquez, *who* was born in 1929 in Colombia, one of sixteen children of an impoverished telegraph operator, is among the most eminent of living Latin American writers.

That refers to people, animals, or things.

> At 19, he began to write stories *that* were rich in myth.

Which refers to animals and things.

> At 25, he moved to Mexico City, *which* is where he built his towering reputation among readers of Spanish literature.

2 Using relative pronouns in essential and nonessential clauses

Use either *that* or *which* depending on whether a clause begun by one of these words is essential or nonessential to the meaning of the noun being modified. Use *that* or *which* (with *no* commas around the dependent clause) to denote an **essential** (or restrictive) **modifier**—a word, phrase, or clause that provides information crucial for identifying a noun.

14e

ref

> As a young man, Márquez advocated many left-wing proposals for reform *that* were not in the end accepted.

or

> As a young man, Márquez advocated many left-wing proposals for reform *which* were not in the end accepted.

As the noun being modified becomes more specific (when it becomes a proper noun, for instance, that identifies a *particular* person, place, or thing), then a modifying clause is no longer essential since the core information of the noun is already established. Use *which* (*with* commas around the dependent clause) to denote a **nonessential** (or nonrestrictive) **modifier.**

> The celebrated *Cien años de soledad* (1967), *which* was published in English as *One Hundred Years of Solitude,* traces the history of a Colombian family through six generations. [Since the novel is titled, any modifying information is nonessential.]

The relative pronoun *who* can begin either an essential or a nonessential clause.

ESSENTIAL One Latin American novelist *who* very effectively mixes elements of fantasy with reality is Gabriel García Márquez. [Since there are many Latin American novelists and none of them is named, the information in the modifying clause is essential.]

NONESSENTIAL Nobel laureate Gabriel García Márquez, *who* was born in 1929 in Colombia, is among the most eminent of living Latin American writers. [Since a *particular* novelist is named, the modifying clause is nonessential.]

See 25d for a full discussion of essential and nonessential modifiers with commas.

EXERCISE 2

Revise the following sentences so that pronouns refer clearly to their antecedents. Place a check beside the sentences that need no revision.

> *Example:* Manic-depressive illness is a disorder characterized by extreme changes in mood between low (or depressed) and high (or manic). They usually are affected by the illness in the third or fourth decade of life.
>
> Manic-depressive illness is a disorder characterized by extreme changes in mood between low (or depressed) and high (or manic). *Manic-depressives* usually are affected by the illness in the third or fourth decade of life.

14e

ref

1. In recent years, the disorder has been called "bipolar affective disorder," because of the two opposite affects—or moods—involved. They say the illness differs from depression, which is termed a "unipolar" illness.
2. The "blue moods" of manic-depressives are characterized by feelings of discouragement, low energy level, and loss of interest in activities usually enjoyed. They tend to think slowly and often have difficulty concentrating.
3. Characteristically, there are other distressing symptoms, such as insomnia, sleeping too much, restless sleep, poor appetite, and often a pervasive anxiety and tension. This usually lasts for weeks or months.
4. The opposite mood is the elated, euphoric, or manic mood, which gives one an abundance of energy and a diminished need for sleep.
5. They say you can recognize a person's manic phase by listening to his or her speech, that is usually fast and pressured in an effort to keep pace with the rapid and shifting flow of ideas.
6. It is common that expansive and grandiose plans preoccupy the manic mind, for it is full of itself and will even put into operation wild business ventures that can end in embarrassment or bankruptcy.
7. The manic state, like the depressive state, can last weeks or months, which can seem a very long time for the family which must live with a manic-depressive.
8. According to recent research, the illness is transmitted in families, though they are not sure how genetic predisposition interacts with environmental factors to trigger manic or depressive episodes.
9. Recent biomedical theories suggest that changes in the level of various chemicals in the brain account for both manic and depressive episodes.
10. The illness's treatment has evolved from electroshock therapy, to antidepressant medication, to the now widespread use of lithium carbonate. It can be managed, as long as individuals are willing to submit themselves to chemical and psychological therapy.

EXERCISE 3

The pronouns *this, that, these, which,* and *it* are often used ambiguously, especially when they refer to ideas, situations, or circumstances not previously identified or clearly explained. In the following sequence of sentences, avoid vagueness by rewriting sentences to provide clear references. Use information from adjoining sentences to provide references.

> *Example:* Archaeology offers a unique approach to studying long-term change in human societies. This has characterized the study of humankind in North America.
>
> Archaeology offers a unique approach to studying long-term change in human societies. *This approach* has characterized the study of humankind in North America.

1. Unfortunately, archaeologists have only recently undertaken it in the context of the European Contact Period.
2. In the past they somewhat rigidly saw it as the ending point of prehistory, when Native Americans came into the orbit of Western civilization.
3. This was apparent especially because archaeologists tended to be preoccupied with the classification of discrete periods in the past, rather than with the processes of cultural change.
4. These were given names such as Paleo-Indian, Archaic, Woodland, etc.
5. In short, these narrowly constrained the interests of archaeologists.
6. Now they are taking a closer look at the phenomenon of European Contact as a part of long-term developments in that society.

14e

ref

CHAPTER 15

Misplaced and Dangling Modifiers

This chair was designed for weekend athletes with extra padding. Get the joke? Who (or what) has extra padding: the chair or weekend athletes? Misplaced, awkward, or dangling modifiers can prompt a smile, certainly; but more often they may confuse readers. Recall that the function of a modifier is to describe a noun, verb, or other modifiers (see 7c). A modifier can be a single word: a *sporty* car; a phrase: Joanne drove *in a sporty car;* or a dependent clause: *After Joanne collected her insurance settlement,* she drove a sporty car.

In order to function most effectively, a modifier should be placed directly next to the word it modifies. If this placement disrupts meaning, then the modifier should be placed *as close as possible* to the word it modifies. These two principles inform the discussion that follows.

MISPLACED MODIFIERS

 15a Position modifiers so that they refer clearly to the words they should modify.

Readers expect a modifier to be linked clearly with the word the writer intended it to modify. When this link is broken, readers become confused or frustrated.

CONFUSING   This chair was designed for weekend athletes with extra padding.

REVISED   This chair with extra padding was designed for weekend athletes.

Here is a more complicated example of a sentence made confusing by a misplaced modifier.

CONFUSING   The behavior of a chemical compound in a laboratory that is put together is similar to the behavior of an identical compound obtained from plants and animals growing in nature.

The example frustrates readers because key elements in the sentence do not seem to fit: Does *in a laboratory* modify *compound* or *behavior*? Is it really the *laboratory* that is *put together,* and if so, how or where? An analysis of the sentence suggests that the writer has misplaced the modifier *in the laboratory.* When the prepositional phrase is repositioned next to the words it should modify, the sentence becomes clear.

REVISED   The behavior of a chemical compound that is put together *in the laboratory* is similar to the behavior of an identical compound obtained from plants and animals growing in nature.

If a phrase or clause beginning a sentence functions as an adjective modifier, then the first words after the modifier—that is, the first words of the independent clause—should include the noun being modified.

CONFUSING   Still plunged in the darkness of the superstition, legends of the mysterious East circulated widely among medieval Europeans. [Who or what is "plunged in the darkness of superstition"—certainly not *legends.*]

15a

mm

REWRITTEN   Still plunged in the darkness of superstition, *medieval Europeans* widely circulated legends of the mysterious East. [The original sentence, *"Legends . . . Europeans,"* has been given a new subject, *medieval Europeans,* that can be modified by the introductory phrase.]

EXERCISE 1

Reorganize or rewrite the following sentences (you may need to add a word or two) so that the misplaced modifier is correctly placed. Place a check mark beside any sentence in which modifiers are used clearly.

> *Example:*   Turning to black subculture as an alternative to homogenized mainstream culture, black slang and music became increasingly common among American teenagers after 1950.
>
> Turning to black subculture as an alternative to homogenized mainstream culture, American teenagers after 1950 began using black slang and listening to black music. [The sentence is given a new subject, *American teenagers,* that can be modified by the introductory phrase.]

1. Black rhythm and blues with its typical twelve-bar structure among white teenagers became rock 'n roll's most common format.
2. Organized by a disc jockey in Cleveland, Ohio, two-thirds of the audience for a stage show featuring black rhythm and blues acts in 1953 were white.
3. Strung down the center of the theater, black and white members of the audience were separated by a rope that was often gone by the end of the performance.
4. Combining elements of black rhythm and blues and white country western music, American teenagers found rock 'n roll attractive.

15b   Position limiting modifiers with care.

In conversation, **limiting modifiers**—words such as *only, almost, just, nearly, even,* and *simply*—are often shifted within a sentence with little concern for their effect on meaning. When written, however, a limiting modifier is taken literally to restrict the meaning of the word placed directly after it. Observe how meaning changes as the position of a limiting modifier changes.

> *Nearly* 90 percent of the 200 people who served in Presidential cabinets from 1897 to 1973 belonged to the social or business elite.

> Ninety percent of the *nearly* 200 people who served in Presidential cabinets from 1897 to 1973 belonged to the social or business elite.

15c

Placement of the limiting modifier *nearly* fundamentally alters the meaning of these sentences. To establish meaning clearly, position limiting modifiers with care.

mm

> EXERCISE 2
>
> Use the limiting modifier in parentheses to rewrite each sentence two ways, giving each version a different meaning.
>
> *Example:*   The Greek astrolabe measured the elevation of the sun or a star. (only)
>
> *Only* the Greek astrolabe measured the elevation of the sun or a star.
>
> The Greek astrolabe measured *only* the elevation of the sun or a star.
>
> 1. When they market new musical trends, major record labels follow rather than lead. (usually)
> 2. The latest hot trend, "world music," is not an exception. (even)
> 3. "There is no one way to decide what to put out," says Roger Armstrong. (simply)
> 4. "By putting out titles you are developing a taste," he claims. (just)

Reposition modifiers that describe two elements simultaneously.

A **squinting modifier** appears to modify two words in the sentence—the word preceding it and the word following it. To convey a clear meaning, the modifier must be repositioned so it can describe only a *single* word.

CONFUSING   The official being questioned aggressively shut the door. [What does *aggressively* describe—how the official was being questioned or how the official shut the door?]

REVISED   The official, who was being questioned aggressively, shut the door. [A clause is set off to become a nonessential modifier of *official*.]

REVISED   The official who was being questioned shut the door aggressively. [*Aggressively* is moved to an unambiguous position and modifies *shut*.]

EXERCISE 3

The following sentences are made awkward by squinting modifiers. Revise each sentence twice so that the modifier describes a different word in each revision.

Example: Sitting in the hot summer sun often accelerates the skin's aging process.

Sitting *often* in the hot summer sun accelerates the skin's aging process. [*Often* modifies *sitting*—the sense being that one must sit in the sun many times to accelerate the skin's aging.]

Often, sitting in the hot summer sun accelerates the skin's aging process. [The sense here is that sitting in the sun even once or a few times can accelerate the aging of the skin.]

1. Going to the movies sometimes makes me wish I were an actress.
2. The equation that Steven thought he had analyzed thoroughly confused him on the exam.
3. The father reprimanding his son angrily pushed the shopping cart down the supermarket aisle.
4. The suspect being questioned thoroughly believed his constitutional rights were being violated.
5. Taking long walks frequently helps me to relax.

15d

mm

15d Reposition a lengthy modifier that splits a subject and its verb.

Meaning in a sentence depends on the link a writer establishes between a subject and its verb. We commonly interrupt or split these elements with adjective phrases and clauses; and provided these modifiers make a distinct modifying unit and do not suspend for too long the link between subject and verb, they need not confuse readers.

Handmade carpets, *woven in Iran by villagers and nomads for thousands of years,* have been exported to Europe since the sixteenth century.

It is also common to find a one- or two-word adverb between a subject and verb.

Groups of three or four weavers *normally* work seven days a week for anywhere between one to two years to produce a single carpet.

Lengthy modifiers, however, disrupt the link between subject and verb and should be repositioned to keep that link clear.

CONFUSING   Carpet production, *whether in the cities or in the tents of wandering tribes, or for that matter in the simple houses of villagers in small, isolated villages around the country,* has been labor intensive.

REVISED   *Whether in the cities or in the tents of wandering tribes, or for that matter in the simple houses of villagers in small, isolated villages around the country,* carpet production has been labor intensive. [An introductory modifier puts a repositioned subject next to its verb.]

REVISED   Carpets were produced *in the cities or in the tents of wandering tribes and in the simple houses of villagers in small, isolated villages around the country.* In all cases, the techniques of carpet production were labor intensive. [The lengthy original sentence has been split into two sentences.]

15d

mm

Avoid Splitting Paired Sentence Elements with Lengthy Modifiers

Each of the five basic sentence patterns (see 7b) presents paired parts of speech that function together to create meaning. Avoid splitting the following elements with lengthy modifiers that disrupt meaning.

		⌐ *Predicate* ¬	
Pattern 1:	Subject	verb	
	Sarah	*arrived.*	

		⌐——— *Predicate* ———¬	
Pattern 2:	Subject	verb (tr.)	direct object
	Sarah	*embraced*	*her family.*

		⌐————— *Predicate* —————¬	
Pattern 3:	Subject	verb (tr.)	indirect object	direct object
	Sarah	*brought*	*them*	*presents.*

		⌐————— *Predicate* —————¬	
Pattern 4:	Subject	verb (tr.)	direct object	object complement
	Sarah	*considered*	*her family*	*a blessed sight.*

		⌐————— *Predicate* —————¬	
Pattern 5:	Subject	verb (linking)	subject complement
	She	*was*	*relieved.*

EXERCISE 4

Reposition modifiers in rearranged, rephrased, or divided sentences to establish clear links between subjects and verbs. Place a check before any sentence in which modifiers are used clearly.

Example: Heraldry, which includes the tracing of pedigrees and establishing the order of persons taking part in important ceremonies, as well as a familiarity with armorial bearings (or "emblems"), the rules regarding their design and use, and their technical description, in its broadest sense, comprises the skills and knowledge necessary to the occupation of *herald*.

Heraldry, in its broadest sense, comprises the skills and knowledge necessary to the occupation of *herald*. These skills include the tracing of pedigrees and establishing the order of persons taking part in important ceremonies, as well as a familiarity with armorial bearings (or "emblems"), the rules regarding their design and use, and their technical description.

1. The origins of heraldry, first of all in clan totems and tribal and national emblems, and in Western civilization in the shield insignia used by Athenian families in the fifth and sixth centuries B.C., are perhaps as old as the human race.
2. Some of the older emblems, whether the eagle of Rome, which reappears as the eagle of the Austrian, German, and Russian emperors, or the white horse of Woden, eventually found their way into medieval heraldry.
3. The absence of any sign of true armorial bearings in the Bayeux tapestry, which was probably woven for Bishop Odo, who was himself present at Hastings, seems to provide conclusive evidence that personal heraldry did not exist as early as the battle of Hastings (1066), pictured in detail in the tapestry.

15e

mm

15e Reposition a modifier that splits a verb and its object or a verb and its complement.

A lengthy adverb phrase or clause can create an awkward sentence if it splits a verb and its object or a verb and its complement. Reposition these adverbs by placing them at the beginning or the end of a sentence.

AWKWARD   A number of presidents have emphasized *in foreign disputes* nonintervention. [The verb and object are split.]

REVISED   A number of presidents have emphasized nonintervention *in foreign disputes.*

AWKWARD   Millard Fillmore became, *after serving eight years as a U.S. representative from New York,* the elected vice president in 1848. [The verb and complement are split.]

REVISED   *After serving eight years as a U.S. representative from New York,* Millard Fillmore was elected vice president in 1848.

Note that one- or two-word adverbial modifiers commonly appear before a direct object or complement.

CLEAR   Zachary Taylor became *in 1848* the twelfth President.

However, when a modifier (or a combination of them) places too great a distance between a verb and its object or complement, the modifier should be repositioned.

AWKWARD   Millard Fillmore became, *on the death of Taylor in 1850,* the thirteenth President of the United States.

REVISED   Millard Fillmore became the thirteenth President of the United States *on the death of Taylor in 1850.*

EXERCISE 5

Reposition modifiers in order to restore clear links between verbs and objects or complements in these sentences. Place a check before any sentence in which modifiers are used correctly.

Example: Heraldic devices became, once a particular design had been associated with a name and a lordship, hereditary.

Heraldic devices became hereditary, once a particular design had been associated with a name and a lordship.

1. Armorial bearings once they became the fashion among the most influential aristocracy spread quickly throughout western Europe.
2. The use of coats of arms, as they became associated with military command and with the warlike games of joust and tourney, was at first confined to those who held their lands by force.
3. The surcoat and standard of a king or baron obviously had, like a modern army uniform, a practical military function, enabling soldiers to find and rally around their commander in the press of battle.
4. It is said that Henry IV had, at the Battle of Shrewbury in 1403, several of his knights wear the royal surcoat, a dangerous honor because Henry's opponents were eager to kill him.

15f Reposition a modifier that splits the parts of an infinitive.

An **infinitive** is the dictionary or **base** form of a verb: *go, walk, see.* In a sentence, the infinitive form is often immediately preceded by the word *to: to go, to walk, to see.* Because the base word of the infinitive is a verb, the words that modify infinitives are adverbs. In conversation, emphasis on a short adverbial modifier sometimes interrupts the two parts of an infinitive: *"Please try to quickly move up."* Such an interruption in long or complex written sentences can be disruptive to the intended meaning.

Move an adverb to a position before or after an infinitive, or rewrite the sentence and eliminate the infinitive.

SPLIT   Many managers are unable *to* with difficult employees *establish* a moderate and reasonable tone.

REVISED   Many managers are unable *to establish* a moderate and reasonable tone with difficult employees.

SPLIT   One of a manager's responsibilities is *to* successfully *manage* conflict.

REVISED   One of a manager's responsibilities is *to manage* conflict successfully.

Occasionally, a sentence with a split infinitive will sound more natural than a sentence rewritten to avoid the split. This will be the case when the object of the infinitive is a long phrase or clause and the adverbial modifier is short.

SPLIT   Some managers like to *regularly* interview a variety of workers from different departments so that potential problems can be identified and averted.

Avoiding the split may become somewhat awkward.

No SPLIT   Some managers like to interview *regularly* a variety of workers from different departments so that potential problems can be identified and averted.

No SPLIT   Some managers like *regularly* to interview a variety of workers from different departments so that potential problems can be identified and averted.

Some readers do not accept split infinitives, whatever the circumstances of a sentence. The safe course for a writer is to revise the sentence and eliminate the infinitive or change the modifier.

No INFINITIVE   *On a regular basis,* some managers like to interview a variety of workers from different departments so that potential problems can be identified and averted.

mm

15g Reposition a lengthy modifier that splits a verb phrase.

A *verb phrase* consists of a main verb and its auxiliary or helping verb. Like an infinitive, a verb phrase is a grammatical unit. Unlike infinitives, verb phrases are commonly split with brief modifiers.

In developed countries, the commitment to children as a natural resource *has* long *been linked* to huge investments in education and health care.

The sense of a verb phrase is disrupted when it is split by a lengthy modifying phrase or clause. Repair the split by relocating the modifier.

CONFUSING   Despite severe economic limitations, many third-world countries *have* in efforts to improve the health, well-being, and education of children *invested* large sums.

REVISED   Despite severe economic limitations, many third-world countries *have invested* large sums in efforts to improve the health, well-being, and education of children.

EXERCISE 6

In the following sentences, reposition modifiers in order to repair split infinitives and restore clear links between auxiliary verbs and main verbs.

> *Example:*   Coats of arms were in ensuing centuries used by bishops and abbots, who ranked as lords in the feudal hierarchy.
>
> Coats of arms were used in ensuing centuries by bishops and abbots, who ranked as lords in the feudal hierarchy.
>
> In ensuing centuries, coats of arms were used by bishops and abbots, who ranked as lords in the feudal hierarchy.

1. They were also, in municipalities and other corporations which held legal powers or lands, widely adopted.
2. The association of armorial bearings with nobility came, as evidence that the user and his descendants had acquired the social status of gentlemen, to symbolize rank.
3. The sporting and military uses of heraldry were with the appearance of both tournaments and closed helmets in the sixteenth century, becoming less important, while its other (social) uses were multiplying.
4. Coats of arms were within a very short span of time carved over doorways, placed in stained glass windows, engraved upon silver, and painted on porcelain dishes and other household articles of the upper class.

dm

DANGLING MODIFIERS

15h   Identify and revise dangling modifiers.

A modifier is said to "dangle" when the word it modifies is not clearly visible in the same sentence. Correct the error by rewriting the sentence, making sure to include the word modified.

1   Give introductory clauses or phrases a specific word to modify.

An introductory phrase or clause will modify a specific word in a sentence, most often a subject or verb. First-draft sentences beginning with long introductory phrases or clauses are in danger of becoming dangling modifiers, perhaps because complex openings lead a writer to assume that the word being modified is obvious. The modified word will *not* be obvious to a reader unless it appears in the sentence that follows the introductory remark. Revision involves asking what the opening clause or phrase modifies and rewriting the sentence to provide an answer.

DANGLING   Dominated though they are by a few artists who repeatedly get the best roles, millions of people flock to the cinemas. [Who or what are dominated? If the *millions* are not, the main clause lacks a visible word to be modified.]

REVISED   Dominated though they are by a few artists who repeatedly get the best roles, *movies* continue to attract millions of people. [With a rewritten main clause, the opening clause is immediately followed by a noun it can modify.]

DANGLING   After appearing in *The Maltese Falcon,* it was clear that Warner Brothers had a box-office star. [Who appeared in the film?]

REVISED   After appearing in *The Maltese Falcon,* <u>Humphrey Bogart</u> became Warner Brothers' box-office star.

2   Rewrite passive constructions to provide active subjects that introductory phrases and clauses can modify.

Often a modifying phrase that begins a sentence will dangle because the independent clause is written in the passive voice (see 9g). Missing from this passive-voice sentence is the original subject, which would have been modified by the introductory phrase or clause. Correct the dangling modifier by rewriting the independent clause in the active voice.

15h

dm

DANGLING   With his weary, sardonic style and his cigarettes lipped loosely, the persona of the private detective was etched into the American psyche. [The persona of the private detective was etched *by whom?*]

REVISED WITH ACTIVE VOICE   With his weary, sardonic style and his cigarettes lipped loosely, <u>Bogart</u> etched the persona of the private detective into the American psyche.

EXERCISE 7

Repair the dangling modifiers that follow by restoring the word modified to each sentence. Place a check in front of any sentence in which modifiers are used correctly.

> *Example:*   Having conquered an area stretching from the southern border of Colombia to central Chile, civilian and military rule was maintained for two hundred years before the Spanish discovery of America.
>
> Having conquered an area stretching from the southern border of Colombia to central Chile, *the Incas* maintained civilian and military rule for two hundred years before the Spanish discovery of America.

1. Centering on the city of Cuzco in the Peruvian Andes, the coastal and mountain regions of Ecuador, Peru, and Bolivia were included.
2. As the only true empire existing in the New World at the time of Columbus, wealth both in precious metals and in astronomical information had been assembled.
3. Knitting together the two disparate areas of Peru, mountain and desert, the Incas achieved an economic and social synthesis.
4. Growing and weaving cotton and planting such domesticated crops as corn, squash, and beans, Peru had been settled dating from before 3000 B.C.

CHAPTER 16

Shifts and Mixed Constructions

*C*onsistency is an essential quality of language, allowing us to learn and master vocabulary and sentence structure. When we open a book, we expect to read words from left to right; different, or suddenly shifting, positioning of sentences on the page would disorient us. Just so, we expect that within sentences writers will adhere to certain patterns or conventions. When these patterns are violated, clear communication suffers. Writers need to maintain the consistency of every sentence by avoiding abrupt shifts and by establishing a clear, consistent sentence structure.

SHIFTS

Aside from the content it communicates, a sentence expresses other important information: whether a singular or plural subject is speaking or being spoken to; whether action takes place in the present, future, or past; whether a subject is acting or being acted on; whether the occasion for writing is formal or informal; and whether a subject is speaking directly or indirectly. Once a writer makes a decision about these matters, that decision should be followed conscientiously within any one sentence. To do otherwise will confuse readers.

16a Revise shifts in person and number.

The term **person** identifies whether the speaker of a sentence is the person speaking (the first person), the person spoken to (the second person), or the person spoken about (the third person). **Number** denotes whether a person or thing is singular or plural. (See 7a-7 and 7a-2.)

Pronoun Forms (Subjective Case)		
	Singular	*Plural*
First Person	I	we
Second Person	you	you
Third Person	he, she, it, one, a person	they, people

1 Revise shifts in person by keeping all references to a subject consistent.

A shift from one person form to another obscures a subject's identity, changing the reference by which the subject is known. Shifts in person often occur when a writer switches from the second person (you) to the first person (I, we) or to the third person (he, she, it). You can avoid this difficulty by recognizing the first-, second-, or third-person orientation of your sentences and by maintaining consistency.

INCONSISTENT A person who is a nonsmoker can develop lung troubles when you live with smokers.

THIRD PERSON A person who is a nonsmoker can develop lung troubles when he or she lives with smokers.

SECOND PERSON If you are a nonsmoker, you can develop lung troubles if you live with smokers.

16a

shift

2 Revise shifts in number by maintaining consistent singular or plural forms.

Shifts in number tend to occur when a writer uses pronouns (see 10b and 14a). Pronouns should agree in number with the nouns for which they substitute. You can avoid shifting number and confusing readers by maintaining a clear plural or singular sense throughout a sentence.

INCONSISTENT At the turn of the century, it was common for a man to come to the United States alone and work to raise money so that family members could later join them.

REVISED At the turn of the century, it was common for a man to come to the United States alone and work to raise money so that family members could later join him.

Any significant words related to a subject or object should match its number.

INCONSISTENT The seven candidates for the judgeship have a liberal record.

REVISED The seven candidates for the judgeship have liberal records.

EXERCISE 1

Correct shifts in person and number in the following sentences.

Example: In the eighth century Vikings launched attacks on the peoples around the Baltic and the North Sea during which we raided churches and monasteries.

In the eighth century Vikings launched attacks on the peoples around the Baltic and the North Sea during which *they* raided churches and monasteries.

1. Viking raids struck terror in the heart of a monk because, as peaceable men, they were ill-prepared to fend off attack.
2. Even Charlemagne reportedly feared the Vikings, and is said to have shed tears over his power to destroy the king's legacy for posterity.
3. For a hit-and-run robber the sea was the best avenue because they could strike their victims without warning, then make a quick get-away.
4. In a Viking invasion, news of your coming usually preceded you, giving a victim time to hide their treasure and disappear.

Revise shifts in tense, mood, and voice.

shift

Tense, mood, and *voice* denote important characteristics of main sentence verbs: when the action of the verb occurs, what a writer's attitude toward that action is, and whether the *doer* or *receiver* of the action is emphasized. When these characteristics are treated inconsistently, readers can be confused.

1 Revise shifts in tense by observing the appropriate sequence of verb tenses.

A verb's **tense** shows when an action has occurred or when a subject exists in a certain state of being. (See 9e and 9f.) The tenses are marked by verb endings and auxiliary verbs.

He walk*ed* home.	He *was* walk*ing* home.
He walk*s* home.	He *is* walk*ing* home.
	He *will be* walk*ing* home.

Tenses are often changed within sentences in regular and consistent patterns (see 9f), as shown in the accompanying box. (The box in 9f shows examples of each pattern.) Shifts in tense that disrupt these patterns strike readers as illogical, especially when the shifts alter the logic or time sequencing within or between sentences.

Sequencing Verb Tenses in a Sentence

See the descriptions and guidelines on tenses of verbs in 8f and 9e.

To establish a relationship between two events, both of which occur in the past:

- Use the simple past tense in the independent clause—and any of the four past tenses in the dependent clause.

- Use the past perfect tense in the independent clause and the simple past tense in the dependent clause.

To establish a relationship between a past event and a future event:

- Use the past tense in the independent clause and the simple future, future progressive, or simple present tenses in the dependent clause.

To establish a relationship between a past event and an acknowledged fact or condition:

- Use the simple past tense for the main clause and the simple present tense in the dependent clause.

- Use the past perfect tense for the main clause and the simple present tense in the dependent clause.

16b

shift

INCONSISTENT   When the Civil War begins, only one American in five was living in a city. By 1915, cities hold half of all Americans. [The tense shifts from present to past and back again for no reason.]

CONSISTENT   When the Civil War began, only one American in five was living in a city. By 1915, cities held half of all Americans. [The past tense is used consistently.]

The "historical present tense" is often used in academic writing to refer to material in books or articles or to action in a film (see 9e-1).

INCONSISTENT   In her article, Karen Wright referred to Marshall McLuhan's global village and asks rhetorically, "Who today would quarrel with McLuhan's prophecy?" [The reference to Wright's work should either be past or "historically" present, but not both.]

CONSISTENT   In her article, Karen Wright refers to Marshall McLuhan's global village and asks rhetorically, "Who today would quarrel with McLuhan's prophecy?"

Occasionally, a shift of tense in one sentence will be needed to establish a proper sequence of events.

ACCEPTABLE   After he *had read* of experiments in electricity, Nathaniel Hawthorne *observed* that the world *was becoming* "a great nerve." [The tenses change from past perfect to past to past progressive. See chapter 9 for a full discussion of tenses.]

2   Revise for shifts in mood.

A verb's **mood** indicates whether a writer judges a statement to be a fact, a command, or an occurrence contrary to fact (see 9h). Sentences in the **indicative mood,** by far the most common, are presented as fact. In the **imperative mood,** writers express commands—addressing them usually to an implicitly understood "you." In the **subjunctive mood,** writers express doubt or a condition contrary to fact (see 9h-1–4). When mood shifts in a sentence, readers cannot be sure of a writer's intended judgment about the information presented. You can avoid confusion by choosing a mood (most often the indicative) and using it consistently.

INCONSISTENT   If the writing process were easy, students will not need to take classes in composition. [The sentence shifts from the "doubtful" subjunctive to the "factual" indicative, leaving readers unsure about what is intended.]

CONSISTENT   If the writing process were easy, students would not need to take classes in composition. [Consistent use of the subjunctive makes the writer's judgment clear.]

16b ⌐3 Revise for shifts in voice.

shift

A **transitive verb**—one that transfers action from a subject to an object—can be expressed in the active or passive voice. The natural state of a verb is the active voice. In the sentence *Mary kicked the ball*, the verb (*kicked*) transfers action from the subject (*Mary*) to the direct object (*the ball*). An **active-voice sentence** emphasizes the *doer* of an action. A rearrangement of words yields a **passive-voice sentence,** which emphasizes the *receiver* of an action: *The ball was kicked by Mary.*

Both the active and passive voices have their uses. (See 9g-1–2.) However, if writers shift from one voice to the other in a single sentence, both emphasizing and deemphasizing a subject (or *doer* of an action), then readers will be confused. Avoid the difficulty by choosing an active *or* a passive voice in any one sentence.

INCONSISTENT   Columbus arrived in the New World and it was believed he had found the coast of Asia. [The shift from active voice to passive leaves doubt about who believed this.]

CONSISTENT   Columbus arrived in the New World and believed he had found the coast of Asia.

EXERCISE 2

Correct the shifts in tense, voice, and mood in the following sentences.

Example: Gradually the Viking raiders became settlers; they find it more convenient to remain in the coastal villages they attack than to return to frigid Scandinavia.

Gradually the Viking raiders became settlers; they *found* it more convenient to remain in the coastal villages they *attacked* than to return to frigid Scandinavia.

1. Norsemen and Northmen became "Normans," and so would give their name to Normandy.

2. The Normans adapted readily to the variety of circumstances in which they found themselves, and were fitted easily into the feudal hierarchy in France and Germany.
3. In England they will help catalyze the process of unification, while in Sicily they acted as mediators among the diverse groups who live there.
4. A Norman, Tancred, led the First Crusade during which Jerusalem was captured and a Norman kingdom was established in Syria.
5. Though adept at migration, the assimilation of peoples, and the cementing of nations, the Normans would have no talent or appetite for exploration.
6. The Norse acquired a reputation as a "fast-breeding" people, and it was speculated by those they conquered that they practice polygamy.

16c   Revise for shifts in tone.

16c

shift

Tone refers to the writer's attitude toward the subject or the audience and is signaled by the qualities that make writing formal or informal, learned or breezy, measured or hysterical. Without doubt, tone is a difficult element to revise since so much determines it: choice and quality of description, verb selection, sentence structure, and sentence mood and voice. Tone changes depending on a writer's audience: You will adopt one tone in a letter to a friend and an altogether different tone when writing a paper for your art history professor. The level of diction used in a writer's choice of words is a major factor affecting tone. See 3c-5 and 21e for more on matching the tone of a paper to your occasion for writing.

In papers that you prepare for your courses, your tone should be characterized by writing that is precise, logical, and formal, though not stuffy or filled with jargon. (See 21e.) Abrupt shifts from any established basic tone in a paper will be disconcerting to readers.

DISCONCERTING   In his famous painting *Persistence of Memory*, Salvador Dalí creates his most haunting allegory of empty space in which time is deader than a doornail. [The final slang expression creates an informal tone inconsistent with a formal analysis.]

CONSISTENT   In his famous painting *Persistence of Memory*, Salvador Dalí creates his most haunting allegory of empty space in which time is at an end. [A more formal expression is consistent with the analysis.]

EXERCISE 3
Correct any shifts in tone in the following sentences so that the sentences are consistent.

Example: Can you name a person who is always in a hurry, is extremely competitive, and blows his stack frequently?

Can you name a person who is always in a hurry, is extremely competitive, and is often angry?

1. In contrast, can you think of someone who is so low key that he's a couch potato, not very competitive, and easy-going in relations with others?
2. You now have in mind two *homo sapiens* who could be described as showing Type A and Type B behavior patterns.
3. Type A individuals get frazzled by stress more easily and tend to suffer more coronary problems than Type Bs.
4. Type Bs have the patience of the blessed saints and perform well under high levels of stress and on tasks involving complex judgments and accuracy.
5. Who would make the better executive, the better spouse, the better party animal?

shift

16d Maintain consistent use of direct or indirect discourse.

Direct discourse reproduces exactly, with quotation marks, spoken or written language. **Indirect discourse** approximately reproduces the language of others, capturing its sense, though not its precise expression. (See 28a-1.)

DIRECT   Lawrence asked, "Is that the telephone ringing?"

INDIRECT   Lawrence asked whether the telephone was ringing.

Mixing discourse in one sentence can disorient a reader by raising doubts about what a speaker has actually said. You can avoid the problem by making a conscious choice to refer to another's speech either directly or indirectly.

INCONSISTENT   In his inaugural speech, John F. Kennedy exhorted Americans to ask what they could do for their country, not "what your country can do for you." [The direct quotation following the indirect discourse raises unnecessary questions about what Kennedy actually said.]

CONSISTENT   In his inaugural speech, John F. Kennedy exhorted Americans to ask what they could do for their country, not what their country could do for them.

CONSISTENT   In his inaugural speech, John F. Kennedy exhorted Americans, "Ask not what your country can do for you, ask what you can do for your country."

EXERCISE 4
Correct the shifts in discourse in the following sentences by making direct quotations indirect.

Example: As a boy in his teens, Albert Einstein asked what our world view would look like if "I rode on a beam of light."

As a boy in his teens, Albert Einstein asked what our world view would be if seen from the perspective of light.

1. The great physicist Niels Bohr nailed a horseshoe on a wall in his cottage because "I understand it brings you luck whether you believe or not."
2. The mystery writer Agatha Christie believed that being married to an archaeologist, a man whose business it was to excavate antiquities, was a stroke of great good luck, because as she got older "he shows more interest in me."
3. In a feverish letter from a battlefield in Italy, Napoleon wrote Josephine that he had received her letters and that "do you have any idea, darling, what you are doing, writing to me in those terms?"

MIXED CONSTRUCTIONS

16e

mix

A **mixed construction** occurs when a sentence takes a reader in one direction by beginning with a certain grammatical pattern and then abruptly changes direction with another pattern. The resulting mix of incompatible sentence parts invariably confuses readers.

16e Establish clear, grammatical relations between sentence parts.

In speech, mixed constructions are common. We can compensate for grammatically inconsistent thoughts in speech with gestures or intonation, and listeners usually understand. But readers work at a disadvantage, for they cannot see or hear our attempts to correct jumbled expressions. More so than listeners, readers are likely to be sensitive to and confused by mixed constructions.

MIXED   If you do not understand a poem is when a lapse into singsong can become a problem as a reader.

This construction, imaginable as a spoken statement, is not a sentence but a fragment—actually two fragments (see 12a). The construction begins with a dependent clause—an *if* clause that readers expect to see followed by and independent *then* clause, which never appears. Instead, the *if* construction is followed by the verb *is* and by a second dependent clause, beginning with *when*. Revise mixed constructions by rearranging words until you create an independent clause.

REVISED   If you do not understand a poem, then the chances are good you will lapse into a singsong when reading it. [An independent clause beginning with *then* now completes the introductory *if* construction.]

REVISED   Lapsing into a singsong can become a problem if you read poems you
do not understand. [The mixed construction is avoided by rearranging
words and by converting the *when* clause to a subject.]

Proofread carefully to identify and correct mixed constructions, which
tend to occur in predictable patterns.

"The fact that"

The expression "the fact that" and words immediately associated with
it result in a mixed construction when writers forget that the expression begins
a noun clause that functions as a subject or object, but not as a complete
sentence.

MIXED   The fact that rhyming makes a poem memorable. [Even though *makes*
is a verb, and *rhyming* functions as a noun, this string of words is not a
sentence. It is a noun clause that takes the place of a noun, either as a
subject or as an object.]

REVISED   The fact that rhyming makes a poem memorable is important to know
when choosing poems to read aloud. [*The fact that* and its associated
words now function as the subject of a sentence.]

REVISED   Rhyming makes a poem memorable. [Deleting the words *the fact that*
converts the dependent noun clause into an independent clause. *Makes*
now functions as the main verb.]

An adverb clause

Adverb clauses begin with subordinate conjunctions—words like *when,
because,* and *although* (see 19b). A mixed construction occurs when the final
word of an introductory adverb clause also serves as the subject (or a word
modifying the subject) of an independent clause.

MIXED   When a poem is rhymed words can stand out unnaturally if emphasized. [The last word of the adverb clause, *rhymed,* is also used to modify
the subject, *words.*]

REVISED   When a poem is rhymed, the rhymed words can stand out unnaturally
if emphasized.

REVISED   Rhymed words in a poem can stand out unnaturally if emphasized.

A prepositional phrase

A prepositional phrase consists of a preposition (*by, of, in,* etc.) and a
noun—the object of the preposition (see 7d-1). A noun functioning as the
object of a prepositional phrase cannot simultaneously function as the subject
of an independent clause.

MIXED   By reading a poem slowly can help your listeners to concentrate. [*Reading a poem slowly* functions as both the object of the preposition *by* and
the subject of the independent clause.]

16e

mix

REVISED   Reading a poem slowly can help your listeners to concentrate. [Eliminating the preposition *by* allows the phrase *reading a poem slowly* to function as the subject of the independent clause.]

REVISED   By reading a poem slowly, you can help your listeners to concentrate. [The prepositional phrase is retained and a new subject, *you*, is added.]

16f   Establish consistent relations between subjects and predicates.

A second type of mixed construction occurs when the predicate part of a sentence does not logically complete its subject. The error is known as **faulty predication** and most often involves a form of the verb *to be*, a linking verb that connects the subject complement in the predicate part of the sentence with the subject. You are familiar with the sentence pattern __A__ is __B__ : *The child is happy.* (See 7b, Pattern 5.) In this sentence the verb functions as an equal sign. If the subject complement, *B*, is logically inconsistent with the subject, *A*, then the predicate is faulty and the sentence will confuse readers.

16f

mix

INCONSISTENT   The resolving power of an electron microscope is keenly aware of life invisible to the human eye. [Can a microscope be keenly aware?]

Only living, sentient beings—mammals, for instance—can be *aware*. The writer and reader know that a microscope (an inanimate object) is not alive and does not have a mind. Therefore it is not logical to assert (or to predicate—hence, faulty predication) that electron microscopes are aware. The imprecise, illogical match between subject and predicate jumbles the sentence and confuses readers. Assuming the sentence is not trying to be science fiction or poetry but informative writing, the predicate and subject must be made logically consistent.

REVISED   The resolving power of an electron microscope helps us to be keenly aware of life invisible to the human eye. [Now it is people (*us*) who have been made aware.]

REVISED   Aided by the resolving power of the electron microscope, we have grown keenly aware of life invisible to the human eye.

Faulty predication occurs in three other constructions involving the verb *to be* and sentence pattern __A__ is __B__ or __A__ = __B__ . If in writing a definition you begin the subject complement (*B*) with the word *when* or *where*, or if in giving a reason you begin the subject complement with *because*, you may create a mixed construction.

FAULTY   Electron illumination is when beams of electrons instead of light are used in a microscope. [In this sentence pattern, the subject (*electron illumination*) must be renamed by a noun or described by an adjective.]

FAULTY   The reason electron microscopes have become essential to research is because their resolving power is roughly 500,000 times greater than the power of the human eye. [In this sentence pattern, the subject (*reason*) must be renamed by a noun or described by an adjective.]

The sentence pattern of *subject / linking verb / subject complement* requires an adjective or a noun to serve as subject complement. The words *when, where,* and *because* begin adverb clauses and, thus, do not fit grammatically into the pattern. Revise a faulty predicate by changing the adverb clause to a noun clause or by changing the verb and reordering the sentence. Usually a revision requires adding and deleting words.

REVISED   Electron illumination is achieved by using beams of electrons instead of light in a microscope.

REVISED   The reason electron microscopes have become essential is that their resolving power is roughly 500,000 times greater than the power of the human eye.

16f

mix

Verbs other than *to be* can assert actions or states that are not logically consistent with a subject. Wherever you find faulty predication, correct it.

FAULTY   The rate of Native American enrollment in institutions of higher learning sees an improvement in the last ten years. [A *rate* cannot see.]

REVISED   The rate of Native American enrollment in institutions of higher learning has improved in the last ten years.

REVISED   Over the last ten years, educators have seen an improvement in the rate of Native American enrollment in institutions of higher learning.

EXERCISE 5

Revise the sentences that follow in two ways, making each consistent in grammar or meaning. Place a check beside any sentence that needs no revision.

Example: Language and the state that have been companions through history.

Language and the state have been companions throughout history.

Throughout history, language and the state have been companions.

1. The fact that ancient Greeks and Romans as well as every other colonial power spread their languages as far as their armies maintained outposts.
2. When the Nazis rose to power was established through military might in support of the Aryan myth.
3. The Aryans were not a race but rather a great variety of peoples who spoke the early Indo-European (also sometimes known as Indo-Aryan) languages.

4. One measure of loyalty is when a nation's citizens speak a single language approved by the state.
5. Even a dialect of the state language finds suspicion in local groups who insist upon speaking their own way, in opposition to the rest of the country.

INCOMPLETE SENTENCES

An **incomplete sentence,** as its name implies, is one that lacks certain important elements. A fragment (see chapter 12), the most extreme case of an incomplete sentence, has no subject or predicate. In less extreme cases, a sentence may lack a word or two, which you can identify and correct with careful proofreading.

16g Edit elliptical constructions to avoid confusion.

Both in speech and in writing, we omit certain words in order to streamline communication. These "clipped" or shortened sentences are called **elliptical constructions,** and, when used with care, they can be concise and economical. But elliptical constructions may confuse readers if a writer omits words that are vital to sentence structure.

1 Use *that* when necessary to signal sentence relationships.

Often, *that* is the word omitted in an elliptical construction. If the omission of *that* does not confuse readers, then the omission is of no consequence.

> Closely related to the unequal treatment of a minority language by a majority language is the unequal treatment (that) many languages give to the two sexes.

If the omission of *that* alters the relationship among words in a sentence, then restore *that* to the sentence.

UNCLEAR   Few people stop to consider our scientific name for both sexes is the word for only one of them, *Homo,* "man" in Latin. [The clipped wording incorrectly points to *our scientific name* as the object of *consider.*]

CLEAR   Few people stop to consider *that* our scientific name for both sexes is the word for only one of them, *Homo,* "man" in Latin. [It is now clear that the noun clause beginning with *that* and ending with *Latin* functions as the object of the verb.]

2 Provide all the words needed for parallel constructions.

Elliptical constructions are found in sentences where words, phrases, or clauses are joined by the conjunction *and* or are otherwise made parallel. Grammatically, an omission is legitimate when a word or words are repeated *exactly* in all compound parts of the sentence, as in the following examples. Omitted words are placed in parentheses.

PARALLEL   According to one widely accepted theory, humans possess sensory (memory), short-term (memory), and long-term memory. [A word is omitted.]

PARALLEL   Information moves from short- (term memory) to long-term memory when we think about its meaning or (when we think) about its relationship to other information already in long-term memory. [A clause is omitted.]

16g

inc

An incomplete sentence results when words omitted in one part of an elliptical construction do not match identically the words appearing in another part.

NOT   Sensory and short-term memory *last* seconds or minutes, while long-
PARALLEL   term memory years or decades.

PARALLEL   Sensory and short-term memory *last* seconds or minutes, while long-term memory *lasts* years or decades.

The omitted word, *lasts*, is not identical to the word in the first part of the parallel structure, *last*. One verb completes a singular subject and the other a plural subject, as in the following example.

NOT   One long-term memory *is triggered* by fleeting sight or smell and others
PARALLEL   by sounds.

PARALLEL   One long-term memory *is triggered* by fleeting sight or smell and others *are triggered* by sounds.

PARALLEL   One long-term memory *may be triggered* by fleeting sight or smell and others by sounds.

3 Use the necessary prepositions with verbs in parallel constructions.

Elliptical constructions also result from the omission of a preposition that functions idiomatically as part of a complete verb phrase: believe *in*, check *in*, handed *in*, hope *in*, hope *for*, looked *up*, tried *on*, turned *on*. When these expressions are doubled by the conjunction *and*, and you wish to omit the second preposition, be sure this preposition is identical to the one remaining in the sentence. (See 18a-2 and 18a-3 on parallel constructions.) In the following example, the doubled preposition is *on*: relied *on* and ultimately thrived *on*.

> In 1914, Henry Ford opened an auto manufacturing plant that relied and ultimately thrived on principles of assembly-line production.

To be omitted from a parallel construction, a preposition must be identical to the one left remaining in the sentence. If the prepositions are not identical, then *both* must appear in the sentence so that the full sense of each idiomatic expression is retained.

FAULTY   Henry Ford believed and relied *on* the assembly line as a means to revolutionize American industry.

REVISED   Henry Ford believed *in* and relied *on* the assembly line as a means to revolutionize American industry.

16h   Make comparisons consistent, complete, and clear.

16h

inc

Writers have many occasions to devote sentences, paragraphs, and even entire essays to writing comparisons and contrasts. To make comparisons effective at any level, you should compare logically consistent elements; you should state comparisons completely; and you should state comparisons clearly. (In chapter 11 you will find more on comparative forms of adjectives and adverbs.)

1   Keep the elements of a comparison logically related.

The elements you compare in a sentence must in fact be comparable—of the same logical class.

ILLOGICAL   Modern atomic theory provides for fewer types of atoms than Democritus, the ancient Greek philosopher who conceived the idea of atoms. [Atoms are being compared with Democritus, a person. The comparison must be made logical.]

LOGICAL   Modern atomic theory provides for fewer types of atoms than did Democritus, the ancient Greek philosopher who conceived the idea of atoms.

2   Complete all elements of a comparison.

Comparisons must be made fully, so that readers understand which elements in a sentence are being compared.

INCOMPLETE   Democritus believed there existed an infinite variety of atoms each of which possessed unique characteristics—so that, for instance, atoms of water were smoother. [Smoother than what?]

COMPLETE   Democritus believed there existed an infinite variety of atoms each of which possessed unique characteristics—so that, for instance, atoms of water were smoother than atoms of fire.

INCOMPLETE   The ideas of Democritus were based more on speculation. [More on speculation than on what?]

COMPLETE   The ideas of Democritus were based more on speculation than on the hard evidence of experimentation.

  3   Make sure comparisons are clear and unambiguous.

Comparisons that invite alternate interpretations must be revised so that only one interpretation is possible.

16h

inc

UNCLEAR   Scientists today express more respect for Democritus than his contemporaries. [Two interpretations: (1) Democritus's contemporaries had little respect for him; (2) scientists respect the work of Democritus more than they respect the work of his contemporaries.]

CLEAR   Scientists today express more respect for Democritus than they do for his contemporaries.

CLEAR   Scientists today express more respect for Democritus than his contemporaries did.

EXERCISE 6

Revise the sentences that follow to eliminate problems with elliptical constructions and comparisons. Place a check beside any sentence that needs no revision.

Example: We have a special reverence and fascination *with* fire.

We have a special reverence *for* and fascination *with* fire.

1. Since ancient times, fire has been regarded more as a transforming element than sheer destructive power.
2. Medieval alchemists believed in fire resided magical properties.
3. Alchemists would impress their patrons by heating the red pigment cinnabar (a sulphide of mercury) to produce exquisite pearls of liquid mercury.
4. In legend, Prometheus's gift of fire made humans better, and for this Prometheus was punished.
5. Humankind has used fire for about 400,000 years, although it is not clear that all people have known how to *make* it.
6. One tribe on the Andaman Islands (south of Burma) carefully tends spontaneous fires because they have no techniques for producing fire.

PART V

Writing Effective Sentences

CHAPTER 17

Being Clear, Concise, and Direct

I have made this letter longer than usual, only because
I have not had time to make it shorter.

—BLAISE PASCAL

Over three hundred years ago, the French mathematician and philosopher Pascal knew what writers know today: writing concisely is a challenge that takes time. Just like Pascal, you face a decision when rereading your first draft sentences: Should you revise? What will you get in return for your efforts at making sentences briefer? Simply put, the answer is *clarity* and directness—writing that gives readers an exact, immediate grasp of your meaning.

Revising sentences for clarity and directness means more than making a correct, complete expression. Revision at this level means making choices about wording that will help your audience to clearly understand your ideas. Your knowledge of an audience's readiness and level of understanding will strongly influence your choices. One audience, with an elementary level of understanding, might need to see basic ideas broken down into many brief, simple sentences; a group of specialists might relish complex sentences with many details. Still others, well informed but impatient, might find those details getting in the way of the "bottom-line" statement they want to hear. In virtually all contexts, it pays to revise first-draft sentences until they exactly express the meaning you want for your audience.

17a Revise to eliminate wordiness.

There are many kinds of wordiness, including the use of empty words and phrases (see 21b-3, 21e-4, 21h-2); passive-voice constructions (see 9g); and buzzwords, redundancy, and unnecessary repetition. When you are revising a first draft, search out wordiness and eliminate it. Try to avoid saying things two different ways or with two words when one will do. Eliminating extra words is a reliable way to give your message direct impact; padded wording never makes writing sound more authoritative. If used as filler to meet the length requirement of an assignment, padded writing will backfire by obscuring your message to readers, causing them to be confused and annoyed.

1   Combine sentences that repeat material.

When writing a first-draft paragraph you are apt to string together sentences that repeat material. When revising your work, combine sentences to eliminate wordiness and to sharpen focus.

WORDY   In this era of Boy George and Grace Jones it might seem that we are moving toward *a unisex style of culture*. Jeans and track suits, normal wear for both men and women, are signs of *a unisex style of culture*. [Two sentences end by repeating the same point.]

COMBINED   In this era of Boy George and Grace Jones, when jeans and track suits are normal wear for both men and women, it might seem that we are moving toward a unisex style of culture. [A single complex sentence can be more efficient and concise.]

2   Eliminate wordiness from clauses and phrases.

Eliminate wordiness by eliminating relative pronouns and by reducing adjective clauses to phrases or single words.

COMPLEX   Josephine Baker, *who was* the first black woman to become an international star, was born poor in St. Louis in 1906. [The clause creates some interruption in this complex sentence.]

CONCISE   Josephine Baker, the first black woman to become an international star, was born poor in St. Louis in 1906. [The phrase creates less of an interruption.]

COMPLEX   Many were drawn by her vitality, *which was* infectious.

CONCISE   Many were drawn by her infectious vitality. [A simple sentence is created.]

OPTION   Her vitality was infectious; many were drawn by it. [Simple independent clauses are created.]

Wordiness can also be eliminated by shortening phrases. When possible, reduce a phrase to a one-word modifer (see 7c, d).

WORDY   *Recent revivals of* Baker's French films have included *re-releases of subtitled versions of* "Zou-Zou" and "Princess Tam-Tam."

CONCISE   *Recently* Baker's French films "Zou-Zou" and "Princess Tam-Tam" have been *re-released with subtitles*. [The phrases are reduced to simpler modifiers.]

3   Revise sentences that begin with expletives.

Expletive constructions (*it is, there is, there are, there were*) fill blanks in a sentence when a writer inverts normal word order. Expletives are almost

17a

w/rep

always unnecessary, and should be replaced with direct, active verbs, whenever possible.

WORDY   *There were many reasons why* Josephine Baker was more successful in Europe than in America. [The expletive is unnecessary here.]

DIRECT   Josephine Baker was more successful in Europe than in America for several reasons.

WORDY   *It is* because Europeans in the 1920s were interested in anything African *that* they so readily responded to Baker's outrageous style. [The expletive is indirect; it also sets up an unnecessary *that* clause.]

DIRECT   Because Europeans in the 1920s were interested in anything African, they readily responded to Baker's outrageous style.

4   Eliminate buzzwords.

17a

w/rep

Buzzwords are vague, often abstract expressions that sound as if they mean something but are only "buzzing" or adding noise to your sentence, without contributing anything of substance. (See 21c, d.) Buzzwords can be nouns: *area, aspect, case, character, element, factor, field, kind, sort, type, thing, nature, scope, situation, quality.* Buzzwords can be adjectives, especially those with broad meanings: *nice, good, interesting, bad, important, fine, weird, significant, central, major.* Buzzwords can be adverbs: *basically, really, quite, very, definitely, actually, completely, literally, absolutely.* Eliminate buzzwords. When appropriate, replace them with more precise expressions.

WORDY   *Those types of major* disciplinary problems are *really quite* difficult to solve. [None of these buzzwords has any meaning.]

CONCISE   Disciplinary problems are difficult to solve.

WORDY   *Basically,* she was *definitely* a *nice* person.

CONCISE   She was friendly [kind, thoughtful, sweet, outgoing, or any other more precise adjective could replace the vague *nice*].

5   Eliminate redundant writing.

Occasional, intentional repetition can be a powerful technique for achieving emphasis. (See chapter 19.) Writers may not realize they are repeating themselves, and the result for readers is usually a tedious sentence. When you spot unintended repetition in your own writing, eliminate it.

REDUNDANT   In *Cinderella,* feminine, lady-like actions and behavior are praised and rewarded.

REVISED   In *Cinderella,* feminine behavior is rewarded.

REDUNDANT Cinderella is a degraded household drudge and her household work demeans her.

REVISED Cinderella is a degraded household drudge.
Cinderella is a drudge degraded by housework.
Housework degrades Cinderella.

Redundant phrases

A **redundant phrase** repeats a message unnecessarily. Redundant phrases include *small in size, few in number, continue to remain, green in color, free gift, extra gratuity, repeat again, combine together, add to each other, final end.* Make your sentences concise by omitting one part of a redundant phrase.

REDUNDANT Cinderella's stepsisters, two in number, continued to remain hateful toward her throughout the story.

CONCISE Cinderella's two stepsisters were hateful to her throughout the story.

REDUNDANT The fairy godmother's free gift of gown and carriage enables Cinderella to achieve a girl's final goal: marriage to the Prince.

CONCISE The fairy godmother's gift of gown and carriage enables Cinderella to achieve her goal: marriage to the Prince.

17a

w/rep

 6 Eliminate long-winded phrases.

Long-winded phrases such as *at this point in time* in no way enhance the meaning or elegance of a sentence. Such expressions are tempting because they come to mind ready-made and seem to endow writing with added formality, sophistication, and authority. But do not be fooled. Using such phrases muddies your sentences, making them sound either pretentious or like the work of an inexperienced writer. Eliminate these phrases and strive for simple, clear, direct expression.

Expressions to Avoid	
Wordy	*Direct*
at this moment (point) in time	now, today
at the present time	now, today
due to the fact that	because
in order to utilize	to use
in view of the fact that	because
for the purpose of	for
in the event that	if
until such time as	until
	(continued)

Expressions to Avoid (continued)

Wordy	Direct
is an example of	is
would seem to be	is
the point I am trying to make*	——
in a very real sense*	——
in fact, as a matter of fact *	——

* These expressions are fillers and should be eliminated.

WORDY   *Due to the fact that* Cinderella is a heroine in *what would appear to be* a fairy-tale world, she is, *in a very real sense,* "rewarded" with marriage to the Prince.

REVISED   Because Cinderella is a fairy-tale heroine, she is rewarded with marriage to the Prince.

As a fairy-tale heroine, Cinderella is rewarded with marriage to the Prince.

In fairy-tale worlds, heroines like Cinderella are rewarded with marriage to the Prince.

17a

w/rep

EXERCISE 1

Revise these sentences to eliminate wordiness by combining repeated material, reducing phrases and adjective clauses, and avoiding expletives.

Example: What type of consumer do you want to advertise to? Specifying the target or consumer that you want to reach with your product is the main step in advertising.

Effective advertising targets specific consumers.

1. When defining the purpose of advertising some experts admit that it is a manipulation of the public while others insist that advertising promotes the general well-being of its audience.
2. Advertising is one of the most eye-catching methods of selling a product. This is because advertising is a medium of information.
3. There are many consumers who are drawn to a product because the advertising campaign has been effectively utilized.
4. There are many qualities which an advertisement must have to lure the public to buy its product. The advertisement must be believable, convincing, informative, and persuasive. With these qualities in the ads, they will be the first ones to sell.
5. Like I mentioned before, it is not only women who are being portrayed sexually. Men are used in many advertisements also.
6. There exists a built-in sexual overtone in almost every commercial and advertisement around.
7. Advertising is one of several communications forces which performs its role when it moves the consumer through successive levels. These levels include unawareness, awareness, comprehension, conviction, and action.

EXERCISE 2

Revise the following sentences to eliminate wordiness.

Example: Early forms of advertisements were messages to inform the consumers of the benefits and the availability of a product.

Originally, advertisements informed consumers of a product's benefits and availability.

1. The producer must communicate with the product's possible customers in a way that is quite personal and quite appealing to the customer.
2. By identifying the product you start to narrow down the range of people you want to buy the product.
3. Advertising is a complex, but not mysterious, business.
4. To summarize a successful advertiser in today's world in one word, it would have to be opportunistic.
5. From campaign to campaign there are many different objectives and goals ads are trying to accomplish.
6. It used to be that women were mainly portrayed in the kitchen or in other places in the home.
7. We find advertising on television, on the radio, in newspapers and magazines, and in the phone book, just to name a few places.

 Use strong verbs.

17b

vb

A verb is like an engine. Strong verbs move sentences forward and precisely inform readers about the action a subject is taking or the condition or state in which the subject exists. One way to improve a draft is to circle all your verbs, revising as needed to ensure that each verb makes a crisp, direct statement.

 Give preference to verbs in the active voice.

Sentences with verbs in the active voice emphasize the actor of a sentence rather than the object that is acted upon (see 9g).

ACTIVE   The state legislature approved a tax hike.

PASSIVE   A tax hike was approved by the state legislature.

PASSIVE   A tax hike was approved. [The actor is not named.]

Unless a writer intends to focus on the object of the action, leaving the actor secondary or unnamed, the active voice is the strongest way to make a direct statement. When the actor needs to be named, a passive-voice sentence is wordier and thus weaker than an active-voice sentence.

PASSIVE   In 1947 the Hollywood Ten, writers and filmmakers, *were cited* for contempt of Congress, tried, and sentenced to prison. [The passive voice obscures the accusers, who are not named here.]

ACTIVE   In 1947 the House Un-American Activities Committee cited, tried and sentenced the Hollywood Ten for contempt of Congress.

PASSIVE   The accused *were known as* "pinkos" while the prosecutors *were identified as* "red baiters." [The passive voice here conceals who promoted these labels.]

ACTIVE   Pro-Committee partisans identified the accused as "pinkos" while defenders of *the accused* identified the prosecutors as "red baiters."

 2 Use forms of *to be* and *to have* as main verbs only when no alternatives exist.

The verb *to be* is essential in forming certain tenses, as in a progressive tense.

During the Red Scare of the early 1950s, the government *was prosecuting* anyone with suspected Communist sympathies.

In a sentence of definition, *to be* functions as an equal sign.

HUAC *is* an abbreviation for the House Un-American Activities Committee.

Beyond these uses, *to be* is a weak verb. When possible, replace it with a strong, active-voice verb.

WEAK   Many people today *are* of the opinion that the government *was not right to have* its own citizens prosecuted for exercising their first amendment rights. [The verbs require weak and wordy constructions.]

STRONGER   Many people today *think* the government *should not have* prosecuted its own citizens for exercising their first amendment rights. [Stronger verbs make more direct, active statements here.]

The verb *to have* functions as an auxiliary in forming the perfect tenses. This verb tends to make a weak and indirect statement when used alone as the main verb of a sentence. Replace forms of *to have* with strong, active-voice verbs.

WEAK   The blacklist *had the effect of getting* people to inform on their friends and families. [The verb produces a vague statement.]

STRONGER   The blacklist *pushed* people to inform on their friends and families. [Replacement with another verb produces a definite statement.]

3 Revise nouns derived from verbs.

A noun can be formed from a verb by adding a suffix: dismiss/dismiss*al*, repent/repent*ance*, devote/devo*tion*, develop/develop*ment*. Often these constructions result in a weak, wordy sentence, since the noun form replaces what was originally an active verb and requires the presence of a second verb. When possible, restore the original verb form of a noun derived from a verb.

WORDY   Many people *found that cooperation* with HUAC *was necessary for survival.* [The noun form, the dependent clause, and the *to be* verb make a weak, redundant sentence.]

DIRECT   Many people eventually *cooperated* with HUAC *to survive.* [The noun form is changed to a verb, producing a stronger statement.]

WORDY   The government *was caught up in a period of intimidating* its own people.

DIRECT   The government intimidated its own people.

Write Clearly, Concisely, Directly

When revising a draft for clarity, conciseness, and directness, be critical of every sentence.

1. Combine repetitive sentences.
2. Reduce an adjective clause to a phrase or to one word.
3. Eliminate relative pronouns whenever possible.
4. Reduce adverbial and prepositional phrases to one word.
5. Eliminate expletives.
6. Eliminate buzzwords.
7. Eliminate redundant writing.
8. Eliminate long-winded phrases.
9. Use verbs in the active voice, not the passive.
10. Substitute strong verbs for *to be* and *to have*.
11. Convert nouns made from verbs back into verbs.

17b

vb

EXERCISE 3

Revise these sentences for clarity and directness by changing passive verbs to active verbs, replacing weak verbs with strong verbs, and converting nouns made from verbs back into verbs.

> *Example:* Both positive and negative reactions to a product should be expected.
>
> Consumers should expect both positive and negative reactions to products.

1. Advertising has always been generally understood as a form of communication between the buyer and the seller.
2. The aim of advertising is to give exposure of a certain product to a targeted audience.
3. Without catalogue viewership the product may be forgotten because the consumer will not have the ability to view it again.

4. There is a discussion of effective marketing in Thomas R. Forrest's article which is entitled "Such a Handsome Face: Advertising Male Cosmetics."

5. It has been noticed that in today's society a man's appearance is thought to be an important factor in his success.

6. There are several aspects of advertising that are seen to be essential to the successful marketing of a product.

7. Five questions should be asked before the implementation of a successful advertising campaign.

8. The association of a product with something that is desirable increases its visibility.

EXERCISE 4

Revise the following first draft of a student paper. Use all the techniques described in this and related chapters to achieve conciseness, clarity, and directness.

Advertising can be displayed in many different ways. One major way that advertisers try to sell their products is through the use of sexism. Sexism is portrayed in the majority of ads lately and it appears to be only getting worse.

It is now over twenty years after the feminist movement and sexism is as big of a problem as ever. Usually in the advertising industry it is the female that is used in the ad that portrays sexism: however, male sexism is found also. The latest problem occurred when Miller Beer tried to hook spring-break college bound kids with an ad insert for campus newspapers about annual trips to Florida that are often taken by college students. The ad included sketches of women in bikinis with hints of ways for these college kids to "pick up women." This ad insert drew a lot of attention from college students, mainly females that were outraged over it. There were even threats to boycott the product. However there were no results because the National Advertising Review Board has not issued guidelines on the use of women in ads since 1978. Also, there are very few agencies that have particular rules or regulations on sexism in ads. This could be due to the fact that the top managements are mostly male.

Everyone knows that sexism is used in advertisements all over the place but the question is, are they avoidable? Many advertising executives say no because they feel that advertisers have to address themselves to such a huge chunk of people that they are never going to be able to make everyone happy. This is why sexism and stereotyping in advertising is such a big problem today.

17b

vb

CHAPTER 18

Maintaining Sentence Parallelism

In writing, **parallelism** involves matching a sentence's structure to its content. When two or more ideas are parallel (that is, closely related or comparable), a writer can emphasize similarities as well as differences by creating parallel grammatical forms.

> Like many other towns on the Great Plains, Nicodemus, Kansas, was founded in the 1870s; unlike any other that still survives, it was founded by black homesteaders.

Parallels are built on repeated structures that make sentences like the preceding one both rhythmically pleasing and easy to read. The moment readers see a word that signals a parallel construction (in the preceding example that word is *unlike*), they prepare themselves for a repeated grammatical structure and closely related content. Parallel structures help sentences to cohere by establishing clear relationships among sentence parts. Through their closely matched word elements, parallel structures present ideas in a logical comparison or contrast. Parallelism in writing thus draws on your skills in creating a logical analogy, a comparison, or a parallel argument (see 6d-2). In the example on black homesteaders, the opening phrases in both parts of the compound sentence are parallel in logic and grammatical structure. Both prepositional phrases modify a subject.

> *Like* many other towns on the Great Plains, Nicodemus, . . .
>
> *unlike* any other that still survives, it . . .

The subjects of both clauses are parallel in content as well as in form: one is a noun, the other a singular pronoun taking the place of that noun.

> *Nicodemus, Kansas,* was founded in the 1870s;
>
> *it* was founded by black homesteaders.

The verb phrases of each clause are exactly parallel in the past tense.

> Nicodemus, Kansas, *was founded* in the 1870s;
>
> it *was founded* by black homesteaders.

To use parallelism effectively, you must become consciously logical and systematic about how you present parallel ideas.

18a   Use parallel words, phrases, and clauses with coordinate conjunctions.

Whenever you use a coordinate conjunction (*and, but, for, or, nor, so, yet*), the words, phrases, or clauses joined form a *pair* or a *series* (a list of three or more related items) and become *compound* elements: compound subjects, objects, verbs, modifiers, and clauses. For sentence parts to be parallel in structure, the compounded elements must share an equivalent grammatical form. Equivalent does not mean identical. If in one part of a parallel structure a verb is modified by a prepositional phrase, then a corresponding verb in the second part of the sentence should also be modified by a prepositional phrase—*but* that phrase need not begin with the same preposition.

In sentences with *faulty parallelism,* elements that should be grammatically equivalent are not. The only indication of faulty parallelism may be that a sentence with a coordinate conjunction (or some other word signaling an attempt at parallelism) makes part of the sentence sound out of place or illogical.

18a

coord

//

NOT PARALLEL   Before the horse, Indians hunted buffalo by chasing them over blind cliffs, up box canyons, or *when they went* into steep-sided sand dunes. [Following the conjunction *or,* the sentence shifts from listing locations to naming a time.]

To revise a sentence with faulty parallelism, *determine which elements should be parallel* (that is, logically comparable), and then *revise the sentence so that these elements share an equivalent grammatical form.* It may help to think of parallel elements as word groupings that complete slots in a sentence. The same grammatical form that you use to complete any one slot in a parallel structure must be used to complete all remaining slots.

Determine the parallel elements.

by chasing them   Slot 1   ,   Slot 2   , and   Slot 3   .
by chasing them *over blind cliffs,*   Slot 2   , and   Slot 3   .

Because Slot 1 is completed with a prepositional phrase (*over blind cliffs*), Slots 2 and 3 should be filled with prepositional phrases. The series *over blind cliffs, up box canyons, or when they went into steep-sided sand dunes* lacks parallel structure because the third element in the series introduces a *when* clause, which is not consistent with the grammatical form of Slot 1.

Revise so that parallel elements have equivalent grammatical form.

PARALLEL   Before the horse, Indians hunted buffalo by chasing them *over blind cliffs, up box canyons,* or *into steep-sided sand dunes.* [All elements now refer to a location in a grammatically parallel form.]

1 Using parallel words

Words that appear in a pair or a series are related in content and should be parallel in form.

NOT PARALLEL According to figures released by the Senate Judiciary Committee in 1991, the United States has the most violence and crime-ridden society in the industrialized world.

Determine the parallel elements.

the United States has the most ___Slot 1___ and ___Slot 2___ society in the industrialized world.

In this sentence, the noun *violence* completes Slot 1 and the adjective *crime-ridden* completes Slot 2. In order for the sentence to be parallel, both slots must show the same part of speech. Both must be nouns or both must be adjectives. In this case, the words should be adjectives, since both are being used to modify the noun *society*.

Revise so that parallel elements have equivalent grammatical form.

PARALLEL According to figures released by the Senate Judiciary Committee in 1991, the United States has the most *violent* and *crime-ridden* society in the industrialized world.

If the elements that should be logically parallel shift their function in a sentence, then they may well shift their part of speech. If the adjectives *violent* and *crime-ridden* are to become nouns—*violence* and *crime*—you should consider them as similar elements in a comparison and treat them as objects of the verb *has*.

PARALLEL According to figures released by the Senate Judiciary Committee in 1991, the United States has the most *violence* and *crime* of any society in the industrialized world. [Two nouns are now comparable in a parallel structure.]

In parallel constructions, idiomatic terms must be expressed completely. (See also 16g-3.)

NOT PARALLEL White people were called "Flop Ears" by some Indians who were both aghast and entertained *by* the way white parents grabbed their children by the ears to discipline them.

Determine the parallel elements.

who were both ___Slot 1___ and ___Slot 2___ the way white parents grabbed their children by the ears to discipline them.

The preposition *at* is necessary for completing the first verb phrase, since the idiom is *aghast at*, not *aghast by*.

18a

coord

//

Revise so that parallel elements have equivalent grammatical form.

PARALLEL   White people were called "Flop Ears" by some Indians who were both aghast *at* and entertained *by* the way white parents grabbed their children by the ears to discipline them. [Each parallel item now has its proper idiomatic preposition.]

2 Using parallel phrases

To echo the idea expressed in a phrase in one part of a sentence, use a phrase with the same grammatical structure in another part.

NOT   Tumbleweeds' main function seems to be poetic, for they roll and
PARALLEL   bounce on the wind, *are flying through the air like weather balloons,* and pile up along fences.

Determine the parallel elements.

for they <u> Slot 1 </u> , <u> Slot 2 </u> , and <u> Slot 3 </u> .

for they *roll and bounce on the wind,* <u> Slot 2 </u> , and <u> Slot 3 </u> .

Slot 1 is completed with two present-tense verbs and a modifying phrase. Slots 2 and 3 need at least one present-tense verb and a modifying phrase. Slot 2 is out of parallel because the verb appears in its *-ing* form with an auxiliary.

Revise so that parallel elements have equivalent grammatical form.

PARALLEL   Tumbleweeds' main function seems to be poetic, for they roll and bounce on the wind, *fly through the air like weather balloons,* and pile up along fences.

PARALLEL   Tumbleweeds' main function seems to be poetic, for they are always *rolling and bouncing* on the wind, *flying* through the air like weather balloons, and *piling* up along fences. [In this revision, all verbs appear in their *-ing* form and, thus, are parallel.]

3 Using parallel clauses

A *clause* is a grouping of words that has a complete subject and predicate. Both independent clauses (that is, sentences) and dependent clauses can be set in parallel, provided they are parallel in content. At times, brief sentences can be used to form items in a series. When choosing such a structure, make sure each sentence is parallel in form.

NOT   Tumbleweeds are a signature of hundreds of old Westerns: the
PARALLEL   saloon doors swing back and forth, a tumbleweed rolls across a
(INDEPENDENT   deserted street, the marshall and the bad guy *walking* slowly
CLAUSES)   toward each other.

18a

coord

//

Determine the parallel elements.

Tumbleweeds are a signature of hundreds of old Westerns: Slot 1 ,
  Slot 2 , and   Slot 3 .

the saloon doors swing back and forth,   Slot 2 , and   Slot 3 .

Slot 1 is completed with a clause that has the following structure: an
article (*the, a*), noun, present-tense verb, modifying phrase: *the saloon doors
swing back and forth.* The final element in the series is not a clause; specifically,
the verb of the third element is not parallel with the two preceding verbs.

Revise so that parallel elements have equivalent grammatical form.

PARALLEL   Tumbleweeds are a signature of hundreds of old Westerns: the
saloon doors *swing* back and forth, a tumbleweed *rolls* across a
deserted street, the marshall and the bad guy *walk* slowly toward
each other.

PARALLEL   Tumbleweeds are a signature of hundreds of old Westerns: the
saloon doors *swinging* back and forth, a tumbleweed *rolling* across
a deserted street, the marshall and the bad guy *walking* slowly
toward each other. [In this revision, the verb of each slot is
changed to its *-ing* form, making each element in the series a
parallel phrase.]

18a

coord
//

In order to maintain parallel structure in sentences that have a pair or
series of dependent relative clauses, you will need to repeat the relative
pronouns *who, whom, which,* and *what.*

NOT
PARALLEL
(DEPENDENT
CLAUSES)   Archimedes was the celebrated mathematician of antiquity *who*
invented the Archimedean screw, *who* explained the theory of the
lever, and *he* defended his native Syracuse against the Romans
with great mechanical skill.

Determine the parallel elements.

Archimedes was the celebrated mathematician of antiquity   Slot 1 ,
  Slot 2 , and   Slot 3 .

Archimedes was the celebrated mathematician of antiquity *who invented the
Archimedean screw,*   Slot 2 , and   Slot 3 .

Slot 1 is completed with a relative clause beginning with the relative
pronoun *who;* Slots 2 and 3 must have the same structure: each slot must be
completed with a clause that begins with the word *who* (but see the variation
immediately following).

Revise so that parallel elements have equivalent grammatical form.

PARALLEL   Archimedes was the celebrated mathematician of antiquity *who*
invented the Archimedean screw, *who* explained the theory of the
lever, and *who* defended his native Syracuse against the Romans
with great mechanical skill.

VARIATION: Brief words that begin a series (for example, a relative pronoun such as *who*, a preposition such as *by* or *in*, and the infinitive *to*) may be written once at the beginning of the first item in the series and then omitted from all remaining items.

PARALLEL   Archimedes was the celebrated mathematician of antiquity *who* invented the Archimedean screw, explained the theory of the lever, and defended his native Syracuse against the Romans with great mechanical skill.

A CAUTION: Should one of these introductory words appear in more than one part of the series but not in *all* parts, the use of parallelism will be faulty.

PARALLEL   I want *to* go home, *to* wash up, and *to* eat.

          I want *to* go home, wash up, and eat.

NOT   I want *to* go home, wash up, and *to* eat.
PARALLEL

18b Use parallelism with correlative conjunctions.

//

Whenever you join parts of a sentence with pairs of words called *correlative conjunctions* (*either/or, neither/nor, both/and, not only/but also*), you must use the same grammatical form in both parts. Once again, think of the conjunction as creating parallel slots in the sentence. Whatever grammatical structure is used to complete the first slot must be used to complete the second.

NOT   After defeating Custer at Little Bighorn, Crazy Horse managed both
PARALLEL to stay ahead of the Army and *escape*.

Determine the parallel elements.

    managed both __Slot 1__ and __Slot 2__ .

    managed both *to stay ahead of the army* and __Slot 2__ .

Slot 2 must take the same form as Slot 1. Each must be a verb in its infinitive form: *to* _____ .

Revise so that parallel elements have equivalent grammatical form.

PARALLEL   After defeating Custer at Little Bighorn, Crazy Horse managed both *to stay* ahead of the Army and *to escape*.

VARIATION: By slightly modifying the sentence—by moving the word *to* outside of the parallel structure created by the correlative conjunction—you can eliminate the word *to* in both of the sentence's parallel slots.

    managed *to* both __Slot 1__ and __Slot 2__ .

    managed *to* both *stay ahead of the army* and __Slot 2__ .

PARALLEL   After defeating Custer at Little Bighorn, Crazy Horse managed *to* both
stay ahead of the Army and *escape*.

 18c ## Use parallelism in sentences with compared and contrasted elements.

When words, phrases, or clauses are compared or contrasted in a single
sentence, their logical and grammatical structures must be parallel (see 16h).
Expressions that set up comparisons and contrasts include *rather than, as
opposed to, on the other hand, not, like, unlike,* and *just as/so too.*

NOT   Several experts explain the Loch Ness Monster as a survivor of an
PARALLEL   otherwise extinct reptile species rather than fulfilling people's need for
a myth. [The noun *survivor* makes a mismatched contrast with the
verbal *fulfilling*.]

Determine the parallel elements.

Several experts explain the Loch Ness Monster as ___Slot 1___ rather than
___Slot 2___ .

Several experts explain the Loch Ness Monster as *a survivor of an otherwise
extinct reptile species* rather than ___Slot 2___ .

Slot 1 consists of an article (*a*) and a noun that is modified (*survivor of
an otherwise extinct reptile species*). Slot 2 should take the same basic form.

Revise so that parallel elements have equivalent grammatical form.

PARALLEL   Several experts explain the Loch Ness Monster as *a survivor of an
otherwise extinct reptile species* rather than *a fulfillment of people's need for
a myth*. [Two modified nouns are now matched in parallel contrast.]

18c

//

EXERCISE 1
The following sentences contain coordinating or correlative conjunctions,
or elements of comparison and contrast. Revise each to correct the faulty
parallel structure.

Example: Native Americans have one of the highest unemployment
rates in the nation, the lowest educational attainment of any
U.S. minority group, and they fare worst in the area of health.

Native Americans have one of the highest unemployment
rates in the nation, the lowest educational attainment of any
U.S. minority group, and *the worst record of health care*. [Each
slot in the series now begins with an adjective in its superlative form: *highest, lowest, worst*. Each adjective is followed by
a noun and each noun by a prepositional phrase.]

1. Designating Asian Americans as the "model minority" is problem-
atic not only because the term obscures the diversity of the group but

they are represented in only a small percentage of top-ranking positions in the U.S.

2. Some sociologists say that racism is rooted in a preference for one's
"own kind" rather than social causes.

3. Conflict theorists feel that racism results from competition for scarce
resources and an unequal distribution of power and racial tension
increases during periods of economic decline.

4. Corporate managers do not tend to wield the political power of
professionals such as lawyers and doctors, nor workers whom they
supervise.

5. Either the percentage of the elderly living below the poverty line has
decreased or to underestimate the number of elderly living in poverty
is prevalent.

Use parallelism among sentences to enhance paragraph coherence.

Because parallel grammatical structures highlight parallel ideas among
sentence parts, parallelism is an excellent device for organizing sentence
content. But parallelism can also help to relate the parts of an *entire paragraph*
by highlighting the logic by which a writer moves from one sentence to the
next. Parallel structures bind a paragraph's sentences into a coherent unit.

18e

dev //

PARALLEL SENTENCES WITHIN A PARAGRAPH

A house divided against itself cannot stand. I believe this government
cannot endure, permanently half slave and half free. I do not expect the
Union to be dissolved. I do not expect the house to fall. But I do expect it
will cease to be divided. It will become all one thing, or all the other.

—ABRAHAM LINCOLN, 1858

In this famous passage, Lincoln uses parallel structures to show relationships not only among single words or phrases, but also among whole
sentences. Elements of the first sentence (*house, divided*) are repeated near the
end of the paragraph. Lincoln repeats the phrase *I do not expect* twice and then
produces a parallel contrast with *But I do expect* in a third repetition. The final
two sentences repeat *it will* with different verbs. The last sentence sets up a
parallel opposition governed by *all*. These parallel repetitions of words,
phrases, and structures help to make the paragraph coherent by highlighting
relationships among sentences. Such relationships could be mapped in parallel "slot" diagrams similar to those used for sentences. Parallel structures
also give the paragraph an emphatic, memorable rhythm.

18e Use parallel entries when writing lists or outlines.

A list or outline divides a single large subject into equal or coordinate
elements. A grocery list is the simplest example: *grocery* is the subject, and all
the subdivisions appear as nouns (*steak, cheese, turnips, ketchup*). However,

lists or outlines may also be written in phrases or clauses. When preparing a paper or taking notes from a book, keep the elements of lists and outlines in equivalent grammatical form. As with parallel elements in a sentence, parallel elements in a list or outline will highlight the logical similarities that underlie parallel content.

 Making lists

A *list* is a displayed series of items that are logically similar or comparable and are expressed in grammatically parallel form. A list that is not parallel can be very confusing.

NOT PARALLEL

Those attending should be prepared to address these issues:

- morale of workers
- Why do we need so much overtime?
- getting more efficient
- We need better sales tools.

A list or outline can be a helpful way to organize your thoughts. To keep the logic of similar or comparable ideas in line, all items of a list should be expressed in equivalent grammatical form. The preceding example shows a list with four forms: a noun phrase, a question, a verb in its *-ing* form, and a sentence. Choosing any one of these forms as a standard for the list would make the list parallel.

PARALLEL

Those attending should be prepared to address these issues:

- morale of workers
- necessity of overtime
- need for efficiency
- need for better sales tools

PARALLEL

Those attending should be prepared to address these issues:

- improving worker morale
- reducing the need for overtime
- improving efficiency
- reevaluating sales tools

2 **Making outlines**

An **outline** is essentially a logically parallel list with further subdivisions and subsections under individual items in the list. To make an outline

18e

dev //

that will help you write a paper or take summarizing notes from a book, follow the guidelines shown in 3g-3. You should keep elements at the same level of generality in the outline parallel in form. Following is an example:

NOT PARALLEL

Chapter Title: Jefferson Takes Power [clause]

    A. The man and his policies [compound nouns]

    B. Buying Louisiana [*-ing* form of a verb]

    C. Jefferson, Marshall, and the courts [compound nouns]

    D. There's trouble on the seas [clause]

      In this outline, the subdivisions within the chapter are written three different ways: as an independent clause, as a noun or noun phrase, and as a verb in its *-ing* form. You need to choose *one* of these grammatical structures to make a logically parallel outline. Any choice can be correct, but one may be preferable for your purposes. Often a compromise choice is to outline entries as nouns or noun phrases.

PARALLEL, WITH A SUBDIVISION

Chapter Title: Jefferson in Power

    A. The man and his policies

    B. The Louisiana Purchase

    C. Jefferson, Marshall, and the courts

    D. Trouble on the seas

        1. The benefits of neutrality

        2. The dangers of neutrality

18e

dev //

      As you expand the outline in greater detail, once again present each entry of the subdivision in parallel form. Within each subdivision, list all parallel items at the same level of generality. If you wanted to subdivide items in the outline to a still more particular level of detail, you would once again make the listed elements of the next subdivision parallel in form.

> EXERCISE 2
>
> In a textbook of your choice, outline the major sections of any one chapter, using the author's subheadings or your own. Then choose one section to outline in detail. Make parallel entries in your outline for every paragraph in that section maintaining a consistent grammatical form.

> EXERCISE 3
>
> Repeat Exercise 2, but use as your source a paper you have recently written. Once you have outlined your paper, use the outline as a tool for evaluating the coherence of your work. Based on your outline, what observations can you make about the structure of your paper?

CHAPTER 19

Building Emphasis with Coordination and Subordination

To emphasize a thought, a writer assigns special weight or importance to particular words in a sentence and to particular sentences in a paragraph. You are in the best position to make decisions about emphasis once you have written a draft and have your main points clearly in mind. Then you can manipulate words, phrases, and clauses to create the effects that will make your writing memorable.

Sentence emphasis does not exist independently of content. While your readers may admire the elegance and force of your writing, they must also be convinced that the content of your sentences and paragraphs is clear and logical as well as grammatical. As they consider what your sentences say, readers will appreciate any efforts you make to convert adequate, unemphatic writing into memorable prose. For example, consider the following two selections. Which do you find more readable, more interesting?

Unemphatic

The story begins when the deceased arrives at the funeral parlor. The deceased person would be surprised to learn how variously his body is manipulated by undertakers in an effort to make it presentable for public viewing.

Emphatic

The drama begins to unfold with the arrival of the corpse at the mortuary.

Alas, poor Yorick! How surprised he would be to see how his counterpart of today is whisked off to a funeral parlor and is in short order sprayed, sliced, pierced, pickled, trussed, trimmed, creamed, waxed, painted, rouged, and neatly dressed—transformed from a common corpse into a Beautiful Memory Picture.

Emphatic writing uses specific, concrete images (21c, d); is concise and direct (chapter 17); employs parallelism (chapter 18); and is varied (chapter 20). Your writing can improve immensely if you apply the techniques discussed here; but remember that no amount of emphasis can salvage sentences that are seriously flawed in content, grammar, usage, or punctuation.

361

COORDINATION

19a Use coordinate structures to emphasize equal ideas.

As a unit of thought, a sentence is naturally emphatic. Like a story, it has a beginning, middle, and end; and by virtue of its form alone—its uppercase letter at the beginning and its concluding period—it calls on the reader to take notice by distinguishing its content from that of the sentences immediately preceding and following. A sentence, of course, can be more or less effective. One important and very common technique for both creating emphasis and eliminating wordiness is **coordination,** combining sentence elements by the use of coordinate and correlative conjunctions and conjunctive adverbs. Elements in a coordinate relationship share equal grammatical status and equal emphasis.

19a

*emph/
coord*

1 Give equal emphasis to elements with coordinate conjunctions.

The **coordinate conjunctions** *and, but, or, nor, so, for, yet* offer an efficient way of joining parallel elements from two or more sentences into a single sentence. The following sentences are parallel in content.

A market allows sellers of goods to interact with buyers.

A market allows sellers of services to interact with buyers.

By using the coordinate conjunction *or,* you can create a compound sentence in which each independent clause has equal grammatical status.

A market allows sellers of goods to interact with buyers, *or* a market allows sellers of services to interact with buyers.

If words are repeated in coordinate clauses, you can economize by coordinating sentence *parts,* in this case the objects of two prepositional phrases. In the following sentence, *goods* and *services* receive equal emphasis.

COMBINED   A market allows sellers of goods *or* services to interact with buyers. [The object of the preposition has been doubled with a coordinating conjunction.]

Coordinate conjunctions express specific logical relations between the elements they join. *Or* and *nor* suggest choice, one positive and the other negative. *And* joins elements by addition. *But* and *yet* join elements by establishing a contrast. *For* suggests a cause of an occurrence. *So* suggests a result of some action. *For* and *so,* when used as coordinate conjunctions, must join entire independent clauses. All other coordinate conjunctions may join sentence elements and entire sentences. Coordinate conjunctions must be used with appropriate punctuation to show that two ideas share the same emphasis.

To ESTABLISH EQUALITY BETWEEN WORDS

Darwin was a pioneer in biology *and* a thinker with an exceptionally fertile mind. [The coordinating conjunction *and* allows the writer to explain two aspects of Darwin in the same sentence.]

To ESTABLISH EQUALITY BETWEEN PHRASES

Darwin theorized that evolutionary changes proceed not in jumps *but* in leaps. [Here *but* contrasts two ideas in prepositional phrases of equal weight.]

To ESTABLISH EQUALITY BETWEEN CLAUSES

Darwin's theory of natural selection was his most daring, *for* it dealt with the mechanism of evolutionary change. [The independent clause after *for* permits the writer to give an explanation or reason for the first clause.]

Evolutionists from Darwin on have always emphasized the continuity of populational evolution, *yet* they have ignored the fact that even continuous evolution is mildly discontinuous. [The independent clause after *yet* permits the writer to establish an exception to the first clause.]

2 Give equal emphasis to elements by using correlative conjunctions.

19a

emph/ coord

Correlative conjunctions are pairs of coordinate conjunctions that emphasize the relationship between the parts of the coordinated construction. The following are the common correlative conjunctions:

either/or	*both/and*	*not only/but*
neither/nor	*whether/or*	*not only/but also*

The first word of the correlative is placed before the first element to be joined, and the second word of the correlative before the second element.

Both supply *and* demand are theoretical constructs, not fixed laws.

3 Use conjunctive adverbs to give balanced emphasis to sentence elements.

Conjunctive adverbs, also called *adverbial conjunctions,* create compound sentences in which the independent clauses that are joined share a logically balanced emphasis. The following conjunctions (as well as others— see the box) provide logical linkages between sentences: *however, otherwise, indeed, nevertheless, afterward,* and *still.* (See 7a-9 and especially 13b-5 for uses of conjunctive adverbs.)

Linked sentences

As the price of a good or service increases, the quantity of the good or service demanded is expected to decrease. *Moreover,* as the price of a good or service decreases, the quantity of the good or service demanded is expected to increase.

Conjunctive adverbs, like most adverbs, can be moved around in a sentence.

> We almost take for granted that rain will replenish whatever amount of water we may use up. Water, *however,* is no longer the infinitely renewable resource that we once thought it was.

In the second sentence, the conjunctive adverb may be moved.

> *However,* water is no longer the infinitely renewable resource that we once thought it was.

NOTE: Because conjunctive adverbs have the force of transitional elements, they are usually set off in a sentence with commas. It is virtually automatic that with the use of a conjunctive adverb one of the joined independent clauses will contain a comma, as in all the preceding examples. (See 13b-4 for avoiding comma splices when using conjunctive adverbs.)

Conjunctive Adverbs and the Relationships They Establish

To show contrast: *however, nevertheless, nonetheless,* and *still*

To show cause and effect: *accordingly, consequently, thus,* and *therefore*

To show addition: *also, besides, furthermore,* and *moreover*

To show time: *afterward, subsequently,* and *then*

To show emphasis: *indeed*

To show condition: *otherwise*

19a

*emph/
coord*

4 Revise sentences that use illogical or excessive coordination.

Problems with coordination arise when writers use conjunctions aimlessly, stringing unrelated elements together without regard for an equal or balanced relationship of ideas in the joined elements.

Faulty coordination

Two elements linked by a conjunction show faulty coordination when they are not logically related. Revise or reorganize sentences to establish groupings that make sense, using coordination for elements of closely related importance.

FAULTY   Newts are salamanders that live on the land and in the water, and they are characterized by a presence of lungs, well-developed eyes, and two rows of teeth on the roof of the mouth. [The writer coordinates these sentences improperly: the topic of the first sentence, the habitat of newts, is not shown to be logically related to the topic of the second sentence, physical characteristics.]

REVISED   Newts are salamanders that live on the land and in the water. They are characterized by a presence of lungs, well-developed eyes, and two rows of teeth on the roof of the mouth. [The first sentence now concerns only the habitat of newts. The second describes their physical characteristics.]

Excessive coordination

Readers look to a writer for signals about logical relationships among ideas, as well as for what is important in a paragraph. If a writer has aimlessly used coordinating conjunctions to join every statement to the next, readers will see no real connections among the ideas; no single idea will stand out. In reviewing first-draft writing, study your use of coordinate and correlative conjunctions and of conjunctive adverbs. Coordinate structures should be retained only when you have deliberately equated main ideas.

FAULTY   The tribe of Iks, a nomadic tribe in northern Uganda, have become celebrities and literary symbols for the ultimate fate of disheartened and heartless mankind at large, for two disastrous things happened to them, and they were compelled to give up hunting and become farmers on poor hillside soil, and an anthropologist detested them, and he wrote a book about them.

19a

REVISED   The Iks, a nomadic tribe in northern Uganda, have become celebrities and literary symbols for the ultimate fate of disheartened and heartless mankind at large. Two disastrous things happened to them. They were compelled to give up hunting and become farmers on poor hillside soil. Also, an anthropologist detested them and wrote a book about them.

emph/
coord

—LEWIS THOMAS, *Lives of A Cell*

The division into sentences is based on the writer's assessment of his most important ideas. The first sentence is a definition. The next three describe two events.

EXERCISE 1

Combine the following sets of sentences so that whole sentences or parts of sentences show equal emphasis. Use coordinate conjunctions, correlative conjunctions, or conjunctive adverbs.

> *Example:* Ostriches grow from egg to 150-pound bird in nine months. A young python of five pounds requires ten to twenty years to reach 120 pounds.
>
> Ostriches grow from egg to 150-pound bird in nine months, but a young python of five pounds requires ten to twenty years to reach 120 pounds.

1. Why living things evolve is only partly understood. How living things evolve is only partly understood.
2. Monkeys, apes, and man are all good manipulators of hand-eye coordination. No mammal can rival the chameleon for eye-tongue coordination.

3. Snake anatomy contains the most clever feeding apparatus. Snake anatomy also contains the most intricately efficient feeding apparatus.
4. The snake opens its jaws. It begins to engulf the monkey. It is not hurried. It is deliberate. It is precise.
5. The Nunamiu Eskimo believe that wolves know where they are going when they set out to hunt caribou. They believe that wolves learn from ravens where caribou might be. They believe certain wolves in a pack never kill. Others, they believe, specialize in killing small game.
6. When the wolves come together, they make squeaking noises. They encircle each other. They rub and push one another. They poke their noses into each other's neck fur. They back away to stretch. They chase each other. They stand quietly together. Then they are gone down a vague trail.
7. Mexico still has a small population of wolves. Large populations remain in Alaska and Canada.

EXERCISE 2

Rewrite the sentences in the following paragraph by using coordinate conjunctions, correlative conjunctions, or conjunctive adverbs along with appropriate punctuation. Remember that you want to show equality between ideas or parts of ideas. Be sure that the revised paragraph is cohesive and coherent.

The word *dinosaur* conjures up a hazy picture of prehistoric creatures. It is a far-from-accurate picture. They were thought to be cold-blooded. Some scientists now believe that dinosaurs were warm-blooded, like birds and mammals. Popular imagination made them out to be slow, clumsy, and stupid. They were not very good at keeping themselves alive either. Scientists now believe that some dinosaurs could run very fast. They think that their legs were suitable for a very active life. They do not think that dinosaurs were any less intelligent than the reptiles of today. Their brains were not so small. Their bodies were unusually large by comparison.

EXERCISE 3

Rewrite the following sets of sentences to correct problems of faulty coordination.

1. An intelligent dog can track a man across open ground by his smell and he can distinguish that man's tracks from those of others, and, more than this, the dog can detect the odor of a light human fingerprint on a glass slide, and he will remember that slide and smell it out from others for as long as six weeks when the scent fades.
2. Bats are obliged to make sounds almost ceaselessly and to sense, by sonar, all the objects in their surroundings, for they can spot with accuracy small insects, and they will home onto things they like with infallibility and speed, for they must live in a world of ultrasonic bat-sound.

SUBORDINATION

19b Use subordinate structures to emphasize a main idea.

Writers use **subordination** within sentences to give more emphasis to one idea than to another. The basic idea always appears in an **independent clause,** a core statement that can stand alone as a sentence in itself. To state another idea closely linked to that core statement writers add a **dependent clause,** which cannot stand by itself. The resulting construction is known as a **complex sentence.** (For more information on dependent clauses, see 7e.)

1 Use subordinate conjunctions to form dependent adverb clauses.

A subordinate conjunction placed at the beginning of an independent clause (a complete sentence) renders that clause *dependent*. Once dependent, this clause can be joined to an independent clause and will function like an adverb. In this new complex sentence, the independent clause will receive the primary emphasis, with the dependent clause closely linked to it in a subordinate relationship. To create a dependent adverb clause, begin with two sentences that you think could be combined.

19b

emph/ sub

> Married women could not leave the home for the twelve-hour work days required in the mills.

> Married women lost their ability to earn income.

Place a subordinate conjunction at the head of the dependent clause, the clause that will function like an adverb in the new complex sentence.

> Because married women could not leave the home for the twelve-hour work days required in the mills,

Join the now dependent clause to the independent clause.

> Because married women could not leave the home for the twelve-hour work days required in the mills, they lost their ability to earn income.

Subordinate Conjunctions and the Relationships They Establish

To show condition: *if, even if, unless,* and *provided that*

To show contrast: *though, although, even though,* and *as if*

To show cause: *because* and *since*

To show time: *when, whenever, while, as, before, after, since, once,* and *until*

To show place: *where* and *wherever*

To show purpose: *so that, in order that,* and *that*

Emphasis and logical sequence determine the placement of a dependent adverb clause.

AT THE BEGINNING

When the first certain ancestor of man walked, it was with a foot almost indistinguishable from the foot of modern man. [The writer wants the reader to know immediately that the era is pre-human; the writer therefore places the dependent clause at the beginning of the sentence.]

IN THE MIDDLE

Scientists concentrate, because it has undergone the most formative changes, on the head. [Here the emphasis is on the final word of the main clause, *head*. The dependent clause interrupts the independent clause to introduce tension or mystery, allowing the end of the sentence to resolve the tension.]

AT THE END

Australopithecus or "Southern Ape" was the name given to a skull found in Africa although it was actually the first non-ape skull ever uncovered. [Here the information in the dependent clause qualifies in a surprising way all the information presented in the main clause.]

19b

emph/ sub

2 Use *that, which,* and *who* to form dependent adjective clauses.

A dependent **adjective clause** modifies a noun in an independent clause. Adjective clauses are introduced by relative pronouns that rename and refer to the nouns they follow. The pronoun *who* can refer to people or to personified divinities or animals. *That* refers to people, animals, or things. *Which* refers to animals and things. To create a dependent adjective clause, begin with two sentences that you think could be combined.

The ancient Turkic Khazars appeared in Transcaucasia in the 2nd century A.D.

The ancient Turkic Khazars subsequently settled in the lower Volga region.

Substitute a relative pronoun for the subject of the dependent clause, the clause that will function like an adjective in the new complex sentence.

who appeared in Transcaucasia in the 2nd century A.D.,

Join the now dependent clause to the independent clause.

The ancient Turkic Khazars, who appeared in Transcaucasia in the 2nd century A.D., subsequently settled in the lower Volga region.

3 Use subordination accurately.

Three errors are commonly associated with subordination: inappropriate and ambiguous use of subordinate conjunctions, illogical subordination, and excessive subordination.

Inappropriate and ambiguous use of subordinate conjunctions

The subordinate conjunction *as* is used to denote both time and comparison.

> As human beings became more advanced technologically, they learned to domesticate animals and plants rather than to forage and hunt.

As is occasionally used to indicate cause: *Mary didn't arrive this morning, as she missed her plane.* This usage is apt to confuse readers, who may expect *as* to indicate time or comparison. When you wish to establish cause and effect, use the subordinate conjunction *because.*

CONFUSING *As* the plough is used as a wedge to divide the soil, it is the most powerful invention in all agriculture.

REVISED *Because* the plough is used as a wedge to divide the soil, it is the most powerful invention in all agriculture. [The reason for the plough's being a powerful invention is given in the adverbial clause, requiring a conjunction that indicates *cause.*]

The preposition *like* is used as a subordinate conjunction in informal speech. In formal writing, use the subordinate conjunction *as* in place of *like* when a conjunction is needed.

NONSTANDARD American agriculture did not have the plough and the wheel *like* Middle Eastern agriculture did.

REVISED American agriculture did not have the plough and the wheel *as* Middle Eastern agriculture did.

Illogical subordination

The problem of illogical subordination arises when a dependent clause does not establish a clear, logical relationship with an independent clause. To correct the problem, reexamine the clauses in question and select a more accurate subordinate conjunction or, if the sentences warrant, a coordinate conjunction.

FAULTY *Although* she was agitated at being shut up in a matchbox for so long, the female scorpion seized the first opportunity to escape.

The subordinate conjunction *although* fails to establish a clear, logical relationship between the dependent and independent clauses. The content of the dependent clause gives no reason for the scorpion's wanting to escape.

REVISED *Because* she was agitated at being shut up in a matchbox for so long, the female scorpion seized the first opportunity to escape. [The dependent clause explains the reason for the scorpion's escape and requires a subordinate conjunction denoting *cause.*]

19b

*emph/
sub*

Excessive subordination

As with coordination, a writer may overuse subordination. When all or most parts of a long sentence are subordinate in structure, readers may have trouble identifying points of particular importance. In your review of a first draft, study your use of subordinate conjunctions and relative pronouns. Retain subordinate structures when you have deliberately made the ideas of one clause dependent on another. Choose some other sentence structure when the clauses you are relating do not exist in a dependent/independent relationship.

FAULTY   As dawn suffuses the heavily shaded forest floor, the colony of army ants is in "bivouac," which means that it is temporarily camped in an exposed position, since the sites most favored for bivouacs are the relatively sheltered spots along the trunks of standing trees or beneath fallen trees, although most of the shelter for the queen is provided by the bodies of the workers themselves.

REVISED   As dawn suffuses the heavily shaded forest floor, the colony of army ants is in "bivouac," meaning that it is temporarily camped in an exposed position. The sites most favored for bivouacs are the relatively sheltered spots along the trunks of standing trees or beneath fallen trees, although most of the shelter for the queen is provided by the bodies of the workers themselves.

19b

emph/ sub

EXERCISE 4

Revise each pair of sentences that follow by creating a complex sentence with one dependent clause and one independent clause. Place the dependent clause in whatever position you think will best demonstrate the relationship of that clause to the main idea.

Example: The Viennese naturalist Konrad Lorenz took a degree in medicine. Later, Konrad Lorenz became director of the Max Planck Institute for behavioral physiology.

After he took a degree in medicine, the Viennese naturalist Konrad Lorenz became director of the Max Planck Institute for behavioral physiology. [A dependent adverb clause is joined to an independent clause to form a complex sentence.]

1. Social animals such as crows will attack or "mob" a nocturnal predator. The nocturnal predator sometimes appears during the day.
2. A fox is followed through the woods by a loudly screaming jay. The fox's hunting is spoiled.
3. Poisonous or foul-tasting animals have chosen the "warning" colors of red, white, and black. Predators associate these with unpleasant experiences.
4. Scent marks of cats act like railway signals. The scent marks prevent collision between two cats.
5. The surroundings become stranger and more intimidating to the animal. The readiness to fight decreases proportionately.

OTHER DEVICES FOR ACHIEVING EMPHASIS

19c Use special techniques to achieve emphasis.

Coordination and subordination are fundamental to the structure of so many sentences that often they go unnoticed as devices for directing a reader's attention. Not so subtle are special stylistic techniques like repetition and contrast, which writers use to achieve highly visible and at times dramatic prose. Precisely because they are so visible, you should mix these techniques both with subordination and coordination and with less emphatic simple sentences in a paragraph.

1 Punctuate, capitalize, and highlight to emphasize words.

Capitalizing a word, especially if it is not a proper name and hence is usually not begun with an uppercase letter, is one sure way to create emphasis. Capitalizing all the letters of a word, as in FIRE, will attract even more attention. So, of course, will **boldfacing** a word. In academic writing, strictly limit your use of these techniques and depend, instead, on the wording of your sentences to create emphasis. Occasionally, however, you might use uppercase letters for effect.

19c

emph

> There does not seem to be any point in my knowing for the rest of my life that, during 1964, 720 tons of soot fell on every square mile of New York City, yet there it is in my notebook, labeled "FACT."

The *exclamation point* was created for the very purpose of giving emphasis to written words. Do not assume, however, that punctuation alone can make a sentence emphatic. Punctuation works in *tandem* with sentence content. Misused with content that is not extraordinary, an exclamation point will make a writer seem excitable and melodramatic. Well used, an exclamation point will sit a reader upright, at attention, to share a writer's amazement, enthusiasm—or, in the following example, contempt. (The sentences that follow also use *italics* to call special attention to individual words.)

> When friends arrived from out of town, I always took them first to the lobby of the Tower. *Pink* marble! An eighty-foot indoor *waterfall!* The first truly American cathedral, dedicated to luxury, to a great blinding opulence, to . . . mammon!

Ending a sentence with a *colon* sets for your reader an expectation that important, closely related information will follow. The words after a colon are emphasized.

> If a cowboy's "a rugged individualist" he's also part of a team: ranch work is teamwork and even the glorified open-range cowboys of the 1880s rode up and down the Chisholm Trail in the company of twenty or thirty other riders.

A *dash*, which you will show on a typewriter or computer as a double hyphen (--), creates a pause in a sentence and the expectation that some significant comment will follow. Used sparingly, a dash is an excellent tool for emphasis. Overused, it creates a choppy effect and will annoy readers.

> A cowboy is someone who loves his work. Since the hours are long—ten to fifteen hours a day—and the pay is minimal, he has to.

Information set within *parentheses* will be viewed by readers as an aside—interesting, useful, but ultimately nonessential information. Parentheses give material special attention, but of a curious sort: parenthetical material limits its own emphasis and says in effect, pay attention, but not *too much*. Thus, material set off in parentheses is simultaneously emphasized and de-emphasized.

> Historically torture has been a tool of legal systems, used to get information needed for a trial or, more directly, to determine guilt or innocence. In the Middle Ages confession was considered the best of all proofs, and torture was the way to produce a confession. In other words, torture didn't come into existence to give vent to human sadism. It is not always private and perverse but sometimes social and institutional, vetted by the government and, of course, the Church. (There have been few bigger fans of torture than Christianity and Islam.) Righteousness, as much as viciousness, produces torture.

19c

emph

2 Repeat words, phrases, and clauses to emphasize ideas.

Intentional repetition is a powerful technique for creating emphasis. With repetition, words echo for a reader. Whatever is repeated, if it is repeated well, will be remembered. When using repetition, it is especially important to maintain parallel structure (see chapter 18) and to avoid overuse. Our language and certain others seem naturally "tuned" to two and three repetitions in any one sentence. Words, phrases, and clauses doubled by coordinate conjunctions create by far the most typical instances of repetition. It is both more emphatic and less wordy to write

> A market allows sellers of goods or services to interact with buyers.

instead of

> A market allows sellers of goods to interact with buyers. A market allows sellers of services to interact with buyers.

Using repetition to triple sentence elements is more dramatic than doubling and will give a sentence an arresting, memorable rhythm. Think of Caesar's "I came, I saw, I conquered"; or the phrasing in the Declaration of Independence: "Life, Liberty and the pursuit of Happiness"; or Lincoln's lines at Gettysburg: "government of the people, by the people, for the people." (In each case, note the parallel structures.) One repetition too many can ruin a sentence, however, transforming a dramatic rhythm into a boring catalogue: *On arriving home, I folded the laundry, cooked dinner, read the paper, bathed my kids, finished the taxes, and went to sleep.*

To summarize, doubled sentence elements are commonplace and slightly emphatic; tripled elements are clearly emphatic; and quadrupled elements can tax a reader's patience, unless the sentence is carefully crafted. Generally, try not to follow one sentence that has a repeated structure with a second sentence of a similar structure. Too much repetition within a sentence or within a paragraph will create an unpleasant, overly balanced effect.

One special case of repetition concerns the *appositive phrase,* used to rename a noun. Although an appositive does not exactly repeat a word, in content the appositive is a technique based on repetition. In the following example, the phrase *a symbolic embodiment of its territorial status* renames (that is, repeats) the noun *flag.*

> Today each nation flies its own flag, a symbolic embodiment of its territorial status.

3 Use contrasts to emphasize ideas.

Contrast, otherwise known as *antithesis* or *opposition,* creates emphasis by setting one element in a sentence off against another, in the process emphasizing both. When using this technique, be sure that the elements you set in contrast have parallel structures.

19c

emph

> More ambiguous than other scientific inventions familiar to modern artists, but no less influential, are the psychoanalytic studies of Freud and his followers.

> If the classroom now begins to seem a stale and flat environment for learning, the inventors of television itself are to blame, not the Children's Television Workshop.

4 Use specialized sentences to create emphasis.

Readers expect sentences to be a certain length. Of course, sentence length is variable and depends both on a writer's preferences and on an audience's needs; still, it is safe to say that readers do not expect a steady diet of four- or five-word sentences. Nor do they expect one-sentence paragraphs. Purposefully violating these (and other) expectations regarding the sentence can create emphasis. (See 20a and 20b.)

The brief sentence

An especially brief sentence located anywhere in a paragraph will call attention to itself. The following paragraph concludes emphatically with a five-word sentence.

> The Red Sox were winners of five of the first fifteen World Series but have not won one since 1918. They have been in Series since then but lost them all—in the seventh games. There have been two one-game playoffs in American League history. The Red Sox lost both.

The one-sentence paragraph

Because it is so rare, a one-sentence paragraph calls attention to itself. Often these emphatic paragraphs begin or conclude an essay. In the following example, the one-sentence paragraph appears mid-essay and is both preceded and followed by long paragraphs.

> . . . Not only are fruit seeds dispersed in the coyote's scat, the seeds' pericarp dissolves in his digestive tract, increasing the chance of germination by 85 percent.
>
> A coyote's breath is rumored to be so rank that he can stun his prey with it.
>
> Most people may never see a coyote—especially if they go looking for one—but everyone can hear them at night. They're most vocal from December to February, during the mating season. . . .

The periodic sentence

Most sentences can be classified as *cumulative*. They begin with a subject and gather both force and detail as one reads, beginning to end. The advantage of a cumulative sentence is that it directly and emphatically announces its business by beginning with its subject.

CUMULATIVE SENTENCE   Most people may never see a coyote—especially if they go looking for one—but everyone can hear them at night.

A *periodic* sentence delays the subject and verb in an effort to pique the reader's interest. Information placed at the head of the sentence draws readers in, creating a desire to find out what happens. Emphasis is given to the final part of the sentence, where the readers' need to know is satisfied.

PERIODIC SENTENCE   Washing machines, garbage disposals, lawn mowers, furnaces, TV sets, tape recorders, slide projectors—all are in league with the automobile to take their turn at breaking down whenever life threatens to flow smoothly for their enemies.

EXERCISE 5

Read the sets of sentences that follow and underline the emphatic elements in each. Label the specific techniques each writer uses: coordination, subordination, punctuation, capitalization, repetition, contrast, or sentence length. Choose one set of sentences to analyze closely. Write your analysis in paragraph form.

[Robert E. Lee] embodied a way of life that had come down through the age of knighthood and the English country squire. America was a land that was beginning all over again, dedicated to nothing much more complicated than the rather hazy belief that all men had equal rights and should have an equal chance in the world. In such a land Lee stood for the feeling that it was somehow of advantage to human society to have a pronounced inequality in the social structure. There should be a leisure class, backed by ownership of land; in turn, society itself should be

---

19c

emph

keyed to the land as the chief source of wealth and influence. It would bring forth (according to this ideal) a class of men with a strong sense of obligation to the community; men who lived not to gain advantage for themselves, but to meet the solemn obligations which had been laid on them by the very fact that they were privileged. From them the country would get its leadership; to them it could look for higher values—of thought, of conduct, or personal deportment—to give it strength and virtue.

—BRUCE CATTON

In books I've read since I was young I've searched for heroines who could serve as ideals, as models, as possibilities—some reflecting the secret self that dwelled inside me, others pointing to whole new ways that a woman (if only she dared!) might try to be. The person that I am today was shaped by Nancy Drew; by Jo March, Jane Eyre and Heathcliff's soul mate Cathy; and by other fictional females whose attractiveness or character or audacity for a time were the standards by which I measured myself.

I return to some of these books to see if I still understand the powerful hold that these heroines once had on me. I still understand.

—JUDITH VIORST

19c

emph

EXERCISE 6

Use the various techniques you have learned in this chapter to combine the short, choppy sentences that follow, rewording them to make an engaging paragraph.

The brain is a tissue. It is complicated. It is intricately woven. It is like nothing else we know of in the universe. It is composed of cells. These are highly specialized cells. They function according to laws. These same laws govern any other cells. The electrical and chemical signals of cells can be detected, recorded and interpreted. Their chemicals can be identified. For this reason, the brain can be studied systematically.

CHAPTER 20

Controlling Length and Rhythm

O nce satisfied that a draft expresses its meaning correctly with the detail and level of emphasis needed to communicate clearly to your audience, you can consider how to make the paper varied and interesting. The benefits of rewriting to achieve variety in sentence length and rhythm are best shown in an example. Consider this set of sentences as if it were an unfinished draft.

> I have been teaching English literature in a university, and I have also been studying literature. I have been doing these things for twenty-five years. Certain questions stick in one's mind in this job; actually, they do in any job. They persist not only because people keep asking them. Such questions stick in one's mind because they are inspired by the very fact of being in a university. First one might ask what is the benefit of studying literature. Then one might ask whether literature helps us think more clearly, or whether it helps us feel more sensitively, or whether literature helps us live a better life than we could if we did not have it.

This draft is correct and clear enough, but the same material could be rewritten to become the more varied and interesting piece the writer actually published.

> For the past twenty-five years I have been teaching and studying English literature in a university. As in any other job, certain questions stick in one's mind, not because people keep asking them but because they're the questions inspired by the very fact of being in such a place. What good is the study of literature? Does it help us think more clearly, or feel more sensitively, or live a better life than we could without it?
>
> —NORTHROP FRYE

The first version is choppy and redundant. It has the bumpy, uncertain rhythm of someone just learning to drive. By contrast, Northrop Frye's sentences are fluid and rhythmically pleasing. When one of his sentences comes to a stop, it does so gently. Frye builds pauses, breathing spaces, into his writing. He knows how to use a comma to slow the reader down and to create emphasis. Are the pleasing rhythms of Frye's work purely a matter of "writer's intuition"? Could someone who produced the first version be taught to produce such rhythms, or is writing that pleases the ear a matter of art reserved for born writers?

There is less art than you might think in creating effective sentences. A writer's intuition is built on very specific skills, which are used so often and are so familiar that they become automatic—or intuitive. A writer's intuition has first to do with content and commitment. Effective sentences like Frye's are always the work of someone who has something to say, who believes in that content, and who therefore will take time to revise so that the sentences are not only accurate and correct but also inviting. If you want to write effective sentences, begin with content worth writing about and to which you are committed. Read books and articles that show commitment, reflect on why these interest you, and observe how the best writing achieves a variety and emphasis that conveys this commitment (see 1e). Try to enjoy or at the very least show interest in what you are writing. Then you will have a reason to learn techniques for varying sentences in length and rhythm and for writing sentences that you and others want to read.

Beyond content and commitment, good writing has much to do with timing: how long a sentence takes to read and what rhythmic effects are encountered along the way. Considerations of length and rhythm alone will not make a sentence memorable. But any significant content, once established, can be expressed with a more or less effective style, and effective style has a great deal to do with sentence length and rhythm (as well as conciseness, parallelism, and emphasis—see chapters 17, 18, and 19).

20a

emph

20a   Monitoring sentence length

1   Track the length of your sentences.

Often, without realizing it, writers will work with favorite sentence patterns. For reasons of personal preference and audience analysis, the average length of one writer's sentences will differ from the average length of those of another writer. Common sense dictates that when a sentence gets so long that readers forget important sentence parts (for instance, the subject), then sentence length should be revised.

Track the length of your sentences. Especially in the late stages of revision, once you are certain of a paper's content, you are in a good position to monitor the length of sentences, which is the first step in varying length and rhythm. *Variety* means variation from an average. If you want to vary sentence length, you must be aware of the average length of your sentences. The information in the following box will help you make that determination.

As you begin tracking sentence length, following a technique like the one suggested here will not be necessary for long. Soon you will develop a writer's intuition about sentence length; you will begin to vary the number of words from sentence to sentence because you *feel* the need. This *feeling* will be based on an analysis similar to the one shown here.

Tracking Sentence Length

Any given sentence in a paragraph is long or short in relation to the *average* number of words per sentence in that paragraph. A simple process of counting and dividing will reveal your average sentence length.

1. Number the sentences in a paragraph and write those numbers in a column on a piece of paper.

2. Count and record the number of words in each sentence.

3. Add the word counts for step 2 to obtain the total number of words in the paragraph.

4. Divide the number of words in the paragraph (step 3) by the number of sentences in the paragraph (step 1): this number is your average sentence length for the paragraph.

Consider a sentence to be *average* in length if it has *five words more or less* than your average. Consider a sentence *long* if it has six or more words than your average and *short* if it has six or fewer words than your average.

5. Return to the listing you made in step 2, and designate each sentence of your paragraph as *average* length, *short*, or *long*. These designations apply to your writing only. They are relative terms, representing different sentence lengths for different writers.

20a

emph

2 Vary sentence length and alternate the length of consecutive sentences.

Two paragraphs follow, showing writers working with different average sentence lengths. In the first paragraph, by biologist Helena Curtis, the average sentence length is longer than those in subsequent examples. The designation *average*, remember, means different lengths for different writers. Regardless of average sentence length, good writers will (1) write sentences in a paragraph that vary from their average and (2) will avoid placing two or more very short or very long sentences consecutively. (See 19c-4.)

Aristotle, the first great biologist, believed that all living things could be arranged in a hierarchy. This hierarchy became known as the *Scala Naturae,* or ladder of nature, in which the simplest creatures had a humble position on the bottommost rung, man occupied the top, and all other organisms had their proper places between. Up until the end of the last century, many European biologists believed in such a natural hierarchy. But whereas to Aristotle living organisms had always existed, the later Europeans, in harmony with the teachings of the Scriptures, believed that all living things were the products of a divine creation. In either case, the concept that prevailed for 2,000 years was that all the kinds, or species (*species* simply means "kinds"), of animals had come into existence in their present form. Even those who believed in spontaneous generation (toads forming from the mud and snakes from a lady's hair dropped in a rain barrel) did not believe that any species had an historical relationship to any other one—any common ancestry, so to speak.

—HELENA CURTIS

(30 word avg.)
1. 16 words (short)
2. 38 words (long)
3. 17 words (short)
4. 32 words (average)
5. 31 words (average)
6. 43 words (long)
   177 words ÷ 6 ≈ 30

Curtis's sentence lengths are varied: two short, two long, two average

- No short sentences are placed consecutively.
- No long sentences are placed consecutively.
- Two sentences of average length are placed consecutively—these are preceded by a short sentence.

For another example, consider the paragraph section you read at the opening of this chapter, by Northrop Frye, a teacher of literature and a literary critic. His sentences, when analyzed like Curtis's for varied length, average twenty words; he has two average sentences (the first and last), one long (the second), and one short (the third). Like Curtis, he varies length and is mindful of alternating length in consecutive sentences.

20a

emph

Varying Sentence Length and Alternating the Length of Consecutive Sentences

While no precise formula exists for determining how many long or short sentences should be used in a paragraph, you may find these general principles helpful:

- Determine the average length of sentences in a paragraph.
- Plan to vary from that average by using short and long sentences.
- Use short sentences to break up strings of longer ones.
- Avoid placing short sentences consecutively unless you are doing so for specific stylistic effect.
- Avoid placing more than two or three long sentences consecutively.
- Avoid placing more than three or four sentences of average length consecutively.

EXERCISE 1

Choose three paragraphs you have written recently (not necessarily from the same paper) and analyze them for sentence length. Follow the steps laid out in the box in 20a-1 above. On finishing your analysis, you should have figured your average sentence length for each paragraph and designated each sentence in the paragraph as *short, average,* or *long.* Write a brief paragraph in which you summarize your findings.

20b Strategies for varying sentence length

Once you have determined the average length of your sentences and the extent to which you vary from that average, you should become familiar with techniques for manipulating sentence length. The techniques discussed here will be helpful *only* if you are working with sentences that are already concise and direct. Sentence length can always be reduced by eliminating wordiness, and revising for conciseness should be your first strategy in managing sentence length. See chapter 17 for advice.

1 Control the use of coordination.

Coordination—the use of coordinate and correlative conjunctions and of conjunctive adverbs to compound sentence elements—is the principal means by which parts of two or more sentences are joined into a single sentence. (See 19a.) In its favor, coordination reduces the overall length of a paragraph by allowing a writer to combine sentence parts (or entire sentences) and eliminate redundancy. The following is a partial paragraph.

> In Puritan Massachusetts the town common had a dual function. It provided for the welfare of the needy. Somewhat incongruously, the town common was the place of public whippings and executions.

The cost of combining sentences with coordination is that the length of the revised sentence will increase. The first sentence in the preceding example has ten words and the set of sentences, thirty-one. In revision, three sentences are combined into one, but that one sentence now has twenty-five words.

> In Puritan Massachusetts the town common *both* provided for the welfare of the needy *and,* somewhat incongruously, was the place of public whippings and executions.

If you decided that the combined sentence made possible by coordination was too long (and you would only know this in relation to the sentences preceding and following it in an actual paragraph), you could break the combined sentence into two.

> In Puritan Massachusetts the town common provided for the welfare of the needy. Somewhat incongruously, it was also the place of public whippings and executions.

In this second revision, the first sentence has thirteen words and the set of sentences, twenty-five—still a reduction in length from the original.

2 Control the use of modifying phrases and clauses.

One way of controlling sentence length is to control the extent to which you use modifying phrases and clauses. (See 7d, e.) Two types of clauses and four types of phrases can function in sentences as adjectives or adverbs.

coord/ sub

20b

Infinitive phrases can function as adjectives or adverbs.

> **ADJECTIVE**   Water is not a resource *to squander.*

> **ADVERB**   Ranchers draw water from the Ogallala aquifer *in order to feed livestock.*

Prepositional phrases can function as adjectives or adverbs.

> **ADJECTIVE**   We assume incorrectly that rain will replenish whatever amount *of water* we may use up.

> **ADVERB**   Ranchers and farmers have begun arguing *over water rights.*

Participial phrases function as adjectives.

> **ADJECTIVE**   *Alarmed by the diminishing supply of water,* rural and municipal leaders have begun serious attempts to find new sources.

Appositive phrases function as adjectives.

> **ADJECTIVE**   In Los Angeles, *a city that has suffered through severe droughts,* engineers have considered building desalination plants.

Clauses with subordinate conjunctions function as adverbs.

> **ADVERB**   *When a city is threatened with water shortages,* rationing often becomes necessary.

Clauses with relative pronouns function as adjectives.

> **ADJECTIVE**   The melting of ice, *which would be towed south from the Arctic Ocean,* is one solution that would supply millions of gallons of fresh water.

Convert modifying clauses to phrases.

If you determine that a sentence is too long in relation to its neighbors, you can reduce sentence length by converting a modifying clause into a phrase.

> *When a city is threatened with water shortages,* drastic actions become necessary.

> *In times of drought,* drastic actions become necessary. [The dependent clause is shortened to two prepositional phrases.]

Move modifying phrases from one sentence to another.

If you determine that a sentence is too long in relation to its neighbors, you may be able to strip a sentence of a modifier, which you can then move to an adjacent sentence (where it may have a new function).

> In Los Angeles, *a city that has suffered through severe droughts,* engineers have considered building desalination plants.

> In Los Angeles, engineers have considered building desalination plants. Recently, *that city has suffered through severe droughts,* and municipal leaders

20b

coord/
sub

are now ready to consider long-term solutions to a persistent problem. [The appositive phrase is converted to a subject and predicate in the new sentence.]

Substitute a single-word modifier for a phrase- or clause-length modifier.

If you determine that a sentence is too long in relation to its neighbors, you may be able to convert phrases or clauses to single-word adjectives or adverbs. In the following example an important detail (about towing icebergs) is lost in the conversion and would need to be added to some other sentence; still, the desired result, a briefer sentence, is achieved.

The melting of ice, *which would be towed south from the Arctic Ocean,* is one solution that would supply millions of gallons of fresh water.

The melting of *arctic* ice is one solution that would supply millions of gallons of fresh water.

3 **Control the use of phrases and clauses used as nouns.**

coord/ sub

Sentences can be combined by converting the key words of one sentence into a phrase or clause that then functions as a noun (as a subject, object, or complement) in a second sentence. The disadvantage of the revision is that the newly combined sentence tends to be long.

Infinitive phrases can function as nouns:

Van Gogh painted peasants in their natural setting.

Van Gogh placed great importance in this painting.

COMBINED   *To paint peasants in their natural settings* was of great importance to Van Gogh. [The infinitive phrase functions as the subject.]

Gerund phrases can function as nouns.

At his uncle's art dealership in Paris, Vincent grew fond of *studying the work of French Barbizon landscapists, especially Millet.* [The gerund phrase functions as the object of a preposition.]

Noun phrases and clauses can function as nouns.

Personal awkwardness and a dislike of business turned Vincent away from dealing in art. [The noun phrase functions as the subject.]

Paris is *where Vincent met Paul Gauguin.* [The noun clause functions as a subject complement.]

If you determine that a sentence is too long in relation to its neighbors, try to identify a phrase or clause functioning as a noun. Revise the sentence, possibly moving the noun phrase or clause into its own sentence.

SENTENCE WITH   The fact that Van Gogh's artistic career lasted only a decade
A NOUN CLAUSE   astonishes most art historians who are familiar with his work.

REVISED   Van Gogh's artistic career lasted only a decade. Art historians familiar with his work are astonished by this fact.

EXERCISE 2

Use any of the strategies discussed thus far in the chapter to combine the following sentences. Vary sentence length and alternate the length of consecutive sentences. Following is a brief listing of conjunctions you may want to use (see 19a, b). *Coordinate conjunctions:* and, but, or, nor, for, so, yet. *Correlative conjunctions:* not only/but also, either/or, both/and. *Conjunctive adverbs:* however, moreover, furthermore, therefore, consequently. *Subordinate conjunctions:* when, although, while, since, because, before. *Relative pronouns:* who, which, that.

We almost take for granted that rain will replenish whatever amount of water we may use up. Water is no longer an infinitely renewable resource. We once thought it was. Water from the Ogallala aquifer stretches nearly 800 miles under eight states. Water in the aquifer is drawn eight times faster than nature can replenish the supply. The demand for water in the aquifer is growing. Ranchers and farmers in states from the Texas panhandle to South Dakota have begun arguing over water rights. Consumers must see the supply of a good or service threatened. Then they awake to the value of that good. What is valued drifts from view. What is valued is taken for granted. Assume the supply of water is drying up. We can expect from the law of demand that price increases will diminish demand. We can expect that price increases will ease the rate at which water is depleted from the aquifer.

20c

emph

EXERCISE 3

Follow the instructions in Exercise 2 and revise the three paragraphs that you analyzed for sentence length in Exercise 1. The aim of your revision is to vary sentence length and to alternate the length of consecutive sentences.

20c Strategies for controlling sentence rhythm

1 Use modifying phrases and clauses to alter sentence rhythm.

Varying sentence openings is the most direct way of varying the rhythm of a sentence or the cadence with which the sentence is read. Sentences consist of a subject, followed by a verb and then an object (if the verb is transitive) or a complement (if the verb is linking). Any of these important elements can be modified, and it is primarily through placement of modifiers that sentences change rhythm. When you want to alter sentence rhythm, revise sentence structure by changing the extent and location of your modifiers. Writers often concentrate modifiers at the beginning, middle, or end of a sentence.

Modifiers concentrated at the *beginning* of a sentence:

> *For years when Andrew Carnegie might have chosen vast personal wealth for himself and his investors,* he funneled profits back into his steel works.

Modifiers concentrated in the *middle* of a sentence:

> Carnegie, *the first industrialist to transfer sophisticated methods of management to manufacturing,* built Carnegie Steel into the world's largest steel producer.

Modifiers concentrated at the *end* of a sentence:

> The United States became a great industrial power by 1900 *in part because of Carnegie, whose mills produced steel more cheaply than any in the world.*

Aside from being related to the extent and location of modifiers, rhythm is also a function of sentence length. A brief sentence with relatively few modifiers has a rhythm altogether different from the preceding sentences.

> Andrew Carnegie was born in Scotland in 1835.

20c

emph

Vary the position of phrases.

Phrases that function as adverbs (see 20b-2) may, like adverbs, be moved around in a sentence. Because such movement can change meaning as well as sentence rhythm, beware of altering the meaning of your sentences when revising for style.

> I reached our new home *on Monday,* wondering whether the movers would arrive.

SHIFTED RHYTHM	*On Monday,* I reached our new home, wondering whether the movers would arrive.
SHIFTED MEANING	I reached our new home, wondering whether the movers would arrive *on Monday.* [The timing of the movers' arrival has now become the issue.]

A phrase that functions as an adjective (see 20b-2) should be placed as close as possible to the noun it modifies to avoid confusion and faulty reference.

FAULTY	Zebulon Pike ventured west to the Rockies, *an explorer of the Mississippi.*
REVISED	Zebulon Pike, *an explorer of the Mississippi,* ventured west to the Rockies.
SHIFTED RHYTHM	*An explorer of the Mississippi,* Zebulon Pike ventured west to the Rockies.

Vary the position of clauses.

Like single-word adverbs and phrases functioning as adverbs, adverb clauses can be moved around in a sentence. An adverb clause that begins a sentence can be shifted to the interior or to the end of the sentence. The placement of the clause determines its punctuation.

> *After so many white settlers had come from England,* it was not surprising that the English language, English customs, and English ways of government dominated America.

> It was not surprising, *after so many white settlers had come from England,* that the English language, English customs, and English ways of government dominated America.

> It was not surprising that the English language, English customs, and English ways of government dominated America *after so many white settlers had come from England.*

Place a dependent clause that functions as an adjective next to the word it modifies. Neglecting to do so may confuse readers. (See chapter 15 on revising to correct misplaced modifiers.)

FAULTY   The Berlin Wall was recently demolished which was 29 miles long.

REVISED   The Berlin Wall, which was 29 miles long, was recently demolished.

SHIFTED   Twenty-nine miles long, the Berlin Wall was recently demolished.
RHYTHM

Vary the position of transitions.

20c

emph

Experienced writers make frequent use of **transitions,** words that like logical bridges help readers move from one idea to another within a sentence, between sentences, or between paragraphs (see 5d-3). Brief transitions include *for instance, for example, on the one hand, on the other hand, in addition,* and *additionally.* Conjunctive adverbs also serve as transitions: *however, moreover, consequently,* and *therefore.* Transitions like these can be moved around in a sentence; when their position changes, sentence rhythm changes.

> Advertising is an ancient art. *For example,* some early advertisements appear about three thousand B.C. as stenciled inscriptions on bricks made by the Babylonians.

> Advertising is an ancient art. Some early advertisements, *for example,* appear about three thousand B.C. as stenciled inscriptions on bricks made by the Babylonians.

2 Revise individual sentences with a disruptive rhythm.

As with the length of a sentence, the rhythm of a sentence should be evaluated both on its own terms and in relation to neighboring sentences. A sentence that starts and stops a reader repeatedly has a disruptive rhythm and should be revised.

DISRUPTIVE   The Boston Common, used originally as pasture land, at one point,
RHYTHM   early in the nineteenth century, because of excessive public drinking, turned into a site of rowdy and indecent exhibitions.

Because its erratic, bumpy rhythm interferes with understanding, this sentence needs revision. Revising in this case might lead to two sentences.

REVISED   The Boston Common has had a long history. Used originally as pasture land, it became in the early nineteenth century the site of excessive public drinking that led to rowdy and indecent exhibitions.

3 Revise groups of sentences to avoid a repetitive rhythm.

The rhythm of a sentence in isolation might be perfectly acceptable. Set in a paragraph, however, this same sentence may have a rhythm that too closely resembles the rhythm of other sentences. Unintentional repetition of sentence structures and rhythms usually results in a stylistically weak paragraph. Revise by restructuring one or more sentences.

UNINTENTIONALLY REPEATING RHYTHM

Used originally as pasture land, the Boston Common became in the early nineteenth century the site of excessive public drinking that led to rowdy and indecent exhibitions. Because of the problem with public drinking, many temperance and drinking ordinances were put into effect. Arising from the needs of Boston's resident population, these ordinances and the Common itself embodied the city's ideals and aspirations.

20c

emph

The sentence structures and rhythms in this paragraph too closely resemble each other: every sentence begins with a modifying phrase or clause. For stylistic reasons, the structure of one or more sentences should be changed.

REVISED   Used originally as pasture land, the Boston Common became in the early nineteenth century the site of excessive public drinking that led to rowdy and indecent exhibitions. So bad was the problem that the city enacted many temperance and drinking ordinances. Boston's resident population was declaring its needs with these new laws. Over time, the Common and the rules that governed its use came to embody Boston's ideals and aspirations.

4 Vary sentence types.

Sentences are classified by structure and function. There are four functional types of sentences (7f-1). The **declarative sentence** is a direct statement: *The driver turned the ignition key.* The **interrogative sentence** is a question: *Was the engine flooded?* The **exclamatory sentence** expresses emotion: *What an awful fire! How terrible!* The **imperative sentence** expresses a command: *Get back! Don't go near that!*

Use occasional questions for variety and focus.

For the most part, academic writing is restricted to declarative and interrogative sentences. Researchers and writers pose questions, conduct investigations, and write responses. The occasional question posed in a paragraph will be important to the content, but a question also introduces a unique rhythm. For an example of how a writer can use questions to create a pleasing sentence rhythm, look again at the passage by Northrop Frye at the beginning of the chapter.

Vary the structure of sentences.

Varying sentence structure, as you have seen in 20c, will vary sentence rhythm. There are four structural types (see 7f-2). Writing that is strong stylistically tends to mix all four types of structure. A **simple sentence** has a single subject and a single verb or predicate. (In the examples that follow, simple subjects will be underlined once and simple predicates, twice.)

> Before the rise of the railroad, most business people based decisions on experience, instinct, and information that was often guesswork.

A **compound sentence,** which has two subjects and two predicates, is created when a writer joins two independent clauses with a conjunction (see 7f-2 and 19a).

> Textile mills used fairly complex methods of planning, but they still relied on preindustrial operations.

A **complex sentence** has one independent clause and one or more dependent clauses (see 7e and 19b). The dependent clause in this example is italicized.

> The system of train control developed by American railroads accomplished a managerial revolution *that brought more change in business decision-making and operational methods in twenty-five years than had occurred in the preceding five centuries.*

A **compound-complex sentence** has at least two independent clauses and one dependent clause. The dependent clause in this example is italicized.

> *When an employee performed badly in a well-managed shop,* the shop lost only that employee's output; no great harm resulted.

20c

emph

Varying Sentence Rhythm

Variety in sentence structures and rhythms is the mark of stylistically strong writing. While no rules govern exactly how a writer should vary rhythm from sentence to sentence, you may find the following general principles helpful.

- Use phrases, clauses, and transitional expressions to vary sentence beginnings.
- Consciously shift the location of phrase- and clause-length modifiers in a paragraph: locate modifiers at the beginning of some sentences, in the middle of others, and at the end of others.

(continued)

> **Varying Sentence Rhythm (continued)**
>
> - Use short sentences to break up strings of long, heavily modified sentences.
>
> - Limit your concentration of phrase- and clause-length modifiers to one and possibly two locations in a sentence. Heavily modifying a sentence at the beginning, middle, *and* end will create a burden stylistically.
>
> - Vary sentence types.

20d Analyzing length and rhythm: A student paragraph

20d

emph

The paragraph analyzed here was written by a student, Jenafer Trahar. (The paper from which this paragraph was excerpted appears at the end of chapter 6.) At twenty words, Trahar's average sentence length is slightly less than that of Northrop Frye, whose paragraph you read at the beginning of this chapter. She, like Frye and other stylistically strong writers, is careful both to vary length and to alternate lengths in consecutive sentences.

[1]One major problem with the commercialization of college sports is the exploitation of student-athletes, many of whom come to school on athletic scholarships. [2]Frequently, student-athletes don't deserve to be admitted to a school. [3]Many colleges routinely lower admissions requirements for their ball players, and some schools will even waive requirements for that exceptional athlete, who without his sports abilities might not have had a place on a college campus. [4]Most kids not interested in academics would normally shun a college education. [5]But for gifted athletes, college appears to be a road that leads to the pros. [6]Or so they think. [7]According to Richard Lapchick of the Center for the Study of Sport in Society, twelve thousand high school athletes participate in sports in any one year, but only one will subsequently play for a professional team.

—JENAFER TRAHAR

Analysis of sentence length

(20 word avg.)
1. 24 words (average)
2. 11 words (short)
3. 36 words (long)
4. 12 words (short)
5. 15 words (average)
6. 4 words (short)
7. 36 words (long)
    $138 \div 7 \approx 20$

Trahar's sentence lengths are varied: three short, two long, two average.

- No short sentences are placed consecutively.

- No long sentences are placed consecutively.

- No sentences of average length are placed consecutively.

Analysis of sentence rhythm

(Structural) type of sentence	Sentence opens with
1. complex	noun phrase functioning as the subject
2. simple	single-word modifier
3. compound-complex	subject
4. simple	subject
5. simple	coordinate conjunction and modifying phrase
6. simple	coordinate conjunction
7. compound	modifying phrase

The preceding analysis may look technical, but peel away the numbers and structural descriptions and you have a paragraph that succeeds in both content and style. Trahar varies sentence lengths in the paragraph, and at no point does she write consecutive sentences of the same length. (The professional writers whose paragraphs you read at the beginning of this chapter do on occasion write two consecutive long or average-length sentences, but note that these are preceded by short sentences.) Trahar regularly alternates short sentences with long or average-length ones. While her sentences are declarative (typical of academic writing), she makes use of all four structural sentence types: simple, compound, complex, and compound-complex. What is more, she nicely varies the openings of her sentences, beginning twice with simple subjects, once with a long phrase that functions as a subject, and the remainder of the time with a modifier or a conjunction.

20d

emph

Jenafer Trahar's paragraph is stylistically sophisticated. Every technique she has used to gain that sophistication has been discussed in this chapter, and you can apply these same techniques to your own writing. Like Jenafer, you will need to begin with a subject you care about. Then you will have the motivation to analyze the length and rhythm of your sentences and to make revisions until you feel the sentences are stylistically effective. When revising for style, you may want to consult other chapters in this section on matters of conciseness (17), parallelism (18), and emphasis (19).

EXERCISE 4

Revise the following paragraph to eliminate the choppiness created by too many short sentences. In your revision, use all the techniques you have learned in this chapter for varying sentence length and rhythm.

Vincent van Gogh was a very ordinary child. At the age of fifteen he abruptly left school. At this school he had become an expert in several languages. His Uncle Cent was a partner in Goupil and Company. Goupil's was the eminent Paris-based art dealership. Goupil's offered him a position at the firm's branch in The Hague. Vincent was working there. He saw the paintings. These were created by some of the leading academic painters of the day. He was most impressed by the French Barbizon landscapists. Millet impressed him especially. It was years before Vincent would become an artist. He developed during this period the idealized image of peasant life. This image was to figure prominently in his early work. It would culminate in his first masterpiece. His first masterpiece was "The Potato Eaters." This painting was of a family gathered around a dinner table. The family was rough-hewn. The painting epitomized van Gogh's attempt to crown the poor with a halo of sanctity.

EXERCISE 5

Choose a paragraph from a book you happen to be reading (this book included), and analyze the component sentences for length and rhythm. Structure your analysis like the analysis of Jenafer Trahar's paragraph in 20d. Be sure to include a paragraph that summarizes your observations.

EXERCISE 6

Reexamine the three paragraphs that you revised for sentence length in Exercise 3. Revise these paragraphs a final time for sentence rhythm, using the techniques you have learned in this chapter.

emph

Using
Effective
Words

CHAPTER 21

Choosing the
Right Word

Your purpose as a writer and your intended audience profoundly affect your **diction**—your choice of words. Like the overall tone of a document, diction can be high or low, formal or informal, or any register between (see 3c-5). The English language usually gives you options in selecting words. For instance, in describing a recent meeting with a professor, which would you write: *The thing that really gets to me about that guy is*— or *What most disturbs me about Professor X is*—? Both phrasings are correct grammatically; yet one, because of its diction, is formal, fit for a letter of complaint to a dean, while the other is informal, appropriate for a letter home to a friend.

Those who choose words with care implicitly *command* respect. Readers have a certain attention span and a certain radar; they know when writers are invested in their work—when, for instance, writers have taken time to state a thought precisely or to render a description vividly. A document that shows little concern for word choice will quickly lose its readers.

21a Learning denotation and connotation

Your first concern in selecting a word is to be sure that its **denotation** or dictionary meaning is appropriate for the sentence at hand. A careless writer might, for instance, state that in performing their jobs diplomats should know when to *precede*. Is this the intended meaning (when to go first), or did the writer mean that diplomats should know when to *proceed* (when to go forward)? Although these words look similar and sound nearly the same, their denotations are very different. Once you are satisfied that you are using a word correctly according to its denotation, consider its **connotations**—its implications, associations, and nuances of meaning. Consider this sentence:

The professor urged *abstinence* in times of emotional stress.

Is *abstinence* the word with the right connotation for this sentence? If you are not sure, consider some possible synonyms. Turning to a dictionary or thesaurus for synonyms may help, but you should realize that to choose among synonyms you will need an awareness of differences in connotation. Some dictionaries are especially helpful in this regard. For instance, *The*

American Heritage Dictionary discusses shades of meaning whenever it offers synonyms for an entry. At *abstinence* you will find the following:

> **Synonyms:** *abstinence, self-denial, temperance, sobriety, continence.* These nouns suggest restraint of one's appetites or desires. *Abstinence* implies the willful avoidance of pleasures, especially of food and drink, thought to be harmful. *Self-denial* suggests resisting one's desires for some higher, moral goal. *Temperance* and *sobriety* both stress avoidance of alcohol, but *temperance* is more often associated with mere curtailment of drinking, while *sobriety* additionally suggests conservative action or manner. *Continence* specifically refers to restraint of sexual activity.

As you read this entry, you are likely to reconsider *abstinence* and choose instead *sobriety* or even *restraint*. The more you care about what you write, the more precise you will want to be with word choice. Consider the following choices:

> Thomas was *electrified* by the news.
> Thomas was *exhilarated* by the news.
> Thomas was *delirious* with the news.
> Thomas was *delighted* with the news.

Electrified, exhilarated, delirious, and *delighted:* the dictionary meanings of these words, their denotations, are roughly the same. Each adjective describes excitement. Nonetheless, the adjectives differ in their connotations. For example, if Thomas is *delirious,* he is (so suggests the connotation) happy to the point of losing his senses, as if his happiness were a powerful narcotic. *Delirious* in other contexts is used to describe someone in the grip of a high fever or someone recovering from anesthesia. If Thomas is *exhilarated,* he is feeling powerful and energetic; but certainly he remains in control of himself, and his mind is clear. *Exhilarated* is also used to describe the effects of vigorous exercise.

If Thomas is *electrified,* not just his emotions and intellect are stimulated by the good news, but seemingly his whole body. Someone who is *electrified* will sit, walk, and see differently than one who is *delirious* or *exhilarated.* (Objects that are electrified move by virtue of some power source outside themselves, and we typically approach and use these objects with caution.) And finally, if Thomas is *delighted,* he is happy, although his happiness seems polite and uninvolved—more like a celebration at someone else's good fortune. Of the four adjectives, *electrified* and *delirious* suggest an excitement at the very edge of control. *Exhilarated* suggests excitement kept firmly in control, while *delighted* implies a happiness not so intensely felt that it could momentarily overwhelm a person. Your choice among these words with their different connotations will make a difference in how your readers react.

21a

ww/k

EXERCISE 1

Given the following set of words, state which word in each set you would prefer someone to use in describing you. Why? Choose one set of words and, in a paragraph, discuss what you understand to be the differences in connotation among words. Use a dictionary, if necessary.

1. thrifty, economical, provident, frugal
2. reserved, inhibited, restrained, aloof
3. strange, bizarre, eccentric, peculiar, weird
4. lively, alert, enthusiastic, pert, spirited, sprightly
5. sentimental, emotional, maudlin, mushy

21b Revising awkward diction

At times you may find the abbreviation *"AWK"* in the margins of your papers, with a line leading to a phrase or to a particular word. *Awkward diction,* or word choice, interrupts the process of communication. It momentarily stops an audience from reading by calling attention to a word that is somehow not quite right for a sentence. How can you avoid this difficulty? Until you have more experience with the ways of words, you will not be able to avoid it entirely. However, you can minimize awkward writing by guarding against four common errors: inappropriate connotation, inappropriate idiom, straining to sound learned, and unintentional euphony (rhyming, etc.).

21b

d/k

1 Choosing words with an appropriate connotation

Frequently, *awkward diction* means that a word's connotation is inappropriate. The sentence in which the word appears is grammatical; the word in question is the right part of speech, but the word's meaning seems only partially correct for the sentence—as in this example from 21a.

AWKWARD The professor urged *abstinence* in times of emotional stress. [Does the writer mean to suggest the avoidance of alcohol only? The sentence seems to suggest something else.]

As the dictionary's usage entry for *abstinence* shows (see 21a), there are synonyms for this word with nearly the same denotation but which might have a less awkward and limited connotation.

REVISED The professor urged *sobriety* in times of emotional stress.

REVISED The professor urged emotional *restraint.* [The revisions do not limit the advice to avoiding alcohol.]

2 Following standard English idioms

An **idiom** is a grouping of words, one of which is usually a preposition, whose meaning may or may not be apparent based solely on simple dictionary definitions. Moreover, the grammar of idioms—particularly the choice of of prepositions used with them—is a matter of customary usage and is often difficult if not impossible to explain. Native speakers of English know intuitively that "running *across* an old letter" is a legitimate phrase (often listed in the dictionary), while "running *in* an old letter" is not. The difference is very difficult to explain, even for native speakers. Often, our attempts at using idioms result in awkwardness.

NOT IDIOMATIC　When the intruder left, the manager *got the courage* to call the police. [Idiomatically, we do not normally *get* courage; we either have it or we do not.]

IDIOMATIC　When the intruder left, the manager *got up the courage* to call the police. [The standard idiom implies that courage is summoned from within when needed.]

To avoid awkwardness, memorize idioms or do not use them at all. You can refer to the detailed listings in a dictionary to find some idioms; for others, you must listen carefully to the patterns of common usage. The following box shows a few of the hundreds of idiomatic expressions in English.

Some Common Idioms in American English

We *arrived at* a conclusion.
We *arrived in* time.
We *arrived on* time.
We *brought in* the cake.
We *brought up* the rear of the parade.
Except for my close friends, no one knows of my plan.
Don't call, *except in* emergencies.
I often *get into* jams.
Get up the courage to raise your hand.
I *got in* just under the deadline.
Good friends will *make up* after they argue.
How did you *make out* in your interview?
We'll *take in* the trash later.
Next week, the Red Sox *take on* the Orioles.
The senate will *take up* the issue tomorrow.
A large crowd *turned out.*
At midnight, we will *turn in.*
The request was *turned down.*

21b

d/k

3　Writing directly rather than straining to sound learned

When you are new to an area of study, or for that matter new to a social group, it is natural to want to fit in and sound as if you know what you are talking or writing about. In academics, this desire shows when students strain to take on the learned diction of professors. Some students try so hard they will use words that do not exist in any dialect of English.

AWKWARD   The character's grief and *upsetion* were extreme. [The word does not exist.]

AWKWARD   *Disconcern* is common among the employees at that factory. [*Disinterest, indifference,* or *unconcern* could be used.]

At times, students straining at sophistication will choose lengthy, complicated phrasings when simpler ones will do; they will favor pretentious language because they believe this is the way learned people express themselves. The following sentence is *not* erudite.

AWKWARD   The eccentricities of the characters could not fail to endear them to this reader.

REVISED   I found the eccentric characters endearing.

4   Listening for unintentional euphony

In a poem, **euphony**—the pleasing sound produced by certain word combinations—is put to literary ends, and the effect can be memorable. A sentence in an essay or report, however, will turn awkward when a writer unintentionally creates rhymes or alliterations (words that begin with the same consonant sound) that distract the reader from a sentence's meaning.

AWKWARD   Particularly in poetry, euphony is put to literary ends. [The rhymes and alliterations distract from the meaning.]

SIMPLIFIED   In a poem, euphony is used for literary ends.

21c

ww/d

The surest way to avoid unintentional rhymes or alliterations is to listen for them as you read your work aloud. Reading aloud forces you to slow down and hear what you have written. It can also help you to become aware of sentence rhythms. Finally, reading aloud can be an aid to proofreading—catching misspelled words, inadvertently misused homonyms (writing *affect* instead of *effect*), omitted words (often a preposition), and doubled words.

21c   Using general and specific language

Specific details, illustrations, and observations are more vivid and more memorable than *general* remarks. To comment that a book about fourteenth-century Europe was *interesting* is so general as to be meaningless. By contrast, to state that you were perplexed by your morbid fascination with Barbara Tuchman's description of bubonic plague in fourteenth-century Europe—*that* is a specific comment.

Successful writers shuttle back and forth between the general and specific, since to dwell at either end of this spectrum for too long will tax a reader's patience. The writer who concentrates on details and will not general-ize gives the impression of being unable to see "the big picture." Conversely, the writer who makes nothing but general claims will seem arrogant and will leave readers restless for specific details that would support these claims. Read the following sets of sentences. One is specific, the other general. Consider the differences.

> The Black Death, as the bubonic plague was called, was a relentless killer that struck swiftly and always with a predictable end. Millions of victims died.

> In October 1347, two months after the fall of Calais, Genoese trading ships put into the harbor of Messina in Sicily with dead and dying men at the oars. The ships had come from the Black Sea port of Caffa (now Feodosiya) in the Crimea, where the Genoese maintained a trading post. The diseased sailors showed strange black swellings about the size of an egg or an apple in the armpits and groin. The swellings oozed blood and pus and were followed by spreading boils and black blotches on the skin from internal bleeding. The sick suffered severe pain and died quickly within five days of the first symptoms. . . . [E]verything that issued from the body—breath, sweat, blood from the buboes and lungs, bloody urine, and blood-black-ened excrement—smelled foul.

As effective as Tuchman's details are, had she provided nothing but details on the symptoms of bubonic plague she would have failed in one of her jobs as historian: to glean from specific facts *general* observations about life and death in another time. Thus, in the paragraphs following the one above, from *A Distant Mirror,* Tuchman pulls back her lens for a broader view. Throughout the discussion, Tuchman regularly makes general claims:

21c

ww/d

> Ignorance of the [plague's] cause augmented the sense of horror.

> To the people at large there could be but one explanation—the wrath of God.

> Efforts to cope with the epidemic availed little, either in treatment or prevention.

> The hostility of man proved itself against the Jews.

Her weaving of general and specific, in fact, offers a model of clear academic writing in the disciplines, where we see the pattern repeated: general claims organize a piece of writing, giving it vision and scope, while specific details substantiate these claims.

EXERCISE 2

Create three lists, the first item of each being a very general word, the next item somewhat less general, the next still less general, and so on. The completed list, top to bottom, will proceed from general to specific.

Example: nation, state, county, city, neighborhood, street, house

EXERCISE 3

Choose a topic that you know well (sports, music, art, etc.) and write a general sentence about it. Then, in support of that sentence, write two additional sentences rich in specific detail.

Example: Topic—Cooking an omelette
General sentence: Making omelettes is a delicate operation.
Specific sentences:
Use a well-seasoned omelette pan—cast iron, well greased, clean but never thoroughly scrubbed.
Scramble the eggs with a splash of water (not milk), scrambling lightly so as not to toughen the cooked eggs.

21d Using abstract and specific language

Like general words, **abstract** words are broad. They name categories or ideas, such as *patriotism, evil,* and *friendship*. **Concrete** expressions (a *throbbing* headache, a *lemon-scented* perfume) provide details that give readers a chance to see, hear, and touch—and in this way to understand how an idea or category is made real. Just as with general and specific language, you should seek a balance between the abstract and concrete. Writers who dwell on the concrete give readers the impression of literal mindedness, perhaps even denseness. Writers who dwell on the abstract give the impression of being vague or aloof.

21d

ww/d

As with the general and specific, balance is the key—and not just in literary writing or autobiography but in all disciplines where writers labor to give concrete meaning to their ideas. See, for example, the balanced use of abstract and concrete terms in the following explanation of a key concept in physics.

Time is a difficult concept to define. (Try it.) A common definition is that time is the forward flow of events. This is not so much a definition as an observation that time has never been known to run backwards (as it might appear to do when you view a film run backwards in a projector). Time is sometimes said to be a fourth dimension, accompanying the three dimensions of space. Thus, if something exists in space, it also exists in time. In any case, events can be used to mark time measurements. The events are analogous to the marks on a meterstick used for length measurements.

The SI[1] unit of time is the **second(s).** The solar "clock" was originally used to define the second. A solar day is the interval of time that elapses between two successive crossings of the same meridian by the Sun, at its highest point in the sky at that meridian. A second was fixed as $1/86{,}400$ of this apparent solar day (1 day = 24 h = 1440 min = 86,400 s). However, the elliptical path of the Earth's motion around the Sun causes apparent solar days to vary in length.

---

[1]The abbreviation **SI** refers to Système International units, agreed-upon standards of measurement used by scientists worldwide.

As a more precise standard, an average, or mean, solar day was computed from the lengths of the apparent solar days during a solar year. In 1956, the second was referenced to this mean solar day. But the mean solar day is not exactly the same for each yearly period because of minor variations in the Earth's motions and a steady slowing of its rate of rotation due to tidal friction. So scientists kept looking for something better.

In 1967, an atomic standard was adopted as a more precise reference. Currently, the second is defined as the duration of 9,192,631,770 cycles (periods) of the radiation associated with a particular transition of the cesium-133 atom.

EXERCISE 4

In the preceding paragraphs on Time, circle all abstract language and underline all examples of concrete language.

EXERCISE 5

Take an abstract word such as *honesty, truth, friendship,* or *chaos,* and, in two or three sentences, link that word with a specific person, place, or event. Then provide concrete, descriptive details that help give meaning to the abstraction.

21e   Using formal English as an academic standard

21e

ww/d

Academic writing is expected to conform to standards of **formal English**—that is, the English described in this handbook. There are many standards, or dialects, of English in this country, all of which are rich with expressive possibilities. Why formal English should be the acknowledged standard is, by some accounts, a purely political tactic orchestrated by the powerful to keep the less powerful disenfranchised. Those who grow up speaking formal English are born (so goes the argument) into an upper-range socioeconomic class that has a vested interest in maintaining its privileges. People who are privileged will admit into their circle only those who speak as they speak and who, presumably, share the same values because they share the same language.

In any case, it is clear that business, government, and academic communication would suffer if there were no accepted norm for language in a society. Some standard of communication is necessary, if only for the sake of efficiency. That the standard happens to be formal English has alienated some, and from a descriptive linguist's perspective it is certainly true that formal English is inherently no more *correct* than any other dialect of English. Linguists teach us that dialects—for instance, ones using the nonstandard *ain't*—are rule governed, just as formal English is rule governed. The diction of formal English is not better; it *is*, however, the only widely accepted standard for communicating among the many groups of English speakers. As a college student, you are learning communication skills that will enable you to reach the widest possible audience, and for that purpose you need to develop skill in formal English.

Academic writing avoids language that by virtue of its private references limits a reader's understanding or limits the audience. Slang, jargon, and regional or ethnic dialect language are examples of writing specific to particular groups. When you write to members of the *same* social group, profession, or region, there are two clear advantages to using in-group language: first, it is efficient, and second, it can help to cement a group's identity. When you address an audience *beyond* the group, slang, jargon, dialect, and regionalisms restrict what that audience can understand.

1   Revise most slang expressions into standard English.

Slang is the comfortable, in-group language of neighborhood friends, coworkers, teammates, or of any group to which we feel we belong. Assume for the moment you do not windsurf, and you happen to overhear a conversation between windsurfers in which someone says that she was *dialed in* or *completely powered*. What do these words mean? To someone not involved with the sport, nothing specific. Slang can be descriptive and precise for those who understand; it can just as readily be confusing and annoying to those who do not. In some cases, slang may mislead: the same expression can have different meanings for different groups. For example, *turbo charged* has distinctly different meanings for computer aficionados and for race-car enthusiasts and is likely to be vague and confusing when used outside of those settings. In the interest of writing accessibly to as many people as possible, avoid slang expressions in academic papers.

21e

ww/d

2   Replace regionalisms and dialect expressions with standard academic English.

Regionalisms are expressions specific to certain areas of the country. Depending on where you were born, you will use the word *tonic, soda, cola,* or *pop* to describe what you drink with your *sub, hoagie, grinder,* or *hero*. In a few states, when you are driving fast and a *smokey* catches up with you, your insurance rates will skyrocket. Words that have a clear and vivid reference in some areas of the country may lack meaning in others or have an unrelated meaning. For instance, *muss* means "to make messy" in some places and "to fight" in others. *Bad* means "good" in some places and "bad" in others.

Dialect expressions are specific to certain social or ethnic groups, as well as regional groups, within a country. Like regionalisms, dialects can use a specialized vocabulary and sometimes a distinctive grammatical system. Especially with respect to verbs (see chapter 9), regional and ethnic dialect usage may regularly differ from standard English in omitting auxiliary verb forms. ("I done everything I can" or "It taken him all day" omit the standard auxiliaries *have, had,* or *has*. "They be doing all right" replaces the standard *are* with the infinitive or base form *be*.) These are grammatically consistent and correct usages within the dialects they represent, but they address their language to a specific and restricted group rather than to a general audience. Like slang, regionalisms and dialect usages are appropriate for the audience that understands them; however, for general audiences in academic writing, they should be avoided.

3 **Reduce colloquial language to maintain clarity and a consistent level of academic discourse.**

Colloquial language is informal, conversational language. Colloquialisms do not pose barriers to understanding in the same way that slang, jargon, and regionalisms do; virtually all long-time speakers of English will understand expressions like *tough break, nitty-gritty,* and *it's a cinch.* In formal English, however, colloquialisms are rewritten or "translated" to maintain precision and to keep the overall tone of a document consistent. A few translations follow.

Colloquial	Formal
it's a cinch	it is certain
tough break	unfortunate
got licked	was beaten

Some of these colloquial expressions are also worn-out figures of speech whose meaning has become vague or obscure (see 21f-3).

21e

4 **Revise to restrict the use of jargon.**

ww/d

Jargon is the in-group language of professionals, who may use acronyms (abbreviations of lengthy terms) and other linguistic devices to take short cuts when speaking with colleagues. When writers in an engineering environment refer to RISC architecture, they mean machines designed to allow for **R**educed **I**nstruction **S**et **C**omputing. RISC is an easy-to-use acronym, and it is efficient—as long as one engineer is writing or speaking to another. (If the in-group that uses these expressions is a prestigious one, the use of jargon can become a form of false or pretentious writing—see section 21h-2). The moment communication is directed outside the professional group, a writer must take care to define terms. The following sentences illustrate highly technical, in-group language among biologists. The writers are addressing upper-division biology majors with language that non-biologists will find difficult to follow.

Writing directed to an in-group audience:

Clostridia are ubiquitous, versatile, anaerobic flagellated microorganisms that generally form spores. As a group, they will ferment almost anything organic except plastics—sugars, amino acids and proteins, polyalcohols, organic acids, purines, collagen, and cellulose.

—Lynn Margulis and Kathlene V. Schwartz

By contrast, in this next passage biologists are addressing a general student population, only a fraction of whom are biology majors.

Writing directed to a general audience:

> Historically, biology has been considered a "soft" science whose subject was more complex and "laws" less rigorous than disciplines such as chemistry and physics. This soft status, however, has been rapidly changing since the medical discovery of the role of microorganisms in disease, Darwin's theory of evolution by natural selection, Mendel's description of the rules by which traits are inherited, and the understanding of the way DNA both duplicates itself and determines the details for the manufacture of proteins that comprise all living things.
>
> —DORIAN SAGAN and LYNN MARGULIS

Language that is specialized by a particular group, for a particular purpose, is universal. Literary critics will speak of *deconstruction*, philosophers of *positivism*, sociologists of *dyads*, and mathematicians of *Sigma functions*. When you become part of a group, academic or otherwise, you will be expected and will find it convenient to use in-group language. You will need to interpret that language for outsiders, of course; but even within the group, if you can communicate precisely without using jargon, do so.

21f

ww/d

EXERCISE 6

Think of a group—social, geographic, or professional—to which you belong and which you know well. Write a paragraph on some subject using in-group language: slang, jargon, or regionalisms. When you are finished, translate your paragraph into formal English, rewriting in-group expressions so that the paragraph can be read and understood by a general audience.

21f   Using figures of speech with care

Similes, analogies, and *metaphors* are **figures of speech,** carefully controlled comparisons that clarify or intensify meaning. Perhaps your spirit *soars* when you read this line of poetry: "Come live with me and be my love." The figurative use of *soar* creates an image of birds in flight, of elevation and clear vision. Literally speaking, birds and planes soar; spirits do not. English allows for the pairing of unlikely, even totally opposite images to help readers feel and see as writers do. In academic writing, figurative language is used across disciplines, though in some disciplines more freely than in others.

Figurative language in the sciences

The author of one well-respected book on scientific writing advises caution in using figures of speech in the life sciences and physical sciences.

"Use [them] rarely in scientific writing. If you use them, use them carefully."[2] Following the logic of this advice, a biologist who is writing to fellow biologists would not report that in the course of an experiment water turned *ice* cold. This figurative language, however suggestive to nonscientists, lacks precision (ice cold water *is* ice). Biologists reading the article will want to know the precise temperature of the water, and they expect that temperature to be given in degrees. However, scientists in control of their writing *do* use figurative language at times, when addressing colleagues but more often when attempting to convey to the general public complicated, specialized knowledge. Thus (as illustrated later) you will find physicists and physicians as well as philosophers and poets using figures of speech, all to the same end: to communicate in ways that literal language, alone, fails to do.

There are many techniques for using language figuratively. As you read in the disciplines, you will encounter three figures most often: *simile, analogy,* and *metaphor.*

1   Using similes, analogies, and metaphors

A **simile** is a figure of speech in which two different things—one usually familiar, the other not—are explicitly compared. The properties of the thing known help to define what is unknown. Similes make comparison very explicit, often using the word *like* or *as* to set up the comparison.

> Plastic is the new protector; we wrap the already plastic tumblers of hotels in more plastic, and seal the toilet seats *like* state secrets after irradiating them with ultraviolet light.
> —LEWIS THOMAS
> Physician, researcher

> The wind whistled in the street and the music ghosted from the piano *as* leaves over a headstone and you could imagine you were in the presence of genius.
> —BRUCE CHATWIN
> Traveler, writer

> A particle of spin 2 is *like* a double-headed arrow: it looks the same if one turns it round half a revolution (180 degrees).
> —STEPHEN HAWKING
> Physicist

21f

ww/d

As with a simile, the purpose of an **analogy** is to make an explicit comparison that explains an unknown in terms of something known. Analogies most often use direct comparison to clarify a process or a difficult concept. An analogy can be developed in a single sentence; extended analogies can be developed over a paragraph or several paragraphs. The primary purpose of an analogy is to clarify.

_____

[2] Robert A. Day, *How to Write and Publish a Scientific Paper,* 3rd ed. (Phoenix: Oryx Press, 1988) p. 155.

Just as a trained mechanic can listen to a ping in a car's engine and then diagnose and correct a problem, so too an experienced writer can reread an awkward sentence and know exactly where it goes wrong and what must be done to correct it.

Extended analogies usually begin and end with certain *cues,* or words that signal a reader that an analogy is about to be offered or concluded. Words that mark a transition to an analogy are *consider, by analogy,* and *just as.* The transition from analogy back to a main discussion is achieved with expressions like *similarly, just so, so too,* and *in the same way.* (See 6d-2 for use of analogies in building an argument.)

Just as with a simile and analogy, a **metaphor** illustrates or intensifies something relatively unknown by comparison with something familiar. In the case of metaphor, however, the comparison is implicit: the thing or idea that is relatively unknown is spoken of in terms closely associated with a significant feature of the thing that is known. The key features of the "known" are attributed directly to the "unknown." In the expression *hand of time,* for instance, the abstract term *time* is given a physical attribute. *Like* and *as* or other signals of explicit comparison are not used in metaphors.

In the mirror of his own death, each man would discover his individuality.

—PHILIPPE ARIÈS
Historian

21f

ww/d

The metaphor suggests that contemplating death allows people to see themselves in revealing ways.

Metaphors are not restricted to poetry or academic writing; they are used everywhere in our daily speech when an abstract or unknown idea, thing, or activity is spoken of in terms associated with something else. When we say "round up everybody," we implicitly compare the activity to a cattle roundup. When we say "Walk the thin line between good and bad," we compare a moral dilemma to a tightrope act. By speaking of people who have been "jerked around" or "left hanging," we compare their general situation to those physical activities. At times, such metaphorical comparisons, if not well matched to the situation, can create more confusion for the reader than clarity.

2 Revise mixed metaphors.

Like all comparisons, metaphors need to match elements that can be compared logically (even if not explicitly). The metaphorical comparison must be consistent. Keep your language focused on a single metaphorical image throughout a sentence. Otherwise, you risk a **mixed metaphor,** which will stop your readers for a hearty laugh—at your expense. You would not, for instance, want to be the author of this:

MIXED METAPHOR   This story weaves a web that herds characters and readers into the same camp. [The comparison mixes spider webs with cattle roundups.]

CONSISTENT   This story weaves a web that tangles characters and readers alike.

3   **Replace worn-out metaphors (clichés) with fresh figures.**

In a famous essay, "Politics and the English Language," writer George Orwell warns against the *worn-out metaphor.*

> A newly invented metaphor assists thought by evoking a visual image, while on the other hand a metaphor which is technically "dead" (e.g., *iron resolution*) has in effect reverted to being an ordinary word and can generally be used without loss of vividness. But in between these two classes there is a huge dump of worn-out metaphors which have lost all evocative power and are merely used because they save people the trouble of inventing phrases for themselves.

Orwell proceeds to offer his list of worn-out metaphors, which can also be termed **clichés.** These include *play into the hands of, no axe to grind, swan song,* and *hotbed.* These trite expressions, current when Orwell's essay was written in 1945, are with us still. Modern-day expressions that can be added to this list of clichés would include *the game of life, counting chickens before they hatch, water over the dam* or *under the bridge, crossing bridges,* and *burning bridges.* Work to create your own metaphors; keep them vivid; and keep them consistent.

21g

ww

> EXERCISE 7
> In a few sentences, use figurative language to describe the approach of a thunderstorm, the effect of a sunny morning on your mood, or the feeling of just having finished your last exam of a long and difficult semester.

21g Eliminating biased, dehumanizing language

Language is a tool; just as tools can be used for building, so too they can be used to dismantle. You have heard and seen the words that insensitive people use to denigrate whole groups. Clearly, any use of *kike, nigger, faggot,* or parallel terms is intolerable. Equally repugnant is language used to stereotype. In discussing the prevalence of crack cocaine in inner cities, the spread of AIDS, or the poverty endemic to certain areas of this country, some writers let creep into their language expressions such as *those people* or *they're the ones who . . .* or *can we really expect more from. . . .* Any language that explicitly or subtly characterizes an individual in terms of a group is potentially offensive. Writers must take care to avoid stereotyping.

Sexism in diction

Sexism in English is a particular problem when value judgments are linked with male or female reference. The issue can become a sensitive one in almost any sentence, since English has no gender-neutral pronoun in the third-person singular. Consider this sentence: *A doctor should wash _____ hands before examining a patient.* English demands that we choose the possessive pronoun *his* or *her* to complete this thought. Until recently, the designated "neutral" pronoun was usually masculine (*his*), but changing times have made this usage potentially offensive. It is obvious that women, along with men, are physicians, engineers, attorneys, construction workers, accountants, realtors, etc. Men, along with women, are elementary school teachers, nurses, cooks, tailors, receptionists, and secretaries. Given these circumstances, it is both offensive and inaccurate to imply by one's choice of a single pronoun that men or women, exclusively, inhabit one or another profession. Gender-offensive language can also be found in such expressions as chair*man*, *man*kind, *man*power, *mother*ing, etc. Reread late drafts of your writing to identify potentially gender-offensive language. Unless the context of a paragraph clearly calls for a gender-specific reference, follow the suggestions given in the box to avoid offending your readers.

21g

ww

Some Potentially Offensive Gender-Specific Nouns

Avoid: stewardess (and generally nouns ending with *-ess*)
Use: flight attendant

Avoid: chairman
Use: chair or chairperson

Avoid: woman driver; male nurse
Use: woman who was driving; driver; nurse; man on the nursing station

Avoid: mankind
Use: people; humanity; humankind

Avoid: workmen; manpower
Use: workers; work force; personnel

Avoid: the girl in the office
Use: the woman; the manager; the typist.

Avoid: mothering
Use: parenting, nurturing

  Rewrite gender-stereotyping nouns as neutral nouns.

SEXIST   A cover letter, along with a résumé, should be sent to the *chairman* of the department. [The male suffix may be taken to imply that the writer expects this person to be male.]

NEUTRAL A cover letter, along with a résumé, should be sent to the department *chair.*

SEXIST *Man's* need to compete may be instinctive. [A generic male noun or pronoun referring to all of humanity is unacceptable.]

NEUTRAL *The human* need to compete may be instinctive.

2 Balance references to the sexes.

SEXIST The *men* and *girls* in the office contributed generously to the Christmas Fund. [A reference singling out females as children in an adult setting is demeaning.]

NEUTRAL The *men* and *women* in the office contributed generously to the Christmas Fund. [In a school setting the reference might be to *boys* and *girls*.]

3 Make balanced use of plural and gender-specific pronouns.

See 10c for five strategies that will help you to correct gender problems with pronoun use.

SEXIST A doctor should wash *his* hands before examining a patient. [Here the generic male pronoun implies that the writer expects most doctors to be male.]

NEUTRAL *Doctors* should wash *their* hands before examining patients. [The plural strategy is used; see 10c.]

21g

ww

EXERCISE 8

Identify gender-offensive language in the following paragraph. Rewrite sentences in whatever way you feel is needed to make the gender references neutral.

A teacher, like a parent, will maintain that she treats children fairly and equally regardless of their sex. Research demonstrates, however, that in practice a teacher typically interacts differently with her female and boy students. In elementary school, for example, a teacher routinely practices sex segregation in her classroom—e.g., by seating girls together and young men together; by having girls and young men form separate lines; and by organizing team competitions, such as spelling bees, by sex. At the other end of academic life, in college, girls—especially minorities—have few same-sex role models and mentors available to them on the faculty and administration. In the classroom, a professor will call on his male students more often than on girls and will interrupt girls more. Sexism, overt and covert, persists beyond college: in the workplace, in the home, and in the political arena.

21h Avoiding euphemistic and pretentious language

Sometimes writers betray an anxious, condescending, or self-inflated attitude through their word choices. These attitudes may arise from a variety of motives, but the result is almost always a loss of clear expression.

1 Restrict the use of euphemisms.

The **euphemism** is a polite rewording of a term that the writer feels will offend readers. Invariably, euphemisms are longer than the words they replace and by definition are less direct: instead of *dead* or *died,* you will find *passed on, passed away, mortally wounded.* You may also find these clichés: *kicked the bucket, bit the dust, didn't make it, met his/her Maker, caught the Last Train, went to the Great Beyond,* and so on. If you are concerned about using expressions that might offend readers, create a context within a sentence or paragraph that may soften a potentially harsh word choice.

EUPHEMISM   No one wanted to tell the child that his dog had gone to the Great Beyond.

REVISED   Breaking the news to the child that his dog had died was very painful.

In nonacademic writing, use discretion in selecting a euphemism. Debate with yourself your use of language and then make your choice.

2 Eliminate pretentious language.

Pretentious language is unnecessarily ornate, puffed-up with its own self-importance, and suggests a writer concerned more with image than with clear communication. See 17a-6 as well as 17a-2 and 4 on eliminating wordiness. Pretentious writers will often choose the windy version of everyday expressions that seem too common.

PRETENTIOUS	DIRECT
It appears to me that	I believe
In the final analysis	In conclusion
The individual who . . .	The person who . . .
utilize	use
demonstrate	show
functionality	function

Because many topics you will study are complex and technical, you should expect to encounter new and difficult vocabularies in your college career. In specialized areas of study, you will find that writers need technical

21h

ww/d

terms to communicate precisely. Writing that requires specialized terms is very different from pretentious writing that is calculated to bolster a writer's ego. In your own work, you can distinguish between a legitimate technical term and a pretentious one by being both a concise and a precise writer.

Distinguishing Pretentious Language from Legitimate Technical Language

Bear in mind two principles when attempting to eliminate pretentious language:

- **Be concise:** use as few words as possible to communicate clearly. Delete whole sentences or reduce them to phrases that you incorporate into other sentences; reduce phrases to single words; choose briefer words over longer ones. (See 17a for a full discussion of conciseness.)

- **Be precise:** make sure your sentences communicate your *exact* meaning. If you need to add clarifying words, add as few words as possible. Use technical language for precision only when no other language will do.

Adhering to these two principles—the one helping you to cut wordiness and the other helping you to maintain precision—should make you aware of pretentious language, which can *always* be cut from a sentence.

21h

ww/d

PRETENTIOUS LANGUAGE	The Australian subcontinent was regarded by the leaders of the British policy-making establishment as the site of penal colonies that could optimize the expressed desire to rid the British Isles of its criminal elements.
DIRECT LANGUAGE	British politicians believed that they could resolve problems of crime at home by transporting criminals to penal colonies in Australia.
SPECIALIZED LANGUAGE (NO REVISION NEEDED)	Index futures differ from other futures contracts in that they are not based on any underlying commodity or financial instrument that can be delivered; therefore, there is no cash market associated with them.

This passage on "index futures" comes from a book on investing. Students of finance would understand, or would be expected to understand, the terms *index futures, futures contracts, commodity, financial instrument*, and *cash market*. None of the words in this legitimately technical passage is calculated to bolster the writer's ego, as was the case in the preceding example.

EXERCISE 9

The following speech was generated by a computer as an example of empty political rhetoric. The professors of speech communication who programmed the computer with a list of set phrases had been alarmed by the growing dominance of style over substance in American political discourse. In the paragraphs of the speech excerpted here, identify what you feel are examples of euphemisms, clichés, and pretentious language. Find other samples of writing, perhaps from a current newspaper, and conduct a similar analysis.

The Middle East is again in a no-war, no-peace stalemate and is likely to remain so for some time. Step-by-step diplomacy, treating all parties with an even hand, is the only means for maintaining a delicate peace in the Middle East.

The United States must ground its China policy in morality. We should work to improve our relationships with her. The People's Republic of China is a sovereign state, but we must not forget to support our ally, The Republic of China, on Taiwan. I believe both governments can learn to live with the reality of each other.

21h

ww/d

CHAPTER 22

Dictionaries and Vocabulary

A living language is continually evolving; it is always shifting and changing; it is flexible and yet precise. English is just such a language. Two thousand years ago nobody spoke English; it did not exist. Today, in the last decade of the twentieth century, it is the first truly global language, more widely spoken and written than any language has ever been. English originally spread through British imperialism to such countries as the United States, Canada, Australia, New Zealand, India, and various African and Caribbean nations. But the demise of the British Empire in no way signaled the demise of English as an international language. Rather, as the novelist Salman Rushdie notes, "English, no longer an *English* language, now grows from many roots; and those whom it once colonized are carving out large territories within the language for themselves. The Empire is striking back." At the same time, the cultural dominance of American English, the international language of multinational corporations, science and technology, rock music, Hollywood films, television, and mass consumerism continues to further the dissemination of English world-wide.[1]

USING DICTIONARIES

The emergence of English as a constantly changing global language raises the question of what constitutes "English" and/or the various Englishes. It is the job, indeed often the life work, of the editors and compilers of dictionaries to help readers understand the most current usages of words in the language. The dictionary will tell you what forms and meanings have become widely used or are in restricted use. On the basis of this information, you must decide which forms and meanings are most precisely suited to your purpose. In the next sections you will find descriptions of what is included in a typical dictionary entry, followed by descriptions of the abridged and unabridged dictionaries which have best met the dual challenge of currency and comprehensiveness.

---

[1]This introduction is based on chapter 1, pages 19–48, of *The Story of English* by Robert McCrum, William Cran, and Robert MacNeil (New York: Elisabeth Sifton Books/Viking, 1986).

22a Exploring dictionaries of the English language

Dictionaries give us far more than a list of words and their meanings. They not only define a given word, but also provide a brief description of its etymology, spelling, division, as well as pronunciation, and related words and forms. Here is a typical set of entries:

Grammatical functions

Word
division   Pronunciation   Grammatical forms

Spelling —**proc·ess**¹ (prŏs′ĕs′, prō′sĕs′) *n., pl.* **processes** (prŏs′ĕs′ĭz, prō′-sĕs′-, prŏs′ə-sēz′, prō′sə-). *Abbr.* **proc. 1.** A system of opera- ⎤
tions in the production of something. **2.** A series of actions, ⎪
changes, or functions that bring about an end or result. ⎪
3. Course or passage of time. **4.** Ongoing movement; progres- ⎬— Meanings
Field label — sion. [**5.** *Law.* **a.** A summons or writ ordering a defendant to ⎪
appear in court. **b.** The total amount of summonses or writs ⎪
issued in a particular proceeding. **c.** The entire course of a judi- ⎪
cial proceeding. **6.** *Biology.* A part extending or projecting ⎦
from an organ or organism; an appendage. **7.** Any of various ⎤— Grammatical
photomechanical or photoengraving methods. —*tr.v.* **proc-** ⎦ functions
essed, -cessing, -cesses. 1. To put through the steps of a prescribed procedure. **2.** To prepare, treat, or convert by sub-
jecting to some special process. **3.** *Law.* To serve with a summons or writ. **4.** To institute legal proceedings against; prose-
cute. —*adj. Abbr.* **proc. 1.** Prepared or converted by a special ⎱— Idioms
Example— treatment: *process cheese.* **2.** Made by or used in photomechanical or photoengraving methods: *a process print.* [Mid- ⎤
dle English *proces(se)*, from Old French *proces*, from Latin ⎬— Etymology
Related   *prōcessus*, from the past participle of *prōcēdere*, to PROCEED.] ⎦
words   —[**proc′es′sor** (prŏs′ĕs′ər, prō′sĕs′-), **proc′es′ser** *n.*
pro·cess² (prə-sĕs′) *intr.v.* **-cessed, -cessing, -cesses.** To move
along or go in or as if in a procession. [Back-formation from
PROCESSION.]

 Understanding standard entry information in dictionaries

Most dictionary entries include more information on words than many people expect. In a typical entry you can find:

- *Spelling* (including variations, especially British versus American spellings—see chapter 23 for more on rules of spelling)

- *Word division* indicating syllabication and where a word should be divided, if necessary

- *Pronunciation* (including variations)

- *Grammatical functions* (parts of speech)

- *Grammatical forms* (plurals, principal parts of irregular verbs, other irregular forms)

- *Etymology* (a given word's history/derivation)

- *Meanings* (arranged either according to currency or frequency of use, or earliest to most recent use)

- *Examples* of the word in context
- *Related words; synonyms* and *antonyms*
- *Usage labels* (see 22a-2)
- *Field labels* (for words that have discipline-specific meanings)
- *Idioms* that include the word

2 Usage labels

Usage refers to how, where, and when a word has been used in speech and writing. Usage labels in a dictionary indicate special restrictions that compilers find operating for a particular meaning of a word. When you see the label *slang* assigned to the entry *prof*, for instance, the dictionary is indicating that in standard, formal English usage that word is not accepted. Aware of this *restriction* on the word, you would probably choose not to use it in formal writing. There are several standard categories of restricted usage, and these are generally listed and explained in the front matter of most dictionaries before the beginning of the alphabetical entries. The following is a list of common usage labels and the restricted usages they describe:

- *Colloquial*: used conversationally and in informal writing
- *Slang*: in-group, informal language; not standard
- *Obsolete*: not currently used (but may be found in earlier writing)
- *Archaic*: not commonly used; more common in earlier writing
- *Dialect*: restricted geographically or to social or ethnic groups; used only in certain places with certain groups
- *Poetic, literary*: used in literature rather than everyday speech

22a

ww/d

EXERCISE 1

Consult your dictionary to answer the following questions about grammatical function.

1. Which of the following nouns can be used as verbs: *process, counsel, dialogue, hamper, instance*?
2. How do you make these nouns plural: *annals, humanity, armor, accountancy, deer, analysis, medium, sister-in-law, knife*?
3. What are the principal parts of these verbs: *hang, begin, break, forbid, rise, set*?
4. What are the comparative and superlative forms of these adverbs and adjectives: *unique, bad, mere, initial, playful*?

EXERCISE 2

Using two different dictionaries, list and comment on the usage restrictions that are recorded for the following words:

1. awesome   3. celebrate   5. ere
2. mews   4. groovy   6. flunk

Example: ain't

Webster's New Collegiate Dictionary (Springfield, MA: G. & C. Merriam, 1974)

> though disapproved by many and more common in less educated speech, used orally in most parts of the U.S. by many educated speakers esp. in the phrase *ain't I*

The American Heritage Dictionary, 2nd College Edition (Boston: Houghton Mifflin, 1982)

> *Ain't* has acquired such a stigma over the years that it is beyond rehabilitation, even though it would serve a useful function as a contraction for *am not* and even though its use as an alternate form for *isn't, hasn't, aren't,* and *haven't* has a good historical justification. In questions, the variant *aren't I* is acceptable in speech to a majority of the Usage Panel, but in writing there is no generally acceptable substitute for the stilted *am I not.*

Comment: *The American Heritage Dictionary* is clearly sympathetic to the word but seems resigned (even disappointed!) that *ain't* will never be acceptable as a standard word in the language. *Webster's* makes a class distinction between the "educated" and "less educated" and seems elitist about the word's usage.

22b Choosing a dictionary

22b

d

Because the English language is constantly changing and is used in so many environments around the world, no dictionary can ever claim to be the final authority on every possible current meaning or correct usage for the words it lists. A dictionary's authority rests mainly on its attempt to be reasonably comprehensive and linguistically accurate in recording the most frequently used meanings of a word. Dictionaries further try to be as balanced as possible in recording the kind of usage and the restrictions on usage that have been observed for each meaning. In addition, dictionaries record a time dimension for changes in meaning: some list the earliest meanings on record first, moving on to the more recent; others reverse the sequence to start with contemporary meanings. All dictionaries record the basic categories of information shown in the previous section.

1 Comparing abridged dictionaries

The most convenient and commonly used dictionaries in households, businesses, and schools are called "abridged"—or shortened. They do not try to be as exhaustive or complete as the "unabridged" dictionaries (described in 22b-2). An abridged dictionary tries to give as much information as possible in one portable volume. You will find that several dictionaries claim the name *Webster's,* after the early American lexicographer Noah Webster. Since his name is in the public domain and is not copyrighted, it appears in the titles of a number of dictionaries with varying characteristics. The following list includes only some of the more widely used abridged dictionaries.[2]

The American Heritage Dictionary (Houghton Mifflin) includes about 200,000 entries. It differs from most other dictionaries in that it presents the most contemporary meaning of a word first, rather than proceeding historically. Guidance to good usage is provided by extensive usage-context indicators and "Usage Notes" which reflect the opinions of a panel of usage experts. The dictionary contains many photographs, illustrations, and maps. Foreign words and the names of mythological and legendary figures appear in the regular listings, while biographical and geographical entries and abbreviations are listed in the back.

The Concise Oxford Dictionary of Current English (Oxford University Press) is the briefest of the abridged dictionaries listed here. It is based on the work for the unabridged *Oxford English Dictionary* (see 22b-2) and includes current usage and illustrative quotations, scientific and technical terms, many colloquial and slang expressions, and both British and American spellings. There are no illustrations, and little front or back matter.

The Random House College Dictionary (Random House) is based on the unabridged *Random House Dictionary of the English Language* (see 22b-2). The dictionary contains about 155,000 entries, and it lists the most common usage of a word first. It indicates informal and slang usage and synonyms and antonyms, and lists recent technical words along with biographical and geographical names as part of its main entries. A manual of style is included as part of its back matter.

Webster's Ninth New Collegiate Dictionary (G. & C. Merriam) is based on *Webster's Third New International Dictionary of the English Language* (see 22b-2) and includes some 160,000 entries emphasizing "standard language." Labels indicating usage occur less frequently than in other desk dictionaries. Entries give full etymologies followed by definitions in chronological order, with the most recent meaning listed last. It includes extensive notes on synonyms and illustrative quotations. Foreign words and phrases, biographical and geographical names, and a manual of style are listed separately as back matter.

Webster's New World Dictionary of the American Language (Prentice Hall) has a contemporary American emphasis and uses a star to indicate Americanisms—words that first became part of the language in the United States. Definitions are listed in chronological order, with the earliest first, and extensive etymologies, synonyms, and usages are provided. Proper names, place names, abbreviations, and foreign phrases are included in the main listings.

22b

d

---

[2]The descriptions of abridged, unabridged, and discipline-specific dictionaries that follow are adapted from entries in Sheehy, Eugene. *Guide to Reference Books*, 10th ed. Chicago: American Library Association, 1986; Strauss, Diane Wheeler. *Handbook of Business Information: A Guide for Librarians, Students and Researchers*. Englewood, CO: Libraries Unlimited, Inc., 1988; and Wynar, Bohdan. *ARBA Guide to Subject Encyclopedias and Dictionaries*. Littleton, CO: Libraries Unlimited, 1986.

EXERCISE 3

Look up the following words in one of the abridged dictionaries listed above. How many different meanings does each word have? From observing older meanings versus the more current meanings, how would you describe the overall shifts in meaning that some words have undergone over time?

1. immure   3. obnoxious   5. luster
2. junk   4. heroic   6. hide

 Comparing unabridged dictionaries

The compilers of unabridged dictionaries attempt to be exhaustive both in recounting the history of a word and in describing its various usages. For quick reference—to check spelling, meaning, or commonplace usage, an abridged dictionary will serve you well. But when you are puzzled by or otherwise curious about a word and its history (for instance, if you wanted to know the route by which the word *farm* has made its way into the language), you will want to consult an unabridged dictionary where the principle for compiling an entry is *thoroughness.*

22b

d

The second edition of *The Oxford English Dictionary* (Oxford: Clarendon Press), prepared by J. A. Simpson and E. S. C. Weiner, was published in 1989 and includes the text of the first edition (1933), the *Supplement* (1972–1986), and almost 5,000 new entries for a total of more than 500,000 words. It is the great dictionary of the English language, arranged chronologically to show the history of every word from the date of its entry into the language to its most recent usage, supported by almost two million quotations from the works of more than 5,000 authors since 1150. The *O.E.D.* is an invaluable source for scholars.

The Random House Dictionary of the English Language (Random House) is considerably briefer than the other unabridged dictionaries listed here, though it is particularly current, and includes extensive usage notes. The back matter includes several foreign word lists and an atlas with colored maps.

Webster's Third New International Dictionary of the English Language (G. & C. Merriam) includes about 450,000 entries, with special attention to new scientific and technical terms. The third edition of 1986 emphasizes the language as currently used (though entries are arranged chronologically, with the earliest uses first), with a descriptive approach to usage, construction, and punctuation. Many obsolete and rare words have been dropped. Although the third edition is widely used as a descriptive standard, some scholars prefer the more prescriptive approach of the second edition of 1959. Most college students will find that the third edition meets their needs and is convenient to use.

EXERCISE 4

Choose two of the words you looked up in Exercise 5 and compare what you found with the entry for the same word in an unabridged dictionary, preferably the *Oxford English Dictionary*. Briefly characterize the history of each word, explaining how its meaning has shifted over time.

22c Using specialized dictionaries of English

Abridged and unabridged dictionaries of the English language can provide you with a wealth of general information about language. However, there will be times when you will need to consult a specialized dictionary which focuses on a specific kind of word or language information, such as slang, etymologies, synonyms, antonyms, and accepted usage. The following are some particularly useful specialized dictionaries.

1 Dictionaries of usage

When your questions regarding the usage of a word are not adequately addressed in a standard dictionary, consult one of the following dictionaries of usage:

A Dictionary of Contemporary American Usage, ed. Bergen Evans and Cornelia Evans

Dictionary of Modern English Usage, ed. H. W. Fowler

Dictionary of American-English Usage, ed. Margaret Nicholson

Modern American Usage, ed. Jacques Barzun

22c

d

2 Dictionaries of synonyms

Dictionaries that present synonyms of words can be a great help for writers wanting to expand vocabulary. A caution, though: while synonyms have approximately the same denotation, their connotations (or nuances of meaning) differ. Before using a synonym, be sure that you thoroughly understand its connotation. See also 22f-3.

Webster's Dictionary of Synonyms

The New Roget's Thesaurus of the English Language in Dictionary Form

3 Other specialized dictionaries

The dictionaries listed here are specialized sources for the historical and social dimensions of word use.

Dictionaries of origins/etymologies

The information on word origins in basic dictionaries can be pursued in more detail in the following specialized references.

Dictionary of Word and Phrase Origins, ed. William Morris and Mary Morris

The Oxford Dictionary of English Etymology, ed. C. T. Onions

Origins: A Short Etymological Dictionary of Modern English, ed. Eric Partridge

Dictionaries of slang and idioms

Many terms omitted or given only brief notice in basic dictionaries are described in great detail in slang dictionaries.

The New Dictionary of American Slang, ed. Robert Chapman

Dictionary of Slang and Unconventional English, ed. Eric Partridge

Dictionary of American Slang, ed. Harold Wentworth and Stuart Berg Flexner

Dictionaries of regionalism or foreign terms

The *Dictionary of American Regional English,* compiled by linguist Frederic Cassidy, is the standard work on regional and dialect expressions in America.

Dictionary of American Regional English, ed. Frederic Cassidy

Dictionary of Foreign Phrases and Abbreviations, ed. Kevin Guinagh. 3rd ed.

Dictionary of Foreign Terms, ed. C. O. Sylvester Mawson and Charles Berlitz. 2nd ed.

Dictionary of Foreign Terms, ed. Mario Pei and Savatore Ramondino

---

EXERCISE 5

Look up the following words in a dictionary of usage and a dictionary of origins. Based on information you find out about the meanings, origins, and uses of each word from these specialized sources, characterize the kind of writing or the kind of audience for which each term seems most appropriate.

1. awesome   3. celebrate   5. ere
2. mews   4. groovy   6. flunk

BUILDING VOCABULARY

You will need a good vocabulary to understand discussions in texts and to follow lectures. As you move from discipline to discipline, vocabularies will change: you will, in effect, learn new languages. As a writer, you will need a good vocabulary to help you write precisely. This said, you should realize that *vocabulary power* alone, notwithstanding the promises of correspondence courses, does not a writer make. A modest but precise vocabulary will suffice in most cases, so long as you use it in sentences that are structured well, in paragraphs that are coherent, and in essays and reports that show a careful development of ideas. Vocabulary does not exist independently from any of these elements.

 22d   Learn root words, prefixes, and suffixes.

Where applicable, the editors of college dictionaries will place in square brackets [ ] abbreviations of languages from which words are derived. Some of the abbreviations (and their spelled out version) include: *F*, French; *Gk*, Greek; *LL*, Late Latin; *L*, Latin; *Heb*, Hebrew; *ME*, Middle English; *Dan*, Danish; *D*, Dutch; *G*, German; *LG*, Low German; *Flem*, Flemish; *Ital*, Italian; *OW*, Old Welsh; *Span*, Spanish; *Skt*, Sanskrit; and *OPer*, Old Persian. There are more than 100 languages from which the half-million words of English are derived. Modern words are often variants of earlier forms that have snaked their way through history, changing outward appearances for different peoples at different times—though retaining a recognizable core or root. The study of the history of words is called **etymology.** In the square brackets of dictionary entries you will usually find either the abbreviation **fr.** or the symbol <, meaning *derived from.*

Once a word enters the language, its core or *root* is often used as the basis of other words that are formed with *prefixes* and *suffixes*—letters coming before, or after, the root. When you can recognize root words, prefixes, and suffixes, often you will be able to understand the meaning of a new word without checking a dictionary.

22d

ww/d

> EXERCISE 6
>
> Using two unabridged dictionaries, research the etymology of a word. In four or five sentences, trace the word's use over time.

1   Becoming familiar with root words

A root anchors a plant or tree in the ground and provides a structural and nutritional base from which it can grow. The **root** of a word anchors it in language, providing a base from which meaning is built. When you encounter an unfamiliar word, try identifying its root; with help from the context of the surrounding sentence, you can often infer an appropriate definition. Consider the following sentence:

Beautiful and *beauteous* are paronymous words.

You have come upon an unfamiliar word, *paronymous.* You might say: "This reminds me of another word—*anonymous.*" Immediately, you sense that the similar sounding words share a root: *nymous.* You know that *anonymous* means "having an unknown name." It is not so tremendous a leap to conclude that the root *nymous* means *name*. Now you examine the sentence once more and make an educated guess, or inference. What do the words *beautiful* and *beauteous* have to do with *names*? The words themselves tell you—that they are built upon a single name: *beauty*. If you guessed that *paronymous* means "derived from the same word (or root)," you would be correct.

Whether you know a root word or make an educated guess about its meaning, your analysis will aid reading comprehension and, in the process, will improve your vocabulary. Many of the root words in English come from Latin and Greek. The following box contains a small sample of root words.

22d

ww/d

Common Root Words

ROOT	DEFINITION	EXAMPLE
acus [Latin]	needle	acute, acumen
basis [Greek]	step, base	base, basis, basement, basic
bio- [Greek]	life	biography, biology, bionic
cognoscere [Latin]	to know	recognize, cognizant, cognition
ego [Latin]	I	ego, egocentric, egotistical
fleure [Latin]	flow	flow, fluid, effluence
grandis [Latin]	large	grandiose, aggrandize
graphein [Greek]	to write	graph, graphic
hypnos [Greek]	sleep	hypnosis, hypnotic
hydro [Greek]	water	hydraulic, dehydrate
jur, jus [Latin]	law	jury, justice
lumen [Latin]	light	illuminate, luminary
manu- [Latin]	hand	manage, management, manual, manipulate
mare [Latin]	sea	marine, marinate, marina, marinara
matr- [Latin]	mother	maternal, matrilineal
pathos [Greek]	suffering	empathy, sympathy
patr- [Latin]	father	paternal, patriarch
polis [Greek]	city	metropolis, police
primus [Latin]	first	primitive, prime, primary
psych [Greek]	soul	psychological, psyche
sentire [Latin]	to feel	sentiment, sentimental, sentient, sense, sensitive
scrib, script [Latin]	to write	describe, manuscript
sol [Latin]	sun	solstice, solar, solarium
solvere [Latin]	to release	solve, resolve, solution, dissolve, solvent
tele [Greek]	distant	telegraph, telemetry
therm [Greek]	heat	thermal, thermos
truncus [Latin]	trunk	trunk, trench, trenchant
veritas [Latin]	truth	verity, verify, veritable
vocare [Latin]	to call	vocal, vocation, avocation

2 Recognizing prefixes

A **prefix**—letters joined to the beginning of a root word to qualify or add to its meaning—illustrates its own definition: the root *fix* comes from the Latin *fixus*, meaning "to fasten"; *pre* is a prefix, also from Latin, meaning "before." The prefix joined to a root creates a new word, the meaning of which is "to place before." Recognizing prefixes can help you isolate root words. The prefix and the root, considered together, will allow you to infer a meaning. Prefixes can indicate number, size, status, negation, and relations in time and space. The following are some frequently used prefixes.

Prefixes indicating number

PREFIX	MEANING	EXAMPLE
uni-	one	unison, unicellular
bi-	two	bimonthly, bicentennial, bifocal
tri-	three	triangle, triumvirate
multi-	many, multiple	multiply, multifaceted
omni-	all, universally	omnivorous, omniscient
poly-	many, several	polytechnic, polygon

Prefixes indicating size

PREFIX	MEANING	EXAMPLE
micro-	very small	microscopic, microcosm
macro-	very large	macroeconomics
mega-	great	megalomania, megalith

22d

ww/d

Prefixes indicating status or condition

PREFIX	MEANING	EXAMPLE
hyper-	beyond, super	hyperactive, hypercritical
neo-	new	neonate, neophyte
para-	akin to	parachute, paramilitary
pseudo-	false	pseudoscience, pseudonym
quasi-	in some sense	quasi-official, quasi-public

Prefixes indicating negation

PREFIX	MEANING	EXAMPLE
anti-	against	antibiotic, antidote, anticlimax
counter-	contrary	counterintuitive, counterfeit
dis-	to do the opposite	disable, dislodge, disagree
mal-	bad, abnormal, inadequate	maladjusted, malformed, malcontent, malapropism
mis-	bad, wrong	misinform, mislead, misnomer
non-	not, reverse of	noncompliance, nonalcoholic, nonconformist, nonessential

Prefixes indicating spatial relations

PREFIX	MEANING	EXAMPLE
circum-	around	circumspect, circumscribe
inter-	between	intercede, intercept
intra-	within	intravenous, intramural
intro-	inside	introvert, intrude

Prefixes indicating relations of time

PREFIX	MEANING	EXAMPLE
ante-	before	antecedent, anterior
paleo-	ancient	Paleolithic, paleography
post-	after	postdate, postwar, posterior
proto-	first	protohuman, prototype

3 Analyzing suffixes

A **suffix**—letters joined to the end of a word or a root—will change a word's grammatical function. Observe how with suffixes a writer can give a verb the forms of a noun, adjective, and adverb.

22d

ww/d

VERB	impress
NOUN	impression
ADJECTIVE	impressive
ADVERB	impressively

The following are some frequently used suffixes.

Noun-forming suffixes

VERB	+	SUFFIX	(MEANING)	=	NOUN
betray		-al	(process of)		betrayal
participate		-ant	(one who)		participant
play		-er	(one who)		player
construct		-ion	(process of)		construction
conduct		-or	(one who)		conductor

NOUN	+	SUFFIX	(MEANING)	=	NOUN
parson		-age	(house of)		parsonage
king		-dom	(office, realm)		kingdom
sister		-hood	(state, condition of)		sisterhood
strategy		-ist	(one who)		strategist
Armenia		-n	(belonging to)		Armenian
master		-y	(quality)		mastery

ADJECTIVE	+	SUFFIX	(MEANING)	=	NOUN
pure		-ity	(state, quality of)		purity
gentle		-ness	(quality of, degree)		gentleness
active		-ism	(act, practice of)		activism

Verb-forming suffixes

NOUN	+	SUFFIX	(MEANING)	=	VERB
substance		-ate	(cause to become)		substantiate
code		-ify	(cause to become)		codify
serial		-ize	(cause to become)		serialize

ADJECTIVE	+	SUFFIX	(MEANING)	=	VERB
sharp		-en	(cause to become)		sharpen

Adjective-forming suffixes

NOUN	+	SUFFIX	(MEANING)	=	ADJECTIVE
region		-al	(of, relating to)		regional
claim		-ant	(performing, being)		claimant
substance		-ial	(of, relating to)		substantial
response		-ible	(capable of, fit for)		responsible
history		-ic	(form of, being)		historic
Kurd		-ish	(of, relating to)		Kurdish
response		-ive	(tends toward)		responsive

VERB	+	SUFFIX	(MEANING)	=	ADJECTIVE
credit		-able	(capable of)		creditable
abort		-ive	(tends toward)		abortive

22d

ww/d

EXERCISE 7

Identify and initially define, without using a dictionary, the roots, prefixes, and suffixes of the following sets of words. Then check your definitions against dictionary entries.

1. photometry
   photogenic
   photograph
   photoelectric

2. excise
   concise
   precise
   incisive

3. conduce
   reduce
   deduce
   produce

4. optometrist
   optician
   ophthalmologist
   optical

5. discourse
   recourse

6. diverge
   converge

7. convert
   pervert
   revert

8. tenable
   tenacious
   retain

9. memoir
   remember

10. remorse
    morsel

22e   Strategies for building a vocabulary

1   Use contextual clues and dictionaries.

In college, you will spend a great deal of your time reading, and reading provides the best opportunities for expanding your vocabulary. When a new word resists your analysis of root and affix (prefix or suffix), reach for a dictionary or let the context of a sentence provide clues to meaning. Contextual clues will often let you read a passage and infer fairly accurate definitions of new words—accurate enough to give you the sense of a passage. Indeed, using a dictionary to look up *every* new word in the name of thoroughness can so fragment a reading that you will frustrate—not aid—your attempts to understand. Focus first on the ideas of an entire passage; circle or otherwise highlight new words, especially repeated words. Then, if the context has not revealed the meaning, reach for your dictionary.

In the passage that follows, possibly unfamiliar vocabulary is set in italics. Do not stop at these words. Note them, but then complete your reading of the entire paragraph, which was written by the noted linguist Benjamin Lee Whorf about the language of the native American Hopi.

22e

ww/d

> [The] Hopi [language] has one noun that covers every thing or being that flies, with the exception of birds, which class is *denoted* by another noun. The former noun may be said to *denote* the class (FC – B)—flying class minus bird. The Hopi [people] actually call insect, airplane, and aviator all by the same word, and feel no difficulty about it. The situation, of course, decides any possible confusion among very *disparate* members of a broad *linguistic class,* such as this class (FC – B). This class seems to us too large and *inclusive,* but so would our class "snow" to an Eskimo.

It is better that you understand the sense of this paragraph than that you look up and remember dictionary-perfect definitions of the italicized words. After all, the purpose of words—of vocabulary—is to convey a meaning. If through context alone you have defined the italicized words well enough to follow two main points in Whorf's discussion, then you have used contextual clues to real advantage.

1. Whorf works a comparison among speakers of Hopi, English, and Eskimo in order to make the following observation:

2. Speakers of different languages use words with varying levels of generality to describe objects in nature. The level of generality will depend on the speakers' relation with (dependence on, familiarity with) that object.

If contextual clues alone do not help you understand unfamiliar words, and if your lack of understanding prevents you from appreciating a passage's main points, then it is time to turn to a dictionary.

EXERCISE 8

Based on context alone, make an educated guess about the italicized words in the paragraph by Benjamin Lee Whorf. Write down the definition you would give each word. Then look up each word in an unabridged dictionary. How do your definitions compare?

2 Collect words—and use them.

If a word is mentioned more than twice, you should know its formal definition since its repeated use indicates that the word is important. Look the word up if you are not sure of its meaning. When attempting to *increase* your vocabulary, proceed slowly when putting newly discovered words to use in your own writing and speech. As an aid to vocabulary building, you may want to create a file of new words, as described in the box.

A Personal Vocabulary File

- Make a list of flash cards with a new word and the sentence in which it appears on one side of the card; place the definition on the other side.

- Review the cards regularly. Categorize them by discipline or by part of speech. Practice changing the vocabulary word's part of speech with suffixes.

- Expand entries in your file when you find a previously filed word used in a new context.

- Consciously work one or two new words into each paper that you write, especially when the new words allow you to be precise in ways you could not otherwise be.

22e

ww/d

3 Use the thesaurus with care.

A thesaurus (literally from the Greek word meaning "treasure") is a reference tool that lists the synonyms of words and, frequently, their antonyms. Because the thesaurus is found in many computerized word processing programs, its use has become dangerously easy. If you find yourself turning to a thesaurus merely to dress up your writing with significant-sounding language, spare yourself the trouble. Unfortunately, sentences like the one that follows are too often written in a transparent effort to impress—and the effect can be unintentionally comical.

PRETENTIOUS   The *penultimate* chapter of this novel left me *rhapsodic.*

This sentence shares many of the problems associated with pretentious diction (see 21h-2). It also suggests how the *diction* (the level) of the two italicized words chosen from the thesaurus is likely to contrast sharply with the diction that characterizes the rest of a paper. Often, the sense of the word (its denotation or connotation) may be slightly off the mark—not precisely what the meaning of the sentence requires (see 21a). In either case, a sentence with such "treasures" usually stands out as awkward (see 21b). A more restrained choice of words would produce a better sentence.

REVISED I was overwhelmed by the next to last chapter of this novel.

By no means should you ignore the thesaurus; it is, in fact, a treasury of language. But when you find a word, make sure you are comfortable with it—that it is *your* word—before appropriating it for use in a paper.

4 Build discipline-appropriate vocabularies.

Each discipline has a vocabulary that insiders, or professionals, use when addressing one another; and one of your jobs as you move from class to class will be to recognize important words and add them to discipline-specific vocabularies that you will develop. The longer you study in a discipline, and especially if you should major in it, the larger and more versatile your specific vocabulary will be. Discipline-specific vocabularies consist of two types of words: those that are unique to the discipline and those that are found elsewhere, though with different meanings. For example, the word *gravity* occurs in contexts outside of the physics classroom. In a newspaper article or essay you might find *gravity* used to suggest great seriousness: *The gravity of the accusations caused Mr. Jones to hire a famous attorney.* Present-day physicists use the word *gravity* with an altogether different sense.

Discipline-specific vocabularies also consist of words unique to a particular field of study. The sheer volume of these words makes it impossible to review them here; suffice it to say that as you see new terms repeated in texts or recurring in the speech of your professors, you should note these words and learn their definitions. As you move from introductory courses in a subject to upper-level courses, the new terms will become more familiar.

EXERCISE 9

Take an informal survey to see if you can identify five words or phrases unique to a particular group of people. Listen to fraternity or sorority members on campus addressing members of their own houses; listen closely in a locker room to members of a team with which you have practiced; or sit in on a campus club meeting or a session of the student government. List the five words or phrases; then define each expression and illustrate its community-specific use in a sentence.

EXERCISE 10

Review your notes and text for one course and identify five words or phrases particular to that subject. The words or phrases might well occur in contexts beyond the course but will, as well, have a course-specific meaning. List the words or phrases; then define each expression and illustrate its discipline-specific use in a sentence.

22e

ww/d

CHAPTER 23

Spelling

English is an eclectic language derived from several different sources, including Old German, Scandinavian, and Norman French, as well as Latin and Greek. With such a mixed vocabulary, it is remarkable how closely most English spellings are associated with the sounds of words. Nevertheless, many words that look or sound alike may in fact derive from different sources, and thus be spelled or pronounced differently. With practice in writing and reading, certain basic patterns emerge that connect spelling to word sounds. Spelling can be mastered by learning a few rules and the exceptions to those rules. Spelling "demons" can be overcome by recognizing the words you most commonly misspell and remembering devices for memorizing their correct spelling.

Why trouble yourself with spelling, especially when writing on computers with dictionary or spell-check programs built in? First, word-processing programs give users choices when checking the spelling of a word. These programs call for you to make decisions, and you will need to understand some basic rules. The second reason you should learn spelling rules has to do with the way you are perceived on the basis of what you write. Spelling is the covering or clothing of words. Just as we are judged by our appearance, so our words are judged by the way they look on the page: misspelled words make a bad first impression, and spelling errors can both detract and distract from what you are trying to say. At the very least, you appear lazy or careless; at worst, uninformed or unconcerned—messages you never want to send. Spelling accurately may be a challenge, but it is a challenge you can master.

23a Overcoming spelling/pronunciation misconnections

Long-time speakers and readers of English have learned basic connections between sounds and letter combinations that help them spell a large number of words. However, for historical reasons certain combinations of letters are not always pronounced in the same way (for example: th*ough*t, b*ough*, thr*ough*, dr*ough*t, etc.). In addition, regional and dialect variations in pronunciation may drop or vary the pronunciation of certain endings of auxiliary verbs. It is safer to try to keep a visual image of a word in your mind, rather than to rely on what you hear to help you to spell a word correctly.

1 Recognizing homonyms and commonly confused words

One of the most common causes of spelling confusion is **homonyms**—words that sound alike, or are pronounced almost alike, but that have different spellings and meanings. The following box lists the most commonly confused homonyms and near homonyms.

23a

sp

Commonly Confused Homonyms and Near Homonyms

accept [to receive]
except [to leave out]

advice [recommendation]
advise [to recommend]

affect [to have an influence on]
effect [result; to make happen]

all ready [prepared]
already [by this time]

bare [naked]
bear [to carry, endure; an animal]

board [piece of wood]
bored [uninterested]

brake [stop, device for stopping]
break [to smash, destroy]

buy [purchase]
by [next to, through]

capital [city seat of government]
capitol [legislative or government building]

cite [quote, refer to]
sight [vision, something seen]
site [place, locale]

complement [something that completes]
compliment [praise]

conscience [moral sense, sense of right/wrong]
conscious [aware]

discreet [respectfully reserved]
discrete [distinct, separate]

dominant [controlling, powerful]
dominate [to control]

elicit [to draw out]
illicit [illegal]

eminent [distinguished]
immanent [inborn, inherent]
imminent [expected momentarily]

fair [just; light-complexioned; lovely]
fare [fee for transportation; meal]

gorilla [ape]
guerilla [unconventional soldier]

heard [past tense of *to hear*]
herd [group of animals]

hole [opening]
whole [entire, complete]

its [possessive form of *it*]
it's [contraction of *it is*]

lead [guide; heavy metal]
led [past tense of *to lead*]

lessen [decrease]
lesson [something learned]

loose [not tight, unfastened]
lose [misplace, fail to win]

moral [object-lesson, knowing right from wrong]
morale [outlook, attitude]

passed [past tense of *to pass*]
past [after; beyond; a time gone by]

patience [forbearance]
patients [those under medical care]

peace [absence of war]
piece [part or portion of something]

personal [private, pertaining to an individual]
personnel [employees]

plain [simple, clear, unadorned; flat land]

plane [carpenter's tool, flat surface, airplane]

presence [attendance, being at hand]
presents [gifts; gives]

principal [most important; school administrator]
principle [fundamental truth, law, conviction]

scene [setting, play segment]
seen [past participle of *see*]

shore [coastline]
sure [certain]

stationary [standing still]
stationery [writing paper]

straight [unbending]
strait [narrow waterway]

than [besides; as compared with]
then [at that time; therefore]

their [possessive form of *they*]
there [opposite of *here*]
they're [contraction of *they are*]

threw [past tense of *throw*]
through [by means of, finished]
thorough [complete]

to [toward]
too [also, in addition to]
two [number following *one*]

weak [feeble]
week [seven days]

weather [climatic conditions]
whether [which of two]

whose [possessive form of *who*]
who's [contraction of *who is*]

your [possessive form of *you*]
you're [contraction of *you are*]
yore [the far past]

EXERCISE 1

From each pair or trio of words in parentheses, circle the correct homonym. Then make up sentences using each of the other word[s] correctly.

1. If (your/you're) going to the store make (shore/sure) you take (your/you're) shopping list and return the (bier/beer) bottles to get the deposit money back.
2. Jean's going to tell Gary (their/they're/there) (through/threw).
3. The (imminent/eminent) author's death was (immanent/imminent).
4. (Your/you're) (illusion/allusion) to Dave's preferring apple pie is an (illusion/allusion); he prefers cherry.
5. We're having trouble (devicing/devising) a (devise/device) to decode this code.

23a

sp

2 Recognizing words with more than one form

A subgroup of homonyms that many people find particularly troublesome consists of words that sometimes appear as one word and other times appear as two words.

We *always* work hard, in *all ways*.

By the time everyone was *all ready* to go, it was *already* too late to catch the early show.

It *may be* a question of etiquette, but *maybe* it's not.

Everyday attitudes are not always appropriate *every day*.

Walking *in to* the theater, he accidentally bumped *into* the usher.

Once we were *all together*, we were *altogether* convinced the reunion had been a wonderful idea.

Unlike *always/all ways* and *already/all ready*, *all right* and *a lot* do not vary: they can be written only as two words.

FAULTY   It's *alright* with me if Sally comes along.

REVISED   It's *all right* with me if Sally comes along.

FAULTY   James has *alot* of homework to do tonight.

REVISED   James has *a lot* of homework to do tonight.

3   Memorizing words with silent letters or syllables

Many words contain silent letters such as the *k* and the *w* in *know* or the *b* in *dumb*, or letters that are not pronounced in everyday speech, such as the first *r* in *February*. The simplest way to remember the spelling of these words is to commit them to memory, mentally pronouncing the silent letters as you do so. Following is a list of frequently used words whose mispronunciation in everyday speech often leads to misspelling.

23a

sp

ai*s*le	Feb*r*uary	paradi*g*m
can*d*idate	foreign	*p*neumonia
clim*b*	gover*n*ment	privi*l*ege
condem*n*	int*e*rest	prob*a*bly

4   Distinguishing between noun and verb forms of the same word

Many spelling problems occur when noun and verb forms of a word have different spellings.

VERB	NOUN
advise	advice
describe	description
enter	entrance
marry	marriage

5   Distinguishing American from British and Canadian spellings

The endings of various words differ depending on whether the American version or the British version of the word is being used. Though each is correct, when in America, do as the Americans do. Above all, you should be consistent. If you are not sure what the correct version of the word is, consult your dictionary, making sure you know whether the dictionary "prefers" English or American variations.

AMERICAN	BRITISH
—or (humor, color)	—our (humour, colour)
—ment (judgment)	—ement (judgement)
—tion (connection)	—xion (connexion)
—ize (criticize, realize)	—ise (criticise, realise)
—er (center, theater)	—re (centre, theatre)
—led (traveled)	—lled (travelled)

Other American/British variations include: gray/grey and check/cheque.

23b Learn basic spelling rules for *ie/ei*.

Despite the troublesome aspects of English spelling detailed previously, there are a number of general rules that greatly simplify the task of spelling words correctly.

The *i* before *e* rule you learned in grammar school still holds true: "*i* before *e* except after *c*, or when pronounced *ay*, as in n*ei*ghbor."

23b

sp

i **before** *e*

achieve	experience	piece
belief/believe	field	relief/relieve
brief	fiend/friend	grief/grieve
chief	niece	

except after *c*

ceiling	deceit/deceive	perceive
conceit	conceive	
receipt/receive		

ei **pronounced** *ay*

beige	neighbor	vein
eight(h)	heinous	weigh(t)
freight		

Learn some exceptions

ancient	foreign	neither
caffeine	height	seize
either	leisure	weird

Finally, if the *ie* is not pronounced as a unit, the rule does not apply: science, conscientious, atheist.

EXERCISE 2

Insert *ie* or *ei* in the following words. If necessary, use a dictionary to confirm your choice.

forf ___ t	s ___ zure	p ___ rce
financ ___ r	f ___ nt	pat ___ nce
consc ___ nce	h ___ ress	counterf ___ t
defic ___ nt	sl ___ ght	r ___ fy

23c Learn rules for using prefixes.

Prefixes are placed at the beginnings of words to qualify or add to their meaning. The addition of a prefix never affects the spelling of the root word: do not drop a letter from or add a letter to the original word.

un + usual = unusual

mis + statement = misstatement

under + rate = underrate

dis + service = disservice

anti + thesis = antithesis

de + emphasize = de-emphasize

23d

The following are also used as prefixes: *en, in, ante, inter, pre, per, pro,* and *over.*

sp

23d Learn rules for using suffixes.

A **suffix** is an ending added to a word in order to change the word's function. For example, suffixes can change a present tense verb to a past tense verb (help, help*ed*); make an adjective an adverb (silent, silent*ly*); make a verb a noun (excite, excite*ment*); or change a noun to an adjective (force, forc*ible*). Spelling difficulties often arise when the root word must be changed before the suffix is added.

1 Learn rules for keeping or dropping a final *e.*

Many words end with a silent *e* (have, mate, raise, confine, procure). When adding a suffix to these words, you can use the following rules.

The basic rule: If the suffix begins with a vowel, drop the final silent *e.*

accuse + ation = accusation

inquire + ing = inquiring

debate + able = debatable

sedate + ive = sedative
cube + ism = cubism
pore + ous = porous

Exceptions
The silent *e* is sometimes retained before a suffix that begins with a vowel in order to distinguish homonyms (dyeing/dying); to prevent mispronunciation (*mileage*, not milage); and especially, to keep the sound of *c* or *g* soft.

courage + ous = courageous
outrage + ous = outrageous
embrace + able = embraceable
notice + able = noticeable

Rule: If the suffix begins with a consonant, keep the final silent *e*.

manage + ment = management
sedate + ly = sedately
blame + less = blameless
acute + ness = acuteness
force + ful = forceful

23d

Exceptions
When the final silent *e* is preceded by another vowel, the *e* is dropped (*argument*, not arguement; *truly*, not truely).

sp

Other exceptions include:

judge + ment = judgment
acknowledge + ment = acknowledgment
awe + ful = awful
whole + ly = wholly

EXERCISE 3
Combine the following words and suffixes, retaining or dropping the final *e* as needed. Check your choices in the dictionary to make sure they are correct.

1. investigate + ive
2. malice + ious
3. due + ly
4. trace + able
5. singe + ing

6. service + able
7. complete + ly
8. mistake + en
9. grieve + ance
10. binge + ing

2 Learn rules for keeping or dropping a final *y*.

When suffixes are added to words that end in a final *y*, use the following rules.

Rule: When the letter immediately before the *y* is a consonant, change the *y* to *i* and then add the suffix.

beauty + ful = beautiful

breezy + er = breezier

worry + some = worrisome

comply + ant = compliant

busy + ness = business

study + ous = studious

Exceptions

Keep the final *y* when the suffix to be added is *-ing.*

study + ing = studying

comply + ing = complying

Keep the final *y* for some one-syllable root words.

shy + er = shyer

wry + ly = wryly

Keep the final *y* when the *y* is the ending of a proper name.

Janey/Janeys

Bobby/Bobbylike

Keep the final *y* when it is preceded by a vowel, and then add the suffix.

journey + ing = journeying

deploy + ment = deployment

spray + ed = sprayed

buoy + ant = buoyant

play + ful = playful

coy + ly = coyly

23d

sp

EXERCISE 4

Combine the following root words and suffixes, changing the *y* to *i* when necessary.

1. supply + er
2. stultify + ing
3. testy + er
4. rarefy + ed
5. joy + ousness

6. convey + ance
7. cry + er
8. Kennedy + s
9. plenty + ful
10. day + ly

3 Learn rules for adding -*ally*.

Rule: Add -*ally* to make an adverb out of an adjective that ends with *ic*.

terrific + ally = terrifically   emphatic + ally = emphatically
caustic + ally = caustically   music + ally = musically
fantastic + ally = fantastically

Exception
public + ly = publicly

4 Learn the rule for adding -*ly*.

Rule: Add -*ly* to make an adverb out of adjectives that do not end with *ic*.

hesitant + ly = hesitantly   fastidious + ly = fastidiously
helpful + ly = helpfully   conscientious + ly = conscientiously
fortunate + ly = fortunately

5 Learn the rule for adding -*cede*, -*ceed*, and -*sede*.

Words that sound like *seed* are almost always spelled -*cede*.

intercede   concede   precede
accede   recede   secede

Exceptions
Only supersede uses -*sede*.
Only exceed, proceed, and succeed use -*ceed*.

6 Learn rules for adding -*able* or -*ible*.

These endings sound the same, but there is an easy way to remember which to use.

Rule: If the root word is an independent word, use the suffix -*able*. If the root is not an independent word, use the suffix -*ible*.

comfort + able = comfortable   audible
advise + able = advisable   plausible
agree + able = agreeable   compatible

Exceptions
culpable, probable, resistible

23d

sp

436 SPELLING

7 **Learn rules for doubling the final consonant.**

A word that ends in a consonant sometimes doubles the final consonant when a suffix is added.

Rule: Double the final consonant when a one-syllable word ends in a consonant preceded by a single vowel.

flip + ant = flippant   slip + er = slipper
flat + en = flatten   split + ing = splitting

Rule: Double the final consonant when adding a suffix to a two-syllable word if a single vowel precedes the final consonant and if the final syllable is accented once the suffix is added.

control + er = controller
concur + ence = concurrence
commit + ing = committing

Rule: Do not double the final consonant when it is preceded by two or more vowels, or by another consonant.

sustain + ing = sustaining
comport + ed = comported
insist + ent = insistent

Rule: Do not double the final consonant if the suffix begins with a consonant.

commit + ment = commitment
fat + ness = fatness

Rule: Do not double the final consonant if the word is *not* accented on the last syllable, or if the accent shifts from the last to the first syllable when the suffix is added.

beckon + ing = beckoning
prefer + ence = preference

23d

sp

EXERCISE 5
Add the correct suffix to the following roots, changing the roots as necessary. Consult a dictionary as needed.

1. benefit + ed
2. realistic + (-ly or -ally?)
3. contempt + (-able or -ible?)
4. parallel + ing

5. proceed + ure
6. reverse + (-able or -ible?)
7. allot + ment

8. occur + ence
9. room + mate
10. control + (-able or -ible?)

23e Learn rules for forming plurals.

There are several standard rules for making words plural.

1 Learn the basic rule for adding -s/-es.

Adding -s

For most words, simply add -s.

gum/gums   automobile/automobiles
season/seasons   investment/investments

Adding -es

For words ending in -s, -sh, -ss, -ch, -x, or -z, add -es.

bus/buses   watch/watches
bush/bushes   tax/taxes
mistress/mistresses   buzz/buzzes

23e

sp

For words ending in -o add -es if the o is preceded by a consonant.

tomato/tomatoes   hero/heroes
potato/potatoes   veto/vetoes

Exceptions
pro/pros, piano/pianos, solo/solos
soprano/sopranos

Add -s if the final o is preceded by a vowel.

patio/patios   zoo/zoos

2 Learn the rule for plurals of words ending in -f or -fe.

To form the plural of some nouns ending in -f or -fe, change the ending to -ve before adding the -s.

half/halves   leaf/leaves
elf/elves   yourself/yourselves

Exceptions
scarf/scarfs/scarves   hoof/hoofs/hooves
belief/beliefs; proof/proofs; motif/motifs

 3   **Learn the rule for plurals of words ending in -*y*.**

For words that end in a consonant followed by -*y*, change the *y* to *i* before adding -*es* to form the plural.

amenity/amenities   enemy/enemies
raspberry/raspberries   mystery/mysteries

Exceptions
proper names such as McGinty/McGintys; Mary/Marys
For words ending in a vowel followed by -*y*, add -*s*.

monkey/monkeys   delay/delays
alloy/alloys   buy/buys

23e

sp

 4   **Learn the rule for plurals of compound words.**

When compound nouns are written as one word, add an -*s* ending as you would to make any other plural.

snowball/snowballs   mailbox/mailboxes
breakthrough/breakthroughs

When compound nouns are hyphenated or written as two words, the most important part of the compound word (usually a noun that is modified) is made plural.

sister-in-law/sisters-in-law   head of state/heads of state
nurse-midwife/nurse-midwives   city planner/city planners

5   **Learn the irregular plurals.**

Some words change internally to form plurals.

woman/women   goose/geese
mouse/mice   tooth/teeth

Some Latin and Greek words form plurals by changing their final *-um*, *-on*, or *-us* to *-a* or *-i*.

curricul*um*/curricul*a*   criteri*on*/criteri*a*
syllab*us*/*syllabi*   medi*um*/medi*a*
dat*um*/dat*a*   stimul*us*/*stimuli*
alumn*a*/alumn*ae*

For some words, the singular and the plural forms are the same.

deer/deer   sheep/sheep
species/species   moose/moose
elk/elk   rice/rice

EXERCISE 6
Make the following words plural. Check your answers in the dictionary.

1. spoonful
2. phenomenon
3. monkey house
4. thesis
5. beauty

6. fish
7. apparatus
8. wolverine
9. attorney general
10. antenna

23f

sp

23f Developing spelling skills

In addition to learning the spelling rules detailed earlier, there are several ways to improve your spelling skills.

- Memorize commonly misspelled words.
- Keep track of the words that give you trouble. See if you can discern a pattern, and memorize the relevant rule.
- Use the dictionary. Check words whose spelling you are not sure of, and add them to your personal list of difficult-to-spell words. If you are not sure of the first few letters of a word, look up a synonym of that word to see if the word you need is listed as part of the definition.
- Pay attention when you read: your mind will retain a visual impression of a word that will help you remember how it is spelled.
- You may also develop mnemonic devices—techniques to improve memory—for particularly troublesome words. For instance, you might use the *-er* at the end of pap*er* and lett*er* as a reminder that station*er*y means writing paper, while station*ar*y means standing still.

- Edit and proofread carefully, paying particular attention to how the words look on the page. You will find as you train yourself that you will begin to recognize spelling errors, and that you actually know the correct spelling but have made an old mistake in haste or carelessness.

- On word processors, use a spell-checker, but realize that this computer aid will only identify misspelled words: if you have used an incorrect homonym, but have spelled it correctly, the spell-checker will not highlight the word.

23f

sp

PART VII

Using Punctuation

CHAPTER 24

End Punctuation

The ending of one sentence and the beginning of the next is a crucial boundary for readers. Sentences provide the primary medium for delivering isolatable, comprehensible chunks of information, and readers are highly sensitive to signals that show when they come to a full stop. When sentence boundaries are blurred, readers have trouble grouping a writer's words into meaningful segments. The end-sentence boundary in English is marked in three ways: with a period, a question mark, and an exclamation point.

THE PERIOD

24a Using the period

The **period** is our workhorse mark of punctuation, the one used most often for noting a full stop—the end of a sentence.

1 Placing a period to mark the end of a statement or a mild command

It is conventional to end statements or mild commands with a period.

Carry that barrel over here.

Four of the first five Presidents of the United States were Virginia men.

We usually call them the "Virginia dynasty."

A restatement of a question asked by someone else is called an **indirect question.** Since it is really a statement, it does not take a question mark.

DIRECT
QUESTION   These presidents asked, "Do Americans have faith in the people?"

STATEMENT   These presidents asked whether Americans have faith in the people.

2 Placing periods in relation to end quotations and parentheses

A period is always placed inside a quotation that ends a sentence.

These presidents basically asserted, "Americans should have faith in the people."

When a parenthesis ends a sentence, place a period outside the end parenthesis if the parenthetical remark is not a complete sentence. If the parenthetical remark is a separate complete sentence, enclose it entirely in parentheses and punctuate it as a sentence—with its own period.

FAULTY   Four of the first five Presidents of the United States were Virginia men (Washington, Jefferson, Madison, and Monroe.).

REVISED   Four of the first five Presidents of the United States were Virginia men (Washington, Jefferson, Madison, and Monroe).

REVISED   Four of the first five Presidents of the United States were Virginia men. (These were Washington, Jefferson, Madison, and Monroe.)

3   Using a period with abbreviations

The following are considered abbreviations that conventionally end with a period:

Mr. Mrs. Ms. (even though this is not an abbreviation)
apt. Ave. St. Dr. Eccles. mgr.

When an abbreviation ends a sentence, use a single period.

FAULTY   The lawyers addressed their questions to Susan Turner, Esq..

REVISED   The lawyers addressed their questions to Susan Turner, Esq.

When an abbreviation falls in the middle of a sentence, punctuate as if the word abbreviated were spelled out.

FAULTY   The award envelope was presented to Susan Turner, Esq. who opened it calmly.

REVISED   The award envelope was presented to Susan Turner, Esq., who opened it calmly.

Use no periods with acronyms or certain long abbreviations.

A number of abbreviations do not take periods—most often *acronyms* (NATO for *N*orth *A*tlantic *T*reaty *O*rganization), the names of large organizations (IBM for *I*nternational *B*usiness *M*achines), or government agencies (FTC for *F*ederal *T*rade *C*ommission). To be sure about the proper abbreviation of a word or organizational name, consult a standard dictionary for general purposes or specialized dictionaries when you are writing in a particular discipline. The following are some typical abbreviations.

ABC   CNN   AT&T   USA   ABM   FAA

24a

EXERCISE 1

Add, delete, or reposition periods in these sentences as needed.

Example: The development of a uranium industry has had serious consequences within South Africa

The development of a uranium industry has had serious consequences within South Africa.

1. In 1957, South Africa became one of the first U.S. partners in an agreement known as "atoms for peace"
2. Under this agreement a U.S. firm, Allis Chalmers, supplied South Africa with its first nuclear reactor in 1961, a large research reactor dubbed "Safari 1".
3. South Africa has developed a uranium enrichment capability with aid from West Germany, and a large nuclear power station is being built at Koeberg, near Capetown, by the French firm Framatome (This firm is partly owned by Westinghouse)
4. These developments were begun under the rubric of "atoms for peace." Yet today South Africa has become a nuclear weapons power (the only one in its region)
5. Both Soviet and American satellites had revealed the preparation of a testing site, and in 1979 a U.S. satellite brought disturbing news, this time of a "small atmospheric nuclear explosion in the South Atlantic".
6. Although these events remain ambiguous, there is no doubt that the government of South Africa does have the capacity to produce nuclear fission weapons There is also no doubt that the nuclear cooperation with Pretoria, begun in order to secure the U.S. uranium supply, has been a major factor in making that possible

24b

? THE QUESTION MARK

24b Using the question mark

1 Using a question mark after a direct question

Why do children develop so little when they are isolated from others?

Why is the crime rate higher in the city than the country, in impoverished areas more than other areas? Why do more males than females, more young people than older people, commit crimes?

NOTE: An indirect question restates a question put by someone else. The indirect question does not take a question mark.

Sociologists Eshleman and Cashion have asked why children develop so little when they are isolated from others.

Requests, worded as questions, are often followed by periods.

Would you pour another glass of wine.

Questions in a series inside a sentence will take question marks if each denotes a separate question.

When an automobile manufacturer knowingly sells a car that meets government safety standards but is defective, what are the manufacturer's legal responsibilities? moral responsibilities? financial responsibilities? [Note that these three "clipped" questions—these incomplete sentences—do not require capitalization.]

When the sense of the questions in a series is not completed until the final question, use one question mark—at the end of the sentence.

Will the agent be submitting the manuscript to one publishing house, two houses, or more?

2 Using a question mark after a quoted question within a statement

Placing the question mark *inside* the end quotation

When the question mark applies directly to the quoted material, place it inside the quotation.

In a dream, Abraham Lincoln remembered a stranger asking, "Why are you so common looking?"

Place the question mark inside the end quotation when the mark applies to *both* the quoted material *and* the sentence as a whole.

Don't you find it insulting that a person would comment directly to a president, "Why are you so common looking?"

Placing the question mark *outside* the end quotation

When the sentence as a whole forms a question but the quoted material does not, place the question mark outside the quotation.

Was it Lincoln who observed, "The Lord prefers common-looking people; that's the reason he makes so many of them"?

NOTE: Do *not* combine a question mark with a period, a comma, or an exclamation point.

24b

?

FAULTY   "Are you going with him?!" asked Joan.

REVISED   "Are you going with him?" asked Joan.

REVISED   "Are you going with him!" shouted Joan.

3   Using a question mark within parentheses to indicate that the accuracy of information is in doubt even after extensive research

The question mark can be used to indicate dates or numerical references known to be inexact. The following are equivalent in meaning.

Geoffrey Chaucer was born in 1340 **(?)**.

Chaucer was born about 1340.

Chaucer was born c. 1340. (The c. is an abbreviation for *circa*, meaning "around.")

NOTE: Do *not* use the question mark in parentheses to make wry comments in your sentences.

FAULTY   We found the play a stimulating **(?)** experience.

REVISED   Martin fell asleep in the play's first act, and I persuaded him to leave at intermission.

EXERCISE 2

Add or delete question marks as needed. If necessary, reword sentences.

Example: The candidates forum provided an illuminating **(?)** hour of political debate.

            The candidates forum failed to provide an illuminating debate.

1. Many people are quick to complain about the quality of political discourse in American politics, so why is it that more thoughtful people aren't running for elected office.
2. When we find that it is polling information, not philosophical conviction, that shapes the public remarks of political figures, is it any wonder that Americans turn cynical, refuse to vote, bemoan the absence of leadership.
3. Political scientists ask why Americans have one of the lowest voter turnouts among democratic nations?
4. Was it Marie Thompson who asked, "Why do we have so much difficulty rising to the challenge of our democratic traditions"?
5. Thompson reaches no firm answers when she concludes, "If the framers of the Constitution assumed an educated, caring citizenry, then we must wonder aloud—have we failed to meet the challenges laid down 200 years ago"?

24b

?

THE EXCLAMATION POINT

24c   Using the exclamation point

In spoken conversation, exclamations are used freely, especially in moments of high passion. For some informal occasions, writers may be tempted to create with exclamation points what their breath cannot show on paper. In academic writing, however, it is far more convincing to create emphasis by the force of your words, as opposed to the force of your punctuation.

1 Using the exclamation point—sparingly—to mark an emphatic statement or command

Overused exclamation points create a none-too-flattering portrait of a "breathy" or "flaky" writer who is highly excitable and not too credible. Save the exclamation point to call special attention to a unique, memorable sentence, the content of which creates its own emphasis. The exclamation point will highlight the emphasis already present.

Enterprising archaeologists visit their dentists regularly, if only to obtain supplies of worn-out dental instruments, which make first-rate fine digging tools!

Please! Let me do it myself! [The use of exclamation points with this emphatic exclamation and command is appropriate for duplicating spoken dialogue.]

2 Marking mild exclamations with periods or commas

Please, let me do it myself.

NOTE: Do not combine an exclamation point with a period, comma, or question mark.

FAULTY   "Leave this room!," demanded the judge.

REVISED   "Leave this room!" demanded the judge.

FAULTY   "Can't you give us some privacy?!" he snarled.

REVISED   "Can't you give us some privacy!" he snarled.

EXERCISE 3

Read the following paragraphs on the subject of blushing and provide periods, question marks, and exclamation points as needed.

Occasionally you may find yourself blushing when you're being flattered The tendency is to interpret this as shyness Before interpreting

24c

!

it in this way, hold on Is your blush possibly saying, "I don't believe they mean it They're flattering me manipulatively" Trust the blush as an automatic aversion response that may be saying far more than just, "I'm shy"

The next time you blush, try saying "I don't like . . . " and finish the sentence with the cause of the blushing (This may also keep you from being a constant target) In other words, "I don't like your asking me that question" See if that then makes sense in helping you understand your blushing problem

24c

!

CHAPTER 25

Commas

One important purpose of punctuation is to help readers identify clusters of related words, both between and within sentences. By far the most common mark used to distinguish one sentence from another is the period. *Within* sentences, the most common mark is the **comma,** and it is used primarily as a signal that some element, some word or cluster of related words, is being set off from a main sentence for a reason. Readers see the comma as a direct instruction from the writer on how to read and understand. Clear instructions will keep readers focused on the words in exactly the way the writer deems necessary. A well-used comma helps to move readers from the beginning of a sentence through to the end, effortlessly and with understanding. Poorly used, a comma will scatter meaning and create confusion. There is much to gain, therefore, in using commas precisely.

In this chapter you will find rules and guidelines for using the comma. Much of the logic of punctuating with commas is tied to the logic of a sentence's structure. See chapter 7 for details.

25a Using commas with introductory and concluding expressions

1 Place a comma after a modifying phrase or clause that begins a sentence.

A sentence may begin with an opening phrase or clause that is neither the subject nor a simple modifier of the subject. If such an introductory element is longer than a few words, set it off from the main part of the sentence with a comma. The comma will signal the reader that the sentence's subject is being delayed.

> According to sociologist Herbert Gans, poverty's function is to provide a low-wage labor pool to do society's necessary dirty work.

> Because the poor seldom have a chance to buy desirable products, they in this way help merchants by purchasing leftovers—dilapidated cars or deteriorated housing.

Option: The comma after an introductory word or brief phrase is optional.

> Perhaps some will be surprised to find that sociologists consider poverty to have an economic function.

25a

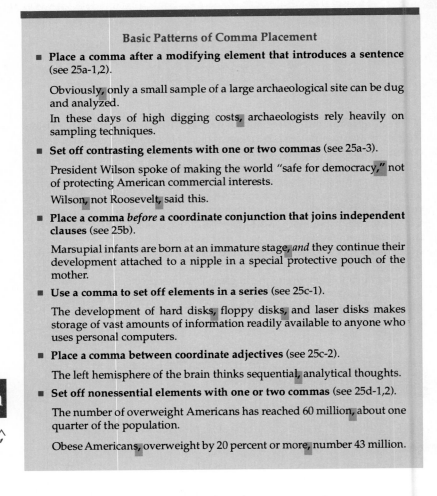

Basic Patterns of Comma Placement

- **Place a comma after a modifying element that introduces a sentence** (see 25a-1,2).

  Obviously, only a small sample of a large archaeological site can be dug and analyzed.

  In these days of high digging costs, archaeologists rely heavily on sampling techniques.

- **Set off contrasting elements with one or two commas** (see 25a-3).

  President Wilson spoke of making the world "safe for democracy," not of protecting American commercial interests.

  Wilson, not Roosevelt, said this.

- **Place a comma *before* a coordinate conjunction that joins independent clauses** (see 25b).

  Marsupial infants are born at an immature stage, *and* they continue their development attached to a nipple in a special protective pouch of the mother.

- **Use a comma to set off elements in a series** (see 25c-1).

  The development of hard disks, floppy disks, and laser disks makes storage of vast amounts of information readily available to anyone who uses personal computers.

- **Place a comma between coordinate adjectives** (see 25c-2).

  The left hemisphere of the brain thinks sequential, analytical thoughts.

- **Set off nonessential elements with one or two commas** (see 25d-1,2).

  The number of overweight Americans has reached 60 million, about one quarter of the population.

  Obese Americans, overweight by 20 percent or more, number 43 million.

When an introductory element consists of two or more phrases, a comma is required.

> Even with our understanding of poverty's root causes, we lack as a society the will to eliminate it. [With two prepositional phrases, the opening needs to be set off from the main sentence.]

NOTE: An opening verbal phrase or clause is set off with a comma if it is used as a modifier; an opening verbal used as a subject is *not* set off.

MODIFIER   Understanding what we do about the root causes of poverty, we lack as a society the will to eliminate it. [The opening modifier needs to be set off.]

SUBJECT Understanding what we do about poverty does not help us gain the will to eliminate it. [The opening verbal functions as the subject of the sentence and is *not* set off.]

2 **Place a comma after a transitional word, phrase, or clause that begins a sentence.**

A transition is a logical bridge between sentences or paragraphs. As an introductory element, it is set off with a comma.

Once division of labor by sex arose, it must have produced several immediate benefits for the early hominids. *First of all,* nutrition would have improved owing to a balanced diet of meat and plant foods. *Second,* each male or female would have become expert in only part of the skills needed for subsistence and have increased his or her efficiency accordingly.

When a transitional element is moved to the interior of a sentence, set it off with a *pair* of commas. At the end of a sentence, the transitional element is set off with a single comma.

Lipid molecules, *of course,* and molecules that dissolve easily in lipids can pass through cell membranes with ease.

Lipid molecules and molecules that dissolve easily in lipids can pass through cell membranes with ease, *to cite two examples.*

3 **Use a comma (or commas) to set off a modifying element that ends or interrupts a sentence *if* the modifier establishes a qualification, contrast, or exception.**

A QUALIFICATION

The literary form *short story* is usually defined as a brief fictional prose narrative, *often involving one connected episode.*

A CONTRAST

The U.S. government located a lucrative project for an atomic accelerator in Texas, *not Massachusetts.*

AN EXCEPTION

The children of the rich are the group most likely to go to private preparatory schools and elite colleges, *regardless of their grades.*

When phrases or clauses of contrast, qualification, and exception occur in the middle of a sentence, set them off with a *pair* of commas.

The government chose Texas, *not Massachusetts,* as the site of a lucrative project for an atomic accelerator.

All seas, *except in the areas of circumpolar ice,* are navigable.

EXERCISE 1

The following sentences contain transitional expressions and modifying words or phrases. Rewrite each sentence so that the transition or modifier will come at the *beginning* of the sentence *or* at the *end*. Use commas as needed.

Example: Some of the Balkan nations of southeastern and south central Europe declared war on the waning Ottoman Empire in 1912.

In 1912, some of the Balkan nations of southeastern and south central Europe declared war on the waning Ottoman Empire.

1. Bulgaria attacked Serbia and Greece in 1913 in a second war over boundaries.
2. Bulgaria was carved up as a result of the 1913 war by its former Balkan allies and Turkey.
3. The assassination of the Archduke Ferdinand of Austria the following year brought on the First World War.
4. A sprawling new nation, Yugoslavia, was formed after the Austro-Hungarian Empire collapsed.
5. The aspirations of Croats and other minorities in Yugoslavia were suppressed under the tenuous domination of the Serbs.
6. The collapse of the Ottoman Empire at the same time left many ethnic Turks subject to their longtime foes the Bulgarians.
7. A million Armenians were slaughtered at the same time as a result of attempts at forging a new Turkish state in Anatolia.
8. Undermined by corrupt and meddling monarchs and by ethnic passions, parliamentary governments of southeastern Europe rose and fell.
9. Stalin was interested in Balkan hatreds not Balkan reconciliations according to a Yugoslav official.
10. There are between 2 and 2.5 million Magyars (ethnic Hungarians) in Romania making them the largest ethnic minority in all of Europe.

25b

∧/coord
,

25b Using a comma before a coordinate conjunction to join two independent clauses

One of the principal ways to join two independent clauses is to link them with a comma and a coordinating conjunction: *and, but, or, nor.* (See 19a-1.)

The changes in *Homo erectus* are substantial over a million years, *but* they seem gradual by comparison with those that went before.

A computer's data and addressing information are stored in flip-flops within the various memory registers, *or* they take the form of an electrical signal that is moving through wires from one register to another.

OPTIONS: You have several options for linking independent clauses: (1) you can separate the clauses and form two distinct sentences—see 24a; (2) you can use a semicolon to link the clauses within one sentence—see 26a,b; (3) you can make one clause subordinate to another—see 19b.

NOTE: When a coordinate conjunction joins two independent clauses, and when one or both of these clauses has internal punctuation, to prevent misreading change the comma appearing before the conjunction to a semicolon.

> Several thousand years ago, probably some lines of Neanderthal man and woman died out; but it seems likely that a line in the Middle East went directly to us, *Homo sapiens.*

25c Using commas between items in a series

One major function of the comma is to signal a brief pause that separates items in a series—a string of related elements.

1 Place a comma between items in a series.

Items joined in a series should be parallel. (See chapter 18.) Items can be single words, phrases, or clauses.

WORDS   A Central Processing Unit contains a large number of special-purpose registers for storing *instructions, addresses, and data.*

PHRASES   Booms and busts have plagued economic activity since the onset of industrialization, *sporadically ejecting many workers from their jobs, pushing many businesses into bankruptcy, and leaving many politicians out in the cold.*

OPTION: Some writers prefer to omit the final comma in a series—the comma placed before the coordinate conjunction *and.* The choice is yours. Whatever your preference, be consistent.

OPTION   Exercise appears *to reduce the desire to smoke, to lessen any tendency toward obesity, and to help in managing stress.*

NOTE: When at least one item in a series contains a comma, use a semicolon to separate items and prevent misreading. (See chapter 26.) For the same reason, use semicolons to separate long independent clauses in a series.

> I believe that the sun is about ninety-three million miles from the earth; that it is a hot globe many times bigger than the earth; and that, owing to the earth's rotation, it rises every morning and will continue to do so for an indefinite time in the future.

25c

∧
,

2 Place a comma between two or more coordinate adjectives in a series, if no coordinate conjunction joins them.

A series of adjectives will often appear as a parallel sequence: the *playful, amusing* poet; an *intelligent, engaging* speaker. When the order of the adjectives can be reversed without affecting the meaning of the noun being modified, the adjectives are called **coordinate adjectives.** Coordinate adjectives can be linked by a comma or by a coordinate conjunction.

SERIES WITH COMMAS

The stomach is a thick-walled, muscular sac that can expand to hold more than 2 liters of food or liquid.

SERIES WITH *AND*

The stomach is a thick-walled *and* muscular sac that can expand to hold more than 2 liters of food or liquid.

SERIES WITH COMMAS

The left hemisphere of the brain thinks sequential, analytical thoughts and is also the center of language.

SERIES WITH *AND*

The left hemisphere thinks sequential *and* analytical thoughts and is also the center of language.

NOTE: The presence of two adjectives beside one other does not necessarily mean that they are coordinate. In the phrase "the wise old lady," the adjectives could not be reversed in sequence or joined by *and;* the adjective *wise* describes *old lady,* not *lady* alone. The same analysis holds for the phrase "the ugly green car." *Green car* is the element being modified by *ugly.* Only coordinate adjectives modifying the same noun are separated by commas.

25c

∧
,

EXERCISE 2

Combine the following sentences with the conjunction indicated in brackets, and decide whether you need to use a comma. Recall that unless a conjunction joins independent clauses, no comma is needed.

Example: Anthropologists are currently investigating whether or not early hominids (proto-humans) ate meat. [and] Did they obtain meat by hunting or scavenging?

Anthropologists are currently investigating whether or not early hominids (proto-humans) ate meat and whether they obtained it by hunting or scavenging.

1. Proto-humans did not walk as well on two feet as we do. They were better than we are at climbing trees and suspending themselves from branches.

2. Ancestors of present-day leopards were contemporary with early hominids. [and] Ancestors of present-day leopards shared the same habitats as early hominids.
3. Leopards cannot defend their kills from scavenging by lions. [so] They store their kills in trees.
4. Archaeologist John Cavallo thinks that early tree-climbing hominids may have fed off leopard kills stashed in trees. [since] Leopards don't guard the carcasses of their kills.

EXERCISE 3

Decide whether the following sentences need commas between adjectives.

Example: Many compelling larger-than-life people figure in the drama of Columbus's "discovery" of America.

Many compelling, larger-than-life people figure in the drama of Columbus's "discovery" of America.

1. Columbus described Native Americans as well-built handsome people.
2. He also reported they were friendly and well dispositioned.
3. Native American culture had not achieved the political and economic sophistication of Western civilization.
4. Yet many Native American civilizations were complex and steeped in richly articulated religious practices.
5. Native Americans were ill equipped to resist the onslaught of a highly individualistic technologically superior civilization.

EXERCISE 4

25c

∧
,

In each sentence, place a comma as needed between items in a series.

Example: Native American societies were based on notions of community mutual obligations and reciprocity and on close ties of kin.

Native American societies were based on notions of community, mutual obligation, and reciprocity and on close ties of kin.

1. They possessed complex religious beliefs symbolic world views radically different from those of Europeans and cultural values Europeans did not understand.
2. Like other native populations "discovered" after them, Native Americans were exploited decimated by exotic diseases robbed of their lands and ultimately stripped of their traditional cultures.
3. Survivors became serfs slaves or subordinate and often tangential elements in the new social order.
4. Therefore, for centuries Native Americans continued to resist Catholic missionaries explorers and settlers from all over Europe.

25d Using commas to set off nonessential elements

1 Identifying essential (restrictive) elements that need no commas

When a modifier provides information necessary for identifying a word, then the modifier is said to be **essential** (or **restrictive**), and it appears in its sentence *without* commas.

> The Vatican theologian *charged with responding to scientific challenges* wanted to suppress the work of Galileo and Copernicus.

There have been many theologians in the Vatican. This sentence refers to the *one* theologian responsible for answering scientific challenges. Without the modifying phrase *charged with responding to scientific challenges,* the subject of this sentence, *the Vatican theologian,* could not be conclusively identified. Therefore, the modifying expression is essential, and no commas are used to set apart the phrase from the sentence in which it appears.

An essential modifier can also be a single word (or single name).

> The Apollo astronaut *Jim Irwin* has devoted a great deal of time and expense to proving the existence of Noah's Ark.

Without the name *Jim Irwin,* we would not know which of the Apollo astronauts has been hunting for Noah's Ark. By contrast, consider the following sentence.

> The first man on the moon, Neil Armstrong, was famous as a pilot who would stay with his craft until the last possible moment.

In this sentence, the modifying information—also the name of an astronaut—is no longer essential because there was only one *first* man on the moon. Thus *Neil Armstrong* is considered nonessential information and is set off by a pair of commas.

An essential modifier can also be a clause.

> The cyclotron is an instrument *that accelerates charged particles to very high speeds.*

The noun modified—*instrument*—could be *any* instrument, and the clause that follows provides information essential to the definition of *which* or *what kind* of instrument.

2 Use a pair of commas to set off nonessential (nonrestrictive) elements.

If a word being modified is clearly defined (as, for instance, a person with a specific name is clearly defined), then the modifying element—though it might add interesting and useful information—is nonessential. When the modifier is not essential for defining a word, use commas to set the modifier apart from the sentence in which it appears.

NONESSENTIAL   Cardinal Bellarmine, *the Vatican theologian charged with responding to scientific challenges,* wanted to suppress the work of Galileo and Copernicus.

The subject of the sentence has already been adequately defined by his name, *Cardinal Bellarmine.* The writer uses the modifying phrase not as a matter of definition but as an occasion to add nonessential information. The meaning of a sentence will change according to whether modifying elements are punctuated as essential or nonessential. The two pairs of sentences that follow are worded identically. Punctuation gives them different meanings.

ESSENTIAL   The miners *who went on strike* gained the support of local newspapers.

NONESSENTIAL   The miners, *who went on strike,* gained the support of local newspapers.

ESSENTIAL   The local newspapers supported the miners *who went on strike.*

NONESSENTIAL   The local newspapers supported the miners, *who went on strike.*

Punctuating Modifying Clauses with *Which, Who,* and *That*

The relative pronouns *who, which,* and *that* begin modifying clauses that can interrupt or end sentences.

WHO
Who can begin a clause that is essential to defining the word modified.

> Formal organizations designate managers *who help administrative units meet their specific goals.*

Who can also begin a nonessential clause. Note the presence of commas in this sentence.

> Frank Smith, *who is an administrative manager,* helps his administrative unit meet its goals.

WHICH
Similarly, *which* can begin an essential or a nonessential modifying clause.

> Two sites *which flourished in the dim yet documented past* are Saxon London and medieval Winchester. [essential]
>
> Some historical archaeologists excavate sites like Saxon London or medieval Winchester, *which flourished in the dim yet documented past.* [nonessential]

THAT
That always denotes an essential clause. Do not use commas to set off a modifying clause beginning with *that.*

> Two sites *that flourished in the dim yet documented past* are Saxon London and medieval Winchester. [essential]

25d

∧
,

The essential modifiers precisely define *which* miners gained the support of the newspapers—*only* those who went on strike. The meaning, then, is that not all of the miners struck. The nonessential modifiers communicate that *all* of the miners struck, and all gained the support of the local newspapers.

3 Use commas to set off parenthetical or repeating elements.

By definition, a parenthetical remark is not essential to the meaning of a sentence. The remark sometimes illuminates the sentence but by no means provides crucial information. Set off parenthetical expressions as you would any nonessential element.

> Revolutionary Boston, *where it was easy to collect a crowd,* became a center of agitation.

OPTIONS: You have the choice of setting off parenthetical elements by using commas, parentheses, or dashes. Any of these options is correct, so base your decision on the level of emphasis you wish to give the parenthetical element. Dashes call the most attention to the element and parentheses the least attention.

Repeating elements

Repetition can both add useful information to a sentence and create pleasing sentence rhythms. By definition, a repeating element is nonessential, so the logic of setting off nonessential elements with commas applies. Set off a repeating element with a *pair* of commas if the element appears in the middle of a sentence. (You may also use a pair of dashes.) Use a comma or a dash and a period if the element concludes the sentence.

> Samuel Adams, *a master of propaganda and mob tactics,* was clever at creating a sensation out of every incident and blaming it all on the British.

> Archaeologists working underwater have exactly the same intellectual goals as their dry-land colleagues—*to recover, reconstruct, and interpret the past.*

> These bare facts have become so familiar, *so essential in the conduct of an interlocking world society,* that they are usually taken for granted.

Appositives

One class of repeating element is called an **appositive phrase,** the function of which is to rename a noun. The phrase is called *appositive* because it is placed in *apposition* to—that is, *side by side* with—the noun it repeats. In the first example, the appositive *a master of propaganda and mob tactics* renames Samuel Adams. The sentence could be rewritten, and repunctuated, as follows.

> *A master of propaganda and mob tactics,* Samuel Adams was clever at creating a sensation out of every incident and blaming it all on the British.

EXCEPTION: When a nonessential appositive phrase consists of a series of items separated by commas, set it off from a sentence with a pair of dashes—not commas—to prevent misreading.

CONFUSING Motion sickness, nausea, dizziness, and sleepiness, is a dangerous and common malady among astronauts.

REVISED Motion sickness—nausea, dizziness, and sleepiness—is a dangerous and common malady among astronauts.

EXERCISE 5

The following sentences include (italicized) modifying phrases or clauses. In a sentence or two, explain the presence or absence of commas in these sentences.

> *Example:* Rock 'n roll, *the dominant popular music form of the last thirty-five years,* has had a profound impact on American culture.
>
> The modifying phrase provides interesting but not essential information. Without the phrase, the sentence is perfectly understandable, since everyone knows what rock 'n roll is.

1. Rock's assimilation of black music and performers into a mainstream art form contributed *in crucial but not often noted ways* to desegregation.
2. In addition rock created a powerful youth culture, *which visibly rebelled against its elders.*
3. Movies and other forms of popular culture during the 1930s, 1940s, and 1950s presented a highly idealized, romanticized picture *of family and national life in America.*
4. Teenagers in the 1950s, *who had to confront an increasingly atomized family life and domestic and international tensions,* scorned this sterile version of American life.

25d

∧
,

EXERCISE 6

Combine the following pairs of sentences. Use commas to set off nonessential modifiers and omit commas when modifiers are essential.

> *Example:* Elvis Presley was a "white boy from across the tracks."
>
> Elvis Presley was a symbol of rebellion in popular music.
>
> Elvis Presley, a "white boy from across the tracks," was a symbol of rebellion in popular music.

1. In the 1950s three films depicted youthful criminals as alienated loners and contributed to teenagers' sense of themselves as different. These three films also influenced the "look" of rock 'n roll.
2. The first film, *City Across the River* (1951), dealt with youth gangs in Brooklyn. It starred Tony Curtis as a hard but honest youth.
3. Curtis's hairstyle started a major trend. Curtis wore his hair in a perfectly sculpted, swept back pompadour later copied by Elvis.

4. The second film, *The Wild One,* featured Marlon Brando as a laconic, distant, rebellious, but ultimately honorable motorcycle gang leader. Brando's character was infinitely more attractive than the ignorant, weak, or brutal adults he had to deal with.

5. James Dean starred in the last of the three films, *Rebel Without a Cause.* The film focused on an alienated teenager trying to find his own truth in a world where adults provide little guidance.

6. Dean's performance electrified the nation, especially teenagers. His performance derived its power from the same rebelliousness that fueled rock 'n roll.

7. Elvis saw *Rebel Without a Cause* more than a dozen times. Elvis could recite whole passages from *Rebel Without a Cause.*

25e Using commas to acknowledge conventions of quoting, naming, and various forms of separation

1   Use a comma to introduce or to complete a quotation.

Commas set a quotation apart from the words that introduce or conclude the quotation. Commas (and periods) are placed *inside* end quotation marks.

The prizefighter Rocky Graziano once said, "I had to leave fourth grade because of pneumonia—not because I had it but because I couldn't spell it."

Early in his career, Winston Churchill sported a mustache. At a fancy dinner, he argued with a woman who snapped, "Young man—I care for neither your politics nor your mustache."
  "Madam," responded Churchill, "you are unlikely to come into contact with either."

(For more on using commas with quotations, see chapter 28.)

2   Use a comma to set off expressions of direct address. If the expression interrupts a sentence, set the word off with a *pair* of commas.

You will most often encounter expressions of direct address when writing dialogue or when quoting speakers addressing their audiences.

"You, Sir, have the sense of a baboon."

"Paul, run to the exit."

"Run to the exit, Paul."

My fellow citizens, I come before you with a heavy heart.

I come before you, my fellow citizens, with a heavy heart.

25e

∧
,

3 Use a comma to mark the omission of words in a balanced sentence.

Sentences are balanced when identical clause constructions are doubled or tripled in a series. So that repeating words in the clauses do not become tedious to a reader, omit these words and note the omission with a comma.

Some southern novelists attribute the character of their fiction to the South's losing the Civil War; others, to the region's special blending of climate and race; and still others, to the salubrious powers of mint juleps.

In this example, the comma and the word *others* substitute for *some southern novelists attribute the character of their fiction.*

 4 Place a comma between paired "more/less" constructions.

Some constructions involve a paired comparison of "more" of one element contrasted against "more" or "less" of another. Separate these elements with a comma to maintain a clear relationship between them.

The more wires a data base contains, the greater the number of bits it can move at a time.

The more some people get, the less they are willing to give.

5 Use a comma to set off tag questions that conclude a sentence.

A **tag question,** a brief question "tagged on" to a statement addressed to someone, should be set off from that statement. Tags are used for a variety of purposes, at times to suggest indecision or hesitancy.

This is the right house, isn't it?

You slipped into the office and read that letter, didn't you?

I have reached the only possible conclusion, haven't I?

25e

∧
,

 6 Use a comma to set off yes/no remarks and mild exclamations.

"Yes, I'll call him right away."

"Oh well, I can put it off for another day."

7 Use commas according to convention in names, titles, dates, numbers, and addresses.

Commas with names and titles

Place a comma directly after a name if it is followed by a title.

Mr. Joe Smith, Executive Editor

Ms. Ann Jacobs, Senior Vice President

Lucy Turner, Ph.D.

Mr. Frank Reynolds, Esq.

Set off a title in commas when writing a sentence.

Mr. Joe Smith, Executive Editor, signed for the package.

Lucy Turner, Ph.D., delivered the commencement address.

Mr. Robert Jones, Sr., attended the ceremony.

Commas with dates

Place a comma between the day of the month and year. If your reference is to a particular month in a year and no date is mentioned, do not use a comma.

January 7, 1992   but   January 1992

When a date is written out, as in an invitation, use the following convention.

the seventh of January, 1992

No commas are used in the military convention for writing dates.

7 January 1992

If you include a day of the week when writing a date, use the following convention.

The package will be delivered on Thursday, January 7, 1992.

Commas with numbers

Place a comma to denote thousands, millions, and so forth.

543   5,430   54,300   543,000   5,430,000   5,430,000,000

Some writers place no comma in four-digit numbers that are multiples of fifty.

2550   1600   but   1,625

Do *not* use commas when writing phone numbers, addresses, page numbers, or years.

Commas with addresses

When writing an address, place a comma between a city (or county) and state.

Baltimore, Maryland   Baltimore County, Maryland

Place no comma between a state and zip code.

Baltimore, Maryland 21215

When writing an address into a sentence, use commas to set off elements that would otherwise be placed on separate lines of the address.

Mr. Abe Stein, Senior Engineer
Stein Engineering
1243 Slade Avenue
Bedford, Massachusetts 01730

The control boards were shipped to Mr. Abe Stein, Senior Engineer, Stein Engineering, 1243 Slade Avenue, Bedford, Massachusetts 01730.

8   **Use commas to prevent misreading.**

Although no rule calls for it, a comma may be needed to prevent misreading. Misreading can occur when numbers are placed together.

| CONFUSING | Down by twenty six members of the squad suddenly woke up. |
| REVISED | Down by twenty, six members of the squad suddenly woke up. |

Misreading can occur when words that are often used as auxiliary verbs (e.g., *will, should,* forms of *to be, to do*) function as main verbs and occur before other verbs.

| CONFUSING | Those who do know exactly what must be done. |
| REVISED | Those who do, know exactly what must be done. |

Misreading can occur when a word that functions both as a preposition and as a modifier (e.g., *after, before, along, around, beneath, through*) is used as a modifier and is followed by a noun.

| CONFUSING | Moments after the room began to tilt. |
| REVISED | Moments after, the room began to tilt. |

Misreading can occur when identical words are placed together.

| CONFUSING | To speak speak into the microphone and press the button. |
| REVISED | To speak, speak into the microphone and press the button. |

25e

$\wedge$
,

EXERCISE 7

Supply the missing commas in the following sentences.

Example: Colette France's best-known woman writer of the twentieth century remarked of her honeymoon "My life as a woman began with this buccaneer a serious match for a country girl."

Colette, France's best-known woman writer of the twentieth century, remarked of her honeymoon, "My life as a woman began with this buccaneer, a serious match for a country girl."

1. A very poetic writer Colette described her birthplace as "a large house solemn somewhat forbidding . . . a house that only smiled on its garden side."
2. "What a pity" Colette's mother once wrote of Colette's father "that he should have loved me so much! It was his love for me that destroyed one after another all his splendid abilities."
3. Engaged at eighteen to a man twice her age Colette noted "the infatuation of a girl in love is neither as constant nor as blind as she tries to believe."
4. "It was a quiet and modest wedding" Colette noted of her nuptials. "I looked quite nice and was rather pale."

EXERCISE 8

Use commas in the following sentences to set off words of direct address or tag questions.

Example: "Dad asked you to shovel the walk didn't he?"

"Dad asked you to shovel the walk, didn't he?"

1. "Frank close the door will you?"
2. "Sir I entreat you to reconsider."
3. "My dear fellow you will reconsider won't you?"
4. "Mrs. Gorbachev do you prefer Barbara Bush to Nancy Reagan or not?"
5. "It's a scorcher isn't it?"

EXERCISE 9

Decide whether commas are needed to clarify meaning in these sentences. Then make up three sentences of your own in which adding a comma will prevent misreading.

1. If you can come join us.
2. The doctor dressed and performed an emergency appendectomy.
3. The doctor dressed and sutured the wound.
4. From beneath the supports began to weaken.
5. By *two*s twenty children walked down the aisle.

25f Editing to avoid misuse or overuse of commas

1 Eliminate the comma splice.

The most frequent comma blunder, the **comma splice,** occurs when a writer joins independent clauses with a comma.

FAULTY   Christopher Columbus is considered a master navigator today, he died in neglect.

To revise a comma splice, see the accompanying box and also chapter 13.

Four Ways to Avoid Comma Splices

1. Separate the two clauses with a period.

   Christopher Columbus is considered a master navigator today. He died in neglect.

2. Join the two clauses with a coordinate conjunction and a comma.

   Christopher Columbus is considered a master navigator today, but he died in neglect.

3. Join the two clauses with a conjunctive adverb and the appropriate punctuation.

   Christopher Columbus is considered a master navigator today; nevertheless, he died in neglect.

4. Join the two clauses by making one subordinate to the other.

   Although Christopher Columbus is considered a master navigator today, he died in neglect.

---

2 Eliminate commas misused to set off essential (restrictive) elements.

As noted in 25d-1, commas are not used with essential elements. The presence of commas can alter the meaning of otherwise identical sentences. Therefore, be sure of your meaning as you decide to punctuate (or not) a modifying element.

25f

ESSENTIAL   The students who signed the petition are eligible. [The *who* clause is essential and restricts the meaning of students to those who signed the petition.]

NONESSENTIAL   The students, who signed the petition, are eligible. [The presence of commas signals that the *who* clause is nonessential. The sense of the sentence is that *all* the students signed the petition and are eligible.]

3 Eliminate commas that are misused in a series.

A comma is not placed before a coordinate conjunction if it connects only two elements in a series.

FAULTY   You cannot learn much about prices, and the amounts of goods traded from demand curves alone.

REVISED   You cannot learn much about prices and the amount of goods traded from demand curves alone.

A comma is *not* used after a second coordinate adjective.

FAULTY   One reason individuals engage in various efforts at self-improvement is that they can imagine alternate, improved, selves.

REVISED   One reason individuals engage in various efforts at self-improvement is that they can imagine alternate, improved selves.

A comma is not placed before the first item in a series or after the last item, unless the comma is required because of a specific rule.

FAULTY   A Central Processing Unit (CPU) is designed with a fixed repertoire of instructions for carrying out a range of tests involving, data manipulation, logical decision making, and control of the computer. [The comma should be eliminated before the first item in this series.]

REVISED   A Central Processing Unit (CPU) is designed with a fixed repertoire of instructions for carrying out a range of tests involving data manipulation, logical decision making, and control of the computer.

4   Eliminate commas that split paired sentence elements.

A comma is not placed between a subject and verb—even if the subject is a lengthy one.

FAULTY   What has sometimes been dramatically termed "the clash of civilizations," is merely the difference in the interpretation given by different societies to the same acts. [The noun clause subject should not be split from its verb *is*.]

25f

REVISED   What has sometimes been dramatically termed "the clash of civilizations" is merely the difference in the interpretation given by different societies to the same acts.

A comma is not placed between a verb and its object or complement, nor between a preposition and its object.

FAULTY   One culture may organize, its social relations around rites of physical initiation. [The comma should not come between the verb and its object.]

REVISED   One culture may organize its social relations around rites of physical initiation.

FAULTY   The principle of mutual respect among, neighboring peoples requires flexibility and tolerance. [The comma should not come between the preposition and its object.]

REVISED   The principle of mutual respect among neighboring peoples requires flexibility and tolerance.

5 Eliminate misuse of commas with quotations.

A comma is not used after a quotation that ends with a question mark or an exclamation point.

FAULTY   "Get out!," cried the shopkeeper.

REVISED   "Get out!" cried the shopkeeper.

FAULTY   "Is this the way home?," asked Arthur.

REVISED   "Is this the way home?" asked Arthur.

A comma is not used to set apart words quoted (or italicized) for emphasis.

FAULTY   The list of, "exemplary," citizens the Governor referred to includes two convicted felons.

REVISED   The list of "exemplary" citizens the Governor referred to includes two convicted felons.

EXERCISE 10

Supply the commas for this dialogue between a young child and her nurse, adapted from Amy Tan's *The Joy Luck Club*.

> I tugged Amah's sleeve and asked "Who is the Moon Lady?"
> "Chang-o" replied Amah "who lives on the moon and today is the only day you can see her and have a secret wish fulfilled."
> "What is a secret wish?" I asked her.
> "It is what you want but cannot ask" said Amah.
> "Then how will the Moon Lady know my wish?" I wanted to know.
> "Because she is not an ordinary person" Amah explained.

EXERCISE 11

Correct the misuse of commas in the sentences that follow (from a parody of an anthropological study). Place a check before the sentences in which commas are used correctly.

> *Example:* The daily body ritual, performed by the Nacirema people includes a mouth-rite.
>
> The daily body ritual performed by the Nacirema people includes a mouth-rite.

1. Despite the fact that these people are so punctilious about the care of the mouth, this rite involves, a practice which strikes the uninitiated stranger as revolting.
2. It was reported to me that the ritual consists of inserting a small bundle of hog hairs into the mouth, along with certain magical powders, and then moving the bundle in a highly formalized series of gestures.

25f

∧
,

3. In addition to the private mouth-rite, the people seek out a holy-mouth-man once, or twice a year.
4. These practitioners have an impressive set of paraphernalia, consisting of a variety of, augers, awls, probes, and prods.
5. The use of these objects in the exorcism of the evils of the mouth involves, almost unbelievable ritual torture of the client.
6. The holy-mouth-man opens the client's mouth and, using the above mentioned tools, enlarges any holes which decay may have created in the teeth.
7. Magical materials are put into, these holes.
8. If there are no naturally occurring holes in the teeth, large sections of one or more teeth are gouged out so that the supernatural substance, can be applied.
9. In the client's view, the purpose of these ministrations is to arrest decay, and to draw friends.
10. The extremely sacred and traditional character of the rite is evident in the fact that the natives return to the holy-mouth-men year after year, despite the fact that their teeth continue to decay.

25f

$\wedge$
,

CHAPTER 26

Semicolons

The main function of a **semicolon** is to separate elements. But as its name suggests, the semicolon serves to make only a "semi" or partial separation that maintains a relationship between independent elements. In its primary use, a semicolon can mark the end of one complete thought and the beginning of another. So can a period or a comma with a coordinating conjunction, of course. But whereas a period is chosen to make a full stop, a semicolon denotes a writer's decision to make a partial break. This chapter shows you the situations in which such a partial break is appropriate and gives you the tools for making such decisions as you write or revise your sentences.

 Use a semicolon, not a comma, to join independent clauses that are intended to be closely related.

26a

Joining independent clauses with a semicolon is one of four basic ways to establish a relationship between clauses, ranging from full separation to subordination of one clause to another. (See the following box.) If the independent clauses are not joined by a comma and a coordinating conjunction (as in Pattern B), a semicolon can be used between the clauses to make a close connection. A comma should never be used to join independent clauses. (See chapter 13 on comma splices.)

FAULTY   Agriculture is one part of the biological revolution, the domestication and harnessing of village animals is the other.

REVISED   Agriculture is one part of the biological revolution; the domestication and harnessing of village animals is the other.

Use semicolons to join closely related independent clauses, not to string unconnected statements together.

Semicolons can be overused. By themselves, they are not enough to make close connections from a series of statements that are simply added together.

OVERUSED   Agriculture was the first part of the biological revolution; the development of crop rotation and irrigation contributed to it; another important part was the harnessing of village animals. [The semicolons add pieces together but do not make the statements closely related.]

REVISED   Agriculture, the first part of the biological revolution, was aided by the development of crop rotation and irrigation. There was also another part of the revolution; this was the harnessing of village animals. [The semicolon joins only closely related statements.]

Linking Clauses—Why Choose the Semicolon?

There are four ways to establish a relationship between clauses.

Pattern A—a closely related separation.
Independent clauses linked by a semicolon:

> Agriculture is one part of the biological revolution; the domestication and harnessing of village animals is the other.

Pattern B—a simple joining of clauses.
Independent clauses linked by a comma and a coordinating conjunction:

> Agriculture is one part of the biological revolution, *and* the domestication and harnessing of village animals is the other.

Pattern C—a full separation of clauses.
Independent clauses separated by a period:

> Agriculture is one part of the biological revolution. The domestication and harnessing of village animals is the other.

Pattern D—one clause dependent on another.
Dependent clause linked by a subordinating conjunction and a comma:

> *While* agriculture is one part of the biological revolution, the domestication and harnessing of village animals is another.

In Pattern D, the subordinate conjunction *while* signals that the first clause is dependent on the second. In Pattern B, the coordinate conjunction *and* establishes the two clauses as equal, but the relationship between clauses is a matter of simple addition. Pattern A uses a semicolon to show that although the clauses are of equal value they are closely related; the semicolon gives a subtle suggestion of unfinished business to follow.

Use a semicolon, not a comma, to join two independent clauses that are closely linked by a conjunctive adverb.

26b

A conjunctive adverb is often used to establish a close connection between independent clauses. (See chapter 19.) With conjunctive adverbs, use a semicolon (or a period) between the clauses, never a comma. (Refer to chapter 13.)

FAULTY   Historical researchers cannot control the events they want to recreate, indeed, they often cannot find enough documentation to learn all the facts of an occurrence. [The comma after *recreate* makes a comma splice; a comma cannot be used to join independent clauses.]

REVISED   Historical researchers cannot control the events they want to recreate; indeed, they often cannot find enough documentation to learn all the facts of an occurrence. [Here the conjunctive adverb creates a very close link between clauses.]

NOTE: When independent clauses are closely connected with a conjunctive adverb, the semicolon always falls between the clauses, no matter where the conjunctive adverb is located.

OPTION: If chlorophyll is extracted from plant cells and exposed to light, it does momentarily absorb light energy; *however*, this energy is almost immediately reradiated as light.

OPTION: If chlorophyll is extracted from plant cells and exposed to light, it does momentarily absorb light energy; this energy is almost immediately reradiated as light, *however*. [The semicolon falls between the independent clauses, even if the adverb is moved to the end of the sentence.]

26b

;

NOTE: The use of a conjunctive adverb does not necessarily mean that there must be a semicolon between clauses. If you feel that the business of the first clause is finished, or that you do not need a sense of anticipation for the next clause, you can always make a full break between clauses with a period.

OPTION: If chlorophyll is extracted from plant cells and exposed to light, it does momentarily absorb light energy. This energy, however, is almost immediately reradiated as light, usually of a different wavelength. [Here the writer intends for the period to mark a sharp boundary between clauses.]

26c Join independent clauses with a semicolon before a coordinate conjunction when one or both clauses contain a comma or other internal punctuation.

Short or uncomplicated independent clauses joined by coordinating conjunctions do not normally use a semicolon. However, internal commas or complicated subordinations within one of the independent clauses can create confusion and misreading; in such cases the clauses need stronger separation with a semicolon before the coordinating conjunction.

> Gorbachev came to power relatively ill-prepared, both by personal temperament and by previous political experience, to deal with the nationalities in question; and he was clearly impatient that such intensely emotional, indeed irrational, sentiments could divert attention from the larger struggle over reform.

 26d Use a semicolon to separate items in a series when each item is long or when one or more items contain a comma.

Short or uncomplicated items in a series are normally separated only by commas (see chapter 25). However, when the units to be separated are further subdivided with internal punctuation or are made up of complex clauses, it is necessary to provide stronger separation with a semicolon.

> Several issues have concerned Gorbachev: the extent to which the national republics in the Soviet federation should enjoy real sovereignty; the legal status of the Baltic republics, annexed as a result of the Molotov-Ribbentrop pact; and the criteria for allocating resources among the regions of the USSR.

26e

; /quot

 26e Place semicolons *outside* of end quotation marks.

A semicolon that separates independent clauses and other major elements is not part of a direct quotation.

> According to political scientist Gail Lapidus, "Traditional assumptions about life in the Soviet Union are now being directly challenged in public debates"; such debates unquestionably complicate Gorbachev's efforts at political and economic reform.

26f Edit to avoid common errors.

1 Use a comma, not a semicolon, after an introductory subordinate clause.

Use semicolons to link independent clauses; never use them to link subordinate to independent clauses. (See chapter 19.)

FAULTY   When a writer begins a new project; the blank page can present a barrier.

REVISED   When a writer begins a new project, the blank page can present a barrier.

2 Use a colon, not a semicolon, to introduce a list.

FAULTY   The writing process consists of three stages; planning, drafting, and revision.

REVISED   The writing process consists of three stages: planning, drafting, and revision.

EXERCISE 1

Join the following pairs of sentences with a semicolon, with a semicolon and conjunctive adverb, or with a period and conjunctive adverb. Explain your decision.

> *Example:* Politics and social realism have not been the hallmarks of the film industry in Hollywood.
>
> Yet there was a time when liberal, conservative, and radical organizations made films for a mass audience aimed at politicizing millions of viewers.
>
> Politics and social realism have not been the hallmarks of the film industry in Hollywood; yet there was a time when liberal, conservative, and radical organizations made films for a mass audience aimed at politicizing millions of viewers.

26f

no ;

The sentences are closely enough related in meaning to warrant their being joined into a single, compound sentence. For this reason, the semicolon is appropriate. The conjunction *yet* is kept to establish the contrasting relationship between clauses. Without the conjunction this relationship might not be obvious to a reader.

1. During the early years of the twentieth century, leisure assumed an increasingly important role in everyday life.
   Amusement parks, professional baseball games, nickelodeons, and dance halls attracted a wide array of people anxious to spend their hard-earned cash.

2. Of all these new cultural endeavors, films were the most important. Even the poorest worker could afford to take his family to the local movie theater.

3. Cinemas took root in urban working-class and immigrant neighborhoods.
   They then spread to middle-class districts of cities and into small communities throughout the country.

4. As early as 1910 the appeal of movies was so great that nearly one-third of the nation flocked to the cinema each week.
   Ten years later, weekly attendance equalled fifty percent of the nation's population.

5. As is true today, early films were primarily aimed at entertaining audiences.
   But then, entertainment did not always come in the form of escapist fantasies.

6. Many of the issues that dominated Progressive-era politics were portrayed on the screen.
   While most of these films were produced by studios and independent companies, a significant number were made by what we might call today "special interest groups."

7. The modest cost of making one- or two-reel films allowed many organizations to make movies to advance their causes.
   Moreover, exhibitors' need to fill their daily bills with new films meant these films would be seen by millions.

EXERCISE 2

In very long sentences semicolons are used in place of commas to prevent misreading. Combine, repunctuate, or otherwise revise the following sentences by using semicolons.

26f

no ;

Example: The traditional view of the diffusion of Indo-European languages over wide areas holds that as nomadic mounted warriors conquered indigenous peoples, they imposed their own proto-Indo-European language, *which,* in turn, evolved in local areas into the various languages we know today.

But many scholars have become dissatisfied with this explanation.

The traditional view of the diffusion of Indo-European languages over wide areas holds that as nomadic mounted warriors conquered indigenous peoples, they imposed their own proto-Indo-European language; *this language,* in turn, evolved in local areas into the various languages we know today. But many scholars have become dissatisfied with this explanation.

1. Linguists divide the languages of Europe into families: the Romance languages include French, Italian, Spanish, Portuguese and Romanian.

The Slavonic languages include Russian, Polish, Czech, Slovak, Serbo-Croat and Bulgarian. The Germanic languages include German, Norwegian, Danish and Swedish.

2. Many archaeologists accept a theory of "Kurgan invasions" as an explanation of the spread of Indo-European languages.
   But others dispute it because the archaeological evidence is not convincing, the core words, which resemble each other from place to place, may have changed meaning over time, and the hordes of mounted warriors would have had no obvious reason for moving west at the end of the Neolithic period.

3. There are four models of how language change might occur according to a process-based view: initial colonization, by which an uninhabited territory becomes populated, linguistic divergence arising from separation or isolation, which some think explains the development of the Romance languages in Europe, linguistic convergence, whereby languages initially quite different become increasingly similar to each other, and, finally, linguistic replacement, whereby indigenous languages are gradually replaced by the language of people coming from the outside.

EXERCISE 3

Correct the misuse of semicolons and, if necessary, the wording in the following sentences. Place a check by any sentence in which a semicolon is used correctly.

> *Example:* Freud remarks in his lecture on the interpretation of dreams that dreams can tell us about the self hidden from conscious view; that they provide unique raw materials for analysis.
>
> Freud remarks in his lecture on the interpretation of dreams that dreams can tell us about the self hidden from conscious view *and* that they provide unique raw materials for analysis.

26f

no ;

1. For Freud, what the dreamer remembers of a dream is not in itself important; it is a substitute for something not immediately available to the person dreaming; just as "slips of the tongue" are spoken for reasons not immediately understood by a speaker.

2. Freud prefers to call what is "hidden" in our psyches as that which is "inaccessible to the consciousness of the dreamer;" that is to say, what is hidden exists and is real but is unconscious at the moment.

3. A dream as a whole is a distorted substitute for something else, something unconscious; and it is the task of dream interpretation to discover these unconscious thoughts.

4. Freud claims we should not concern ourselves with the surface meaning of a dream; whether it be reasonable or absurd, clear or confused; since it does not in any way constitute the unconscious thoughts of the dreamer; which is what the interpreter really seeks.

CHAPTER 27

Apostrophes

The **apostrophe** (') is used to show possession, mark the omission of letters or numbers, and mark plural forms. In speech, keeping these matters straight poses no problem. In writing, however, the three uses of the apostrophe very nearly overlap with certain words, creating confusion for the reader. Therefore, try to distinguish carefully among the uses of the apostrophe.

27a Using apostrophes to show possession with single nouns

1 For most nouns and for indefinite pronouns, add an apostrophe and the letter *s* to indicate possession.

Bill's braces	the government's solution
history's verdict	somebody's cat
Susan's basketball	everyone's business

For singular nouns ending with the letter *s, show possession by adding an apostrophe and s if this new construction is not difficult to pronounce.*

Ellis's Diner   hostess's menu   Orson Welles's movie

NOTE: The possessive construction formed with 's may be difficult to read if it is followed by a word beginning with an *s* or *z* sound. If this is the case, you have the option of dropping the *s* after the apostrophe.

ACCEPTABLE Ellis' zipper   or   Ellis's zipper

Whichever convention you adopt, be consistent.

2 Eliminate apostrophes that are misused or confused with possessive pronouns.

Personal pronouns have their own possessive case forms (see chapters 7 and 8); they *never* use apostrophes to show possession.

POSSESSION WITH PERSONAL PRONOUNS

its	the book's binding	*its* binding
whose	Who owns the book?	*Whose* book is this?
your	the book owned by you	*your* book
yours	the book owned by you	The book is *yours.*
their	a book owned by Bob and Sue	*their* book
theirs	a book owned by Bob and Sue	The book is *theirs.*
her	a book owned by Sue	*her* book
hers	a book owned by Sue	The book is *hers.*
our	a book owned by us	*our* book
ours	a book owned by us	The book is *ours.*
his	a book owned by Bob	*his* book
his	a book owned by Bob	The book is *his.*

Distinguish personal pronouns in their possessive form from personal pronouns that are contractions.

For readers, the most annoying possible mixup with apostrophes occurs when personal pronouns meant to show possession are confused with personal pronouns that are contractions formed with the verb *be*, as shown here. (See the guidelines for making contractions in 27c.)

PERSONAL PRONOUNS: CONTRACTIONS FORMED WITH *BE*

it's	*It is* doubtful he'll arrive.	*It's* doubtful he'll arrive.
who's	*Who is* planning to attend?	*Who's* planning to attend?
you're	*You are* mistaken.	*You're* mistaken.
there's	*There is* little to do.	*There's* little to do.
they're	*They are* home.	*They're* home.

Edit to eliminate apostrophes from personal pronouns that are meant to show possession, not contraction.

FAULTY   You're order has arrived.

REVISED   Your order has arrived.

27a

′
∨

3 **For a plural noun ending with *s*, add only an apostrophe to indicate possession. For a plural noun not ending with *s*, add an apostrophe and the letter *s*.**

bricklayers' union	teachers' strike
dancers' rehearsal	men's locker
children's games	cattle's watering hole

EXERCISE 1

Read the following sentences. Use either an apostrophe or an apostrophe with the letter *s* to make possessive each noun or pronoun in parentheses.

> *Example:* (Apple Corporation) Macintosh computers can transfer files with an IBM PC in a variety of ways.
>
> Apple Corporation's Macintosh computers can transfer files with an IBM PC in a variety of ways.

1. You can connect a PC and a Mac with electronic mail software, such as (CE Software) QuickMail.
2. Networks are fast and convenient; they allow both camps access to the (other) hard disk.
3. But networks are rather expensive, and could tie up the linked (computers) memory systems.
4. Online information networks are another alternative. (Dow Jones) Desktop Express for the Macintosh can help download IBM files from a communications service.
5. Direct modem file transfers are inexpensive, but there needs to be an operator at both (owners) computers to ensure problem-free transfers.
6. Graphics files do not transfer as easily as text, so it is important to know your graphics (files) language codes.
7. (Microsoft Word) software can read documents written in both IBM and Mac formats on either computer.
8. Not too long ago it was thought that a Macintosh would never work with (IBM) programs.
9. Yet there are programs available today that can emulate and run almost any IBM software on a (Macintosh) configuration.
10. It is projected that over the next few years, the increased ease in transferring files from one computer system to another will help boost alternative (systems) sales.

27b

' ∨

27b Using apostrophes to show possession with multiple nouns

Multiple nouns showing possession can be tricky to punctuate, since the apostrophe and the letter *s* will indicate who—and how many people—own what, either separately or together. Because establishing possession is so important (especially in our culture), take care when using the apostrophe with multiple nouns. Punctuate so that your sentences express your exact meaning.

 To indicate possession when a cluster of words functions as a single noun, add an apostrophe and the letter *s* to the last word.

Executive Vice President's role   Chief Executive Officer's salary

brother-in-law's car   First Deck Officer's watch

2 To indicate possession of an object owned jointly, add an apostrophe and the letter *s* to the last noun (or pronoun) named.

Smith and Thompson's interview notes are meticulous. [The notes belong jointly to, they were gathered jointly by, Smith and Thompson.]

Mary and Bill's car needs a muffler. [The car belongs jointly to Mary and Bill.]

3 To indicate individual possession by two or more people, add an apostrophe and the letter *s* to each person named.

Judy's and Rob's interview notes are meticulous. [The reference is to two sets of notes, one belonging to Judy and the other to Rob.]

27c Using apostrophes in contractions to mark the omission of letters and numbers

When you join or compress words into a contraction, you omit letters to indicate a more rapid, informal pace of pronunciation. The omission *must* be marked in writing with an apostrophe. Similarly, when you omit numbers in a date, use an apostrophe. Because many readers consider contractions an informality, you may want to avoid using them in academic writing. When in doubt about the appropriateness of contractions and the register they indicate in a particular document, check with the professor who will be reading your work.

27c

1 Use an apostrophe to indicate the omission of letters in a contraction.

can't = can not   won't = will not   you've = you have

2 Use an apostrophe to indicate the omission of numbers in a date.

the '60s   the '80s   the '90s

3 Eliminate apostrophes from verbs in their -*s* form.

The -*s* ending used in regular verb formation does *not* involve the omission of any letters (see 9a). Any apostrophe that creeps into such verb endings should be eliminated.

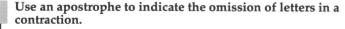

FAULTY   He walk's with a limp.   A cat eat's mice.

REVISED   He walks with a limp.   A cat eats mice.

EXERCISE 2

Correct the use of apostrophes in the following sentences by adding or deleting apostrophes as needed. Place a check by the sentences in which apostrophes are used correctly.

Example: Rough weather sailing can be exciting, but only if you're crew is well prepared for it.

Rough weather sailing can be exciting, but only if your crew is well prepared for it.

1. Bad weather inevitably puts you're crew's lives in danger.
2. Obviously their likely to be wetter and colder; foul weather gear should be available and distributed *before* the first splash lands in the cockpit.
3. Its equally important to take precautions to prevent risk of injury to limbs and body.
4. Those who normally lead a sedentary life are much more liable to injuries than those whose muscles are well exercised to withstand rubs, bumps, and twists.
5. Inadequate footwear, or none at all if you're feet are not hardened to such treatment, can lead to real pain if a toe is stubbed against a deck bolt or stanchion.
6. Make sure you have a working man-overboard pole—you're attention to safety could save someone's life.
7. Bad weather is particularly tiring and can result in seasickness; keep a watch to see whose becoming sick.
8. Seasickness and exhaustion combined can lead to a state of not caring what happens next to your boat and crew.
9. An exhausted sailor huddled in a wave- and windswept cockpit, peering into the murk, can easily come to see Poseidon, whose lashing the waves to fury out of spite.
10. Perhaps the easiest precaution to avoid problems in raw weather is to bring a crew whose not afraid of the tense environment faced while sailing in rough seas.

27d Using apostrophes to mark plural forms

As readers, we expect the letter *s* or letters *es* placed at the end of a word to show that the word is plural. Yet if we were to follow that convention with letters or symbols, we would quickly create a puzzle of pronunciation: *How many les in Lilliputian?* We avoid the confusion by adopting a different convention to form the plurals of letters, symbols, and so on.

1 Use an apostrophe and the letter *s* to indicate the plural of a letter, number, or word referred to as a word.

The letter, number, or word made plural should be underlined if typewritten or set in italics if typeset. Do *not* underline or italicize the apostrophe or the letter *s*.

Standard for Typewriter Usage:

```
Mind your p's and q's.

How many 5's in sixty?

The frequent in's and with's reduced the effectiveness
of his presentation.
```

Standard for Typeset Usage:

Mind your *p*'s and *q*'s.

How many *5*'s in sixty?

The frequent *in*'s and *with*'s reduced the effectiveness of his writing.

EXCEPTION: When forming the plural of a proper noun (e.g., someone's name), omit the apostrophe but retain the letter *s*.

Standard for Typewriter Usage:

```
At the convention I met three Franks and two Maudes.
```

Standard for Typeset Usage:

At the convention I met three *Frank*s and two *Maude*s.

Using an apostrophe in this case would mistakenly suggest possession and thus confuse a reader.

 2 **Use an apostrophe and the letter *s* to indicate the plural of a symbol, an abbreviation with periods, and years expressed in decades.**

 27d

Do *not* underline or italicize the symbol, the abbreviation, or the decade.

Joel is too fond of using &'s in his writing.
With all the M.D.'s at this conference, I feel safe.
Computer assisted software engineering will be important in the 1990's.

OPTION: Some writers omit the apostrophe before the letter *s* when forming the plural of decades, abbreviations without periods, and symbols.

1900s   or   1900's
IBMs   or   IBM's
%s   or   %'s

Whichever convention you adopt, be consistent.

 3 **Eliminate any apostrophes misused to form regular plurals of nouns.**

For a regular noun, an apostrophe is never used to create a plural form; rather, the apostrophe indicates possession (see 7a-2).

POSSESSIVE	the cat's meow	that idea's beginning
FAULTY PLURAL	Cat's eat meat.	Idea's begin in thought.
REVISED PLURAL	Cats eat.	Ideas begin.

EXERCISE 3

Follow the instructions in parentheses after each sentence to clarify possession.

> *Example:* The *governor office personnel* have formed some close friendships. (Use apostrophes to indicate that the people who have become friends work in the office of the governor.)
>
> The governor's office personnel have formed some close friendships.

1. Jane O'Leary works at the State House as the *governor spokesperson.* (Use apostrophes to indicate that the spokesperson for the governor is Jane O'Leary.)
2. *Mrs. O'Leary and her husband Bob house* is replete with pictures of government officials posing with the O'Leary family. (Use apostrophes to indicate that Mrs. O'Leary and Bob own their house together.)
3. The governor lives around the corner, in the *Governor Mansion.* (Use apostrophes to indicate that the governor lives in the mansion.)
4. *Jane O'Leary and the governor homes* are decorated similarly, both in a colonial style. (Use apostrophes to indicate that two different homes are being referred to.)
5. Often they'll have dinner together, cooked by *Jane and the governor husbands.* (Use apostrophes to indicate that two husbands cook together.)

27d

EXERCISE 4

Decide whether an apostrophe is needed to form plurals for the following letters, numbers, or words.

> *Example:* b
>
> b's (or *b*'s if typeset)

1. &   2. 42   3. 7   4. j   5. d   6. Karen

EXERCISE 5

Read the following paragraph on Donald Duck. Provide apostrophes and rewrite words as needed.

> Theirs one basic product never stocked in Disneys store: parents. Disneys is a universe of uncles and grand-uncles, nephews and cousins. The male-female relationships existence is found only in eternal fiancés. Donald Duck and Daisy relationship, like Mickey Mouse and Minnie relationship, is never consummated or even legitimized through the all-American institution of marriage. More troubling, though, is the

origin of all of the nephews and uncles in the Disney Comics worlds. Huey, Dewey, and Louie Uncle Donald is never known to have a sister or sister-in-law. In fact, most of Donald relatives are unmarried and unattached males, like Scrooge McDuck. Donalds own parents are never mentioned, although Grandma Duck purports to be the widowed ancestor of the Duck family (again no husband-wife relationship). Donald and Mickey girlfriends, Daisy and Minnie, are often accompanied by nieces of their own. Since these women are not very susceptible to men or matrimonial bonds, Disney's "families" are necessarily and perpetually composed of bachelors accompanied by nephews, who come and go. A quick look at Walt Disneys own biography demonstrates a possible reason for his comics anti-love, anti-marriage sentiments: Disney's mother is rarely mentioned, and his wifes role in his life was minimal at best. As for the future of the Magic Kingdoms demographic increases, it is predictable that they will be the result of extra-sexual factors.

27d

ˇ∨

CHAPTER 28

Quotation Marks

Quoting the words of others is a necessary, essential fact of academic life, both for professors and for students. As a writer you will make claims, cite the words and work of others, and then respond to those words. For the sake of both accuracy and fairness, your quotations must be managed precisely. (See 34d on quoting sources in research.) If you quote to help make a point, you must do so accurately since readers count on you for a faithful transcription of what another has written. (See chapter 36 for conventions on citing sources in various disciplines.) This chapter will discuss the conventions for quoting as well as the stylistic tricks for smoothly incorporating quoted language into your work.

28a Quoting prose

1 **Use double quotation marks (" ") to set off a short direct quotation from the rest of a sentence.**

Short quotations—those that span four or fewer lines of your manuscript—may be incorporated into your writing by running them in with your sentences as part of your normal paragraphing. When quoting a source, reproduce exactly the wording and punctuation of the quoted material. For the most part, when you enclose the material in quotation marks, you will do so to indicate **direct discourse,** the exact recreation of words spoken or written by another person. Direct discourse places another person's language directly before readers as if you (the writer) were not present.

DIRECT   "To us," write scholars Douglas C. Wilson and William L. Rathje, "modern garbage deserves as much of our attention as does ancient garbage."

Indirect discourse occurs when you quote the words of someone inexactly, and from a distance.

INDIRECT Douglas C. Wilson and William L. Rathje believe that modern garbage deserves as much archaeological attention as ancient garbage.

Indirect discourse inserts your voice into the quotation: you mediate the quotation, or create the frame through which your readers perceive it.

484

ALTERING A QUOTATION: **Quotation marks** denote the *exact* reproduction of words written or spoken by someone else. Changes that you make to quoted material (such as words omitted or added) must be announced as such—either with brackets or ellipses (see 29d and e).

Use single quotation marks (' ') to set off quoted material—or the titles of short works—within a quotation enclosed by double (" ") marks.

The use of single quotation marks can be shown by a comparison of original passages with quotations.

ORIGINAL PASSAGES (with words to be quoted italicized)

> *The Soviet leadership, and Gorbachev in particular, clearly failed to anticipate that the process of reform would inevitably reignite the "nationalities question,"* and then they underestimated its potential explosiveness.

> Read *"Gorbachev Faces Soviet Nationalism,"* an important article in this magazine.

QUOTATIONS

> Political scientist Gail W. Lapidus feels that the "Soviet leadership, and Gorbachev in particular, clearly failed to anticipate that the process of reform would inevitably reignite the 'nationalities question.' "

> "Read 'Gorbachev Faces Soviet Nationalism,' " said Professor Lapidus.

If you find it necessary to quote material within single quotation marks, use double marks once again.

> Historian Beth Bailey cites popular magazines as one source of information. "In *Mademoiselle*'s 1938 college issue," writes Bailey, "a Smith college senior advised incoming freshmen to 'cultivate an image of popularity' if they wanted dates. 'During your first term,' the senior wrote, 'get "home talent" to ply you with letters, invitations, and telegrams.' "

Use commas to enclose explanatory remarks that lie outside the quotation.

A comma is placed after an explanatory remark that introduces a quotation.

> According to Bailey, "Competition was the key term in the formula—remove it and there was no rating, dating, or popularity."

When a remark interrupts a quotation, a pair of commas or a comma and a period should be used. The conventions for punctuation are as follows: The first comma enclosing an explanatory remark notes the (temporary) ending of the quoted material and is placed inside the quotation. If the sentence continues past the explanatory comment, a second comma is placed before the quote is reintroduced. If the sentence ends with an explanatory mark, a period is placed after that remark. In this case, when the quotation is resumed in a new sentence, the first letter of the quotation is capitalized.

> "Rating, dating, popularity, competition," writes Bailey, "were catch-words hammered home, reinforced from all sides until they seemed a natural vocabulary."
>
> "You had to rate in order to date, to date in order to rate," she adds. "By successfully maintaining the cycle, you became popular."

NOTE: When the word *that* introduces a direct quotation, or when an introductory remark has the sense of a "that" construction but the word itself is omitted, do not use a comma to separate the introduction from the quoted material. In addition, do not capitalize the first letter of the quotation.

FAULTY   Bailey discovered that, "The Massachusetts *Collegian* (the Massachusetts State College student newspaper) ran an editorial against using the library for 'datemaking.' "

REVISED   Bailey discovered that "the Massachusetts *Collegian* (the Massachusetts State College student newspaper) ran an editorial against using the library for 'datemaking.' "

4 **Display—that is, set off from text—lengthy quotations. Quotation marks are *not* used to enclose a displayed quotation.**

28a

" "

Quotations of five or more lines are too long to run in with sentences in a paragraph. Instead they are displayed in a block format in a narrower indentation, without being enclosed by quotation marks.

> In his remarks at the March 1989 Mary and Jackson Burke Distinguished Lecture Series, Bill Bradley spoke on the impressive economic growth of East Asia:
>
> > East Asia is quickly becoming the richest, most populous, most dynamic area on earth. Over the last quarter century, the East Asian economies grew at an average real growth rate of 6 percent annually while the economies of the United States and the countries of the European Community grew at 3 percent. East Asia's share of gross world product has more than doubled during the last twenty years, rising from 8 percent to 20 percent.

Manuscript Form

Double space the displayed quotation and indent ten spaces from the left margin. Punctuate material as in the original text. Quotation marks inside a displayed quotation remain double (" ") marks. If one paragraph is being displayed, do not indent the first word of the paragraph. If multiple paragraphs are being displayed, indent the first word of each paragraph three additional spaces (that is, thirteen spaces from the left). However, if when quoting multiple paragraphs the first sentence quoted does not begin a paragraph in the original source, then do not indent the first paragraph in your paper.

A displayed quotation is best introduced with a full sentence, ending with a colon. The colon provides a visual cue to the reader that a long quotation follows.

5 Place periods and commas inside the end quotation mark.

"The big question is whether this kind of growth is sustainable," says Bradley.

He adds, "Because American trade deficits must shrink in the years ahead, Asian nations can no longer count as heavily on expanding exports to the United States to fuel their growth."

EXCEPTION: When a pair of parentheses enclosing some comment or page reference appears between the end of the quotation and the end of the sentence, use quotation marks to note the end of the quoted text, place the parentheses, and then close with a period.

CONFUSING   He adds, "Because American trade deficits must shrink in the years ahead, Asian nations can no longer count as heavily on expanding exports to the United States to fuel their growth. (1)"

REVISED   He adds, "Because American trade deficits must shrink in the years ahead, Asian nations can no longer count as heavily on expanding exports to the United States to fuel their growth" (1).

6 Place colons, semicolons, and footnotes outside end quotation marks.

COLON   Bradley directly asserts that "the futures of Asia and the United States are inextricably intertwined": Asian countries profited by U.S. growth in the 1980s, and the U.S. must profit by Asian growth in the '90s and beyond.

SEMICOLON   Bradley believes that the United States must look to the East with the intention of forming a "strong, lasting partnership"; moreover, he states that we must do so without the condescension that has for so long characterized our relations with countries like Japan and South Korea.

FOOTNOTE   Bradley believes that the United States must look to the East with the intention of forming a "strong, lasting partnership."[4]

7   **Place question marks and exclamation points inside or outside end quotation marks, depending on meaning.**

Place a question mark or exclamation point *inside* the end quotation when the mark applies to the quoted material only or when it applies to both the quoted material and the sentence as a whole. Place the mark *outside* the end quotation mark when the sentence as a whole forms a question or exclamatory remark but the quoted material does not.

MARK APPLIES TO QUOTED MATERIAL ONLY

Naturalist José Márcio Ayres began his field work on the ukaris monkey of the upper Amazon with this question: "How do these primates survive almost exclusively on the pulp and seeds of fruit, when the forests in which they live are flooded much of the year?"

MARK APPLIES BOTH TO QUOTED MATERIAL AND TO SENTENCE AS WHOLE

How can we, sitting comfortably in living rooms and libraries, appreciate the rigors of field research when even Ayres remarks, "Is the relative protection of the ukaris habitat at all surprising in light of the enormous swarms of mosquitoes one encounters in all seasons and at all hours of the day?"

MARK APPLIES TO SENTENCE AS A WHOLE BUT NOT TO QUOTATION

Bachelor ukaris looking for mates behave as badly as hooligans at a soccer match. Ayres reports that fights are frequent and that "after all this trouble, copulation may last less than two minutes"!

8   **Place dashes inside quotations only when they are part of the quoted material.**

PART OF QUOTED MATERIAL

Would-be competitors like "brocket deer, peccaries, agoutis, armadillos, and pacas—mammals common in upland habitats—"do not inhabit the ukaris forest, most likely because of the Amazon's annual flooding. This is one reason the ukaris has survived.

SEPARATE FROM QUOTED MATERIAL

Once the flood waters recede, each afternoon the ukaris descend from the upper canopy of trees—"where the temperature is uncomfortably high"— to forage for seedlings, which they dig up and eat.

EXERCISE 1

Use double quotation marks (" ") and single quotation marks (' ') to punctuate the sentences that follow. Words to be quoted are underlined.

Example: Michel Foucault describes 18th-century discipline methods as a festival of punishment.

Michel Foucault describes 18th-century discipline methods as "a festival of punishment."

1. At a public execution before the Church of Paris in 1757, a man was condemned to make the *amende honorable*, a form of lethal torture.
2. According to the official record of the event, the flesh will be torn from his breasts, arms, thighs, and calves with red-hot pincers.
3. Foucault quotes from a diary by an eyewitness, who wrote: The excessive pain made him utter horrible cries, and he often repeated: My God, have pity on me!
4. Foucault uses the example of the 18th-century execution to introduce one of his major themes, the disappearance of torture as a public spectacle.
5. Although the public execution was no longer an acceptable practice by the 19th century, the use of prisoners in public works, such as cleaning city streets, still brought criminals into the public eye to be humiliated and often debased by townspeople.
6. By the end of the 19th century, the parading of the chain-gang across France was replaced with inconspicuous black-painted cell-carts.
7. The reason for ending public executions was to keep the delineation between good and evil readily apparent. Foucault notes that as early as 1764, Beccaria remarked: The murder that is depicted as a horrible crime is repeated in cold blood, remorselessly (Beccaria 101). The public execution is now seen as a hearth in which violence bursts again into flame.

28b Quoting poetry, dialogue, and other material

1 Run-in brief quotations of poetry with your sentences. Indicate line breaks in the poem with a slash (/). Quote longer passages in displayed form.

A full quotation of or a lengthy quotation from a poem is normally made in displayed form (see 28a-3).

The Black Riders

42

I walked in a desert.
and I cried:
"Ah, God, take me from this place!"
A voice said: "It is no desert."
I cried, "Well, but—
The sand, the heat, the vacant horizon."
A voice said: "It is no desert."

—STEPHEN CRANE

When quoting a brief extract—four lines or fewer—you can run the lines into the sentences of a paragraph, using the guidelines for quoting prose (see 28a); however, line divisions are shown with a slash (/) with one space before and one space after.

Stephen Crane's bleak view of the human condition is expressed in lyric 42 of his series "The Black Riders." Walking in a desert, his narrator cries: " 'Ah, God, take me from this place!' / A voice said: 'It is no desert.' "

2   Use quotation marks to quote—or write—dialogue.

When quoting or writing dialogue, change paragraphs to note each change of speaker. Explanatory comments between parts of the quotation are enclosed with two commas. The first, signaling the (temporary) ending of the quoted material, is placed *inside* the end quotation mark. The second comma, signaling the end of the explanatory remark, is placed before the quotation mark that opens the next part of the quotation. When the quotation resumes, its first letter may be capitalized only if a new sentence has been started (in which case the comma concluding the explanatory material is changed to a period).

> "Do you remember what I told you?" I asked.
> She nodded.
> "Can you tell me?"
> "That Dad'll come to see me right when we get to the new house in Cambridge. Right the day when."
> "That's right, honey," I said. I leaned forward and began to splash water gently on her soap-slicked body.
>
> —SUE MILLER

In a speech of two or more paragraphs, begin each new paragraph with opening quotation marks to signal your reader that the speech continues. Use closing quotation marks *only* at the end of the final paragraph, to signal that the speech has concluded.

28b

" "

3   Indicate the titles of brief works with quotation marks: chapters of books, short stories, poems, songs, sections from newspapers, essays, etc.[1]

I read the "Focus Section" of the *Boston Sunday Globe* every week.

"The Dead" is, perhaps, Joyce's most famous short story.

"Coulomb's law" is the first chapter in volume two of Gartenhaus's text, *Physics: Basic Principles.*

Manuscript Form

When placed on the title page of a paper you are submitting to a professor or your peers, the title of your work should *not* be put in quotation

---

[1]The titles of longer works—books, newspapers, magazines, long poems—are underlined in typewritten text and italicized in typeset text. (See chapter 36.)

marks. Only when you are quoting a title (yours or anyone else's) *in* a paper do you use quotation marks. However, if a title itself contains a title—a reference to some other work, you must quote appropriately. If the title of your own paper included a reference to a poem, the title would look like this.

Images of the Quest in Tennyson's "Ulysses"

This same title, referred to *in* a sentence:

In her paper "Images of the Quest in Tennyson's 'Ulysses,' " Donna Smith defines heroism as a forward-looking state of mind, not as a series of great (but already accomplished) deeds.

When a title is included in any other quoted material, double quotation marks (" ") change to single marks (' ').

4   **Use quotation marks, occasionally, to emphasize words or to note invented words.**

An uncommon usage of a standard term or a new term that has been invented for a special circumstance can be highlighted with quotation marks. Once you have emphasized a word with quotation marks, you need not use the marks again with that word.

In the mid-1960s, when relaxed restrictions dramatically increased Asian immigration to the United States, the popular press, politicians, and others assigned Asian Americans the role of "model minority."

Words that will be defined in a sentence, or words that are referred to as words, are usually italicized, though they are sometimes set in quotations. Definitions themselves, especially if they provide a translation of a word or phrase in another language, are placed in quotation marks.

The sense of the Latin *quid pro quo* is that "one thing is given in fair exchange for another."

Some of the ancient literature (e.g., Ezekiel 31:1–18) places Eden, "the Garden of God," in the mountains of Lebanon.

28c   **Eliminating misused or overused quotation marks**

1   **Eliminate phrases using quotation marks to note slang or colloquial expressions.**

If your use of slang is appropriate for and important (as slang) in your paper, then no quotation marks are needed. If, on the other hand, you are uncomfortable with slang or colloquial expressions and choose to show your discomfort by using quotation marks, then find another, more formal way to express the same thoughts.

OVERUSED   Kate promised she would "walk that extra mile" for Mark. [The quote does not excuse the use of a cliché here.]

REVISED   Kate promised to help Mark in any way she could.

 2   Eliminate phrases using quotation marks to make ironic comments.

When possible, express your thoughts directly through word choice.

MISUSED   Dean Langley called to express his "appreciation" for all I had done.

REVISED   Dean Langley called to complain about the accusations of bias I raised with reporters.

 3   Eliminate quotations used to emphasize technical terms.

Assume your readers will note technical terms as such and will refer to a dictionary if needed.

MISUSED   "Electromagnetism" is a branch of physics.

REVISED   Electromagnetism is a branch of physics.

 4   Eliminate quotations that are overused to note commonly accepted nicknames.

OVERUSED   "Bob" Dole is a powerful senator.

REVISED   Bob Dole is a powerful senator.

 Reserve your use of quotation marks for unusual nicknames, which often appear in parentheses after a first name. Once you have emphasized a name with quotation marks, you need not use the marks again with that name.

> Ralph ("The Hammer") Schwartz worked forty years as a longshoreman in San Francisco and was fond of saying, "Don't end your life face down at the bottom of a bird cage."

28c

EXERCISE 2

Correct the use of quotations to emphasize specific words in the following paragraph. Two of the eight expressions in quotation marks are emphasized correctly.

> "Don" Vito Corleone was a man to whom everybody came for help, and never were they disappointed. No matter how poor or powerless the supplicant, "Don" Vito Corleone would take that man's

troubles to his heart. And he would let nothing stand in the way to a solution of that man's "woe." His reward? Friendship, the respectful title of "Don," and sometimes the more "affectionate" title of "Godfather." And perhaps, to show respect only, never for profit, some "humble gift"—a gallon of homemade wine or a basket of peppered taralles specially baked to grace his Christmas table. It was understood, it was mere "good manners," to proclaim that you were in his debt and that he had the right to call upon you at any time to redeem your debt by some small service.

—MARIO PUZO

EXERCISE 3

Following is a passage on World Cup soccer by John Eisenberg. Quote from the paragraph, as instructed here.

1. Introduce a quotation with the word *that.*
2. Introduce a quotation with a phrase and a comma. End the quotation with a page reference noted in parentheses.
3. Introduce a quotation with a sentence and a colon.
4. Interrupt a quotation with the phrase "Eisenberg states."
5. Follow a quotation with an explanatory remark.

Had England's David Platt not fielded a difficult pass and blasted the ball past the Belgian goalkeeper, the game would have come down to a round of penalty kicks and the English might well have been knocked out of the World Cup in the second round, an ending that would not have sat well back home. But now they are in the quarterfinals, officially one of the eight best teams in the world. The English now only have to beat a long shot, Cameroon, to reach the semifinals. "We have proved our place in the world," announced Bobby Robson, the English coach.

28c

" "

CHAPTER 29

Other Marks

This chapter reviews the conventions for using colons, dashes, parentheses, brackets, ellipses, and slashes. Of these marks, the first three are the most frequently used. The colon, the dash, and parentheses are important marks for the writer concerned with style: they significantly alter and thereby vary the rhythm of sentence structures. Brackets and ellipses are marks you will need to know when incorporating quotations into your papers.

THE COLON

29a Using the colon

The **colon** is the mark of punctuation generally used to make an announcement. In formal writing, the colon follows only a *complete* independent clause and introduces a word, phrase, sentence, or group of sentences (as in a quotation). For readers, the colon gives an important cue about the relationship of one part of your text to another: the sentence before the colon leads directly to the word or words after, in the fashion of an announcement.

1   Edit to eliminate colons misused within independent clauses.

In formal writing, a colon must always follow a complete statement or independent clause. The mark must never be used as a break inside an independent clause.

FAULTY   For someone who is depressed, the best two things in life are: eating and sleeping.

REVISED   For someone who is depressed, the best two things in life are eating and sleeping.

REVISED   For someone who is depressed, only two things in life matter: eating and sleeping.

2   Use a colon to announce an important statement or question.

You create emphasis in a paragraph when you write one sentence to introduce another. Greater emphasis is created when you conclude that introduction with a colon.

The mind's deepest desire, even in its most elaborate operations, parallels man's unconscious feeling in the face of the universe: it is an insistence upon familiarity, an appetite for clarity.

Dramatic changes now occurring in the !Kung culture are illuminating a major problem in anthropology: Why did most hunting and gathering societies disappear rapidly after coming in contact with societies that kept domesticated animals and plants?

3 Use a colon to introduce a list or a quotation.

If at the conclusion of an independent clause you want to introduce a list or a quotation, do so with a colon.

A LIST

According to Cooley, the looking-glass self has three components: how we think our behavior appears to others, how we think others judge our behavior, and how we feel about their judgments.

A QUOTATION

A New England soldier wrote to his wife on the eve of the First Battle of Bull Run: "I know how great a debt we owe to those who went before us through the Revolution. And I am willing, perfectly willing, to lay down all my joys in this life, to help maintain this government, and to pay that debt."

A colon can introduce either a list or a quotation that is set off and indented.

29a

:

A New England soldier wrote to his wife on the eve of the First Battle of Bull Run:

I know how great a debt we owe to those who went before us through the Revolution. And I am willing, perfectly willing, to lay down all my joys in this life, to help maintain this government, and to pay that debt.

Chip designers use increased packing density of transistors in one of two ways:

1. They increase the complexity of the computers they can fabricate.
2. They keep the complexity of the computer at the same level and pack the whole computer into fewer chips.

NOTE: Both when lists and quotations are run in with sentences and when they are set off, the expression *as follows* or some variant often precedes the colon. If this expression is tagged onto a complete sentence, it is preceded by a comma.

There are three reasons to reject the theory of spontaneous generation, as follows:

 4 **Use a colon to set off an appositive phrase, summary, or explanation.**

Appositive

Food sharing, in which individuals provision other members of a group, is extremely rare in mammals. In addition to bats, only a few species are known to display such behavior: wild dogs, hyenas, chimpanzees, and human beings.

Summary

A number of recent studies reveal that female vampire bats cluster together during the day but at night reassort themselves, creating a fluid social organization that is maintained for many years: vampire bats are remarkably social.

Explanation

When Calais surrendered, King Edward (of England) threatened to put the city to the sword, then offered the people a bargain: he would spare the city if six of the chief burghers would give themselves up unconditionally.

5 **Use a colon to distinguish chapter from verse in Biblical citations, hours from minutes, and titles from subtitles or subsidiary material.**

29a

:

Biblical citation

It is an irony that almost none of the literature of the people who gave us the alphabet has been preserved. Fragments of Phoenician poetry have survived in the Psalms, where the mountains are described as "a fountain that makes the gardens fertile, a well of living water" (Song of Songs 4:15).

Hours from minutes

8:15 A.M.   12:01 P.M.

Titles from subtitles or subsidiary material

"Gorbachev's Problem: The U.S.S.R. and Its Nationalities"

6 **Use a colon after the salutation in a formal letter, and in bibliographic citations.**

Dear Ms. King:
Dear Dr. Hart:
Bikai, Patricia. "The Phoenicians." *Archaeology* Mar./Ap. 1990: 30.

EXERCISE 1

Correct the use of colons in these sentences. Add or delete colons as needed.

> *Example:*   The links between the military and national policy making continue to grow out of control the military budget of today resembles those of times when we are at war.
>
> The links between the military and national policy making continue to grow out of control: the military budget of today resembles those of times when we are at war.

1. A structural clue to the power elite today lies in the enlarged and military state that clue becomes evident in the military ascendancy.
2. Virtually all political and economic actions are now judged in terms of military definitions the higher warlords have ascended to a firm position within the power elite.
3. In part at least this has resulted from one simple historical fact: pivotal for the years since 1939: the focus of elite attention has been shifted from domestic problems, centered in the 1930s around slump, to international problems, centered in the '40s and '50s around war.

EXERCISE 2

Write brief sentences, as instructed.

1. Write a sentence with a colon that introduces a list.
2. Write a sentence with a colon that announces an emphatic statement.
3. Write a sentence with a colon that sets off an appositive phrase, summary, or explanation.

29b

THE DASH

29b Using dashes for emphasis

—

On the typewritten page, the dash is written as two hyphens (--). The space between these hyphens closes when the dash is typeset (—).

1 Use dashes to set off nonessential elements.

Use dashes to set off brief modifiers, lengthy modifiers, and appositives. In contrast to pairs of commas and parentheses, dashes emphasize the nonessential element set off in a sentence (see 25d). If dashes are the most emphatic interrupting marks and parentheses the least emphatic, commas offer a third, middling choice—neither emphatic nor fully parenthetical.

When Do Writers Need Dashes?

Sentence constructions rarely *require* the use of dashes. The dash is a stylist's tool, an elective mark. It halts the reader within a sentence by creating a cha-cha, dance-like syncopation. On seeing the dash, readers pause; then they speed up to read the words you have emphasized. Then they pause once more before returning to the main part of your sentence:

EFFECTIVE   Zoologist Uwe Schmidt discovered that shortly after birth, vampire bat pups are given regurgitated blood—in addition to milk—by their mothers.

Use the single dash to set off elements at the beginning or end of a sentence and a pair of dashes to set off elements in the middle. When elements are set off at the end of a sentence or in the middle, you have the choice of using commas or parentheses instead of dashes. Whatever punctuation you use, take care to word the element you set off so that it fits smoothly into the structure of your sentence. For instance, in the following sentence the nonessential element would be awkward.

AWKWARD   Zoologist Uwe Schmidt discovered that shortly after birth, vampire bat pups are given regurgitated blood—they drink milk too—by their mothers.

BETTER   Bat pups are given regurgitated blood—in addition to milk—by their mothers.

29b

Brief modifiers in mid-sentence

Seven to thirty percent of vampire bats in a cluster fail to obtain a sufficient blood meal on any given night. By soliciting regurgitated blood from a roostmate, a bat can fend off starvation—at least for one more night—and so have another chance to find a meal. [The phrase acts as an adverb, modifying *fend off.*]

Lengthy modifiers

Within the past ten years, a new generation of investigators—armed with fresh insights from sociobiology and behavioral ecology—have learned much about social organization in the birds of paradise. [The phrase acts as an adjective, modifying *investigators.*]

Appositives

We study history to understand the present. Yet sometimes the present can help us to clarify the past. So it is with a San-speaking people known as the !Kung—a group of what were once called African Bushmen. [The appositive phrase renames the noun *!Kung.*]

NOTE : Use dashes to set off appositives that contain commas. Recall that a nonessential appositive phrase can also be set off from a sentence by a pair of commas (see 25d). When the appositive is formed by a series, the items of which are already separated by commas, dashes prevent misreading.

CONFUSING   Since the turn of the century, the percentage of information workers, bankers, insurance agents, lawyers, science journalists, has gone from a trickle to a flood.

REVISED   Since the turn of the century, the percentage of information workers—bankers, insurance agents, lawyers, science journalists—has gone from a trickle to a flood.

2 **Use dashes to set off a significant repeating structure or an emphatic concluding element.**

Repeating structure

To me the color, movement, and sound of the bird of paradise's mating display was—and continues to be—one of nature's most thrilling sights. [The verb is repeated.]

Emphatic concluding remark

Once disposed of in the landfill, garbage is supposed to remain buried for eternity. So it was in Collier County, Florida—until we found several good reasons to dig it up again. [The dash sets off a sharply contrasting element, in this case a subordinate clause that functions as an adverb.]

Use dashes—with care. [This brief qualifying tag, a prepositional phrase, functions as an adverb.]

29b

—

3 **Use a dash to set off an introductory series from a summary or explanatory remark.**

Strategic spots on the Boston Common are occupied by regiments of lunch-hour workers, and the Common is still the preferred site for political rallies. Pocket change, ball-point pens, campaign buttons—humanity's imprint continues to be recorded on the grassy slopes of the Boston Common. [This sentence structure, which begins with a series, is relatively rare.]

4 **Use a dash to express an interruption in dialogue.**

A dash used in dialogue shows interruption—speakers interrupting themselves or being interrupted by others. The dash used in dialogue also shows a change of thought or an uncompleted thought, a change in tone, or a pause.

Adam studied his brother's face until Charles looked away. "Are you mad at something?" Adam asked.

"What should I be mad at?"

"It just sounded— "

"I've got nothing to be mad at. Come on, I'll get you something to eat."

—JOHN STEINBECK

 5   **Use a dash to set off an attribution (by name), following an epigram.**

At blows that never fall you falter,
And what you never lose, you must forever mourn.

—GOETHE

Dashes used in this fashion often follow epigrams—succinct, provocative quotations placed at the beginning of a paper as a vehicle for the introduction. Typically, the writer opens such a paper with a direct reference to the epigram and its author: "In these lines from *Faust,* the main character laments his limited human powers. . . ."

29b

—

EXERCISE 3

Add a dash or a pair of dashes to the following sentences.

Example: The emptiness of our middle-class futures made us willing to risk our lives to a degree in actions against racism, against repression, against the war.

The emptiness of our middle-class futures made us willing to risk our lives—to a degree—in actions against racism, against repression, against the war.

1. We had grown up in America's most seductive image of itself the suburban, consuming world you see on TV.
2. Most working people did not share the unusual source of our particular radicalism a privileged rejection of the middle-class life that Americans are supposed to strive for.
3. The early 1970s saw the end of this mass radical movement of white students and youth the end of great numbers of people self-consciously taking action as part of a group of people like themselves taking similar actions across the country.

EXERCISE 4

Write brief sentences, as instructed.

1. Write a sentence with a nonessential series placed mid-sentence, set off by a pair of dashes.
2. Write a sentence in which a nonessential element is set off at the end by a dash.
3. Write a sentence in which a dash or pair of dashes sets off a significant repeating structure or emphatic statement.

PARENTHESES

<table>
<tr><td>**29c**</td><td>Using parentheses to set off nonessential information</td></tr>
</table>

Parentheses ( ) are used to enclose and set off nonessential dates, words, phrases, or whole sentences that provide examples, comments, and other supporting information. The remark enclosed by parentheses is the ultimate nonessential modifier; it presents the reader with an aside, an interesting but by no means crucial bit of information. To give nonessential remarks more emphasis, use commas or dashes.

1 Use parentheses to set off nonessential information: examples, comments, appositives.

Examples

The ground beetle *Pterostichus pinguedineus* vanished from Iowa 15,300 years ago, but today it survives in Alaska, in the Yukon, and in a series of isolated alpine refuges in the northern Appalachians (for example, the peak of Mt. Washington in New Hampshire).

Comments—explanatory or editorial

Beetles (especially those species that scavenge or that prey on other arthropods) are rapid colonizers and are among the first organisms to invade terrain opened up to them by changing climates.

Appositives

The information content of a slice of pizza (advertising, legal expenses, and so on) accounts for a larger percentage of its cost than the edible content does, according to Henry Kelley and Andrew W. Wyckoff of the Congressional Office of Technology Assessment.

29c

( )

2 Use parentheses to set off dates, translations of non-English words, and acronyms.

Dates

Thomas Aquinas (b. 1225 or 1226, d. 1274) is regarded as the greatest of scholastic philosophers.

Translations

The look on the faces of the Efe tribesmen made it clear that they could think of nothing worse than to have a *muzungu* (foreigner) living with them for even a day.

Acronyms

Lucy Suchman, staff anthropologist of Xerox's Palo Alto Research Center (better known as PARC), watches workers in an airline operations room at San Jose International Airport to learn how they extract particular information from a chaotic assortment of radio, telephone, text, and video feeds. [Typically, an acronym is placed in parentheses directly after the first mention of a term or title subsequently referred to by its acronym.]

3 **Use parentheses to set off numbers or letters that mark items in a series, when the series is run-in with a sentence.**

Chip designers use increased packing density of transistors in one of two ways: (1) they increase the complexity of the computers they can fabricate, or (2) they keep the complexity of the computer at the same level and pack the whole computer into fewer chips.

When the series appears in list form, parentheses are omitted.

Chip designers use increased packing density of transistors in one of two ways:
1. They increase the complexity of the computers they can fabricate.
2. They keep the complexity of the computer at the same level and pack the whole computer into fewer chips.

4 **Punctuate parentheses according to convention.**

Words enclosed by parentheses should be punctuated according to standard practice. When a parenthetical remark forms a sentence, the remark should begin with an uppercase letter and end with an appropriate mark (period, question mark, or exclamation point) placed *inside* the end parenthesis. In all other cases, end punctuation should be placed outside the end parenthesis, and punctuation that would normally be placed directly after a word should be placed directly after the parenthetical remark.

29c

( )

FAULTY   Like other nomads, the Bakhtiari think of themselves as a family, the sons of a single founding-father. (as did the ancient Jews)

REVISED   Like other nomads, the Bakhtiari think of themselves as a family, the sons of a single founding-father (as did the ancient Jews).

FAULTY   According to J. Bronowski, the Bakhtiari "think of themselves as a family, the sons of a single founding-father." (60)

REVISED   According to J. Bronowski, the Bakhtiari "think of themselves as a family, the sons of a single founding-father" (60).

EXERCISE 5

Add parentheses to the following sentences to enclose nonessential information.

Example: Nearly all twin-lens reflex cameras and a few single-lens reflex SLR cameras are designed to accommodate roll film somewhat wider than 35 millimeters.

Nearly all twin-lens reflex cameras and a few single-lens reflex (SLR) cameras are designed to accommodate roll film somewhat wider than 35 millimeters.

1. Because of their size and the "look-down" viewing systems, twin-lens reflexes are not good for quick action candid shooting. An SLR is best in these situations.
2. The look-down viewing system is better for carefully composed photographs in a studio or home for example when time is not of the essence.
3. For my money, the Canon AE-1 originally designed in 1971 remains one of the best and most flexible workhorse cameras that an amateur photographer could want.
4. I still cannot understand why any amateur photographer would want anything besides a good, reliable, single-lens reflex camera usually referred to as an SLR.

BRACKETS

29d Using brackets for editorial clarification

Use brackets [ ] to clarify or insert comments into quoted material. Throughout this section the following passage will be altered to demonstrate the various uses of brackets.

29d

[ ]

> Elephant sounds include barks, snorts, trumpets, roars, growls, and rumbles. The rumbles are the key to our story, for although elephants can hear them well, human beings cannot. Many are below our range of hearing, in what is known as infrasound.
>
> The universe is full of infrasound: It is generated by earthquakes, wind, thunder, volcanoes, and ocean storms—massive movements of earth, air, fire, and water. But very low frequency sound has not been thought to play much of a role in animals' lives. Intense infrasonic calls have been recorded from finback whales, but whether the calls are used in communication is not known.
>
> Why would elephants use infrasound? It turns out that sound at the lowest frequency of elephant rumbles (14 to 35 hertz) has remarkable properties—it is little affected by passage through forests and grasslands. Does infrasound, then, let elephants communicate over long distances?

1 Use brackets to insert your own words into quoted material.

Recall that quotation marks denote an *exact* reproduction of someone else's writing or speech. When you alter the wording of a quotation either by adding or deleting words, you must indicate as much to your reader with appropriate use of punctuation.

Brackets to clarify a reference

When quoting a sentence with a pronoun that refers to a word in another, nonquoted, sentence, use brackets to insert a clarifying reference into the quotation. Delete the pronoun and add bracketed information; or, if wording permits (as in this example), simply add the bracketed reference.

> According to Katherine Payne, "Many [elephant rumbles] are below our range of hearing, in what is known as infrasound."

Brackets to weave quoted language into your sentences

The stylistic goal of quoting material in your papers is to make the fit between quoted language and your language seamless. To do this, you will sometimes need to alter a quotation if its structure, point of view, pronoun choices, or verb forms differ from those of the sentence into which you are incorporating the quotation. Show any changes to quoted text in brackets.

> The human ear can discern a wide band of sounds, but there are animals we can't hear without special equipment. Elephants emit inaudible (that is, to humans), very low-frequency rumbles called infrasound. At frequencies of 14 to 35 hertz, elephant rumbles have "remarkable properties—[they are] little affected by passage through forests and grasslands" (Payne 67).

The bracketed verb and pronoun have been changed from their original singular form to plural in order to agree in number with the plural *elephant rumbles*. The original subject of the quoted sentence was singular (*sound*). Quoting without brackets would have resulted in an awkward construction: *Elephant rumbles have "remarkable properties—it is. . . ."*

29d

[ ]

Brackets to show your awareness of an error in the quoted passage

When you quote a sentence that contains an obvious error, you are still obliged to reproduce exactly the wording of the original source. To show your awareness of the error and to show readers that the error is the quoted author's, not yours, place the bracketed word *sic* (Latin, meaning "thus") after the error.

> "Intense infrasonic calls have been recorded from finback whales, but weather [sic] the calls are used in communication is not known."

Brackets to note emphasis

You may wish to underline or italicize quoted words. To show readers that the emphasis is yours and not the quoted author's, add the bracketed expression *emphasis added, italics added,* or *italics mine.*

"The universe is *full* of infrasound: It is generated by earthquakes, wind, thunder, volcanoes, and ocean storms—massive movements of earth, air, fire, and water [italics mine]."

2 Use brackets to distinguish parentheses inserted within parentheses.

Katherine Payne reports that "sound at the lowest frequencies of elephant rumbles (14 to 35 hertz [cycles per second]) has remarkable properties—it is little affected by passage through forests and grasslands."

ELLIPSES

29e Using an ellipsis to indicate a break in continuity

Just as you will need to add words in order to incorporate quotations into your sentences, so too you will need to delete words. **An ellipsis,** noted as three spaced periods (. . .), shows that you have deleted either words or entire sentences from a passage you are quoting. Throughout this section the following passage will be altered to demonstrate the various uses of ellipses.

> First, for Americans, the human cost of the Civil War was by far the most devastating in our history. The 620,000 Union and Confederate soldiers who lost their lives almost equaled the 680,000 American soldiers who died in all the other wars this country has fought combined. When we add the unknown but probably substantial number of civilian deaths—from disease, malnutrition, exposure, or injury—among the hundreds of thousands of refugees in the Confederacy, the toll of the Civil War may exceed war deaths in all the rest of American history.
>
> The ghastly toll gives the Civil War a kind of horrifying but hypnotic fascination. As Thomas Hardy once put it, "War makes rattling good history; but Peace is poor reading." The sound of drum and trumpet, the call to arms, the clashing of armies have stirred the blood of nations throughout history. As the horrors and the seamy side of a war recede into the misty past, the romance and honor and glory forge into the foreground.

29e

. . .

1 Know when *not* to use an ellipsis.

Do *not* use an ellipsis to note words omitted from the beginning of a sentence. In the following example, three words are deleted.

FAULTY   James McPherson observes that ". . . the human cost of the Civil War was by far the most devastating in our history."

REVISED   James McPherson observes that "the human cost of the Civil War was by far the most devastating in our history."

Do *not* use an ellipsis if the passage you quote ends with a period and ends your sentence as well.

FAULTY   James McPherson believes that "the toll of the Civil War may exceed war deaths in all the rest of American history. . . ."

REVISED   James McPherson believes that "the toll of the Civil War may exceed war deaths in all the rest of American history."

 2 **Use an ellipsis to indicate words deleted from the middle of a sentence.**

If you have deleted words mid-sentence from an original passage, indicate the deletion with an ellipsis. If the words omitted directly follow an internal mark of punctuation (comma, dash, colon, semicolon), retain that mark and then add the ellipsis.

"[T]he human cost of the Civil War was . . . the most devastating in our history," writes James McPherson.

"The sound of drum and trumpet, . . . [has] stirred the blood of nations throughout history."

3 **Use an ellipsis to indicate words deleted from the end of a sentence.**

You may delete the end of a sentence from a quoted passage while your own sentence continues. If so, retain any internal mark of punctuation (comma, dash, colon, semicolon) that directly follows the last quoted word. Then add the ellipsis.

29e

Though the "6,500 men killed and mortally wounded in one day near Sharpsburg were nearly double the number of Americans killed and mortally wounded in combat in all the rest of the country's nineteenth-century wars combined—. . ." (McPherson 42), many in the twentieth century continue to view the Civil War as a romance.

You may want to end your sentence with a quotation that does not end a sentence in the original. If so, whatever mark of punctuation (if any) follows the last quoted word in the original should be deleted. Then add a period and an ellipsis, following one of two conventions. If you *do not* conclude your sentence with a citation, place the sentence period after the final letter of the quotation; place the ellipsis; and conclude with the end quotation mark.

Official mortality figures for the Civil War do not include the "probably substantial number of civilian deaths—from disease, malnutrition, exposure, or injury. . . ."

If you *do* conclude your sentence with a citation, skip one space after the final letter of the quotation; place the ellipsis and follow with an end quotation mark; skip one space and place the citation; and then place the sentence period.

> Official mortality figures for the Civil War do not include the "probably substantial number of civilian deaths—from disease, malnutrition, exposure, or injury . . ." (McPherson 42).

4   **Use an ellipsis to show a pause or interruption.**

In dialogue

"No," I said. I wanted to leave. "I . . . I need to get some air."

In prose

When I left the seminary, I walked long and thought hard about what a former student of divinity might do. . . . My shoes wore out, my brain wore thin. I was stumped and not a little nervous about the course my life would take.

THE SLASH

29f   Using the slash

1   **Use slashes to separate the lines of poetry run in with the text of a sentence.**

Retain all punctuation when quoting poetry. Leave a space before and after the slash when indicating line breaks.

29f

/

> The "hermit" of Robert Bly's poem of the same name "is a man whose body is perfectly whole. / He stands, the storm behind him, / And the grass blades are leaping in the wind. / Darkness is gathered in folds / About his feet. / He is no one."

2   **Use slashes to show choice.**

Use slashes, occasionally, to show alternatives, as with the expressions *and/or* and *either/or*. With this use, do not leave spaces before or after the slash.

Either/Or is the title of a philosophical work by Kierkegaard.

As a prank, friends entered the Joneses as a husband/wife team in the *Supermarket Sweepstakes*.

If your meaning is not compromised, avoid using the slash; instead, write out alternatives in your sentence.

Send a telegram and/or call to let us know you're well.

The sense, here, is that there are three options: send a telegram, call, *or* send a telegram *and* call. If two options are intended, then the sentence should be rewritten one of two ways.

> Send a telegram and call to let us know you're well.

> Send a telegram or call to let us know you're well.

3 Use a slash in writing fractions or formulas to note division.

The February 1988 index of job opportunities (as measured by the number of help wanted advertisements) would be as follows:

$$(47,230/38,510) \times 100 = 122.6$$

$$1/2 \quad 5/8 \quad 20\ 1/4$$

EXERCISE 6

Construct sentences, as directed, in which you quote from the following passage by Sigmund Freud.

[1]As to the origin of the sense of guilt, the analyst has different views from other psychologists; but even he does not find it easy to give an account of it. [2]To begin with, if we ask how a person comes to have a sense of guilt, we arrive at an answer which cannot be disputed: a person feels guilty (devout people would say "sinful") when he has done something which he knows to be "bad." [3]But then we notice how little this answer tells us. [4]Perhaps, after some hesitation, we shall add that even when a person has not actually *done* the bad thing but has only recognized in himself an *intention* to do it, he may regard himself as guilty; and the question then arises of why the intention is regarded as equal to the deed. [5]Both cases, however, presuppose that one had already recognized that what is bad is reprehensible, is something that must not be carried out. [6]How is this judgement arrived at?

Example: Quote sentence 1, but delete the phrase "As to the origin of the sense of guilt. . . ."

According to Sigmund Freud, "the analyst has different views from other psychologists; but even he does not find it easy to give an account of it."

1. Quote sentence 2, beginning with "a person feels. . . ." Delete the parenthetical note.
2. Quote sentence 4 but delete the end of the sentence, beginning with "and the question. . . ."
3. Quote sentence 1 and use a bracketed reference to clarify the second use of the pronoun *it*.
4. Quote sentence 5 and show your awareness of the spelling error.

29f

/

PART VIII

Using Mechanics

CHAPTER 30

Capitals
and Italics

Capitals and italics are primarily graphic devices that give readers cues on how to read: where to look for the beginning of a new thought, which words in a sentence are emphasized, which words form titles or proper names, and so on. Capitals and italics are also very useful for special designations that can only be shown in writing.

CAPITALS

Before the late nineteenth century, printers manually composed words by placing molded letters in type holders, taking letters from individual compartments, or type cases, set on a nearby wall. Letters used most often (vowels, for instance) were kept on the wall's lower cases, within easy reach. Letters used less often (capital letters, for instance) were kept in a slightly less convenient location in upper cases. In spite of innovations that have made manual typesetting obsolete, we still retain the printer's original designations, upper and lower case, when referring to the appearance of type on a page. Readers depend on capital (uppercase) letters, in contrast to lowercase letters, as cues to help recognize when sentences begin and when a noun refers to a particular person, place, or thing.

30a Capitalize the first letter of the first word in every sentence.

The most basic use of capitals is to signal the start of sentences.

When a box of mixed-grain-and-nut cereal is shaken, large particles always rise to the top—for the same reason that, over time, stones will rise to the top of a garden lot or field.

1 Reproduce capitalization in a quoted passage.

Capitalize the first word of quoted material when you introduce a quotation with a brief explanatory phrase.

According to archaeologist Douglas Wilson, "Most of what archaeologists have to work with is ancient trash."

"Most of what archaeologists have to work with is ancient trash," according to archaeologist Douglas Wilson.

Do not capitalize the first word of a quotation run into the structure of your sentence. When you change capitalization in a quoted text, indicate the change with brackets.

Wilson says that archaeologists who dig through modern trash must come "[e]quipped with rubber gloves, masks, and booster shots."

2 **Capitalize the first word in a parenthetical statement if the remark is a sentence.**

Once a sleepy suburban town whose workers commuted to Chicago every morning, Naperville, Illinois, has acquired its own employment base. (It has become an "urban village," a "technoburb.")

If the parenthetical remark forms a sentence but is placed inside another sentence (this is a relatively rare occurrence), *do not* capitalize the first word after the parenthesis and *do not* use a period. However, do use a question mark or exclamation point if the parenthetical remark requires it.

Naperville grew robustly (the population nearly quadrupled!), as Amoco and companies large and small erected what Governor James R. Thompson would later term "The Illinois Research and Development Corridor."

3 **In a series of complete statements or questions, capitalize the first word of each item.**

When a series is formed by phrases or incomplete questions, capitalization of the first word is optional.

CAPITALS   What causes air sickness? Is it inner-ear disturbance? Is it brain waves?

OPTIONAL   Air-Force scientists want to know what causes motion sickness. Is it inner-ear disturbance? brain wave anomalies? disorienting visual signals?

OPTIONAL   Air-Force scientists want to know what causes motion sickness. Is it inner-ear disturbance? Brain wave anomalies? Disorienting visual signals?

In a series of phrases run-in with a sentence, the phrases are *not* capitalized.

The program for low-input sustainable agriculture that has emerged from a recent federal study has three objectives: (1) to reduce reliance on fertilizer, pesticide, and other purchased resources to farms; (2) to increase farm

30a

cap

profits and agricultural productivity; and (3) to conserve energy and natural resources.

In a displayed series, capitalization of the first word is optional.

OPTIONAL   The program for low-input sustainable agriculture that has emerged from a recent federal study has three objectives:
1. To reduce reliance on fertilizer, pesticide, and other purchased resources to farms.
2. To increase farm profits and agricultural productivity.
3. To conserve energy and natural resources.

The word *to* could also be in lowercase letters in each number of the displayed series.

4   Capitalizing the first word of a sentence following a colon is optional.

OPTIONAL   The program has two aims: The first is to conserve energy.

OPTIONAL   The program has two aims: the first is to conserve energy.

30b   Capitalize words of significance in a title.

Capitalize all words of significance in the titles of books, journals, magazines, articles, and art works. *Do not* capitalize articles (*a, an, the*) or conjunctions and prepositions that have four or fewer letters, except at the title's beginning. *Do* capitalize the first and last words of the title (even if they are articles, conjunctions, or prepositions), along with any word following a colon or semicolon.

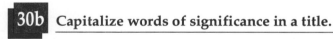

Pride and Prejudice	*Great Expectations*
The Sound and the Fury	*The Joy Luck Club*
Much Ado About Nothing	*West with the Night*

"The Phoenicians: Rich and Glorious Traders of the Levant"

Do not capitalize the word *the* if it is not part of a title or proper name.

the Eiffel Tower	*The Economist*
the Mediterranean Sea	*The Brothers Karamazov*

The first word of a hyphenated word in a title is capitalized. The second word is also capitalized, unless it is very short.

"The Selling of an Ex-President"   *Engine Tune-ups Made Simple*
"Belly-down in a Cave: A Spelunker's Weekend"

30b

cap

30c Capitalize the first word in every line of poetry.

Lines of poetry are conventionally marked by initial capitals. The interjection *O*, restricted for the most part to poetry, is always capitalized. The word *oh* is capitalized only when it begins a sentence.

> Break, break, break,
>   On thy cold gray stones, O Sea!
> And I would that my tongue could utter
>   The thoughts that arise in me.
>
> —TENNYSON, *from "Break, Break, Break"*

> . . . Oh, oh,
> It makes me mad to see what men shall do
> And we in our graves!
>
> —ROBERT BROWNING, *from "Fra Lippo Lippi"*

NOTE: Some poets begin lines with lowercase letters—e.e. cummings, for instance. Others write verse that deliberately shifts some standard conventions. When quoting such poets, retain the capitalization of the original.

30d Capitalize proper nouns—people, places, objects; proper adjectives; and ranks of distinction.

Capitalizing the first letter of a noun helps to establish its identity. In general, capitalize any noun that refers to a *particular* person, place, object, or being that has been given an individual, or proper, name.

30d

cap

1 Capitalize names of people or groups of people.

Names of people are capitalized, as are titles showing family relationships *if* the title is part of the person's name.

George Bush	Martha Washington
Aunt Millie	Uncle Ralph

Names of family relations—brother, aunt, grandmother—are not capitalized if not used as part of a particular person's proper name.

> He phoned his grandmother, Bess Truman.
> I saw my favorite aunt, Janet, on a trip to Chicago.

Names of political groups and of formal organizations are capitalized.

Democrats	the Left
Republicans	the Right
Communists	Socialists

 2   Capitalize religions, religious titles and names, and nationalities.

Religions, their followers, and their sacred beings and sacred documents are capitalized.

Judaism	Jew	the Bible
Catholicism	Catholic	the New Testament
Islam	Muslim	the Koran
God	Allah	Buddha

Nations and nationalities are capitalized.

America	Americans	Native Americans
Liberia	Liberians	Hispanic Americans
Czechoslovakia	Czechs	

NOTE: The terms *black* and *white,* when designating race, are usually written in lowercase, though some writers prefer to capitalize them (by analogy with other formal racial designations such as Mongolian and Polynesian).

3   Capitalize places, regions designated by points on the compass, and languages.

Places and addresses

Cascades	Asia
Idaho	England
Joe's Diner	Philadelphia
Main Street	Elm Boulevard

NOTE: Capitalize common nouns such as *main* or *center* when they are part of an address.

30d

cap

Names of regions and compass points designating the names of regions

Appalachia	the frozen Northwest
the Great Lakes	the Sun Belt
the sunny South	Mid-Atlantic

NOTE: A compass point is capitalized only when it functions as a noun and serves as the name of a particular area of the country. As a direction, a compass point is not capitalized.

NO CAPITALS   I'll be driving northeast for the first part of the trip. [The word *northeast* in this sentence is a modifier and indicates a direction, not a region.]

We made a course to the northeast, but soon turned to the north. [These are compass points, not the names of regions.]

CAPITALS   I'll be vacationing in the Northeast this year. [The word *Northeast* is the name of an area of the country.]

Names of languages

English	Arabic	Swahili
Spanish	Greek	Italian

4   **Capitalize adjectives formed from proper nouns, and titles of distinction that are part of proper names.**

Proper adjectives formed from proper nouns

English tea	French perfume
Cartesian coordinates	Balinese dancer

NOTE: Both *Oriental* and *oriental* are considered correct, though the capitalized form is more common. Both *Biblical* and *biblical* are considered correct.

Titles of distinction

Capitalize a title of distinction when no words separate it from a proper noun. Do not capitalize most title designations if they are followed by the preposition *of*.

30d

Governor Cuomo	Mario Cuomo, governor of New York	*cap*
Mayor Dinkins	David Dinkins, mayor of New York	

NOTE: When titles of the highest distinction are paired with proper names for a specific office—President, Prime Minister—they often remain capitalized, even if followed by a preposition and even if not paired with a specific name.

George Bush, President of the United States
John Major, Prime Minister of Great Britain
The President arrived at two o'clock.
The Secretary of State flew to Geneva.

The Prime Minister's role is to lead both party and government.
A prime minister may do as she pleases. [A specific office is not being named.]

Capitalize titles and abbreviations of titles when they follow a comma—as in an address or closing to a letter.

Martha Brand, Ph.D.   Fred Barnes, Sr.
Sally Roth, M.D.   David Burns, Executive Vice-President

 5 **Capitalize the names of days, months, holidays, and historical events or periods.**

Monday   New Year's Day
Saturday   Columbus Day
December   Revolutionary War
January   Paleozoic Era
Christmas   Middle Ages

NOTE: When written out, centuries and decades are not capitalized.

the nineteenth century   the fifties   the twenty-third century

Seasons are capitalized only when they are personified.

spring semester   Spring's gentle breath
                         [The season is personified.]

6 **Capitalize particular objects and name-brand products.**

Mount Washington   USS *Hornet*
Jefferson Memorial   Sam Rayburn Building
Aswan Dam

Bic pen   Ford Taurus
Whopper   Apple computer
Sony television

30d

cap

7 **Use capitals with certain abbreviations, prefixes, or compound nouns.**

Capitalize abbreviations only when the words abbreviated are themselves capitalized.

Mister James Wolf   Mr. James Wolf
Apartment 6   Apt. 6
1234 Rockwood Avenue   1234 Rockwood Ave.
Silver Spring, Maryland Silver Spring, Md.

Capitalize acronyms and abbreviations of companies, agencies, and treaties.

FAA (Federal Aviation Administration)
ABM Treaty (Anti-Ballistic Missile Treaty)
DEC (Digital Equipment Corporation)

The prefixes *ex, un,* and *post* are capitalized only when they begin a sentence or are part of a proper name or title.

a post-Vietnam event	the Post-Vietnam Syndrome
an un-American attitude	the Un-American Activities Committee

Capitalize a number or the first word in a compound number that is part of a name or title.

Third Avenue
the Seventy-second Preakness

EXERCISE 1

Correct the capitalization in these sentences. When needed, change lower-case letters to uppercase and change uppercase to lowercase. Place a check before the two sentences in which the use of capitals is correct.

Example: The civil war soldier was going into action just when techni-cal improvements in the design of weapons had created a great increase in fire power.

The Civil War soldier was going into action just when tech-nical improvements in the design of weapons had created a great increase in fire power.

1. The basic all-important weapon was the infantry musket, and the standard of the war was the rifled springfield.
2. at a moderately long range the old springfield lacked penetrating power.
3. Drill on the target range began with the command, "load in nine times: load!"
4. The "Nine-times" meant that nine separate and distinct operations were involved in loading a piece.
5. The bullet was the Minie, named for the french captain who had invented it.
6. The damage wrought by the Minie ball was frightful; as one army surgeon wrote long afterwards: "Early experience taught surgeons that amputation was the only means of saving life."

30d

cap

ITALICS

A word set in italics calls attention to itself. On the typewritten (or handwritten) page, words that you would italicize are underlined. Italics have three principal uses: they give emphasis; they mark the plural forms of letters and numbers; and they denote titles of long works and certain names.

30e Underline or italicize words if they need a specific emphasis.

Words that you underline or set in italics are given particular emphasis. As a stylistic tool, italicizing will work well only if you do not overuse it.

Cultural relativity does *not* mean that a behavior appropriate in one place is appropriate everywhere.

Italicized words can be useful to create emphasis and change meaning in sentences, especially when writing attempts to duplicate the emphasis of speech.

"*You're* going to the movies with him?"
"You're going to the movies with *him*?"
"You're going to the *movies* with him?"

NOTE: The best way to create emphasis in your writing is not to simulate emotion with punctuation or with typeface, but to make your point with words. Italics should be saved for rare occasions and for a specific purpose. Overuse devalues the emphasis of italics and makes your writing appear overexcited and unconvincing.

OVERUSED   The Phoenicians were *masters* of the sea and with the cities they founded, like Tyre and Carthage, they became commercial *giants.* But Rome *envied* the Phoenician wealth. The angry prophet Isaiah called the Phoenicians *sinners,* and the heroic poet Homer thought they were *sly.* Ultimately, these many hatreds *crushed* the Phoenicians.

REWORDED   During the hundreds of years that they dominated the seas, the Phoenicians made enemies, the sort of enemies that are inevitable when you are commercially successful. Homer's heroic poems described the Phoenicians as slippery and as swindlers. Isaiah called Tyre a whore. The Romans depicted the Carthaginians as treacherous. In the end, the Phoenicians and Carthaginians lost to those enemies and were completely crushed, militarily and culturally.

30f

ital

 30f Underline or italicize words, letters, and numbers to be defined or identified.

 1 Use italics for words to be defined.

Words to be defined in a sentence are usually underlined or set in italics. Occasionally, such a word is set in quotation marks.

OPTION   The *operating system* runs a computer as a sort of master organizer that can accept commands whenever no specific program is running.

OPTION   The remarkable permanence of color in certain statues at the Acropolis is due, partly, to the technique of "encaustic," in which pigment is mixed with wax and applied to the surface while hot.

2 Use italics for expressions recognized as foreign.

Underline or italicize foreign expressions that have not yet been assimilated into English but whose meanings are generally understood. The following is a brief sampling of such words.

amore [Italian]	*Doppelgänger* [German]
enfant terrible [French]	*esprit de corps* [French]
e pluribus unum [Latin]	*hombre* [Spanish]
goyim [Hebrew]	*post hoc* [Latin]
pâté [French]	

No underlines or italics are used with foreign expressions that have been assimilated into English. The following is a brief sampling of such words.

alter ego [Latin]	blitz [German]
ex post facto [Latin]	fait accompli [French]
hoi polloi [Greek]	fellah [Arabic]
guru [Sanskrit]	kayak [Eskimo]
kibitz [Yiddish]	machete [Spanish]
maestro [Italian]	memorabilia [Latin]

3 Use italics to designate words, numerals, or letters referred to as such.

Underline or italicize words when you are calling attention to them as words.

Many writers have trouble differentiating the uses of *lie* and *lay*.

The word *the* is not capitalized in a title, unless it is the first word of the title or follows a colon or semicolon.

Italicize letters and most numerals when they are referred to as letters or numerals.

She crosses the *t* in *top*.

Shall I write a *1* or a *2*?

The combination of italics (or underlining) and an apostrophe with the letter *s* is used to make numbers and letters plural.

Cross your *t*'s and dot your *i*'s.

We saw *1*'s on the scoreboard each inning—a good sign.

30f

ital

30g

Use underlining or italics for titles of book-length works separately published or broadcast, as well as for individually named transport craft.

1 Use italics for books, long poems, and plays.

Love in the Ruins [novel]   *The Joy Luck Club* [novel]
A Discovery of the Sea [book]   *Twelfth Night* [play]
Antigone [play]   *The Odyssey* [long poem]
The Rime of the Ancient Mariner [long poem]

The titles of sacred documents (and their parts) as well as legal or public documents are frequently capitalized (see 30d) but are not set in italics.

the Bible   the New Testament
the Magna Carta   the Bill of Rights
the Koran   Book of Exodus

2 Use italics for newspapers, magazines, and periodicals.

the *Boston Globe*   the *New York Times*
Brookline *Citizen*   *Times*
the *Georgia Review*   *Archaeology*

With newspapers, do not capitalize, underline, or set in italics the word *the*, even if it is part of the newspaper's title. Italicize or underline the name of a city or town only if it is part of the newspaper's title. Titles of particular selections in a newspaper, magazine, or journal are set in quotation marks.

30g

ital

3 Use italics for works of visual art, long musical works, movies, and broadcast shows.

Rodin's *The Thinker*   *The Last Judgment*
Van Gogh's *The Starry Night*   the *Burghers of Calais*
Mozart's *The Magic Flute*   the *German Requiem*

NOTE: Underline or set in italics the article *the* only when it is part of a title.

Movies and television or radio shows are italicized.

As the World Turns   *A Prairie Home Companion*
Latenight with David Letterman *All Things Considered*
Batman   *Dick Tracy*

4 Use italics for individually named transport craft: ships, trains, aircraft, and spacecraft.

USS *Hornet* (a ship)   *Atlantis* (a spacecraft)
HMS *Bounty* (a ship)   the *Montrealer* (a train)
Apollo X (a spacecraft)   *Spirit of St. Louis* (an airplane)

Do not underline or italicize USS or HMS in a ship's name.

EXERCISE 2

Correct the use of italics in these sentences. Circle words that should not be italicized. Underline words that should be italicized. Place a check beside any sentence in which italics are used correctly.

Example: The most important tool of the navigator is an ⟨*accurate,* *current*⟩ chart, without which it is virtually impossible to navigate successfully.

1. Navigation is the art of staying *out* of trouble.
2. You can keep your charts as current as possible by subscribing to Local Notices to Mariners, a weekly publication of the U.S. Coast Guard.
3. The key to successful navigation is to navigate *continuously*, that is, *always* be able to determine the position of your boat on the chart.
4. *Landmarks* (smokestacks, water towers, buildings, piers, *etc.*) and *aids to navigation* (beacons, lighthouses, buoys) help relate what you see from your boat to items found on the chart.
5. Aids to navigation are installed and maintained by the Coast Guard *specifically* to help you relate your surroundings to the appropriate symbols on the chart.
6. A *beacon* will be denoted on the chart by a triangle and the letters *Bn.*

30g

ital

CHAPTER 31

Abbreviations and Numbers

The root word of *abbreviation* is the Latin *breviare*, from which comes the familiar *brief, briefing,* and *brevity.* We use an **abbreviation**—the shortened form of a word followed (for the most part) by a period—only in restricted circumstances. Most often these circumstances are formal and prescribed by standardized conventions, as in titles, forms of address, designations of units or of businesses, familiar acronyms, and numerical specifications in restricted settings such as charts or tables that report data in various disciplines. Most disciplines and professions use very specific sets of abbreviations to present their data and their numbers; this chapter can give only a sample of some of them. Writers working in an unfamiliar discipline should consult the standard manuals of reference, style, and documentation for guidance in using abbreviations and numbers in the field. Many such reference works are listed in chapter 36, Research Documentation, with conventions shown in chapters 37–39 on writing in each of the major discipline areas.

ABBREVIATIONS

Abbreviating titles of rank both before and after proper names

The following titles of address are usually abbreviated before a proper name.

Mr.   Mrs.   Ms.   Dr.

Though not an abbreviation, *Ms.* is usually followed by a period.

Abbreviations for titles of rank or honor are usually reserved for the most formal references and addresses in connection with a person's full name and title. Mention of a person's title or rank in a less formal context does not call for an abbreviation. Typically, the abbreviations *Gen., Lt., Sen., Rep.,* and *Hon.* precede a full name—first and last.

FAULTY	Gen. Eisenhower		Sen. Dole
REVISED	General Eisenhower		Senator Dole
REVISED	Gen. Dwight D. Eisenhower		Sen. Bob Dole

The following abbreviated titles or designations of honor are placed *after* a formal address or listing of a person's full name.

B.A.	M.A.	M.S.	Ph.D.	C.P.A.
Jr.	Sr.	M.D.	Esq.	

Place a comma after the surname, then follow with the abbreviation. If more than one abbreviation is used, place a comma between abbreviations.

Lawrence Swift, Jr., M.D.

Abbreviations of medical, professional, or academic titles are *not* combined with the abbreviations *Mr.*, *Mrs.*, or *Ms.*

FAULTY	Ms. Joan Warren, M.D.	Ms. Mindy Lubber, Ed.D.
REVISED	Dr. Joan Warren	Mindy Lubber, Ed.D.
	or Joan Warren, M.D.	*or* Dr. Mindy Lubber

Other than for direct reference to academic titles such as *Ph.D.* (Doctor of Philosophy), *M.A.* (Master of Arts), and *M.S.* (Master of Science), do not use freestanding abbreviated titles in a sentence that have not been paired with a proper name.

ACCEPTABLE	Jane Thompson earned her Ph.D. in biochemistry [A degree is referred to separately.]
FAULTY	Marie Lew is an M.D. [The degree should either be referred to separately or attached to the person's title.]
REVISED	Marie Lew is a physician.
REVISED	Marie Lew was awarded an M.D. degree from Harvard.
FAULTY	John Kraft is a C.P.A.
REVISED	John Kraft is a certified public accountant.
REVISED	John passed the C.P.A. examination yesterday.

31b

ab

31b Abbreviating specific dates and numbers

With certain historical or archaeological dates, abbreviations are often used to indicate whether the event occurred in the last two thousand years.

Ancient times (prior to two thousand years ago)

B.C.   (before the birth of Christ)

B.C.E.   (before the common era)

Both abbreviations follow the date.

Modern times (within the last two thousand years)

C.E.   (of the common era)

A.D.   (*Anno Domini*, "in the year of the Lord," an abbreviation that
        precedes the date)

Augustus, the first Roman Emperor, lived from 63 B.C. (*or* B.C.E.) to A.D. 14
(*or* C.E.).

When the context of a paragraph makes clear that the event occurred
in the last two thousand years—suppose you are writing on the Industrial
Revolution—it would be redundant, even insulting, to write "A.D. 1820."

Clock time, indicated as prior to noon or after, uses abbreviations in
capitals or in lowercase.

5:44 P.M. (or p.m.)

5:44 A.M. (or a.m.)

When typeset, A.M./P.M. often appear in a smaller type size as capital
letters: 5:44 P.M.

When numbers are referred to as specific items (such as numbers in
arithmetic operations or as units of currency or measure), they are used with
standard abbreviations.

No. 23 or no. 23   2 + 3 = 5
$23.01   99 bbl. [barrels]
54%

31b

ab

**Abbreviations for time, numbers, units, or money should be used
only with reference to specific dates or amounts.**

Numerical concepts must be fully written out as part of a sentence, not
given shortened treatment with abbreviations, unless they are attached to
specific years, times, currencies, units, or items.

FAULTY   We'll see you in the A.M.

REVISED   We'll see you in the morning.

FAULTY   Let's wait until the nos. are in before we make a decision.

REVISED   Let's wait until the numbers are in before we make a decision.

FAULTY   This happened in the B.C. era.

REVISED   This happened almost three thousand years ago.

FAULTY   Please tell me the % of dropouts for the year.

REVISED   Please tell me the percentage of dropouts for the year.

31c Using acronyms, upper-case abbreviations, and corporate abbreviations

An **acronym** is the upper-case, pronounceable abbreviation of a proper noun—a person, organization, government agency, or country. Periods are not used with acronyms. If there is any chance that a reader might not be familiar with an acronym or abbreviation, spell it out on first mention, showing the acronym in parentheses.

Medical researchers are struggling to understand the virus that causes Acquired Immune Deficiency Syndrome (AIDS).

The following are some familiar acronyms.

NATO   North Atlantic Treaty Organization

MADD   Mothers Against Drunk Driving

NASA   National Aeronautics and Space Administration

NOW   National Organization for Women

Helping Readers to Understand Acronyms

Unless an acronym or upper-case abbreviation is common knowledge, courtesy obligates you to write out the full word, term, or organizational name at its first mention. Then, in a parenthetical remark, you give the abbreviation. In subsequent references to the person, word, or organization, use the abbreviation—as is illustrated in the beginning of this article from the journal *Archaeology*.

> To the end of the Early Intermediate Period (EIP), the appearance of stunning, elaborately decorated ceramics . . . suggests that tribal leaders possessed and exchanged prestige items as a way of consolidating their claims to political power.

In lengthy documents where you will be using many upper-case abbreviations and acronyms, consider creating a glossary in addition to defining abbreviations the first time you use them. The glossary, which is placed at the end of the paper as an appendix, provides one convenient place to make identifications, sparing readers the trouble of flipping through pages and hunting for an abbreviation's first defined use.

31c

ab

Other upper-case abbreviations use the initial letters of familiar persons or groups to form well-known "call letter" designations conventionally used in writing.

JFK   John Fitzgerald Kennedy

SEC   Securities and Exchange Commission

ISBN   International Standard Book Number

NAACP   National Association for the Advancement of Colored People

MVP   Most Valuable Player

VFW   Veterans of Foreign Wars

USA (or U.S.A.)   United States of America

USSR (or U.S.S.R.)   Union of Soviet Socialist Republics

Abbreviations used by companies and organizations vary according to the usage of the organization. When referring directly to a specific organization, use its own preferred abbreviations for words such as *Incorporated (Inc.)*, *Limited (Ltd.)*, *Private Corporation (P.C.)*, or *Brothers (Bros.)*. Some companies will abbreviate the name of a city or state or the words *Apartment (Apt.)*, *Post Office (P.O.) Box*, *Avenue (Ave.)*, *Street (St.)*, or *Boulevard (Blvd.)* in their formal return addresses; others will not. In a sentence that does not refer directly to a specific corporation, do not abbreviate such terms, but spell out all the pronounceable words.

FAULTY   I mailed it to a corp. out on the blvd.

REVISED   I mailed it to a corporation on the boulevard.
           I mailed it to The Impax Corp., Zero Wilshire Blvd.

31d Using abbreviations for parenthetical references

31d

ab

From Latin, the traditional language of international scholarship, we have inherited conventional expressions used in research to make brief references or explanations. These are conventionally used in footnotes, documentation, and sometimes in parenthetical comments. All of these Latin expressions should be replaced in a main sentence by their English equivalents.

e.g. (*exempli gratia*)	for example
et al. (*et alii*)	and others
i.e. (*id est*)	that is
N.B. (nota bene)	note well
viz. (*videlicet*)	namely
cf. (*confer*)	compare
c. or ca. (*circa*)	about
etc. (*et cetera*)	and such things; and so on

The extremely vague abbreviation *etc.* should be avoided unless a specific and obvious sequence is being indicated, as in *They proceeded by even numbers (2, 4, 6, 8, etc.).* Even here the phrase *and so on* is preferable. When used in parenthetical or bibliographical comments, these Latin abbreviations are not underlined or italicized since they are commonplace in English. Typically, these expressions introduce a parenthetical remark in an informal aside.

INFORMAL   A growing portion of our National Income is composed of government transfer payments (e.g., welfare payments).

FORMAL   A growing portion of our National Income is composed of government transfer payments (for example, welfare payments).

Bibliographical abbreviations are commonly used in documentation to provide short forms of reference citations, but they should not be used in sentences of a paragraph. The following are some of the most frequently used abbreviations.

p.	page	Jan.	January
pp.	pages	Feb.	February
ed./eds.	editor(s)	Mar.	March
f./ff.	the following (pages)	Apr.	April
n.d.	no date (for a publication	Aug.	August
	lacking a date)	Sep./Sept.	September
ch./chs.	chapter(s)	Oct.	October
ms./mss.	manuscript(s)	Nov.	November
col./cols.	column(s)	Dec.	December
vol./vols.	volume(s)		

Each discipline has specific conventions for abbreviations in documentation, for example, the months May, June, and July are not abbreviated in MLA style; other conventions are discussed in chapter 36.

Revise to eliminate all but conventional abbreviations from sentences.

31e

ab

In sentences, no abbreviations are used for the names of days or months, units of measure, courses of instruction, geographical names, and page/chapter/volume references. These abbreviations are reserved for specific uses in charts and data presentations that require abbreviated treatment in each discipline.

FAULTY   Come see me on the first Mon. in Aug.

REVISED   Come see me on the first Monday in August.

FAULTY   He weighed 25 lbs.

REVISED   He weighed 25 pounds.

EXCEPTION: Abbreviations of standard, lengthy phrases denoting measurement are common in formal writing: miles per hour (mph or m.p.h.) and revolutions per minute (rpm or r.p.m.).

FAULTY   We enrolled in bio. and soc. next semester.

REVISED   We enrolled in biology and sociology next semester.

FAULTY   NYC is a haven for writers.

REVISED   New York City is a haven for writers.

FAULTY   The reference can be found in Vol. 6, sec. 5, p. 1. [These are used in bibliographies and documentation only.]

REVISED   The reference can be found in Volume 6, section 5, page 1.

Writing in the Disciplines

Conventions differ in the disciplines about when and how much writers should use abbreviations—and about which abbreviations are common knowledge and need not be defined. Across disciplines, abbreviations are avoided in titles. For specific abbreviations lying beyond common knowledge, writers follow the convention of defining the abbreviation on first use. As a demonstration, a sketch of conventions for abbreviating in some of the science disciplines is provided here. For detailed information about conventions in a specific discipline, see the style manuals recommended in chapters 37–39, section e, or consult your professor.

- In scientific writing, courtesy dictates that writers define words that are later abbreviated.

  Some 800 species of bats live in diverse habitats and vary greatly in behavior and physical characteristics. Their biosonar pulses also differ, even among species within the same genus. Nevertheless, these pulses can be classified into three types: constant frequency (CF), frequency modulated (FM), and combined (CF-FM).

- Units of measure are generally abbreviated when they are paired with specific numbers. When not thus paired, the units are written out.

  In the next stage, 14 g were added.
  Several grams of the material were sent away for testing.

- Abbreviations of measurements in scientific writing need not be defined on first use.

- Symbol abbreviations are standardized, and you will find lists of accepted abbreviations in the *CBE Style Manual* published by the Council of Biology Editors. Generally, the use of abbreviations in titles is not accepted in science writing. Limited abbreviations—without definition—are accepted in tables.

31e

ab

EXERCISE 1

Correct the use of abbreviations in these sentences. When appropriate, write out abbreviations.

> *Example:* In Ap. 1977, the Interfaith Ctr. on Corp. Responsibility announced that some of its subscribing members owned stock in Texaco and in SoCal (Standard Oil Company of California).
>
> In April 1977, the Interfaith Center on Corporate Responsibility announced that some of its subscribing members owned stock in Texaco and in Standard Oil Company of California (SoCal).

1. These members decided to introduce shareholders' resolutions at the next annual stockholders' meeting of Texaco and SoCal that would require the companies and their affiliates to terminate operations in S. Africa.

2. The effort to get Texaco out of South Africa was primarily directed by Tim Smith, project dir. of the Interfaith Ctr. on Corp. Responsibility.

3. The managements of Texaco and SoCal both opposed the resolution by citing their adherence to the Sullivan Principles, a code of conduct drafted by the Rev. Sullivan, a civil rights activist and minister of Phila.'s large Zion Baptist Church.

4. S. African blacks had in fact benefited from the presence of U.S. and other firms as evidenced by the dramatic 118% increase in black incomes between 1970 and 1975 followed by a 30% rise in the subsequent five year period.

5. In addition, the gap between blk. and white incomes had narrowed between 1970 and 1976.

NUMBERS

31f

31f	**Write out numbers that begin sentences and numbers that can be expressed in one or two words.**	*num*

One to ninety-nine

nineteen	seventy-six
twenty-six	ninety-nine

Fractions

five-eighths	three-fourths
two and three-quarters	seven-sixteenths

Large round numbers

twenty-one thousand   fifteen hundred

Decades and centuries

the sixties   or   the '60s
the twenty-first century   or   the 21st century

Numbers that begin sentences should be written out.

FAULTY   57 percent of those attending the meeting fell asleep.

REVISED   Fifty-seven percent of those attending the meeting fell asleep.

REVISED   Of those attending the meeting, 57 percent fell asleep.

When it is awkward to begin a sentence by writing out a long number, rearrange the sentence.

AWKWARD   Forty-two thousand eight hundred forty-seven was the paid atten-
            dance at last night's game.

REVISED   The paid attendance at last night's game was 42,847.

31g Use figures in sentences according to convention.

Numbers longer than two words

1,345   2,455,421

num

Units of measure

Rates of speed	Temperature	Length
60 mph	32°F	17.6 nanometers
33 rpm	0°C	24¹/₄ in.

Weight	Money	
34 grams	$.02 2¢	
21 pounds	$20.00	
	$1,500,000	$1.5 million

Amounts of money that can be written in two or three words can be spelled out.

two cents
twenty dollars
one and a half million dollars

Scores, Statistics, Ratios

The game ended with the score 2–1.

In the past presidential election, less than 50 percent of the eligible population voted.

The odds against winning the weekly lottery are worse than 1,000,000 to 1.

A mean score of 72 can be expected on the exam.

Addresses

Apartment 6	2nd Avenue
231 Park Avenue	East 53rd Street
New York, New York 10021	

Telephone numbers

301-555-1212

Volume, page, and line references

Volume 6	act 1 scene 4 line 16
page 81	pages 120–133

Military units

the 41st Tactical Squadron	the 6th Fleet

Dates

70 B.C.	A.D. 70
from 1991 to 1992	1991–1992
1991–92	

Time

Write out numbers when using the expression *o'clock*.

10:00 a.m. but ten o'clock in the morning
10:02 p.m. but two minutes past ten in the evening

31h

num

Edit to eliminate numbers and figures mixed together in one sentence, unless these have different references.

FAULTY   A spacecraft orbiting Earth travels at seventeen thousand miles per hour; but because of the craft's distance from the planet, the images of continents and oceans seen through its window appear to be moving not much faster than images seen through the windshield of a car traveling 60 mph.

REVISED   A spacecraft orbiting Earth travels at 17,000 mph; but because of the craft's distance from the surface, the images of continents and oceans seen through its window appear to be moving not much faster than images seen through the windshield of a car traveling 60 mph.

ACCEPTABLE   For two months before its closing, the U-Trust Savings and Loan advertised wildly fluctuating interest rates in an effort to secure new cash: 9 percent one month and 15 percent the next. [Both numbers referring to advertised rates are presented as figures; the numbers *two* and *one*, referring to measures of time, are written out.]

EXERCISE 2

Correct the use of numbers in these sentences. Write out numbers in some cases; use figures in others.

Example: 6,000,000 of its cars are sold annually, making Ford Motor Company the second largest automobile producer.

Six million of its cars are sold annually, making Ford Motor Company the second largest automobile producer.

1. Ford was the subject of one of the most famous product liability controversies in the nineteen seventies as a result of problems with its Pinto.
2. Although the normal preproduction testing and development of an automobile takes about forty-three months, the Ford teams managed to bring the Pinto to production in a little over 2 years.
3. Styling preceded engineering, which resulted in the Pinto's gas tank being placed behind the rear axle, leaving only 9 or ten inches of crush space between the rear axle and rear bumper.
4. Subsequent crash-test results showed that striking a Pinto from the rear at twenty-one miles-per-hour caused the gas tank to be punctured, creating a fuel leak that could easily be ignited by any stray spark.
5. Other test results showed that design improvements needed to prevent the fuel leakage problem would have cost eleven dollars per vehicle.

31h

num

CHAPTER 32

Hyphens

A small but important mark, the hyphen (-) has two uses: to join compound words and to divide words at the end of lines. You will find advice on word divisions in any dictionary, where each entry is broken into syllables. If you write on a computer, the odds are your word-processing software will suggest word divisions. As for compounds, these will require more discernment on your part, for relocating a simple hyphen can alter meanings entirely.

> The museum show included twenty first century examples of foundry art.

Two thousand years separate the two possible meanings of this sentence, and only the presence of a hyphen could settle whether you would expect ancient (twenty *first-century*) or futuristic (*twenty-first* century) examples of foundry art on visiting the museum. Small as they are, hyphens make a difference. Each of the following sentences has a distinct meaning.

> The cross reference helped me to understand the passage.

> The cross-reference helped me to understand the passage.

The first sentence concerns a literary reference to a *cross;* the second, a note that refers readers to some other page in an article or text.

32a Using hyphens to make compound words

Compound words are created when two or more words are brought together to create a distinctive meaning and to function grammatically as a single word. Many compounds occur together so often that they have become one word, formed without a hyphen.

> sandbox   outline   casework   aircraft

Many other words appearing in pairs remain separate. Two-word compounds often become one word over time, so consult a current dictionary when you are uncertain about spelling.

> sand toys   out loud   case study   air conditioning

Use a hyphen to link words when a compound expression would otherwise confuse a reader, even if only momentarily.

CONFUSING   Helen's razor sharp wit rarely failed her. [Helen's *razor* is not the subject; Helen's *wit* is.]

CLEAR   Helen's razor-sharp wit rarely failed her. [With the hyphen, meaning is clear.]

The conventions for forming compounds with hyphens are as follows.

1   Form compound adjectives with a hyphen to prevent misreading when they precede the noun being modified.

The following hyphenations make compound or multiple-word modifiers out of words that might otherwise be misread.

low-interest loan   state-of-the-art technology   hoped-for success

Note that when a **compound adjective** is positioned *after* the noun it modifies, it does not need hyphenation. Placed after a noun, the first word of the adjective does not compete for the reader's attention as the subject or object in the sentence.

Helen's wit was razor sharp.

A compound modifier is not hyphenated when its first word ends with the distinctive suffix of a modifier.

Helen's impressively sharp wit rarely failed her.

Because of its ending, the first word in this compound modifier is not misread. In this case, the *-ly* suffix marks *impressive* as an adverb, and the reader knows that *impressively* will not function as the subject. Thus, the suffix in effect instructs the reader to move forward in search of the sentence's first noun—*wit*, which is in fact the subject. Because there is no possibility of misreading, no hyphen is used. The same analysis holds when the first word of the compound is a modifier ending with a comparative or superlative suffix *-er* or *est* form (see 11e). In the following examples, the reader knows that *least* and *sweetest* are modifiers because of their endings.

The least expensive item in that store cost more than I could afford.
The sweetest sounding voice in the choir belonged to a child of ten.
[*By contrast:* The sweet-sounding voice belonged to a child of ten.]

2   Form compound nouns and verbs with a hyphen to prevent misreading.

Use a hyphen with **compound nouns** and **compound verbs** when the first word of the compound invites the reader to regard that word, alone, as a noun or verb. Hyphenated nouns and verbs are marked as such in a dictionary.

cross-reference (n)   cross-examine (v)   runner-up (n)   shrink-wrap (v)

Hyphenating the compound forms makes reading the following sentence easier.

CONFUSING   The runner up staged a protest. [What is intended: *runner-up* or *up-staged*?]

REVISED   The runner-up staged a protest.

3   Use hanging hyphens in a series of compound adjectives.

Hang—that is, suspend—hyphens after the first word of compound adjectives placed in a parallel series. In this usage, observe that the second word of the compound as well as the noun being modified is mentioned *once*.

The eighth-, ninth-, and tenth-grade classes went on the trip. [The second word of the compound, *grade*, and the noun modified, *classes*, are mentioned once.]

4   Follow conventions in hyphenating numbers, letters, and units.

Hyphenate fractions and the numbers twenty-one through ninety-nine.

Place a hyphen between the numerator and denominator of a fraction, unless one of these (or both) is already hyphenated.

one-fourth   seven-thousandths   seven one-thousandths
forty-six   seventy-one

Hyphenate figures and letters joined with words to form nouns or modifiers.

4-minute mile   B-rated   U-turn

Hyphenate units of measure.

light-year   kilowatt-hour

32a

hyph

5 Hyphenate compounds formed by prefixes or suffixes according to convention.

Use a hyphen with the prefixes *ex, quasi,* and *self,* with the suffix *elect,* and with most uses of *vice.* (Consult a dictionary for specifics.)

ex-President   quasi-serious   self-doubt

Use a hyphen with the prefixes *pro, anti,* and *pre* only when they are joined with proper nouns.

NO HYPHEN	HYPHEN WITH PROPER NOUN
prochoice	pro-Democracy
antimagnetic	anti-Maoist

But use a hyphen with a prefix or suffix that doubles a vowel or that triples a consonant.

NO HYPHEN	HYPHEN WITH PROPER NOUN
antiseptic	anti-intellectual
childlike	bell-like

6 Hyphenate to avoid misreading.

re-form (to form an object—such as a clay figure—again)
reform (to overhaul and update a system)

EXERCISE 1

Use hyphens in the sentences that follow to form compound adjectives; to mark prefixes or suffixes; to note fractions, numbers less than one hundred, or words formed with figures; and to prevent misreading. Place a check beside any sentence in which hyphens are used correctly.

Example: Following WWII, Pepsi Cola Company succeeded in recruiting Alfred N. Steele, a tough talking, two fisted, pinstriped warrior with a unique grasp of the mood of the fifties.

Following WWII, Pepsi-Cola Company succeeded in recruiting Alfred N. Steele, a tough-talking, two-fisted, pinstriped warrior with a unique grasp of the mood of the fifties.

1. Steele was uniquely qualified to lead the Pepsi Cola Company when it began to falter because of its outdated marketing campaign; he had been educated at the world's greatest soft drink institution—the Coca Cola Company.
2. Beginning his career running a circus, he moved into advertising and then jumped to a vice presidency at Coca Cola.
3. Subsequently, Steele accepted the more lucrative offer from Pepsi-Cola, though in his first quarter at the company it lost $100,000 as Coca-Cola pulverized the entire industry with a 67% stranglehold on the soft drink market.

32a

hyph

4. Coca Cola was the darling of the ever expanding middle class, while Pepsi was a favorite of the downtrodden who couldn't afford to sacrifice Pepsi's extra ounces for Coke's prestige.
5. Thus, Steele set his sights on getting Pepsi into America's living rooms, and to that end redesigned Pepsi's standard 12 ounce bottle.

32b Using hyphens to divide a word at the end of a line

To the extent possible, avoid dividing words at the end of a line. For those times when you must divide words, do so only at syllable breaks (as noted in a dictionary). Even when given suggestions for hyphenation by word-processing software, you often face a choice concerning hyphenation that could make a difference in clarity. The following conventions improve comprehension.

Divide compound words at the hyphen marking the compound.

When hyphens join compound words, it is unnecessary and confusing to divide the word at any place other than the compound. (See the discussion on writing compounds in 32a.)

UNNECESSARY   The mouthparts of many insects are exquisitely adapted to the nectaries (*nectar-hold-ing* organs) of special flowers.

CLEARER   The mouthparts of many insects are exquisitely adapted to the nectaries (*nectar-holding* organs) of special flowers.

Divide words at a prefix or suffix.

Hundreds of words are formed in English by adding prefixes and suffixes to root words. (See 22e-2, 3.) Divide these words, when possible, between prefix and root word or between suffix and root word. Thus, *un-necessary* would be preferable to *unne-cessary*.

A number of prefixes—such as *pro, anti, quasi, vice,* and *ex*— require the use of a hyphen. Divide these words at the hyphen.

AWKWARD   In the election of 1848, the "Free-Soil" party nominated Charles Francis Adams for *Vice-Presi-dent.*

REVISED   In the election of 1848, the "Free-Soil" party nominated Charles Francis Adams for *Vice-President.*

32b

hyph

Eliminate hyphenations that hang a single letter at the beginning or end of a line.

To avoid misleading your readers, you would not divide these words: *e-nough* (it is misleading) or *tast-y*.

CONFUSING   Inflation creates fractures in the implicit and explicit *a-greements* that bind people together.

REVISED   Inflation creates fractures in the implicit and explicit *agree-ments* that bind people together.

Eliminate misleading hyphenations.

The first syllable of a word is sometimes itself a word (for instance, *break-fast, arch-angel, in-stall, match-less*). Confusion results when the first syllable, left hyphenated at the end of a line, fits a sentence's content and suggests one meaning while the full, undivided word suggests another.

Single-syllable words are never hyphenated.

To prevent misleading the reader, you would not, for example, divide any of these words; *ceased, doubt, friend, freeze, though*.

Abbreviations, contractions, or multiple-digit numbers are not hyphenated.

Abbreviations (*apt., IBM, NATO*) and contractions (*can't, won't, they're*) are already shortened forms. To shorten them further by a word division will confuse your readers. A multiple-digit number divided at the end of a line is also confusing.

32b

hyph

PART IX

Writing the Research Paper

CHAPTER 33

Understanding the Research Process

Each discipline you study is based on a body of knowledge that is continually growing and changing. Your professors have a good deal to do with this change. In their own research they challenge assumptions; make discoveries about the physical world; and find meaningful patterns in human behavior and human artifacts, past and present. Researchers gain entrance into this world of making and revising knowledge gradually. At first their efforts focus on the library, where they develop habits of investigation important to all researchers, beginners and experts alike. In many of your courses you will be asked to write papers based on library research.

Four chapters constitute the section of this book devoted to research. The present chapter introduces you to a process of conducting library research that will lead you to pertinent sources on your topic. Chapter 34 is devoted to the ways in which you will *use* these sources: taking notes, summarizing, paraphrasing, and quoting. Chapter 35 will provide guidance on arranging materials and writing your paper. And chapter 36 will acquaint you with the process of documenting sources—acknowledging in your papers that you have drawn on the work of others.

33a Investigating the world through research

Since people in colleges and universities spend a good deal of time conducting research, and since college instructors are the ones who will evaluate your research efforts, you can gain from learning how faculty view their own research. How do their ideas develop into research questions? How are research questions pursued? How are new ideas communicated? How does new research generate discussion and even controversy?

Observe how professional researchers approach the issues.

Recently, two researchers at the University of California, Santa Barbara—Judith Kirscht and John Reiff, of the Writing Program—interviewed some of their colleagues from other departments to learn the answers to these questions. For example, they asked professor of psychology Diane Mackie about how her research projects begin. Professor Mackie replied:

> I guess most of the ideas really come out of interacting with other people. When colleagues are talking, or when you're talking with students about something, and somebody just says, "I don't follow how these people came to that conclusion," or "Didn't somebody do something else that was inconsistent with that?" And we're sitting there and we're thinking . . . yes, that seems inconsistent and . . . what could we do to see which one is right, or which one is wrong . . . or is one right under different circumstances? And it seems to me that's where the majority of our ideas come from.

Kirscht and Reiff interviewed other professors who spoke about levels of personal commitment to their work. Julia C. Allen, who has published extensively in the field of geography and environmental studies, spoke of how she grew interested in the subject of forest management. On a trip to Tanzania, she was "so struck by the deforestation in the country that [she] decided . . . to do a Ph.D. . . . on the problem of managing forests and the environmental effects of that process." In an interview, Professor "R," an historian, explained his personal commitment to research projects this way:

> Basically, I think I've always chosen research topics that respond to something I personally am looking for. I've always tried to construct a coherent, philosophical world view for myself, and I'm always interested in topics that help me better understand basic questions I'm asking.

Also interviewed was anthropologist Napoleon Chagnon, whose years of field research on the Yanomamo Indians of Venezuela resulted in the best-selling monograph ever written in anthropology—*Yanomamo: The Fierce People.* For Professor Chagnon, clearly expressing the results of research is important:

> Even though I pride myself on being hard-nosed and quantitative and meticulous and testing hypotheses by chi-squares [a statistical technique] and other things, I think, also, a lot of my publications reflect an interest in and a genuine respect for being able to state things clearly and in an interesting way.

Chagnon's research into the causes of warfare also got him embroiled in controversy, not an uncommon experience in the academic world. From this fact follows a cautionary note on academic research that you may find surprising:

33a

> I think it's important for students who are going to get involved in research to understand that the academic world is not one big, altruistic, happy family where scholars and academics make decisions on whose theory is better than someone else's theory on the basis of logic, reason, methods, science, etc.; that the behavior of scientists and academics is often vicious, nasty, unpleasant, and downright political.

What conclusions can you draw from comments such as these? First, academic researchers write on topics important to them for personal reasons, professional reasons, or both. Second, colleagues discuss their work or the work of other researchers with one another, and these discussions sometimes lead to ideas for future research. Third, the products of one's research must be communicated clearly and engagingly to one's audience. Finally, researchers will sometimes disagree with one another, sometimes quite heatedly.

Find your own "burning question."

In conducting and reporting on your own research, you can put these conclusions to work. Just as your professors do, you should have a *reason* for researching a topic aside from your obligation to complete an assignment. Choose a "burning question," one that you feel you must find an answer to. Once engaged by your work, you will want to discuss your progress—and frustrations—with friends and teachers; you will be committed enough to defend or challenge certain points of view; and you will be committed enough to want, as Professor Chagnon wants, to "state things clearly and in an interesting way."

1   Using essay writing as a foundation for research writing

The process of writing a research paper is very similar to that of writing an essay. In chapters 3 and 4 of this book, a diagram was used to model the writing process (see pages 54, 75, and 99). This illustration shows writing and thinking as circular, recursive activities. *Recursive* means looping back on itself. The term as applied here suggests that although a writer will identify purpose and define audience, will generate ideas and organize information, and will produce a first draft, in no way will these activities represent a straight-line progression from the beginning of a paper to the end. For instance, well into developing the first draft of a research report, you may discover the need for new information. When this happens, you will need to interrupt your work on the draft and return to your notes, to the lab, or to the library for the necessary material. That is, to move forward you may sometimes need to pause and loop backward to an earlier stage in the process of writing and research.

33a

Be a critical thinker.

In the discussion that follows, you will learn a strategy that will help you generate information for your research papers in most courses. Conducting research requires that you work with source materials, reading with a critical eye. Give your work a boost by becoming familiar with the material in chapter 1, "Critical Thinking and Reading," where you will find specific strategies for reading to comprehend sources, to evaluate them, and to relate them to each other and to your unique point of view. See also chapter 2,

"Critical Thinking and Writing," where you will learn the types of writing—especially synthesis—essential to working with source materials.

EXERCISE 1

Interview two of your professors. Ask what kinds of research they do and why their research interests them personally. Ask what, if any, "burning questions" have directed their research. Why do these questions burn for them? Take notes during the interviews. Then review these notes and write three paragraphs: two paragraphs devoted to summarizing the interviews; and one paragraph in which you make observations about the research your professors do and their personal relationships to that research.

33b Defining the scope of your paper

1 Determining the research assignment

What you write about in your research paper—the kind of subjects you pursue—is determined primarily by the discipline in which you are working. A paper on the incidence of alcoholism among student athletes would be suitable for a sociology course, but not for a literature or business course. A paper on the genetic factor in crack cocaine addiction would be suitable for a biology course, but not for a sociology course. The following examples show some representative research assignments in the major disciplinary areas; they concern general topics that can be adapted to a wide variety of particular subjects.

Social Science

Describe and discuss a particular behavioral pattern or syndrome among a definable social group. The group may be defined by social class, ethnicity, gender, occupation, age, or some other factor. You may also wish to compare the behaviors of this group with corresponding behaviors of one or more other groups.

Humanities

Examine several works by a particular playwright or novelist, focusing on a single feature or device characteristic of this artist. Explain how and why this feature manifests itself in different forms in various works and perhaps how it develops over the artist's career. Draw on the interpretations of critics and literary scholars to help illuminate your discussion.

Science

Scientists frequently find themselves drawn into controversies when their research tends either to support or to refute the views of particular groups or of social critics. For example, Darwin and his followers were embroiled

33b

in conflicts with creationists; physicists have been involved in controversies over the safety of nuclear power plants. Select a particular scientific discovery or line of research and explore the ways in which it has generated controversy among scientists and nonscientists alike.

Business

In recent years, much attention has been focused on the ethical aspects of business decisions. Research and discuss a particular business practice that has raised significant ethical questions. Show, by means of case studies, the kind of controversies and problems that have arisen as a result of such practices, and discuss and evaluate some of the recommended solutions to these problems.

2 Formulating initial questions

In preparing to write a paper on the general subject of drug abuse, what kind of questions might you ask?

The following are some questions from the perspective of the *social sciences.*

How do various cultures differ in their approach to drug abuse? How do drugs and alcohol affect the behavior and mental functioning of those who take them? To what extent does the incidence of drug abuse vary with age, sex, race, ethnicity, religion, family history, or educational level? How effective are prevention programs? What is the incidence of drug abuse among college or professional athletes?

The following are some questions from the perspective of the *humanities.*

How has drug abuse been treated in works of art—novels, short stories, plays, films, poetry? How have particular artists succumbed to drug abuse? To what extent have important historical personalities and events been affected by drug abuse? To what extent do organized religions see drug use as a problem?

The following are some questions from the perspective of the *sciences.*

What are the physiological effects (long term, short term) of drugs and alcohol on the human body and its various systems and organs? How effective has modern medicine been in dealing with the effects of drug abuse? Is alcoholism a disease? Should it be approached—both by society and by medical professionals—as if it *were* a disease, that is, without moral condemnation or punishment?

The following are some questions from the perspective of *business.*

How is productivity affected by drug abuse? What are the costs of developing and implementing drug prevention and treatment programs in the workplace? How effective are such programs? Should there be random drug testing of employees—particularly employees in sensitive positions (such as air traffic controllers)? How reliable are such tests?

Most of these questions are too broad as they now stand; you would have to narrow them down considerably to make them more suitable for a paper of ten to twenty-five pages. In looking at the question of how race is related to drug abuse, for example, you might focus on differences among alcohol consumption between Asians and Caucasians, or on drinking practices among Jews, or on substance abuse among Native American adolescents.

Before you narrow the focus too sharply, however, it would be wise to do some preliminary research on the subject. Otherwise, you may overlook aspects that you would have found particularly interesting. This preliminary research could involve reading an encyclopedia or magazine article, a section of a textbook, or possibly even a short book on the subject. Such reading may raise particular questions in your mind—"burning" questions that you feel compelled to pursue. Afterward, you will be in a better position to narrow your focus—and you will do this primarily by searching your sources to discover the answer to one primary *research question*. This research question may be one of the questions posed here, or it may be another question that was raised in the course of your preliminary reading. The advantage of a question, as opposed to a thesis, at this point, is that you are acknowledging that you still have to discover the answer(s), rather than just to find evidence to support a prematurely established conclusion.

EXERCISE 2
Select one question from each of the disciplinary groups covered in the previous section and narrow it down to a more particular question that you could deal with in a short research paper. Focus on *particulars*—particular social groups, artists, physical effects, companies, programs, and so on.

33c Generating ideas for the paper

Perhaps you have selected a broad subject, which you may have already begun to narrow down. Or you may have started with a "burning question" and have begun to follow it up with further questions. Here, we will consider ways of further narrowing your focus and of searching for information sources about your topic. Specifically, we will consider (1) how to keep a research log of your ongoing ideas; (2) how to develop a search strategy for preliminary reading; and (3) how to develop a search strategy for more focused reading, leading toward the development of your working thesis.

1 Keep a research log.

Many students find it valuable to keep track of their ideas in a research log. They write down their initial questions in this log and update it as often as possible. The log becomes a running record of all their inspirations, false starts, dead ends, second thoughts, breakthroughs, self-criticisms, and plans.

One technique that is particularly useful at the outset of a project is called *nonstop writing*. Nonstop writing (sometimes called *brainstorming* or *freewriting*) requires you to put pen to paper, consider your topic, and write down anything that occurs to you. Do not stop to revise, fix punctuation or spelling, or cross out bad ideas. Do not even stop to think what to say next—just write. The goal is to generate as many ideas as you possibly can within a limited period of time—say, ten or fifteen minutes. At the end of a session of nonstop writing, you may (or may not) have some useful ideas that you want to pursue.

Here, for example, are some initial ideas generated by nonstop writing sessions about alcohol and drugs. Note the difference in personal styles: the first is a stream-of-consciousness entry; the second is a list; the third is a rough plan for designing a questionnaire.

1. bad dangerous alcohol related accidents kill a lot of people drugs also kill and are one of the leading causes of violent crime alcohol is bad for the liver brain cells die with drugs, lungs, emotional problems, family problems begin because of alcohol and drug abuse, kids die, genetics are messed up miscarriage or deformations occur.

2. Cocaine, Crack, Heroin, Pot, Ludes, Sinsemilla
   Drugs can kill.
   Too many kids use drugs. Peer pressure
   AIDS from shared needles
   Alcohol is a drug
   Drinking and driving

3. There are many things to write about concerning drug and alcohol abuse. If I were to do a research paper that was interesting, I would probably make out questionnaires and survey people. That way the info. I get would be personal, not from a book. I would ask people if, when, why, and how much they drink or smoke. Then, also, if they think of themselves as an alcoholic or drug abuser. Of course, I would have to do research into the effects of alcohol and drug abuse. That could be interesting . . .

33c

Even though these ideas are in crude form, you can see some papers beginning to take shape here. As you proceed with your research, keep your log updated. You will want to do this not just to preserve a record of your research (often valuable in itself), but also to allow you to return to initially discarded ideas which, at a later stage in the paper, may assume new relevance or importance.

Researchers use a log for other purposes, as well.

1. To jot down *sources* and possible sources—not only library sources, but also names and phone numbers of people to interview.

2. To freewrite their *reactions* to the material they are reading and to the people they are interviewing; these reactions may later find their way into the finished paper.

3. To jot down *questions* that occur to them in the process of research, which they intend to pursue later. (For example, how much money does the federal government allocate to drug education? What percentage of large U.S. companies have drug testing programs?)

4. To try out and revise ideas for *theses*, as their research progresses.

Do not use your log for actually taking notes on your sources; it is best to do this on note cards.

Generating Ideas for Your Paper

The following are three additional strategies for generating ideas. Each will help you consider ways in which to divide a broad topic into smaller, more manageable parts. You will probably be more specific and imaginative in thinking about *parts* of a topic than you will in thinking about the topic as a whole.

- **Reading:** Read general works that survey your topic. The survey will suggest subdivisions. Some encyclopedia entries begin with an outline of the discussion. A research project appropriate for a term paper would focus on *part* of that outline.

- **Brainstorming:** Place your topic at the top of a page and, working for five or ten minutes continuously, list any related phrases or words that come to mind. Work quickly. After generating your list, group related items. Groups with the greatest number of items indicate areas that should prove fertile in developing your paper.

- **Listing attributes:** In a numbered list, jot down all of the attributes, or features, that a broad topic possesses. Then ask of every item on your list: What are its uses? What are its consequences?

---

2   Talk with your instructor or with other authorities.

33c

Before you start your research, do not neglect another important resource: your professor. Schedule a conference or visit your professor during office hours. You may have little or no idea about what kind of paper you would like to write, but during the course of discussion, something may occur to your professor or to you that piques your curiosity, that becomes the equivalent of the "burning question." Your conference may turn into a kind of verbal freewriting session, with several unresolved questions remaining at the end of the session—one of which may become the focus of your paper.

3 Work toward a thesis.

You have now focused on a particular research question; you have done some preliminary reading and perhaps have talked to one or two authorities on the subject; and you have begun generating some written ideas. At this point—having begun to formulate some informed opinions on the subject—you are ready to venture a thesis. If you had attempted to develop the thesis any earlier, you might not have been ready. You might have reached a conclusion that could not be supported by additional research. Or you might have proceeded to assemble a mass of supporting material without being sufficiently aware of whether or not you were missing sources in related areas that could enhance (or even refute) your thesis. On the other hand, do not wait too long to formulate a thesis. If you do, your research is likely to be unfocused, and your supporting material may not provide a coherent answer to your central research question. Remember that having selected a thesis, you are under no obligation to zealously guard it against all changes. Quite possibly, you will need to adjust your focus—and therefore your thesis—as your research and your thinking on a subject develop.

EXERCISE 3

Choose a subject—either one of your own or one of the subjects discussed here—and develop some ideas about it, using one or more of the strategies discussed in this section. Read at least two relevant sources, and then develop a tentative thesis for a research paper on the subject.

33d Library research: Preliminary reading

Research logs and other strategies can be useful for getting down on paper ideas and information that you already have. Conferences with your professor can help get you thinking about a subject. Obviously, though, there are numerous aspects of that subject of which you are not yet aware, and one of these aspects may interest you enough to become your final topic. The best way to discover some of the possibilities is to use a systematic library search strategy.

33d

1 Develop a preliminary search strategy.

A good search strategy begins with the most general reference sources: encyclopedias, bibliographic listings, biographical works, and dictionaries. The accompanying diagram shows a skeleton view of such a library search strategy. By consulting such sources at the outset, you will be able to narrow your subject to a manageable scope—that is, to one that you can cover in adequate depth within the length specified.

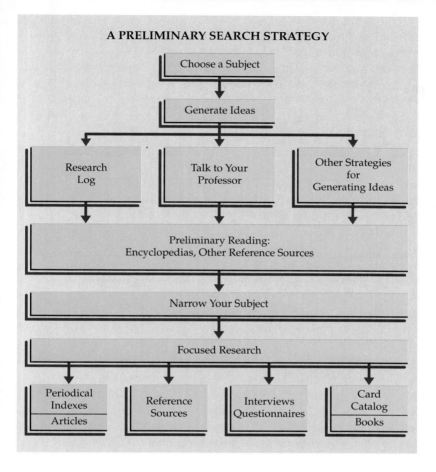

A PRELIMINARY SEARCH STRATEGY

Choose a Subject

Generate Ideas

Research Log

Talk to Your Professor

Other Strategies for Generating Ideas

Preliminary Reading: Encyclopedias, Other Reference Sources

Narrow Your Subject

Focused Research

Periodical Indexes
Articles

Reference Sources

Interviews Questionnaires

Card Catalog
Books

33d

Having narrowed your subject, you can then locate additional information, both from (1) periodicals and newspapers, which you locate through indexes and abstracts and/or computer search; and (2) books, which you locate through the card catalog and/or computer search. During this part of your search, you may further narrow your topic, and you can consult additional books and articles as necessary, along with additional reference sources such as biographical dictionaries, specialized dictionaries, and book reviews.

The following diagram illustrates how the narrowing down process might proceed.

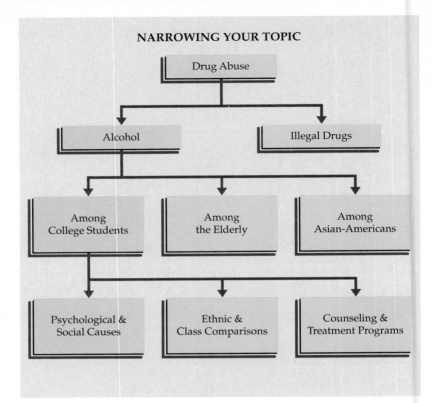

NARROWING YOUR TOPIC

Drug Abuse

Alcohol

Illegal Drugs

Among College Students

Among the Elderly

Among Asian-Americans

Psychological & Social Causes

Ethnic & Class Comparisons

Counseling & Treatment Programs

This diagram illustrates the process of a student who wants to write a paper on the drug problem. After some idea-generating strategies, she decides to focus on alcohol abuse. Since this subject is obviously still too broad for a relatively short paper, she does some preliminary reading and considers whether to focus on alcohol abuse among college students, among the elderly, or among a particular ethnic group, such as Asian-Americans. After some additional reading, she decides to concentrate on alcohol abuse among college students. But finding that even this narrowed-down topic is too broad, she finally decides on a paper dealing with the psychological and social causes of alcoholism among college students.

You should recognize that any diagram of the search strategy or of the narrowing-down procedure makes these processes look neater than they generally are. In practice, they are often considerably less systematic. What is crucial is to keep in mind the kind of resources and procedures that are available to you, and—given the constraints on your time—to use as many as you can.

33d

As you proceed, you will discover that research is to some extent a self-generating process. That is, one source will lead you—through references in the text, citations, and bibliographic entries—to others. Authors will refer to other studies on the subject; and frequently, they will indicate which ones they believe are the most important, and why. At some point you will realize that you have already looked at most of the key research on the subject. This is the point at which you can be reasonably assured that the research stage of your paper is nearing its end.

2 Use librarians as a resource.

We list "librarians" as a primary source, because they are a *major* resource too frequently overlooked both by harassed students *and* by professors. As one of our colleagues has remarked, "Librarians—especially reference librarians—are a *godsend.*" Librarians have made it their career's work to know how to find information quickly and efficiently. This does not mean that they will do your research for you. It means they will be happy to direct you to the tools with which to do your own research. Frequently, the key to getting the information you need is simply knowing where to look. The next section will provide some assistance in this area. Your reference librarian will be able not only to supplement our list of sources, but also to tell you which ones are best for your purposes.

3 Look into the general sources.

General sources, such as general encyclopedias and biographical dictionaries, are designed for people who want to familiarize themselves relatively quickly with the basic information about a particular subject. Authors of general sources assume that their readers have little or no prior knowledge of the subjects covered and of the specialized terminology used in the field. Thus, if they use specialized terminology, they are careful to define it. General sources are also comprehensive in their coverage.

On the other hand, general sources tend to lack depth. They typically cover a subject in less detail than does a specialized source, such as an encyclopedia of music or a business periodical index. They also cover fewer subjects in a given field. Thus, while a student interested in a major film director such as Alfred Hitchcock would probably find an appropriate article in a general encyclopedia, someone beginning research on a less well-known director such as Leo McCarey would be better advised to consult a specialized encyclopedia of film. And, in fact, this specialized encyclopedia would probably have a more extensive article on Hitchcock than the general encyclopedia. In this section we will review some of the most useful general sources.

33d

Encyclopedias

A general encyclopedia is a comprehensive, often multivolume work that covers events, subjects, people, and places across the spectrum of human knowledge. The articles, usually written by specialists, offer a broad overview of the subjects covered. From an encyclopedia you may be able to discover a particular aspect of the subject that interests you and to see how that aspect relates to the subject in general. Encyclopedia entries on major subjects frequently include bibliographies.

Keep in mind that encyclopedias—particularly general encyclopedias—are frequently not considered legitimate sources of information for college-level papers. Thus while you may want to use an encyclopedia article to familiarize yourself with the subject matter of the field and to locate specific topics within that field, you probably should not use it as a major source, or indeed, for anything other than background information.

One disadvantage of encyclopedias is that since new editions are published only once every several years, they frequently do not include the most up-to-date information on a subject. Naturally, this is of more concern in some areas than others: if you are writing on the American Revolution, you are on safer ground consulting an encyclopedia than if you are writing on whether doctors consider alcoholism a disease. Still, the nature of scholarship is that *any* subject—including the American Revolution—is open to reinterpretation and the discovery of new knowledge, so use encyclopedias with due caution.

Following are some of the most frequently used general encyclopedias:

American Academic Encyclopedia
Collier's Encyclopedia
Columbia Encyclopedia
Encyclopedia Americana
Encyclopædia Britannica

Biographical sources

Frequently you may have to look up information on particular people. Note that some biographical sources are classified according to whether the person is living or dead. The following are some of the most common biographical sources:

33d

FOR PERSONS STILL LIVING

American Men and Women of Science
Contemporary Authors: A Biographical Guide to Current Authors and Their Works
Current Biography
Directory of American Scholars
International Who's Who

FOR PERSONS LIVING OR DEAD

American Novelists Since World War II
Biography Almanac
American Poets Since World War II
Contemporary American Composers: A Biographical Dictionary
McGraw-Hill Encyclopedia of World Biography
National Academy of Sciences, Biographical Memoirs
Webster's Biographical Dictionary

Dictionaries

Dictionaries enable you to look up the meaning of particular terms. As with encyclopedias, dictionaries may be either general or specialized in scope. Some of the more common dictionaries are listed in 22b-1.

Other sources of information

In addition to encyclopedias, biographical sources, and dictionaries, you may find the following sources useful:

Guides to the literature enable you to locate and use reference sources within particular disciplines. Here are five examples:

Reference Books: A Brief Guide
How and Where to Look It Up: A Guide to Standard Sources of Information
Sources of Information in the Social Sciences
Guide to Historical Literature
Business Information Sources

Handbooks provide facts and lists of data for particular disciplines. Here are several examples:

Handbook of Chemistry and Physics
The Allyn and Bacon Handbook (covers grammar and style)
Handbook of Basic Economic Statistics
Statistical Abstract of the United States
Gallup Poll: Public Opinion

Almanacs also provide facts and lists of data, but are generally issued annually:

Information Please Almanac (general)
The World Almanac (general)
Almanac of American Politics
Congressional Quarterly Almanac
Dow Jones Irwin Business Almanac

33d

Yearbooks, issued annually, update data already published in encyclopedias and other reference sources:

Americana Annual

Britannica Book of the Year

Statesman's Yearbook

Atlases and gazetteers provide maps and other geographical data:

National Atlas of the United States of America

Times Atlas of the World

Citation indexes indicate when and where a given work has been cited *after* its initial publication; these are useful for tracing the influence of a particular work:

Social Science Citation Index

Humanities Citation Index

Science Citation Index

Book review indexes provide access to book reviews; these are very useful for evaluating the scope, quality, and reliability of a particular source:

Book Review Digest (includes excerpts from reviews)

Book Review Index

Government publications are numerous and frequently offer recent and authoritative information in a particular field:

American Statistics Index

Congressional Information Service

The Congressional Record

Government Manual

Guide to U.S. Government Publications

Information U.S.A.

Monthly Catalogue of U.S. Government Publications

Consult your librarian for information on guides to the literature, almanacs, and other reference guides relevant to your subject.

33d

Bibliographic Index

Although we will cover periodical indexes in a later section of this chapter, it is appropriate here to mention the *Bibliographic Index* as an excellent research tool both for browsing through some of the subtopics of a subject and for directing you to additional sources. The *Bibliographic Index* is an annual bibliography of bibliographies (that is, a bibliography that lists other bibliographies), arranged by subject. Here, for example, is part of the listing under "Alcoholism" in the 1990 *Bibliographic Index*.

Main heading — **Alcoholism**
        See also
Entries under other main headings —
    Alcoholics
    Drinking of alcoholic beverages
    Korsakoff's syndrome
       See also subhead Alcohol use under classes of persons and ethnic groups

Ackerman, Robert J. Children of alcoholics; a bibliography and resource guide. 3rd ed Health Communications 1987 82p

Advances in alcohol and substance abuse. Haworth Press. See issues

Author — Ellis, R. J. and Oscar-Berman, M. Alcoholism, aging, and functional cerebral asymmetries. *Psychol Bull* 106:143-7 — Volume: Page numbers
Date of Periodical — Jl '89

Kline, R. B. The relation of alcohol expectancies to drinking patterns among alcoholics: generalization across gender and race. *J Stud Alcohol* 51:181-2 Mr '90

Room, R. Alcoholism and Alcoholics Anonymous in U.S. films, 1945-1962: the party ends for the "wet generations".
Title of Periodical — *J Stud Alcohol* 50:382-3 Jl '89

Wallace, John. Alcoholism; new light on the disease. Edgehill Publs. 1990 p149-55

Wallace, John. John Wallace; writings. Edgehill Publs. 1989 — Publisher and date
incl bibl

Subheading — **Genetic aspects**
Stabenau, J. R. Additive independent factors that predict risk for alcoholism. *J Stud Alcohol* 51:172-4 Mr '90

Government policy
Great Britain
Preventing alcohol and tobacco problems; v. 2, Manipulating consumption: information, law and voluntary controls; edited by Christine Godfrey and David Robinson. Avebury 1990 incl bibl

History
Lender, Mark E., and Martin, James Kirby. Drinking in America; a history. rev & expanded ed Free Press; Collier Macmillan 1987 p207-19 annot — Entries are annotated

Cross-reference — **Physiological aspects**
See Alcohol—Physiological effect

Prevention
Gonzalez, G. M. An integrated theoretical model for alcohol and other drug abuse prevention on the college campus. *J Coll Stud Dev* 30:501-3 N '89

Milgram, Gail Gleason. The facts about drinking; coping with alcohol use, abuse, and alcoholism; [assisted by] the editors of Consumer Reports Books. Consumers Union of U.S. 1990 p165-73 — Number of pages

O'Gorman, Patricia A., and Oliver-Diaz, Philip. Breaking the cycle of addiction; a parent's guide to raising healthy kids. Health Communications 1987 p155-62

Preventing alcohol and tobacco problems; v. 2, Manipulating consumption: information, law and voluntary controls; edited by Christine Godfrey and David Robinson. Avebury 1990 incl bibl

33d

Each of these listings represents a bibliography that appears in another source—a book, a pamphlet, or an article. In most cases, the bibliography appears as a source of additional reading at the conclusion of the book, the chapter, or the article. In some cases, however, the bibliography stands by itself as an independent publication. If you browse through a few successive years of listings on a subject, you will probably discover some topics that interest you, as well as a source of readings on that topic.

Using General Sources

- Use *encyclopedias* to get a broad overview of a particular subject.
- Use *biographical sources* to look up information about persons living or dead.
- Use *general dictionaries* to look up the meaning of particular terms.
- Use *guides to the literature* to locate reference sources in particular disciplines.
- Use *handbooks* to look up facts and lists of data for particular disciplines.
- Use *almanacs* to look up annually updated facts and lists of data.
- Use *yearbooks* to find updates of data already published in encyclopedias and other reference sources.
- Use *atlases* and *gazetteers* to find maps and other geographical data.
- Use *citation indexes* to trace references to a given work after its initial publication.
- Use *book review indexes* to look up book reviews.
- Use *government publications* to look up recent and authoritative information in a given field.
- Use *bibliographic sources* to locate books and articles on a particular subject.

EXERCISE 4

Select a subject you are interested in learning more about. Look up information about this subject in various general sources, keeping a record of (1) the *sources* used (give full bibliographic information); (2) the *location* of the relevant information (give page numbers); and (3) the *type* of information you find (give brief descriptions).

33e Devising a working thesis

During your preliminary reading you began to focus on a *research question*. For example: should private companies require drug testing of their employees? As you continue to read about this subject—including arguments on both sides of the issue, anecdotal and statistical information about the experiences of certain individuals and certain companies—you should begin to develop your own ideas about your subject. Many of these ideas may have found their way into your journal. Perhaps as you reflect on the experiences you have read about, and as you review your journal entries, one side's argument begins to seem considerably stronger than that of the other side. Or perhaps it is not a case of one argument being stronger than another, but a combination of various circumstances that makes testing advisable in some cases and inadvisable in others. Such observations and reflections on your part should eventually come into focus as a *working thesis*. This thesis is, of course, subject to change as you come across new material and as your thinking about the subject develops further. For now, however, this working thesis is the main idea that shapes your thinking. The working thesis will also influence the focused reading of your subsequent research since, by defining relevant areas and eliminating irrelevant ones, it narrows the scope of your search for supporting evidence.

For the sake of example, let's consider four working theses. First, we will consider the narrower topics developed from the main subject:

> For a paper in the *social sciences*, the topic is alcoholism among college students.
>
> For a paper in the *humanities*, the subject is the motif of drug and alcohol abuse in the works of American playwright Eugene O'Neill.
>
> For a paper in *science*, the subject is whether alcoholism should be considered a disease.
>
> For a paper in *business*, the issue is drug testing in the workplace.

So far, these are only *topics*—not theses. To develop a working thesis from each of these topics, you will need to make a *statement* about the topic (after surveying a good deal of source material). Here are four statements that can be used as working theses:

> *Social Science:* Alcoholism among college students is an increasingly serious problem, but there are workable solutions.
>
> *Humanities:* Alcoholism and drug abuse are important elements of O'Neill's later plays; these elements are grounded in O'Neill's own life.
>
> *Science:* Alcoholism should be considered a disease, rather than an immoral behavioral syndrome.
>
> *Business:* In certain occupations drug testing is necessary to ensure public safety.

Note that while each thesis requires that the writer support his or her opinion, the first two theses tend to be *descriptive*, while the second two tend to be *argumentative*. That is, in each of the first two cases, the writer will attempt to describe a situation that she or he believes to be true. But the thesis itself is not a particularly controversial one; it is not a proposition that normally generates strong emotions. After considering the evidence, most people would probably agree with the thesis. In the latter two cases, however, the writer will argue one side of a fairly controversial issue. These are issues on which it is sometimes difficult to get people to change their minds, even after considering the evidence, because they have strong underlying feelings about them. To take an example from another area: a *descriptive* thesis would

33e

be "Abortion rights have been a decisive factor in many recent state elections." (One could provide enough evidence to show that this was the case.) An *argumentative* thesis would be "Abortions should be readily available to those who want them." (For those whose religious or moral convictions make abortion unacceptable, it would be difficult to find any evidence that would change their minds—though it may be possible to find evidence and lines of argument that would persuade those who are more or less undecided on the subject.)

> **EXERCISE 5**
> Based on your preliminary reading in general sources (Exercise 4), develop two working thesis statements about your topic: a *descriptive thesis* and an *argumentative thesis*. Make sure that each thesis takes the form of a *statement* about the topic.

33f Doing focused reading

If you have looked through a number of general sources, you have probably also developed a working thesis. At this point, you have some basic knowledge about your subject and some tentative ideas about it. But there are limits to your knowledge—which correspond to the limits of the kind of sources you have relied on so far. You need more specific information to pursue your thesis.

1 Looking for specific sources

General sources are not intended to provide in-depth knowledge, nor can they explore more than a few of the often numerous aspects of a subject. Refer back to the diagram on page 550. If you were researching the subject of alcoholism among college students, your general sources might be sufficient to get you down to the third level of the diagram, but the sources' inherent limitations would prevent them from taking you any further. For more detailed information about the kind of topics on the fourth level—the psychological and social causes of alcoholism among college students, ethnic and class comparisons, counseling and treatment programs—you would need to do more focused reading. You need a strategy for locating information in articles and books.

2 Finding what you need in focused sources

An overview of available sources will help you focus on the ones that best address your thesis. This overview will start with articles in order to emphasize the fact that periodical indexes are often preferable to the card catalogue as a first step in conducting focused research.

General periodical indexes: Magazines

Periodicals are magazines and newspapers published at regular intervals—quarterly, monthly, daily. Periodical articles often contain information available from no other source and are generally more up-to-date than books published during the same period. You are probably familiar with the *Reader's Guide to Periodical Literature* as a means of locating magazine articles, but there are numerous other periodical reference guides.

For example, consider *Ulrich's International Periodicals Directory*. This is not a periodical index, but rather a subject guide to periodicals, that is, it directs you to periodicals on a given subject. To find out more about the nature or scope of a particular magazine, check *Katz's Magazines for Libraries*. This reference tool lists the most commonly used magazines and offers basic descriptive and evaluative information about each.

Like encyclopedias, periodical indexes are of two types: *general* and *specialized*. The most commonly used general periodical index is, of course, the *Reader's Guide to Periodical Literature,* which indexes magazines of general interest such as *Time, Newsweek, U.S. News and World Report, The New Republic, Sports Illustrated, Commonweal.* Here, for example, is a recent *Reader's Guide* entry for "Drug Abuse."

DRUG ABUSE
     See also
     Alcoholics and alcoholism
     Children of drug addicts
     Cocaine
     Crack (Cocaine)
     Drug education
     Drugs and authors
     Drugs and blacks
     Drugs and infants
     Drugs and politicians
     Drugs and sports
     Drugs and the aged
     Drugs and women
     Drugs and youth
     Heroin
     Marijuana
The drug dilemma: manipulating the demand [cocaine]
    M. E. Jarvik. bibl f *Science* 250:387-92 O 19 '90 — *Title of article*
Drug policy: striking the right balance. A. Goldstein
    and H. Kalant. bibl f il *Science* 249:1513-21 S 28
    '90 — *Includes picture*
The drug war [cover story; special section] il *The
    Humanist* 50:5-30+ S/O '90
Just say whoa [J. Bennett resigns as drug czar] il por — *Subject of article (if not clear from title)*
    Time 136:91 N 19 '90 — *Volume: pages*

          Rehabilitation
     See also
     Church work with drug addicts
The cure: researchers say a nonaddictive painkiller stops
    cravings for cocaine and heroin [buprenorphine] K.
    McAuliffe. il *Omni (New York, N.Y.)* 13:20 D '90 — *Date of issue*
Meharry gets $2.8 million to treat drug-using moms.
    Jet 79:28 N 5 '90
Perinatal substance abuse and public health nursing
    intervention. B. A. Rieder. bibl f il *Children Today* — *Title of Periodical*
    19:33-5 Jl/Ag '90
          Testing — *Subheading*
Hairy problems for new drug testing method [Psy-
    chemedics Corp.'s use of radioimmunoassay] C. Holden. — *Author*
    il por *Science* 249:1099-100 S 7 '90

33f

Another useful general periodical index is the *Essay and General Literature Index,* which indexes (by subject, author, and sometimes by title) articles and essays which have been collected into books. The index is especially useful in that it gives you access to material that might not otherwise have surfaced in your search. These articles and essays generally would be classified under the humanities, but some deal with social science issues as well.

Computerized periodical indexes

Note that many periodical indexes are also available through computer. Indexes may be *on-line:* your library may provide access to off-campus electronic databases, such as DIALOG, WILSONLINE, PSYCHINFO, BIOSIS, or INFOTRAC. DIALOG is the name of a commercial database vendor— and of the software—used to retrieve records from 300 bibliographic databases. WILSONLINE is another such general database. PSYCHINFO is a specialized index for psychological articles; BIOSIS is a specialized index for biological articles. INFOTRAC provides access to articles in over 900 business, technological, and general-interest periodicals, as well as the *New York Times* and the *Wall Street Journal.* Some on-line databases (such as INFOTRAC) are available at no cost to the user. Other on-line database searches can be expensive (as much as $75.00 per hour) because they involve access to a national network. Therefore they are generally not used for undergraduate research.

The library may also have information on CD-ROM (compact disc, read-only-memory). CD-ROM searches involve no additional expense, since the library has already purchased the CDs. Since one CD can store several years worth of indexes, a CD-ROM search takes less time and effort than a search through several bound volumes of printed indexes.

General periodical indexes: Newspapers

33f

Most libraries have back issues of important newspapers on microfilm. The *New York Times Index* may be used to retrieve articles in the *Times* as far back as 1913. There are also indexes for the *San Francisco Chronicle,* the *Los Angeles Times,* and the *Wall Street Journal* (an important source of business news). The *Newspaper Index* lists articles from the *Chicago Tribune,* the *New Orleans Times-Picayune,* the *Los Angeles Times,* and the *Washington Post.* You can print out "hard copies" (from microfilm) of articles you need. If you're looking for articles in newspapers other than these, check dates of stories in the *New York Times Index,* or see whether the newspaper has a search service.

Here is a sample entry on "Drug Addiction and Alcohol Abuse" from a recent *New York Times Index:*

Major stories in bold face

Brooklyn man who waged campaign against drug dealers in his Sunset Park neighborhood is run over and killed by furious van driver; family and neighbors of victim, Ceferino Viera, say killing was in retaliation for his persistence in ordering drug dealers, addicts and prostitutes off block; note that Viera had refused to move even as crack dealing drove many of his neighbors away; police say they have no strong evidence that Viera was killed for his anti-crime stand, but his neighbors and friends are convinced that that was cause; photo (M), Ap 18,A,1:1 **Manhattan grand jury indicts defense lawyer Lynne F Stewart for criminal contempt for refusing to disclose source and amount of legal fees she got for defending drug dealer Donald Maldonado;** her trial is expected to underscore growing legal battle in United States over lawyer-client confidentiality; special narcotics prosecutor Sterling Johnson sought unusual indictment; photo (M), Ap 18,B,1:5

Description of story

James J Dolan Jr, suspended police chief of Hudson, NY, is sentenced to five years probation and fined $8,000 for obstructing justice by intefering with drug investigations by other law-enforcement agencies (M), Ap 19,B,4:4
Florida appeals court upholds first conviction in nation of woman charged with delivering cocaine to her newborn baby through umbilical cord; decision is first time state appeals court had approved prosecution strategy of charging new mothers whose babies are born with traces of cocaine in their blood under laws designed to punish drug dealers who give drugs to children under 18; mother, Jennifer Clarise Johnson, 25 years old, of Orlando, is sentenced to 14 years' probation and participation in drug-treatment program; photo (M), Ap 20,I,6:4

Date of story, section no., page no. , column no.

Dates of relevant stories are in chronological order

The card catalogue

Most libraries have now computerized their card catalogues; if this process is not yet complete, some of the older books may be accessible only through the traditional 3 × 5 card files. But whether on-line or on cards, a given item in the catalogue will be classified in three ways—by *author*, by *title*, and by *subject*. Browsing through some of the subject cards is a good way of locating books on your topic; but before you do this, you should have at least begun to narrow your subject. Otherwise, you could be overwhelmed with the sheer number of books available. (There may be several hundred books on various aspects of the drug problem.)

Notice the call number in the upper left-hand corner of the cards. One or more letters preceding the number indicates that the book has been catalogued according to the Library of Congress System, the most common cataloguing system for larger libraries. Smaller libraries use the Dewey Decimal System, which always begins with a number.

Shown on pages 562 and 563 are three catalogue cards for *Alcohol and Old Age* by Brian L. Mishara and Robert Kastenbaum. The library's on-line computer database would have equivalents to these cards in printout form. If you are doing literary research, most of the books you will need will have call numbers beginning with "PR" or "PS"; if you are working on a political science paper, you will probably be looking in the "E" section. If you are working with the Dewey Decimal System, literary books are in the 800 series and political science books are in the 300 series. Check the reference desk at your library for a key to the cataloguing system.

33f

SUBJECT CARD

```
            ALCOHOLISM.
    RC
    451.4  Mishara, Brian L.
    .A5      Alcohol and old age / by Brian L.
    M57    Mishara and Robert Kastenbaum. -- New
           York : Grune & Stratton, c1980.
            ix, 220 p. ; 24 cm. -- (Seminars in
           psychiatry)

            1. Geriatric psychiatry. 2. Aged--
           Psychology. 3. Alcohol--Physiological
           effect. 4. Alcohol--Psychological
           aspects. 5. Alcoholism.
```

AUTHOR CARD

```
    RC
    451.4  Mishara, Brian L.
    .A5      Alcohol and old age / by Brian L.
    M57    Mishara and Robert Kastenbaum. -- New
           York : Grune & Stratton, c1980.
            ix, 220 p. ; 24 cm -- (Seminars in
           psychiatry)
            Includes bibliographies and index.

            1. Geriatric psychiatry. 2. Aged--
           Psychology. 3 Alcohol--Physiological
           effect. 4. Alcohol--Psychological
           aspects. 5. Alcoholism.
           I. Kastenbaum, Robert, joint author.
           II. Title
```

33f

TITLE CARD

```
           Alcohol and old age
RC
451.4   Mishara, Brian L.
.A5       Alcohol and old age / by Brian L.
M57     Mishara and Robert Kastenbaum. -- New
           York : Grune & Stratton, C1980.
            ix, 220 p. ; 24 cm. -- (Seminars in
           psychiatry)
```

Library of Congress Subject Headings

If you have not narrowed down your subject by the time you begin your catalogue search, you should probably check the *Library of Congress Subject Headings*. This is a set of volumes that indicates how the subjects listed according to the Library of Congress System are broken down. For example, drug abuse is broken down into such subtopics as "religious aspects," "social aspects," and "treatment." You can use the *Library of Congress Subject Headings* as you used the encyclopedia entries or the *Bibliographic Index*. First, you can survey the main aspects of that subject. Second, you can select a particular aspect that interests you. Third, you can focus your subject search (both in the book and periodical indexes) on the particular aspect or subtopic that interests you, since these subtopics indicate the headings to look under in these indexes.

Book Review Digest

An invaluable source for determining the quality of books is the *Book Review Digest*. This publication, collected into annual volumes, indexes many of the most important books published during a given year by author, title, and subject. More important, it provides lists of reviews of those books, as well as brief excerpts from some of the reviews. Thus, you can use the *Book Review Digest* to quickly determine not only the scope of a given book (each entry leads off with an objective summary) but also to determine how well that book has been received by reviewers. If the reviews are almost uniformly good, that book will be a good source of information. If they're almost uniformly bad, stay away. If the reviews are mixed, proceed with caution.

33f

Trade bibliographies and bibliographies of books

For books too recent to have been acquired by your library or which the library does not have, you may wish to consult *Books in Print* and

Paperbound Books in Print. These volumes, arranged by author, title, and subject, are available in some libraries and in most bookstores. For books that your library does not have, but which may be in other libraries, consult the *Cumulative Book Index* and the *National Union Catalog.*

Focused Reading

- To locate articles in general-interest magazines, use *The Reader's Guide to Periodical Literature,* the *Reader's Guide CD-ROM index,* INFOTRAC, or another database index.

- To locate articles in newspapers, use the *New York Times Index* or other indexes for particular newspapers.

- To identify periodicals specializing in a given subject, use *Ulrich's International Periodicals Directory.*

- To determine the scope of a particular magazine, use *Katz's Magazines for Libraries.*

- To locate books and government publications, use the *card catalogue* or the library's *on-line catalogue.*

- To determine how a given subject is subclassified in card catalogues, use the *Library of Congress Subject Headings Index.*

- To locate reviews of books, see the *Book Review Digest.*

---

3   Working with non-library research

33f

Although you will probably conduct most of your research in the college library, remember that professional researchers do most of their work *outside* the library—in the field, in labs, in courthouses, and in government and private archives. Consider the possibilities of conducting original research for your own paper, by (1) interviewing knowledgeable people; (2) devising and sending out questionnaires; (3) making your own observations or experiments, in the appropriate settings; (4) seeking out unpublished letters, diaries, or personal papers; and (5) looking through government records in federal, state, county, or local files.

For example, in conducting research on alcoholism among college athletes, you might seek out and talk to students who are willing to discuss their alcohol problems. (Of course, you must assure them that their identities will remain strictly confidential.) You might also talk to medical professionals who treat such students. For a paper on the value of drug testing by private business, you could talk, or send questionnaires, to business executives, to employees who have had to submit to such testing, or to lawyers who are involved in the legal issues behind such testing. For a paper dealing with therapy for those with drug problems, you could seek permission to attend a session for recovering addicts. Consider, also, that many subjects have been extensively discussed by experts on television news programs, talk shows, and documentaries. It may be possible (either by calling or writing to the station, or simply by checking with the library) to borrow videocassettes or to obtain printed transcripts of such programs.

EXERCISE 6

Researching either the topic you selected in Exercise 4, or some other topic, locate at least five books and ten articles on the subject. Provide complete bibliographic information for these sources (see 34b). Locate several reviews of at least one of the books, and in a paragraph summarize the main responses.

Choosing the best sources

At some point during your research, you will probably realize that you have accumulated more sources than you can possibly read, let alone use in your paper. How do you sort through all of this material? How do you distinguish the valuable from the useless? Here are a few worthwhile techniques:

- *Skim* through the material. At first, read only the introductions and conclusions, the section headings, and the topic sentences; skim the rest. If you are looking at a book, skim the preface, the table of contents, and selected topics that you locate through the index. If what you have skimmed seems useful and interesting, you can begin reading more carefully.

- Generally, if you have two or more sources that cover the same ground, then you should prefer the most *recent* source. Recent sources frequently incorporate important previous work—and refute earlier mistakes and misjudgments. Of course, certain older sources may be important for their distinctive viewpoints, for their thorough coverage of the subject, or for other reasons. However, you can often determine the "classic" sources in a particular field because their titles will keep turning up in bibliographies and in references by other authors you have read.

- If your source is a book (particularly a book on which you plan to rely heavily), look up the reviews in the *Book Review Digest* or the *Book Review Index*. If the reviews are largely negative, drop the source (or use it with due caution).

- Check the credentials of the author by means of a biographical index such as *Contemporary Authors* or *Who's Who in America*.

33g

- Use your own judgment to determine whether an author is reliable. (See 1c, Reading to evaluate a source.) Ask yourself: How reliable, accurate, significant, or representative is the evidence cited by the author? Assess the author's logic. How well has the author defined key terms? How reliable are the author's assumptions? Admittedly, it is not always easy to answer such questions; after all, you are not an expert on the subject. But as you read more and more sources, you will gain expertise, and this will help you make the kind of critical judgments that enable you to separate good sources from bad ones.

Having narrowed down your list of sources, your next task is making the best possible use of them, a task discussed in chapter 34.

33g

CHAPTER 34

Using Sources

Researchers in a college community work with written sources, and the library, home to these sources, is the hub of academic life. Each discipline has its specialized journals in which the latest research is reported, and each discipline has a multitude of specialized books devoted to its study. When researchers want to know what work has been done in an area, they conduct a search, or literature review, that reveals the varieties of inquiry into the area, the names of investigators, and the possibilities for further research. Without the benefit of prior work, researchers would be left to begin every inquiry from the beginning. Having to re-invent the wheel, so to speak, as if no one else had ever studied a particular problem, would be a wasted effort. The ability to read well, to *use* sources, is a crucial skill for researchers.

34a Reading with care

A search process that generates sources is useful only if you can work with them: only if you can read and understand, evaluate, respond to, and forge relationships among several selections on a related topic. Strategies for conducting a close, active reading are discussed at length in chapter 1, "Critical Thinking and Reading." Chapter 1 offers advice for strategic reading; it discusses how to search for and distinguish an author's facts from his or her opinions, and provides techniques for evaluating both facts and opinions. It shows how to recognize and evaluate an author's assumptions— bedrock beliefs about the world and the way it works, the beliefs on which the author builds arguments. And it provides a strategy for making inferences among your sources, for seeing the multiple ways in which Source A is related to Sources B, C, and D. In conducting and reporting on your research, you will need to make such relationships explicit.

Your ability to write a research paper depends on your ability to use sources. And your ability to use sources, the subject of this chapter, depends *entirely* on your ability to read well. Because effective reading is a foundational skill on which the success of all research rests, you should turn to chapter 1 if you are not fully comfortable with the prospect of reading to understand, respond, and forge relationships. Close, strategic reading is a skill you can teach yourself; once learned, it will serve you well both in college and in your career.

Characteristics of a Careful, *Critical* Reader

- **Read with a strategy.** Before reading, preview a selection and pose questions. During reading, make notes and monitor your progress. After reading, review notes, highlight the important passages, and organize questions.

- **Distinguish facts from opinions and evaluate both.** Recognize the differences between facts (statements that can be checked for accuracy) and opinions (statements that are interpretations). Question each.

- **Identify assumptions.** Whether they are stated explicitly or not, identify assumptions and determine the extent to which you agree with them and, subsequently, the arguments built on them.

- **Infer relationships among sources.** While you are reading one source, bear in mind other sources you have read on the same topic. Cross-reference your sources, noting where one author refers to ideas discussed by other authors. Identify the relationship of one source to others. When possible, establish a comparison, contrast, definition, example, process, or cause and effect.

- **Respond personally.** Invest yourself sufficiently in your reading to react. Write your reactions as "comment notes" that you make while reading. Refer to these notes when you begin to write, for often a personal response will help you to formulate a thesis for a research paper.

34b Creating a working bibliography

Your **working bibliography** is a list of all of the sources you locate in preparing your paper. This includes books, articles, entries from biographical sources, handbooks, almanacs, and the various other kinds of sources cited in chapter 33. The bibliography should also include sources you locate in indexes that you intend to check later. Your working bibliography differs from your **final bibliography** in that it is more comprehensive: the final bibliography consists only of those sources that you actually use in writing the paper.

It is absolutely essential that you prepare your working bibliography *at the same time* that you are compiling and consulting your sources. That way you can be sure to have accurate and complete information when the time comes to return to your sources to obtain more information or to double-check information, and to compile your final bibliography. It is enormously frustrating to be typing your list of references (quite possibly the night before your paper is due!) and to suddenly realize that your notes do not contain all the information necessary.

We recommend that you compile a working bibliography on 3" × 5" index cards. A card file allows you to easily alphabetize entries or to arrange them in any other order (such as by topic and subtopic order, or by sources you have already examined and ones you have not) that is most useful to you during the research and writing process. As you consult each new source, carefully record key information:

1. full name of author (last name first),
2. title (and subtitle),
3. publication information:
   a. place of publication
   b. name of publisher
   c. date of publication
4. inclusive page numbers

In case you have to relocate the source later, indicate the library call number (in the upper right-hand corner) and the name and date of the index where you located the source (at the bottom). It is also a good idea to include (either below the publication information or on the back of the card) a brief annotation, in which you describe the contents of that source or the author's main idea, and indicate your reaction to the source and how you might use it in your paper. By surveying your annotations as you proceed with your research, you will quickly be able to see how much you have already found on your subject and what else you still need to look up. Your annotations may also help prevent you from wasting time looking up the same sources twice. Finally, you should assign a code number to each bibliographic entry. Then, when you are taking notes on the source (perhaps on 4" × 6" note cards), you can simply put that code number in the upper right-hand corner of the note card, which saves you from having to recopy your complete bibliographic information.

When the time comes to prepare your final bibliography, you can simply arrange the cards for the sources you used in alphabetical order and type up the pertinent information as a list. Here's a sample bibliography card for a book.

4. Berger, Gilda, *Drug Testing.* New York: Franklin Watts, 1987.

HV58235
U5B47
1987

Considers the U.S. drug crisis and issues of drug testing in various public & private sectors. Chapter 7 deals with drug testing in private industry — includes several specific cases.

34b

Here's a sample card for an article.

⑱ Gilmore, Thomas B. "The Iceman Cometh and PI
the Anatomy of Alcoholism" Comparative C6184
Drama, 18.4 (winter 1984-85): 335-47.

Focuses on Hickey. Thesis: "throughout the play the
principles of AA [Alcoholics Anonymous] provide an
excellent means of analysis for examining Hickey's
salesmanship in order to determine the quality of
his new product or line, sobriety" (336)
1984 MCA Bib. 1:10436

A note on *photocopying*: frequently, you will not be able to check periodicals out of the library, so you may find yourself photocopying stacks of
articles. In recent years many journals have begun to include complete
bibliographic information at the bottom of the first page of each article. But if
some or all of this information is not already there, *make sure you carefully and
immediately record the bibliographic data on the first page of the photocopy*. To
provide additional backup for documentation, you may find it useful to
photocopy those pages of the bibliographic indexes from which you located
sources; keep in mind, however, that these pages often indicate the authors'
first names only by initials.

If you are photocopying a section of a book, it is a good idea to also
photocopy the book's title page, which contains all the bibliographic information, except the date of publication (that is located on the reverse side of
the title page). Whether copying articles or books, double-check to make sure
that you have copied *all* of the text on each page—including the page number
(you may have to write these in). Finally, if you are photocopying text that
includes footnotes, remember to also copy the corresponding footnote references at the end of the article, the chapter, or the book. Again, taking the time
to do all of this now—at the photocopy machine—may save you hours of time
later if you have to relocate the item.

34b

EXERCISE 1

Compile a working bibliography—both books and articles—of twenty to
twenty-five items for one of the subjects you have been researching for the
previous chapter. Or if you prefer, research a new subject. Record key

information (as indicated above) on 3" × 5" cards or in your electronic database (if the latter, you will need a printout). Include content annotations for at least five items.

Taking notes

Use 4" × 6" cards for taking notes. You could use other materials, of course, but you will have difficulty sorting through and rearranging individual entries. Notecards solve this problem and allow you to add or drop entries with ease.

Researchers use various formats for notecards, but the following elements are most important:

1. a *code number* (corresponding to the code number on your bibliography card) *or* the bibliographic reference;
2. A *topic* or *subtopic* label (these enable you to easily arrange and rearrange the cards in topical order);
3. the *note* itself;
4. a *page reference*.

Do not attempt to include too much information on a single notecard. For example, do not summarize an entire article or chapter on one card, particularly if you are likely to use information from a single card in different places in your paper. By limiting each card to a single point or illustration, you make it easier to arrange your cards according to your outline, and to rearrange them later if your outline changes. A sample notecard for Gilda Berger's *Drug Testing* appears on page 572. (For comparison's sake, it is placed directly after the bibliography card for the same source.)

---

④ Berger, Gilda, *Drug Testing.* New York :
Franklin Watts, 1987.

HV58235
U5847
1987

34c

Considers the U.S. drug crisis and issues of drug testing in various public & private sectors. Chapter 7 deals with drug testing in private industry — includes several specific cases.

Test Accuracy ④

The accuracy of drug testing is open to serious question. Berger states that "out of every twenty people in a workplace tested for drugs, the chances are that one will get a false positive result" (p. 88). And while testing labs claim error rates of less than one percent, one study revealed that "Known samples submitted to thirteen drug laboratories showed error rates as high as 100 percent for certain drugs." (p. 88)

There are three methods of notetaking: *summarizing, paraphrasing,* and *quoting.* These methods can be used either singly or in combination. *Summarizing* is used when there is a relatively long passage of text from which you need to extract one or two main points; these points would probably be used as background information for your own paper. *Paraphrasing* is used with a relatively brief passage of important material that is central to your discussion or argument. *Quoting* is used if the person being quoted has made a point in a particularly dramatic or incisive way, or if the reputation of this person would enhance the credibility of your presentation. The preceding notecard on drug testing used a combination of quotation and summary.

To illustrate how each of these methods of notetaking would show up in the final paper, we will use as an example the final two paragraphs of an article called "Jar Wars" by William Saletan, which appeared in the October 2, 1989, *New Republic.*

34c

> Conyers's campaign chairman told reporters that he and other Conyers officials were "philosophically opposed" to the drug test but took it anyway just to quash the issue. "The conventional wisdom now is to acquiesce, to get it out of the arena right away," explains one GOP consultant. But in jar wars, like nuclear wars, everybody loses. Take Atlanta. In 1986 rumors of drug abuse by Bond provided at least a bare context for making testing an issue. In 1989 even that basis was lacking, but both candidates volunteered for the test anyway. Several other local officeholders have also begrudgingly taken the test to immunize themselves against suspicion. Local consultants say widespread capitulation has made the test, in effect, a mandatory ritual. Elsewhere consultants say more and more candidates are keeping test results at hand, just in case they're needed.

> Every politician who takes a drug test justifies it as a way to send a message to the public, particularly to the young. But the trouble is that it sends the wrong message: if you won't take the test, you're suspect. Not only are your agenda and your political record irrelevant, but so is your conduct, which is the only defensible basis for requiring a drug test of a political candidate. The only way to reverse this trend is to reverse the test. The message from voters to politicians must be: if you value substance above stunts, and if you respect yourself and your constituents, offer us your platform and your record, not your urine.

Here is how the information in that passage might turn up in the final paper. Markings indicate those sections summarized, paraphrased, and quoted from the original.

Summary {
> Many candidates for public office have been feeling pressure both from their political opponents and from the anti-drug atmosphere to submit to drug testing as a way of proving themselves drug free (Saletan 14). But self-imposed drug testing of politicians is not necessarily a good trend. As Saletan remarks, "in jar wars, like

Quotation {
> nuclear wars, everybody loses" (14). The message sent by these tests, notes Saletan, is if you don't agree to take one you may be

Paraphrase {
> guilty, and that your political philosophy and your past performance have no bearing on your qualifications for office.

1   Summarizing sources

A *summary* is a relatively brief, objective account, in your own words, of the main ideas in a source passage. As mentioned previously, you would summarize a passage when you wanted to extract the main ideas and use them as background material in your own paper. For details on the process of writing summaries, see 2a.

Suppose you were preparing the paper dealing with drug-taking among college students. You decided in the early part of this paper to do a brief survey of drug use in various cultures as one means of establishing the "normality" of such practices among college students. From an anthropology course you recall studying a tribe of Indians known as the Yanomamo who live in Venezuela and Brazil and for whom the regular taking of hallucinogenic drugs is an important part of tribal culture. Unfortunately you have sold your textbook, so you go to the library and check out a copy of *Yanomamo: The Fierce People* by Napoleon A. Chagnon (New York: Holt, 1968). You locate the following two sections dealing with hallucinogenic drug-taking.

34c

> HALLUCINOGENIC DRUGS Another useful plant provided by the jungle is the *ebene* tree. The inner bark of this tree is used in the manufacture of one kind of hallucinogenic drug. The bark is scraped from the trunk after the exterior layer of bark is removed, or is scraped from the inside of the bark surface itself. This material, which is fairly moist, is then mixed with wood ashes and kneaded between the palms

of the hands. Additional moisture is provided by spitting periodically into the pliable wad of drug. When the drug has been thoroughly mixed with saliva and ashes, it is placed on a hot piece of broken clay pot and the moisture driven out with heat. It is ground into a powder as it dries, the flat side of a stone axe serving as the grinding pestle. The dried, green powder, no more than several tablespoons full, is then swept onto a leaf with a stiff feather. The men then gather around the leaf containing the drug, usually in the late afternoon, and take it by blowing the powder into each other's nostrils. . . . A small quantity of the powder is introduced into the end of a hollow cane tube some 3 feet long. The tube is then flicked with the forefinger to scatter the powder along its length. One end of the tube is put into the nostril of the man taking the drug, and his helper then blows a strong blast of air through the other end, emitting his breath in such a fashion that he climaxes the delivery with a hard burst of air. Both the recipient and the blower squat on their haunches to do this. The man who had the drug blown into his nostrils grimaces, groans, chokes, coughs, holds his head from the pain of the air blast, and duck-waddles off to some leaning post. He usually receives two doses of the drug, one in each nostril. The recipient usually vomits, gets watery eyes, and develops a runny nose. Much of the drug comes back out in the nasal mucus that begins to run freely after the drug has been administered. Within minutes after the drug has been blown into the man's nose, he begins having difficulties focusing his eyes and starts to act intoxicated. The drug allegedly produces colored visions, especially around the periphery of the visual field, and permits the user to enter into contact with his particular *hekura,* miniature demons that dwell under rocks and on mountains. The man begins to chant to the *hekura* when the drug takes effect, inviting them to come and live in his chest.

The men of the host group had finished their preparations for the feast; they were all painted in red and black, bearing colorful feathers. They had cleaned the debris from their houses, had finished hauling out the weeds they had picked from the village clearing, and had brought in quantities of food to give their guests. Now, it was time for them to take *ebene,* their hallucinogenic drug. They separated into several groups and began blowing the brownish-green powder up each other's nostrils with 3-foot long hollow tubes. As the drug would be administered, each recipient would reel from the concussion of air, groan, and stagger off to some convenient post to vomit. Within ten minutes of taking the drug, the men would be bleary-eyed and wild, prancing around in front of their houses, stopping occasionally to vomit or to catch their breath. In each group there would be one man particularly adept at chanting to the *hekura,* the mountain demons, and he would soon take over the show, while the others retired to the sidelines in a stupor, green slime dripping from their nostrils. Should there be sick people in the village, the adept chanters—the *shabori*—would cure them by chanting, massaging, sucking, and vomiting out the evil spirit that caused the sickness. Otherwise, they would chant about other things, perhaps sending their *hekura* to enemy villages to eat the souls of children, or enjoining them to prevent

34c

their enemies from doing the same. Occasionally, one of the men takes too much of the drug and becomes violent. On this particular occasion, Shiimima, one of Kaobawä's brothers, grabbed his bow and arrows and ran to the center of the village. This caused a minor sensation for a moment, but one of the men managed to catch and disarm him, hiding his weapons so he could not find them. Things returned to normal again, and the other participants in the drug-taking began chanting to Shiimima to restore him to his senses. The chanting lasted for an hour or so, and the participants, one by one, returned to their houses to clean up their paint jobs; most of them had smeared their careful work by vomiting all over themselves.

Here is a sample summary from this source.

> DRUG USE IN PRIMITIVE CULTURES. Among the Yanomamo Indians, halluci-
> nogenic drug-taking is a regular and accepted habit. The drug is a powder
> derived from the bark of the ebene tree, and is administered through hollow,
> 3-foot long cane tubes. One man blows the powder with sharp bursts
> through the tube into the nostril of another. The man who has received the
> drug will stagger away, then vomit; and his nose will begin running with
> mucus containing the drug residue. He will begin to act intoxicated, to see
> visions, and to chant to his demons (hekura) (pp. 23-24). If he takes too much
> ebene, he may become violent and will have to be restrained and disarmed
> (p. 109).

2   Paraphrasing sources

A *paraphrase* is a restatement, in your own words, of a passage of text. Its structure reflects the structure of the source passage. Paraphrases are sometimes the same length as the source passage, sometimes shorter. In certain cases—particularly if the source passage is written in densely con-structed or jargon-laden prose—the paraphrase may be even longer than the original. You would paraphrase a passage when you want to preserve all of the points in the original, both major and minor, and when—perhaps for the sake of clarity—you want to communicate the ideas in your own words. Keep in mind that only an *occasional* word (but not whole phrases) from the original source appears in the paraphrase, and that a paraphrase's sentence structure does not reflect that of the source.

The following is a paraphrase of the first section of the passage on the hallucinogenic drugs taken by the Yanomamo.

34c

> The Yanomamo make a hallucinogenic drug from the bark on the *ebene* tree.
> After scraping the outer bark off the tree trunk, they shave off the inner bark
> and mix it with wood ashes and saliva, while kneading the mixture in their
> hands. Then they place the mixture on a piece of hot clay pot, drying it and
> grinding it to a powder with the flat side of an ax, and finally depositing
> the dried powder onto a leaf. Next, the men gather around the leaf and take
> turns blowing the drug into each other's nostrils with a long, hollow tube.

The process as described here has almost as much detail as the original, but the wording is the student's own.

Sometimes you may wish to paraphrase a passage whose dense language makes it somewhat difficult to understand. Here, for example, is a paragraph from an article entitled "Cross-Cultural Perspectives on Developmental Stages in Adolescent Drug Use," by Israel Adler and Denise B. Kandel, which appeared in the *Journal of Studies on Alcohol*, 42 9 (1981): 701–15.

> The identification of a developmental sequence in adolescent drug use has important implications for understanding the phenomena of drug use and for policy making. A developmental sequence in drug use bridges the seeming gap between legal and illegal behaviors. Even though one cannot argue, as will be pointed out later, that there is a cause-and-effect relationship between the use of legal drugs and the use of illegal drugs, the link between the two types of behavior implies that they should be studied in conjunction with each other. Robins and Wish (3) go further, placing drug use within more general sequences of child development. They link drug behavior, through a series of cumulative events, to other behaviors that point to childhood deviance.

You might paraphrase this passage as follows.

```
              The "developmental sequence"


It's important to understand that adolescents follow a regular

pattern in the way they progress from legal drugs to illegal

drugs. This pattern is called a "developmental sequence." It's

not necessarily true that if adolescents begin with wine or

beer, they will inevitably proceed to marijuana and then to hard

drugs. These behaviors are related, however, not only to each

other, but also to childhood development in general. (p. 702)
```

EXERCISE 2
Write a 250–400 word summary of one of the sources you have located for your working bibliography (Exercise 1). Then write a paraphrase of several sentences from a section of text in the same source.

34d Quoting sources

You may choose to quote from a passage when the author's language is particularly well chosen, lively, dramatic, or incisive, and when you think you could not possibly express the same idea so effectively. Or you may choose to quote when you want to bolster the credibility of your argument with the reputation of your source. By the same token, you may occasionally choose to discredit an idea by quoting a discredited or notorious source.

1 Avoiding over-quoting

Knowing how much to quote is an art in itself. If you under-quote, your paper may come across as dry and second-hand. If you over-quote, your paper may come across as an anthology of other people's statements ("a scissors-and-paste job"), rather than an original work. Some professors have developed rules of thumb on quoting. One such rule is that for a ten-page paper, there should be no more than two extended quotations (i.e., indented quotations of more than 100 words); and each page should contain no more than two short quotations. If this rule of thumb makes sense to you (or your professor), adopt it; otherwise, modify it to the extent you think reasonable.

2 How to quote

Suppose you are working on a paper on drug testing in certain occupations. Here is the concluding section from one source, "Testing for Drugs and Alcohol: Proceed with Caution," by Rusch O. Dees, Esq. (an attorney for management), which appeared in the magazine *Personnel* (Sep. 1986): 53–55.

> The precise legal status of drug and alcohol testing remains undefined. An employer's use of testing can be fraught with potential liabilities. The "quick fix" envisioned through random drug or alcohol testing intrudes too far into the area of individual privacy to be condoned. However, courts as well as arbitrators have upheld employee testing programs where such programs have fallen within the more limited framework and scope discussed above.
>
> To date, too many employers have begun testing without first making essential policy decisions on what standards must be met to warrant testing and deciding what action will be taken with the results. A drug-and-alcohol testing program must not be approached in a cavalier manner when an individual's career, a company's image, and legal liabilities are at stake.

The following note contains the most useful quotation.

```
        Cautions about drug testing


"A drug-and-alcohol testing program must not be approached in a
cavalier manner when an individual's career, a company's image,
and legal liabilities are at stake." (p. 55)
```

34d

Sometimes you may wish to quote a passage that has itself been quoted by your source author. For example, in researching the acceptability of alcohol in earlier periods of American history, you locate Jack H. Mendelson and Nancy K. Mello's *Alcohol: Use and Abuse in America* (Boston: Little, Brown, 1985). In a chapter on "Alcohol Use in Colonial Times," you find an interesting quotation concerning the extent to which the authorities frowned on excessive alcohol consumption:

> Almost nothing is known about alcohol use during the first years, but in a time of constant scarcity it is unlikely that alcohol was readily available in any form. However, the Colonists' concern with social order was soon extended to include alcohol intoxication. By 1633, in Plymouth Colony, a John Holmes was censured for drunkenness. His penalty–"to sit in the stocks, and was amerced forty shillings." In 1629, the governor of the Massachusetts colony was advised by his English superior that "We pray yow endeavor, though ther be much *strong waters* sent for sale, yett see to order it, as that the salvages may not for or lucre sake bee induced to excessive use or rather abuse of it, and, at any hand, take care or people give us ill example; and if any shall exceed in that inordinate kind of drinking as to become drunck, wee hope you will take care his punishment be made exemplary for all others."

If you decide to use only the quotation by the "English superior" (and not Mendelson and Mello's commentary), your notecard would look like this.

Colonial attitudes toward excessive drinking [note #8]

Admonition to governor of Massachusetts colony from his English superior:
"We pray yow endeavor, though ther be much strong waters sent for sale, yett see to order it, as that the salvages may not for or lucre sake bee induced to excessive use or rather abuse of it, and, at any hand, take care or people give us ill example; and if any shall exceed in that inordinate kind of drinking as to become drunck, wee hope you will take care his punishment be made exemplary for all others." (pp. 7-8)

Note that these are the *exact* words from the original. The student has added nothing, omitted nothing, and changed nothing.

3 Using brackets and ellipses in quotations

34d Sometimes for the sake of clarity, conciseness, or smoothness of sentence structure, you will need to make additions, omissions, or changes to quotations. For example, suppose you wanted to quote a passage beginning with the following sentence: "In 1979, one week after receiving a 13.3% pay raise, she was called on the carpet." To clarify the pronoun *she*, you would need to replace it with the name of the person in question enclosed in a pair of brackets: "In 1979, one week after receiving a 13.3% pay raise, [Virginia Rulon-Miller] was called on the carpet." (See 29d.)

Suppose you also decided that the 13.3% pay raise was irrelevant for your purpose in quoting the material. You could omit this phrase, and indicate the omission by means of an *ellipsis*—three spaced dots: "In 1979 . . . [Virginia Rulon-Miller] was called on the carpet." (See 29e.) Note that, when using brackets, you do not need to use the ellipsis to indicate that the pronoun (*she*) has been omitted; brackets surrounding proper nouns imply that one word (or set of words) has replaced another. For more on altering quotations with ellipses and brackets, see chapters 28 and 29, sections d and e.

Sometimes you need to change a capital letter to a lowercase one in order to smoothly integrate the quotation into your own sentence. For example, suppose you want to quote the following sentence: "Privacy today matters to employees at all levels, from shop-floor workers to presidents." You could smoothly integrate this quotation into your own sentence by altering the capitalization, as follows.

> The new reality, as John Hoerr points out, is that "[p]rivacy today matters to employees at all levels, from shop-floor workers to presidents."

4   Smoothly integrating quotations into your text

Whether or not you alter quotations by means of ellipses or brackets, you should strive to smoothly integrate them into your own text. Suppose, for example, you decide to use the following sentence from *Heavy Drinking: The Myth of Alcoholism as a Disease* by Herbert Fingarette.

> The classic disease concept of alcoholism is unquestionably a hindrance rather than a help in addressing the broad problems of heavy drinking in our society (University of California Press, 1988).

You could integrate this quotation in any of several ways.

1. According to Fingarette, "The classic disease concept of alcoholism is unquestionably a hindrance rather than a help in addressing the broad problems of heavy drinking in our society" (4).

2. Fingarette puts it bluntly: "The classic disease concept of alcoholism is unquestionably a hindrance rather than a help in addressing the broad problems of heavy drinking in our society" (4).

3. "The classic disease concept of alcoholism," claims Fingarette, "is unquestionably a hindrance rather than a help in addressing the broad problems of heavy drinking in our society" (4).

4. "The classic disease concept of alcoholism is unquestionably a hindrance rather than a help in addressing the broad problems of heavy drinking in our society," claims Fingarette (4).

5. According to Fingarette, looking at alcoholism as a disease is "a hindrance rather than a help" (4).

34d

After attributive phrases such as "According to Fingarette," a comma is inserted. In the second example, a colon is the appropriate punctuation (to avoid a comma splice or run-on sentence). The first, third, and fourth examples differ only in the location of the attributive phrase: at the beginning, the middle, or the end of the sentence. In the fifth example, the original sentence has been largely paraphrased, rather than quoted.

5   Using attributive phrases with quotations

Note that single, quoted sentences should never stand by themselves, without an attributive phrase like "According to Fingarette, . . ." For example, you would not write

> Fingarette thinks this way of looking at alcoholism is part of the problem. "The classic disease concept of alcoholism is unquestionably a hindrance rather than a help in addressing the broad problems of heavy drinking in our society" (4).

Even though it ends with a citation, the quotation needs to be integrated with the previous material. You could do this by substituting a *colon* for the period after "part of the problem," or by inserting a phrase like "As he points out," before the quotation. (See the box below for other variations.)

Verbs That Help You Attribute Quotations

Attributive phrases use verbs in the present tense. To vary attributive phrases, you might consider verbs such as these:

adds	denies	rejects
agrees	derides	relates
argues	disagrees	reports
asks	disputes	responds
asserts	emphasizes	reveals
believes	explains	says
claims	finds	sees
comments	holds	shows
compares	illustrates	speculates
concedes	implies	states
concludes	insists	suggests
condemns	maintains	thinks
considers	notes	warns
contends	observes	writes
declares	points out	
defends	refuses	

34d

Note that all of the attributive verbs in the box are in the *present* tense (see 9e-1). Even though your source has already been written (and so technically, the author has already decla*red* or stat*ed* or conclud*ed*), when quoting sources you should use the present tense (declares, states, concludes). This applies even if you are discussing a literary work; thus you would say that Hamlet ponders: "To be or not to be. . . ." The only exception to the use of the present tense would be if you were reporting the historical progress of some development or debate and you wished to emphasize that certain things were said at a particular point in time. ("The Senator asserted: 'I do not intend to dignify these scurrilous charges by responding to them.' ")

6 Using block quotations

You should integrate most quotations into your own text, using quotation marks. If a quotation runs longer than four lines, however, you should set it apart from the text by indenting it ten spaces from the left margin. Quotation marks are not required around block quotations. Block quotations should be double spaced, like the rest of the text.

The following box reviews the discussion on summarizing, paraphrasing, and quoting sources.

When to Summarize, Paraphrase, or Quote a Source

Summarize

- to present the main points from a relatively long passage
- to condense information essential to your discussion

Paraphrase

- to clarify complex ideas in a short passage
- to clarify difficult language in a short passage

Quote

- when the language of the source is particularly important or effective
- when you want to enhance your credibility by drawing on the words of an authority on the subject

---

EXERCISE 3

Write a short section of a paper based on several of the sources you have located for exercises in the last two chapters. Summarize, paraphrase, and quote your sources. In particular, carefully select material that you believe deserves quotation, rather than summary or paraphrase. Your quotations should be of varying lengths: perhaps one block quotation, some sentence-length quotations, and others of phrase or clause length. In one or two cases, use ellipses and brackets to modify the quoted material. In all cases, smoothly integrate quotations into your own text, using a variety of attributive phrases.

34d

34e   Eliminating plagiarism

Plagiarism is an unpleasant subject, but one that must be confronted in any discussion of research papers. In its most blatant form, **plagiarism** is an act of conscious deception: an attempt to pass off the ideas or the words of another as your own. To take an extreme example, a student who buys a research paper from a commercial "paper mill" and turns it in for academic credit is guilty of the worst kind of plagiarism. Only slightly less guilty is the student who copies into his paper passages of text from his sources without giving credit or using quotation marks.

The penalties for plagiarism can be severe—including a failing grade in the course or even a suspension from school. Graduate students guilty of plagiarism have been dropped from advanced degree programs. Even professionals no longer in school can see their reputations damaged or destroyed by charges of plagiarism. During the 1988 presidential campaign, a Democratic candidate was forced to drop out of the race when it was revealed that some of the material in his campaign speeches was copied from a speech by a prominent British politician.

Much plagiarism is unintentional. Students may not intend to pass off as their own the work of others; but either through ignorance of the conventions of quotation, attribution, and citation, or simply through carelessness, they may fail to distinguish adequately between their own ideas and words and those of their sources.

Here are two general rules to help you avoid unintentional plagiarism:

1. Whenever you *quote* the exact words of others, place these words within quotation marks and properly cite the source.

2. Whenever you *paraphrase* or *summarize* the ideas of others, do not use whole phrases, many of the same words, or sentence structures similar to the original. You must identify the source of the paraphrased or summarized material: do not assume that you are under no obligation to credit your source if you simply change the wording of the original statement or alter the sentence structure. The only exception to this rule is if the information is common knowledge. For example, you need not cite the source of the information that General Lee commanded the Confederate forces during the Civil War, or the fact that Mars is the fourth planet from the sun, or the fact that Ernest Hemingway wrote *The Sun Also Rises*. (As you read more sources about your subject, you will gradually learn what is considered common knowledge on that subject and what is not. If the same fact is repeated in several sources, it is probably common knowledge.)

Here is a sample passage of text, followed by several student versions of the ideas represented. The passage is from Steven F. Bloom's "Empty Bottles, Empty Dreams: O'Neill's Use of Drinking and Alcoholism in *Long*

Day's Journey into Night," which appears in *Critical Essays on Eugene O'Neill,* edited by James J. Martine (Boston: G.K. Hall, 1984).

> In *Long Day's Journey Into Night,* O'Neill captures his vision of the human condition in the figure of the alcoholic who is constantly and repeatedly faced with the disappointment of his hopes to escape or transcend present reality. As the effects of heavy drinking and alcoholism increase, the alcoholic, in his attempt to attain euphoric forgetfulness, is repeatedly confronted with the painful realities of dissipation, despondency, self-destruction, and ultimately, death. This is the life of an alcoholic, and for O'Neill, this is the life of modern man.

1 Identifying blatant plagiarism of a source

Here is one student version of this passage.

> *Long Day's Journey into Night* shows O'Neill's vision of the human condition in the figure of the alcoholic who is constantly faced with the disappointment of his hopes to escape. As the effects of heavy drinking and alcoholism increase, the alcoholic, in his attempt to attain forgetfulness, is repeatedly confronted with the painful realities of dissipation, self-destruction, and, ultimately, death. This is the life of an alcoholic, and for O'Neill, this is the life of modern man.

This is the most blatant form of plagiarism. The student has copied the passage almost word for word and has made no attempt to identify the source of either the words or the ideas. Even if the author *were* credited, the student's failure to use quotation marks around quoted material would render this version unacceptable.

2 Avoiding unintentional plagiarism of a source

Here is another version of the same passage.

> The figure of the disappointed alcoholic who hopes to escape reality represents the human condition in *Long Day's Journey into Night.* Trying to forget his problems, the alcoholic, while drinking more and more, is confronted with the realities of his self-destructive condition, and, ultimately, with death. For Eugene O'Neill, the life of the alcoholic represents the life of modern man.

34e

In this version, the writer has attempted (for the most part) to put the ideas in his own words; but the result still so closely resembles the original in sentence structure, in the sequence of ideas, and in the use of key phrases ("confronted with the realities") that it is also unacceptable. Note that this would hold true even if the author *were* credited; that is, had the first sentence begun, "According to Steven F. Bloom, . . ." The student may not have intended to plagiarize—he may, in fact, believe this to be an acceptable rendition—but it would still be considered plagiarism.

3 Making legitimate use of a source

Here is another version.

> According to Steven F. Bloom, alcoholism in *Long Day's Journey into Night* is a metaphor for the human condition. The alcoholic drinks to forget his disappointments and to escape reality, but the more he drinks, the more he is faced with his own mortality. "This is the life of an alcoholic," asserts Bloom, "and for O'Neill, this is the life of modern man" (177).

This version is entirely acceptable because the student has carefully attributed both the paraphrased idea (in the first part of the passage) and the quotation (in the second part) to the source author, Steven Bloom. The student has also taken special care to phrase the idea in her own language.

Of course, you cannot avoid keeping *some* key terms: obviously, if you are going to paraphrase the ideas in this passage, you will need to use words and phrases like "alcoholic," "heavy drinking," "the human condition," and so on. However, what you say *about* these terms should be said in your own words.

It is crucial that you give your readers no cause to believe that you are guilty either of intentional or unintentional plagiarism. When you are summarizing or paraphrasing a particular passage, you must do more than change a few words. You must fully and accurately cite your source, by means of parenthetical citations or by means of attributive phrases, such as "According to Bloom, . . ."

4 Quoting accurately

When you do quote material directly, be certain that you quote it accurately. For example, consider a student quotation of the preceding passage (which follows the student's introduction).

> *Long Day's Journey into Night* is O'Neill's "vision of the human condition," according to Steven F. Bloom:
>
>> As the effects of his heavy drinking and alcoholism increase, the alcoholic, attempting to achieve forgetfulness, is repeatedly confronted with all the painful realities of dissipation, self-destruction, and death. This is the life of an alcoholic for O'Neill and it is also the life of modern man.

At first glance, this quotation may seem to be accurate. But it is not. The student has *omitted* some words that were in the source passage (in the first sentence, "euphoric" and "despondency"; in the second sentence, "and"); has *changed* other words (in the first sentence, "attempting to achieve," instead of "in his attempt to attain"; in the second, "it," instead of "this"); has *added* some words that were not in the original (in the first sentence, "all"; in the second sentence, "also"); and has also omitted punctuation (in the second sentence, the comma after "O'Neill").

34e

These changes may seem trivial and may not seem to essentially change the meaning of the passage, but once you place a passage within quotation marks, you are obligated to copy it *exactly*. Deleted material should be indicated by an ellipsis (. . .); your own insertions should be indicated by brackets ([   ]). Otherwise, the material within your quotation marks must be word for word, punctuation mark for punctuation mark, *identical* to the original.

EXERCISE 4

Paraphrase a short passage from one of the sources you have located during your research. Then write a short paragraph explaining what you have done to eliminate all possibility of inadvertent plagiarism in your paraphrase.

34e

CHAPTER 35

Writing the Research Paper

Aside from the discussion on organizing notecards, the material in this chapter parallels that in chapters 3, 4, and 5 on planning, writing, and revising an essay. Because the *process* of writing a research paper is in so many (but not all) respects similar to that of writing an essay, the discussion here will be brief and will be cross-referenced with earlier sections of the book.

35a Refining the thesis

As you complete your research and prepare to write a paper, you probably will have more information than you can possibly absorb. How will you get from those stacks of 4" × 6" notecards to a finished paper? This is the moment—between generating sources and starting a first draft—when chaos begins coalescing into order. If you feel intimidated and overwhelmed by the quantity of your notes, rest easy: probably every writer of research reports feels the same way at this particular moment in the process.

You will do well to remember the "burning question" that launched your project (see 33a-1). Ask yourself: What do I want to accomplish in this paper? Why write it in the first place? Why write on *this* subject, on this *aspect* of the subject? Such questions should help you to clear away extraneous details and refocus your attention. In 33e you saw the need for a researcher to devise a working thesis. The writer of any first draft needs a working thesis—a statement that will help to plan the first draft. With a working thesis, a writer has a principle on the basis of which to exclude or include information (see 3f).

In 33e you saw examples of working theses from four perspectives—the social sciences, the humanities, the sciences, and business—concerning the use of alcohol and drugs. For the purposes of the following discussion we will assume that you have decided to pursue one of these theses. The first thesis, for a course in the social sciences, was as follows.

INITIAL WORKING THESIS

Alcoholism among college students is an increasingly serious problem, but there are workable solutions.

As you progressed in your note-taking, you probably proceeded to gather information on the seriousness of the problem of alcoholism among college students and on the workable solutions. Perhaps all of this informa-

Characteristics of a Working Thesis

- The subject of the thesis is *narrow* enough in scope that you can write a detailed paper without being constrained by the page limits of the assignment. (See 3f-1.)

- The predicate of the working thesis communicates an inference you have made about your subject, based on your understanding of the information you have generated. (See 3f-2.)

- The main inference of your thesis involves one or more (but not many more) of the following relationships: sequential order, definition, classification, comparison, contrast, generalization, or causation. (See 3f-3.)

- The thesis clearly suggests the patterns of development you will be pursuing in your paper. (The types of paragraphs you write in your paper will be directly related to the inferences you make in your thesis. See 3f-4.)

- The thesis will clearly communicate your intellectual ambitions for the paper. (See 3f-5.)

tion confirmed your working thesis and you see no reason to change it. You may still reserve the right to change it later, once you start writing the paper, but for now you leave your working thesis unchanged.

On the other hand, in the course of your research, you may have shifted direction, so that your working thesis is no longer accurate. Perhaps you discover that alcoholism among college students, while serious, is not increasing. Such a discovery would require only the deletion of "increasingly" from your provisional thesis. Or suppose you decide to focus exclusively on solutions to the problem of student alcoholism (you can deal with the seriousness of the problem in one or two paragraphs in the introduction), and then discover that these solutions are not as workable as you first suspected. You could consequently adjust your thesis to read as follows.

REFINED WORKING THESIS

Health care professionals have learned that while they can help some student alcoholics, there are no easy solutions to the problem.

35a

The change of thesis may be even more dramatic. Recall from chapter 35 the passage dealing with the ritual use of the drug from the *ebene* tree from Napoleon A. Chagnon's book on the Yanomamo Indians. This subject may have fascinated you so much that you decided to shift your focus entirely from the problems of student alcoholism to a survey of drug use in various cultures. In this case, your working thesis would have to be abandoned and a new thesis would emerge from the results of your research.

The same process applies to the other working theses. For example, consider the thesis of a student taking a humanities course: "Alcoholism and drug abuse are important elements of O'Neill's later plays; these elements are grounded in O'Neill's own life." Such a thesis would require a consideration of O'Neill's most well-known later plays, *The Iceman Cometh* and *Long Day's Journey into Night.* In the course of your research it may become obvious that you will have your hands full dealing with just *one* of these plays. So you change your thesis to include only one play—and regretfully, but decisively, put all of your notecards on the other play in the "inactive" file. (Do not discard them; they may come in handy for a subsequent paper.)

Or consider the working thesis of a student taking a science course: "Alcoholism should be considered a disease, rather than an immoral behavior syndrome." Suppose that a reading of Herbert Fingarette's *Heavy Drinking: The Myth of Alcoholism as a Disease* and several articles supporting Fingarette's position persuades you that alcoholism should not, in fact, be considered a disease—even if you still do not consider alcoholism an "immoral behavior syndrome." You would need to adjust your thesis accordingly.

The final provisional thesis for a paper in the business disciplines reads this way: "In certain occupations drug testing is necessary to assure public safety." The rest of this chapter will focus on the composition of a paper on this subject. Assume that in the course of your research you became convinced that drug testing is—in most cases—*not* necessary to assure public safety.

35b Developing a plan

At this point in your preparations for writing, your main task is to review the notes you have taken and to consolidate them into categories that will help you to refine your thesis and support it. See 3e for a discussion on how to select, organize, and analyze information by working with categories.

If you have been conscientiously applying headings to each of your notecards, your task will be considerably easier. Stack the cards into piles according to their headings. For example, you may have devised this heading: "Extent of the Problem," referring to all cards that summarize, paraphrase, or quote material that provides numbers on how many employees are thought to have a drug problem and on how many major companies administer drug tests. You may have a heading, "Arguments for Drug Testing," to cover all the defenses commonly offered to justify the use of drug testing.

If you have not already written headings on your cards, write them as you review your notes. There are two ways to do this. Either you can draft a provisional outline and then write the appropriate headings and subheadings on the notecards, or you can write headings on the individual cards and then draft an outline based on groupings of cards.

Outlines come in all shapes and sizes. Informal outlines generally have only two levels: one level for topics and another for subtopics. For example:

Drug testing in the workplace
 —public sector
 —private sector

Formal outlines have several levels. The most common type employs a combination of Roman and Arabic numerals and letters.

I. Major topic
   A. Subtopic
      1. Minor subtopic
         a. sub-subtopic (or illustration)
            (a) illustration, example, explanation
            (b) illustration, example, explanation
      2. Minor subtopic
   B. Subtopic
II. Major topic

For more information on how to write outlines, see 3g-3; for a discussion on how to work from outlines as you write a first draft, see 4a.

35c Drawing on your sources

After you have developed your outline and arranged notecards to correspond to the outline, you will probably discover that in some areas you have more information than you need, while in other areas you do not have enough. In the latter case, go back to the library to fill in the gaps or take another look at material you have already gathered. In the former case (too much information), you will have to make some hard decisions. After accumulating so much material, you may be tempted to use it *all*. Resist that temptation. Your goal is to fulfill the purpose you have set for yourself in writing the paper, not to overwhelm readers. Select information for your paper according to your purpose. Focus on your working thesis and bear in mind the ways in which a thesis limits the types of information in a paper. Once you have provided readers with enough explanation and examples of a particular point, move on.

As discussed in chapter 34, there are three ways of dealing with source material: summary, paraphrase, and quotation. However, your paper should not simply be a collection of summarized, paraphrased, and quoted material. After all, you are not compiling an anthology; you are presenting your own viewpoint on a particular subject, a viewpoint supported by evidence of various types from your sources. Keep in mind that you have conducted your research in an attempt to come to some understanding of the subject, and that you will use the sources to *support* that understanding.

To give your paper the feel of a coherent discussion, you need to establish the connections among various pieces of evidence by means of your own *commentary*, your own critical evaluations of your sources. You also need to establish *transitions* between ideas, both within paragraphs and from paragraph to paragraph. (See 5d-3 for a review of transitions.)

35c

35d Determining your voice

As an author, how do you want to come across to your readers? As an authority, lecturing to the uninitiated? As an old friend, casually discussing your observations on a subject? As serious? cynical? excited? warm? distant? The option you select determines the *voice* that comes across in the paper.

Consider, for example, the voice of the following passage written by Jon D. Bible, a professor of business law, for an article that appeared in *Labor Law Review.*

> Most opponents of urine testing accept the employers' right to try to rid their workplaces of drugs. Their concerns focus on the appropriateness of urinalysis as a means to this end. Tests can be untrustworthy, they note, and even sound ones may produce erroneous results because of mistakes in the testing process. Tests may also yield positive results because of drug use occurring days or weeks earlier, which raises questions about an employer's right to proscribe usage that does not directly affect one's present ability to perform his job. Opponents also claim that tests compromise personal security and dignity, especially when given randomly or on a mass basis. Finally, they assert that urine testing violates the principle that people are to be presumed innocent of wrongdoing until proven guilty.

The voice of this passage is serious, systematic, somewhat dry, and impersonal. The author seems to make little attempt to engage his readers and certainly none to entertain them. But engagement and entertainment are not his purpose. This is a lawyer writing to other lawyers (or to management/labor professionals) who need to understand how the Fourth Amendment applies to drug testing. Though it may be dry, Bible's writing is clear and to the point.

Now consider the following passage, by William Saletan, which first appeared in *The New Republic* on October 2, 1989.

> Jar wars are back. Three years ago, to dramatize their "Just Say No" campaign, President Reagan and Vice President Bush led the way to the water closet, and dozens of candidates for lower office followed. This year Bush is riding the drug issue again, and politicians campaigning in four major cities have already submitted to drug tests. In 1986 some politicians resisted this nonsense. This year resistance has disappeared. Drug testing has become almost a standard part of political campaigns.

35d

The difference in voice between the two passages could hardly be greater. Saletan uses word play ("Jar wars"), off-color images ("led the way to the water closet"), and unusually blunt language ("nonsense"). Clearly, the audience for *The New Republic* (*TNR*) is quite different from the audience for *Labor Law Review*: while *TNR* readers also tend to be highly educated, they appreciate both witty language and plain speaking, and they are decidedly irreverent toward the powers-that-be. Saletan's voice, however, is not superior to Bible's—though more readers may prefer it. Each author's voice is suitable for its intended purpose and audience.

Think of your readers as intelligent people who are interested in the issue on which you are writing, but who still expect to be engaged, as well as informed, by what you have to say. Although they may *have* to read your paper, do not make them resent the effort. Be serious and informative, but not dull. A good academic paper should be like one side of an intelligent conversation—a conversation in which both participants take pleasure. (See 2d for more on determining your own voice.)

 ## Writing a draft

Sections 4a-c and 5a provide detailed discussions of strategies that will help you to write a first draft. You will need a method for working (or not working) from your outline, for writing a group of related paragraphs at a single sitting, and for recognizing and responding to obstacles as they arise.

You are finally ready to write. You have conducted systematic research on a subject in which you are interested; you have accumulated a stack of notecards, on which you have summarized, paraphrased, and quoted relevant material; you have developed and revised a thesis; and you have prepared an outline, on the basis of which you have organized your notecards: in short, you have become something of an expert on the subject. There is no reason to be anxious at this point: you are not writing the final draft; you are simply preparing a rough draft that will be seen by no one but yourself (and possibly some friends whose advice you trust). You will have plenty of opportunity to revise the rough draft.

To avoid overreliance on sources, as well as to clarify the main lines of a paper's argument, some researchers write their first draft referring only to their outlines—and not to their notecards. As they write, they note the places where source material (in summarized, paraphrased, or quoted form) will later be inserted. Drafts written in such a manner are simply scaffolds, of course. But by examining the scaffold, you can easily see whether your logic stands up. Does the argument make sense to you? Does one part logically follow from another? It should, even without the material on your notecards. The evidence, after all, is for your readers' benefit, not yours.

At some point in the drafting process, however, you will need to turn to your notecards. Arrange them in the order in which you intend to use them; but do not simply transcribe your notes onto your rough draft. Keep your mind on your purpose and on your audience: tell them—as if you were in conversation with them—what they should know about the subject and why you believe as you do. If you think you have made your point, move on, and skip any additional, unused notecards on the topic or subtopic (or substitute a particularly effective point from one of these unused notecards for a less effective point from a notecard already used).

To avoid having to transcribe lengthy quotations from the notecards onto your draft, you may want to consider taping or stapling these notecards (or photocopies of the quotations) directly onto the appropriate spots on the draft. When you do incorporate your quotations, summaries, and paraphrases, remember to transfer your bibliographic codes and page numbers as well, so that later you can enter the correct citations.

Many writers skip the introduction on the rough draft and get right into the body of the paper. These writers believe that they are in a better position to draft the introduction when they know exactly what they are introducing and when they have overcome the writer's block that frequently grips writers facing that first page. If this approach works for you, fine. However, if you believe that you must begin at the beginning and work systematically all the way through, then do that. Whichever approach you take (and neither one is inherently preferable), remember that this is only a *rough* draft; nothing at this stage is final.

35f Revising and editing

In sections 4d–j, you will find a discussion on strategies for revising and editing. You may wish to review this material after you compose your rough draft. Perhaps the main point to keep in mind is that revision literally means "re-seeing." You should not consider revision simply a matter of fixing up punctuation and spelling errors and improving a word or phrase here and there. It is, rather, a matter of looking at the whole essay, from top to bottom, and trying to determine whether you have presented your material in the most effective way possible. Some writers think of revision as a two-fold process: *macro-revision*—concerning the essay as a whole and its larger component units, such as the section and the paragraph, and *micro-revision*—concerning sentence structure, grammar, punctuation, and mechanics. Others consider revision to be a four-stage process: (1) the essay as a whole; (2) individual paragraphs; (3) individual sentences; and (4) individual words. These strategies are means toward the same goal: ensuring that you consider *every* component of your essay, from the largest to the smallest, as you work to improve it.

When you begin to revise your paper, get as much feedback as possible from others. It is difficult even for professional writers to get perspective on what they have written immediately after they have written it. You are likely to be too close to the subject, too committed to your outline or to the particular words you have written, to be very objective at this point. Show your draft to a friend or classmate whose judgment you trust and to your instructor. Obtain reactions on everything from the essay as a whole to the details of word choice.

35g Understanding the elements of documentation

There are several systems of documentation that writers can use to credit their sources (see chapter 36). The system used depends on the discipline in which they are writing—social sciences, humanities, science and technology, or business (see chapter 36) or on the preferences of the person or persons to whom the writing is addressed.

Using documentation to give fair credit and to assist your reader

Why go to the trouble to document your sources? Perhaps the first reason is to avoid charges of plagiarism. You certainly do not want to give your readers the impression that you are claiming credit for ideas or words that are not yours. The second reason is to allow your readers to gauge the accuracy and reliability of your work. Any research paper will stand or fall according to how well (how resourcefully, perceptively, accurately, or selectively) you use sources. The third reason turns on the word *credit* itself—that is, you should give credit where it is merited. Your sources have done a great deal of work for you; by acknowledging them, you acknowledge the value of their work. The fourth reason for giving credit is to allow the reader who is interested in a particular point in your paper, or in a particular source that you have employed, to return to the original document.

Placing documentation references

Documentation is provided in two places: (1) *in the text*, to identify and credit a source immediately following its use; and (2) *following the text*, in the form of a list of references that readers can pursue in more detail. In-text citations are usually placed within parentheses (although the footnote and endnote systems are still sometimes used, particularly in the humanities).

It is important that *all* information and ideas be documented—not simply the ones that you quote directly. Summaries or paraphrases also require source acknowledgment. The only exception to this rule is that *common knowledge* need not be documented. For the particular documentation form in the discipline areas, see chapter 36.

35h A sample paper: "Drug Testing in the Workplace"

The following research paper demonstrates the process of research and writing discussed in these chapters. The student writer, Michael Arai, chose the topic of "Drug Testing in the Workplace" because a friend and his coworkers had recently been required to take periodic tests for substance abuse, even though no one at this particular job had ever demonstrated a problem. In talking with his friend, Arai discovered a "burning question": Why should people who have never had problems with drugs be required to take drug tests as a condition of employment? Arai's paper conforms to Modern Language Association (MLA) documentation style.

COVER-PAGE FORMAT

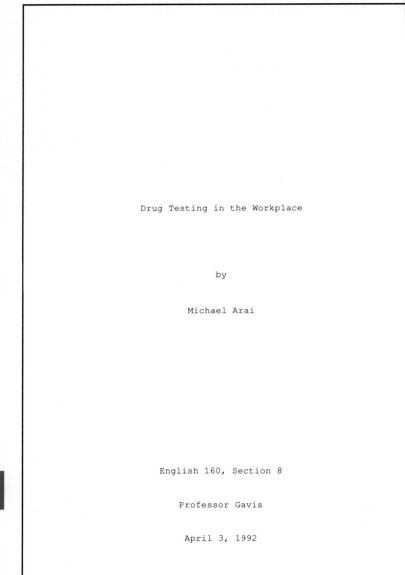

Drug Testing in the Workplace

by

Michael Arai

English 160, Section 8

35h

Professor Gavis

April 3, 1992

Cover page: Center the title of your paper approximately one-third down the page. Skip four lines and center the preposition *by.* Skip another two lines and center your name. Skip approximately ten lines and center your course number and section. Then follow with your professor's name and the date submitted as shown.

Binding: Professors reading a stack of papers often find transparent folders to be a nuisance. Use a staple or paper clip to bind your paper at the upper-left corner.

35h

FIRST-PAGE FORMAT FOR A PAPER
WITHOUT A COVER PAGE

1

Michael Arai

Professor Gavis

English 160, Section 8

April 3, 1992

                    Drug Testing in the Workplace

    In 1986 President Reagan's federal commission on organ-
ized crime called for widespread, random drug testing of American workers (Weiss 56). Two clear reasons prompted this
call, the first being money: in 1983 businesses lost up to
$100 billion as a result of drugs (Weiss 56). Concerns for
public safety have also prompted the call for mandatory testing. On January 4, 1987, a Conrail locomotive near Baltimore
collided with an Amtrak train, killing 16 people and wounding
176. Investigators later discovered that the engineer was
under the influence of marijuana at the time of the accident
(Sanders 10). Similarly infuriating stories abound of drug-
dulled employees endangering an unsuspecting public. Advocates of drug testing claim that testing employees improves
public safety. According to Peter Bensinger, former head of
the Drug Enforcement Administration, "As a result of drug
testing in American industry, the number of job-related incidents is beginning to go down. . . . It's saving lives" ("Interview" 58).

35h

First-page format: Here is the first-page format for a paper *without* a cover page. Provide double-spaced information, flush with the left margin, as above. Skip two lines and center your title. Skip four lines and begin your paper. Number the page, *without* your name, in the upper-right corner as shown. Beginning with page 2, place your name before the page number.

First page: See page 600 for the first-page format of a paper *with* a cover page. You will see that while the first page is numbered at the upper-right corner, no name appears. Your name and page number appear beginning with page 2. (If you are working on a computer, your word processing program probably has the capability to run "headers." Consult your user's manual.)

Outline (pages 598 and 599): Some professors will ask that you submit a formal outline with your completed paper—for two reasons. For professors, your outline is a previewing tool. Professors will read the outline and quickly gain a sense of your paper's scope and direction. For you, the outline serves as a final check that the paper is unified and coherent. Papers that do not outline easily may suffer from organizational problems.

> **Outline placement and form:** Papers with outlines should begin with a cover page. Place the outline immediately after the cover page. Number the outline in the upper-right corner with lowercase roman numerals, beginning with *i*.

> **Outline in sentences:** The following outline is written in sentences. If you choose not to write in sentences, your entries should be parallel (see chapter 18). Begin with a statement of your paper's thesis. Follow with major section headings (I, II), subsections (A, B), and supporting points (1, 2). Place your thesis first in the outline, regardless of its actual location in the paper. (In the sample paper—an argument with an inductive arrangement—the thesis and conclusion appear together at the end.)

35h

Outline

Thesis statement: Random, sweeping drug testing as espoused
by the government commission and proponents such as Peter
Bensinger functions more as a propaganda tool in the overall
"War on Drugs" than as a serious attempt to address the issues of productivity and safety in the workplace.

 I. Review of the controversy: For the most part, experts
    disagree on the value and legality of mandatory drug
    testing.

    A. Proponent Peter Bensinger says that drug-related ac-
       cidents are a major problem--but are decreasing be-
       cause of drug testing.

    B. Opponents claim that mandatory tests violate an
       employee's civil rights.

       1. The Fourth Amendment to the Constitution pro-
          tects citizens from "unreasonable searches and
          seizures."

       2. Ira Glasser and Norma Rollins of the American
          Civil Liberties Union emphasize the American
          tradition of fairness and of assuming innocence
          unless circumstances prove otherwise.

    C. Proponents and opponents of mandatory drug testing
       agree that in certain occupations tests are justi-
       fied.

 II. Drug testing is a bad idea: neither the extent of the
     problem of on-the-job drug use nor the benefits or accu-
     racy of mandatory testing are clear.

    A. Statistics from different sources dramatically dis-
       agree about the cost of on-the-job drug use to Amer-
       ican business.

    B. Companies that test employees cite gains in produc-
       tivity and safety, but these gains are reported by
       the companies themselves, not by impartial research-
       ers.

    C. Tests are inaccurate and costly.

35h

Arai ii

    1. First-round tests can be inaccurate by as much as 100 percent.

    2. Second-round tests are much more accurate but are very costly.

III. Drug testing is a bad idea: mandatory drug testing has created legal problems and may negatively affect worker productivity.

    A. Accusations of drug use against employees have led to court suits.

    B. The courts have generally ruled in favor of employees.

    C. Mandatory tests may negatively affect productivity in the workplace.

        1. One consultant predicts that testing will destroy employee morale.

        2. Another observer believes that companies that trust employees get more from them.

IV. Conclusion: mandatory drug testing is a flawed policy in any business where the work of employees does not directly affect public safety.

    A. Only people in high-risk jobs should be tested, and even then with more accurate and sensitive tests than are currently used.

    B. In all other cases, employees should be tested under two conditions.

        1. An employee should first demonstrate a drug-related problem.

        2. Tests should be administered to help that employee.

35h

1

Drug Testing in the Workplace

In 1986 President Reagan's federal commission on organized crime called for widespread, random drug testing
of American workers (Weiss 56). Two clear reasons
prompted this call, the first being money: in 1983 businesses lost up to $100 billion as a result of drugs
(Weiss 56). Concerns for public safety have also
prompted the call for mandatory testing. On January 4,
1987, a Conrail locomotive near Baltimore collided with
an Amtrak train, killing 16 people and wounding 176. Investigators later discovered that the engineer was under
the influence of marijuana at the time of the accident
(Sanders 62). Similarly infuriating stories abound of
drug-dulled employees endangering an unsuspecting public. Advocates of drug testing claim that testing employees improves public safety. According to Peter
Bensinger, former head of the Drug Enforcement Administration, "As a result of drug testing in American industry, the number of job-related incidents is beginning to
go down. . . . It's saving lives" ("Interview" 58).

Opponents of drug testing argue that testing vio-
lates American civil liberties, particularly the liberties guaranteed by the Fourth Amendment to the
Constitution. This amendment guarantees that "[t]he   A
right of the people to be secure in their persons . . .
against unreasonable searches and seizures, shall not be
violated." The Fourth Amendment also specifies that such
searches may only be conducted on the basis of "probable
cause" and under the authority of a signed warrant specifying the place to be searched and the items being
searched for.

Ira Glasser, executive director of the American
Civil Liberties Union, represents the opposition in saying that "[t]he tradition in America is that you don't   B
hang them all to get the guilty. You can search people

Quoting and Paraphrasing Sources

Paragraph A (Quotation and paraphrase—common knowledge): The quotation in paragraph A, taken from the Fourth Amendment to the U.S. Constitution, is not cited because the amendment is common knowledge and is widely available in a variety of sources. Note the use of an ellipsis (. . .), three spaced dots, to indicate that some material has been omitted from the quotation. Following the quotation, Arai paraphrases material from the second part of the amendment ("under the authority of a signed warrant specifying the place to be searched and the items being searched for").

35h

. . . only if you have some reason to believe that a specific individual is committing an offense" ("Interview"
58). Norma Rollins, an official of the New York Civil
Liberties Union, believes that drug testing should be directed only at the relatively few employees whose job
performance suggests possible trouble with substance
abuse. Opponents of drug testing believe that mandatory
testing is un-American and must be challenged at every
opportunity. Even so, opponents say that in some cases--
those involving public safety--drug testing is justified. George S. Odiorne, a professor of management at
Eckard College, and an opponent of drug testing, defends
the practice for high-risk jobs:

B

> Would I favor random testing for anybody? Yes.
> The kids in missile silos: two 19-year-old kids
> sitting 80 feet underground with their hands on
> the triggers of 12 Minuteman missiles that
> could blow up Minsk, Kapinsk and Moscow. (qtd.
> in Gordon 59)

Apparently, 6.6 million working Americans are alcoholics, and 6 million are regular drug users. Thirteen
percent of American workers have abused drugs on the
job--most of the 14 to 18 percent of Americans who abuse
drugs or alcohol in general (Gordon 26). These statistics alone would seem to justify drug testing, even with
the myriad problems associated with testing programs.
But the statistics must be examined.

James Wrich, writing for the Harvard Business Review, claims that the cost of drug abuse to businesses
is $100 billion annually (120). This astonishing figure
appears less than exact, however, for research shows
that no two authorities agree on the annual dollar cost
of drug abuse. For instance, Philip Weiss, writing for
Harper's, puts the cost at $33 billion (56). Another
group, Research Triangle Institute (RTI), puts the
annual cost of drug abuse at $25.7 billion (Gordon 26).

C

35h

Paragraph B (Quotation—attributed and run in with text): In paragraph B, the quotation by Ira Glasser includes an ellipsis (. . .). Note that the original text of this quotation began as follows: "The tradition in America is that you don't hang them all to get the guilty." Arai has changed the uppercase *T* in *The* to a lowercase *t* in order to integrate the quotation smoothly into his own sentence. Notice the use of brackets [   ] to indicate the change.

Paragraph B (Paraphrase): Arai originally quoted a sentence from Rollins, as follows: "A fair program should focus on those individuals who exhibit drug dependence on the job, rather than forcing tests on thousands of innocent people . . ." (qtd. in Chapman 58). On rereading his draft, Arai decided that the paragraph had one too many quotations, and he therefore decided to paraphrase instead of quote Rollins.

Paragraph B (Block quotation—attributed): At the end of paragraph B, the lengthy quotation of George Odiorne has been indented ten spaces from the left margin. Notice that the citation for a block quotation is set *outside* the final period. In this case, Arai found the quotation quoted by another author and has noted this in the citation.

35h

Arai 3

RTI has been cited elsewhere as putting the figure of
drug and alcohol abuse at $16 billion. Which authority
is one to believe? The numbers create anything but a
clear picture of the extent of the problem. Nobody really knows how much drug or alcohol abuse costs business. Richard Bickerton of the Employee Assistance Program believes that these estimates are fictions and
that "the figures you're given often depend on the self-
interest of the people giving you the figures" (Gordon
26).

     C

    What, then, can one make of claims regarding the
benefits of drug testing? In support of their position,
proponents of testing on the one hand cite cost estimates like $100 billion and on the other cite success
stories as evidence that drug testing works. For instance, Southern Pacific Railroads has reported a reduction in their accident rate by 67 percent and in their
"lost time" and injuries by 25 percent (Berger 94). Com-
monwealth Edison has reported 25 to 30 percent lower ab-
senteeism since they instituted their drug testing
program. Georgia Power has reported a sharp drop in
accidents (Kupfer 133).

    Yet these figures on productivity and safety ad-
vances due to testing are supplied largely by private
companies conducting the tests, not by impartial research institutes. The companies might have an interest
in justifying their testing programs. These same companies have admitted that their testing programs are only
one part of an entire program of managerial reforms (Kupfer 133). The fact is that no conclusive relationship exists between drug testing and productivity or safety
gains.

    Various accuracy studies conducted by independent
research groups have shown truly embarrassing rates of
error at testing centers across the country. One study
revealed that "known samples submitted to thirteen drug

35h

Revising the Paper

In revision, the following three rough-draft paragraphs were combined to yield the final paragraph (C):

Let's examine as an example one organization one organization's claim that the annual cost of drug abuse to business is $100 billion (Gordon 26). The actual numbers or dources behind these claims provied inconclusive. *is astonishing figure* The impressive $100 billion price tag on workplace *less than exact, however,* drug use appears to be little more than statistical fiction, for in my research no two sources agreed on the *annual dollar cost of drug abuse.* *Shows* figure--in fact, the wide discrepencies called the concept of quantifying the cost into question. James *Begin # here*

Wrich, writing for the Harvard Business Review, quoted *annually* $100 billion (120), but Philip Weiss, writing for *For instance,* Harper's, found the cost more like $33 billion (56).

Too confusing. Keep focus on various dollar amounts.

Furthermore, from where do these statistics come? The $100 billion was attributed to an organization called the Research Institute of America (RIA). It, in turn, cited "varrious estimates" for its numbers (Gordon 26). But RIA puts out inconsistent and cnofusing reports. For example, it has also stated flatly that alcohol presents the greatest threat to productivity and safety in the workplace. However, in the same report RIA estimated that the annual cost of alcohol abuse was only $10 billion. Another research group, Research Triangle *puts* Institute (RTI), estimated the annual coast of drug abuse at $25.7 billion, "about half of what alcohol abuse costs" (Gordon 26). But RTI has been cited else- *as* where putting the the figure of drug and alcohol use com- *al* bined at $16 billion. *which authority is one to believe?*

The point? Nobody really knows how much drug or alcohol abuse costs business. Says Richard Bickerton of *believes that these estimates are* the Employee Assistance Program: "The truthy is, nobody *fictions and that,* knows . . . the figures you're given often depend on the self-interest of the people giving you the figures" (Gordon 26). Fortune magazine concurs, concluding that the figures "rely on a lot of guesswork. Pinning down the cost more precisely is almost impossible" (Chapman 59). *one note is enough*

35h

Arai 4

laboratories showed error rates as high as 100 percent
for certain drugs" (Berger 88). Legal substances such as
Contac, Sudafed, diet pills, asthma medications, cough
syrup, antibiotics, painkillers, poppy seeds, and herbal
teas will all register as illegal drugs (O'Keefe 35).
Testing proponents like Bensinger agree that drug-test-
ing companies must double-check their results, and to
their credit the confirmation tests boast a 95 percent
accuracy rate. But they also cost up to $100--five times
as much as the initial tests. The Center for Disease Con-   D
trol (CDC) has reported that most companies are failing
to double-check tests that initially are positive for
drug use (Chapman 60). Even though some companies do follow up with accuracy checks, nationally companies will
falsely accuse one employee of every twenty tested (Berger
88). Companies are firing their employees and ruining
careers on the basis of test results that are as scatter-
shot as if the testers had simply flushed the samples down
the toilet and flipped a coin--as one CDC doctor put it.

      Predictably, less-than-reliable testing procedures
have resulted in legal problems. The jury is still out
regarding the current legal status of drug testing in
the private workplace. Urine testing has been pronounced
"search and seizure," but Fourth Amendment restrictions
apply only to governmental drug testing. "Private employers currently have an unfettered right to test, but do
have limits on disciplinary actions based on test results," according to Brian Heschizer and Jan Muczyk (356).
Firing somebody because of a failed drug test is almost
certain to bring down a lawsuit upon a company.

      The courts have in most cases ruled in favor of em-
ployees. Management lawyer Rusch O. Dees advises extreme
caution concerning the drug testing of an ordinary
worker: "The further removed from the public safety con-   E
cerns a particular job may be, the more difficult it becomes to establish the reasonableness of the test

Incorporating Your Notes into the Paper

Paragraph D. Following are two cards that Michael Arai made as he read Gilda Berger's *Drug Testing*. The first card is his bibliography card; the second, one of several notecards. The first time Arai refers to this note on test accuracy, he quotes Berger. In his second reference, he paraphrases her.

④ Berger, Gilda, *Drug Testing*. New York: Franklin Watts, 1987.

HV58235
U5B+7
1987

Considers the U.S. drug crisis and issues of drug testing in various public & private sectors. Chapter 7 deals with drug testing in private industry — includes several specific cases.

Test Accuracy ④

The accuracy of drug testing is open to serious question. Berger states that, "out of every twenty people in a workplace tested for drugs, the chances are that one will get a false positive result," (p. 88). And while testing labs claim error rates of less than one percent, one study revealed that "known samples submitted to thirteen drug laboratories showed error rates as high as 100 percent for certain drugs." (p. 88)

35h

program" (54). A management law firm survey revealed that jury verdicts in invasion of privacy cases are increasing--and averaging $316,000 (Hoerr 62). These large awards are in part the result of several cases in which employers used drug testing as a weapon against whistle-blowers. In Philadelphia, companies have tested "troublesome" union leaders as often as five times in three months. Clearly, testing has the potential to be misused.

    Drug and alcohol use <u>have</u> caused problems for American companies. Debates may exist over the extent of the problem and the accuracy of the tests, but no one can deny the fact that thousands of employees show up to work every day impaired and not fit to work at full productive capacity. Surely a company has the right to be concerned with employee productivity. The difficult question is how this concern should be translated into action. Should drug tests be mandated for all employees? Based on a review of the findings just presented, the answer is <u>no</u>. Proponents of drug testing prop their arguments on guesswork, hazy statistics, and blind faith in an extremely inexact science. There exists no conclusive relationship between drug testing and gains in productivity or safety. Moreover, the tests themselves are notoriously unreliable, and testing can too readily become a weapon in the hands of unscrupulous employers.

    Granting for the moment that these serious objections to drug testing could be overcome, there remains a final, compelling reason to reject mandatory testing: a possible <u>decline</u> in worker productivity. A consultant in Raleigh, North Carolina, predicts that testing will destroy employee morale. "I imagine it would be a matter of [employees] not putting themselves out," he says (Gordon 24-25). In other words, if management all but admits its distrust of employees by requiring drug tests, why should employees give an extra measure of effort to meet management's objectives?

    Ultimately, the decision of whether or not to test rests on a philosophy of management and involves two opposing views on how a company achieves higher productivity

E

F

35h

G

Paragraph E (Citation logic): In paragraph E, Arai cites two sources. In the first case, he mentions the author's name in preparing for a quotation, the reason being that he thinks it useful for the reader to know that the quotation's originator is a lawyer for management. With Rusch O. Dees mentioned in the sentence, there is no need to cite him again in the parenthetical note. The reader has enough information to locate the source of the quotation in the Words Cited. In the sentence that ends with the second citation, Arai makes no mention of the author (Arai is focusing on information); therefore, he must note the author's last name in the parentheses.

Paragraph F (First explicit mention of the thesis): Until this point in the paper, Arai has discussed several ways in which the arguments favoring mandatory drug testing are flawed. In paragraph F, he summarizes his arguments and draws them together in a conclusion: that drug testing should not be mandated for all employees. The paragraph serves as a preparation for a final, compelling argument that Arai believes will sway his readers.

35h

Arai 6

from its employees. Some employers prefer to crack the whip, telling their employees exactly how to do their jobs, establishing strict rules, and imposing harsh disciplinary measures for infractions. Other employers prefer to motivate their employees by treating them decently and fairly, by giving them autonomy in doing their jobs, and by praising them for work well done. Jack Gordon, summarizing management theory, calls the first approach "Theory X" and the second, "Theory Y" (27-28). According to Gordon, who is editor of the journal Training, Theory Y management results in greater productivity than Theory X management. If Gordon is correct, then companies that impose drug testing programs to achieve greater productivity may in fact be operating counterproductively.

Random, sweeping drug testing as espoused by the government commission and proponents such as Peter Bensinger functions more as a propaganda tool in the overall "War on Drugs" than as a serious attempt to address the issues of productivity and safety in the workplace. The only cases in which I would recommend random drug testing are the so-called "high risk" jobs of airline pilot, Secret Service agent, nuclear reactor operator, and so on. And even then I would demand more appropriate and sensitive tests than are usually given.

In all other cases, I would recommend a management program of training and encouragement that better evaluates employee performance. Following the reasoning that "you don't need a chemist to tell you to fire somebody who spends ten or twenty weeks a year in bed," I advise reaction to specific problems, not a near-futile search for drug use that may or may not be causing those problems ("Your Boss" 8). Responsibly applied drug testing serves only one purpose in the case of the problem employee: pinpointing the problem in order to offer that employee treatment. To conclude more specifically, I suggest several guidelines regarding testing: Employees must have demonstrated a clear job-performance problem before any tests are administered; all positive tests must be confirmed; results must remain confidential; and use of urinalysis must be accompanied by drug rehabilitation (Berger 99).

G

35h

Using Sources—But Ensuring That Your Voice Predominates

Paragraph G is based on the following material, found in Jack Gordon's "Drug Testing as a Productivity Booster?" (in *Training*, 22 March 1987).

Theory X and Theory Y are, of course, terms coined by Douglas McGregor in the 1950s to represent two basic philosophies by which managers may view their subordinates. In a nutshell, the Theory X manager assumes that workers are untrustworthy—they won't show up for work, do their jobs properly, refrain from robbing the company fund, control their dark urges to turn into dope fiends, etc.—unless and until they prove otherwise. The Theory Y manager assumes the opposite—that unless a worker proves otherwise, he or she probably is honest, at least semi-competent, and willing to do a good job.

The body of management theory rooted in Theory Y says basically that while it's true the Egyptians got the pyramids built with Theory X methods, they would have gotten better, faster and even cheaper pyramids had they 1) dropped their whips and 2) enlisted the hearts and minds of the labor force in the project by giving them well-targeted praise, rewards, responsibility, authority, training, and not least, trust.

Another theory comes into play here. It's called the Pygmalion Effect. In essence, it says that if you treat employees as if you believe they are honest, trustworthy people who want to do a good job, most of them will behave like honest, trustworthy people who want to do a good job. If you treat them as if you believe they're thieves, incompetents and malingerers, constantly on the lookout for ways to abuse their positions, many will,

indeed, start looking for ways to abuse their positions.

Participative management techniques and other methods grounded in a Theory Y view of employees have been consistently pushed forward as responses to virtually every "workplace crisis" of the '80s: the productivity crisis, the international-competition crisis, the "How in the world are we going to cope with the accelerating pace of change?" crisis, the "declining loyalty toward employers" crisis, and so on. Theory Y techniques are strongly recommended for managers who want to keep their companies "union-free." Without Theory Y assumptions, there is no such thing as "intrapreneuring." Theory Y is the basis for the HRD emphasis on team building. To a large extent, it's the basis for the popular view that "leadership" is something different from "management," and that effective leaders draw their power not from their rank in the company hierarchy but from their ability to win the hearts and minds of their peers and subordinates.

If management theory for the past two decades tells us nothing else, it tells us that if we want productivity, Theory Y is the way to go.

If you say nothing else about a policy stating that employees under no particular suspicion of anything will be subjected to urine inspections to prove that they aren't dope fiends, you have to say that it is, by definition, a Theory X policy. And a pretty dramatic one at that.

35h

While most of paragraph G summarizes the passage here, the first and the last sentences serve as the writer's own critical commentary which sets the summarized material in the context of a larger issue (first sentence) and also provides the writer's own viewpoint (last sentence). This viewpoint is consistent with the writer's thesis, stated directly in the paragraph following. Michael Arai puts his summaries (as well as paraphrases and quotations) to his own purpose and ensures that his voice, not the voices of his sources, predominates in the paper.

Arai 7

Works Cited

Berger, Gilda. _Drug Testing_. New York: Franklin Watts, 1987.

Chapman, Fern Schumer. "The Ruckus Over Medical Testing."
    Fortune 19 Aug. 1985: 57-62.

Dees, Rusch O. "Testing for Drugs and Alcohol: Proceed with
    Caution." _Personnel_ Sept. 1986: 53-55.

Gordon, Jack. "Drug Testing As a Productivity Booster?" _Train-_
    ing 22 Mar. 1987: 22-28+.

Heschizer, Brian and Jan P. Muczyk. "Drug Testing at the Work-
    place: Balancing Individual, Organizational, and Societal
    Rights." _Labor Law Journal_ 39 (1988): 342-57.

Hoerr, John, Katherine M. Hafner, Gail DeGeorge, Anne R.
    Field, and Laura Zinn. "Privacy." _Business Week_ 28 Mar.
    1988: 61-68.

"Interview with Ira Glasser." _U.S. News & World Report_ 17
    Mar. 1986: 58.

"Interview with Peter Bensinger." _U.S. News & World Report_ 17
    Mar. 1986: 58.

Kupfer, Andrew. "Is Drug Testing Good or Bad?" _Fortune_ 19
    Dec. 1988: 133-39.

O'Keefe, Anne Marie. "The Case Against Drug Testing." _Psychol-_
    ogy Today Jun. 1987: 34-38.

Sanders, A. L. "Boost for Drug Testing." _Time_ 3 Ap. 1989: 62.

Weiss, Peter. "Watch Out: Urine Trouble." _Harper's_ Jun.
    1986: 56-57.

Wrich, James T. "Beyond Testing: Coping with Drugs at Work."
    Harvard Business Review 66 (1988): 120-130.

"Your Boss Is Not a Cop." _The New Republic_ 6 Jun. 1988: 7-9.

35h

Format for the list of references (Works Cited). See chapter 36 for explanations and examples of the proper form for each entry. The entries are alphabetical and double spaced; the heading is centered an inch from the top of the page. Each new entry begins at the left margin; subsequent lines in the entry are indented five spaces.

35h

Documenting Research

Any time you use material derived from specific sources, whether quoted passages or summaries or paraphrases of fact, opinion, explanation, or idea, you are ethically obligated to let your reader know who deserves the credit. Further, you must tell your readers precisely where the material came from so that they can locate it for themselves. Often readers will want to trace the facts on which a conclusion is based, or to verify that a passage was quoted or paraphrased accurately. Sometimes readers will simply want to follow up and learn more about your subject.

There are basically two ways for a writer to show a "paper trail" to sources. The format most used today is the parenthetical reference, also called an *in-text citation*. This is a telegraphic, short-hand approach to identifying the source of a statement or quotation. It assumes that a complete list of references appears at the end of the paper. Each entry in the list of references includes three essential elements: authorship, full title of the work, and publication information. In the references, entries are arranged, punctuated, and typed to conform to the bibliographic style requirements of the particular discipline or of the instructor. With this list in place, the writer is able to supply the briefest of references—a page number or an author's name—in parentheses right in the text, knowing that the reader will be able to locate the rest of the reference information easily in the list of references.

For more detailed information on the conventions of style in the humanities, social sciences, and sciences, refer to the style manuals listed below.

- Gibaldi, Joseph, and Walter S. Achtert. *MLA Handbook for Writers of Research Papers*. 3rd ed. New York: MLA, 1988.
- *Publication Manual* (of the American Psychological Association). 3rd ed. Washington, DC: APA, 1983.
- *CBE Style Manual*, 5th ed. Bethesda, MD: CBE, 1983.

36a Using the MLA system of documentation

36a

MLA

The Modern Language Association (MLA) publishes a style guide that is widely used for citations and references in the humanities. This section gives detailed examples of how the MLA system of parenthetical references provides in-text citation. In addition, a later subsection (36a-3) will show how to use the alternative footnote or endnote system of documentation, where complete information on each source is given every time a source is cited.

In a research paper, either of these systems of source citation is followed at the end by a list of references. In the MLA system, the list of references is called "Works Cited." Keep in mind that the complete information provided in the list of references will be the basis of your in-text citations. The parenthetical form provides minimal information and sends the reader to the list of references to find the rest. By contrast, the footnote or endnote system virtually duplicates the information in the list of references but uses a slightly different arrangement of the elements in the entry. Following is an index to this section on the MLA system of documentation.

36a

MLA

36a

MLA

1 Making in-text citations in the MLA format

When you make a parenthetical in-text citation, you assume that your reader will look to the list of "Works Cited" for complete references. The list of references at the end of your paper will provide three essential pieces of information for each of your sources: author, title, and facts of publication. Within your paper, a parenthetical citation may serve either of two purposes: to point to a source considered as a whole, or to point to a specific page location in a source. Here is an example of an MLA in-text citation referring to a story as a whole.

> In "Escapes," the title story of one contemporary author's book
> of short stories, the narrator's alcoholic mother makes a public
> spectacle of herself (Williams).

The next example refers to a specific page in the story. In the MLA system, no punctuation is placed between a writer's last name and a page reference.

> In "Escapes," a story about an alcoholic household, a key moment
> occurs when the child sees her mother suddenly appear on stage
> at the magic show (Williams 11).

Here is how the references to the Williams story would appear as described in the list of references or "Works Cited."

> Williams, Joy. "Escapes." Escapes: Stories. New York: Vintage,
> 1990. 1-14.

Deciding when to insert a source citation and what information to include is often a judgment call rather than the execution of a mechanical system. Use common sense. Where feasible, incorporate citations smoothly into the text. Introduce the parenthetical reference smoothly at a pause in your sentence, at the end if possible. Place it as close to the documented point as possible, making sure that the reader can tell exactly which point is being documented. When the in-text reference is incorporated into a sentence of your own, always place the parenthetical reference *before* any enclosing or end punctuation.

36a

MLA

> In Central Africa in the 1930s, a young girl who comes to town
> drinks beer with her date because that's what everyone does (Les-
> sing 105).

> In a realistic portrayal of Central African city life in the
> 1930s (Lessing), young people gather daily to drink.

When a quotation from a work is incorporated into a sentence of your own, the parenthetical reference *follows* the quotation marks, yet precedes the enclosing or end punctuation.

```
At the popular Sports Club, Lessing's heroine finds the "ubiqui-
tous glass mugs of golden beer" (135).
```

EXCEPTION: When your quotation ends with a question mark or exclamation point, keep these punctuation marks inside the end quotation marks, then give the parenthetical reference, and end with a period.

```
Martha's new attempts at sophistication in town prompted her to
retort, "Children are a nuisance, aren't they?" (Lessing 115).
```

Naming an author in the text

When you want to emphasize the author of a source you are citing, incorporate that author's name into your sentence. Unless you are referring to a particular place in that source, no parenthetical reference is necessary in the text.

```
Biographer Paul Mariani understands Berryman's alcoholism as one
form of his drive toward self-destruction.
```

Naming an author in the parenthetical reference

When you want to emphasize information in a source but not especially the author, omit the author's name in the sentence and place it in the parenthetical reference.

```
Biographers have documented alcohol-related upheavals in John
Berryman's life. Aware, for example, that Dylan Thomas was in an
alcohol-induced coma, dying, Berryman himself drank to escape
his pain (Mariani 273).
```

When you are referring to a particular place in your source and have already incorporated the author's name into your sentence, place only the page number in parentheses.

```
Biographer Paul Mariani describes how Berryman, knowing that his
friend Dylan Thomas was dying in an alcohol-induced coma, him-
self began drinking to escape his pain (273).
```

Documenting a block quotation

For block quotations, set the parenthetical reference—with or without an author's name—*outside* of the end punctuation mark.

36a

MLA

The story graphically portrays the behavior of Central African
young people gathering daily to drink:

> Perry sat stiffly in a shallow chair which looked as if it
> would splay out under the weight of his big body . . . while
> from time to time--at those moments when laughter was jerked
> out of him by Stella--he threw back his head with a sudden
> dismayed movement, and flung half a glass of liquor down his
> throat. (Lessing 163)

A work by two or three authors

If your source has two or three authors, name them all, either in your
text or in a parenthetical reference. Use last names, in the order they are given
in the source, connected by *and.*

Critics have addressed the question of whether literary artists
discover new truths (Wellek and Warren 33-36).

One theory claims that the alcoholic wants to "drink his environment in" (Perls, Hefferline, and Goodman 193-194).

A work by four or more authors

For a work with four or more authors, name all the authors, or use the
following abbreviated format with *et al.* to signify "and others."

Some researchers trace the causes of alcohol dependence to
"flawed family structures" (Stein, Lubber, Koman, and Kelly 318).

Some researchers trace the causes of alcohol dependence to
"flawed family structures" (Stein et al. 318).

Stein et al. trace the causes of alcohol dependence to "flawed
family structures" (318).

Reference to two or more sources with the same authorship

When you are referring to one or two or more sources written by the
same author, include in your in-text citation a shortened form of each title so
that references to each text will be clear. The following example discusses how
author Joy Williams portrays the drinking scene in her fiction. Note that a
comma appears between the author's name and the shortened title.

```
She shows drinking at parties as a way of life in such stories
as "Escapes" and "White Like Midnight." Thus it is matter of
course that Joan pours herself a drink while people talk about
whether or not they want to survive nuclear war (Williams,
"White" 129).
```

Distinguishing two authors with the same last name

Use one or more initials to supplement references to authors with the same last name.

```
It is no coincidence that a new translation of Euripides' The
Bacchae should appear in the United States (Williams, C. K.) at
a time when fiction writers portray the use of alcohol as a
means of escape from mundane existence (Williams, J.).
```

Two or more sources in a single reference

Particularly in an introductory summary, you may want to group together a number of works that cover one or more aspects of your research topic. Separate one source from another by a semicolon.

```
Studies that confront the alcoholism of literary figures di-
rectly are on the increase (Mariani; Dardis; Gilmore).
```

A corporate author

A work may be issued by an organization or government agency with no author named. Cite the work as if the name given is the author's. Since the name of a corporate author is often long, try incorporating it into your text rather than using a parenthetical note. In this example the corporate author of the book is Alcoholics Anonymous. The book will be listed alphabetically under "Alcoholics" in Works Cited.

```
Among publications that discuss how to help young people cope
with family problems, Al-Anon Faces Alcoholism, put out by Alco-
holics Anonymous, has been reissued frequently since 1974 (117-
124).
```

36a

MLA

A multivolume work

When citing a page reference to a multivolume work, specify the volume by an arabic numeral followed by a colon and the page number. The Trevelyan history is in four volumes.

```
Drunkenness was such a problem in the first decades of the eigh-
teenth century that it was termed "the acknowledged national
vice of Englishmen of all classes" (Trevelyan 3: 46).
```

A literary work

Well-known literary works, particularly older ones now in the public domain, may appear in numerous editions. When referring to such a work or a part of one, give information for the work itself rather than for the particular edition you are using, unless you are highlighting a special feature or contribution of the edition.

For a play, supply act, scene, and line number in arabic numerals, unless your instructor specifies using Roman numerals for act and scene (II. iv. 118–119). In the following example, the title of the literary work includes numerals referring to the first of two plays that Shakespeare wrote about Henry IV, known as parts 1 and 2.

```
Shakespeare's Falstaff bellows, "Give me a cup of sack, rogue.
Is there no virtue extant?" (1 Henry IV 2. 4. 118-119).
```

To cite a modern editor's contribution to the publication of a literary work, adjust the emphasis of your reference. The abbreviation *n.* stands for *note.*

```
Without the editor's footnote in the Riverside Shakespeare ex-
plaining that lime was sometimes used as an additive to make
wine sparkle, modern readers would be unlikely to understand
Falstaff's ranting: "[Y]et a coward is worse than a cup of sack
with lime in it. A villainous coward!" (1 Henry IV 2. 4. 125-
126n.).
```

Material quoted in your source

Often you will want to quote and cite material that you are reading at second hand—in a work by an intermediate author. Quote the original material and refer to the place where you found it.

```
Psychoanalyst Otto Fenichel included alcoholics within a general
grouping of addictive personalities, all of whom use addictive
substances "to satisfy the archaic oral longing, a need for secu-
rity, and a need for the maintenance of self-esteem simulta-
neously" (qtd. in Roebuck and Kessler 86).
```

36a

MLA

An anonymous work

A work with no acknowledged author will be alphabetized in a list of references by the first word of its title. Therefore cite the anonymous work in the same way in your parenthetical reference. The title in this example is *The Hidden Alcoholic in Your Midst.*

```
People who do not suffer from addiction often can be thought-

less and insensitive to the problems of those around them. That

is the message of an emotional and thought-provoking pamphlet

(Hidden), whose author writes anonymously about the pain of keep-

ing his alcoholism secret.
```

2 Preparing a list of references in the MLA format

In research papers following MLA format, the list of references is called "Works Cited" when it includes those sources you have referred to in your paper. Be aware that some instructors request a more comprehensive list of references—one that includes every source you consulted in preparing the paper. That list would be titled "Bibliography."

The examples in this section show how entries in the "Works Cited" list consist of three elements essential for a list of references: authorship, full title of the work, and publication information. The basic format for each entry requires the first line to start at the left margin, with each subsequent line to be indented five typed spaces from the left margin.

Not every possible variation is represented here. In formatting a complicated entry for your own list, you may need to combine features from two or more of the examples. The MLA "Works Cited" list begins on a new page, after the last page of your paper, and continues the pagination of your paper. Entries in the list are alphabetized by the author's last name. An anonymous work is alphabetized by the first word in its title (but disregard *A*, *An*, and *The*).

Listing books in the MLA "Works Cited" format

The MLA "Works Cited" list presents book references in the following order:

36a

MLA

1. Author's name: Put the last name first, followed by a comma and the first name (and middle name or initial) and a period. Omit the author's titles and degrees, whether one that precedes a name (Dr.) or one that follows (Ph.D.). Leave two typed spaces after the period.

2. Title of the book: Underline the complete title. If there is a subtitle, separate it from the main title by a colon and one typed space. Capitalize all important words, including the first word of any subtitle. The complete title is followed by a period and two typed spaces.

3. Publication information: Name the city of publication, followed by a colon and one typed space; the name of the publisher followed by a comma; the date of publication followed by a period. This information appears on the title page of the book and the copyright page, on the reverse side of the title page.

If the city of publication is not well known, add the name of the state, abbreviated as in the zip code system. Shorten the name of the publisher in a way that is recognizable. "G. P. Putnam's Sons" is shortened to "Putnam's." For university presses use "UP" as in the example "U of Georgia P." Many large publishing companies issue books under imprints that represent particular groups of books. Give the imprint name first, followed by a hyphen and the name of the publisher: Bullseye-Knopf.

Any additional information about the book goes between author and title or between title and publication data. In the examples that follow, you will notice the kinds of information that can be added to an entry. Observe details of how to organize, abbreviate, and punctuate this information.

A book with one author

The basic format for a single-author book is as follows:

```
Mariani, Paul.  Dream Song: The Life of John Berryman.   New
     York: Morrow, 1990.
```

A book with two or three authors

For a book with two or three authors, follow the order of the names on the title page. Notice that first and last name are reversed only for the lead author. Notice also the use of a comma after the first author.

```
Roebuck, Julian B., and Raymond G. Kessler.  The Etiology of Al-
     coholism: Constitutional, Psychological and Sociological Ap-
     proaches.  Springfield: Thomas, 1972.
```

36a

MLA

A book with four or more authors

As in the example under in-text citations (see 36a-1), you may choose to name all the authors or to use the abbreviated format with *et al.*

```
Stein, Norman, Mindy Lubber, Stuart L. Koman, and Kathy Kelly.
     Family Therapy: A Systems Approach.  Boston: Allyn, 1990.
Stein, Norman, et al. Family Therapy: A Systems Approach.  Bos-
     ton: Allyn, 1990.
```

A book that has been reprinted or reissued

In the following entry, the date 1951 is the original publication date of the book, which was reprinted in 1965.

> Perls, Frederick, Ralph F. Hefferline, and Paul Goodman.   Ge-
>
>   stalt Therapy: Excitement and Growth in the Human Personal-
>
>   ity.   1951. New York: Delta-Dell, 1965.

A dictionary or encyclopedia

If an article in a reference work is signed (usually by initials), include the name of the author, which is spelled out elsewhere in the reference work (usually at the beginning). The first example is unsigned. The second article is signed (F.G.H.T.).

> "Alcoholics Anonymous."   Encyclopaedia Britannica: Micropaedia.
>
>   1991 ed.
>
> Tate, Francis G. H.   "Rum."   Encyclopaedia Britannica. 1950 ed.

A selection from an edited book or anthology

For a selection from an edited work, name the author of the selection and enclose the selection title in quotation marks. Underline the title of the book containing the selection, and name its editor(s). Give the page numbers for the selection at the end of your entry.

> Davies, Phil. "Does Treatment Work?   A Sociological Perspec-
>
>   tive."   The Misuse of Alcohol.   Ed. Nick Heather et al.   New
>
>   York: New York UP, 1985.   158-177.

When a selection has been reprinted from another source, include that information too, as in the following example. State the facts of original publication first, then describe the book in which it has been reprinted.

> Bendiner, Emil.   "The Bowery Man on the Couch."   The Bowery Man.
>
>   New York: Nelson, 1961.   Rpt. in Man Alone: Alienation in
>
>   Modern Society.   Ed. Eric Josephson and Mary Josephson.   New
>
>   York: Dell, 1962.   401-410.

Two or more works by the same author(s)

When you cite two or more works by the same author(s), you should write the author's full name only once, at first mention, in the reference list. In subsequent entries immediately following, substitute three hyphens and a period in place of the author's name.

> Heilbroner, Robert L.   The Future as History.   New York: Harper
>
>   Torchbooks-Harper, 1960.
>
> ---.   An Inquiry into the Human Prospect.   New York: Norton, 1974.

36a

MLA

A translation

When a work has been translated, acknowledge the translator's name after giving the title.

```
Kufner, Heinrich, and Wilhelm Feuerlein.  In-Patient Treatment

    for Alcoholism: A Multi-Centre Evaluation Study.  Trans. F.

    K. H. Wagstaff.  Berlin: Springer, 1989.
```

A corporate author

If authorship is not individual but corporate, treat the name of the organization as you would the author. This listing would be alphabetized under "National Center."

```
National Center for Alcohol Education.  The Community Health

    Nurse and Alcohol-Related Problems: Instructor's Curriculum

    Planning Guide.  Rockville: National Institute on Alcohol

    Abuse and Alcoholism, 1978.
```

Signaling publication information that is unknown

If a document fails to state place or date of publication or the name of the publisher, indicate this lack of information in your entry by using the appropriate abbreviation.

```
Missing, Andrew.  Things I Forgot or Never Knew.  n.p.: n.p.,

    n.d.
```

In the above example, the first *n.p.* stands for "no place of publication." The second *n.p.* means "no publisher given" and *n.d.* stands for "no date."

An edition subsequent to the first

Books of continuing importance may be revised substantially before reissue. Cite the edition you have consulted just after giving the title.

```
Scrignar, C. B.  Post-Traumatic Stress Disorder: Diagnosis,

    Treatment, and Legal Issues.  2nd ed.  New Orleans: Bruno,

    1988.
```

36a

MLA

A book in a series

If the book you are citing is one in a series, include the series name (no quotation marks or underline) followed by the volume number and a period before the publication information. You need not give the name of the series editor.

```
Schuckit, Marc A., ed.  Alcohol Patterns and Problems.  Series

    in Psychological Epidemiology 5.  New Brunswick: Rutgers UP,

    1985.
```

An introduction, preface, foreword, or afterword

When citing an introductory or concluding essay by a "guest author" or commentator, begin with the name of that author. Give the type of piece—Introduction, Preface—without quotation marks or underline. Name the author of the book after giving the book title. At the end of the listing, give the page numbers for the essay you are citing. If the author of the separate essay is also the author of the complete work, repeat that author's last name, preceded by *By,* after the book title.

> Fromm, Erich. Foreword. <u>Summerhill: A Radical Approach to Child Rearing</u>. By A. S. Neill. New York: Hart, 1960. ix-xiv.

In this book, the editors also wrote the introduction to their anthology.

> Josephson, Eric, and Mary Josephson. Introduction. <u>Man Alone: Alienation in Modern Society</u>. Ed. by Josephson and Josephson. New York: Dell, 1962. 9-53.

An unpublished dissertation or essay

An unpublished dissertation, even of book length, has its title in quotation marks. Label it as a dissertation in your entry. Naming the university and year will provide the necessary publication facts.

> Reiskin, Helen R. "Patterns of Alcohol Usage in a Help-Seeking University Population." Diss. Boston U., 1980.

Listing periodicals in the MLA "Works Cited" format

A *periodical* is any publication that appears regularly over time. A periodical can be a daily or weekly newspaper, a magazine, or a scholarly or professional journal. As with listings for books, a bibliographical listing for a periodical article includes information about authorship, title, and facts of publication. Authorship is treated just as for books, with the author's first and last name reversed. Citation of a title differs in that the title of an article is always enclosed in quotation marks rather than underlined; the title of the periodical in which it appears is always underlined. Notice that the articles *a, an,* and *the,* which often begin the name of a periodical, are omitted from the bibliographical listing.

The facts of publication are the trickiest of the three elements because of the wide variation in how periodicals are dated, paginated, and published. For journals, for example, the publication information generally consists of journal title, the volume number, the year of publication, and the page numbering for the article cited. For newspapers, the listing includes name of the newspaper, full date of publication, and full page numbering by both section and page number(s) if necessary. The following examples show details of how to list different types of periodicals. With the exception of May, June, and July, you should abbreviate the names of months in each "Works Cited" entry (see 31d).

36a

MLA

A journal with continuous pagination through the annual volume

A continuously paginated journal is one that numbers pages consecutively throughout all the issues in a volume instead of beginning with page 1 in each issue. After the author's name (reversed and followed by a period and two typed spaces), give the name of the article in quotation marks. Give the title of the journal, underlined and followed by two typed spaces. Give the volume number, in arabic numerals. After a typed space, give the year, in parentheses, followed by a colon. After one more space, give the page number(s) for the article, including the first and last pages on which it appears.

```
Kling, William.  "Measurement of Ethanol Consumed in Distilled

    Spirits."  Journal of Studies on Alcohol  50 (1989): 456-460.
```

In a continuously paginated journal, the issue number within the volume and the month of publication are not included in the bibliographical listing.

A journal paginated by issue

```
Latessa, Edward J., and Susan Goodman.  "Alcoholic Offenders: In-

    tensive Probation Program Shows Promise."  Corrections Today

    51.3 (1989): 38-39+.
```

This journal numbers the pages in each issue separately, so it is important to identify which issue in volume 51 has this article beginning on page 38. The plus sign following a page number indicates that the article continues after the last-named page, but after intervening pages.

A monthly magazine

This kind of periodical is identified by month and year of issue. Even if the magazine indicates a volume number, omit it from your listing.

```
Waggoner, Glen. "Gin as Tonic."  Esquire  Feb. 1990: 30.
```

Some magazines vary in their publication schedule. *Restaurant Business* publishes once a month or bimonthly. Include the full date of publication in your listing. Give the day first, followed by an abbreviation for the month.

```
Whelan, Elizabeth M.  "Alcohol and Health."  Restaurant Business

    20 Mar. 1989: 66+.
```

36a

MLA

A daily newspaper

In the following examples, you see that the name of the newspaper is underlined. Any introductory article (*a, an,* and *the*) is omitted. The complete date of publication is given—day, month (abbreviated), year. Specify the edition if one appears on the masthead, since even in one day an article may be located differently in different editions. Precede the page number(s) by a colon and one typed space. If the paper has sections designated by letter (A, B, C), include the section before the page number.

If the article is unsigned, begin your entry with the title, as in the second example ("Alcohol Can Worsen . . .").

```
Welch, Patrick. "Kids and Booze: It's 10 O'Clock--Do You Know
     How Drunk Your Kids Are?" Washington Post  31 Dec. 1989: C1.
```

The following entry illustrates the importance of including the particular edition of a newspaper.

```
"Alcohol Can Worsen Ills of Aging, Study Says." New York Times
     13 June 1989, national ed.: 89.
"Alcohol Can Worsen Ills of Aging, Study Says." New York Times
     13 June 1989, late ed.: C5.
```

A weekly magazine or newspaper

An unsigned article listing would include title, name of the publication, complete date, and page number(s). Even if you know a volume or issue number, omit it.

```
"A Direct Approach to Alcoholism." Science News  9 Jan. 1988:
     25.
```

A signed editorial, letter to the editor, review

For these entries, first give the name of the author. If the piece has a title, put it within quotation marks. Then name the category of the piece—Letter, Rev. of (for Review), Editorial—without quotation marks or underline. If the reference is to a review, give the name of the work being reviewed with underline or quotation marks as appropriate.

```
Fraser, Kennedy.  Rev. of Stones of His House: A Biography of
     Paul Scott, by Hilary Spurling.  New Yorker  13 May 1991:
     103-110.
James, Albert. Letter.  Boston Globe  14 Jan. 1992: 61.
Stein, Norman.  "Traveling for Work."  Editorial. Baltimore Sun
     12 Dec. 1991: 82.
```

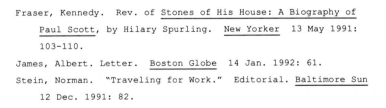

36a

Other sources in the MLA "Works Cited" format

An abstract of an article

Libraries contain many volumes of abstracts of recent articles in many disciplines. If you are referring to an abstract you have read rather than to the complete article, list it as follows.

```
Corcoran, K. J., and M. D. Carney.  "Alcohol Consumption and
     Looking for Alternatives to Drinking in College Students."
     Journal of Cognitive Psychotherapy  3 (1989): 69-78.  Abstr.
     in Excerpta Medica  Sec. 32 Vol. 60 (1989): 40.
```

A government publication

Often, a government publication will have group authorship. Be sure to name the agency or committee responsible for writing a document.

```
United States Congress.  Senate.  Subcommittee to Investigate
     Juvenile Delinquency of the Committee on the Judiciary.
     Juvenile Alcohol Abuse: Hearing.  95th Cong., 2nd sess.
     Washington: GPO, 1978.
```

An unpublished interview

A listing for an unpublished interview begins with the name of the person interviewed. If the interview is untitled, label it as such, without quotation marks or underlining. Name the person doing the interviewing only if that information is relevant.

```
Bishop, Robert R.  Personal interview.  5 Nov. 1987.
```

An unpublished letter

Treat an unpublished letter much as you would an unpublished interview. Designate the recipient of the letter. If you as the writer of the paper were the recipient, refer to yourself as "the author."

```
Bishop, Robert R.  Letter to the author.  8 June 1964.
```

If a letter is housed in a library collection or archive, provide full archival information.

```
Bishop, Robert R.  Letter to Jonathan Morton.  8 June 1964.
     Carol K. Morton papers.  Smith College, Northampton.
```

A film or videotape

Underline the title, and then name the medium, the distributor, and the year. Supply any information that you think is useful about the performers, director, producer, or physical characteristics of the film or tape.

```
Alcoholism: The Pit of Despair.  Videocassette.  Gordon Jump.
     AIMS Media, 1983.  VHS and Beta.  20 min.
```

A television or radio program

If the program you are citing is a single episode with its own title, supply the title in quotation marks. State the name and role of the foremost

36a

MLA

participant(s). Underline the title of the program, identify who produced it, and list the station on which it first appeared, the city, and the date.

```
"The Broken Cord."  Interview with Louise Erdrich and Michael

     Dorris. Dir. and prod. Catherine Tatge.  A World of Ideas

     with Bill Moyers.  Exec. prod. Judith Davidson Moyers and

     Bill Moyers. Public Affairs TV. WNET, New York.  27 May 1990.
```

A live performance, lecture

Identify the "who, what, and where" of a live performance. If the "what" is more important than the "who," as in a performance of an opera, give the name of the work before the name of the performers or director. In the following example, the name of the speaker, a cofounder of AA, comes first.

```
Wilson, Bill.  "Alcoholics Anonymous: Beginnings and Growth."

     Presented to the NYC Medical Society.  New York, 8 Apr.

     1958.
```

A work of art

Underline the title of a work of art referred to, and tell the location of the work. The name of the museum or collection is separated from the name of the city by a comma.

```
Manet, Edouard.  The Absinthe Drinker.  Ny Carlsberg Glyptotek,

     Copenhagen.
```

Electronic material

Information services. Listings in indexes, volumes of abstracts, and bibliographies on computer often have identification numbers. If you are citing such a listing, whether you located it in print or in a computer database, add the name of the source and the identification number of your entry. The "ED" number for each item in ERIC (Educational Resources Information Center) will represent one document.

```
Weaver, Dave.  "Software for Substance Abuse Education: A Criti-

     cal Review of Products."  Portland: Northwest Regional Educa-

     tional Lab, 1988.  ERIC ED 303 702.
```

36a

MLA

Computer software. Like a printed book, computer software has authorship, a title, and a publication history. Include this in any bibliographical listing, along with relevant information for your reader about the software and any hardware it requires. Underline the title of the program. Identify the title as computer software. In the example, the name of the author and the location of the company would be added if they were known.

```
Alcohol and Pregnancy: Protecting the Unborn Child.  Computer
    software.  Student Awareness Software, 1988.  48K Apple II
    and 256K IBM PC.
```

A separately issued map, chart, or graph

Even a free-standing map or poster generally tells something about who published it, where, and when. Give the title, underlined, and any identifying information available. Use the abbreviation *n.d.* any time a date is lacking in publication information.

```
Roads in France.  Map.  Paris: National Tourist Information
    Agency, n.d.
```

3 Making in-text citations in MLA footnote format

The parenthetical reference mode of in-text citation is neat and easy to use. The physical and biological sciences, as well as the social sciences, have used it for decades. In the humanities, however, it has long been common practice for writers to make their citations by means of the note—whether a footnote at the bottom of the page containing the cited material, or an endnote placed at the end of the chapter or of the entire work. When the Modern Language Association, with its widely used *MLA Handbook for Writers of Research Papers,* adopted the parenthetical note as its norm in its 1984 edition, custom changed. Still, some instructors and some disciplines continue to prefer the note method of citation.

Check with your instructor regarding use of notes. He or she may prefer the in-text citation form or may prefer endnotes to footnotes. Some instructors may not require a separate list of references if you use footnotes or endnotes.

To use footnotes or endnotes, signal a citation in the text by a raised numeral (superscript) at the appropriate point, preferably just after a comma or period. Place the citation information that you have signaled in a separate note with matching number. Place a footnote at the bottom of the page; collect endnotes at the end of your paper, just before the list of references.

To type a footnote, leave two double spaces below the text. Single-space the note, but double-space between notes. Indent the start of each note 5 typewriter spaces. Begin with the superscript numeral, followed immediately by the first word of the note. To continue the note on subsequent lines, return to the left margin, as in this example.

```
    3Paul Mariani, Dream Song: The Life of John Berryman (New
York: Morrow, 1990) 45-49.
```

A citation note contains essentially the same information—author, title, publication facts—as an entry in a list of references, but there are differences

36a

MLA

in order and punctuation between the two. Notice that the note, unlike an entry in a list of references, concludes with a page reference. A note need not tell the span of pages of a source article or essay because that information is provided in the list of references.

There are two key features of the footnote and endnote format in the MLA system:

1. An author's name appears in normal (not inverted) order and is followed by a comma.

2. Publishing information is contained in parentheses and follows the book title with no intervening period.

Making the first and subsequent references in notes

The first time you cite a source in your paper, you will give complete information about it. If you refer to that source again, you need give only the briefest identification. Usually, this is the author's name and a page reference.

In the following sample paragraph, the first note refers to an entire book. The second note cites a particular passage in a review, and refers to that page only. The third note refers to a work already cited in note 2.

> Alcohol has played a destructive, painful role in the lives of numerous twentieth-century writers. Among poets, Dylan Thomas is often the first who comes to mind as a victim of alcoholism. John Berryman, too, suffered from this afflic-tion.[1] Among novelists who battled alcohol was the great British writer Paul Scott, author of the masterpiece The Raj Quartet. A reviewer of a new biography of Scott faults the biographer for not understanding fully the effect of alcohol-ism on Scott and his wife and daughters.[2] Scott's own mother, out of a kind of bravado, encouraged Paul to drink gin at the age of six.[3]

> [1]Paul Mariani, Dream Song: The Life of John Berryman (New York: Morrow, 1990).
> [2]Kennedy Fraser, rev. of Stones of His House: A Life of Paul Scott, by Hilary Spurling. New Yorker 13 May 1991: 110.
> [3]Fraser 108.

36a

MLA

Compare the format of these footnotes with their corresponding entries in the "Works Cited" list.

Mariani, Paul. Dream Song: The Life of John Berryman. New York: Morrow, 1990.

Fraser, Kennedy. Rev. of Stones of His House: A Biography of Paul Scott, by Hilary Spurling. New Yorker 13 May 1991: 103-110.

Following the note format in citing books

A book with two or three authors

[1]Julian B. Roebuck and Raymond G. Kessler, The Etiology of Alcoholism: Constitutional, Psychological and Sociological Approaches (Springfield, IL: Thomas, 1972) 72.

A book with four or more authors

Name each author, or use the *et al.* format.

[2]Norman Stein et al., Family Therapy: A Systems Approach (Boston: Allyn, 1990) 312.

A corporate author

[3]National Center for Alcohol Education, The Community Health Nurse and Alcohol-Related Problems: Instructor's Curriculum Planning Guide (Rockville: National Institute on Alcohol Abuse and Alcoholism, 1978) 45-49.

A multivolume work

[4]G.M. Trevelyan, Illustrated English Social History, vol. 3 (Harmondsworth: Pelican-Penguin, 1964) 46.

Two sources cited in one note

[5]Joy Williams, Escapes (New York: Vintage, 1990) 57-62; C. K. Williams, The Bacchae of Euripides: A New Version (New York: Farrar, 1990) 15.

An edition subsequent to the first

[6]C.B. Scrignar, Post-Traumatic Stress Disorder: Diagnosis, Treatment, and Legal Issues, 2nd ed. (New Orleans: Bruno, 1988) 23-28.

A selection in an edited book or anthology

[7]Emil Bendiner, "The Bowery Man on the Couch," Man Alone: Alienation in Modern Society, ed. Eric Josephson and Mary Josephson (New York: Dell, 1962) 408.

36a

MLA

An introduction, preface, foreword, or afterword

> [8]Erich Fromm, foreword, <u>Summerhill: A Radical Approach to Child Rearing</u>, by A.S. Neill (New York: Hart, 1960) xii.

Following the note format in citing periodicals and other sources

A journal with continuous pagination through the annual volume

> [9]William Kling, "Measurement of Ethanol Consumed in Distilled Spirits," <u>Journal of Studies on Alcohol</u> 50 (1989): 456.

A monthly magazine

> [10]Glen Waggoner, "Gin as Tonic," <u>Esquire</u> Feb. 1990: 30.

A weekly magazine

> [11]"A Direct Approach to Alcoholism," <u>Science News</u> 9 Jan. 1988: 25.

A daily newspaper

> [12]"Alcohol Can Worsen Ills of Aging, Study Says," <u>New York Times</u> 13 Jun. 1989, late ed.: C5.

A dissertation abstract

> [13]Helen R. Reiskin, "Pattern of Alcohol Usage in a Help-Seeking University Population," <u>DAI</u> 41 (1983): 6447A (U of Vermont).

Computer software

> [14]<u>Alcohol and Pregnancy: Protecting the Unborn Child</u>, computer software, Student Awareness Software, 1988.

A government document

> [15]United States Senate, Subcommittee to Investigate Juvenile Delinquency of the Committee on the Judiciary, <u>Juvenile Alcohol Abuse: Hearing</u>. 95th Cong., 2nd sess. (Washington: GPO, 1978) 3.

36a

MLA

36b Using the APA system of documentation

The American Psychological Association's *Publication Manual* has set documentation style for psychologists. Writers in other fields, especially those in which researchers report their work fairly frequently in periodicals and edited collections of essays, also use the APA system of documentation. Whichever style of documentation you use in a given research paper, use only one; do not mix features of APA and MLA (or any other format) in a single paper.

APA documentation is similar to the MLA system in coupling a brief in-text citation, given in parentheses, with a complete listing of information about the source at the end of the paper. In the APA system this list of references is called "References." In the in-text citation itself, APA style differs by including the date of the work cited. The publication date is often important for a reader to have immediately at hand in psychology and related fields, where researchers may publish frequently, often modifying conclusions reached in prior publications. Date of publication also serves to distinguish readily among publications for authors who have many titles to their name. Following is an index to this section on the APA system of documentation.

1   Making in-text citations in the APA format

For every fact, opinion, or idea from another source that you quote, summarize, or otherwise use, you must give credit. You must also give just enough information so that your reader can locate the source. Whether in the text itself or in a parenthetical note, APA documentation calls for you to name the author and give the date of publication for every work you refer to. When you have quoted from a work, you must also give the page or page numbers (preceded by *p.* or *pp.*, in APA format). When you summarize or paraphrase, as well, it is often helpful to supply exact location of the source material by page number as part of the parenthetical reference. Supply the page number(s) immediately following a quotation or paraphrase, even if the sentence is not at a pause point.

In the sample paragraphs that follow, you will find variations on using APA in-text citation. Notice that, wherever possible, reference information is incorporated directly into the text and parentheses are used as a supplement to information in the text. Supply the parenthetical date of publication immediately after an author's name in the text. If you refer to a source a second time within a paragraph, you need not repeat the information if the reference is clear. If there is any confusion about which work is being cited, however, supply the clarifying information. If in your entire paper you are citing only one work by a particular author, you need give the date only in the first reference. If the page number for a subsequent reference differs from the earlier page number, supply the number. Separate items within a parenthetical reference by commas.

Dardis's study (1989) examines four twentieth-century Ameri-

can writers—three of them Nobel Prize winners—who were alcohol-

ics. Dardis acknowledged (p. 3) that American painters too

include a high percentage of addicted drinkers. Among poets, he

36b

APA

```
concludes (p. 5) that the percentage is not so high as among
prose writers.
```
```
      However, even a casual reading of a recent biography of poet
John Berryman (Mariani, 1990) reveals a creative and personal
life dominated by alcohol. Indeed, "so regular had [Berryman's]
hospital stays [for alcoholism] become . . . that no one came to
visit him anymore" (Mariani, p. 413). Berryman himself had no il-
lusions about the destructive power of alcohol. About his friend
Dylan Thomas he could write, "Dylan murdered himself w. liquor,
tho it  took years" (qtd. in Mariani, p. 274). Robert Lowell and
Edna St. Vincent Millay were also prominent American poets who
had problems with alcohol (Dardis, p. 3).
```

A work by two authors

To join the names of two authors of a work, use *and* in text but use the ampersand (&) in a parenthetical reference. Notice how the parenthetical information immediately follows the point to which it applies.

```
Roebuck and Kessler (1972) summarized the earlier research (pp.
21-41).
```

```
A summary of prior research on the genetic basis of alcoholism
(Roebuck & Kessler, 1972, pp. 21-41) is our starting point.
```

Two or more works by the same author

If the work of the same author has appeared in different years, distinguish references to each separate work by year of publication. If, however, you refer to two or more works published by the same author(s) within a single year, you must list the works in alphabetical order by title in the list of references, and assign each one an order by lowercase letter. Thus,

```
(Holden, 1989a)
```

could represent Caroline Holden's article "Alcohol and Creativity," while

```
(Holden, 1989b)
```

would refer to the same author's "Creativity and Craving," published in the same year.

A work by three to five authors

Use names of all authors in the first reference, but subsequently give only the first of the names followed by *et al.* Use the *et al.* format for six or more authors.

36b

APA

```
Perls, Hefferline, and Goodman (1965) did not focus on the addic-
tive personality. Like other approaches to the study of the mind
in the '50s and '60s, Gestalt psychology (Perls et al.) spoke of
addiction only in passing.
```

A work by a corporate author

Give a corporate author's whole name in a parenthetical reference. If the name can be readily abbreviated, supply the abbreviation in brackets in the first reference. Subsequently, use the abbreviation alone.

```
Al-Anon Faces Alcoholism (Alcoholics Anonymous [AA], 1974) has
been reissued many times since its initial publication.
```

```
One of the books most widely read by American teenagers (AA,
1974) deals with alcoholism in the family.
```

Distinguishing two authors with the same last name

Distinguish authors with the same last name by including first and middle initials in each citation.

```
(J. Williams, 1990)
(C. K. Williams, 1991)
```

Two or more sources in a single reference

Separate multiple sources in one citation by a semicolon. List authors alphabetically within the parenthesis.

```
We need to view the alcoholic in twentieth-century America from
many perspectives (Bendiner, 1962; Dardis, 1989; Waggoner, 1990)
in order to understand how people with ordinary lives as well as
people with vast creative talent can appear to behave identi-
cally.
```

36b

APA

2   Preparing a list of references in the APA format

In research papers following the APA system, the list of references (which is alphabetized) is called "References." Within an entry, the date is separated from the other facts of publication. The APA list of references includes only those works referred to in your paper.

Listing books in the APA format

Leave two typed spaces to separate items in an entry. Double space the list throughout. Start each entry at the left margin; if the entry runs beyond one line, indent subsequent lines three typewriter spaces. The following order of presentation is used:

1. Author's name(s): Put the last name first, followed by a comma. Use first—and middle—initial instead of spelling out a first or middle name.

2. Date: Give the year of publication in parentheses followed by a period. If your list includes more than one title by an author in any one year, distinguish those titles by adding a lowercase letter (a, b, etc.) to the year of publication (as in 1989a and 1989b).

3. Title of the book: Underline the complete book title. Capitalize only the first word in a title or subtitle, in addition to proper names.

4. Publication information: Name the city of publication, followed by a colon. Give the full name of the publisher, but without the "Co." or other business designation.

```
Dardis, T. (1989).  The thirsty muse: Alcohol and the American
     writer.  New York: Ticknor & Fields.
```

A book with two authors

Invert both names; separate them by a comma. Use the ampersand (&).

```
Roebuck, J. B., & Kessler, R. G. (1972).  The etiology of
     alcoholism: Constitutional, psychological and sociological
     approaches. Springfield, IL: Charles C. Thomas.
```

A book with three or more authors

List *all* authors, treating each author's name as in the case of two authors. Use the ampersand before naming the last. (This book was first published in 1951, then reissued without change.)

```
Perls, R., Hefferline, R. F., & Goodman, P. (1965).  Gestalt psy-
     chology: Excitement and growth in the human personality.
     New York: Delta-Dell.  (Originally published 1951)
```

36b

APA

A selection from an edited book or anthology

Underline the title of the book. The selection title is not underlined or enclosed in quotation marks. (In APA style, spell out the name of a university press.)

```
Davies, P.  (1985).  Does treatment work?  A sociological per-
     spective.  In N. Heather (Ed.), The misuse of alcohol (pp.
     158-177).  New York: New York University Press.
```

A corporate author

Alphabetize the entry in the references list by the first significant word in the name, which is given in normal order.

National Center for Alcohol Education. (1978). The community health nurse and alcohol-related problems: Instructor's curriculum planning guide. Rockville, MD: National Institute on Alcohol Abuse and Alcoholism.

An edition subsequent to the first

Indicate the edition in parentheses, following the book title.

Scrignar, C. B. (1988). Post-traumatic stress disorder: Diagnosis, treatment, and legal issues (2nd ed.). New Orleans: Bruno.

A dissertation

In contrast with MLA style, the title of an unpublished dissertation or thesis is underlined.

Reiskin, H. R. (1980). Patterns of alcohol usage in a help-seeking university population. Unpublished doctoral dissertation, Boston University.

If you are referring to the abstract of the dissertation, the style of the entry differs because the abstract itself appears in a volume (volume number underlined).

Reiskin, H. R. (1980). Patterns of alcohol usage in a help-seeking university population. Dissertation Abstracts International, 40, 6447A.

36b

Listing periodicals in the APA format

APA

A journal with continuous pagination through the annual volume

The entry for a journal begins with the author's last name and initial(s), inverted, followed by the year of publication in parentheses. The title of the article has neither quotation marks nor underline. Only the first word of the title and subtitle are capitalized, along with proper nouns. The volume number, which follows the underlined title of the journal, is also underlined. Use the abbreviations *p.* or *pp.* when referring to page numbers in a magazine or newspaper. Use no abbreviations when referring to the page numbers of a journal.

```
Kling, W.   (1989).   Measurement of ethanol consumed in distilled
     spirits.   Journal of Studies on Alcohol, 50, 456-460.
```

A journal paginated by issue

In this example, the issue number within volume 51 is given in parentheses. Give all page numbers when the article is not printed continuously.

```
Latessa, E. J., & Goodman, S.   (1989).   Alcoholic offenders: In-
     tensive probation program shows promise.   Corrections Today,
     51(3), 38-39, 45.
```

A monthly magazine

Invert the year and month of a monthly magazine. Write the name of the month in full. (For newspapers and magazines use the abbreviations *p.* and *pp.*)

```
Waggoner, G.   (1990, February).   Gin as tonic.   Esquire, p. 30.
```

A weekly magazine

If the article is signed, begin with the author's name. Otherwise, begin with the article's title. (You would alphabetize the following entry under *d.*)

```
A direct approach to alcoholism.   (1988, January 9).   Science
     News, p. 25.
```

A daily newspaper

```
Welch, P. (1989, December 31).   Kids and booze: It's 10 o'clock--
     Do you know how drunk your kids are?   Washington Post, p. C1.
```

A review or letter to the editor

Treat the title of the review or letter as the title of an article, without quotation. Use brackets to show that the article is a review or letter. If the review is untitled, place the bracketed information immediately after the date.

36b

APA

```
Fraser, K. (1991, May·13).   The bottle and inspiration [Review
     of Stones of his house: A biography of Paul Scott].   New
     Yorker, pp. 103-110.
```

Two or more works by the same author in the same year

If you refer to two or more works published by the same author(s) within a single year, list the works in alphabetical order by title in the list of references, and assign each one an order by lowercase letter.

Chen, J. S., & Amsel, A. (1980a). Learned persistence at 11-12
days but not at 10-11 days in infant rats. Developmental
Psychobiology, 13, 481-492.

Chen, J. S., & Amsel, A. (1980b). Retention under changed-
reward conditions of persistence learned by infant rats.
Developmental Psychobiology, 13, 469-480.

Listing other sources in the APA format

An abstract of an article

Show where the abstract may be found, at the end of the entry.

Corcoran, K. J., & Carney, M. D. (1989). Alcohol consumption
and looking for alternatives to drinking in college students. Journal of Cognitive Psychotherapy, 3, 69-78. (From
Excerpta Medica, 1989, 60, Abstract No. 1322)

A government publication

Senate subcommittee to investigate juvenile delinquency of the
committee on the judiciary. (1978). [Hearing, 95th Congress, 2nd sess.] Juvenile Alcohol Abuse. Washington, DC:
U.S. Government Printing Office.

A film or videotape

For nonprint media, identify the medium in brackets just after the title.

Jump, G. (1983). Alcoholism: The pit of despair [Video-
cassette, VHS and Beta]. New York: AIMS Media.

A television or radio program

Erdrich, L., & Dorris, M. (1990, May 27). The broken cord
[Interview]. A world of ideas with Bill Moyers [Television
program]. New York: Public Affairs TV. WNET.

An information service

Weaver, D. (1988). Software for substance abuse education: A
critical review of products. Portland, OR: Northwest Regional Educational Lab. (ERIC Document Reproduction Service
No. ED 303 702)

36b

APA

Computer software

Begin your reference to a computer program with the name of the
author or other primary contributor, if known.

Cohen, L. S. (1989). Alcohol testing: Self help [Computer
program]. Baltimore, MD: Boxford Enterprises.

36c Using the CBE Systems of Documentation

The Council of Biology Editors (CBE) systems of documentation are standard for the biological sciences and, with minor or minimal adaptations, are also used in many of the other sciences. You will find many resemblances between the CBE styles of documentation and the APA style, which was derived from the conventions used in scientific writing. As in APA and MLA styles, any in-text references to a source are provided in shortened form in parentheses. For complete bibliographic information, readers expect to consult the list of references at the end of the document. Following is an index to this section on the CBE systems for documentation.

36c

CBE

1 Making in-text citations in the CBE formats

The CBE Style Manual presents three formats for citing a source in the text of an article. Your choice of format will depend on the discipline in which you are writing. Whatever format you choose, remain consistent within any one document.

The name-and-year system

The CBE convention that most closely resembles the APA conventions is the name-and-year system. In this system a writer provides in parentheses the name of an author and the year in which that author's work was published. Note that, in contrast to the APA system, no comma appears between the author's name and the year of publication.

```
Slicing and aeration of quiescent storage tissues induces a

rapid metabolic activation and a development of the membrane sys-

tems in the wounded tissue (Kahl 1974).
```

If an author's name is mentioned in a sentence, then only the year of publication is set in parentheses.

```
Jacobsen et al. found that a marked transition in respiratory

substrate occurs in sliced potato tissue that exhibits the phe-

nomenon of wound respiration (1974).
```

If your paper cites two or more works published by the same author in the same year, assign a letter designation (a, b, etc.) to inform the reader of precisely which piece you have cited. This form of citation applies both to journal articles and to books.

```
Chen and Amsel (1980a) obtained intermittent reinforcement ef-

fects in rats as young as eleven days of age. Under the same con-

ditions, they observed that the effects of intermittent

reinforcement on perseverance are long lived (Chen and Amsel

1980b).
```

When citing a work by an organization or government agency with no author named, use the corporate or organizational name in place of a reference to an individual author. Provide the year of publication following the name as indicated previously.

```
Style guides in the sciences caution that the "use of nouns

formed from verbs and ending in -tion produces unnecessarily

long sentences and dull prose (CBE Style Manual Committee 1983).
```

36c

CBE

The number systems

The briefest form of parenthetical citation is the number system, a convention in which only an arabic numeral appears in parentheses to identify a source of information. There are two variations on the number system. With references *in order of first mention,* you assign a reference number to a source in the order of its appearance in your paper. With references *in alphabetized order,* you assign each source a reference number that identifies it in the alphabetized list of references at the end of the paper.

Citation for a reference list in order of first mention

> According to Kahl et al., slicing and aeration of quiescent stor-
> age tissues induces a rapid metabolic activation and a develop-
> ment of the membrane systems in the wounded tissue (1). Jacobson
> et al. found that a marked transition in respiratory substrate
> occurs in sliced potato tissue that exhibits the phenomenon of
> wound respiration (2).

Citation for a reference list in alphabetized order

> According to Kahl et al., slicing and aeration of quiescent stor-
> age tissues induces a rapid metabolic activation and a develop-
> ment of the membrane systems in the wounded tissue (2). Jacobson
> et al. found that a marked transition in respiratory substrate
> occurs in sliced potato tissue that exhibits the phenomenon of
> wound respiration (1).

These numbered text citations are linked to corresponding entries in a list of references. The reference list may be numbered either in the order of first mention or alphabetically.

2 Preparing the list of references using CBE systems

In the sciences the list of references appearing at the end of the paper is often called "Literature Cited." If you adopt the name-and-year system for in-text citation (see 36c-1), the entries in your list of references are alphabetized, much as with the APA system, rather than numbered. Like the list of references in the APA system, the "Literature Cited" list is double-spaced; each entry starts at the left margin and the second or subsequent lines are indented three typewriter spaces.

If you adopt one of the numbered systems for in-text citation (see 36c-1), you will either number entries alphabetically or in order of appearance in the paper. A numbered entry, beginning with the numeral, starts at the left margin. Place a period after the number, skip two spaces, and list the author's last name followed by the rest of the entry. For the spacing of the second or subsequent lines of a numbered entry, there are two conventions: either align the second line directly beneath the first letter of the author's last name, or indent the second and subsequent lines five spaces from the left margin. Select a convention depending on the preference of your professor. For style guides in the specific sciences, see 39e-1. The following are some of the basic formats for listing sources in the CBE systems.

36c

CBE

Listing books in the CBE format

In preparing a list of references in the CBE format, leave two typed spaces between each item in an entry. Sequence the items in an entry as follows:

- Number: Assign a number to the entry if you are following a numbered system.
- Author's name: Put the last name first, followed by a comma and the initials of the first and middle names.
- Title of the book: Do not use underlining or italics. Capitalize the first letter of the first word only. End the title with a period. If the work is a revised edition, abbreviate the edition as 2d, 3d, 4th, etc.
- Publication information: Name the city of publication (and state, if needed to clarify). Place a colon and give the full name of the publisher. Place a semicolon, and give the year of publication followed by a period.

If you refer to more than one work published by the same author(s) in the same year, list the works in alphabetical order by title in the list of references, and assign each one a lowercase letter according to its order.

Books by individual or multiple authors

For a book with one author follow the conventions immediately above. For a book with multiple authors, place a semicolon after each coauthor.

1. Beevers, H. Respiratory metabolism in plants. Evanston, IL: Row, Peterson and Company; 1961.
2. Goodwin, T. W.; Mercer, E. I. Introduction to plant biochemistry. Elmsford, NY: Pergamon Press; 1972.

Books by corporate authors

3. CBE Style Manual Committee. CBE style manual. 5th ed. Bethesda, MD: Council of Biology Editors; 1983.

Books by compilers or editors

4. Smith, K. C., editor. Light and plant development. New York: Plenum Press; 1977.

Dissertation or thesis

5. Reiskin, H. R. Patterns of alcohol usage in a help-seeking university population. Boston: Boston Univ.; 1980. Dissertation.

36c

CBE

Listing periodicals in the CBE format

Leave two typed spaces between each item in an entry. Sequence the items as follows:

- Number: Assign a number to the entry if you are using a numbered system.

- Author's name: Put the last name, followed by a comma and the initials of the first and middle names. If there are multiple authors, see the convention for books above.

- Title of the article: Do not use underlining or quotation marks. Capitalize the first letter of the first word only.

- Journal name: Abbreviate the name, unless it is a single word, without underlining. For example, The Journal of Molecular Evolution would be abbreviated as J. Mol. Evol.

- Publication information: Put the volume number, followed by a colon, followed by page numbers (use no abbreviations), followed by a semicolon and the year of publication.

Articles by individual and multiple authors

6. Kling, W. Measurement of ethanol consumed in distilled spirits. J. Stud. Alcohol. 50:456-460; 1989.

7. Coleman, R. A.; Pratt, L. H. Phytochrome: immunological
   assay of synthesis and destruction in plants. Planta
   119:221-231; 1974.

Newspaper articles

8. Welch, P. Kids and booze: it's 10 o'clock--do you know how
   drunk your kids are? Washington Post. 1989 Dec. 21:C1.

Listing other references in the CBE format

Media materials

9. Jump, G. Alcoholism: the pit of despair [Videocassette].
   New York: AIMS Media; 1983. VHS; Beta.

Electronic materials

10. Alcohol and pregnancy: protecting the unborn child [Computer
    program]. New York: Student Awareness Software; 1988.

36c

CBE

PART X

Writing and Reading in the Disciplines

CHAPTER 37

Writing and Reading in the Humanities

The *humanities*—traditionally considered as the disciplines of literature, history, and philosophy—address many puzzles of life and human nature, frequently by posing "large," difficult questions to which there are seldom definite answers. Those who study the humanities ask in distinctive ways such questions as these: Who are we? What are our responsibilities to ourselves? To others? What is a *good* life? In what relation do we stand to the past? What do we owe future generations? Difficult questions lend themselves to difficult answers, and answers in the humanities change from one culture to the next and from one generation to the next. Still, the questions remain largely the same. In the humanities, we are united by questions more than by answers.

In this longstanding quest for answers, philosophers from Plato in ancient times to Richard Rorty today have continued to ask what it means to be an educated human. Two thousand years ago Homer's *Ulysses* told of a Mediterranean hero's search for identity and fulfillment, while James Joyce set his story on the same theme in modern-day Dublin. Thucydides in ancient Greece and Barbara Tuchman today have asked the historian's questions of how we as humans can interpret the events of the past. Such quests for meaning require readers and writers to judge evidence, to develop responsible opinions, to interpret events, and above all to appreciate the value of multiple perspectives.

The humanities are *text*-centered disciplines. In literature courses, your texts will be imaginative works: poems, plays, novels, and films. In philosophy courses, your texts will often be the works of those who, with rigorous and careful reasoning, have reflected on ideas important to understanding human nature. In history courses, your texts will be the records of men and women who have documented public and private lives and events in letters, government files, voting records, newspaper articles, radio and television broadcasts, and photographs. In related disciplines—art, music, and drama— you will work with texts more broadly defined: paintings, sculptures, dramas, and symphonies. In each of these areas, you will read (or observe) closely in order to understand, you will respond, and you will relate individual texts to each other and to events in the world. The humanities are reactive in the sense that they interpret documents that already exist. It falls to the humanities to "comment on and appraise" texts, based on a faith that as we study the important artifacts of culture we grow more aware of who we are and what we have done (Frankel 8–9).*

37a Writing in the humanities

1 Expressing and informing in the humanities

Students in the humanities write for many purposes, two of which are to inform and to express. Expressive writing often begins as a personal response to an individual text. Section 1e, "Reading to Reflect on a Source," discusses questions like the following that can help you to articulate your reactions: What do I feel when reading this material? Why do I feel this way? How am I changed or how could I imagine myself changing in response to this text? Because literary artists, historians, and philosophers often bring great rhetorical and emotional force to their work, readers may find themselves so moved by a text that they want to respond in writing. You might consider keeping a reading journal in which you record responses to texts and, based on your entries, develop ideas for papers. Much of what is best about informative and persuasive writing in the humanities begins as a personal response.

All writing in literature, history, and philosophy courses is, at least in part, informative. Working as an historian, you may need to sift through documents in order to establish a *sequence* to events on which to base a narrative—perhaps the story of how your grandparents came to this country. As a student of literature, you may *compare* and *contrast* works of the same author, responding to assignments such as this: *Choose two of Hawthorne's short stories and discuss his treatment of the origins and consequences of sin.* In a philosophy course, you might be asked to *classify* discussions on a topic, such as education, according to the types of argument authors are making. In informing readers, you will often *define* and illustrate a term by referring to specific passages in a text.

2 Making arguments

Frequently, you will put your informative writing in the humanities to use in making arguments. The purpose of making arguments in literature, history, and philosophy is to *interpret* texts and to *defend* interpretations as

37a

*In-text citations in this chapter refer to the Works Cited list at the end of the book.

reasonable.[1] No one will expect your arguments to end all discussion of a question, but as in any discipline, your arguments should be compelling and well supported. The purpose of reading stories, of retelling the past, or of puzzling through large questions is not to arrive at agreement (as in the sciences), but to deepen individual perception and to realize that we are part of a larger human community. The goal of an argument in the humanities is reached when readers can make this or a similar acknowledgement: "I understand your point of view. You've explained yourself clearly." You should therefore not expect to read—or write—a single, correct interpretation of a play. History professors will urge you to reject single, apparently definitive versions of the past. Philosophy professors will urge you to reject the notion that any one answer to the question *What is a good life?* could satisfy all people.

Consensus is not the goal of arguments in the humanities. But this is not to say that all arguments are equally valid. Arguments must be supported and well reasoned. They can be plainly wrong and they can be irresponsible, as when someone insists: "Since discussions in this course are based on personal opinions, my opinion is as good as anyone else's." Not true. One interpretation, argued well, can be clearly superior to and more compelling than another. In each of the humanities this is so, notwithstanding the fact that students of literature, history, and philosophy pose different questions and examine texts using different methods. As a student of literature, you might investigate living conditions during the Great Depression by reading novels like *The Grapes of Wrath*. In a history class, you might work with oral accounts such as the one compiled by Studs Terkel in *Hard Times: An Oral History of the Great Depression*. In a philosophy course, you might read and debate discussions of a society's obligations to its poor. You would in every case be arguing for an interpretation, and in every case your argument would be more or less convincing, in light of the conventions for arguing in that discipline. You can help yourself focus on the purpose of argumentation in your humanities classes by posing these questions:

- What sorts of questions will I investigate in this course?
- What sorts of texts will I be reading?
- To what extent will I be making interpretations?

Claims, inferences, evidence

Claims in the humanities commit you to making interpretations. An important part of any claim is an *inference*, a pattern of relation that you believe

37a

---

[1]This discussion is based directly on the work of Stephen Toulmin, Richard Rieke, and Allan Janik in *Introduction to Reasoning* (New York: Macmillan, 1979). See chapter 12, their "Introduction" to fields of argument, 195–202; and chapter 15, "Arguing about the Arts," 265–282. For a related discussion, see Richard D. Rieke and Malcolm O. Sillars, *Argumentation and the Decision Making Process*, 2nd ed. (Glenview: Scott, 1984).

gives meaning to your subject (see 3f and 6d-1). What is the importance of the Mississippi as a symbol in the *Adventures of Huckleberry Finn*? In response to such a question you would make a claim—that is, offer an interpretation based on patterns you infer in Twain's novel. Perhaps you believe that "To Huck, the Mississippi represents freedom." If this is your claim, you would justify it to readers by referring them to specific passages in the text. Each such reference would count as *evidence* in support of your claim. Especially in literature and history, evidence usually involves a reference to some primary source—a poem, a novel, a letter, a journal entry, and so on. In these disciplines, there is a common pattern of claim and support:

1. Writers make a claim that commits them to an interpretation.
2. Writers support the claim by referring to a source.
3. Optionally, writers comment on the source, linking it to the claim.

Consider the following three examples of how claims are made and supported in major areas of the humanities.

A literary study. In support of her claim for an interpretation of Wallace Stevens's poetry, literary critic Helen Vendler refers to and quotes part of a poem—a primary source.

> Desire, for Stevens, is always savage and always fierce: to look into one's own heart, to come home to oneself, is to start anew each time at the ground zero of desire:
>
> ... Home
> Was a return to birth, a being born
> Again in the savagest severity,
> Desiring fiercely, the child of a mother fierce
> In his body, fiercer in his mind, merciless
> To accomplish the truth in his intelligence
> (*Esthétique du Mal*, X)
>
> Stevens is the poet of this overmastering and mercilessly renewed desire. Each moment of reflection, for him, is a rebirth of impulse toward fulfillment, as desire reaches for its object....
>
> —HELEN VENDLER, *Wallace Stevens: Words Chosen Out of Desire*

Vendler makes a claim ("Desire, for Stevens, is always savage and always fierce") and then a comment to reinforce the link between the poetry and her claim: "Stevens is the poet of this overmastering and mercilessly renewed desire." This statement is a complex one, built on the work of a challenging poet, Wallace Stevens. In this brief example, Vendler demonstrates the cycle of claim, reference, and comment that is basic to writing about literature. *To make a claim about literature, make an interpretation. Then focus on an imaginative work and discuss how certain passages are related to your interpretation.* An analysis of a literary text (see 37c-1) is built by linking many such cycles according to an overall plan, or thesis.

37a

An historical study. The historian Joanna Stratton supports a claim in the following passage by referring to a source (information from a letter or journal) but does not comment on the source in the same way Vendler does for a literary text.

> For the most part, the cavelike dugout provided cramped and primitive quarters for the pioneering family. Damp and dark year round, it was practically impossible to keep clean, for dirt from the roof and the walls sifted onto everything. Although its thick earthen walls did afford warm insulation from the cold and strong protection from the wind, in rain the dugout became practically uninhabitable.
>
> "Father made a dugout and covered it with willows and grass," wrote one settler, "and when it rained, the water came through the roof and ran in the door. After the storms, we carried the water out with buckets, then waded around in the mud until it dried up. Then to keep us nerved up, sometimes the bull snakes would get in the roof and now and then one would lose his hold and fall down on the bed, then off on the floor. Mother would grab the hoe and there was something doing and after the fight was over Mr. Bull Snake was dragged outside. Of course there had to be something to keep us from getting discouraged."
>
> JOANNA L. STRATTON, *Pioneer Women*

Often in an historical account the writer wants to maintain focus on the narrative or story, and so withholds immediate comment on a source quotation except in footnotes or in specialized analysis. *To make a claim in history, writers make interpretations of available records from the past and try to reconstruct them into a meaningful pattern.*

Sometimes the presentation of a claim in historical writing may seem not to be an interpretation at all:

> [I]n the rain the dugout became practically uninhabitable.

This claim reads as a fact, but actually it is a generalization Joanna Stratton has reached based on available evidence, one example of which she provides with a supporting quotation. Other historians examining the same or different evidence might reach a different conclusion. The importance of an historian's interpretations becomes obvious when you read the conflicting accounts of the events immediately before and after Lincoln's assassination. If these conflicting accounts were based on eyewitness testimony, you would realize that historians must interpret evidence as well as gather it. While Lincoln *was* shot at Ford's Theatre on April 14, 1865, the precise circumstances of and reason for the shooting are subject to historical debate—or interpretation.

37a

A philosophical study. The philosopher Ludwig Wittgenstein makes a claim in the following passage without reference to any written text, but rather to the meaning that is attached to a word and to the patterns of human activity that can be observed in connection with that word. In the process, Wittgenstein himself created a philosophical text, one that later became the subject of interpretation and claim by other philosophers.

Consider for example the proceedings that we call "games". I mean board-games, card-games, ball-games, Olympic games, and so on. What is common to them all?—Don't say: "There *must* be something common, or they would not be called 'games' "—but *look and see* whether there is anything common to all.—For if you look at them you will not see something that is common to *all*, but similarities, relationships, and a whole series of them at that. To repeat: don't think, but look!—Look for example at board-games, with their multifarious relationships. Now pass to card-games; here you find many correspondences with the first group, but many common features drop out, and others appear. When we pass next to ball-games, much that is common is retained, but much is lost.—Are they all 'amusing'? Compare chess with noughts and crosses. Or is there always winning and losing, or competition between players? Think of patience. In ball games there is winning and losing; but when a child throws his ball at the wall and catches it again, this feature has disappeared. Look at the parts played by skill and luck; and at the difference between skill in chess and skill in tennis. Think now of games like ring-a-ring-a-roses; here is the element of amusement, but how many other characteristic features have disappeared! And we can go through the many, many other groups of games in the same way; can see how similarities crop up and disappear.

And the result of this examination is: we see a complicated network of similarities overlapping and criss-crossing: sometimes overall similarities, sometimes similarities of detail.

I can think of no better expression to characterize these similarities than "family resemblances"; for the various resemblances between members of a family: build, features, colour of eyes, gait, temperament, etc. etc. overlap and criss-cross in the same way.—And I shall say: 'games' form a family.

—LUDWIG WITTGENSTEIN, *Philosophical Investigations*

This passage has generated enormous discussion on the meaning and significance of "family resemblances." For example, some might argue that "amusement" is common to all games and might proceed to define that concept. As a student of philosophy, you will sometimes generate your own evidence for arguments; but more often, you will refer to and build on the work of the philosophers you are studying. Learning to make claims in philosophy can be especially demanding for those with little experience in the discipline. In literature and history, sources and what one writes about them are connected in concrete ways to a story, imagined or actually lived. Philosophy has no elements of story as such. *To support a claim in philosophy, you will focus on ideas and their relation to other ideas.* Arguments, consequently, can become quite abstract.

The three examples of claims made by Vendler, Stratton, and Wittgenstein do not begin to represent the variety of claims you will encounter in your study of literature, history, and philosophy. These examples are meant to suggest that variety and to suggest, as well, a common concern in the humanities: interpretation. As you read and study in your courses, try to

37a

identify the specific types of claims that are made and the methods of evidence used to support them. To aid this process, pose these questions: What sorts of claims (interpretations) do people make in this subject? In what ways do writers use sources to support their claims?

37b Reading in the humanities

1 Sources

When you read a poem, a story, a letter, or an autobiography, you are working with a **primary source**. Of the preceding examples, only the one by Wittgenstein is a primary source. The writings of Vendler and Stratton are examples of **secondary sources**, the work of scholars who themselves have interpreted particular poems, stories, or letters. If you were writing a paper on the poet Wallace Stevens, you might refer to Vendler's interpretations. In doing so, you would need to read with care in order to understand and evaluate her ideas (see 1b and 1c) and to distinguish them from your own. In deciding whether to cite Vendler in your paper, you might ask: What point is she making? How well does she make it? Is her observation well grounded in the text that she quotes? On what basis do I agree or disagree with her?

A given source or text in the humanities can be studied from several perspectives within a discipline or across disciplines. Some writers look at a work as a whole, in a broad context of events or ideas surrounding it; others look closely at individual parts of the source, analyzing it independently of its original surroundings. For example, consider how differently Benjamin Franklin's *Autobiography* is studied in the following examples: as literary or cultural expression, as political philosophy, or as an historical event.

The novelist D. H. Lawrence voiced his reaction to American culture in a series of essays, *Studies in Classic American Literature,* one of which focuses on a particular passage from the *Autobiography.* Here Franklin listed his thirteen simple rules for success in life, as part of his "bold and arduous project of arriving at moral Perfection."

1. TEMPERANCE   Eat not to fulness; drink not to elevation.

2. SILENCE   Speak not but what may benefit others or yourself; avoid trifling conversation.

3. ORDER   Let all your things have their places; let each part of your business have its time.

4. RESOLUTION   Resolve to perform what you ought; perform without fail what you resolve.

5. FRUGALITY   Make no expense but to do good to others or yourself— i.e., waste nothing.

6. INDUSTRY   Lose no time, be always employed in something useful; cut off all unnecessary action.

7. SINCERITY   Use no hurtful deceit; think innocently and justly, and, if you speak, speak accordingly.

8. JUSTICE   Wrong none by doing injuries, or omitting the benefits that are your duty.

9. MODERATION   Avoid extremes, forbear resenting injuries as much as you think they deserve.

10. CLEANLINESS   Tolerate no uncleanliness in body, clothes, or habitation.

11. TRANQUILITY   Be not disturbed at trifles, or at accidents common or unavoidable.

12. CHASTITY   Rarely use venery but for health and offspring, never to dulness, weakness, or the injury of your own or another's peace or reputation.

13. HUMILITY   Imitate Jesus and Socrates.

In reaction to Franklin's ambition for moral perfection, Lawrence began his essay derisively: "The Perfectability of Man! Ah heaven, what a dreary theme!" Focusing on the thirteen rules, Lawrence continued in the same acid tone:

> This is Benjamin's barbed wire fence. He made himself a list of virtues, which he trotted inside like a grey nag in a paddock. . . .
>   A Quaker friend told Franklin that he, Benjamin, was generally considered proud, so Benjamin put in the Humility touch as an afterthought. The amusing part is the sort of humility it displays. "Imitate Jesus and Socrates," and mind you don't outshine either of these two. One can just imagine Socrates and Alcibiades roaring in their cups over Philadelphian Benjamin, and Jesus looking at him a little puzzled, and murmuring: "Aren't you wise in your own conceit, Ben?"
>   "Henceforth be masterless," retorts Ben. "Be ye each one his own master unto himself, and don't let even the Lord put His spoke in." "Each man his own master" is but a puffing up of masterlessness.
>   Well, the first of Americans practised this enticing list with assiduity, setting a national example. He had the virtues in columns, and gave himself good and bad marks according as he thought his behaviour deserved. Pity these conduct charts are lost to us. He only remarks that Order was his stumbling block. He could not learn to be neat and tidy.
>   Isn't it nice to have nothing worse to confess?
>   He was a little model, was Benjamin. Doctor Franklin. Snuff-coloured little man! Immortal soul and all!

Lawrence's argument addresses the arrogance of what he considers Franklin's typically American theme, the ambition to achieve individual perfection. The focus on theme is one basic approach to a literary analysis (see the box at 37c-1). Notice that Lawrence follows the pattern discussed in 37a-2 of making a claim, referring to a primary source, and offering a comment that connects the claim and the source.

37b

Using a different approach, philosopher Ralph Ketchem looks at the *Autobiography* as a total work, analyzing how it expresses Franklin's philosophy on the power of individual initiative in politics.

> As a public philosopher, Franklin assumed that the traditional personal values have political relevance. He shared the Aristotelian belief that government exists for the sake of the good life and that its powers can be used to that end. A good citizen, guided by the virtues Franklin encouraged in *Poor Richard's Almanack* and in his *Autobiography*, would undertake civic improvement and participate disinterestedly in government. In an expanding country filled with opportunity, Franklin saw individual initiative as the essential engine of progress, but he did not hesitate to seek whatever seemed required for the public good through government. His confidence in the virtue of the citizens of the United States caused him to favor government by consent, but he was not a simple democrat who believed majority will should be omnipotent. He accepted democracy because he thought it would yield good government; if it did not, he readily rejected it.

Ketchem shows how the *Autobiography* was part of Franklin's overall ambition to promote the role of the individual and of personal values as a force in political life. He supports his claims by focusing on Franklin's ideas about individual values in relation to other ideas about the role of government.

Still another viewpoint, from Franklin's biographer Carl Van Doren, looks at how parts of the *Autobiography* were written and read in their own time and afterward. While literary or philosophical analysts see the work as a self-contained expression of current or ongoing American ideas, the historian looks at the concrete events of the work's arrival and reception.

> The two copies went off to England and France to set in train the complex textual history of this simple book: of which three parts appeared first in French, and of which the earliest English editions were retranslations from the French, and of which [the author's son] Temple Franklin published as authorized in 1818, the copy sent to Le Veillard instead of Franklin's original, which was not published entire, as Franklin wrote it, till 1868. At some time after the copies [of the original manuscript] were made, Franklin, in the six painful months left to him, wrote the fragmentary fourth part and then broke off. It seems likely that he himself had made the revisions which in the copy tamed the original. He could no longer trust his taste and could now and then prefer round academic phrases to his own natural sharp, homely ones. He had lived too long, and put off writing too late, to be able to do justice to himself in a book. His greatest years would have to stay unwritten. He might truly have reflected that this was not altogether the loss it seemed. Plenty of other men could find materials for the story of his latest years. Only he had known about his obscure youth, which could never again be obscure. (767–68)

37b

Van Doren's claims and interpretations try to establish how and where the work came into existence, and the extent to which it reflected Franklin's public versus private personality. The argument follows the pattern of interpreting records to reconstruct a meaningful pattern of events for Franklin's life.

Lawrence, Ketcham, and Van Doren interpret a single text differently, according to their separate disciplinary perspectives. If all three were literary critics, philosophers, or historians, they might just as likely offer different interpretations, since each of the humanities has its subdisciplines or subfields, each of which in turn is guided by a unique perspective. When you work with a primary source in the humanities, you should be clear about the perspective from which you are working. As a student of literature, you will ask certain sorts of questions; as a student of philosophy or history, you will ask other questions.

The more experienced you become in any of these disciplines, the more you will differentiate among perspectives *within* disciplines. For instance, as a student in advanced literature courses you may read and write about literature in different ways. In one class you may investigate the psychological life of an author. In another class, you may be taught to focus only on the text and to reject any appeal to sources *outside* the text. In still another class you may examine a work by investigating the historical and economic conditions existing at the time of its creation. There is no single way to read and write about literature, philosophy, or history. *Perspective* within and between disciplines determines how you will read, what questions you will pursue, and what interpretations you will make.

2   Audiences

As in any discipline, effective writers in literature, philosophy, and history vary the form and tone of their writing according to their purpose and the needs and expectations of their audience. Consider, for example, the work of novelist, literary critic, and essayist Joyce Carol Oates. When writing to readers of literary criticism, Oates (who is a professor of literature at Princeton University) maintains a rigorous, formal tone. The following passage appears in an essay entitled "The Tragedy of Existence: Shakespeare's *Troilus and Cressida*," the first chapter of her book *The Edge of Impossibility: Tragic Forms in Literature*. Oates assumes in her readers a familiarity with Western philosophy and such specialized terms as *a priori* (Latin, meaning "from the former").

> In act 2, scene 2, the Trojans have a council of war, and Troilus and Hector debate. What they say is much more important than why they say it, a distinction that is also true about Ulysses' speeches:
>
> HECTOR
> Brother, she is not worth what she doth cost
> The holding.
> TROILUS
> What is aught but as 'tis valued?

37b

HECTOR

> But value dwells not in particular will;
> It holds his estimate and dignity
> As well wherein 'tis precious of itself
> As in the prizer. (2.2.51–56)

Questions of "worth," "cost," and "value" permeate the play. Human relationships are equated with business arrangements—the consummated love of Troilus and Cressida, for instance, is a "bargain made," with Pandarus as legal witness. Here, it is Helen who is held in question, but clearly she is incidental to this crisis: Hector insists, along with most Western philosophers, that there is an essential value in things or acts that exists prior to their temporal existence and their temporal relationship to a "particular will." They are not created by man but exist independently of him. In other words, men do not determine values themselves, by will or desire or whim. Values exist *a priori*; they are based upon certain natural laws, upon the hierarchy of degree that Ulysses speaks of in the first act. Hector parallels Ulysses in his belief that "degree, priority, and place,/ Insisture, course, proportion, season, form,/ Office, and custom" (1. 3 86–88) are observed not only by man but by the natural universe.

Aside from the formal tone and vocabulary, notice the way in which Oates patterns her discussion in a way common to literary criticism (see 37a-2). She makes a claim: "What [Troilus and Hector] say is much more important than why they say it, a distinction that is also true about Ulysses' speeches"; she refers to a text; and she makes a comment about the text, linking it back to her claim. This is the pattern of claim and support that readers of literary criticism expect. Observe now the change in the vocabulary and structure of Oates's writing as her purpose and audience change. The following passage appears in *On Boxing,* a series of reflective essays directed at the general reader.

> I have no difficulty justifying boxing as a sport because I have never thought of it as a sport.
>
> There is nothing fundamentally playful about it; nothing that seems to belong to daylight, to pleasure. At its moments of greatest intensity it seems to contain so complete and so powerful an image of life—life's beauty, vulnerability, despair, incalculable and often self-destructive courage—that boxing *is* life, and hardly a mere game. During a superior boxing match (Ali-Frazier I, for instance) we are deeply moved by the body's communion with itself by way of another's intransigent flesh. The body's dialogue with its shadow-self—or Death. Baseball, football, basketball—these quintessentially American pastimes are recognizably sports because they involve play: they are games. One *plays* football, one doesn't *play* boxing.

37b

In this excerpt, Oates is concerned not with interpreting literary texts but with reflecting on an idea. Her essay assumes an educated reader (note the difficult phrasing "the body's communion with itself by way of another's intransigent flesh"); but Oates does not expect, as she does when writing for the *Shakespeare Quarterly*, that readers will possess specialized literary knowledge. She does make and support a claim in her essay ("I have no difficulty justifying boxing as a sport"), but she does so *without* referring to a text. As a fiction writer, Oates's purpose for writing changes again, as do her assumptions about the reader. The following paragraph opens the much anthologized short story "Where Are You Going, Where Have You Been?"

> Her name was Connie. She was fifteen and she had a quick nervous giggling habit of craning her neck to glance into mirrors, or checking other people's faces to make sure her own was all right. Her mother, who noticed everything and knew everything and who hadn't much reason any longer to look at her own face, always scolded Connie about it. "Stop gawking at yourself, who are you? You think you're so pretty?" she would say. Connie would raise her eyebrows at these familiar complaints and look right through her mother, into a shadowy vision of herself as she was right at that moment: she knew she was pretty and that was everything. Her mother had been pretty once too, if you could believe those old snapshots in the album, but now her looks were gone and that was why she was always after Connie.

Now Oates is writing a primary text, a work of literature that will be read and commented on by critics. In her fiction, she does not make demands on the reader with respect to vocabulary or specialized knowledge. Nor does she make claims as she does in her essays or scholarship. Rather, Oates writes to suggest and to create a mood. You would not find her being so direct as to write that "Connie was a vain adolescent," even though this assertion accurately describes the character. In a work of fiction, the writer leaves it to the audience to make these claims.

Joyce Carol Oates knows that with a change in audience comes a change in the tone and form that writing will take. You can act on this same knowledge by gauging the needs and expectations of your readers. Does an assignment in your humanities course call for you to write to your peers? to a professor? to a family member? To what extent does the assignment require that you support claims with references to texts? Will you be creating a primary source (a relatively rare occurrence in academic writing) or a secondary one? As a writer, take time before writing to consider the needs of your audience. And as a reader, ask yourself: what does this writer expect of me? What does this writer assume that I will expect of him or her?

L Types of writing assignments in the humanities

The assignments you will most often write in your humanities courses—close analyses of texts, research papers, and book reviews—have in a general way been addressed in chapter 2, "Critical Thinking and Writing." The discussion here will introduce the special requirements of these assignments in the humanities and will refer you to pertinent sections in chapter 2.

1 The analysis

An **analysis** is a close, careful reading in which you study parts of a text in order to see how it functions as a whole. Analysis attempts to explain and make clear. It is an interpretation that you are obliged to support, in most instances with direct evidence to a text (see 37a-2). As a writer, your job is to identify and discuss particular parts, or features, of the text that you feel are especially meaningful. In analyzing a short story or novel, for instance, you might focus on characters, themes, plot, or structure. You might analyze a poem for its rhymes, meter, or symbols (see the box in this section). These features, which are mutually reinforcing, give literary texts their meaning—though the meaning of a work will never be a simple sum of its analyzed parts. Good literature invites and can sustain multiple analyses without ever being "explained away."

Historical events similarly invite a variety of interpretations. As one teacher of history has put it, "[H]istorians like to argue. In fact, they disagree to a greater or lesser extent in their views of personalities and events in every major period in United States History, from Captain John Smith to William Westmoreland, from the American Revolution to the computer revolution" (O'Reilly 281). Historians argue—they present conflicting analyses—in order to understand as fully as possible the causes of events. These causes are usually complex and resist (as mature works of literature resist) a single, definitive explanation.

As a student of literature, philosophy, and history, you will use features specific to these disciplines in conducting your analyses. You have seen previously (in 37b-1) that one text can be analyzed as a work of literature, philosophy, or history, depending on a writer's perspective. Perspective determines the way in which a writer divides a text into analyzable parts. The more you study in a discipline, the more you will learn which features of a text are important to that discipline and, hence, which are worth analyzing.

The following general pattern serves as a model for writing an analysis, regardless of discipline:

- Introduce the work being analyzed and the interpretation you will make (your claim).
- Introduce the features you will use to analyze the text. Your choice of features will depend on the discipline in which you are writing.
- Conduct your analysis by discussing one feature of a text (or idea) at a time. For literary texts, quote specific passages and *comment* on the ways the passage supports your interpretation (see 37a-2).
- Conclude by summing up the evidence for your interpretation. Show how the features you have discussed separately reinforce one another in creating the effect or quality you have argued for.

37c

Section 2c discussed analysis as an investigation conducted by systematically applying a set of *principles*. In introductory courses to literature, this set of principles will be general if you are interpreting a poem or story according to standard features such as *theme*. (Other standard features are listed in the following box.) In advanced literature courses, and also in philosophy and history courses, you may be asked to analyze a text or some situation by applying a much-discussed theory. In a philosophy course, for example, you might be asked to apply Wittgenstein's notion of "family resemblances" to some activity other than games. In this instance, your professor would be asking that you analyze a situation, based on principles laid out in a specific source.

An example of this more complex type of analysis can be found in chapter 1—Harvey Greenberg's analysis of *The Wizard of Oz* according to the principles of Freudian psychology. While the principles guiding your analysis

---

Features to Consider When Conducting a Literary Analysis

You will be able to observe at least several of the following features in the poetry, fiction, and plays that you read. Conduct your analysis of a literary text by reading closely and identifying passages that illustrate one or more of these features. Discussions of specific features should reinforce one another so that your analysis is unified and presents a single, coherent interpretation.

Characterization Who are the main characters? What are their qualities? Is each character equally important? Equally well developed?

Language What devices such as rhyme (identical sounds), meter (carefully controlled rhythms), and pauses does the author use to create special emphasis? How does the author use metaphors and choose words to create visual images? In what ways are these images tied to the meaning of the text?

Narrator, Point of View Who is speaking? What is the narrator's personality and how does this affect the telling? Is the narrator omniscient in the sense that he or she can read into the thoughts of every character? If not, how is the narrator's vision limited?

Plot How does the writer sequence events so as to maintain the reader's attention? Which actions are central? How are other, subsidiary actions linked to the central ones? What patterning to the plot do you see? Are there ways in which the plot's structure and theme are related?

Structure In what ways can you (or does the author) divide the whole poem or story into component parts—according to theme? Plot? Setting? Stanza? How are these parts related?

Setting Where does the story take place? How significant is the setting to the meaning of the text?

Symbolism Are any symbols operating, any objects that (like a flag) create for readers emotional, political, religious, or other associations? If so, how do these symbols function in the poem, story, or play?

Theme What large issues does this text raise? Through which characters, events, or specific lines are the questions raised? To what extent does the text answer these questions?

37c

may be very general or highly specialized, in both cases an analysis will focus on a single text and will argue for a specific interpretation, which *you* will determine.

2   The book review

You may be asked to read and review a book for your courses, both inside and outside of the humanities. The purpose of a review is to make a judgment about the worth of a text and to communicate and justify that judgment to a reader. See 2b for an extended discussion on preparing and writing a review (which in 2b is called an *evaluation*). Before writing to evaluate you should *read* to evaluate. That is, you should understand what an author has written so that you can summarize main points (see 1b and 2a); you should distinguish an author's facts from opinions (see 1c-1); and you should distinguish your assumptions from those of the author (1c-2). Your overall assessment of a book will rest largely on the extent to which you and the author share assumptions about the subject being discussed. You will find a format for preparing a book review on page 33.

3   The research paper

A research paper calls on you to investigate some topic, using both primary and secondary sources. Often, a research paper in the humanities is an analysis (see 37c-1) that you set in a broader context. In writing an analysis, you typically read and interpret a single text—in the paper that follows, it is a short story ("Counterparts") by James Joyce. Broadening your effort into a research paper, you would analyze the story and also draw on available scholarship as an aid to your analysis. For her paper on "Counterparts," Sarika Chandra turned to the work of a Joyce scholar, Richard Ellman, and to the work of a sociologist who has investigated patterns of drinking among Irish men. Chandra also consulted Joyce's nonfiction writing, compiled by Ellman into a collection called *Critical Writings*. In a research paper, you remain responsible for developing and supporting an interpretation. You draw on sources, as needed, to help make your points.

Gathering sources on a topic and using them judiciously, according to a plan, is the activity central to writing a research paper. In section 2d you will find a discussion on writing a synthesis based on multiple sources. To write an effective research paper in the humanities, you must be able to read multiple sources on a topic, understand the main points of each, and then link these points to one another and to your own guiding interpretation, or thesis. In short, you must read source materials effectively. (See chapter 1, "Critical Thinking and Reading.") If you are uncertain of your ability to draw on and refer to multiple sources, also see chapters 33, 34, and 35 on the research process. In chapter 36, you will find a discussion on how to cite sources when writing a paper. In the humanities, you will generally follow the MLA form for documenting sources.

37c

37d

Sample student paper: "The Power of Alcohol and the Church in Joyce's 'Counterparts' "

In the following research paper, Sarika Chandra examines the ways in which a character in a short story by James Joyce uses alcohol in virtually the same way his wife uses the Church—both of them to gain power. Throughout the paper, you will find Chandra following the pattern of claim and support common in literary criticism: Chandra makes a claim, refers to a passage, and then comments on the passage in order to cement its relationship to the claim. She carefully develops an interpretation of the story and, when she finds a broadening of the context useful, draws on secondary sources. This paper is one of three discipline-specific papers relating to the topic of alcohol. See 38d for a lab report on the fermentation of wine and 39d for a sociological paper on women alcoholics.

1″

↕ 1/2″
Chandra 1

Sarika Chandra

Dr. Robert Crooks

English 204

15 May 1991   ⬜ Double space

Indent
5 spaces   The Power of Alcohol and the Church
                    in Joyce's "Counterparts"

⬅→ "Counterparts" tells the story of a man named

Farrington, who will not do his job right and takes abuse   1″
                                                              ⬅→
1″ from his boss for that. Farrington spends a long time
⬅→
drinking after work and when he gets home beats his son.

However, Joyce tells much more in eleven pages than just

another story about an abusive alcoholic. "Counterparts" is

about power--about how Farrington uses alcohol to gain it

and how his wife and children use the church.   The thesis

        The story opens with a scene in which Farrington is

being summoned to the office of Mr. Alleyne, his boss.

Farrington copies documents for a living, and this element

of the story appears to have some basis in Joyce's child-

hood. Richard Ellman notes that "calligraphy enabled   A reference to   **37d**
                                                           a secondary
[Joyce's father, John] to work for a solicitor named   source that
                                                           broadens the   *MLA*
Aylward" (39). Calligraphy is similar in nature to   context of the
                                                           analysis.

Chandra 2

Farrington's job of copying documents. Further, Ellman points out that "Aylward's office is probably that described in 'Counterparts,' where his name is changed to Alleyne" (39). However, nothing in Joyce's biography explains the complexity of "Counterparts."

Farrington sits in Alleyne's office, powerless, listening to this man berate him for some job poorly done. Apparently, mistakes and the resulting humiliation are regular occurrences in this office. Aside from the abuse that he must take from Alleyne, Farrington is made powerless by the very nature of his profession. As a copyist, not even his work is his own: he must labor all day at copying someone else's words. Farrington is trapped, immediately by his boss and more generally by his job.

The first part of the thesis examined

After work, Farrington looks forward to drinking, which he does every time he is humiliated. After the scene in Alleyne's office, he wants to go to the pub but he realizes that he has no money. Suddenly, he thinks of his watch and pawns it for six shillings. Now nothing else matters, for he is in the position to buy himself some power. At the pub, Farrington relates the incident in Alleyne's office to his companions. He claims that he looked coolly at Mr. Alleyne and said, "I don't think that that's a fair question to put to me" (93). Nosey Flynn and Davy Byrne say that this was the smartest thing they have heard. Farrington is pleased and he "[stands] a drink in his turn" (93). He repeats the same story to O'Halloran and Paddy Leonard and they too agree that the story was smart. Farrington stands another round of drinks. Higgens comes to the bar and praises Farrington for being cool in front of Mr. Alleyne.

Reference to the primary source

Here Farrington is trying to get himself some power by buying people drinks and repeating his story in order to believe that he had some control at the office (which he didn't) and that he has control at the pub. But buying drinks leads to no real power or respect, since peo-

Comments on the parts of the source just referenced

37d

MLA

Chandra 3

ple take interest in Farrington for only so long as he
pays for the whiskey. Nevertheless, interest for whatever reason pleases Farrington very much. Later, when
the conversation strays away from his story, he buys another round. At the end of the evening, when all his
money is gone, he is defeated at arm wrestling by Weath-
ers. Again, Farrington is humiliated: "He had lost his
reputation as a strong man, having been defeated twice
by a mere boy" (97).

Frustrated, he goes home, where yet another attempt
to gain power fails. He walks into a dark room in his
house and "a little boy [comes] running down the stairs"
(97). It is one of his five children, Tom, who says that
his mother is at the chapel. Farrington responds,
"That's right.... Did she think of leaving any dinner
for me?" (97). Again, Farrington feels out of control,
and this makes him nervous. He wants his wife home to
serve him since a "servant" gives service to someone who
by definition is powerful. But his wife is not home.
Worse, he has to be informed of her absence by his young
son. Farrington becomes a mimic and grows enraged: "At
the chapel. At the chapel, if you please!" (97-98) and
then tries to assert control by beating Tom, who cries
"O pa! ... Don't beat me, pa! And ... I'll say a Hail
Mary for you ..." (98).

Tom's attempt to save himself by offering a false
prayer shows the influence of the church and of
Farrington's wife on the home. Whereas Farrington escapes to a pub to gain power, his wife has only the
chapel as a means of escape and a path to power. The
Catholic church is extremely influential in Irish life.
As Joyce put it, "Ireland has been ... the most faithful
daughter of the Catholic church .... Its faith was never
once shaken seriously" (Critical Writings 169). In
Joyce's day, women were welcome in church but certainly
not in a pub. Married men were expected to socialize.

Continued
references to
the primary
source

Comments on
the parts of
the source just
referenced

The second
part of the
thesis
continues

37d

MLA

Chandra 4

According to one sociologist, pub life "was a means of
enforcing the religiously inspired segregation of men
and women that even marriage did not break down" (Stivers 86). Ability to drink was not only a display of
manliness but also of a solidarity among men that ex-
cluded women:

> Indent
> 10 spaces

The men drink heavily.... The public houses
are drab and uncomfortable. There is no provision but for hard drinking, and a respect-
able woman would not set foot inside one of
these places. (Stivers 87)

> References to
> a secondary
> source that
> broadens the
> context of the
> analysis

Farrington's wife, unable to go to a pub, turns to
the church both as a source of strength and as a source
of control over her husband. Evidence for this control
can be found in the story even though Farrington's wife
is not directly present. Tom offers to say a prayer for
his father, the implication being that his father needs
help. A helper is someone in control, someone who has
power and is willing to use it. In this case, power
flows from the church, not from a bottle. Farrington's
wife has done well in teaching her children how to
combat a brutish father. As a child, Tom has only one
weapon to fend off this man who has hit him "viciously"
with a stick. Tom has the church, which he uses in an
effort to save himself. This offer to make a prayer is
false in the sense that it is motivated by self defense.
But we see also that Farrington is a man whose soul in
fact needs help, so perhaps a prayer--any prayer--is
legitimate.

In attempting to get power, Farrington uses alcohol
and his wife and children use the chapel. It is hard to
say which is more powerful from Joyce's point of view.
In "Counterparts," alcohol is generally ineffective, but
still it is strong enough an influence to evoke Tom's
cry. Yet the story also shows that the chapel is effec-

> Conclusion

37d

MLA

Chandra 5

tive in that it frustrates Farrington's desire for authority in his own home. But effective is not quite the
right word, for Joyce has created a man who is powerless
in his job and a home in which the wife "bullied her husband when he was sober and was bullied by him when he
was drunk" (97). The characters in "Counterparts" are
locked in a struggle for power, a struggle that everyone
seems to be losing.

1/2″
1″   Chandra 6

Works Cited

1″

Ellman, Richard. James Joyce. Oxford: Oxford UP, 1982.

Joyce, James. "Counterparts." Dubliners. Ed. Robert

Indent 5 spaces   Scholes and A. Walton Litz. New York: Cornell UP,

1989.

---. The Critical Writings. Ed. Ellsworth Mason and Richard

Ellman. New York: Cornell UP, 1989.

Stivers, Richard. A Hair of the Dog: Irish Drinking and

American Stereotype. University Park, PA: Pennsylvania

State UP, 1976.

Reference materials in the humanities

Style guides

The following sources offer discipline-specific guidance for writing in
the humanities.

37e

Barnet, Sylvan. *A Short Guide to Writing About Literature.* 5th ed.
  Glenview: Scott, 1985.
Blanshard, Brand. *On Philosophical Style.* Bloomington: Indiana
  UP, 1954.

Daniels, Robert V. *Studying History: How and Why.* 3rd ed. Englewood Cliffs, NJ: Prentice, 1981.

Specialized references

The following specialized references will help you to assemble information in a particular discipline or field within a discipline.

Encyclopedias provide general information useful when beginning a search.

Cassell's Encyclopedia of World Literature rev. ed.
Encyclopedia of American History
Encyclopedia of Art
Encyclopedia of Bioethics
Encyclopedia of Dance and Ballet
Encyclopedia of Philosophy
Encyclopedia of Religion and Ethics
Encyclopedia of World Art
An Encyclopedia of World History: Ancient, Medieval, and Modern
International Encyclopedia of Film
International Standard Bible Encyclopedia
The New College Encyclopedia of Music
Oxford Companion to Art
Oxford Companion to Film
Oxford Companion to Canadian Literature (there are also *Oxford Companion* volumes for Classical, English, French, German, and Spanish Literature)
Oxford Companion to Music
Penguin Companion to American Literature (there are also *Penguin Companion* volumes for English, European, Classical, Oriental, and African Literature)
Princeton Encyclopedia of Poetry and Poetics

Dictionaries provide definitions for technical terms.

A Handbook to Literature
Concise Oxford Dictionary of Ballet
Dictionary of American History
Dictionary of Films
Dictionary of Philosophy
Harvard Dictionary of Music

37e

Interpreter's Dictionary of the Bible
McGraw-Hill Dictionary of Art
New Grove Dictionary of Music and Musicians

Periodical indexes list articles published in a particular discipline over a particular period. *Abstracts,* which summarize the sources listed and involve a considerable amount of work to compile, tend to be more selective than indexes.

Abstracts of English Studies
America: History and Life
Art Index
Arts and Humanities Citation Index
British Humanities Index
Cambridge Bibliography of English Literature and *New Cambridge Bibliography of English Literature*
Essay and General Literature Index
Film Literature Index
Historical Abstracts
Humanities Index
Index to Book Reviews in the Humanities
International Index of Film Periodicals
MLA International Bibliography of Books and Articles on Modern Languages and Literatures
Music Index
New York Times Film Reviews
Philosopher's Index One: Periodicals
Religion Index
Year's Work in English Studies

37e

CHAPTER 38

Writing and Reading in the Social Sciences

S ocially, as well as individually, organization is indispensable to growth," observed Herbert Spencer, a nineteenth-century pioneer of social science (59).* Today, the inheritors of that view—psychologists, sociologists, economists, political scientists, and anthropologists—attempt to discover patterns in human behavior that illuminate the ways in which we behave as members of groups: as members of family or community groups; as members of racial, ethnic, or religious groups; and as members of political or economic groups.

The belief that behavior is patterned suggests that a person's actions in his or her social setting are not random but instead are purposeful—whether or not the actor explicitly understands this. Social scientists do not claim that human behavior can be known absolutely—that, for instance, given enough information we can plot a person's future. They speak, rather, in terms of how and why a person or group is likely to behave in one set of circumstances or another. Social science is not mathematically precise in the manner of the natural sciences, and yet it is similar to those disciplines in the way that claims are based on what can be observed. Social scientists share the following broad theories:

- Human behavior is patterned, rule-governed behavior that can be described and explained.

- Individuals exist in a complex array of social systems, large and small. Individuals within systems interact; systems themselves interact and are dynamic, evolving entities.

- Individuals and social systems evolve—they change over time. Present behaviors can be traced to prior causes.

At any given moment, each of us exists in a broad constellation of systems: economic, political, cultural, psychological, and familial. The fabric of our lives is so complex that, in order to speak meaningfully and in detail about how we interact, social scientists carve up the social world according to the separate systems that constitute it. But no one of the social sciences is

---

*In-text citations in this chapter refer to the Works Cited list at the end of the book.

dominant: each contributes a partial understanding to what we know of human society.[1]

38a Writing in the social sciences

1 Writing to inform

Before significance can be found in social behavior, behavior must be accurately described and, when appropriate, objectively measured. A great deal of what social scientists do when they write is to *inform* readers with precise descriptions. Consider, for instance, an anthropologist's account of ritual drug-taking among the Yanomamo Indians of Venezuela and Brazil. (For a fuller description of the practice, see 34c-1.)

> Another useful plant provided by the jungle is the *ebene* tree. The inner bark of this tree is used in the manufacture of one kind of hallucinogenic drug. The bark is scraped from the trunk after the exterior layer of bark is removed, or is scraped from the inside of the bark surface itself. This material, which is fairly moist, is then mixed with wood ashes and kneaded between the palms of the hands. Additional moisture is provided by spitting periodically into the pliable wad of drug. When the drug has been thoroughly mixed with saliva and ashes, it is placed on a hot piece of broken clay pot and the moisture driven out with heat. It is ground into a powder as it dries, the flat side of a stone axe serving as the grinding pestle. The dried, green powder, no more than several tablespoons full, is then swept onto a leaf with a stiff feather. The men then gather around the leaf containing the drug, usually in the late afternoon, and take it by blowing the powder into each other's nostrils.

As in other disciplines, informative writing in the social sciences is built on recognizable patterns (see 3f-3), one such pattern being a *process* by which some activity takes place. Napoleon Chagnon's account of the process by which a hallucinogenic drug is prepared is precise and authoritative—in a word, informative. Similarly informative accounts can be found in any of the disciplines in the social sciences. A psychologist, for instance, might *compare* and *contrast* the different motivations people have for joining groups. In the course of this discussion, the psychologist might *classify* types of people according to their need for group identity. Such a discussion might begin or end with an attempt to *define* the term *group*. All of the techniques discussed in chapter 3 for informing writers are put to use in social science writing.

38a

---

[1]To the extent that historical inquiry is based on an interpretation of texts, history is regarded as one of the humanities. Many historians, though, consider themselves to be social scientists in that they use procedures like statistical analysis to find meaningful patterns in the past. In this book, history is discussed as one of the humanities. See chapter 37.

2 Making arguments

When social scientists report their findings in journals, they make arguments. Achieving general agreement about the determinants of human behavior may be a distant goal of researchers, but achieving this goal is unlikely inasmuch as the subjects that social scientists study—humans—are willful beings whose behavior is determined by millions of variables. Researchers acknowledge the complexity of human behavior by avoiding cause-and-effect statements and preferring, instead, to express findings in terms of their *probability* of being correct.

Arguments are the means by which knowledge is built in the social sciences. Various subdisciplines within each discipline carry on these arguments, and each one frames questions differently, uses distinctive methods, and subscribes to different theories. For instance, the discipline of anthropology is broadly understood as the study of humankind in its physical and cultural setting. There are two broad divisions of anthropology: physical anthropology and cultural anthropology. Physical anthropologists study humans as a biological species that evolved in certain environments from earlier forms (such as *Australopithecus*) to its present form (*Homo sapiens*). Cultural anthropologists investigate the artifacts of civilization in an effort to understand how various peoples have organized their lives socially, economically, technologically, or linguistically. Ethnographers, ethnologists, geographers, linguists, archaeologists, and other specialists in the discipline can all be termed anthropologists in that they share basic assumptions—for instance, about the value of studying the physical and/or cultural development of humankind. Nonetheless, both within and between subfields of anthropology, researchers will disagree on how to study human culture or biology. As a student in one of the social sciences, you will learn to read, think, and write in the context of arguments made in a particular field. The more courses you take in a discipline, the more you will learn how to produce arguments and to think like researchers in that discipline.

Claims, inference, and evidence

A *claim* is an arguable statement that a writer is obliged to support with evidence. *Claims in the social sciences will often commit you to observing the actions of individuals or groups and to stating how these actions are significant, both for certain individuals and for the people responding to them* (Braybrooke 11). The variety of human behavior is, of course, vast, and researchers have developed methods for gathering data both in controlled laboratory settings and in field settings. The interview and the survey are two widely used techniques that allow researchers to observe aspects of behavior that remain largely invisible such as attitudes, beliefs, and desires. Researchers carefully develop questionnaires, trying not to skew responses by the way questions are framed. If

38a

successfully developed and administered, questionnaires yield information about behavior that can be quantified and grouped into categories. These categories, in turn, can be analyzed statistically so that logical and reliable comparisons or contrasts can be drawn. Statistics can then be used as *evidence* in social scientific arguments to show whether a proposed connection between behaviors is significant.

The type of *inference* made—the logic by which social scientists argue and connect evidence to claims (see 3f and 6d-1)—will also depend on the method of investigation. Following is a sketch of two social scientific arguments, excerpts of which you will read in 38b-1. You will see in each the interplay of method of observation, type of evidence, and type of inference that connects evidence to a claim.

Study 1: "Factors Influencing the Willingness to Taste Unusual Foods"

PURPOSE:	Psychologist Laura P. Otis investigates the factors that influence a person's willingness to taste unusual foods.
METHOD:	Laboratory experiment—Otis showed students at a Canadian university various unusual foods (e.g., octopus), which they were led to believe they might eat. At various points during the experiment, subjects responded to questionnaires.
EVIDENCE:	Statistical, based on frequency of responses to a questionnaire.
TYPE OF INFERENCE:	An argument from correlation or sign (see 6d-2); one pattern of responses is shown to be closely associated with another pattern—one pattern indicates the presence of another.
CLAIM:	The older a person is, the more likely it is that he or she will experiment with unusual foods. Food preference is generally unrelated to an individual's willingness to engage in novel or risky activities.

Study 2: "The Story of Edward: The Everyday Geography of Elderly Single Room Occupancy Hotel Tenants"

PURPOSE:	Ethnographer Paul A. Rollinson "seeks to provide a rich description of the everyday geography of an often overlooked population in contemporary urban America: elderly tenants of Single Room Occupancy Hotels."
METHOD:	Participant observation—Rollinson spends extended periods of time visiting run-down hotels in a section of Chicago where elderly tenants rent rooms. He tape records his conversations with tenants and forms a close and trusting relationship with one such man, 70-year-old Edward.

38a

EVIDENCE : Personal observations

TYPE OF INFERENCE : An argument from generalization (see 6d-2); the observations made are shown to form a pattern. The observer suggests that this pattern may form a general principle describing conditions for other individuals in similar circumstances.

CLAIM : "The problems faced by elderly tenants of SRO hotels are numerous and often life-threatening. Their treasured independence is encumbered by their poverty-level incomes, their wide range of chronic disabilities, and their inappropriate housing environments." [The generalization of this particular field study extends only to elderly tenants in SRO hotels. While still a generalization, the claim is kept relatively narrow. As you will see, Rollinson is seeking to inform with his discussion as much as to argue.]

These two studies, excerpts of which follow, represent two distinct strains of social scientific research—one quantitative (number-based) and the other qualitative (observation-based). Social scientists have developed methods for investigating human behavior and, accordingly, many types of evidence are used in a variety of arguments. You can help orient yourself to your courses in the social sciences by understanding the special characteristics of arguments. Pose these questions in each of your courses:

- What questions about human behavior are studied in this discipline?
- What methods of investigation do researchers in this discipline use to study these questions?
- How are claims that researchers make related to methods of investigation?
- In this discipline, what types of information count as evidence in support of a claim?

Expect a variety of answers to these questions, even when you ask them of a single discipline. Given the many subspecialties in the social sciences, you are likely to find researchers using several methods to investigate a particular question. For instance, sociologists wanting to clarify the relationship between violence on television and the activities of children might set up several studies. One might be a lab experiment in which a group of children, closely monitored for their reactions, watch violent and nonviolent programs; a second study might take researchers into the field to videotape children watching television programs at home; a third study might collect, analyze, and draw conclusions about the state of published research on television violence and behavior of children (Rieke and Sillars 245–46). Each of these studies would properly be described as "sociological," but each would have its own distinct method and would, accordingly, lead to different claims and different sorts of evidence offered in support of these claims.

38a

38b   Reading in the social sciences

1   Sources

The sources you read in the social sciences will represent the variety of investigations carried out by researchers. Aside from textbooks and other general surveys of the disciplines, you will read reports of carefully controlled laboratory experiments as well as field and case studies. These two broad categories of source types parallel two major strategies for generating information in the social sciences: quantitative (number-based) and qualitative (observation-based) research.

Experimental (quantitative) reports

One method that social scientists have developed for studying human behavior is to conduct controlled experiments in a laboratory. Experimental researchers seek evidence for their claims by making careful observations and measurements in a lab. Based on statistical evidence (often questionnaire responses represented numerically), researchers are able to argue that a nonrandom relationship exists between two or more variables. Equally important can be the finding that no relationship exists between variables. For example, in the following report of a laboratory experiment, psychologist Laura Otis makes the claim displayed previously in Study #1 (38a-2).

Otis began her study with a specific question about human behavior: "Why do some people apparently prefer to eat novel or unusual foods?" Her report represents a particular instance of a social scientist observing the actions of individuals and stating how these actions are significant. Note that whenever Otis makes a direct statement concerning preferences for food, she cites literature and thereby situates herself in a tradition of experimental research. Her opening section and the Methods section are reproduced entirely. Most of her highly technical Results and Discussion section has been omitted, although it is in this technical discussion that Otis conducts her statistical analysis, which she then uses as evidence in support of her claims.

Factors Influencing the Willingness to Taste Unusual Foods

LAURA P. OTIS

York University

Summary.—Factors associated with willingness to taste 12 unusual foods were examined among 42 mature university students in a realistic taste testing situation. Low or nonsignificant correlations were found between subjects' willingness to taste the different foods and their scores on personality measures of sensation seeking as well as their ratings of familiarity with each food. Unexpectedly, age was a significant factor, with the older subjects being somewhat more willing to taste the unusual foods. Only a scale of items dealing specifically with food habits was highly correlated with subjects' willingness to try the unusual foods. The results suggest that food adventurousness is best accounted for by highly specific attitudes about food rather than general personality measures.

Both humans and animals have strong preferences for familiar rather than novel foods (Barnett, 1956; Domjan, 1977; Hall & Hall, 1939; Hill, 1978; Maslow, 1933, 1937; Meiselman & Waterman, 1978; Peryam, 1963; Pliner, 1982; Rozin, 1976). Typically, the animal research on this topic has been interpreted in terms of the "learned safety" hypothesis (Kalat & Rozin, 1973) while research with humans has been interpreted in terms of the "familiarity breeds liking" hypothesis (Zajonc, 1968).

However, neither hypothesis is sufficient to explain the full range of human selection of food. For example, why do some people apparently prefer to eat novel or unusual foods? One possibility is that the desire for novelty in food is a consequence of the negative effects of monotony (Balintfy, Duffy, & Sinha, 1974; Brickman & D'Amato, 1975; Kamen & Peryam, 1961; Siegel & Pilgrim, 1958). Further, it may be that preference for unfamiliar food is a reflection of some personality trait which predisposes some people toward novelty or sensation seeking. In fact, the item "I like to try new foods that I have never tasted before" is included in Zuckerman's Sensation Seeking Scale (Zuckerman, Kolin, Price, & Zoob, 1964) on the assumption that trying new foods reflects a general preference for engaging in risky and exciting kinds of activities.

Only a very few studies have actually investigated the relationship between sensation seeking and food preferences. Kish and Donnenwerth (1972) found a significant, although very modest relationship between sensation seeking and preference for sour, crunchy, and spicy foods. Similarly, Brown, Ruder, Ruder, and Young (1974) report a low but significant correlation between scores on the Change Seeker Index and preference for spicy food. But Rozin and Schiller (1980) conclude that sensation seeking is not related to preference for hot chili pepper. The only other evidence of a relationship between sensation seeking and food preference is provided by Back and Glasgow (1981) who noted that self-proclaimed gourmets scored significantly higher than vegetarians on measures of the General Sensation Seeking Scale and the Experience Seeking subscale of the Sensation Seeking Scale.

It is difficult to draw any clear conclusions regarding the relationship between sensation seeking and food preferences from the existing literature. An obvious omission in the research to date is that no study has looked specifically at the relationship between sensation seeking and preference for *novel* foods. The purpose of the present study was to look specifically at the relationship between personality measures of sensation seeking and preference for unfamiliar and unusual foods. Also, since most previous studies used only verbal measures of acceptance of food, the present study employed a realistic food-choice situation. Finally, the Neary-Zuckerman

38b

Sensation Seeking and Anxiety State Scale (Zuckerman, 1979) was included to assess the contribution of situational reactions to preference for unusual foods.

Method

Subjects

The subjects were 42 students enrolled in a summer session Introductory Psychology class at Glendon College, York University, Toronto. Their ages ranged from 17 to 50 yr., with a mean age of 30 yr. Many of the subjects were public school teachers.

Materials and Procedures

As part of a special class exercise, students were given a brief introduction to the present study which was described as research about attitudes towards foods. Questionnaires were distributed and students were asked to fill in the first two sections of the questionnaire. Section one, entitled "General Interest and Preference Survey" was made up of three subscales of Zuckerman's Sensation Seeking Scale (Form V), the Experience Seeking subscale, the Boredom Susceptibility subscale, and the Thrill and Adventure Seeking subscale (Zuckerman, 1979). The second section, entitled "Food Preference Survey" was made up of 13 items dealing specifically with attitudes towards trying new foods. These items were developed and pretested in an earlier pilot study. The survey included statements such as "I consider myself an adventurous eater," "I don't like eating unusual food because it might upset my stomach," and "I often try new brands of food on the chance of finding something different or better." Each statement was answered on a five-point scale going from 1 (not at all) to 5 (very much) according to how much each statement reflected the respondent's own eating habits. While these sections of the questionnaire were being completed, the food display table in the front of the room was set up. Bite-size pieces of 12 different foods (octopus, hearts of palm, seaweed, soya bean milk, blood sausage, Chinese sweet rice cake, pickled watermelon rind, raw fish, quail egg, star fruit, sheep milk cheese, and black beans) were placed on separate paper plates. Each plate was clearly labeled and the product container or intact fresh example of the product was placed beside the food sample plate. When students had finished the Sensation Seeking Scale and the Food Preference Survey they were instructed to leave their seats and walk around the display table where they were to look at but not yet taste the different foods. Students were led to believe that they would be tasting some of the samples at a later time. They were asked not to talk or communicate their feelings about the foods in any way. Students then returned to their seats and completed the third section of the questionnaire, the Sensation Seeking and Anxiety State Scale. The last section of the questionnaire asked students for three kinds of food evaluation. First, they actually ate and then rated the appearance, taste, and preference for an unfamiliar Japanese snack food. Next, they indicated their willingness to try each of the 12 different food items. These two evaluations were made on a five-point scale going from 1 (not at all) to 5 (very much). They then rated their familiarity with each of the 12 foods on a five-point scale from

38b

1 ("I have never heard of it or seen it before") to 5 ("I have tasted it often"). Finally, students were asked to indicate their age, sex, and whether or not they followed any special diet. At the end of the study, students were given a complete explanation of the purpose of the research and were told that they would not be required actually to eat any of the food samples. Of the 42 participants in the study, 32 indicated at this point that they fully believed that they would be expected to taste some of the food items.

Results and Discussion

The data are discussed in terms of the relationship between each of the main predictor variables (familiarity, trait and state measures of Sensation Seeking, the Food Preference Survey, and age) and the subjects' willingness to taste the unusual foods. A multiple regression analysis showing the relative contribution of each of these factors is also described.

• • •

Conclusions

In exploring a number of factors associated with food adventurousness, several surprises were found. An expected positive relationship between familiarity and food adventurousness was not confirmed. On the other hand, an unanticipated positive relationship between food adventurousness and age was noted. Consistent with previous research, personality measures did not appear to play a very significant role in individual food selections. In conclusion, this study suggests that willingness to taste unusual foods is best predicted by specific attitudes about food and is largely unrelated to preferences for engaging in other kinds of novel or risky activities.

Field (qualitative) studies

Quite different from experimental research, which takes place in the controlled conditions of a laboratory and generates quantifiable data, field studies situate researchers among people in a community in order to observe life as it is lived in its natural social context. The result is a *qualitative* study built on an observer's descriptions and interpretations of behavior. Based on observations, the field worker writes reports and discusses the possible general significance of the behavior he or she has seen, offering what in many cases is a fascinating glimpse into exotic cultures both foreign and local.

Following are excerpts from a field study of an elderly population living in Single Room Occupancy (SRO) hotels in Chicago. You will notice that author Paul Rollinson bases his claims either on prior participant-observer research or on his own observations. Rollinson maintains a distance from his subject that allows him an analytical stance, yet at the same time he is able to enter into the lives of the population he has observed. His report is qualitative, based on personal observations that he then interprets in the context of scholarly work in his discipline. As testament to the impact field studies can have on a researcher, Rollinson dedicates his article to the principal subject of

38b

his study, Edward, who (says Rollinson) "taught me infinitely more valuable lessons than my formal academic training."

The Story of Edward

The Everyday Geography Of Elderly Single Room Occupancy (SRO) Hotel Tenants

PAUL A. ROLLINSON

This article seeks to provide a rich description of the everyday geography of an often overlooked population in contemporary urban America: elderly tenants of Single Room Occupancy (SRO) hotels. The term SRO is a recent one, originally coined to describe apartment dwellings that had been subdivided into single rooms in New York City (Shapiro 1966). SRO's have also been described as "flophouses" and "fleabag hotels" (Eckert 1979). These buildings, originally designated as transient facilities, have evolved into largely permanent residences for the single poor of all ages. Today, SRO hotels, which are typically located in dilapidated and deteriorating inner city areas, have been characterized as the nation's least desirable housing (Kasinitz 1984).

• • •

The scope of the problem facing the elderly living in these SRO hotels throughout the nation is great; at least 400,000 are estimated to live in such accommodations (Eckert 1983). Previous ethnographic studies have brought attention to the unique socio-demographic characteristics of this population. Elderly tenants of SRO's are overwhelmingly single males (Eckert 1980; Mackelman 1961; Stephens 1976) who exist in a state of poverty (Tissue 1971). They are not newcomers to the inner city (Erickson and Eckert 1977; Lally et al. 1979), and Shapiro (1971), Siegal (1978), and Sokolovsky et al. (1978) have all found evidence to suggest the presence of considerable ties among elderly SRO tenants. However, little attention has been paid to this population's involvement in the built environment, their geographical movement, the places that are vital to these men and women, and the barriers that constrain them (Stutz 1976). It is the purpose of this description to pay attention to the elderly tenants' involvement in the built environment within a framework of the geography of everyday experience, defined as "the sum total of a person's first-hand involvements with the geographical world in which he or she typically lives" (Seamon 1979, 15–16). The primary focus of this framework is on understanding and conveying the everyday geographical experience in a "lived" form with as little a priori structuring as possible (Reinharz and Rowles 1988). SRO hotels have, in the past, been portrayed romantically as allowing this population to live independent lives (Eckert 1979; Stephens 1976). In reality, the findings of this exploration suggest that these hotels offer anything but independence. The elderly men and women in this study were caught in an environment that exacerbated their isolation and withdrawal from society. In this research, I portray this unique and vulnerable elderly population's everyday geography.

38b

Methods

The methodology I used aligns itself with a lengthy tradition of participant-observation studies in exploratory social science research (Clark 1965; Gans 1962; Hill 1986; Jackson 1980; Ley 1974; Rowles 1978; Suttles 1968; Whyte 1943; Zorbaugh 1929).

• • •

The Everyday Geography of Edward

This is the story of Edward, an elderly SRO tenant. I compare Edward to the other elderly tenants in the study, briefly describe his life history, how he viewed the SRO hotel and the neighborhood environment, and I discuss his everyday geography and concerns about the future. I met Edward in the lobby of one of the four hotels in August of 1985. Initially, he simply agreed to answer some of my questions. Later, he invited me to his room and subsequently to spend time with him traveling around the neighborhood.

Edward was similar to the majority of the elderly SRO tenant population I saw. The elderly SRO tenant population in the study had a mean age of 70 years, was predominantly white (92%), and male (58%). Edward was a 62-year-old white male. Overall, the elderly tenants had a low educational attainment; almost three-quarters (73%) had achieved education levels of high school or lower. Edward, in contrast, had completed two years of college. Elderly SRO tenants were extremely poor; Edward's yearly income ($4,620 in 1986) was even less than the mean of the elderly tenants in the study ($5,559) and well below the mean poverty level ($5,360). Accompanying his low income was a higher than average rent burden of 69% (compared to the already high mean of 46% for all those I interviewed), which exacerbated the tenuousness of Edward's already critical financial status. Nationally, the accepted normal rent-to-income ratio was 30%. Like 62% of his fellow elderly tenants, Edward received most of his income from Social Security. He was fortunate in that he had some savings to rely upon in times of financial need, as only 10% of all the elderly tenants interviewed had any savings.

• • •

Conclusions

The elderly tenants of SRO hotels had few resources or alternatives, and they lived there out of necessity. The SRO hotel environments were largely unsuited to the needs of this population. These hotels were deteriorating, dirty, and dangerous. In the winter, the heating systems were nonfunctional for days at a time. In the summer, the hotels were unbearably hot. The rooms, bathrooms, hallways, and elevators were not designed to accommodate the functionally impaired elderly tenants. It is very important to remember that the hotels in this study represented the least dilapidated and more conscientiously managed of the hotels, both in the study neighborhood and in the city of Chicago. The elderly tenants were overlooked by social scientists, social service providers, and planners because the majority were trapped inside their hotels and

38b

not visible to the wider society. This isolation should not be confused with independence. . . .

The problems faced by elderly tenants of SRO hotels are numerous and often life-threatening. Their treasured independence is encumbered by their poverty-level incomes, their wide range of chronic disabilities, and their inappropriate housing environments. Their desire to make choices and remain independent is all-important to these men and women. Their residence in the SRO hotels was not a genuine choice. Policymaker and social service agencies must strive to create a genuine choice for these men and women and they must also honor the right of this population to choose their unique and independent life-style. Given the fact that this elderly population had few resources and alternatives, the current and rapid decline in the SRO housing stock poses a serious threat to their ability to secure shelter. SRO hotels were inappropriate to the needs of the elderly tenants, but they did provide shelter at a time when homelessness was on the rise throughout the nation. Tenants of SRO hotels are labelled both deviant and undesirable, as "bums" or "derelicts." These men and women suffer greatly as a result of these inaccurate labels and they are consequently left in isolation, and the hotels are allowed to be removed from the housing stock. Edward noted: "[To] whoever is out there I'd like to say that one day you are going to be old. You will never know what it's like until it happens. A lot of us thought that there would always be someone to look out for us. It's a shock to us all to be in this situation."

2 Audience

The choices that you make concerning the content and presentation of a report are determined partly by the needs of your audience. You may in your courses be asked to prepare some assignment as if it were being submitted to a journal. You might direct other assignments to nonexperts. When an audience consists of specialists (for instance, when you are writing to your professor), your vocabulary will be more specialized and your tone more formal (see 21e). Unless the purpose of your writing is to provide definitions and explanations, as in certain essay exams, you can assume in an audience of experts a level of understanding that frees you from defining terms or explaining concepts. When an audience consists of interested nonspecialists, take care to make your writing accessible, defining specialized terms when you use them and adopting a less formal tone. The work of psychologist B. F. Skinner (1904–1990) provides an excellent example of how flexible writers can be with their presentations, depending on the needs of their audience. Skinner was a prolific and versatile writer who wrote to fellow psychologists in professional journals and to the general public in magazines as varied as *Scientific American, Atlantic Monthly,* and *Ladies Home Journal.* Publication in different magazines resulted in Skinner's altering his tone and the length and shape of his sentences. Here he is writing to colleagues in the *Journal of General Psychology* on the subject of conditioned behavior.

38b

A conditioned reflex is said to be conditioned in the sense of being dependent for its existence or state upon the occurrence of a certain kind of event, having to do with the presentation of a reinforcing stimulus. A definition which includes much more than this simple notion will probably not be applicable to all cases. At almost any significant level of analysis a distinction must be made between at least two major types of conditioned reflex. These may be represented, with examples, in the following way (where S = stimulus, R = response, $(S-R)$ = reflex, $\rightarrow$ = "is followed by," and [ ] = "the strength of" the enclosed reflex):

TYPE 1

$$S_0 \text{———} R_0 \text{————→} S_1 \text{———} R_1$$

(A) lever ——— pressing   food ——— salivation, eating
(B) "   ———   "   shock ——— withdrawal, emotional change

In this paragraph, Skinner addresses his colleagues with language that is formal and precise, cast in a specialized vocabulary that Skinner knows his audience will understand. For nonpsychologists, the language is technical, even intimidating. Now observe the change in Skinner's language when he addresses a general audience—the readers of *Scientific American*. Once again, Skinner is writing on the topic of conditioned behavior—this time, however, without using forbidding technical language. When he does use a term of special interest to psychologists (*reinforcement*), he is careful to define it.

It takes rather subtle laboratory conditions to test an animal's full learning capacity, but the reader may be surprised at how much he can accomplish even under informal circumstances at home. Since nearly everyone at some time or other has tried, or wished he knew how, to train a dog, a cat, or some other animal, perhaps the most useful way to explain the learning process is to describe some simple experiments which the reader can perform himself.

"Catch your rabbit" is the first item in a well-known recipe for rabbit stew. Your first move, of course, is to choose an experimental subject. Any available animal—a cat, a dog, a pigeon, a mouse, a parrot, a chicken, a pig—will do. (Children or other members of your family may also be available, but it is suggested that you save them until you have had practice with less valuable material.) Suppose you choose a dog.

The second thing you will need is something your subject wants, say food. This serves as a reward or—to use a term which is less likely to be misunderstood—a "reinforcement" for the desired behavior.

38b

Writers in each of the social sciences develop specialized vocabularies to help them communicate precisely. When addressing colleagues, they assume a shared language and make no effort to translate technical terms into language appropriate for nonscientists. This is not to say that social scientific writing must be dense; it should be *precise* and *objective*, however, and when the need arises this requirement is met with a specialized vocabulary. Still, the most accomplished writers are versatile enough to shape their language and methods depending on the needs of their readers.

38c Types of writing assignments in the social sciences

The assignments you will most often be given in your social sciences courses have in a general way been addressed in chapter 2, "Critical Thinking and Writing," as well as in other chapters. The discussion here will introduce the special requirements of assignments in the social sciences and will cross-reference you to pertinent sections.

1 The lab report (quantitative research)

Experimental researchers in the social sciences have patterned their writing of lab reports on those done in the sciences. Section 39c-1 discusses the general requirements of each section of the standard lab report: introduction, methods, results, and discussion. In the social sciences, you will encounter more variability than in the sciences in titling the various sections of a research report.

The opening. Depending on the conventions in a discipline (check with your professor), a paper's first section may be titled "Introduction," "Theoretical Background," "Previous Work," or may appear with no heading at all, as is the case of the example report you read by Laura Otis on pages 677–680. Whatever you call your introduction, make sure it orients your reader to the perspective from which you are conducting research. This can be done by reviewing the history of the question you are investigating and by citing pertinent sources.

The Methods section. This section describes how you conducted your study. In the social sciences, the Methods section is divided into subsections as needed to provide a full and accurate accounting of an experiment. Standard subsections include "Subjects," "Measures," "Apparatus," "Procedures," and "Design." In the Methods section, the researcher discusses any instruments that were used, such as questionnaires, in generating data for the experiment.

The Results section. This section presents the data generated by your research. If you have used surveys in your research, you will probably compress your results numerically and run one or more statistical programs, the results of which will provide the evidence for whatever claims you are making.

The Discussion section. This section calls a reader's attention to significant patterns that emerge from your statistical analysis. Your discussion will interpret your results for the reader and lead to a statement of your claims. The discussion will often end with a note on the significance of your research and, if appropriate, suggestions for future research.

Manuscript Form for Research Reports in the Social Sciences

- A research paper should have its own (unnumbered) title page. One-third of the way down the page, center your title. Do *not* place it in quotation marks. Center a line below the title and then center your name: first name, middle initial, last name. Below your name, center the name of the department in which you are taking the course. On the next line, center the name of your college or university. On the next line, center the address of your college or university (Solomon 19, 31).

- Give the abstract its own numbered page following the title page. (The abstract is the first numbered page of the report.) Center the word Abstract, skip a line, and begin, writing the abstract as a single paragraph.

- The heading, Method, is given its own line and is centered. Skip a line to begin the first subsection, Subjects. Each subheading—such as Subjects, Measures, Apparatus, Procedure, and Design—is given its own line, is underlined, and is placed flush to the left margin.

- Each table or figure should be numbered and titled and placed on its own page at the end of the report, after the Reference list. (In a published article, tables and figures appear in the body of the report.) When referring in your report to a particular table or figure, capitalize the *T* and *F*.

2   The field report and case study (qualitative research)

Many inquiries in the social sciences do not lend themselves to statistical analysis but rather to observations of social interactions in the communities where they occur. Researchers who conduct qualitative research go into the "field," a closely defined area of study that may be as exotic as the Trobriand Islands or as commonplace as an urban pool hall. The investigator, informed by a particular disciplinary point of view, collects data by directly observing and in many cases participating in social life. Then the researcher sifts through notes and conducts an analysis (see 2c). At the beginning of research, an observer or participant-observer may purposely try *not* to make predictions, as quantitative researchers do, so as to approach the novel social environment with as few preconceived ideas as possible (Richlin-Klonsky and Strenski 90–91; Rollinson 189). One outcome of field research is the field report, which provides a rich and detailed description of the behaviors observed as well as an analysis that discusses the possible significance of those behaviors. In Paul Rollinson's "Story of Edward," you read a field report—which is also called an *ethnography*.

A set of field observations may be put to other uses. When they concern a "relatively short, self-contained episode or segment of a person's life," field notes may be used in a *case study*, a focused narrative account that becomes the occasion for an analysis (Bromley 1). The case may provide the basis for making a recommendation: for example, concerning the placement of a drunk driver in a rehabilitation program (as opposed to jail) or concerning the placement of a child in an appropriate class. You will find case studies used as the basis of recommendations in most disciplines, but especially in the social sciences and the business and medical disciplines. You may also be given cases to analyze. In this instance, your professor will present a snapshot narrative of some behavior in its social context: perhaps observations of a child in a daycare setting or observations about employee morale at a business. Your job will be to sort through the information presented just as if you had made and recorded the observations yourself. Then you select the most important information to include in your case analysis, based on a theoretical approach recently read or reviewed in class.

If you go into the field to conduct research, you will keep a notebook or journal in which to record observations. Your professor will review particular methods for observing and making field notes. One challenge of writing your report will involve choosing and organizing the particular observations you want to discuss. The following categories of information often appear in case or field reports, and the categories can be useful for note taking. (In brief reports, the researcher may not write on each of these categories.)

- An introduction that sets the question or problem that you have studied in a context of prior research and that establishes your question or problem as *worthy* of research
- Information on the subjects studied and the environment in which you observed them
- Your theoretical perspective
- Your method of making observations
- Your analysis of significant behaviors
- Your conclusions

3 The library research paper

Just as in other disciplines, your library research paper in the social sciences should be guided by a central "burning" question. (See 33a-1 and, generally, chapter 33 on "The Research Process.") You will base your library research on secondary sources of the sort you found illustrated in 38b-1. Depending on your topic, you will read journal articles and books that are both qualitative and quantitative in their method. As you choose a topic, be aware that you will need to narrow it so that you can reasonably manage your discussion in an allotted number of pages. Also, be aware that professors will want you to use sources to support a thesis, or claim, of your own design (see 3f and 33c-3). In a research paper, you will read sources and relate them to each other and to your thesis. As you synthesize material, try to arrange your discussion by *topic* or *idea*, not by source (see 2d). If you need help in

38c

conducting your library research, consult chapters 33, 34, and 35 on writing research papers. For suggestions of discipline-specific sources you might turn to when conducting library research, see 38e. And for the conventions of documenting sources in the social sciences, see 36b.

38d Sample student paper: "Women Alcoholics: A Conspiracy of Silence"

The following library research paper, written by a student for her sociology class, investigates why women alcoholics in this country are largely an unrecognized population. Kristy Bell read several sources in order to support her thesis that the denial surrounding the problems of women alcoholics "amounts to a virtual conspiracy of silence and greatly complicates the process of diagnosis and treatment." Notice that Bell organizes her material by *idea*, not by source—one clear indication of which is her use of headings in the paper. Each heading develops one part of her thesis. Notice as well her use of the American Psychological Association's (APA's) format for documenting sources. This paper is one of three discipline-specific papers relating to the topic of alcohol. See 37d for a paper on the uses of alcohol in a short story by James Joyce, and see 39d for a lab report on the fermentation of wine.

Women Alcoholics: A Conspiracy of Silence

Kristy Bell

Behavioral Sciences Department

Bentley College

Waltham, Massachusetts

November 4, 1991

Information
centered on
title page

38d

APA

Bell 1

Currently, in the United States, there are at least two million women alcoholics (Unterberger, 1989, p. 1150). Americans are largely unaware of the extent of this debilitating disease among women and the problems it presents. Numerous women dependent on alcohol remain invisible largely because friends, family, coworkers and the women themselves refuse to acknowledge the problem. This denial amounts to a virtual conspiracy of silence and greatly complicates the process of diagnosis and treatment.

Introduction: women alcoholics will be studied in their social context

Thesis

Silence: The Denial of Family, Friends and Employers

First section of paper develops first part of thesis

Although the extent of the problem of alcoholism among women is slowly being recognized, a tremendous stigma still accompanies the disease for women. The general public remains very uncomfortable in discussing the topic. A primary reason that women alcoholics remain invisible is that they are so well protected. Family and friends, even if aware of the seriousness of the addiction, suffer pain and embarrassment and generally protect their loved one rather than suggesting that she seek professional counseling. By not confronting the issue, family and friends hope the problem will correct itself. According to Turnbull (1988), "The initial response of those close to the alcoholic woman is usually to deny the problem right along with her" (p. 366). Spouses, friends, relatives and even employers tend to protect the alcoholic rather than help her initiate treatment. "A husband will nervously protect his wife's illness from friends and neighbors" (Sandmaier, 1980, p. 8). Family and friends experience a great deal of guilt and responsibility that, in turn, causes them to deny or hide the problem (Grasso, 1990, p. 32).

APA format for documenting sources

In addition to being ignored, numerous female alcoholics are often abandoned by their spouses or lovers.

38d

APA

Bell 2

The reasons for abandonment generally include guilt, embarrassment and fear of confrontation. The husband tires of the domino effect that drinking has had on his life, the lives of his children, and of those around him (Sandmaier, p. 111). According to Turnbull (1988), "Alcoholic women are more likely to have a problem-drinking spouse or lover than non-alcoholic women and they are more likely to be left by a non-alcoholic spouse" (p. 365). For security and companionship, alcoholic women then gravitate toward men who accept their drinking as normal (Grasso, p. 14).

Women dependent upon alcohol are also ignored in their careers. Employers are unable to confront the problem, in part, due to their having no prior experience with alcoholic women. The conspiracy of silence thus perpetuates itself in the workplace. Employers tend generally to dodge confrontation by simply firing the alcoholic woman on an unrelated charge rather than steering her to an employee assistance program (Sandmaier, p. 131).

Silence: Self-Denial Among Women Alcoholics

Women not only fail to seek treatment because they are ignored and abandoned, but also because they deny the extent of the problem themselves. Sandmaier believes that in "responding to survey questions, women may be more likely than men to minimize alcohol-related problems because of more intense guilt and shame" (p. 73). Thus, statistics published concerning women's dependence upon alcohol understate the extent of the problem. Once again, guilt and pain can be directly related to unfamiliarity with the issue—this time the woman alcoholic's own awareness that alcoholism among women is a debilitating and growing problem. Women alcoholics suffer from the same feelings of guilt and embarrassment felt by family members and friends. Obviously, these feelings

Claims in the paper supported by references to social science literature

A new section also develops the first part of the thesis

38d

APA

Bell 3

are incredibly more intense in the actual alcoholic and
tend to force the woman to be driven underground by her
drinking problem. Unterberger observes that "[m]ore
often than men, female alcoholics turn their anger on
themselves rather than on others, with anxiety and guilt
being the result" (p. 1150).

At second and subsequent references to an author, no date needed in citation

A common feeling among women alcoholics is that
they are disrupting their lives and that any wrongdoing
is their fault. More so than the male, claims Sandmaier,
they tend to feel guilty about their drinking habits because they realize the effects it can have on family,
home and career: "Both recovered alcoholic women and
treatment specialists attest to the intense guilt and
self-hatred borne by alcoholic women because of society's
judgement that they have failed as wives and mothers"
(p. 17). Specialists in the field of alcoholism believe
that there is an inherent trait among women to ignore
the value of their own lives. Unfortunately, a woman today
is rarely taught nor is she able to properly take care
of herself first (Grasso, p. 40). As soon as she marries,
in most cases, she is expected to "take care" of her husband. With the arrival of children she is required to
take care of them. Often, if parents are aged, she will
feel responsible for their well-being. Grasso firmly believes that women not only ignore and deny their problem, but never really think enough about themselves to
realize that they are in trouble with and becoming very
dependent on alcohol. Sandmaier says this feeling is especially true among housewives due to the close identification with their dual roles of wife and mother.

Difficulties in Treatment and Diagnosis

Many women avoid treatment because of concern for
the well-being of their children. A rehabilitation
program including hospital care cannot be considered

New heading signals development of second part of thesis

38d

APA

Bell 4

because the woman is unable to be absent from home for
an extended period. Feelings of obligation to a husband
and children are extremely powerful for a woman, especially one whose emotions are intensified by alcohol.
Turnbull (1988) believes that "child-care services need
to be provided to allow women to seek and remain in
treatment" (p. 369). Treatment would be considerably easier and progress much more quickly if the woman was confident that her children would receive proper care.

> Date contin-
> ues to be cited
> in this refer-
> ence since
> Turnbull has
> written two ar-
> ticles that are
> referred to in
> this paper

Professionals in the field of social work are not
yet experienced enough to recognize alcoholism by its
preliminary characteristics. Because female alcoholism
has really never been a well-defined problem, health specialists do not have the experience needed to detect it
when a woman approaches them with an alcohol-related
problem. Frequently, the alcoholic woman is dismissed as
being "just depressed" or under stress (Turnbull, 1989,
p. 291). Moreover, she is not likely to announce the
problem directly:

> An alcoholic woman is unlikely to come into her
> doctor's office announcing her drinking problem,
> but she is apt to seek medical attention for a wide
> range of problems commonly associated with alcohol
> abuse, including depression, anxiety, stomach trou-
> ble, and injuries from alcohol-related accidents or
> physical abuse. (Sandmaier, p. 207)

On numerous occasions, many alcoholic women have
had personal contacts with health professionals during
which opportunities for intervention went unobserved or
ignored (Turnbull, 1988, p. 369).

Conclusion

Society is now realizing that there is and has been
a definite alcohol problem among women. The problem now
lies in learning to recognize the symptoms and help

38d

APA

Bell 5

women to seek treatment. Many believe that women should be screened routinely at the onset of any kind of treatment program. This would allow for identification of alcohol problems much earlier and would facilitate treatment before problems grow out of control. Social workers, as well, should include screening for drinking problems in all female clients. Some specialists believe that routine screening for substance abuse should become a mandatory part of all gynecological examinations as well as job orientations (Turnbull, 1988, pp. 366-68).

As the recognition of alcoholism among women grows, changes are being initiated to help make these women more visible to themselves, to health care professionals and to society at large. "Public education programs must be strengthened to counter the fear of social stigma that inhibits women from seeking treatment" (Turnbull, 1988, p. 369). The public must be made aware of the severity of the problem of alcoholism.

Bell 6

References

Grasso, A. (1990). Special treatment needs of the chemically dependent woman. Syracuse: Crouse-Irving Memorial School of Nursing.

Sandmaier, M. (1980). The invisible alcoholics. New York: McGraw-Hill.

Turnbull, J. (1988). Primary and secondary alcoholic women. Social Casework: The Journal of Contemporary Social Casework, 36, 290-298.

Turnbull, J. (1989). Treatment issues for alcoholic women. Social Casework: The Journal of Contemporary Social Casework, 47, 364-370.

Unterberger, G. (1989, December 6). Twelve steps for women alcoholics. The Christian Century, pp. 1150-1152.

38d

APA

38e Reference materials in the social sciences

Style guides

The following sources offer general or discipline-specific guidance for writing in the social sciences.

Bart, Pauline, and Linda Frankel. *The Student Sociologist's Handbook.* 4th ed. New York: Random House, 1986.

Becker, Howard S. with a chapter written by Pamela Richards. *Writing for Social Scientists: How to Start and Finish Your Thesis, Book, or Article.* Chicago: University of Chicago Press, 1986.

Cuba, Lee J. *A Short Guide to Writing About Social Science.* Glenview: Scott, Foresman, 1988.

Jolley, Janina M., Peter A. Keller, and J. Dennis Murray. *How to Write Psychology Papers: A Student's Survival Guide for Psychology and Related Fields.* Sarasota: Professional Resource Exchange, 1984.

McCloskey, Donald. *The Writing of Economics.* New York: Macmillan, 1987.

Publication Manual of the American Psychological Association. 3rd ed. Washington: American Psychological Association, 1983 (Revisions, 1984).

Richlin-Klonsky, Judith, and Ellen Strenski, coordinators and eds. *A Guide to Writing Sociology Papers.* New York: St. Martin's, 1986.

Specialized references

The following specialized references will help you to assemble information in a particular discipline or field within a discipline.

Encyclopedias provide general information that is useful when beginning a search.

Editorial Research Reports (current events)
Encyclopedia of Crime and Justice
Encyclopedia of Education
Encyclopedia of Human Behavior
Encyclopedia of Psychology
Encyclopedia of Social Work
Encyclopedia of Sociology
Guide to American Law
International Encyclopedia of Higher Education

38e

International Encyclopedia of Psychiatry, Psychology, Psychoanalysis and Neurology

International Encyclopedia of the Social Sciences

Dictionaries provide definitions of technical terms.

Black's Law Dictionary

Dictionary of the Social Sciences

McGraw-Hill Dictionary of Modern Economics: A Handbook of Terms and Organizations

The Encyclopedic Dictionary of Psychology

The Prentice-Hall Dictionary of Business, Finance and Law

Periodical indexes and abstracts list articles published in a particular discipline over a particular period. *Abstracts*, which summarize the sources listed and involve a considerable amount of work to compile, tend to be more selective than indexes.

Abstracts in Anthropology

Current Index to Journals in Education (CIJE)

Education Index

Key to Economic Science

Psychological Abstracts

Public Affairs Information Service (PAIS)

Social Sciences Citation Index

Social Science Index

Social Work Research and Abstracts

Sociological Abstracts

Women's Studies Abstracts

38e

CHAPTER 39

Writing and Reading in the Sciences

S cientists work systematically to investigate the world of nature—at scales so small that they are invisible to the naked eye and at scales so vast that they are equally invisible. A scientist's investigations are always built on observable, verifiable information, known as **empirical** evidence. Scientific investigations often begin with questions like these:

- What kinds of things are there in the world of nature?
- What are these things composed of, and how does this makeup affect their behavior or operation?
- How did all these things come to be structured as they are?
- What are the characteristic functions of each natural thing and / or its parts? (Toulmin, Rieke, and Janik 231)*

At one point or another, we have all asked these questions and speculated on answers. Scientists do more than speculate. They devise experiments in order to gather information and, on the basis of carefully stated predictions, or **hypotheses,** they conduct analyses and offer explanations. All scientists share two fundamental assumptions about the world and the way it works: that "things and events in the universe occur in consistent patterns that are comprehensible through careful, systematic study" and that "[k]nowledge gained from studying one part of the universe is applicable to other parts" (American Association 25). On the strength of these assumptions, scientists pose questions and conduct experiments in which they observe and measure. Then they make claims (usually) of fact or definition, about *whether* a thing exists and, if it does, *what* it is or *why* it occurs. Questions that cannot be answered by an appeal to observable, quantifiable fact may be important and necessary to ask (for example, "What makes *Moby Dick* a great novel?" or "What are a society's responsibilities to its poor?") but these are not matters for scientific investigation.

---

*In-text citations in this chapter refer to the Works Cited list at the end of the book.

39a Writing in the sciences

1 Writing to inform

A major role of scientific writing is to *inform* readers. All writers want to be precise with their information. When appropriate, scientists write with *mathematical* or *quantifiable* precision. A researcher would report the temperature of water as 4 °C, not as "near freezing"—an inexact expression, the meaning of which would change depending on the observer. Precise measurements taken from a thermometer or some other standard laboratory instrument help readers of scientific literature to know exactly what has been observed or what procedures have been followed.

As in other disciplines, informative writing in science is built on recognizable patterns (see 3f-3). One of the ways in which a scientist may inform is by writing a precise *description*—for example, of experimental methods and materials or of observations made in the lab or field. A description may involve presenting a *sequence* of events—perhaps the sequence by which volcanic islands are born. Presenting information can also take the form of a *comparison and contrast*—for example, between the organization of the human brain and that of a computer. Scientists also *classify* the objects they study. When entomologists report on newly discovered insects, they will identify each discovery with respect to a known species of insect. If no closely related species exists, researchers may attempt to *define* a new one.

When contributors bring different specialties to a project, researchers very often work and write collaboratively. Look in any journal and you will find a number of multiauthored articles. The great advantage of working collaboratively is that researchers can put the power of several minds to work on a particular problem. The challenge in writing collaboratively is to make a final report read as though *one* person had written it, even if several people have had a hand in its creation. If you are part of a group assigned to write a paper, be sure to meet with group members before any writing takes place. Agree on a structure for the document and then assign parts to individual group members. (See 4j for details on how to manage the logistics of collaborative writing.)

2 Arguing in the sciences

A scientist's efforts to inform readers are very often part of a larger attempt to *persuade*. In every discipline arguments are built on claims, evidence, and inferences. But the characteristics of these elements change from one discipline to the next and also *within* disciplines as theoretical perspectives change.[1] Geneticists working on techniques of tissue analysis argue differently than astronomers. Each discipline uses different methods and different tools of investigation. Each asks different questions and finds meaning in different sorts of information. Within any one discipline you will find that multiple perspectives give rise to competing communities or schools of thought. Within any one scientific community the purpose of argument will be to achieve agreement about the way in which some part of the universe works.

The process of scientific inquiry generally goes like this: Once investigators make their observations in a laboratory or in a natural setting, they report their findings to colleagues in articles written for scientific and technical journals. The scientific community will not accept these reports as dependable until independent researchers can re-create experiments and observe similar findings. As scientists around the world try to replicate the experiments and confirm results, a conversation—an argument—develops in which researchers might publish a challenge or addition to the original findings. In this way, a body of literature grows.

At times, scientific debates can grow heated—for instance, when one person attempts to demonstrate why a particular theory is flawed and should be replaced. Revolutions in scientific thinking may upend whole schools of thought and threaten careers of those who have built reputations on outmoded theories. At any one moment, agreement (if it exists) is provisional and will last only until some new challenge is put to conventional thinking—perhaps by a researcher who has observed some new fact that cannot be explained by existing knowledge. As an undergraduate student in the sciences, you will be introduced to scientific thinking and to the ways in which scientists argue. In each of your science classes, try to identify the purposes of argumentation. Pose these questions:

- In this area of science, what are the particular issues around which researchers seek to gain agreement?
- What questions do researchers pose and why are these questions useful?

Claims

Scientific arguments often involve two sorts of claims: the first concerning a definition and the second a fact. In this pattern, the first claim takes the form *X is a problem* or *X is somehow puzzling*. This claim establishes some issue as worthy of investigation, and it is on the basis of this claim (which must be supported) that experiments are designed. Recognizing what counts as a problem or a puzzle requires both experience and creativity. Assume it is early October. One evening the temperature drops and you have the first hard frost

39a

---

[1]This discussion is based directly on the work of Stephen Toulmin, Richard Rieke, and Allan Janik in *Introduction to Reasoning* (New York: Macmillan, 1979). See chapter 12, their "Introduction" to fields of argument, 195–202; and chapter 14, "Argumentation in Science," 229–263. For a related discussion, see Richard D. Rieke and Malcolm O. Sillars, *Argumentation and the Decision Making Process*, 2nd ed. (Glenview: Scott, Foresman, 1984).

of the season. The following day you notice that most of the flowers and vegetables in your garden have wilted—but one particular grouping of flowers (your mums) and one vegetable (your turnips) seem as healthy as ever. You and your neighbor both notice this fact. Your neighbor passes it by with a shrug, but you wonder *why*. You have noticed a *difference,* an anomaly. If you were scientifically inclined, you might begin an investigation into why a certain plant or flower is frost resistant.

Recognizing a difference or anomaly often begins the process of scientific investigation. The process continues when you make a second claim that attempts to explain the anomaly. Such a claim takes this form: *X can be explained as follows.* If in a book on horticulture you did not find an answer to your puzzle about frost heartiness, you might conduct a study in which you examined the leaf and root structures of the various plants in your garden. Based on your research you might develop an educated guess, or hypothesis,

Tense in Scientific Writing

There is one special convention of writing scientific papers that is very sticky. It has to do with *tense,* and it is important because proper usage derives from scientific ethics.

When a scientific paper has been validly published in a primary journal, it thereby becomes knowledge. Therefore, whenever you quote previously published work, ethics requires you to treat that work with respect. You do this by using the *present* tense. It is correct to say "Streptomycin inhibits the growth of *M. tuberculosis* (13)." Whenever you quote or discuss previously published work, you should use the present tense; you are quoting established knowledge.

Your own present work must be referred to in the *past* tense. Your work is not presumed to be established knowledge until *after* it has been published. If you determined that the optimal growth temperature for *Streptomyces everycolor* was 37 °C, you should say "*S. everycolor* grew best at 37 °C." If you are citing previous work, possibly your own, it is then correct to say "*S. everycolor* grows best at 37 °C."

In the typical paper, you will normally go back and forth between the past and present tenses. Most of the Abstract should be in the past tense, because you are referring to your own present results. Likewise, the Materials and Methods and the Results sections should be in the past tense, as you describe what you did and what you found. On the other hand, most of the Introduction and much of the Discussion should be in the present tense, because these sections usually emphasize previously established knowledge.

39a

Source: Robert Day. *How to Write and Publish a Scientific Paper.* 3rd ed. (Phoenix: Oryx Press, 1988) 158–159.

to explain why certain plants are frost resistant. To test your hypothesis you might design an experiment in which you exposed several plants to varying temperatures. Based on your results, you might claim that frost resistance in plants depends on two or three specific factors. Generally, when you are reading or writing in the sciences, these questions will help you to clarify how arguments are made:

- What is the question being investigated? What problem or anomaly is said to exist?

- What explanation is offered in response to this problem or anomaly?

Inferences and evidence

An **inference** is a logical pattern of relation that a writer uses to examine raw data and to select *particular* information as significant. All researchers and writers make inferences about their material. (See 3f and 6d.) The variety of inferences that scientists make in their research and writing is vast and complex, and if you major in a science it will be the purpose of your entire undergraduate career to train you in making valid inferences. For purposes of demonstration, observe the application of one common inference—concerning *type*. Watch how certain kinds of evidence are assembled on the basis of this inference.

Investigations begin with a puzzle or anomaly.

All the flowers and vegetable in my garden—except for mums and turnips—have wilted after the first hard frost. Why weren't these harmed?

A variety of information is available.

This is an above-ground garden, 3 feet deep, 5 feet wide, and 10 feet long. The garden gets full morning sun but is largely shaded each afternoon. I grow tomatoes, beans, peas, cucumbers, turnips, table flowers, geraniums, mums, and morning glories. The soil tests slightly acidic, and it is well fertilized. Turnips are my sweetest crop, high in sugar. All the plants except the turnips grow above ground. The mums differ from the other above-ground plants in that their crown is located below ground. I water the garden twice daily, morning and evening.

A specific statement can be used as a logical principle (or inference) by which to study available information.

39a

Horticulturists know that frost-resistant plants share two or three of these features: (1) The plant is high in sugar content; solutions high in sugar resist freezing. (2) The cell walls of the leaves are thick and fibrous and are not easily punctured by ice crystals. (3) The crown—the portion of the plant from which the above-ground plant grows—is located below ground and is not harmed until the temperature drops to 25° F.

An investigator uses a well-defined inference to determine that certain information is significant.

> Based on the principle above, I see that mums exhibit features 2 and 3, while turnips exhibit features 1 and 3.

Working with an inference and carefully selected evidence, a writer can support a claim (or conclusion).

> Of all the *types* of plants in my garden, only mums and turnips can be classified as frost resistant in that only they exhibit two of the three features characteristic of frost-resistant plants.

Every inference motivates the researcher to look for a certain patterning among available information. You can better understand the workings of a science by identifying the varieties of inferences and evidence that researchers use in making arguments. As a student reading or writing in a scientific discipline, pose these questions:

- What logical principles (or inferences) are used in this discipline to make meaningful, supportable connections between observed facts and claims?
- How do inferences help a researcher to select among available information to form meaningful patterns?
- What observable, measurable evidence can (in light of a specific inference) help to support a scientific claim?

39b Reading in the sciences

1 Sources

Scientists work with written sources all the time. Accurate written records of experiments are essential in the process of reaching consensus about questions of scientific interest. As a student of science, you will read journal articles and textbooks, and you will do well to establish a strategy for reading both. First of all, adopt the general strategies suggested in chapter 1 of this book, especially in 1b, "Reading to understand a source."

Journal articles

Journal articles are written by researchers for colleagues, not for students, and you can expect the language, concepts, and methodologies in journals to be challenging. The use of equations and sophisticated statistical techniques in a study's results section may leave you baffled. But you can still develop a general, useful understanding of an article (if not a critical response to the author's research methodology) by reading as follows: read the article's Abstract, the Introduction, and the Discussion—in this order. If these sections

39b

prove interesting, then read the middle sections (the Materials and Methods, and the Results), which will probably contain the article's most technical elements. As you read, pose these questions:

- What is the purpose of this study?
- What is the researcher's perspective—for instance, biologist, chemist, or electrical engineer—and how does this influence the study?
- What is the researcher's claim or conclusion?
- What seems significant about this research?

The following Abstract, Introduction, and Discussion are sections of a scientific report on mummified human tissue. The authors employ a sophisticated DNA analysis in their study—techniques far too complicated for anyone but specialists to follow. But by reading selected sections of the article, any persistent reader can gain a good sense of how the study develops and why the authors think their work is significant. Written by Ingolf Thuesen and Jan Engberg, "Recovery and Analysis of Human Genetic Material from Mummified Tissue and Bone" appeared in the *Journal of Archaeological Science* 17 (1990): 679–689.

ABSTRACT

Using sensitive techniques of molecular biology, we have been able to demonstrate the presence of genomic material of human origin in samples of mummified human tissue and bone from selected archaeological sites in Greenland. This result has far-reaching consequences for both evolutionary and archaeological studies of past human populations.

INTRODUCTION

Using sensitive techniques of molecular biology, we have investigated the possibility of recovering and analyzing genetic materials (deoxyribonucleic acid, DNA) from mummified human tissue and bone from selected archaeological sites in Greenland. Simple extraction procedures of both skin and bone samples yielded DNA material in purified form. Using human specific probes, we demonstrated that a minor, but distinct, portion of the purified DNA material was of human origin. Further analysis showed the remaining portion of the isolated DNA to consist mainly of DNA of fungal origin. The findings of DNA of human origin in mummified skin and bone samples, in particular, opens up the possibility for detailed anthropological genetic studies.

DISCUSSION

Recovery and analysis of ancient tissue and bone of human origin has long been intensively investigated. With the rapid advances within molecular biology in recent years, we have seen the first successful extraction of DNA from archaeological and anthropological materials (Higuchi *et al.*, 1984; Pääbo 1985*a*, *b*; Doran *et al.*, 1986). The perspective arising from those results and results of the reported work are indeed fascinating. The potential in establishing libraries of ancient DNA is obvious and prepares the road not only for the study of biological evolution (Thomas *et al.*, 1989), but also for research into human cultural history.

Within the archaeological discipline the information that may be recovered from survived fragments of DNA may concern inherited diseases, ethnic or racial associations and even sex and lineage. With the successful extraction of DNA from bones, we are also stabilizing and expanding the interpretative basis of the method. Bones are much more abundant in museum magazines and excavations than soft tissue fragments whether from artificially or naturally mummified bodies. According to our results bones are not contaminated in the same way as is skin tissue. An example of future research topics generated by the present project would be a search for the Eskimo–Norseman ethnic relationship and/or the occurrence of inherited diseases, based on successful extraction of DNA from bone material, which is abundantly available in the collections.

Despite being a time-consuming task, the extraction and identification of relevant fragments of ancient DNA should be a challenge for many anthropologists or evolutionists. In particular, after the appearance of the PCR technique, this task no longer seems out of reach (Pääbo & Wilson, 1988). The study of ancient DNA has already been suggested as a subdiscipline to paleoanthropology (Perizonius *et al.*, 1989). As a curiosity we may mention, that during our work, which has also involved other mummified tissues such as Danish bog people, Nubian cemetery samples (natural mummification) and artificially mummified Egyptians, the project was nicknamed GAP, Genetic Archaeology Project.

The lengthy and highly technical Materials and Methods, and Results sections (omitted here) are sufficiently detailed that other molecular biologists can repeat the authors' DNA analysis. As a student in an introductory course, surely replication will not be your purpose for reading journal articles. Read for other reasons: to see issues important to particular scientists raised and addressed from a particular perspective; to see the process of scientific inquiry at work; and to share in a researcher's excitement.

Textbooks

In introductory courses your reading will be primarily in textbooks, where the writing is directed to students and should, therefore, be more accessible than the writing in journal articles. In the sciences, textbooks play a special role in synthesizing available knowledge in an area and presenting it, with explanations, to students. The material in texts will grow increasingly technical as you move from introductory to specialized courses. Read your texts in science courses closely (see 1b), monitoring your progress frequently to ensure that you understand the material. Highlight any concepts or terms that confuse you and seek clarification from classmates or a professor.

39b

2 Audiences

Scientists report their findings to many audiences, both expert and nonexpert. Like any writer committed to communicating effectively, scientists shape the language and format of their reports depending on the needs of the readers. Observe how an accomplished writer of science changes tone and vocabulary depending on his audience. Stephen Jay Gould, paleontologist and evolutionary biologist, is well known for his theories on evolution. He is equally well known for books written to lay (that is, *non*scientific) audiences. Reporting in the journal *Evolution,* he and coauthor David Woodruff describe the shell of the snail *Cerion,* found in the Florida Keys.

> *Cerion* possesses an ideal shell for biometrical work. . . . It reaches a definitive adult size with a change in direction of coiling and secretion of a thickened apertural lip; hence, ontogenic and static variation are not confounded. (1026)

Now observe Gould writing for a lay audience, readers of his *Hen's Teeth and Horse's Toes: Further Reflections in Natural History.* Gould's writing remains lively and direct. But, realizing that he is addressing primarily nonscientists, he is careful to avoid technical terms.

> In personal research on the West Indian land snail *Cerion,* my colleague David Woodruff and I find the same two morphologies again and again in all the northern islands of the Bahamas. Ribby, white, or solid-colored, thick and roughly rectangular shells inhabit rocky coasts at the edges of banks where islands drop abruptly into deep seas. Smooth, mottled, thinner, and barrel-shaped shells inhabit calmer and lower coasts at the interior edges of banks, where islands cede to miles of shallow water. (143)

Scientists in every discipline develop specialized terms so that they may speak and write with great precision. When communicating with colleagues, they assume a shared vocabulary. This is not to say that scientific writing need be dense; it must be *precise,* however. This requirement is often met with technical terminology (which you are most likely to find in the "Methods" or "Results" sections of the standard research report, as is the case with Gould and Woodruff's technical language in the first quotation). When the requirement of precision can be met without a specialized vocabulary, good writers will communicate in plain, accessible English.

39c Types of writing assignments in the sciences

As an undergraduate, you will most often be assigned two kinds of writing: a report of a laboratory experiment and a literature review. The purpose of writing in both cases will be to introduce you to methods of scientific thinking and ways that scientists argue.

1 The lab report

A laboratory experiment represents a distinct (empirical) strategy for learning about the world. Experimental researchers agree on this basic premise: that research must be *replicable*—that is, repeatable. Knowledge gained through experiment is based on what can be *observed;* and what is observed, if it is going to be accepted universally as a fact, must be observed by others: hence the need for *reporting on* and *writing* original research. Reports of experimental research usually consist of four parts: Introduction, Methods, Results, and Discussion. Even when scientific papers do not follow this structure, they will mirror its problem-solution approach. Robert A. Day, author of a highly readable and authoritative guide to writing scientific papers, characterizes the logic of the four-part form this way:

> What question (problem) was studied? The answer is the Introduction. How was the problem studied? The answer is the Methods. What were the findings? The answer is the Results. What do these findings mean? The answer is the Discussion. (7)

Introduction

The Introduction of a scientific paper should clearly define the problem(s) or state the hypothesis you are investigating, as well as the point of view from which you will be investigating it. Establishing your point of view will help readers to anticipate the type of experiment you will be reporting on, as well as your conclusions. Your Introduction should also state clearly your reasons for investigating a particular subject. This is common practice in journal articles, where researchers will cite pertinent literature in order to set their current project in a context. In referring to prior work in which the same or similar problems or processes have been reported, you will cite sources. (See 36c for the conventions on citing and documenting sources in the sciences.) These references will help you to establish a context as well as a need for the present experiment.

Materials and methods

The Methods section of the lab report is given slightly different names in different discipline areas: Experimental Details, Experimental Methods, Experimental Section, or Materials and Methods (American Chemical Society [ACS] 6); and Subjects, Materials, and Methods (CBE 21). Whatever heading your professor prefers, it is in the Materials and Methods section that you provide readers with the basis on which to reproduce your experimental study. Unless you have some reason for not doing so, describe your experimental methods chronologically. When reporting on the Materials and Methods of *field studies* (investigations carried out beyond the strictly controlled environment of the lab), describe precisely *where* you conducted your study,

39c

Keeping a Laboratory Notebook

The notebook should reflect a daily record of work. It is best to make entries explaining the results expected from each stage of the investigation. Entries should be in chronological order, and so thorough and comprehensive that they can be understood by the corroborating witnesses. Each page should be signed by the inventor or researcher below the last entry, and by one or preferably two witnesses. Full names should be used and the signatures dated.

• • •

1. Use a *bound* notebook, if possible.

2. If a loose leaf notebook is preferred, the pages should be numbered in advance and a record kept of the numbered pages given to each laboratory worker. The point is to rebut any inference that a worker may have inserted a page at a later date.[1]

3. Do not remove any pages or any part of a page. Pages missing from a notebook will seriously weaken a case in the Patent Office, or in cases that go to court for litigation.

4. Record all entries directly and legibly in solvent-resistant black ink.

5. Define the problem or objective concisely. Make entries consistently as the work is performed.

6. All original work, including simple arithmetical calculations, should be performed in the notebook. If you make a mistake, recalculate—**do not erase.**

7. Never use correction fluid or paste-overs of any kind. If you decide to correct an error, place a single line through the mistake, sign and date the correction, and give a reason for the error. Take care the underlying type can still be read. However, even the practice of drawing a line through numbers entered in error is discouraged in many companies. Instead, workers are asked simply to make a new entry, correcting the error when possible.

8. Do not leave blank spaces on any page. Instead, either draw diagonal lines or a cross through any portion of the page you don't use.

9. Date and sign what you have written on the day of entry. In addition, have each notebook page read, signed, and dated by a qualified witness—someone who is not directly involved in the work performed, but who understands the purpose of the experiment and the results obtained.

10. Extra materials such as graphs and charts should be inserted, signed, and witnessed in the same way as other entries.

11. All apparatus should be identified. Schematic sketches should be included.

39c

12. Head each entry with a title. If you are continuing on the next page, say so at the bottom of the page before you continue.

These rules have received a popular formulation as, "Record it. Date it. Sign it. Have it witnessed."

[1]1976 Patent Institute. "A Continuing Seminar of New Developments in Law and Practice," College of Business Administration, Fairleigh Dickinson University, Madison, NJ.

Source: Anne Eisenberg, "Keeping a Laboratory Notebook," *Journal of Chemical Education* 59 (1982): 1045–46.

what you chose to study, the *instruments* you used to conduct the study, and the *methods of analysis* you employed.

As you set up and conduct your experiment, keep detailed records that will allow you to report precisely on your work when the time comes for writing. Both student and professional experimenters keep a *lab notebook* for this purpose. Even though you may be tempted to make quick, shorthand entries, write in precise and complete sentences that will allow you to retrace your steps. The notebook should be complete, containing the information necessary to write your lab report.

Results

The Results section of your paper should precisely set out the data you have accumulated in your research. The statements you make in this section will provide the basis on which you state conclusions in the Discussion section to follow; your presentation of results, therefore, must be both clear and logically ordered. (Professors will usually review in class what constitutes clear and logical ordering of results in their disciplines. For more general advice, see 3g.) As in the Materials and Methods section, when your discussion of results is lengthy, use subheadings to organize the presentation.

Discussion

The purpose of the Discussion section in your report is to interpret experimental findings and to discuss their implications. In the Discussion, your main task is to address the *So what?* question. Readers should know, clearly, what you have accomplished (or failed to accomplish) and why this is significant. Directly address the question or problem that prompted the experimental study, and state the extent to which your data adequately answers the initial question(s). If you believe your research findings are significant, say so and give your reasons. If appropriate, suggest directions for future study. As in the Introduction, set your experimental findings in a

39c

context by relating them to the findings of other experiments. When your results differ from those you expected or from results reported by others, explain the difference.

The Abstract

The Abstract is the *briefest possible* summary of an article. In some journals, articles conclude with a Summary (marked as such). It is more common to find the Abstract appearing at the beginning. An article published in a scientific journal will usually have the complete text of its Abstract reproduced on an electronic database. Researchers scanning the database will read the Abstract to determine whether an article is related to their own work and, thus, worth retrieving in its entirety. Abstracts must therefore be concise and self-contained. Typically, they include the following:

- The subject of the paper, its purpose and objectives
- The experiment's materials and methods, including the names of specific organisms, drugs, and compounds
- Experimental results and their significance

Most often, the Abstract excludes the following:

- References to literature cited in the paper
- Any reference to equations, figures, or tables (AIP 5; CBE 20)

When writing the Abstract of your lab report, consider devoting one sentence of summary to each of the major headings (Introduction, Materials and Methods, Results, and Discussion). If necessary, follow your four-sentence Abstract with a concluding sentence.

Title page and manuscript form

Every research report should have a precise, descriptive title. The title, along with the Abstract, will be read first, so if you want to pique interest, this is the place to begin. Check with your professor about the form your lab report should take. All text—including the Abstract, footnotes, and the reference list—should be double spaced. Generally, all pages of a manuscript are numbered consecutively, *beginning* with the title page. The Abstract page follows, then the body of your report. Each major heading—Introduction, Materials and Methods, Results, and Discussion—should be centered on its own line. (Some professors will want to see each major section begin on a new page.) Subheadings should be placed flush to the left margin; after each, skip one line and begin your text. Place the reference list at the end of the report and follow with your tables and figures if you do not incorporate them into the text of your paper. Each table and figure should be titled and placed on a separate page.

39c

2 The Literature Review

The Literature Review, a prominent and important form of writing in science, synthesizes current knowledge on a topic. Unlike a term paper, which draws on a limited number of sources in order to support a thesis, a literature review covers and brings coherence to the range of studies on a topic. A review may also evaluate articles, advising readers pressed for time about which articles merit attention. While every experimental report begins with a review of pertinent literature, only the Literature Review makes this discussion its main business.

Professors assigning review papers will not ask that you conduct an exhaustive search of literature on a topic. Your search should be limited in such a way that it will both introduce you to a topic and acquaint you with scientific ways of thinking. Your topic should not be so broad that you overwhelm yourself with vast amounts of reading material. For general advice on the skills necessary for conducting a Literature Review, see "Reading to evaluate a source" (1c), "Reading to infer relationships among sources" (1d), and "Writing a synthesis: A paper based on sources" (2d).

Writing the paper

Writing a Literature Review in the sciences involves several steps. Once you have a topic in mind, you will need to read widely so as to learn enough that you can ask a pointed question and can begin to conduct more focused library research. Reading scholarly review articles is an excellent place to begin, since by definition they survey a great many potential sources for you and, better still, point out themes and raise questions that you can take up in your own review. Review articles are published for most of the sciences. Locate them by searching for the word *review* in the various publications that abstract and index journal articles, such as *Microbiological Abstracts, Chemical Abstracts, Engineering Index Annual, Physics Abstracts,* and *Science Abstracts.*

If you are unfamiliar with the process of conducting research, then before attempting a Literature Review you might skim chapter 33, where you will find general strategies for writing a research paper. A Literature Review, like any good synthesis or research paper, is usually organized by *ideas,* not by sources. (See the discussion in 2d-1, on "Ensuring that your voice is heard.") In Literature Reviews, you will not find a simple listing of summaries: these are the substance of annotated bibliographies, which are themselves useful tools to researchers. The review should represent your best effort at inferring themes, problems, trends, and so on. When referring to sources, use the citation form appropriate to your discipline. See 36c for information on citing and documenting sources in the sciences.

39c

39d Sample student paper: "Comparison of Two Strains of Wine-Producing Yeasts"

Following is a lab report on the fermentation of wine. The microbiological processes involved in wine production have been known for nearly 150 years, and the student writing this report has added no new knowledge to our understanding of how wine is made. But creating new knowledge was not the purpose of the assignment. Clarence S. Ivie met his professor's objectives by successfully planning and carrying out an experiment, by making careful observations, and by thinking and writing like a biologist. This paper is the third of three discipline-specific papers relating to the topic of alcohol. (See 37e for a literary analysis of alcohol use in a short story by James Joyce and 38d for a sociological paper on women alcoholics.)

Comparison of Two Strains of Wine-Producing Yeasts

Clarence S. Ivie III

Microbiology 314

Department of Biological Sciences

University of South Alabama

Mobile, Alabama 36688

Professor Burke Brown

4 March 1991

39d

CBE

1

Comparison of Two Strains of Wine-Producing Yeasts

The purpose of this experiment was to determine
which strain of yeast produced the most favorable
wine. Wine yeast, <u>Saccharomyces cerevisiæ</u> var.
<u>ellipsoideus</u> and Fleishman's baker's yeast,
<u>Saccharomyces cerevisiæ</u>, were used to make two sam-
ples of wine. The wines were then compared with one
another to determine which yeast created the best
wine based on smell, taste, and alcohol content.
The results of the experiment indicated that the
wine yeast produced a better wine.

Fermentation is a process whereby a strain of yeast
metabolizes sugar to produce alcohol. Wine is most commonly produced from grape juice by the process of fermentation. Grapes are crushed to acquire the juice. Sugar
is then added to the grape juice. The grape juice, or
<u>must</u>, is then inoculated with yeast and allowed to fer-
ment, a process that takes around fourteen days. The end
product is an alcoholic beverage which has been valued
by man for centuries. It is not known when the first
wines were created. However, throughout the history of
wine making, man has constantly made attempts at improving the quality of the wine he made (2). In this experiment, the strain of yeast that produced the best wine
was determined on the basis of smell, taste, and alcohol
content.

Materials and Methods

Two 1.9L bottles were used in this experiment. Each
bottle contained 1.7L of grape juice. Two hundred thirty
(230) grams of table sugar was added to each bottle of
grape juice. Bottle #1 was then inoculated with one package of <u>Saccharomyces</u> var. <u>ellipsoideus</u>. Bottle #2 was inoculated with one package of Fleishman's baker's yeast.

The abstract consists of one-sentence summaries of the report's major sections.

In some disciplines, "Introduction," as a heading, is omitted from the lab report.

The introduction sets the study in a larger context and establishes the research perspective: microbiology.

The author provides exact information so that readers can replicate the study.

39d

CBE

Ivie 2

The mixtures were then shaken to dissolve their contents. Initial measurements were immediately taken, including: pH, specific gravity, and temperature.
Subjective observations, such as the mixture's color,
were also made. A pH meter was used to measure pH, a hy-
drometer was used to measure specific gravity, and a
thermometer was used to measure temperature. After the
initial measurements were taken, both bottles were then
sealed and allowed to ferment. Periodically CO_2 gas production rates were measured for each experimental wine
fermentation procedure. This was done by measuring the
volume of displacement, due to the gas production. As
the wine continued to ferment, these measurements were
made daily throughout the 20 day duration of the experiment. On the eighteenth day of the experiment, both bottles were inoculated with a bisulphite to stop the
fermentation process.

Results

After the fermentation process was halted, the specific gravity changes of bottles 1 and 2 were compared.
The specific gravities of both wine experiments decreased, but the most substantial decrease occurred in
bottle #1. These results indicated that the wine yeast
metabolized the sugar more efficiently than the
Fleishman's baker's yeast (Fig. 1).

The results of the pH change, in each case, fluctu-
ated daily. There was, however, an overall increase in
both samples.

The temperatures of both samples remained more or
less constant at 22.5 degrees Celsius throughout the entire fermentation process.

The gas production measurements showed that the
wine yeast produced more carbon dioxide than the baker's
yeast. Gas production is directly related to yeast

The author provides a specific criterion, or test, by which to analyze the two samples.

The author provides three additional criteria by which to analyze the samples.

39d

CBE

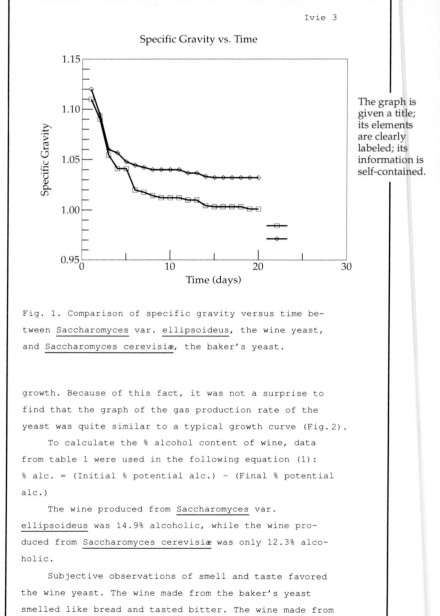

Ivie 3

The graph is given a title; its elements are clearly labeled; its information is self-contained.

Fig. 1. Comparison of specific gravity versus time between Saccharomyces var. ellipsoideus, the wine yeast, and Saccharomyces cerevisiæ, the baker's yeast.

growth. Because of this fact, it was not a surprise to find that the graph of the gas production rate of the yeast was quite similar to a typical growth curve (Fig. 2).

To calculate the % alcohol content of wine, data from table 1 were used in the following equation (1):

% alc. = (Initial % potential alc.) − (Final % potential alc.)

The wine produced from Saccharomyces var. ellipsoideus was 14.9% alcoholic, while the wine produced from Saccharomyces cerevisiæ was only 12.3% alcoholic.

Subjective observations of smell and taste favored the wine yeast. The wine made from the baker's yeast smelled like bread and tasted bitter. The wine made from the wine yeast smelled like wine and tasted sweet.

39d

CBE

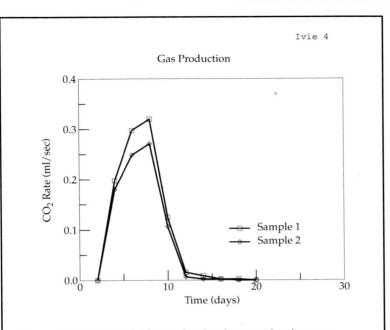

Ivie 4

Fig. 2. Comparison of CO_2 production between Saccharomyces var. ellipsoideus and Saccharomyces cerevisiæ.

Discussion

   Wine is the product of yeast fermentation. The purpose of this experiment was to determine which type of
yeast produced the best wine. The basis by which the
wines made in the experiment were judged included taste,
smell, and alcohol content. It was clearly evident that
the wine yeast created a more pleasant smelling and tasting wine than did the baker's yeast. The wine produced
by the baker's yeast had a harshly overpowering smell
which resembled the smell of bread. Its taste was extremely bitter. Overall, on the basis of taste and
smell, the baker's yeast created an undesirable wine
while the wine yeast created a pleasant smelling and
more desirable tasting wine. On the basis of alcohol content, it is clearly seen from the results of this experiment that the wine yeast produced a more alcoholic wine

The author's discussion is *not* a mere repetition of the results.

39d

CBE

Ivie 5

Table 1. Relations between specific gravities and

% potential alcohol

Specific Gravity	% Potential Alcohol
1.000	0
1.010	0.9
1.020	2.3
1.030	3.7
1.040	5.1
1.050	6.5
1.090	7.8
1.080	10.6
1.090	12.0
1.100	13.4
1.110	14.9
1.120	16.3
1.130	17.7

The information in the table is clearly displayed and is self-contained. The table provides the standards by which alcohol percentages are determined in the experiment.

than the baker's yeast. The wine yeast proved to be more efficient in the metabolism of sugar than the baker's yeast. Evidence of this is seen in the specific gravity measurements. The wine yeast also achieved a greater rate of fermentation as seen in the gas production measurement. From this experiment, it can be concluded that the use of wine yeast, Saccharomyces var. ellipsoideus, is far more advantageous than the use of baker's yeast in making wine.

Each of the author's claims is supported by evidence gathered during the experiment.

Ivie 6

Literature Cited

1. Case and Johnson. Laboratory experiments in microbiology. Reading, MA: The Benjamin/Cummings Publishing Company; 1984.

2. Prescott, Harley, and Klein. Microbiology, Dubuque, IA: Wm. C. Brown Publishers; 1990.

3. Stryer and Lubert. Biochemistry. New York: W. H. Freeman and Company; 1988.

39d

CBE

39e Reference materials in the sciences

Style guides

A source of excellent general advice for writing papers in the sciences is Robert Day's *How to Write and Publish a Scientific Paper*, 3rd ed. (Phoenix: Oryx Press, 1988). For discipline-specific advice on writing, consult the following works:

> *AIP [American Institute of Physics] Style Manual*. 4th ed. New York: AIP, 1990.
>
> CBE [Council of Biology Editors] *Style Manual*. 5th ed. Bethesda: CBE, 1983.
>
> Dodd, Janet S., et al. *The ACS [American Chemical Society] Style Guide: A Manual for Authors and Editors*. Washington: ACS, 1986.
>
> Michaelson, Herbert B. *How to Write and Publish Engineering Papers and Reports*. 2nd ed. Philadelphia: ISI Press, 1986.

Specialized references

The following specialized references will help you to assemble information in a particular discipline or field within the discipline.

Encyclopedias provide general information useful when beginning a search.

> *Cambridge Encyclopedia of Astronomy*
> *Encyclopedia of Biological Sciences*
> *Encyclopedia of Chemistry*
> *Encyclopedia of Computer Science and Engineering*
> *Encyclopedia of Computer Science and Technology*
> *Encyclopedia of Earth Sciences*
> *Encyclopedia of Physics*
> *Grzimek's Animal Life Encyclopedia*
> *Grzimek's Encyclopedia of Ecology*
> *Harper's Encyclopedia of Science*
> *Larousse Encyclopedia of Astronomy*
> *McGraw-Hill Encyclopedia of Environmental Science*
> *McGraw-Hill Yearbook of Science and Technology*
> *Stein and Day International Medical Encyclopedia*
> *Universal Encyclopedia of Mathematics*
> *Van Nostrand's Scientific Encyclopedia*

39e

Dictionaries provide definitions of technical terms.

Computer Dictionary and Handbook
Condensed Chemical Dictionary
Dictionary of Biology
Dorland's Medical Dictionary
Illustrated Stedman's Medical Dictionary
McGraw-Hill Dictionary of Scientific and Technical Terms

Periodical indexes list articles published in a particular discipline over a particular period. *Abstracts,* which summarize the sources listed and involve a considerable amount of work to compile, tend to be more selective than indexes.

Applied Science and Technology Index
Biological Abstracts
Biological and Agricultural Index
Cumulative Index to Nursing and Allied Health Literature
Current Abstracts of Chemistry and Index Chemicus
Engineering Index
General Science Index
Index Medicus
Index to Scientific and Technical Proceedings
Science Citation Index

Computerized periodical indexes are available for many specialized areas and may be faster than leafing through years of bound periodicals. Access to these databases may be expensive.

Science and Technology Databases
Agricola (agriculture)
Biosis Previews (biology, botany)
CA Search (chemistry)
Compendix (engineering)
NTIS (National Technical Information Search)
ORBIT (science and technology)
SciSearch
SPIN (physics)

Writing for Special Occasions

CHAPTER 40

Writing in a Business Environment

In a business environment, much is accomplished—meetings are attended, information is shared, agendas are set, arguments are settled—based on writing alone. When you enter this environment by writing a letter or memo, you must understand that people are not obligated to answer you (rude as this might seem). Business people have many demands placed on them simultaneously. When reading, they must know a writer's purpose and they must be given a motivation for continuing to read. Lacking either of these qualities, a document will not represent itself as *important* enough to merit attention, and the reader will simply turn to more pressing concerns.

You will significantly improve your chances of readers acting on your letters and memos if you begin by appreciating the constraints on their time. Think of your readers as busy people inclined to help if your writing is direct, concise, and clearly organized. A *direct* letter or memo will state in its opening sentence your purpose for writing. A *concise* letter or memo will state your exact needs in as few words as possible. A *well-organized* letter or memo will present only the information that is pertinent to your main point, in a sequence that is readily understood.

The writing process in a business environment

Direct, concise, and clearly organized writing takes time, of course, and is seldom the effort of a single draft. Writing a document in a business setting involves a process, just as your writing a research paper in an academic setting involves a process. It may seem counterintuitive, but you will spend less time writing a letter twice (producing both rough and revised drafts) than you will trying to do a creditable job in a single draft. Generally, you will do well to follow the advice in chapters 3 and 4 on planning, developing, drafting, and revising a paper. For every document that you write, aside from the simplest two- or three-line notes, you should prepare to write, write a draft, and then revise.

Standard formats, spacing, and information in a business letter

Standard formats

Use unlined, white bond paper ($8\frac{1}{2}$ x 11) or letterhead stationery for your business correspondence. Prepare your letter on a typewriter or word processor, and print on one side of the page only. Format your letter according to one of three conventions: full block, block, and semi-block—terms describing the ways in which you indent information. The six basic elements of a letter—return address, inside address and date, salutation, body, closing, and abbreviated matter—begin at the left margin in the *full block* format. Displayed information such as lists begins five spaces from the left margin. In the *block* format, the return address and the closing are aligned just beyond the middle of the page, while the inside address, salutation, new paragraphs, and abbreviated matter each begin at the left margin. (See the "Letter of Inquiry" in 40b for an example of block format.) The *semi-block* format is similar to the block format except that each new paragraph is indented five spaces from the left margin and any displayed information is indented ten spaces. (See the "Letter of Application" in 40d for an example of a semi-block format.)

Standard spacing

Maintain a one-inch margin at the top, bottom, and sides of the page. Single space the document for all but very brief letters (two to five lines), the body of which you should double space. Skip one or two lines between the return address and the inside address; one line between the inside address and the salutation (which is followed by a colon); one line between the salutation and opening paragraph; one line between paragraphs; one line between your final paragraph and your complimentary closing (which is followed by a comma); four lines between your closing and typewritten name; and one line between your typewritten name and any abbreviated matter.

Standard information

RETURN ADDRESS AND DATE

Unless you are writing on letterhead stationery (on which your return address is preprinted), type as a block of information your return address—street address on one line; city, state, and zip code on the next; the date on a third line. If you are writing on letterhead, type the date only, centered one or two lines below the letterhead's final line.

INSIDE ADDRESS

Provide as a block of information the full name and address of the person to whom you are writing. Be sure to spell all names—personal, company,

40a

and address—correctly. Use abbreviations only if the company abbreviates words in its own name or address.

SALUTATION

Begin your letter with a formal greeting, traditionally *Dear___*: Unless another title applies, such as *Dr.* or *Senator,* address a man as *Mr.* and a woman as *Miss* or *Mrs.*—or as *Ms.* if you or the person addressed prefer this. When in doubt about a woman's marital status or preferences in a salutation, use *Ms.* If you are not writing to a specific person, avoid the gender-specific and potentially insulting *Dear Sirs.* Many readers find the generic *Dear Sir or Madam* and *To whom it may concern* to be equivocal, and you may want to open instead with the company name, *Dear Acme Printing,* or with a specific department name or position title: *Dear Personnel Department* or *Dear Personnel Manager.* See the discussion at 31a for the conventions on abbreviating titles in a salutation or an address.

BODY OF THE LETTER

Develop your letter in paragraph form. State your purpose clearly in the opening paragraph. Avoid giving your letter a visually dense impression. When your content lends itself to displayed treatment (if, for instance, you are presenting a list), indent the information. You may want to use bullets, numbers, or hyphens. (See, for example, the "Letter of Inquiry" in 40b.)

CLOSING

Close with some complimentary expression such as *Yours truly, Sincerely,* or *Sincerely yours.* Capitalize the first word only of this closing remark and follow the remark with a comma. Allow four blank lines for your signature, then type your name and, below that, any title that applies.

ABBREVIATED MATTER

Several abbreviations may follow at the left-hand margin, one line below your closing. If someone else has typed your letter, abbreviate initials as follows: Capitalize your initials, place a slash, then place the typist's initials in lowercase—*LR/hb.* If you are enclosing any material with your letter, type *Enclosure* or *Enc.* If you care to itemize this information, place a colon and align items as in the example letter in 40d. If you are sending copies of the letter to other readers (known as a *secondary audience*), write *cc:* (for *carbon copy*) and list the names of the recipients of the copies, as in the example letter in 40f.

THE SECOND PAGE

Begin your letter's second page with identifying information so that if the first and second pages are separated the reader will easily be able to match them again. The blocked information should consist of your name, the date, and the page number presented in a block at the upper left-hand corner of the page.

40a

```
Jon Lipman
January 7, 1992
Page 2

and in the event of your coming to Worcester, I would be
happy to set up an interview with you here. Perhaps the
week of May 20 would be convenient, since I will be travel-
ing to eastern Massachusetts.
```

ENVELOPE

Single-space all information. If you are not using an envelope with a preprinted return address, type your return address at the upper left-hand corner. Center between the right- and left-hand sides the name and address of the person to whom you are writing. Vertically, type the address just below center.

```
Jon Lipman
231 Gray Street
Worcester, Massachusetts 01610




                    Ms. Hannah Marks
                    Equipment Design, Inc.
                    1254 Glenn Avenue
                    Arlington, Massachusetts 02174
```

40b Letters of inquiry

A letter of inquiry is based on a question you want answered. Presumably, you have done enough research to have identified a person knowledgeable in the area concerning you. Do not ask for too much information or for very general information that you could readily find in a library. Avoid giving your reader the impression that you are asking him or her for basic information that you should have managed to locate yourself. If you are inquiring about price or product information, simply ask for a brochure.

- Begin the letter with a sentence that identifies your need. State who you are, what your general project is (if the information is pertinent), and the reason for your writing.

- Follow with a sentence devoted to how you have learned of the reader or the reader's company and how this person or company could be of help to you.

- Pose a few *specific* questions. Frame these questions in such a way that you demonstrate you have done background research.

- State any time constraints you may have. Do not expect your reader to respond any sooner than two or three weeks.

- Close with a brief statement of appreciation. If you feel it would expedite matters, you might include a self-addressed, stamped envelope.

Block Format

40b

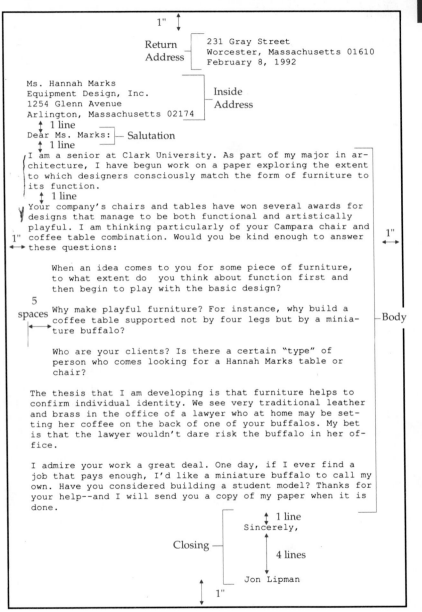

Return Address

231 Gray Street
Worcester, Massachusetts 01610
February 8, 1992

1"

Ms. Hannah Marks
Equipment Design, Inc.
1254 Glenn Avenue
Arlington, Massachusetts 02174

Inside Address

1 line

Dear Ms. Marks: — Salutation

1 line

I am a senior at Clark University. As part of my major in architecture, I have begun work on a paper exploring the extent to which designers consciously match the form of furniture to its function.

1 line

Your company's chairs and tables have won several awards for designs that manage to be both functional and artistically playful. I am thinking particularly of your Campara chair and coffee table combination. Would you be kind enough to answer these questions:

1"

When an idea comes to you for some piece of furniture, to what extent do you think about function first and then begin to play with the basic design?

5 spaces

Why make playful furniture? For instance, why build a coffee table supported not by four legs but by a miniature buffalo?

Body

Who are your clients? Is there a certain "type" of person who comes looking for a Hannah Marks table or chair?

The thesis that I am developing is that furniture helps to confirm individual identity. We see very traditional leather and brass in the office of a lawyer who at home may be setting her coffee on the back of one of your buffalos. My bet is that the lawyer wouldn't dare risk the buffalo in her office.

I admire your work a great deal. One day, if I ever find a job that pays enough, I'd like a miniature buffalo to call my own. Have you considered building a student model? Thanks for your help--and I will send you a copy of my paper when it is done.

Closing —

1 line

Sincerely,

4 lines

Jon Lipman

1"

40d

40c Letters of complaint

When you have a problem that you want remedied, write a letter of complaint. No matter how irate you may be, keep a civil but firm tone and do not threaten. If the time comes to take follow-up action, write a second letter in which you repeat your complaint and state your intentions. Your letter of complaint should be clear on the following points:

- Present the problem.
- State when and where you bought the product in question (if this is a consumer complaint). Provide an exact model number. If this is a complaint about poor service or ill-treatment, state when and where you encountered the unacceptable behavior.
- Describe precisely the product failure or the way in which a behavior was unsatisfactory.
- Summarize the expectations you had when you bought the product or when you engaged someone's services. State succinctly how your expectations were violated and how you were inconvenienced (or worse).
- State exactly how you want the problem resolved.

40d Letters of application

Whether you are applying for summer-time work or for a full-time job after graduation, your first move probably will be to write a letter of application in which you ask for an interview. A successful letter of application will pique a prospective employer's interest by achieving a delicate balance: on the one hand you will present yourself as a bright, dependable, and resourceful person while on the other you will avoid sounding like an unabashed self-promoter. Your goal is to show a humble and earnest confidence. As you gather thoughts for writing, think of the employer as someone in need of a person who can be counted on for dependable and steady work, for creative thinking, and for an ability to function amiably as a member of a team. Avoid presenting yourself merely as someone who has a particular set of skills. You are more than this. Skills grow dated as new technologies become available. You want to suggest that your ability to learn and to adapt will never grow dated.

- Keep your letter of application to one typewritten page.
- Open by stating which job you are applying for and where you learned of the job.
- Review your specific skills and work experience that make you well-suited for the job.

- Review your more general qualities (in relation to work experience, if appropriate) that make you well-suited for the job.
- Express your desire for an interview and note any constraints on your time: exams, jobs, and other commitments. Avoid statements like "you can contact me at. . . ." You will provide your address and phone number on your résumé.
- Close with a word of appreciation.

When you have written a second draft of your letter, seek out editorial advice from those who have had experience applying for jobs and particularly from those who have been in a position of reading letters of application and setting up interviews. Here are a few questions you can put to your readers: What sort of person does this letter describe? Am I emphasizing my skills and abilities in the right way? How do you feel about the tone of this letter? Am I direct and confident without being pushy? Based on editorial feedback, revise. Proofread two or three times so that your final document is direct, concise, well organized, and letter-perfect with respect to grammar, usage, and punctuation. Write your letter in a block or semi-block format on bond paper that has a good, substantial feel to it. Use paper with at least a twenty-five percent cotton fiber content, which you will find at any stationery store. Use an envelope of matching bond paper.

Semi-Block Format

40d

231 Gray Street
Worcester, Massachusetts 01610
March 30, 1992

Ms. Hannah Marks
Equipment Design, Inc.
1254 Glenn Avenue
Arlington, Massachusetts 02174

Dear Ms. Marks:

5 spaces

I would like to apply for the marketing position you advertised in <u>Architectural Digest</u>. As you know from our previous correspondence, I am an architecture major with an interest in furniture design. As part of my course work I took a minor in marketing, with the hope of finding a job similar to the one you have listed.

For the past two summers I have apprenticed myself to a cabinetmaker in Berkshire County, Massachusetts. Mr. Hiram Stains is 70 years old and a master at working with cherry and walnut. While I love working in a shop, and have built most of the furniture in my own apartment (see the photographic enclosures), I realize that a craftsman's life is a bit too solitary for me. Ideally, I would like to combine in one job my woodworking skills, my degree in architecture, and my desire to interact with people.

Your job offers precisely this opportunity. I respect your work immensely and am sure I could represent Equipment Design with enthusiasm. Over time, if my suggestions were welcomed, I might also be able to contribute in terms of design ideas.

I would very much like to arrange an interview. Final exams are scheduled for the last week of April. I'll be preparing the week before that, so I'm available for an interview anytime aside from that two-week block. Thank you for your interest, and I hope to hear from you soon.

Sincerely,

Jon Lipman

Jon Lipman

enc.: photographs
      writing sample

Align
itemized
enclosures

40e Résumés

A résumé highlights information that you think employers will find useful in considering you for a job. Typically, résumés are written in a clipped form. Although word groups are punctuated as sentences, they are, strictly speaking, fragments. For instance, instead of writing "I supervised fund-raising activities" you would write "Supervised fund-raising activities." Keep these fragments parallel: keep all verbs either in the present or in the past tense; begin all fragments with either verbs or nouns.

NOT PARALLEL Supervised fund-raising activities. Speaker at three area meetings on the "Entrepreneurial Side of the Art World." [The first fragment begins with a verb; the second begins with a noun.]

PARALLEL Supervised fund-raising activities. Spoke at three area meetings on the "Entrepreneurial Side of the Art World." [Both fragments begin with a verb in the past tense.]

A résumé works in tandem with your job application. The letter of application establishes a direct communication between you and your prospective employer. Written in your voice, the letter will suggest intangible elements such as your habits of mind and traits of character that make you an attractive candidate. The résumé, by contrast, works as a summary sheet or catalogue of your educational and work experience. The tone of the résumé is neutral and fact-oriented. The basic components are these:

■ Your name, address, and telephone number—each centered on its own line at the top of the page.

Provide headings, as follows:

■ *Position Desired* or *Objective*. State the specific job you want.

■ *Education*. Provide your pertinent college (and graduate school) experience. List degrees earned (or to be earned); major; classes taken, if pertinent; and your grade point average, if you are comfortable sharing this information.

■ *Work Experience*. List your jobs, including titles, chronologically, beginning with your most recent job.

■ *Related Activities*. List any clubs, volunteer positions, or activities that you feel are indicative of your general interests and character.

■ *References*. Provide names and addresses if you expect the employer to contact references directly. If you are keeping references on file at a campus office, state that your references are available upon request.

40e

Jon Lipman
231 Gray Street
Worcester, Massachusetts 01610
508-555-8212

Objective: Marketing position in an arts-related company

Education: Clark University, Worcester, Massachusetts
                  Bachelor of Arts in Architecture, May 1992
                  Minor in Marketing, May 1992
                  Grade point average (to date) 3.3/4.0

Work   September 1991-present: Directed marketing
Experience: campaign for campus-based artists' collec-
                  tive and supervised fund raising. Spoke at
                  three area meetings on the "Entrepreneurial
                  Side of the Art World." Generated community
                  interest in the work of campus artists by or-
                  ganizing a fair and a direct mail program.

                  May 1991-August 1991: Studied cabinet making
                  with Hiram Stains, master cabinetmaker in
                  Berkshire County, Massachusetts. Prepared
                  wood for joining, learned dove-tail tech-
                  nique, and applied design principles learned
                  in school to cabinet construction.

                  September 1990-April 1991: Organized
                  artists' collective on campus and developed
                  marketing plan.

                  May 1990-August 1990: Studied cabinet making
                  with Hiram Stains. Learned tool use and main-
                  tenance.

Related   Supervised set design for theater produc-
Activities: tions on campus. Donated services as carpen-
                  ter to local shelter for the homeless.
                  Designed and built virtually all furniture
                  in my apartment.

References: Mr. Hiram Stains
                  Route 16
                  Richmond, Massachusetts 01201

                  Ms. Amanda Lopez
                  Center Street Shelter
                  Worcester, Massachusetts 01610

                  Dr. Edward Bing
                  Department of Architecture
                  Clark University
                  Worcester, Massachusetts 01610

40f Memoranda

Memoranda, or memos, are internal documents written from one employee to another in the same company. The reasons for writing memos are many: you may want to announce a meeting, summarize your understanding of a meeting, set a schedule, request information, define and resolve a problem, argue for funding, build consensus, and so on. Because they are written "in-house," memos tend to be less formal in tone than business letters; still, they must be every bit as direct, concise, and well organized, or readers will ignore them. When writing a memo longer than a few lines, follow the process discussed earlier of preparing to write, writing, and revising. A memo will differ from a business letter in the following ways:

- The memo has no return address, no inside address, and no salutation. Instead, the memo begins with this information:

    (Date)
    To:
    From:
    Subject:

- The memo follows a full block format, with all information placed flush to the left margin.

- The memo is often divided into headings that separate the document into readily distinguished parts.

- Portions of the memo are often displayed—that is, set off and indented when there are lists or other information lending itself to such treatment.

- Some companies highlight the information about distribution of memo copies to others, either placing the *cc:* line under the *To:* line or adding a subsection titled *Distribution:* with the opening section.

If your memo is three-quarters of a page or longer, consider highlighting its organization with headings, as in the example memo below. Headings work in tandem with the memo's subject line and first sentence to give readers the ability to scan the memo and quickly—within thirty seconds—understand your message. Once again, realize that your readers are busy; they will appreciate any attempt to make their job of reading easier.

40f

February 14, 1992

TO: Linda Cohen

FROM: Matthew Franks

SUBJECT: Brochure production schedule

Thanks for helping to resolve the production schedule for our
new brochure. Please review the following production and distribution dates. By return memo, confirm that you will commit
your department to meeting this schedule.

Production dates

Feb. 19	1992	First draft of brochure copy
March 1	1992	First draft of design plans
March 8	1992	Second draft of brochure copy and design
March 15	1992	Review of final draft and design
March 17	1992	Brochure to printer

Distribution dates

April 4	1992	First printing of 10,000 in our warehouse
April 11	1992	Mailing to Zone 1
April 14	1992	Mailing to Zone 2
April 17	1992	Mailing to Zones 3 and 4

Please let me hear from you by this Friday. If I haven't,
I'll assume your agreement and commitment. It looks as though
we'll have a good brochure this year. Thanks for all your help.

cc: Amy Hanson

CHAPTER 41

Writing Essay Exams

Increasingly, professors across the curriculum are using essay exams to test student mastery of important concepts and relationships. A carefully conceived exam will challenge you not only to recall and organize what you know of a subject but also to extend and apply your knowledge. Essay exams will require of you numerous responses; but the one response to *avoid* is the so-called information dump in which at first glimpse of a topic you begin pouring onto the page *everything* you have ever read or heard about it. A good answer to an essay exam question requires that you be selective in choosing the information you discuss. What you say about that information and what relationships you make with it are critical. As is often the case with good writing, less tends to be more—provided that you adopt and follow a strategy.

41a A strategy for taking essay exams

Prepare

Ideally, you will have read your textbooks and assigned articles with care *as* they were assigned during the period prior to the exam. If you have read closely, or "critically" (see 1b and 1c), your preparation for an exam will amount to a *review* of material you have already thought carefully about. Skim assigned materials and pay close attention to notes you have made in the margins or have recorded in a reading log. Take new notes based on your original notes: highlight important concepts from each assignment. Then reorganize your notes according to key ideas that you think serve as themes or focus points for your course. List each idea separately and beneath each, list any reading that in some way comments on or provides information about that idea. In an American literature course this idea might be "nature as a character" or "innocence lost." In a sociology course the idea might be "social constructions of identity." Turn next to your class notes (you may want to do this *before* reviewing your reading assignments), and add information and comments to your lists of key ideas. Study these lists. Develop statements about each idea that you could, if asked, support with references to specific information. Try to anticipate your professor's questions.

41a

Read the entire exam before beginning to write.

Allot yourself a certain number of minutes to answer each essay question, allowing extra time for the more complex questions. As you write, monitor your use of time.

Adopt a discipline-appropriate perspective.

Essay exams are designed in part to see how well you understand particular ways of thinking in a discipline. If you are writing a mid-term exam in chemistry, for instance, appreciate that your professor will expect you to discuss material from a chemist's perspective. That is, you will need to demonstrate not only that you know your information but also that you can *do* things with it: namely, think and reach conclusions in discipline-appropriate ways.

Adapt the writing process according to the time allotted for a question.

Assuming that you have thirty minutes to answer an essay question, spend at least five minutes of this allotted time in plotting an answer.

- Locate the assignment's key verb and identify your specific tasks in writing. (See the box that follows.)

- Given these tasks, list information you can draw on in developing your answer.

- Examine the information you have listed and develop a thesis (see 3f), a statement that directly answers the question and that demonstrates your understanding and application of some key concept associated with the essay topic.

- Sketch an outline of your answer. In taking an essay exam, you have little or no time for writing to discover. Know before you write what major points you will develop in support of your thesis and in what order.

Spend twenty minutes of your allotted time on writing your answer. When you begin writing, be conscious of making clear, logical connections between sentences and paragraphs. Well-chosen transitions (see 5d-3) not only will help your professor follow your discussion but also will help you to project your ideas forward and to continue writing. As you do in formal papers, develop your essay in sections, with each section organized by a section thesis (see 5a). Develop each section of your essay by discussing *specific* information.

Save five minutes to reread your work and ensure that its logic is clear and that you address the exam question from a discipline-appropriate point of view. Given the time constraints of the essay exam format, professors understand that you will not submit a polished draft. Nevertheless, they will expect writing that faces the question and that is coherent, unified, and grammatical. Again, avoid an information dump. Select information with care and write with a strategy.

41b   The importance of verbs in an essay question

41b

In reading an essay assignment, you will need to identify a specific topic and purpose for writing. Often, you can identify exactly what a professor expects by locating a key verb in the assignment such as *illustrate, discuss,* or *compare.* Following is a guide to students on "Important Word Meanings" in assignments. Developed by the History Department at UCLA, this guide was intended to help students develop effective responses to essay questions. The guide will serve you well in any of your courses.

Important Word Meanings

Good answers to essay questions depend in part upon a clear understanding of the meanings of the important directive words. These are the words like *explain, compare, contrast,* and *justify,* which indicate the way in which the material is to be presented. Background knowledge of the subject matter is essential. But mere evidence of this knowledge is not enough. If you are asked to *compare* the British and American secondary school systems, you will get little or no credit if you merely *describe* them. If you are asked to *criticize* the present electoral system, you are not answering the question if you merely *explain* how it operates. A paper is satisfactory only if it answers directly the question that was asked.

The words that follow are frequently used in essay examinations:

summarize   sum up; give the main points briefly. *Summarize the ways in which man preserves food.*

evaluate   give the good points and the bad ones; appraise; give an opinion regarding the value of; talk over the advantages and limitations. *Evaluate the contributions of teaching machines.*

contrast   bring out the points of difference. *Contrast the novels of Jane Austen and William Makepeace Thackeray.*

explain   make clear; interpret; make plain; tell "how" to do; tell the meaning of. *Explain how man can, at times, trigger a full-scale rainstorm.*

describe   give an account of; tell about; give a word picture of. *Describe the Pyramids of Giza.*

define   give the meaning of a word or concept; place it in the class to which it belongs and set it off from other items in the same class. *Define the term "archetype."*

compare   bring out points of similarity and points of difference. *Compare the legislative branches of the state government and the national government.*

discuss   talk over; consider from various points of view; present the different sides of. *Discuss the use of pesticides in controlling mosquitoes.*

(continued)

41b

	Important Word Meanings (continued)
criticize	state your opinion of the correctness or merits of an item or issue; criticism may approve or disapprove. *Criticize the increasing use of alcohol.*
justify	show good reasons for; give your evidence; present facts to support your position. *Justify the American entry into World War II.*
trace	follow the course of; follow the trail of; give a description of progress. *Trace the development of television in school instruction.*
interpret	make plain; give the meaning of; give your thinking about; translate. *Interpret the poetic line, "The sound of a cobweb snapping is the noise of my life."*
prove	establish the truth of something by giving factual evidence or logical reasons. *Prove that in a full-employment economy, a society can get more of one product only by giving up another product.*
illustrate	use a word picture, a diagram, a chart, or a concrete example to clarify a point. *Illustrate the use of catapults in the amphibious warfare of Alexander.*

Source: Andrew Moss and Carol Holder, *Improving Student Writing: A Guide for Faculty in All Disciplines* (Dubuque, Iowa: Kendall/Hunt, 1988), 17–18.

Writing
with a Computer

If a computer's word processing software only relieved writers of tedium, this benefit in itself would be enormous. In the bad old days, only fifteen years ago, a student would need to retype an entire page for the sake of some small correction, like a spelling error. Today, only a few keystrokes are needed to enter changes and command a printer to reproduce a corrected page. Of greater significance than this ease of correction is the difference a computer can make in the composing and revising process. If you have written much at all, and if you have followed the advice in this handbook, you know that good writing is the result of *re*writing. In brief, the view that writing is a process suggests that a first draft is never complete and that refinements in a writer's thinking come as a consequence of revision. First drafts are created to be revised: paragraphs will be restructured and sentences reworked until they are direct and concise. Here are some ways computers can help you become a more efficient writer:

- Computers can help you assemble ideas quickly and transfer your best ones electronically to an outline or sketch.
- Computers can help you create multiple outlines with ease.
- Computers can help you produce a first draft quickly, with the knowledge that your first draft, once entered onto an electronic file, can be reworked.
- Computers can help you revise repeatedly, maintaining your focus on your document, not on the tedium of retyping.
- Computers can help you edit your document with the aid of spell checkers and other programs.
- Computers, ultimately, can help engender in you a positive attitude toward writing.

A computer is a machine, referred to as *hardware,* that uses silicon chip technology to process information. Without instructions, a computer can do nothing at all. It relies on commands from a user, who will use *software* (a computer program) to instruct the machine to perform various tasks. Of the hundreds of thousands of software programs available, *word processing programs* are among the most widely used. A word processor combines with a computer to create a tool of extraordinary power.

A1 Word processing commands

If you are working in an IBM environment, you will execute word processing commands by keystroking some combination of your keyboard's *control, shift,* or *alternate keys* along with one of the computer's ten or twelve *function keys.* The *block* command will highlight a set of words that you can then *cut* (or delete) and *paste* (move to a new location). The *search* command enables you to search a document forward or backward to find a particular word or string of words. The *retrieve* or *load* command allows you to call up to the screen your documents, which are called *files.* The *save* command saves your work on a *floppy disk,* which you store outside of the computer, or on a *hard disk,* a disk with large storage capacity located within the computer. The *print* command will print any part or all of a document.

In learning to work with a word processor, you will repeatedly use several keys: the *arrow* keys will move the *cursor* around the screen. The cursor is the blinking line or block that shows you where on the screen letters or numbers will appear as you type them. The *backspace* key will move the cursor from right to left and erase characters. Some combination of keys will move the cursor to the top or bottom of a page or to the beginning or end of a document. The *cancel* key will instruct the computer to ignore a command—such as *delete*—that you have given inadvertently.

If you are working in a Macintosh environment, with a *mouse,* many of the commands otherwise achieved with keystrokes can be accomplished using the mouse and the menus at the top of the screen. Consult your software manual for instructions.

ALERT: Save your work often! When working on a document, use the *save* command every fifteen minutes or so to ensure that in the event of a computer failure your work will not be lost. At the end of a work session, print a copy of your paper and create a *backup file* so that you always have one paper copy and two electronic copies, each on a separate disk.

A2 Computers and the writing process

1 Preparing to write

The computer can be enormously helpful in preparing to write. As you read a writing assignment, focus on two key questions: What do you know about your topic? What do you want to say to your audience? Subsequent decisions will depend on your answers, and you can use the power of word processing to make flexible entries and notes that can be rearranged to suit your changing purpose.

Generating ideas and organizing your thoughts

If you use the computer to generate ideas and to keep notes, you can put your word processing software to work by creating an outline of your paper and then moving into that outline all the pertinent information you have generated or collected. With the computer's *block move* or *cut/paste* commands you can rearrange material and sketch your paper in any number of ways, allowing you to compare possible strategies. In this way, the computer can help free you from any inclination to think that only one plan for a paper exists. Any paper can be structured in a variety of ways. The more flexible you are in experimenting with different outlines, the more likely it is you will arrive at one that represents a strong, creative synthesis of possible approaches.

A2

Writing collaboratively

If your computer is hooked into a network, you can share your ideas for a paper with classmates and friends. Send them an electronic letter in which you describe the general approach you want to take in the paper and ask for reactions. As you work through the writing process, use a network for conducting research, revising, and editing. (See A2-3.)

Conducting library research

If you are writing a research paper, you can take your "to do" list with you to the library as you begin the general search process (see chapter 33). If your computer is hooked into a network, you may not need to travel to the library to check its holdings since these may exist on file in the college's main computer, which you can access over the phone lines. Some colleges will even have general references on a mainframe computer, and you will be able to peruse these references and do your initial reading while seated at your own computer. You can take notes at the computer, too, by creating files that divide your research topic into important categories. If categories get too large or ill defined, you can split them into separate files. When the time comes for sketching a plan for your paper, you can print out your notes, laying before you all the information that you have to work with.

2   Writing a first draft

Some people need the physical connection of hand to pen to paper when writing. Some can draft certain sorts of documents—say, business correspondence—on a computer but must write longer efforts by hand. Whatever your preferences, remember that the purpose of a first draft is to get a version of your document written—quickly. If you can work on a computer, all the better. Even if you are a poor typist, a computer keyboard encourages speed. Once you are open to the idea of writing a first draft, making large and small refinements later, you free yourself to write quickly, even furiously. The clear advantage of working on a computer at this stage is having your draft on file, ready and waiting for the work of revision.

A2

3   Revising

Computers greatly facilitate the process of revision. One strategy that many writers find effective is to work consistently from a *hard copy*, or printed page. Read and make changes to words on a page, using a pencil or pen to do so. Once you are satisfied with your changes, turn to the computer and transfer them to your file. Then print your revised document and reread— again with a pen in hand. By making several such passes through your document, you will work steadily toward a final draft.

Revising for purpose, content, and structure

The first order of business in revising is to determine whether you have written the paper you intended (see 4d). Working from hard copies of your paper, revise your working thesis (see 4d); use your final thesis to revise for unity and coherence (see 4e); and revise for balance (see 4f), making sure that the structure of your paper is sound and that parts are developed according to their importance. After you make one or more passes through your paper and revise for content, logic, and balance, enter your changes onto the computer and create a solid second draft.

Writing collaboratively

Writers are always in need of good, critical readers who can offer advice; and certainly writing on a computer facilitates the author/editor relationship. Once you have a complete second draft of your paper, consider sending it over a network or providing both a hard copy and an electronic copy (on floppy disk) to a classmate. Some word processing programs have a feature that allows an editor to suggest deletions and additions without destroying any of your text. When your editor returns the document, suggestions will show up on your screen marked in two distinctive ways. In some programs, additions are shaded and deletions are underlined. Similar markings will also appear on a printed copy. Working from a draft that has been edited in this way, you can get the full benefit of a colleague's close reading of your paper. Of course you have the prerogative to accept or reject editorial advice: you can alter the suggested additions or deletions and then, with a few keystrokes, enter into your work those suggestions you find most helpful. Once again, print out the document so that you can review it with pen in hand.

Revising to achieve concise and direct expression

Having settled on the content and structure of your paper, turn to sentence-level clarity. You probably will have stopped to revise particular sentences during prior stages of writing, but you will not have devoted systematic, document-wide attention to the construction of your sentences. A word processor encourages you to be a wordsmith—to quibble with word choices and to experiment with alternate phrasings. Ultimately, the goal is to achieve a concise, spare style (see chapter 17) that allows you to communicate your content in as few words as possible.

A2

Editing for grammar, punctuation, and style

Toward the final stages of writing, when you have assured yourself that the content of your paper is solid and that the writing is direct, your word processor provides an opportunity to rework small matters that can make a big difference to readers: grammar, usage, and punctuation. Make your changes and, again, enter them into the computer and print out a clean draft. You may want to work collaboratively at this stage, asking a colleague to read your work for matters of punctuation, grammar, and usage.

Proofreading

You have worked too hard on your paper to let trivial errors of spelling, doubled words, or inadvertently used homonyms mar the end product. Now is the time to engage your word processor's *spell check program*. If your software package does not include such a program, you are sure to find a reasonably priced one at a local retailer's or in a catalog of public domain software. With its dictionary of 200,000 words or more, a spell checker compares every word of your paper against the words in its memory. When no match can be found, the computer highlights the word and prompts you to make a decision regarding possible replacements. Remember that a computer cannot identify the word or meaning that is right for a sentence. The best a computer can do is call attention to apparent inconsistencies between its word database and what is shown on the screen. No computer will highlight as incorrect the contraction *it's*, even when the context of your sentence requires using the possessive pronoun *its*. Once again, you must rely on your good judgment as a writer.

Printing

When you have proofread your document, print two final copies: one each for you and your instructor. Word processors have *formatting commands* that allow you to set the margins and spacing for a paper. Generally, conform to the guidelines for manuscript preparation in Appendix B.

NOTE: Save your drafts as proof of your hard work. When the paper is graded and returned, collect your drafts and take them to a recycling center.

A3   Specialized software for writers

A3

Aside from spell checkers, several types of computer programs are available to writers. *Database programs* can prove very useful to researchers who take a great many notes or who constantly arrange and rearrange notes. If you have a portable computer that you can carry with you to the library, these programs allow you to take notes electronically while researching and then to call on these notes, later, while writing. *Prewriting* programs can prompt you to think about a topic in multiple ways and then to organize your thoughts into an outline. *Style checkers* will count the number of words in sentences and sentences in paragraphs, advising you with prompts on the screen to vary sentence length and rhythm. Style checkers will also highlight prepositions and uses of *to be* as a main verb, in both cases prompting you to consider revisions. *Thesaurus* programs are sometimes helpful for locating synonyms; see 22f-3. *Grammar checkers* will analyze the text of your papers and highlight word sequences that apparently do not match its programs for identifying normal or correct sentences. The programs will then suggest with a prompt that you reread these apparently incorrect sentences for any errors that may be present. As with spelling programs, all that such "checker" programs can do is count occurrences and identify patterns that do not precisely match data in the program; they are never a substitute for even the most casual reading for meaning. For instance, a grammar checker would regard the following sentence as correct: *Running down the street, the book dropped out of her hands.* You know perfectly well that books do not run down streets. Yet the computer does *not* know this, primarily because the software is not programmed to distinguish between animate nouns (that can do things like run) and inanimate ones. When artificial intelligence is developed and becomes available on personal computers, such distinctions may become possible. Even if that day arrives, you will have to rely on your own knowledge to make important decisions about writing and revising. The computer is a tool, and a powerful one. But the computer is no match, and was never meant to be a substitute, for your own sound judgment.

APPENDIX B

Manuscript Form and Preparation

Before readers register a word of your writing, they form an impression based on your paper's appearance. If you are committed enough to a paper to have revised it several times, surely you will want to give it a crisp appearance. A clean, well-prepared, typed manuscript is a sign of an attentive attitude taken toward all the stages of writing. Careful manuscript preparation implicitly shows respect for your readers, who will certainly appreciate any efforts to make their work easier.

Style guides in the disciplines recommend slightly different conventions for preparing manuscripts, and you should consult the specialized guides listed in 37e, 38e, and 39e when writing in the humanities, social sciences, and sciences. Consult your professor as well. The recommendations here follow the guide commonly used in the humanities, the *MLA [Modern Language Association] Handbook for Writers of Research Papers*, 3rd ed.

B1 Paper and binding

Prepare your work on plain white, twenty-pound paper that measures $8\frac{1}{2}$ x 11 inches. For economy's sake, you might consider buying a ream (500 sheets) if you are typing the manuscript or are preparing it on a laser printer. If you are working with a dot matrix printer, buy a box of 500 or 1000 sheets of fanfold paper. Unless your professor advises otherwise, avoid onion skin or erasable paper, both of which will easily smudge. (For ease of preparation, though, you might type your work on erasable paper and submit a photocopy, which will not smudge.) Make a copy of your final paper to keep for your files, and submit the original to your professor. In binding pages, affix a single paper clip to the upper left-hand corner. To ease your reader's handling of your paper, do *not* place multiple staples along the left margin, and avoid plastic folders unless otherwise directed.

B2 Page layout

Whether you adopt conventions for page layout suggested by the *MLA Handbook* or by other style guides, maintain consistent margins and spacing.

Your paper's first page, subsequent pages, and reference-list page(s) should be designed according to standard practice in a discipline.

Margins and line spacing

Type on one side of a page, double spacing all text (including footnotes and endnotes). Maintain double spacing between paragraphs and between lines of text and any displayed quotations. Leave a one-inch margin on the top and bottom of a page and a one-inch margin on both sides of a page. If you are working on a computer, set the margins as well as the running head (your last name and a page number) automatically. With each new paragraph, indent five spaces (on a computer, press the Tab key). For displayed quotations (see 28a-4), indent ten spaces and maintain that indentation for the length of the quotation.

Design of first page

Following the MLA format, you do not need to prepare a separate title page for your research papers. (This convention differs in the sciences and social sciences. See the box on page 686 as well as the example research paper on 711.) Observe the spacing of headings and title in the following example.

```
                                                                  ↕ 1/2"
                          ↓ 1"                                Chandra 1  1"
           1"                                                          ←→
          ←→ Sarika Chandra

            Dr. Robert Crooks     ⌐ Double space
            English 204
            15 May 1991           ⌐ Double space
 Center            The Power of Alcohol and the Church   ⌐ Double
 title                  in Joyce's "Counterparts"          space
            Indent five spaces
              ←→ "Counterparts" tells the story of a man named Farrington,   ⌐ Double
            who will not do his job right and takes abuse from his boss       space
            for that. Farrington spends a long time drinking after work
            and when he gets home beats his son. However, Joyce tells
```

Design of subsequent pages

Observe the position of the running head and the first line of text on a paper's second or subsequent page.

```
                    ↕1/2"  1"
      ↓1"          Chandra 2  ←→
 1"
←→ Farrington sits in Alleyne's office, powerless, listening to
   this man berate him for some job poorly done. Apparently,   Running
                                                               head: name
   mistakes' and the resulting humiliation are . . .           and page
                                                               number
                                                               (without
                                                               comma
                                                               or p.)
```

B2

Design of "Works Cited" page

Observe the position of the running head, the title "Works Cited," and the indentation of the reference entry's second line.

```
                                      ↕1/2"  1"
                    ↓1"              Chandra 6  ←→

  1"                     Works Cited ⎤ Double space
←→ Ellmann, Richard. James Joyce. Oxford: Oxford UP, 1982.

       Joyce, James. "Counterparts." Dubliners. Ed. Robert Scholes
5 spaces ←→ and A. Walton Litz. New York: Cornell UP, 1989.

       ---. The Critical Writings. Ed. Ellsworth Mason and Richard
          Ellmann. New York: Cornell UP, 1989.

       Stivers, Richard. A Hair of the Dog: Irish Drinking and
          American Stereotype. University Park, Pa.: Pennsyl-
          vania State UP, 1976.
```

B3 Text preparation

Printing a manuscript on a word processor

Print on one side of the page and, if possible, use a laser printer. If none is available, use a dot matrix printer with a fresh enough ribbon that readers will have no trouble reading your text. Keep the right-hand edge of your text ragged, or *un*justified. If your dot matrix machine is printing a light page, you may be able to improve the product by photocopying the page with the photocopier adjusted to a darker than normal setting.

Printing a manuscript on a typewriter

Type on one side of a page with standard typewriter fonts. Avoid typefaces giving the appearance of script, since these are difficult to read. Use a fresh ribbon with black ink.

Hand writing a manuscript

Not all professors accept handwritten papers. If yours does, use lined, white $8\frac{1}{2}$ x 11 inch paper. Do not use spiral-bound notebook paper with its ragged edges. Write neatly and legibly in pen, on one side of the page, using dark blue or black ink. Consult your professor, who may ask you to skip every other line to allow room for editorial comments.

B4 Alterations

In a final review of your paper, when you are working away from your typewriter or word processor, you may find it necessary to make minor changes to your text—perhaps to correct a typographical error or to improve your wording. Make corrections *neatly*. When striking out a word, do so with a single line. Use a caret (∧) to mark an insertion in the text, and write your correction or addition above the line you are altering. If time permits and you have worked on a word processor, enter the changes into your file and reprint the affected pages. Retype or reprint a page when you make three or more handwritten corrections on it. If your typewriter or computer keyboard lacks a particular symbol or mark that you need, handwrite that symbol on the page.

"Counterparts" tells the story of a man ∧who will not do his job right and takes abuse from his boss for that.

B5 Punctuation and spacing

Observe the following standard conventions for spacing before and after marks of punctuation.

ONE SPACE BEFORE
  beginning parenthesis or bracket
  beginning quotation mark
  period in a series denoting an omission—see ellipses, 29e

NO SPACE BEFORE (EXCEPT AS NOTED)
comma	colon
period[1]	semicolon
exclamation point	end quotation mark
question mark	hyphen or dash
apostrophe	

NO SPACE AFTER (EXCEPT AS NOTED)
  hyphen[2] or dash
  beginning parenthesis or bracket
  apostrophe[3]

ONE SPACE AFTER (EXCEPT AS NOTED)
  comma
  semicolon
  colon[4]
  apostrophe denoting the possessive form of a plural
  end parenthesis or bracket that does not end a sentence
  end quotation within a sentence
  period in a series denoting an omission—see ellipses, 29e
  period marking an abbreviated name or an initial

TWO SPACES AFTER THE FOLLOWING MARKS WHEN THEY CONCLUDE A SENTENCE
  period
  question mark
  exclamation
  closing quotation
  end parenthesis or bracket

EXCEPTIONS (AS NOTED ABOVE)
  [1]Unless the period occurs in a series denoting omission—see 29e.
  [2]Unless the hyphen denotes one in a pair or series of delayed adjectives, as in *a first-, second-, or third-place finish.*

[3]Unless the apostrophe denotes the possessive form of a plural, as in *boys'*, in which case skip one space.

[4]Unless the colon denotes a ratio, as in 3:2.

B5

Glossary of Usage

This glossary is intended to provide definitions and descriptions of selected word usages current in formal academic writing. In consulting this kind of glossary, writers should be prepared to make informed decisions about the meaning and the level of diction that is most appropriate to their writing project.

Many entries in this glossary consist of commonly confused homonyms—words that are pronounced almost alike but have different meanings and spellings. A comprehensive listing of often-confused homonyms appears in section 23a-1 in the spelling chapter.

a, an Use *a* when the article precedes a noun beginning with a consonant. For example, *At last we found a hotel.* Use *an* when the article precedes a word beginning with a vowel or an unpronounced *h*. *It was an honor to receive an invitation.* (See 7a.)

accept, except Use *accept* when your meaning is "to receive." Use *except* when you mean an exception, as in *He invited everyone except Thuan.* You can also use *except* as a verb which means "to leave out," as in *The report excepted the two episodes of misconduct.*

adverse, averse Use *averse* when you mean a person's feelings of opposition. Use *adverse* when you refer to a thing that stands in opposition or is opposed to someone or something, as in *I was not averse to taking the roofing job, but the adverse circumstances of a tight deadline and bad weather almost kept me from it.*

advice, advise Use *advice* as a noun meaning "a recommendation," as in *Longfellow gave excellent military advice.* Use *advise* as a verb meaning "to recommend," as in *Many counselors advise students to declare a double major.*

affect, effect If your sentence requires a verb meaning "to have an influence on," use *affect*. If your sentence requires a noun meaning "result," use *effect. Effect* can also be a verb, however. Use *effect* as a verb when you mean "to make happen," as in *He was able to effect a change in how the city council viewed the benefits of recycling.*

aggravate, irritate In formal writing, use *aggravate* when you mean "to make worse," as in *The smoke aggravated his cough.* Use *irritate* when you mean "to bother," as in *He became irritated when the drunken driver said the accident was not her fault.*

ain't Do not use *ain't* in formal writing. Use *is not, are not,* or *am not* instead.

all ready, already Use *all ready* when you mean "prepared" as in *He was all ready for an expedition to Antarctica.* Use *already* when you mean "by this time," as in *The ushers at Symphony Hall will not seat you if the concert has already started.*

all right Do not use *alright.* It is simply a misspelling.

all together, altogether Use *all together* when you mean "as a group" or "in unison," as in *Once we got the family all together, we could discuss the estate.* Use *altogether* when you mean "entirely," as in *Some of the stories about Poe's addictions and personal habits are not altogether correct.* (See 23a.)

allude, elude Use *allude* when you mean "to refer indirectly to." Use *elude* when you mean "to avoid or escape."

allusion, illusion Use *allusion* when you mean "an indirect reference," as in *The children did not understand the allusion to Roman mythology.* Use *illusion* when you mean "false or misleading belief or appearance," as in *Smith labored under the illusion that he was a great artist.*

C

gl/us

a lot Do not use *a lot* in formal writing. Use a more specific modifier instead. When you use *a lot* in other contexts, remember that it is always two words.

among, between Use *between* when you are expressing a relationship involving two people or things, as in *There was general agreement between Robb and Jackson on that issue.* Use *among* when you are expressing a relationship involving three or more separable people or things, as in *He failed to detect a link among the blood cholesterol levels, the red blood cell counts, and the T-cell production rates.*

amongst Do not use *amongst* in formal writing. Instead, use *among.*

amount, number Use *amount* when you refer to a quantity of something that cannot be counted, as in *The amount of effort put into finding the cure for AIDS is beyond calculation.* Use *number* when you refer to something that can be counted, as in *The number of people who want to run the Boston Marathon increases yearly.*

an, and Use *an* when the article precedes a noun beginning with a vowel or an unpronounced *h.* Use *and* when your sentence requires a conjunction that means "in addition to."

and etc. Avoid using *etc.* in formal writing. When you must use *etc.* in non-formal writing, do not use *and. Etcetera* means "and so forth"; therefore, *and etc.* is redundant.

and/or Use *and* or *or,* or explain your ideas by writing them out fully. But avoid *and/or,* which is usually too ambiguous to meet the demands of formal writing.

anxious, eager Use *anxious* when you mean "worried" or "nervous." Use *eager* when you mean "excited or enthusiastic about the possibility of doing something."

any more, anymore   Use *any more* to mean "no more," as in *I don't want any more of those plums.* Use *anymore* as an adverb meaning "now," as in *He doesn't work here anymore.*

anybody, any body; anyone, any one   Use *anybody* and *anyone* when the sense of your sentence requires an indefinite pronoun. Use *any body* and *any one* when the words *body* and *one* are modified by *any*, as in *The teacher was careful not to favor any one student* and *Any body of knowledge is subject to change.*

anyplace   Do not use *anyplace* in formal writing. Use *anywhere* instead.

anyways, anywheres   Do not use *anyways* and *anywheres* in formal writing; use *anyway* and *anywhere* instead.

apt, liable, likely   Use *apt* when you mean "having a tendency to," as in *Kruschev was apt to lose his temper in public.* Use *likely* when you mean "probably going to," as in *We will likely hear from the Senator by Friday.* Use *liable* when you mean "in danger of," as in *People who jog long distances over concrete surfaces are liable to sustain knee injuries.* Also use *liable* when you are referring to legal responsibility, as in *The driver who was at fault was liable for the damages.*

C

gl/us

as, like   Use *as* as either a preposition or a conjunction, but use *like* as a preposition only. If your sentence requires a preposition, use *as* when you are making an exact equivalence, as in *Edison was known as the wizard of Menlo Park.* Use *like* when you are referring to likeness, resemblance, or similarity, as in *Like Roosevelt, Reagan was able to make his constituency feel optimism.*

as, than   When you are making a comparison, you can follow both *as* and *than* with a subjective or objective-case pronoun, depending on meaning. For example, *We trusted O'Keeffe more than him [we trusted Smith]* and *We trusted O'Keeffe more than he [Jones trusted O'Keeffe].* *O'Keeffe was as talented as he [was talented]* and *We found O'Keeffe as trustworthy as [we found] him.* (See 8g.)

as to   Do not use *as to* in formal writing. Rewrite a sentence such as *The president was questioned as to his recent decisions in the Middle East* to read *The president was questioned about his recent decisions in the Middle East.*

assure, ensure, insure   Use *assure* when you mean "to promise" as in *He assured his mother that he would return early.* Use *ensure* when you mean "to make certain," as in *Taking a prep course does not ensure success in the SATs.* Use *insure* when you mean "to make certain" in a legal or financial sense, as in *He insured his boat against theft and vandalism.*

at   Do not use *at* in a question formed with *where*. For example, rewrite a sentence such as *Where is the class at?* to read *Where is the class?*

a while, awhile   Use *awhile* when your sentence requires an adverb, as in *He swam awhile.* If you are not modifying a verb, but rather want a noun with an article, use *a while*, as in *I have not seen you in a while.*

bad, badly Use *bad* as an adjective, as in *Bad pitching changed the complexion of the game.* Use *badly* as an adverb, as in *The refugees badly needed food and shelter.* Use *bad* to follow linking verbs that involve appearance or feeling, as in *She felt bad about missing the party.* (See 11d.)

being as, being that Do not use either *being as* or *being that* to mean "because" in formal writing. Use *because* instead.

beside, besides Use *beside* as a preposition meaning "next to." Use *besides* as an adverb meaning "also" or "in addition to" as in *Besides, I needed to lose the weight.* Use *besides* as an adjective meaning "except" or "in addition to," as in *Rosa Parks seemed to have nothing besides courage to support her.*

better, had better; best, had best Do not use *better, had better, best,* and *had best* for *should* in formal writing. Use *ought* or *should* instead.

between, among See *among, between.*

breath, breathe Use *breath* as a noun; use *breathe* as a verb.

bring, take Use *bring* when you are referring to movement from a farther place to a nearer one, as in *The astronauts were asked to bring back rock samples.* Use *take* for all other types of movement.

broke Use *broke* only as the past tense, as in *He broke the Ming vase.* Do not use *broke* as the past participle; for example, instead of writing *The priceless vase was broke as a result of careless handling,* write *The priceless vase was broken as a result of careless handling.*

bunch Use *bunch* to refer to "a group or cluster of things growing together." Do not use *bunch* to refer to people or a group of items in formal writing.

burst, bust Use *burst* when you mean "to fly apart suddenly," as in *The pomegranate burst open.* (Notice that the example sentence doesn't say *bursted;* there is no such form of the verb.) (See 9b.)

but however, but yet When you use *however* and *yet,* do not precede them with *but* in formal writing. The *but* is redundant.

but that, but what When you use *that* and *what,* do not precede them with *but* in formal writing. The *but* is unnecessary.

calculate, figure, reckon If your sentence requires a word that means "imagine," use *imagine.* Do not use *calculate, figure,* or *reckon,* which are colloquial substitutes for "imagine."

can't hardly, can't scarcely See *not but, not hardly, not scarcely.*

can't help but Use *can't help* by itself; the *but* is redundant.

can't, couldn't Do not use these contractions in formal writing. Use *cannot* and *could not* instead.

can, may Use *can* when you are writing about the ability to do something, as in *He can jump six feet.* Use *may* when you are referring to permission, as in *He may rejoin the team when the period of probation is over.*

censor, censure Use *censor* when you mean editing or removing from the public eye on the basis of morality. Use *censure* when you mean "to give a formal or official scolding or verbal punishment."

center around Do not use *center around* in formal writing. Instead, use *center on.*

chose, choose Use the verb *choose* in the present tense for the first and second person and for the future tense, as in *They choose [or will choose] their teams carefully.* Use *chose* for the past tense, as in *The presidential candidate chose a distinguished running mate.*

compare to, compare with Use *compare to* to note similarities between things, as in *He compared the Chinese wine vessel to the Etruscan wine cup.* Use *compare with* to note similarities and contrasts, as in *When comparing market-driven economies with socialist economies, social scientists find a wide range of difference in the standard of living of individuals.*

complement, compliment Use *complement* when you mean "something that completes," as in *The wine was the perfect complement for the elegant meal.* Use *compliment* when you mean "praise," as in *The administrator savored the compliment on her organizational skills.*

conscience, conscious Use *conscience* when your sentence requires a noun meaning "a sense of right or wrong." Use *conscious* as an adjective to mean "aware of" or "awake."

consensus of opinion Do not use *consensus of opinion* in formal writing. Use *consensus* instead to avoid redundancy.

continual, continuous Use *continual* when you mean "constantly recurring," as in *Continual thunderstorms ruined their vacation days at the beach.* Use *continuous* when you mean "unceasing," as in *The continuous sound of a heartbeat, unceasing and increasing in volume, haunted the narrator.*

could of, would of, should of, might of, may of, must of In formal writing, avoid combining modal auxiliaries (*could, would, should, might, may,* and *must*) with *of.* Instead, write *could have, would have, should have, might have, may have,* and *must have.*

couple, couple of Do not use *couple* or *couple of* to mean "a few" in formal writing. Instead, write *a few.*

criteria Use *criteria* when you want a plural word referring to more than one standard of judgment. Use *criterion* when you are referring to only one standard of judgment.

C

gl/us

data Use *data* when you are referring to more than one fact, statistic, or other means of support for a conclusion. When you are referring to a single fact, use the word *datum* in formal writing, or use *fact, figure,* or another term that is specific to the single means of support.

different from, different than Use *different from* when an object or phrase follows, as in *Braque's style is different from Picasso's.* Use *different than* when a clause follows, as in *Smith's position on the deficit was different when he was seeking the presidency than it was when he was president.*

differ from, differ with Use *differ from* when you are referring to unlike things, as in *Subsequent results of experiments in cold fusion differed radically from results first obtained in Utah.* Use *differ with* to mean "disagree," as in *One expert might differ with another on a point of usage.*

discreet, discrete Use *discreet* to mean "respectfully reserved," as in *He was always discreet when he entered the synagogue.* Use *discrete* to mean "separate" or "distinct," as in *The essay was a discrete part of the examination and could be answered as a take-home assignment.*

disinterested, uninterested Use *disinterested* to mean "impartial," as in *An umpire should always be disinterested in which team wins.* Use *uninterested* to mean "bored" or "not interested."

doesn't, don't Do not use *doesn't* and *don't* in formal writing; instead, use *does not* and *do not.* In other contexts, use *don't* with the first and second person singular, as in *I don't smoke* and with the third person plural, as in *They don't smoke.* Use *doesn't* with the third person singular, as in *He doesn't ride the subway.*

done Use *done* when your sentence requires the past participle; do not use done as the simple past. For example, rewrite a sentence such as *Van Gogh done the painting at Arles* to read *Van Gogh did the painting at Arles.*

due to, due to the fact that Use *due to* to mean "because" only when it follows a form of the verb *be,* as in *The sensation of a leg falling asleep is due to pooling of the blood in the veins.* Do not use *due to* as a preposition, however. Also, do not use *due to the fact that* in formal writing because it is wordy. (See 17a.)

eager, anxious See *anxious, eager.*

effect, affect See *affect, effect.*

elicit, illicit Use *elicit* to mean "to draw out," as in *The social worker finally elicited a response from the child.* Use *illicit* to mean "illegal," as in *Illicit transactions on the black market fuel an underground Soviet economy.* (See 23a.)

emigrate, immigrate, migrate Use *emigrate* to mean "to move away from one's country." Use *immigrate* to mean "to move to another country." Use *migrate* to mean "to move to another place on a temporary basis."

ensure, assure, insure See *assure, ensure, insure.*

enthused, enthusiastic Use *enthusiastic* when you mean "excited about" or "showing enthusiasm." Do not use *enthused* in formal writing.

especially, specially Use *especially* when you mean "particularly," as in *Maria Mitchell was especially talented as a mathematician.* Use *specially* when you mean "for a specific reason," as in *The drug was intended specially for the treatment of rheumatism.*

et al., etc. Do not use *et al.* and *etc.* interchangeably. *Et al.* is generally used in references and bibliographies and is Latin for "and others." *Etcetera* is Latin for "and so forth." Like all abbreviations, *et al.* and *etc.* are generally not used in formal writing, except that *et al.* is acceptable in the context of a citation to a source.

etc. Do not use *etc.* in formal writing. Use *and so forth* instead. Or, preferably, be as specific as necessary to eliminate the phrase.

everybody, every body Use *everybody* when you mean "everyone." Use *every body* when you are using *body* as a distinct word modified by *every,* as in *Is every body of water in Canada contaminated by acid rain?*

every day, everyday Use *everyday* when your sentence requires an adjective meaning "common" or "daily," as in *Availability of water was an everyday problem in ancient Egypt.* Use *every day* when you are using the word *day* and modifying it with the adjective *every,* as in *Enrico went to the art gallery every day.*

everywheres Do not use *everywheres* in formal writing. Use *everywhere* instead.

except for the fact that In formal writing prefer the less wordy *except that.*

except, accept See *accept, except.*

explicit, implicit Use *explicit* when you mean "stated outright," as in *The Supreme Court rules on issues that are not explicit in the Constitution.* Use *implicit* when you mean "implied," as in *Her respect for the constitution was implicit in her remarks.*

farther, further Use *farther* when you are referring to distance, as in *He was able to run farther after eating carbohydrates.* Use *further* when you are referring to something that cannot be measured, such as *Further negotiations are needed between the central government and the people of Azerbaijan.*

fewer, less Use *fewer* when you are referring to items that can be counted, as in *There are fewer savings accounts at the branch office this year.* Use *less* when you are referring to things that cannot be counted, as in *The East German people have less confidence in the concept of unification than they had one year ago.* (See 11e.)

figure See *calculate, figure, reckon.*

fixing to Do not use *fixing to* in formal writing. Use *intend to* instead.

C

gl/us

former, latter   Use *former* and *latter* only when you are referring to two things. In that case, the former is the first thing, and the latter is the second. If you are referring to more than two things, use *first* for the first and *last* for the last.

get   Do not overuse *get* in formal writing. Prefer more precise words. For example, instead of *get better*, write *improve*; instead of *get*, write *receive, catch,* or *become*; instead of *get done*, write *finish* or *end*.

good and   Do not use *good and* in formal writing. Use *very* or, preferably, a more precise modifier instead.

good, well   Use *good* as an adjective, as in *Astaire gave a good performance, but not one of his best.* Use *well* as an adverb, as in *He danced well.* You can also use *well* as an adjective when you refer to good health, as in *She felt well* or *She is well today.* (See 11d.)

gone, went   Use *gone* when your sentence requires the past participle of to go, as in *They had gone there several times.* Use *went* when your sentence requires the past tense of to go, as in *They went to the theater Friday.*

got, have; has/have go to   Do not use *got* in place of *have* in formal writing. For example, rewrite a sentence such as *I got to lose weight* to read *I have to [or I must] lose weight.*

half   When you refer to half of something in formal writing, use *a half* or *one-half,* but do not use *a half a.* For example, rewrite a sentence such as *He had a half a sandwich for dinner* to read *He had a half sandwich for dinner.*

had better, better; had best, best   See *better, had better.*

had ought   Do not use *had ought* in formal writing. Use *ought* by itself instead.

hanged, hung   Use *hanged* for the action of hanging a person, as in *The innocent man was hanged by an angry mob.* Use *hung* for all other meanings, such as *The clothes were hung on the line* and *The chandelier hung from a golden rope.* (See 9b.)

he, she; he/she; his, her; his/her; him, her; him/her   When you are using a pronoun to refer back to a noun that could be either masculine or feminine, you might use *he or she* in order to avoid language that is now considered sexist. For example, instead of writing *A doctor must be constantly alert; he cannot make a single mistake* to refer generally to doctors, you could write *A doctor must be constantly alert; he or she cannot make a single mistake.* Or you could recast the sentence in the plural to avoid this problem: *Doctors must be constantly alert; they cannot make a single mistake.* (See 10c and 21g for specific strategies on avoiding gender-offensive pronoun references.)

herself, himself, myself, yourself   Use pronouns ending in *-self* when the pronouns refer to a noun that they intensify, as in *The teacher himself could not pass the test.* Do not use pronouns ending in *-self* to take the place of subjective- or objective-case pronouns. Instead of writing, for example, *Joan and myself are good friends,* write *Joan and I are good friends.* (See 7a.)

gl/us

himself   See *herself, himself, myself, yourself.*

his/her   See *he/she.*

hisself   Do not use *hisself* in formal writing. In a context such as *He hisself organized the picnic*, recast the sentence to read *He himself organized the picnic.*

hopefully   Use *hopefully* when you mean "with hope," as in *Relatives watched hopefully as the first miners emerged after the fire.* Avoid using *hopefully* as a modifier for an entire clause or to convey any other meaning. For example, avoid *Hopefully, a cure for leukemia is not far away.*

hung, hanged   See *hanged, hung.*

if, whether   Use *if* to begin a subordinate clause when a stated or implied result follows, as in *If the court rules against the cigarette manufacturers, [then] thousands of lawsuits could follow.* Use *whether* when you are expressing an alternative, as in *Economists do not know whether the dollar will rebound or fall against the strength of the yen.*

gl/us

illicit, elicit   See *elicit, illicit.*

illusion, allusion   See *allusion, illusion.*

immigrate   See *emigrate, immigrate, migrate.*

impact   Use *impact* when you are referring to a forceful collision, as in *The impact of the cars was so great that one was flattened.* Do not use *impact* as a verb meaning "to have an effect on." Instead of writing *Each of us can positively impact waste reduction efforts*, write *Each of use can reduce waste.*

implicit, explicit   See *explicit, implicit.*

imply, infer   Use *imply* when you mean "to suggest without directly stating," as in *The doctor implied that being overweight was the main cause of my problem.* Use *infer* when you mean "to find the meaning of something," as in *I inferred from her lecture that drinking more than two cups of coffee a day was a health risk.*

in regards to   Do not use *in regards to* in formal writing. Generally, you can substitute *about* for *in regards to.*

in, into   Use *in* when you are referring to location or condition. Use *into* to refer to a change in location, such as *The famous portrait shows a man going into a palace.* (See 23a.) In formal writing, do not use *into* for "interested in." For example, avoid a statement such as *I am into repairing engines.*

incredible, incredulous   Use *incredible* to mean "unbelievable," as in *Some of Houdini's exploits seem incredible to those who did not witness them.* Use *incredulous* to mean "unbelieving," as in *Many inlanders were incredulous when they heard tales of white people capturing men, women, and children who lived on the coast.*

individual, person, party Use *individual* when you are referring to a single person and when your purpose is to stress that the person is unique, as in *Curie was a tireless and brilliant individual.* Use *party* when you mean a group, as in *The party of eight at the next table disturbed our conversation and ruined our evening.* The word *party* is also correctly used in legal documents referring to a single person. Use *person* for other meanings.

infer, imply See *imply, infer.*

inside of, outside of Use *inside* and *outside,* without *of,* when you are referring to location, as in *The roller blades were stored inside the garage.* In formal writing, do not use *inside of* to replace *within* in an expression of time. For example, avoid a sentence such as *I'll have that report inside of an hour.*

insure, assure, ensure See *assure, ensure, insure.*

irregardless, regardless Do not use *irregardless.* Use *regardless* instead.

is when, is where Do not use *is when* and *is where* when you are defining something. Instead of writing *Dinner time is when my family relaxes,* write *At dinner time, my family relaxes.*

its, it's Use *its* when your sentence requires a possessive pronoun, as in *Its leaves are actually long, slender blades.* Use *it's* only when you mean "it is." (See 23a.)

-ize Do not use the suffix *-ize* to turn a noun into a verb in formal writing. For example, instead of writing *He is finalizing his draft,* write *He is finishing his draft* or *He is working on his final draft.*

kind of, sort of Do not use these phrases as adjectives in formal writing. Instead, use *rather* or *somewhat.*

kind, sort, type Do not precede the singular words *kind, sort,* and *type* with the plural word *these.* Use *this* instead. Also, prefer more specific words than *kind, sort,* and *type.* (See 17a.)

later, latter Use *later* when you refer to time, as in *I will go to the concert later.* Use *latter* when you refer to the second of two things, as in *The latter of the two dates is better for my schedule.* (See also *former, latter.*)

latter, former See *former, latter.*

lay, lie Use *lay* when you mean "to put" or "to place," as in *She lays the present on the table.* Use *lie* when you mean "recline," as in *She lies awake at night* or when you mean "is situated," as in *The city lies between a desert and a mountain range.* Also, remember that *lay* is a transitive verb that takes a direct object. (See 9d.)

learn, teach Do not use *learn* to mean "teach." For example, rewrite a sentence such as *Ms. Chin learned us Algebra* to read *Ms. Chin taught us Algebra.*

leave, let   Use *leave* to mean "depart." Use *let* to mean "allow." You can use either *leave* or *let* when the word is followed by *alone*, as in *Leave her alone* or *Let him alone.*

less, fewer   See *fewer, less.*

liable   See *apt, liable, likely.*

lie, lay   See *lay, lie.*

like, as   See *as, like.*

like, such as   Use *like* to make a comparison, as in *Verbena is like ageratum in size and color.* Use *such as* when you are giving examples, as in *Many small flowers, such as verbena, ageratum, and alyssum, can be combined to create decorative borders and edgings.*

likely   See *apt, liable, likely.*

C

gl/us

lose, loose   Use *lose* as a verb meaning "to misplace" or "to fail to win." Use *loose* as an adjective meaning "not tight" or "unfastened." You can also use *loose* as a verb meaning "to let loose," as in *They loosed the enraged bull when the matador entered the ring.* (See 23a.)

lots, lots of   Do not use *lots* or *lots of* in formal writing. Use *many, very many, much,* or choose a more precise word instead.

man, mankind   Do not use *man* and *mankind* to refer to all people in general. Instead, consider using *people, men and women, humans,* or *humankind.* (See 21g.)

may be, maybe   Use *maybe* to mean "perhaps." Use *may be* as a verb (or auxiliary verb), as in *William may be visiting tomorrow.* (See 23a.)

may, can   See *can, may.*

may of   See *could of, would of, should of, might of, may of, must of.*

media   Use a plural verb with *media*, as in *The media are often credited with helping the consumer win cases against large companies. Medium* is the singular form.

might of   See *could of, would of, should of, might of, may of, must of.*

migrate   See *emigrate, immigrate, migrate.*

moral, morale   Use *moral* when you mean "an object lesson" or "knowing right from wrong." *What is the moral to the story?* Use *morale* when you mean "outlook" or "attitude." *The team's morale was high.* (See 23a.)

Ms.   Use *Ms.* to refer to a woman when a title is required and when you either know that she prefers this title or you do not know her marital status. An invented title, *Ms.* was intended to address the issue of discrimination or judgment based on marital status. In research writing, use last names alone, without any title, as in *Jenkins recommends* . . . . In this case, do not use a title for either a man or a woman.

must of   See *could of, would of, should of, might of, may of, must of.*

myself   See *herself, himself, myself, yourself.*

nor, or   Use *nor* and *or* to suggest a choice. Use *nor* when the choice is negative; use *or* when the choice is positive. (See 7f.)

not but, not hardly, not scarcely   Do not use *not* to precede *hardly, scarcely,* and *but* in formal writing. Because *but, hardly,* and *scarcely* already carry the meaning of a negative, it is not necessary or correct to add another negative.

nothing like, nowhere near   Do not use *nothing like* and *nowhere near* in formal writing. Instead, use *not nearly.*

nowheres   Do not use *nowheres* in formal writing. Use *nowhere* instead.

number, amount   See *amount, number.*

off of   Do not use *off of* in formal writing. Use *off* or *from* alone instead, as in *She jumped off the bridge* or *He leaped from the rooftop.*

Ok, okay, O.K.   Do not use *Ok, okay,* or *O.K.* in formal writing as a substitute for *acceptable.*

on account of   Do not use this as a substitute for *because.* Use *because* instead.

on, upon   Use *on* instead of *upon* in formal writing.

or, nor   See *nor, or.*

outside of, inside of   See *inside of, outside of.*

party, individual, person   See *individual, person, party.*

people, persons   Use *people* to refer to a general group, as in *The people will make their voices heard.* Use *persons* to refer to a (usually small) collection of individuals, as in *The persons we interviewed were nearly unanimous in their opinion.*

per   Do not use *per* in formal writing. For example, instead of writing *The package was sent per your instructions,* it is better to write *The package was sent according to your instructions. Per* is acceptable in technical writing or when used with data and prices, as in *Charging $75 per hour, the consultant earned a handsome salary.*

percent (per cent), percentage   Use *percent* (or *per cent*) with a specific number. Use *percentage* with specific descriptive words and phrases, such as *A small percentage of the group did not eat meat.* Do not use *percentage* as a substitute for *part;*

C

gl/us

for example, rewrite a sentence such as *A percentage of my diet consists of complex carbohydrates* to read *Part of my diet consists of complex carbohydrates.*

person, party, individual   See *individual, person, party.*

plenty   Do not use *plenty* as a substitute for *quite* or *very*. For example, instead of writing *The Confederate troops were plenty hungry during the winter of 1864*, write *The Confederate troops were hungry [or starving] during the winter of 1864.*

plus   Avoid using *plus* as a conjunction joining independent clauses or as a conjunctive adverb. For example, rewrite *Picasso used color in a new way plus he experimented with shape; plus, he brought new meaning to ideas about abstract painting* to read *Picasso used color in a new way and he experimented with shape; moreover, he brought new meaning to ideas about abstract painting.* It is acceptable to use *plus* when you need an expression meaning "in addition to," as in *The costs of day care, plus the costs of feeding and clothing the child, weighed heavily on the single parent's budget.*

practicable, practical   Use *practicable* when you mean "capable of putting into practice," as in *Although it seemed logical, the plan for saving the zoo was very expensive and turned out not to be practicable.* Use *practical* when you mean "sensible," as in *Lincoln was a practical young man who studied hard, paid his debts, and dealt with people honestly.*

precede, proceed   Use *precede* when you mean "come before," as in *The opening remarks precede the speech.* Use *proceed* when you mean "go forward," as in *The motorists proceeded with caution.*

pretty   Do not use *pretty*, as in *pretty close*, to mean "somewhat" or "quite" in formal writing. Use *somewhat, rather*, or *quite* instead.

previous to, prior to   Avoid these wordy expressions. Use *before* instead.

principal, principle   Use *principal* when you refer to a school administrator or an amount of money. Use *principle* when you are referring to a law, conviction, or fundamental truth. You can also use *principal* as an adjective meaning "major" or "most important," as in *The principal players in the decision were Sue Marks and Tom Cohen.*

quotation, quote   Use *quotation* when your sentence requires a noun, as in *The quotation from Nobel laureate Joseph Goldstein was used to lend credence to the theory.* Use *quote* when your sentence requires a verb, as in *She asked Goldstein whether she could quote him.*

raise, rise   Use *raise* when you mean "to lift." Use *rise* when you mean "to get up." To help you understand the difference, remember that *raise* is transitive and takes a direct object; *rise* is intransitive. (See 9d.)

rarely ever   Do not use *rarely ever* in formal writing. Use *rarely* or *hardly ever* instead.

real, really   Use *real* as an adjective and use *really* as an adverb.

C

gl/us

reason is because   Do not use *reason is because* in formal writing. Rewrite your sentence to say, for example, *The real reason that the bomb was dropped was to end the war quickly* or *The bomb was dropped because Truman wanted to prevent Soviet influence in the Far Eastern settlement.*

reckon   See *calculate, figure, reckon.*

regarding, in regard to, with regard to   In formal writing that is not legal in nature, use *about* or *concerning* instead of these terms.

regardless, irregardless   See *irregardless, regardless.*

respectfully, respectively   Use *respectfully* when you mean "with respect," as in *He respectfully submitted his grievances.* Use *respectively* when you mean "in the given order," as in *The chief of police, the director of the department of public works, and the director of parks and recreation, respectively, submitted their ideas for budget cuts.*

right   Do not use *right* as an intensifier in formal writing. For example, instead of writing that *The farmer was right tired after milking the cows,* write *The farmer was tired [or exhausted] after milking the cows.*

rise, raise   See *raise, rise.*

seen   Do not use *seen* without an auxiliary such as *have, has,* or *had.* For example, rewrite a sentence such as *I seen the film* to read *I have seen the film.*

set, sit   Use *set* when you mean "to place." *Set* is a transitive verb that requires an object, as in *I set the book on the table.* Do not use *set* to mean "to sit" in formal writing. (See 9d.)

shall, will   Use *shall* instead of *will* for questions that contain the first person in extremely formal writing, as in *Shall we attend the meeting?* In all other cases, use *will.*

should of   See *could of, would of, should of, might of, may of, must of.*

should, would   Use *should* when you are referring to an obligation or a condition, as in *The governor's mansion should be restored.* Use *would* when you are referring to a wish, as in *I would like to see it repainted in its original colors.*

sit, set   See *set, sit.*

so   Do not use *so* in formal writing to mean "very" or "extremely," as in *He is so entertaining.* Use *very, extremely,* or, preferably, a more specific intensifier instead. Or follow *so* with an explanation preceded by *that,* as in *The reaction to the Freedom Riders was so violent that Robert F. Kennedy ordered a military escort.*

some   Do not use *some* to mean either "remarkable" or "somewhat" in formal writing. For example, rewrite a sentence such as *Babe Ruth was some hitter* to read *Babe Ruth was a remarkable hitter,* or use another more precise adjective to modify *hitter.* Also, rewrite a sentence such as *Wright's mother worried some about the kinds of building blocks her young child used* to read *Wright's mother worried a bit [or was somewhat worried about] the kinds of building blocks her young child used.*

somebody, some body; someone, some one   Use the indefinite pronouns *somebody* and *someone* when referring to a person, such as *There is someone I admire.* Use *some body* and *some one* when the adjective *some* modifies the noun *body* or *one,* as in *We will find the answer in some body of information.*

sometime, sometimes, some time   Use *sometime* when you mean "an indefinite, later time." Use *sometimes* when you mean "occasionally" or "from time to time." Use *some time* when *some* functions as an adjective modifying *time,* as in *His eyes required some time to adjust to the darkened room.*

sort   See *kind, sort, type.*

specially, especially   See *especially, specially.*

stationary, stationery   Use *stationary* to mean "standing still." Use *stationery* to mean "writing paper."

such   Do not use *such* to mean "very" or "extremely" unless *such* is followed by *that.* For example, rewrite a sentence such as *It had such boring lyrics* to read *It had extremely boring lyrics* or *It had <u>such</u> boring lyrics <u>that</u> I almost fell asleep half way through the song.*

such as, like   See *like, such as.*

supposed to, used to   Do not use *suppose to* or *use to* in formal writing. Use *supposed to* or *used to* instead.

sure and, sure to; try and, try to   Do not use *sure and* and *try and* in formal writing. Instead, use *sure to* and *try to.* For example, rewrite the sentence *Be sure and bring your computer* to read *Be sure to bring your computer.*

sure, surely   Use *surely* instead of *sure* when your sentence requires an adverb. For example, rewrite a sentence such as *Robert Fulton was sure a genius* to read *Robert Fulton was surely [or certainly] a genius.*

take, bring   See *bring, take.*

than, as   See *as, than.*

than, then   Use *than* when you mean "as compared with," as in *The violin is smaller than the cello.* Use *then* when you are stating a sequence of events, as in *First, he learned how to play the violin. Then he learned to play the cello.* Also use *then* when you mean "at that time" or "therefore." (See 23a.)

that there   See *this here, these here, that there, them there.*

C

gl/us

that, which Use *that* or *which* in an essential (or restrictive) clause, or a clause that is necessary to the meaning of the sentence, as in *This is the book that explains Locke's philosophy.* Use *which* in a nonessential (nonrestrictive) clause, or one that is not necessary to the meaning of the sentence, as in *My library just acquired Smith's book on Locke, which is not always easy to find.* (See 14e.)

their, there, they're Use *their* as a possessive pronoun, as in *Their father prevented William and Henry James from being under the control of any one teacher for more than a year.* Use *there* to refer to a place, as the opposite of *here.* Use *they're* to mean "they are."

theirselves Do not use *theirselves* in formal writing. Rewrite a sentence such as *They treated theirselves to ice cream* to read *They treated themselves to ice cream.*

them there See *this here, these here, that there, them there.*

then, than See *than, then.*

these here See *this here, these here, that there, them there.*

these kind See *kind, sort, type.*

this here, these here, that there, them there Do not use *this here, these here, that there,* and *them there* in formal writing. Use *this, that, these,* and *those* instead.

thru Do not use *thru* in formal writing. Use *through* instead.

thusly Do not use *thusly* in formal writing. Use *thus* instead. (*Thus,* which is already an adverb, does not need an *-ly* ending.)

till, until, 'til Do not use *'til* or *till* in formal writing. Prefer *until.*

to, too, two Use *to* as a preposition meaning "toward"; use *too* to mean "also"; and use *two* as a number. (See 23a.)

toward, towards Use *toward* instead of *towards* in formal writing. *Towards* is the British form.

try and, try to See *sure and, sure to; try and, try to.*

type of Do not use *type* in formal writing when you mean "type of." For example, rewrite a sentence such as *He is an anxious type person* to read *He is an anxious type of person.* (See also *kind, sort, type.*)

uninterested, disinterested See *disinterested, uninterested.*

unique Do not modify *unique* in formal writing. Because *unique* is an absolute, you should not write, for example, *most unique* or *very unique.*

until See *'til, till, until.*

use, utilize When you need a word that means "use," prefer *use*. *Utilize* is a less direct choice with the same meaning. (See 17a.)

used to See *supposed to, used to*.

very Avoid using *very* as an intensifier. Sometimes you will want to replace more than one word in order to eliminate *very*. For example, in the sentence *It was a very nice painting*, you could substitute more precise language, such as *It was a colorful [or provocative or highly abstract] painting*. (See 17a.)

wait for, wait on Unless you are referring to waiting on tables, use *wait for* instead of *wait on* in formal writing. For example, rewrite *We grew tired as we waited on Sarah* to read *We grew tired as we waited for Sarah*.

ways Do not use *ways* in formal writing to mean "way." Use *way* instead.

well, good See *good, well*.

whether, if See *if, whether*.

where at See *at*.

which, that See *that, which*.

which, who Use *which* when you are referring to things. Use *who* when you are referring to people.

who's, whose Do not use *who's* in formal writing. Use *who is* instead. Use *whose* to show possession, as in *Whose computer did you use?* (See 8f.)

who, whom Use *who* when a sentence requires a subject pronoun, as in *Who can answer this question?* Use *whom* when a sentence requires an object pronoun, as in *Whom did you invite?* (See 8f.)

will, shall See *shall, will*.

-wise Do not attach the suffice *-wise* to nouns or adjectives to turn them into adverbs in formal writing. For example, instead of writing *I am not doing well grade-wise*, you could recast the sentence to read *My grades are falling* or *My grades are low*.

would of See *could of, would of, should of, might of, may of, must of*.

would, should See *should, would*.

your, you're Do not use *you're* in formal writing. Use *you are* instead. Use *your* to show possession, as in *Your CD player is broken*. (See 8f.)

yourself See *herself, himself, myself, yourself*.

C

gl/us

Glossary of Terms: Grammar and Composition

abbreviation The shortened form of a word, usually followed by a period.

absolute phrase See *phrase*.

abstract expression An expression that refers to broad categories or ideas (*evil, friendship, love*).

abstract noun See *noun*.

acronym The uppercase, pronounceable abbreviation of a proper noun—a person, organization, government agency, or country. Periods are not used with acronyms (*ARCO, WAVES*). (See 31c.)

active voice See *voice*.

adjective A word that modifies or describes a noun, pronoun, or group of words functioning as a noun. Adjectives answer the questions: which, what kind, and how many. A single-word adjective is usually placed before the word it modifies. Pure adjectives are not derived from other words. (See 7a-5; chapter 11).

adjective clause See *clause*.

adjective forms Adjectives change form to express comparative relationships. The **positive form** of an adjective is its base form. The **comparative form** is used to express a relationship between two elements. The **superlative form** is used to express a relationship between three or more elements. Most single-syllable adjectives and many two-syllable adjectives show comparisons with the suffix *-er* (tall*er*) and superlatives with the suffix *-est* (tall*est*). Adjectives of three or more syllables change to the comparative and superlative forms with the words *more* and *most*, respectively (*more beautiful, most beautiful*). Negative comparisons are formed by placing the words *less* and *least* before the positive form (*less interesting, least interesting*). (See 11e.)

adverb A word that modifies a verb, an adjective, another adverb, or an entire sentence. Adverbs describe, define, or otherwise limit the words they modify, answering the questions when, how, where, how often, to what extent, and to what degree. Adverbs (as words, phrases, or clauses) can appear in different places in a sentence, depending on the rhythm the writer wants to achieve. Most adverbs are formed by adding the suffix *-ly* to an adjective. (See 7a-6; chapter 11.)

adverb clause   See *clause.*

adverb forms   The change of form that adverbs undergo to express comparative relationships. The **positive form** of an adverb is its base form. The **comparative form** is used to express a relationship between two elements. The **superlative form** is used to express a relationship among three or more elements. Most single-syllable adverbs show comparisons with the suffix *-er* (*nearer*) and superlatives with the suffix *-est* (*nearest*). Adverbs of two or more syllables change to comparative and superlative forms with *more* and *most,* respectively (*more beautifully, most beautifully*). Negative comparisons are formed by placing the words *less* and *least* before the positive form (*less strangely, least strangely*). (See 11e.)

adverbial conjunctions   See *conjunctive adverbs.*

agreement   The grammatical relationship between a subject and a verb, and a pronoun and its antecedent. If one element in these pairs is changed, the other must also be changed. Subjects and verbs must agree in number and person; pronouns and antecedents must agree in number, person, and gender. (See chapter 10.)

analogy   A figure of speech that makes a comparison between two apparently unrelated people, objects, conditions, or events in order to clarify a process or a difficult concept. The unknown entity is explained in terms of the more familiar entity. (See 5e-2; 6d-2; 21f-1.)

analysis   A close, careful reading of a text in which parts are studied to determine how the text as a whole functions. In a written analysis, in most instances the author is obliged to support his or her interpretation with direct evidence to a text. (See 37c-1.)

antecedent   A noun (or occasionally a pronoun) that a pronoun refers to and renames. A pronoun and its antecedent must agree in number, person, and gender. (See 10b; chapter 14.)

antonym   A word whose denotation (dictionary meaning) is opposite that of another word.

apostrophe   A punctuation mark used to show possession, mark the omission of letters or numbers, and mark plural forms. (See chapter 27.)

appositive   A word or phrase that describes, identifies, or renames a noun in a sentence. (See 8e-2.)

appositive phrase   See *phrase.*

article   The words *a, an,* or *the.* The **indefinite articles,** *a* or *an,* introduce a generalized noun. *A* appears before nouns beginning with a consonant; *an* is placed before nouns beginning with a vowel or an unpronounced *h.* The **definite article,** *the,* denotes a specific noun. Also called *determiners.*

D

gl/gr

assumption   A core belief, often unstated, that shapes the way people perceive the world. A **descriptive assumption** gives an account about how the world in fact works. A **definitional assumption** provides definitions of key terms on which a presentation rests. A **value assumption** presents beliefs about what the world ought to be and the way people ought to behave. (See 1c-2.)

audience   The person or people who will be reading a piece of writing. Writing that takes a particular audience's needs and experience into consideration is most effective.

auxiliary verb   The verbs *be, will, can, have, do, shall,* or *may,* combined with the base form of another verb, or its present or past participle. Such auxiliary verbs are used to establish tense, mood, and voice in a sentence. Also called *helping verbs.* (See 7a-3; chapter 9.)

base form   The infinitive form of a verb (*to be, to go*) from which all changes are made. Also called the *dictionary form.*

bibliography   The list of sources used in writing a paper. A **working bibliography** includes all of the sources located in researching a paper. A **final bibliography** consists of only those sources used in the actual writing of a paper. In Modern Language Association (MLA) format, the bibliography is titled *Works Cited;* in American Psychological Association (APA) format, it is called *References;* and in Council of Biology Editors (CBE) format it is called *Literature Cited.* (See 34b; chapter 36.)

D

gl/gr

brackets   Punctuation marks used to clarify or insert remarks into quoted material. (See 29d.)

brainstorming   A technique of idea generation in which the writer quickly jots down words or phrases related to a broad subject. When the time limit (five or ten minutes) is reached, related items are grouped; groupings with the greatest number of items indicate potential topics for composition. (See 3d-2.)

buzzwords   Vague, often abstract expressions that sound as if they have meaning, but do not contribute anything of substance to a sentence. (See 17a-4.)

case   The change in form of a noun or pronoun, depending on its function in a sentence. The three cases are the subjective, objective and possessive forms. Nouns and indefinite pronouns take all three cases, but change form only when they show possession (with the addition of an apostrophe and *s*). Pronouns change form in all three cases. The **subjective case** is used when a pronoun functions as a subject, subject complement, or as an appositive that renames a subject. The **objective case** is used when a pronoun functions as the object of a preposition, as the object or indirect object of a verb, as the object of a verbal, or as the subject of an infinitive. The **possessive case** of a noun or pronoun indicates possession or ownership. (See chapter 8.)

chronological arrangement   A method of organizing a paper in which the writing begins at one point in time and proceeds in sequence, forward or backward, to some other point. (See 3g-2; 5d-1.)

clause A grouping of words that has a subject and a predicate. An **independent clause** (or *main clause*) is a core statement that can stand alone as a sentence. A **dependent clause** (or *subordinate clause*) cannot stand alone as a sentence; it is joined to an independent clause by either a subordinate conjunction or a relative pronoun. There are four types of dependent clauses. **Adverb clauses** begin with subordinate conjunctions (*when, because, although*) and modify verbs, adjectives, and other adverbs. **Adjective clauses** begin with relative pronouns (*which, that, who, whom, whose*) and modify nouns or pronouns. **Noun clauses** are introduced by pronouns (*which, whichever, who, whoever, whom, whomever,* or *whose*) and the words *how, when, why, where, whether,* or *whatever* and function as subjects, objects, complements, or appositives. **Elliptical clauses** have an omitted word or words (often relative pronouns or the logically parallel second parts of comparisons), but the sense of the sentence remains clear. (See 7e; 16e.)

cliché A trite expression that has lost its impact. (See 21f-3.)

coherence The clarity of the relationship between one unit of meaning and another. (See 4e-2.)

collective noun See *noun.*

colloquial Informal, conversational language. (See 21e-3.)

colon A punctuation mark (:) generally used to make an announcement. In formal writing, the colon follows only a complete independent clause and introduces a word, phrase, sentence, or group of sentences. (See 29a.)

comma A punctuation mark (,) used to signal that some element, some word or cluster of related words, is being set off from a main clause for a reason. (See chapter 25.)

comma splice The incorrect use of a comma to mark the boundary between two independent clauses. (See chapter 13; 25f-1.)

common noun See *noun.*

comparative form See *adjective forms, adverb forms.*

complement A word or group of words that completes the meaning of a subject or direct object by renaming it or describing it. A **subject complement** follows a linking verb and can be a noun, pronoun, adjective, or group of words substituting for an adjective or noun. An **object complement** typically follows verbs such as *appoint, call, choose, make,* or *show* and can be a noun, adjective, or group of words substituting for a noun or adjective.

complete predicate See *predicate.*

complete subject See *subject.*

complex sentence See *sentence.*

compound adjective Two or more words that are combined to modify a given noun. Often, when a compound adjective precedes a noun it is hyphenated to prevent misreading; when it follows the noun it modifies, it does not need hyphenation. (See 32a-1; 32a-3.)

compound-complex sentence   See *sentence*.

compound noun   Two or more words that are combined to function as a single noun. Hyphens are used when the first word of the compound could be read alone as a noun (*cross-reference*). (See 32a-2.)

compound predicate   Two or more verbs and their objects and modifiers that are joined with a coordinate conjunction to form a single predicate.

compound sentence   See *sentence*.

compound subject   Two or more nouns or pronouns and their modifiers that function as a single subject.

compound verb   Two or more verbs that are combined to function as a single verb. Hyphens are used when the first word of the compound could be read alone as a verb (*shrink-wrap*). (See 32a-2.)

compound words   Nouns, adjectives, or prepositions created when two or more words are brought together to form a distinctive meaning and to function grammatically as a single word. (See 32a.)

concrete expression   A vivid, detailed expression (*a throbbing headache*).

concrete noun   See *noun*.

conjunction   A word that joins sentence elements or entire sentences by establishing a coordinate or equal relationship among combined parts, or by establishing a subordinate or unequal relationship. **Coordinate conjunctions** (*and, but, or, nor, for, so, yet*) join complete sentences or parallel elements from two or more sentences into a single sentence and express specific logical relationships between these elements. **Correlative conjunctions** (*both/and, neither/nor, either/or, not only/but also*) are pairs of coordinate conjunctions that place extra emphasis on the relationship between the parts of the coordinated construction. The parts of the sentence joined by correlative conjunctions must be grammatically parallel. **Subordinate conjunctions** (*when, while, although, because, if, since, whereas*) connect dependent clauses to independent clauses. (See 7a-9; 18b; 19a-1, 2.)

conjunctive adverb   An adverb (such as *however, therefore, consequently, otherwise,* or *indeed*) used to create a compound sentence in which the independent clauses that are joined share a logically balanced emphasis. Also called *adverbial conjunction*. (See 7a-9; 19a-3; 26b.)

connotation   The implications, associations, and nuances of a word's meaning. (See 21a.)

coordinate adjectives   Two or more adjectives in a series, whose order can be reversed without affecting the meaning of the noun being modified. Coordinate adjectives are linked by a comma or by a coordinate conjunction (*an intelligent, engaging speaker*). (See 25c-2.)

coordinate conjunction See *conjunction*.

coordination The combining of sentence elements by the use of coordinate and correlative conjunctions and conjunctive adverbs. Elements in a coordinate relationship share equal grammatical status and equal emphasis. (See 19a; 20b-1.)

correlative conjunction See *conjunction*.

count noun See *noun*.

cues Words and phrases that remind readers as they move from sentence to sentence that (1) they continue to read about the same topic and (2) ideas are unfolding logically. Four types of cues are pronouns, repetition, parallel structures, and transitions. (See 5d-2.)

cut To delete sentences because they are off the point or because they give too much attention to a subordinate point. (See 4f.)

dangling modifier A word, phrase, or clause whose referent in a sentence is not clearly apparent. (See 15h.)

dash A punctuation mark (—) used to set off and give emphasis to brief or lengthy modifiers, appositives, repeating structures, and interruptions in dialogue. (See 29b.)

D

gl/gr

dead metaphor A metaphor that has been used so much it has become an ordinary word.

declarative sentence See *sentence*.

definitional assumption See *assumption*.

demonstrative pronoun See *pronoun*.

denotation The dictionary meaning of a word. (See 21a.)

dependent clause See *clause*. Also called *subordinate clause*.

descriptive assumption See *assumption*.

determiner See *article*.

dialect Expressions specific to certain social or ethnic groups as well as regional groups within a country. (See 21e-2.)

diction A writer's choice of words. (See chapter 21.)

dictionary form See *base form*.

direct discourse The exact recreation, using quotation marks, of words spoken or written by a person. Also called *direct quotation*. (See 28a-1; 34d.)

direct object See *object*.

direct quotation See *direct discourse*.

documentation The credit given to sources used in a paper, including the author, title of the work, city, name of publisher, and date of publication. There are different systems of documentation for various disciplines; three frequently used systems include the Modern Language Association (MLA), American Psychological Association (APA), and the Council of Biology Editors (CBE) systems of documentation. (See chapter 36.)

double comparative An incorrect method of showing the comparative form of an adverb or adjective by adding both the suffix *-er* to the word and placing the word *more* before the adverb or adjective. Only one form should be used. (See 11f.)

double negative An incorrect method of negation in which two negative modifiers are used in the same sentence. Only one negative should be used. (See 11f.)

double superlative An incorrect method of showing the superlative form of an adverb or adjective by adding both the suffix *-est* to the word and placing the word *most* before the adverb or adjective. Only one form should be used. (See 11f.)

drafting The stage in the composition process in which the writer generates the first form of a paper from a working thesis or outline. (See 4a, b, c, h; 35e.)

editing The stage in the composition process in which the writer examines and, if necessary, alters the work's style, grammar, punctuation, and word choice. (See 4i; 35f.)

ellipses Punctuation marks (. . .) consisting of three spaced periods that indicate the writer has deleted either words or entire sentences from a passage being quoted. (See 29e.)

elliptical clause See *clause.*

elliptical construction A shortened sentence in which certain words have been omitted deliberately in order to streamline communication. (See 16g.)

essential modifier A word, phrase, or clause that provides information crucial for identifying a noun; this type of modifier appears in its sentence without commas. The relative pronoun *that* is only used in essential clauses (*who* or *which* may also be used). Also called a *restrictive modifier.* (See 14e-2; 25d-2.)

etymology The study of the history of words. (See 22c.)

euphemism A polite rewording of a term that the writer feels will offend readers.

euphony The pleasing sound produced by certain word combinations.

exclamation point A punctuation mark (!) used to indicate an emphatic statement or command. (See 24c.)

exclamatory sentence See *sentence.*

expletive A word that fills the space left in a sentence that has been rearranged. The words *it* and *there* are expletives (filler words without meaning of their own) when used with the verb *to be* in sentences with a delayed subject.

faulty parallelism An error in a sentence where elements that should be grammatically equivalent are not. Faulty parallelism is indicated in a sentence when the use of a coordinate conjunction makes part of the sentence sound out of place or illogical. (See 18a.)

faulty predication An error in a sentence indicated when the predicate part of a sentence does not logically complete its subject. Faulty predication often involves a form of the linking verb *to be.*

figure of speech A carefully controlled comparison that intensifies meaning. See *simile, analogy,* and *metaphor.*

final thesis See *thesis.*

first person See *person.*

formal English The acknowledged standard of correct English. (See 21e.)

formal writing The writing of professional and academic worlds. Formal writing is precise and concise, avoids colloquial expressions, is thorough in content, and is highly structured. (See 3c-5.)

freewriting A technique of idea generation in which the writer chooses a broad area of interest and writes for a predetermined amount of time or in a prescribed number of pages, without pausing to organize or analyze thoughts. In *focused freewriting,* the same process is followed, but a specific topic is prescribed. (See 3d-3.)

D

gl/gr

fused sentence The joining of two independent clauses without a coordinate conjunction or proper punctuation. Also called a *run-on sentence.* (See chapter 13.)

future perfect progressive tense See *tense.*

future perfect tense See *tense.*

future progressive tense See *tense.*

gender The labeling of nouns or pronouns as masculine, feminine, or neuter.

generalization A statement about a group that applies to individual members of that group. (See 6d-2.)

gerund The *-ing* form of a verb without its helping verbs; gerunds function as nouns.

gerund phrase See *phrase.*

helping verbs See *verbs.*

historical present tense The present tense form used when referring to actions in an already existing work (a book, a movie). (See 9e-1.)

homonyms Words that sound alike or are pronounced alike but that have different spellings and meanings. (See 23a-1.)

hyphen A punctuation mark (-) used to join compound words and to divide words at the end of lines.

hypothesis A carefully stated prediction.

idiom A grouping of words, one of which is usually a preposition, whose meaning may or may not be apparent based solely on simple dictionary definitions. The grammar of idioms is often a matter of customary usage and is often difficult to explain. (See 21b-2.)

imperative mood See *mood.*

imperative sentence See *sentence.*

indefinite pronoun See *pronoun.*

independent clause See *clause.*

indicative mood See *mood.*

indirect discourse The inexact quotation of the spoken or written words of a person. Indirect discourse inserts the writer's voice into the quotation. Also called *indirect quotation.* (See 28a-1.)

indirect object See *object.*

indirect question A restatement of a question asked by someone else. An indirect question uses a period as punctuation, not a question mark.

indirect quotation See *indirect discourse.*

inference An unstated conclusion that is based on and is consistent with available evidence. (See 1c-2; 3f-3.)

infinitive The base form of a verb, which is often preceded by the word *to.* Also called the *dictionary form.*

infinitive phrase See *phrase.*

informal writing The more colloquial, casual writing of personal correspondence and journals. (See 3c-5.)

intensive pronoun See *pronoun.*

interjection An emphatic word or phrase. When it stands alone, an interjection is frequently followed by an exclamation point. As part of a sentence, an interjection is usually set off by commas. (See 7a-10.)

interrogative pronoun See *pronoun.*

interrogative sentence See *sentence.*

intransitive verb See *verb.*

irregular verb   A verb that changes its root spelling to show the past tense and form the past participle, as opposed to adding *-d* or *-ed.*

jargon   The in-group language of professionals, who may use acronyms and other linguistic devices to take short-cuts when speaking with colleagues. (See 21e-4.)

limiting modifier   A word that restricts the meaning of another word placed directly after it (*only, almost, just, nearly, even, simply*).

linking verb   See *verb.*

list   A displayed series of items that are logically similar or comparable and are expressed in grammatically parallel form.

logical arrangement   A method of organizing a paper in which the topic is divided into its constituent parts, and the parts are discussed one at a time in an order that will make sense to readers. (See 3g-2; 5d-1.)

main clause   See *independent clause.*

mapping   A visual method of idea generation. The topic (word or phrase) is circled and from the circle are drawn spokes labeled with the "journalists' questions" (*who, what, where, when, how, why*). The answer to each question is then queried with the journalists' questions again. This method groups and subordinates ideas, thus assisting in generating main ideas and supporting information. (See 3d-7.)

D

gl/gr

mass noun   See *noun.*

metaphor   A figure of speech that illustrates or intensifies something relatively unknown by comparing it with something familiar. (See 21f-1.)

misplaced modifier   A word, phrase, or clause whose position confuses the meaning of a sentence. A misplaced modifier is not placed next to the word(s) it is meant to modify. (See 15a.)

mixed construction   A confused sentence structure that begins with a certain grammatical pattern and then abruptly changes direction with another grammatical pattern.

mixed metaphor   An illogical comparison of two elements. (See 21f-2.)

modal auxiliary   A verb that is paired with the base form of a verb to express urgency, obligation, likelihood, or possibility (*can, could, may, might, must, ought to, should, would*). (See 9c-1.)

modifier   An adjective or adverb, in the form of a single word, phrase, or clause, that adds descriptive information to a noun or verb. A single-word adjective is often positioned directly before the noun it modifies. Adverbs can be shifted to any part of a sentence. Depending on its location, an adverb will change the meaning or rhythm of a sentence, so care must be taken to ensure that an adverb modifies the word intended. (See 7c.)

mood The form of a verb that indicates the writer's attitude about an action. The **indicative mood** expresses facts, opinions, or questions. The **imperative mood** expresses commands. The **subjunctive mood** expresses a recommendation, a wish, a requirement, or a statement contrary to fact. (See 9h.)

narrative Writing that recounts for readers a story that will have a point pertinent to the larger essay. Narratives are often sequenced chronologically. (See 5e-2.)

nonessential modifier A word, phrase, or clause that provides information that is not essential for defining a word. Commas are used to set the clause apart from the sentence in which it appears. The relative pronouns *who* or *which* may be used in nonessential clauses. Also called *nonrestrictive modifier*. (See 14e-2; 25d-2.)

nonrestrictive modifier See *nonessential modifier*.

noun A noun names a person, place, thing, or idea. Nouns change their form to show number; the plural is usually formed by adding *-s* or *-es*. Possession is indicated with the addition of an apostrophe and usually an *s*. **Proper nouns,** which are capitalized, name particular persons, places, or things. **Common nouns** refer to general persons, places, or things. **Mass nouns** denote items that cannot be counted. **Count nouns** denote items that can be counted. **Concrete nouns** name tangible objects. **Abstract nouns** name intangible ideas, emotions, or qualities. **Animate** versus **inanimate nouns** differ according to whether they name something alive. **Collective nouns** are singular in form and have either a singular or plural sense, depending on the meaning of the sentence. (See 7a-2; 10a-5.)

noun clause See *clause*.

noun phrase See *phrase*.

number A change in the form of a noun, pronoun, or verb that indicates whether it is singular or plural. (See 16a.)

object A noun, pronoun, or group of words substituting for a noun that receives the action of a transitive verb (**direct object**); is indirectly affected by the action of a transitive verb (**indirect object**); or follows a preposition (**object of a preposition**). (See 7b.)

object complement See *complement*.

objective case See *case*.

object of a preposition See *object*.

outline A logically parallel list with further subdivision and subsections under individual items in the list. (See 18e-2.)

paragraph A group of related sentences organized by a single, controlling idea. (See chapter 5.)

paraphrase A restatement of a passage of text. The structure of a paraphrase reflects the structure of the source passage. (See 34c-2.)

D

gl/gr

parallel case   An argument that develops a relationship between directly related people, objects, events, or conditions.

parallelism   The use of grammatically equivalent words, phrases, and sentences to achieve coherence and balance in writing. (See 5d-2; chapter 18.)

parentheses   Punctuation marks used to enclose and set off nonessential dates, words, phrases, or whole sentences that provide examples, comments, and other supporting information. (See 29c.)

participial phrase   See *phrase.*

participle   A verb form. The **present participle** (the *-ing* form) functions as a main verb of a sentence and shows continuing action when paired with *to be;* functions as an adjective when paired with a noun or pronoun (*the loving parent*), and functions as a noun when used as a gerund (*studying takes time*). (See *gerund.*) The **past participle** (the past tense *-d, -ed, -n,* or *-en* forms) functions as the main verb of a sentence when paired with *to have* (*I have studied for days*); forms a passive construction when paired with *to be* (*The rock was thrown*); and functions as an adjective when paired with a noun or pronoun (*the contented cow*).

parts of speech   The categories into which words are grouped according to their grammatical function in a sentence: nouns, verbs, verbals, adjectives, adverbs, pronouns, prepositions, conjunctions, interjections, and expletives. (See glossary entries for each category and 7a-2–11.)

D

gl/gr

passive voice   See *voice.*

past participle   See *participle.*

past perfect progressive tense   See *tense.*

past perfect tense   See *tense.*

past progressive tense   See *tense.*

past tense   See *tense.*

perfect progressive tense   See *tense.*

period   A punctuation mark (.) that denotes a complete stop—the end of a sentence. (See 24a.)

person   The form of a pronoun or a noun that identifies whether the subject of a sentence is the person speaking (the **first person**); the person spoken to (the **second person**); or the person spoken about (the **third person**). (See 16a.)

personal pronoun   See *pronoun.*

phrase   A grouping of words that lacks a subject and predicate and cannot stand alone as a sentence. **Verbal phrases** consist of infinitive phrases, gerund phrases, and participial phrases—all of which are built on verb forms not functioning as verbs in a sentence, along with associated words (objects and modifiers). **Infinitive phrases** consist of the infinitive form, often preceded by *to;* they function as adjectives, adverbs, or nouns. **Gerund phrases** consist of the *-ing* form of a verb and function as nouns—as subjects, objects, or complements. **Participial phrases** consist of the present or past participle of a verb and function as adjectives. **Verb phrases** consist of the combination of an auxiliary and the base form, or present or past participle, of a verb. **Noun phrases** consist of a noun accompanied by all of its modifying words. A noun phrase may be quite lengthy, but it always functions as a single noun—as a subject, object, or complement. **Absolute phrases** consist of a subject and an incomplete predicate; they modify entire sentences, not individual words. **Appositive phrases** rename or further identify nouns and are placed directly beside the nouns they refer to. (See 7d; 12c; 29a-4; 29b-1.)

plagiarism A conscious attempt to pass off the ideas or the words of another as one's own. (See 34e.)

popular writing The writing typical of most general-interest magazines. The language is more conversational than formal writing, but all conventions of grammar, usage, spelling, and punctuation are adhered to. (See 3c-5.)

positive form See *adjective forms, adverb forms.*

possessive case See *case.*

predicate A verb, and other words associated with it, that states the action undertaken by a subject or the condition in which the subject exists. A **simple predicate** consists of the verb and its auxiliaries. A **complete predicate** consists of the simple predicate and its modifiers and objects. A **compound predicate** consists of two verbs and their associated words which are joined with a coordinate conjunction and share the same subject. (See 7a-1.)

prefix A group of letters joined to the beginning of a root word to form a new, derived word. Prefixes indicate number, size, status or condition, negation, and relations in time and space. (See 22e-1; 23c.)

preposition A word (*in, at, of, for, on, by, above, under*) that links a noun, pronoun, or word group substituting for a noun to other words in a sentence—to nouns, pronouns, verbs, or adjectives. (See 7a-8.)

prepositional phrase See *phrase.*

present participle See *participle.*

present perfect progressive tense See *tense.*

present perfect tense See *tense.*

present progressive tense See *tense.*

primary source An original document or artifact that may be referred to in a paper, such as a story, letter, or autobiography.

principal parts The forms of a verb built from the infinitive, from which the tenses are formed: past tense, present participle, and past participle.

pronoun   A word that takes on the meaning of and substitutes for a noun (referred to as the pronoun's *antecedent*). Pronouns show number (singular or plural) and change case depending on their function in a sentence. **Personal pronouns** (*I, me, you, us, his, hers . . .*) refer to people or things. **Relative pronouns** (*who, which, that . . .*) introduce dependent clauses that usually function as adjectives. The pronouns *who, which,* and *that* rename and refer to the nouns they follow. **Demonstrative pronouns** (*this, that, these, those*) point to the nouns they replace. **Interrogative pronouns** (*who, which, what, whose*) form questions. **Intensive pronouns** (*herself, themselves*) are formed with the suffix *-self* or *-selves* to repeat and emphasize a noun or pronoun. **Reflexive pronouns** (*herself, ourselves*) are formed with the suffix *-self* or *-selves* and rename or reflect back to a preceding noun or pronoun. **Indefinite pronouns** (*one, anybody*) refer to general or nonspecific persons or things. **Reciprocal pronouns** (*one another, each other*) refer to the separate parts of a plural noun. (See 7a-7; chapter 8; chapter 14.)

proofreading   The final stage in the composition process in which the writer rereads the final paper to identify and correct misspelled words; words (often prepositions) omitted from sentences; words that have been doubled; punctuation that may have been forgotten; and homonyms. (See 4k-2.)

proper noun   See *noun.*

quotation   See *direct discourse.*

reciprocal pronoun   See *pronoun.*

redundant phrase   An expression that repeats a message unnecessarily.

reflexive pronoun   See *pronoun.*

regionalism   An expression whose meaning is specific to certain areas of the country. Use of such expressions is inappropriate in formal writing. (See 21e-2.)

register   The level of language or tone used in a paper. (See *formal writing, informal writing, popular writing.*)

regular verbs   Verbs that change form in predictable ways, taking the suffix *-ed* to show the past tense and the past participle.

relative pronoun   See *pronoun.*

restrictive modifier   See *essential modifier.*

revision   A stage in the composition process in which the writer examines the first draft to clarify the purpose or thesis; rewrites to achieve unity and coherence; and adjusts to achieve balance by expanding, condensing, or cutting material. (See 4d, e, f; 35f.)

root word   The base form of a word that contains its core meaning. Suffixes and prefixes are added to a root word to form additional words.

run-on sentence   See *fused sentence.*

D

gl/gr

second person See *person.*

section A grouping of paragraphs that constitutes part of the larger document. (See 5a-1.)

section thesis See *thesis.*

secondary source The work of scholars who have interpreted the writings of others.

semicolon A punctuation mark (;) used to denote a partial separation between independent elements. (See chapter 26.)

sentence A fully expressed thought consisting of a complete subject and a complete predicate. A sentence begins with a capital letter and ends with a period, question mark, or exclamation point. The four functional types of sentences include declarative, interrogative, exclamatory, and imperative sentences. A **declarative sentence** makes a statement or assertion about a subject. An **interrogative sentence** poses a question and is formed either by inverting a sentence's usual word order or by preceding the sentence with words such as *who, which, when, where,* and *how.* An **exclamatory sentence** is used as a direct expression of a speaker's or writer's strong emotion. An **imperative sentence** expresses a command. The four structural types of sentences are simple, compound, complex, and compound-complex sentences. A **simple sentence** has a single subject and a single predicate. A *compound sentence* has two subjects and two predicates. A **complex sentence** has an independent clause and one or more dependent clauses. A **compound-complex sentence** has at least two independent clauses and one dependent clause.

sentence fragment A partial sentence punctuated as if it were a complete sentence, with an uppercase letter at its beginning and a period, question mark, or exclamation point at its end. A sentence fragment lacks either a subject or a predicate, and sometimes both. It can also be a dependent clause that has not been joined to an independent clause.

sexism In writing, the use of inappropriate gender-specific words (*a biologist in his lab*) that creates biased or inaccurate characterizations linked with a male or female reference. (See 21g.)

simile A figure of speech in which two different things, one usually familiar, the other not, are explicitly compared. The properties of the known thing help to define the unknown thing. Similes often use the words *like* or *as* to set up the comparison. (See 21f-1.)

simple future tense See *tense.*

simple past tense See *tense.*

simple predicate See *predicate.*

simple present tense See *tense.*

simple sentence See *sentence.*

D

gl/gr

simple subject See *subject.*

slang The informal language peculiar to a culture or subculture; inappropriate for formal writing.

slash A punctuation mark (/) used to separate lines of poetry run-in with the text of a sentence; to show choice, as in *either/or;* and to note division in fractions or formulas. (See 29f.)

spatial arrangement A method of organizing a paper in which the subjects are described according to their relative positions; for example, for a photograph, the foreground, middle ground, and background might be described. (See 3g-2; 5d-1.)

split infinitive The insertion of an adverbial modifier between the two parts of an infinitive—the word *to* and the base form—which can disrupt to the intended meaning (. . . *to* successfully *attempt*). (See 15f.)

squinting modifier A word, phrase, or clause that ambiguously appears to modify two words in a sentence—both the word preceding and following it.

subject A noun, pronoun, or group of words substituting for a noun, that engages in the main action of a sentence or is described by the sentence. A **simple subject** consists of a single noun or pronoun. A **complete subject** consists of a simple subject and its modifiers. A **compound subject** consists of a multiple subject created by using the coordinate conjunction *and.*

subjective case See *case.*

subject complement See *complement.*

subjunctive mood See *mood.*

subordinate clause See *clause, dependent clause.*

subordinate conjunction See *conjunction.*

subordination A method for linking words, phrases, or clauses that is used to give more emphasis to one idea than to another in a sentence. The words in a dependent (subordinate) clause cannot stand alone as a sentence. (See 19b.)

suffix A group of letters joined to the end of a root word. Suffixes change the grammatical function of words and can be used to indicate tense.

summary A brief, objective account of the main ideas of a source passage. (See 34c-1.)

superlative form See *adjective forms, adverb forms.*

synonym A word that has approximately the same denotation (dictionary meaning) as another word.

synthesis A presentation that draws together material from several sources. (See 2d.)

D

gl/gr

tag question   A brief question attached to a statement, set off by a comma. Tag questions consist of a helping verb, a pronoun, and frequently the word *not* (*He won the match, didn't he?*). (See 25e-5.)

tense   The change in form of a verb that shows when an action has occurred or when a subject exists in a certain state of being. Tenses are marked by verb endings and auxiliary verbs. (See 9e, f; 16b-1.) The **simple present tense** indicates an action taking place at the writer's present time. The verb's base form is used for singular or plural first- and second-person subjects, as well as for plural third-person subjects (*I go, you go, they go*). The verb for a third-person singular subject ends with the suffix *-s* (*she goes*). The **simple past tense** indicates an action completed at a definite time in the past. Regular verbs form this tense by adding *-d* or *-ed* to the base form. The **simple future tense** indicates an action or state of being that will begin in the future. All other tenses build on these basic tenses by using auxiliaries. See chapter 9 for more information on the present, past, and future perfect tenses; the present, past, and future progressive tenses; and the perfect progressive tenses.

thesis   A general statement about a topic that crystallizes the main purpose of a writing and suggests its main parts. A **section thesis** explicitly announces the point to be addressed in a section and either directly or indirectly suggests what will be discussed relating to this point. (See 5a-2.) A **working thesis** is a statement that should prove to be a reasonably accurate summary of what will be written. A **final thesis** is an accurate, one-sentence summary of a work that will appear in the final draft. (See 3f; 33e; 35a.)

third person   See *person.*

tone   The expression of a writer's attitude toward the subject or audience. Tone is determined by word choice and quality of description, verb selection, sentence structure, and sentence mood and voice. The tone of a piece changes depending on the audience. (See 3c-5; 16c.)

topic   The subject of a piece of writing. (See 3b.)

topic sentence   A paragraph's central, controlling idea. (See 5c.)

topical development   The expansion of statements about a topic announced in the opening sentence of a paragraph. After its opening announcement, the topic is divided into two or three parts, each of which is developed at a different location in the paragraph. (See 5e-2.)

transition   A word, sentence, or paragraph devoted to building a smooth, logical relationship between ideas in a sentence, between sentences, between paragraphs, or between whole sections of an essay. (Phrases include: *for example, on the other hand, in addition.*) (See 4e-2; 5d-3; 20c-1.)

transitive verb   See *verb.*

usage   The prevailing, customary conditions describing how, where, and when a word is normally used in speech and writing. Usage labels in a dictionary, such as *colloquial, slang, archaic,* or *dialect,* indicate special restrictions on the conditions for using a particular meaning or form of a word.

D

gl/gr

value assumption See *assumption.*

verb The main word in the predicate of a sentence expressing an action or occurrence or establishing a state of being. Verbs change form to demonstrate tense, number, mood, and voice. **Transitive verbs** (*kick, buy*) transfer the action from an actor—the subject of the sentence—to a direct object—a person, place, or thing receiving that action. **Intransitive verbs** (*laugh, sing, smile*) show action that is limited to the subject; there is no direct object that is acted upon. (*The rock fell.*) The same verb can be transitive in one sentence and intransitive in another. (*She runs a good business. She runs every day.*) **Linking verbs** (*is, feel, appear, seem*) allow the word or words following the verb to complete the meaning of the subject. (*Joan is a lawyer.*) (See 7a-3; chapter 9.)

verbal A verb form that functions in a sentence as an adjective, an adverb, or a noun. Verbals include infinitives, participles, and gerunds. (See *infinitive, participle, gerund;* 7a-4; 7d-2.)

verbal phrase See *phrase.*

verb phrase See *phrase.*

voice The form of a transitive verb in a sentence that shows whether emphasis is given to the actor or to the object acted upon. **Active-voice** sentences emphasize the doer of an action. **Passive-voice** sentences emphasize the object acted upon or de-emphasize an unknown subject. In passive-voice sentences the words are rearranged so that the object occupies the first position. This construction requires the use of a form of the verb *to be* and the preposition *by.* (*The house was designed by Frank Lloyd Wright.*)

working thesis See *thesis.*

D

gl/gr

REFERENCES *and* WORKS CITED

CHAPTER 5: REFERENCES

The illustrative paragraphs in this chapter are attributed in the text as they occur; they are drawn from the following sources (presented here alphabetically with page references provided for ease of reference):

Baron, Robert A., and Jerald Greenberg. *Behavior in Organizations.* 3rd ed. Boston: Allyn and Bacon, 1990, 240–242.

Becker, Carl L. "Everyman His Own Historian." *American Historical Review,* XXXVII (January 1932): 221–236. Rpt. in *The Historian as Detective: Essays on Evidence.* Ed. Robin W. Winks. New York: Harper Torchbooks, 1968, 6–7.

Berry, Wendell. "The Rise." *Recollected Essays 1965–1980.* San Francisco: North Point Press: 1981, 7.

Boorstin, Daniel, and Brooks Mather Kelley. *A History of the United States.* Englewood Cliffs, NJ: Prentice, 1989, 499.

Bronowski, J. *The Ascent of Man.* Boston: Little, Brown, 1973, 115.

Brownlee, Shannon. "First It Was 'Save the Whales,' Now It's 'Free the Dolphins.' " Rpt. in *Elements of Argument.* 2nd ed. Ed. Annette E. Rottenberg. New York: Bedford, 1988, 268.

Burke, Daniel, "In Defense of Fraternities." Student essay. *Aims of the Essay.* Ed. Don Knefel. Boston: Allyn and Bacon, 1991, 213.

Carson, Rachel. *Silent Spring.* Boston: Houghton, 1962, 39, 105, 136.

Catton, Bruce. "Grant and Lee: A Study in Contrasts." Rpt. in *The Longwood Reader.* Ed. Edward A. Dornan and Charles W. Dawe. Boston: Allyn and Bacon, 1991, 236.

Chang, Semoon, *Modern Economics.* Boston: Allyn and Bacon, 1990, 38, 39.

Clarke, Arthur C. "Electron Tutors." *Omni Magazine* 1980. Rpt. in *Writing and Reading Across the Curriculum.* Ed. Laurence Behrens and Leonard Rosen. Boston: Little, Brown, 1982, 273.

Cohen, Paul S., and Milton A. Rothman. *Basic Chemistry.* Boston: Allyn and Bacon, 1986, 45.

Costello, Kevin. "Long Odds: How a Bill Becomes Law." Student essay. *Aims of the Essay.* Ed. Don Knefel. Boston: Allyn and Bacon, 1991, 154.

Curtis, Helena. *Biology.* 2nd ed. New York: Worth, 1975, 47.

Daniels, Robert V. *Studying History: How and Why.* 3rd ed. Englewood Cliffs: Prentice, 1981.

Dillard, Annie. *An American Childhood.* New York: Harper, 1987, 53–54.

Farb, Peter. *Humankind.* Boston: Houghton, 1978, 53.

Farber, Stephen. *The Movie Rating Game.* Public Affairs Press, 1972. Rpt. in *Writing and Reading Across the Curriculum.* 3rd ed. Ed. Laurence Behrens and Leonard Rosen. Glenview: Scott, 1987, 177.

Fagan, Brian M. *Archaeology: A Brief Introduction.* 3rd ed. Glenview: Scott, 1988, 37–38.

Gardner's Art Through the Ages. 5th ed. Revised edition by Horst de la Croix and Richard Tansey. New York: Harcourt, 1970, 40.

Hannan, Sean. "The Win Justifies the Means." Student essay. Quoted by permission of the author.

Huneven, Michelle. "Living Well Is the Best Revenge—Just Ask the Urban Coyote." Rpt. in *The Longwood Reader*. Ed. Edward A. Dornan and Charles W. Dawe. Boston: Allyn and Bacon, 1991, 19.

Janis, Irving L. "Groupthink." Rpt. in *Writing and Reading Across the Curriculum*. 3rd ed. Ed. Laurence Behrens and Leonard Rosen. Glenview: Scott, 1987, 266.

Jones, Beau Fly, Annemarie Sullivan Palincsar, Donna Sederburg Ogle, and Eileen Glynn Carr. *Strategic Thinking and Learning: Cognitive Instruction in the Content Areas*. Alexandria: ASCD, 1987, 22–23.

Jones, Rachel L. "What's Wrong with Black English." *Newsweek*, "My Turn," 27 Dec. 1982: 7. Rpt. in *Effective Argument*. Ed. J. Karl Nicholas and James R. Nicholl. Boston: Allyn and Bacon, 1991, 157, 159.

Hawking, Stephen. *A Brief History of Time*. New York: Bantam, 1988, 2–3.

Keller, Helen. *The Story of My Life*. New York: Doubleday, 1954, 35–37.

Morreall, John. *Taking Laughter Seriously*. New York: State University of New York Press, 1983. Rpt. in *Writing and Reading Across the Curriculum*. 3rd ed. Ed. Laurence Behrens and Leonard Rosen. Glenview: Scott, 1987, 365–366.

Nilsen, Alleen. "Sexism in English: A 1990s Update." *The Longwood Reader*. Ed. Edward A. Dornan and Charles W. Dawe. Boston: Allyn and Bacon, 1991, 209.

Roddy, Jim. "Images of America in Doctorow's *Ragtime*." Student essay. *Aims of the Essay*. Ed. Don Knefel. Boston: Allyn and Bacon, 1991, 256.

Sagan, Carl. *The Dragons of Eden: Speculations on the Evolution of Human Intelligence*. New York: Random, 1977, 45–46.

Shanahan, Daniel. "We Need a Nationwide Effort to Encourage, Enhance, and Expand Our Students' Proficiency in Language." *The Chronicle of Higher Education*, 31 May 1989: 40. Rpt. in *Effective Argument*. Ed. J. Karl Nicholas and James R. Nicholl. Boston: Allyn and Bacon, 1991, 244.

Sheils, Merril, et al. "And Man Created the Chip." *Newsweek*, 30 June 1980. Rpt. in *Writing and Reading Across the Curriculum*. Ed. Laurence Behrens and Leonard Rosen. Boston: Little, Brown, 1982, 256.

Shapiro, David. *Neurotic Styles*. New York: Basic Books, 1965, 44–45.

Singer, Peter. "Animal Liberation." Rpt. in *Elements of Argument*. 2nd ed. Ed. Annette E. Rottenberg. New York: Bedford, 1988, 250.

Sullivan, Anne. Letter in Helen Keller, *The Story of My Life*. New York: Doubleday, 1954, 256–257.

Stratton, Joanna L. *Pioneer Women: Voices from the Kansas Frontier*. New York: Simon and Schuster–Touchstone, 1981, 45.

Trachtenberg, Alan. *Brooklyn Bridge: Fact and Symbol*. Chicago: Chicago UP, 1979, preface.

Trahar, Jenafer. "Athletes and Education." Student essay. Quoted by permission of the author.

Warner, William. *Beautiful Swimmers*. Boston: Little, Brown, 1976.

Watts, James, and Allen F. Davis, eds. *Your Family in Modern American History*. 2nd ed. New York: Knopf, 1978. Rpt. in *Writing and Reading Across the Curriculum*. Ed. Laurence Behrens and Leonard Rosen. Boston: Little, Brown, 1982, 136.

Whiteside, Thomas. *Selling Death: Cigarette Advertising and Public Health*. New York: Liveright, 1971.

CHAPTER 37: WORKS CITED

Frankel, Charles. "Why the Humanities?" *The Humanist as Citizen*. Ed. John Agresto and Peter Riesenberg. Chapel Hill: N. Carolina UP, 1981.

Franklin, Benjamin. *The Autobiography and Other Writings*. New York: Penguin, 1987.

Ketchem, Ralph. "Benjamin Franklin." *Encyclopedia of Philosophy*. Rpt. 1972 ed.

Lawrence, D. H. "Benjamin Franklin." *Studies in Classic American Literature*. 1923. New York: Viking, 1964.

Oates, Joyce Carol. *The Edge of Impossibility: Tragic Forms in Literature.* New York: Vanguard, 1972.

———. *On Boxing.* Garden City: Dolphin, 1987.

———. "Where Have You Been? Where Are You Going?" *The Wheel of Love.* New York: Vanguard, 1970.

O'Reilly, Kevin. "Teaching Critical Thinking in High School History." *Social Education* Ap. 1985: 281.

Rieke, Richard D., and Malcolm O. Sillars. *Argumentation and the Decision Making Process.* 2nd ed. Glenview: Scott, 1984.

Stratton, Joanna L. *Pioneer Women.* New York: Touchstone, 1981.

Toulmin, Stephen, Richard Rieke, and Allan Janik. *An Introduction to Reasoning.* New York: Macmillan, 1979.

Van Doren, Carl. *Benjamin Franklin.* New York: Viking, 1938.

Vendler, Helen. *Wallace Stevens: Words Chosen Out of Desire.* Knoxville: Tennessee UP, 1984.

Wittgenstein, Ludwig. *Philosophical Investigations.* 3rd ed. Trans. G.E.M. Anscombe. New York: Macmillan, 1968.

CHAPTER 38: WORKS CITED

Braybrooke, David. *Philosophy of Social Science.* Prentice-Hall Foundations of Philosophy Series. Englewood Cliffs: Prentice, 1987.

Bromley, D. B. *The Case-study Method in Psychology and Related Disciplines.* Chichester, Great Britain: John Wiley, 1986.

Otis, Laura P. "Factors Influencing the Willingness to Taste Unusual Foods." *Psychological Reports* 54 (1984): 739–745.

Richlin-Klonsky, Judith, and Ellen Strenski, coordinators and eds. *A Guide to Writing Sociology Papers.* New York: St. Martin's, 1986.

Rieke, Richard D., and Malcolm O. Sillars. *Argumentation and the Decision Making Process.* 2nd ed. Glenview: Scott, 1984.

Rollinson, Paul A. "The Story of Edward: The Everyday Geography of Elderly Single Room Occupancy (SRO) Hotel Tenants." *Journal of Contemporary Ethnography* 19 (1990): 188–206.

Skinner, B. F. "Two Types of Conditioned Reflex and a Pseudo-type." *The Journal of General Psychology* 12 (1935): 66–77. Rpt. in B.F. Skinner, *Cumulative Record: A Selection of Papers.* 3rd ed. New York: Appleton, 1972, 479.

———. "How to Teach Animals." *Scientific American* 185 (1951): 26–29. Rpt. in B.F. Skinner, *Cumulative Record: A Selection of Papers.* 3rd ed. New York: Appleton, 1972, 539.

Solomon, Paul R. *A Student's Guide to Research Report Writing in Psychology.* Glenview: Scott, 1985.

Spencer, Herbert. *The Study of Sociology.* Ann Arbor: U of Michigan P, 1961.

CHAPTER 39: WORKS CITED

AIP [American Institute of Physics] Style Manual. 4th ed. New York: AIP, 1990.

American Association for the Advancement of Science. *Project 2061: Science for All Americans.* Washington: AAAS, 1989.

CBE [Council of Biology Editors] Style Manual. 5th ed. Bethesda: CBE, 1983.

Day, Robert. *How to Write and Publish a Scientific Paper.* 3rd ed. Phoenix: Oryx Press, 1988.

Gould, Stephen Jay. *Hen's Teeth and Horse's Toes: Further Reflections on Natural History.* New York: Norton, 1983.

Thuesen, Ingolf, and Jan Engberg. "Recovery and Analysis of Human Genetic Material from Mummified Tissue and Bone." *Journal of Archaeological Science* 17 (1990): 679–689.

Toulmin, Stephen, Richard Rieke, and Allan Janik. *An Introduction to Reasoning.* New York: Macmillan, 1979.

Woodruff, David S., and Stephen Jay Gould, "Fifty Years of Interspecific Hybridization: Genetics and Morphometrics of a Controlled Experiment on the Land Snail *Cerion* in the Florida Keys." *Evolution* 41 (1987): 1026.

CREDITS

Robert A. Baron and Jerald Greenberg, excerpts from *Behavior in Organizations,* Third Edition. Copyright © 1990 by Allyn and Bacon. Reprinted with permission.

Carl L. Becker, excerpts from "Everyman His Own Historian," *American Historical Review,* vol. XXXVII, January 1932, pp. 221–236. Reprinted by permission of the American Historical Association.

Wendell Berry, excerpt from "The Rise." Excerpted from *Recollected Essays 1965–1980,* copyright © 1969, 1981 by Wendell Berry. Published by North Point Press and reprinted by permission.

Bibliographic Index. Entry from *Bibliographic Index,* 1986, p. 21. Copyright © 1985, 1986 by The H. W. Wilson Company. Reprinted by permission of the publisher.

Book Review Digest. Entry from *Book Review Digest,* 1988, pp. 556–557. Copyright © 1988, 1989 by The H. W. Wilson Company. Reprinted by permission of the publisher.

Bruce Catton, excerpts from "Grant and Lee: A Study in Contrasts." Copyright 1956, renewed 1984, United States Capitol Historical Society. All rights reserved. Reprinted by permission.

Napoleon A. Chagnon, excerpt from *Yanomamo: The Fierce People* by Napoleon Chagnon, copyright © 1968 by Holt, Rinehart and Winston, Inc., reprinted by permission of the publisher.

Semoon Chang, excerpts from *Modern Economics.* Copyright © 1990 by Allyn and Bacon. Reprinted with permission.

Robert A. Day, "Tense in Scientific Writing." Reprinted from *How to Write and Publish a Scientific Paper,* 3rd ed., by Robert A. Day. Oryx Press, 4041 N. Central at Indian School Rd., Phoenix, AZ 85012. Copyright 1988 by Robert A. Day. Used by permission of The Oryx Press.

Annie Dillard, excerpt from *An American Childhood* by Annie Dillard. Copyright © 1987 by Annie Dillard. Reprinted by permission of HarperCollins Publishers Inc.

Anne Eisenberg, "Keeping a Laboratory Notebook." Reprinted by permission from the *Journal of Chemical Education,* 59 (1982): 1045–46. Published 1982 by the American Chemical Society.

General Science Index. Entry from *General Science Index,* June 1988-May 1989, p. 56. Copyright © 1988, 1989 by The H. W. Wilson Company. Reprinted by permission of the publisher.

Jack Gordon, excerpt from "Drug Testing as a Productivity Booster?" Reprinted by permission from the March 1987 issue of *Training* Magazine. Copyright 1987, Lakewood Publications, Inc., Minneapolis, MN, (612) 333-0471. All rights reserved.

Harvey Greenberg, excerpts from © 1975 *Movies on Your Mind* by Harvey Greenberg, M.D. published by Saturday Review Press/E.P. Dutton. Reprinted by permission.

Rachel L. Jones, excerpts from "What's Wrong with Black English?" *Newsweek,* December 27, 1982. Copyright © 1982 by Rachel L. Jones. Reprinted by permission of the author.

D. H. Lawrence, from "Benjamin Franklin" in *Studies in Classic American Literature*. Copyright 1923 by Thomas Seltzer, Inc. Copyright renewed 1951 by Frieda Lawrence. Copyright © The Estate of the late Frieda Lawrence, 1961. Reprinted by permission of the publisher, Viking Penguin, a division of Penguin Books USA Inc.

MLA International Bibliography. Entry reprinted by permission of the Modern Language Association of America from *MLA International Bibliography* (Subject Index), 1984, pp. G30–31. Copyright © 1985 by The Modern Language Association of America.

Andrew Moss and Carol Holder, "Important Word Meanings" from *Improving Student Writing: A Guide for Faculty in All Disciplines*, Kendall/Hunt Publishers. Copyright © 1988 by the Trustees of the California State University. Reprinted by permission.

The New York Times Index. Entry from *The New York Times Index*, 1989. Copyright © 1989 by The New York Times Company. Reprinted by permission.

Laura P. Otis. Reproduced with permission of the author and publisher from "Factors influencing the willingness to taste unusual foods," *Psychological Reports*, 1984, 54, 739–745.

Reader's Guide to Periodical Literature. Entry from *Reader's Guide to Periodical Literature*, 1989. Copyright © 1989, 1990 by The H. W. Wilson Company. Reprinted by permission of the publisher.

Paul A. Rollinson, excerpted selection from "The Story of Edward: The Everyday Geography of Elderly Single Room Occupancy (SRO) Hotel Tenants," *Journal of Contemporary Ethnography*, Vol. 19, No. 2, July 1990, pp. 188–206. © 1990 by Sage Publications, Inc. By permission.

William Saletan, excerpt from "Jar Wars." Reprinted by permission from *The New Republic*, 2 October 1989. Copyright © 1989 by The New Republic, Inc.

Social Sciences Index. Entry from *Social Sciences Index*, April 1989-March 1990. Copyright © 1989, 1990 by The H. W. Wilson Company. Reprinted by permission of the publisher.

Sociological Abstracts. Entry from *Sociological Abstracts*, 1989, p. 2268. Reprinted with permission of Sociological Abstracts, Inc. Copyright 1989 Sociological Abstracts, Inc. All rights reserved.

Wallace Stevens, lines from "Esthetique du Mal." From *The Collected Poems of Wallace Stevens* by Wallace Stevens. Copyright 1947 by Wallace Stevens. Reprinted by permission of Alfred A. Knopf, Inc.

Joanna L. Stratton, excerpts from *Pioneer Women: Voices from the Kansas Frontier*. Copyright © 1981 by Joanna L. Stratton. Reprinted by permission of Simon & Schuster, Inc.

Ingolf Thuesen and Jan Engberg, excerpts from "Recovery and Analysis of Human Genetic Material from Mummified Tissue and Bone," *Journal of Archaeological Science* 17 (1990): 679–689. © 1990 Academic Press Limited. Reprinted by permission.

Carl Van Doren, from *Benjamin Franklin*. Copyright Carl Van Doren, 1938. Copyright renewed Anne Van Doren Ross, Margaret Van Doren Bevans, and Barbara Van Doren Klaw, 1966. Reprinted by permission of the publisher, Viking Penguin, a division of Penguin Books USA Inc.

Nicholas Wade, excerpt from "New Light on an Old Fraud," *The New York Times* (Book Review), 11 November, 1990. Copyright © 1990 by The New York Times Company. Reprinted by permission.

Ludwig Wittgenstein, excerpt from *Philosophical Investigations*. Reprinted with permission of Macmillan Publishing Company and Blackwell Publishers from *Philosophical Investigations* by Ludwig Wittgenstein, translated from the German by G.E.M. Anscombe. Copyright 1953 and renewed © 1981 by Macmillan Publishing Company.

INDEX